Historical Foundations of
Modern Psychology

Historical Foundations of Modern Psychology

Howard H. Kendler
University of California, Santa Barbara

Temple University Press
Philadelphia

Dedicated to my son Kenneth whose life has continually enriched my own.

Preface

Before embarking on the arduous task of writing a history of psychology, one should justify the effort, at least to oneself. The history courses I took, first as an undergraduate and then as a graduate student, fell far short of offering a coherent view of the discipline to which I would dedicate my career. The impression students received from those courses was that the total history of psychology was much less than the sum of its parts. Various systematic approaches in psychology (e.g., structuralism, Gestalt, psychoanalysis, behaviorism) did not "hang together"; some conceptions appeared to be completely independent and irrelevant to others. Why?

The answer gradually emerged from my experiences in psychology—as a research and theoretical psychologist, author of an introductory text and a book on methodology, and briefly as a clinical psychologist and an applied experimental psychologist. Such experiences validated the Kantian notion that the history of science without a philosophy of science is blind, while a philosophy of science without the history of science is empty. My *Historical Foundations of Modern Psychology* is based upon the assumption that an integrated view of the development of psychology as an independent discipline can only be achieved by employing a common methodological frame of reference for all systematic conceptions. By so doing, the similarities and differences, continuities and discontinuities became related parts of a historical pattern instead of a sequence of isolated episodes.

My impression of traditional historical analyses of psychology is that attention is focused almost exclusively on the big picture while the nitty-gritty details of empirical evidence are mostly, if not completely, ignored. As a consequence, theoretical notions are severed from their empirical moorings, thus offering an incomplete and, of necessity, distorted picture of psychological theories. Some empirical analyses must accompany descriptions of theoretical systems if they are to be understood. I have tried to satisfy this requirement.

Oversimplifications are an inevitable consequence of attempting to report the history of psychology within the confines of a book of this size. Oversimplifications always carry the threat of serious distortions. I have tried to minimize such a consequence by self-consciously adopting the goal of "communicative accuracy" (Weaver, 1967). If successful, my audience may not be aware of all the subtleties of many complex issues in the history of psychology, but nevertheless will move closer to a deeper and fuller understanding.

This volume owes many debts which I gratefully acknowledge. The major one is to my wife and colleague, Tracy S. Kendler, who offered many helpful suggestions and whose constructive criticism elevated the quality of this book. Carl Duncan and Wendell Jeffrey were generous with assistance and encouragement. The contributions of my close friend and former student, Roy Lachman, are also acknowledged. Correspondence and unpublished papers from Arthur Blumenthal and M. Brewster Smith proved most useful. So were the suggestions of my colleague John Foley. Rand B. Evans offered penetrating comments that helped clarify several complex issues. In many ways, my former teachers assisted in the preparation of this book. And my students also played a role; while it was being written, the chapters were used in both my undergraduate and graduate history courses. Class discussions and individual comments frequently led to clarifications and improvements of the text. Acknowledging the assistance of others in no way reduces my complete responsibility for the views expressed in this book.

I appreciate the care that JeNeal Bradford, Geri Servi, George Skworcow, and Elaine Smith devoted to the typing of parts of the manuscript.

Howard H. Kendler

Contents

List of Figures and Tables

1

Psychology from a Historical Perspective

You cannot understand contemporary psychology without comprehending its past. Only by an acquaintance with its history can a coherent view of modern psychology be achieved. These bold statements, simply and directly, justify the study of the history of psychology. It would be unfortunate, however, if the need to comprehend the historical foundations of psychology is perceived only as another obstacle to overcome. Instead it should be considered as an invitation to learn about one of the most fascinating chapters in the history of human thought: the search to understand human experience and action.

Justifying the study of the history of psychology fails to suggest how such an effort should be organized. Several ways are possible. A history of psychology can be a chronicle of events: Francis Galton in 1869 published a book entitled *Hereditary Genius,* in which he tried to demonstrate that outstanding intellectual ability was inherited; Wilhelm Wundt established the first psychological laboratory at the University of Leipzig in 1879; Sigmund Freud in 1882 became familiar with the case of Fraulein Anna O., a woman of twenty-one who, in the absence of any known medical reasons, developed a host of dramatic symptoms: paralysis of the limbs, difficulties in seeing and speaking, a distressing cough, nausea, and confusion.

A chronological listing of historical events has obvious limitations. First, it fails to offer a coherent account of history. Each event is separate and distinct from every other one. They are related only in the order of the time of occurrence. Second, a chronological listing ignores an event's significance. Its true significance does not depend on an event's position in time but, instead, on its contribution to knowledge. Galton's book, for example, encouraged the study of individual differences: how and why people differ from each other and the significance of these differences for individuals and society. By establishing the first psychology laboratory, Wundt created an independent science of psychology that sought answers to questions about the mind, not by armchair speculations but, instead, by experimental investigations. The case of Fraulein Anna O. influenced Freud's thinking and contributed, along with other clinical evidence, to the formulation of his dramatic theory of personality development that assumed humans are driven by motives of which they are unaware.

Ralph Waldo Emerson (1803–1882), brilliant American essayist and poet, said that "There is properly no history, only biography." Some psychologists share this view, believing that the history of their discipline can be reduced to the lives of great psychologists. If we study their biographies, we can learn about all the important ideas in psychology. This orientation is based upon the *great man theory of history:* all important contributions are made by a few geniuses, and if we understand the lives of these men and women, we will be able to comprehend the origins and substances of their great ideas.

The great man theory is superficial. It ignores the contributions of the near-great and not-so-great, whose efforts often pave the way for the triumphs of the great. The great man theory also overlooks the central role the intellectual climate of a given era plays in the accomplishments of scientific geniuses. Take the case of Charles Darwin's theory of evolution. The idea of evolution, that existing animals and plants develop by a process of change from previous forms, was "in the air" in England during the middle of the nineteenth century. Without this stimulus, Darwin, in spite of his immense talents, would not have formulated his theory of evolution. To justify this claim, consider the consequences of Darwin having been born one hundred years before or after his birthdate in 1809.

If Darwin had been born a century earlier, he would not have profited from Jean Baptiste Lamarck's theory of evolution, which was a forerunner of Darwin's own. Nor would he have read Thomas Malthus's *An Essay on the Principle of Population* (1872/1976), which triggered Darwin's conception of evolution. If Darwin had been born a century later, his formulation of the theory of evolution would have been preceded by Alfred Wallace (1823–1913), a contemporary of Darwin, who independently developed an evolutionary theory similar to Darwin's. Thus, the independent discoveries of Darwin and Wallace suggest that the *Zeitgeist,* a German word meaning the spirit of the times, plays a role in the creation of great ideas. A *great man* interpretation of the history of psychology is, therefore, incomplete because it ignores the powerful influence of the *Zeitgeist* prevailing at a given time.

The history of psychology can be organized around the development and formulation of significant ideas, such as: Psychology is a natural science employing the same methods as physics, chemistry, and biology;

Psychology is the science of the mind and its purpose is to describe the nature of conscious experience; Psychology is a human science that can reveal a true picture of the human potential. But only by tracing the historical development of significant ideas to their present conception will a deep understanding of modern psychology become possible. This book is committed to this approach. It will deal with major ideas, particularly those associated with the methods psychologists employ, that have shaped the historical course of psychology.

A HISTORY OF IDEAS: WHERE TO BEGIN?

The first issue that confronts a historian of psychology is to decide where to begin. This problem is highlighted by a remark of Hermann Ebbinghaus (1850–1909), the first psychologist who experimentally investigated human memory that "Psychology has a long past, but only a short history." Although man's interest in his own experience and behavior has been a dominant theme in recorded history, the first psychology laboratory was not established until 1879. The history of psychology, therefore, begins before psychology officially began.

The search for the origins of ideas that have dominated psychology inevitably draws us back to ancient times. Consider the notion that psychology should be a natural science. To understand the origin of this idea requires knowing something about the development of the scientific method. Several centuries before Christ, the Chaldeans, an ancient Semitic people who inhabited Babylonia, discovered that similar eclipses of the sun occur approximately every eighteen years and eleven days. Not only did this knowledge help them predict the occurrences of solar eclipses, it also encouraged a shift in their view of the world. Before the realization that they occurred in a repetitive cycle, eclipses were believed to be an expression of some arbitrary outside interference with sunlight. Only prayer or incantations or other ritualistic practices could restore the hidden light. The basic conception was that worldly phenomena, like solar eclipses, occurred in an unplanned, irrational, unintelligible fashion. Knowing that eclipses appeared in a repetitive cycle encouraged the belief that they and other natural phenomena were comprehensible because they operated according to some orderly plan. Gradually the view of the world shifted from *supernaturalism* to *naturalism:* Natural events were not miraculous occurrences controlled by outside forces but expressions of processes within nature.

Naturalism did not immediately, or ever completely, overthrow supernaturalism. Naturalism ultimately evolved into modern science that led to a rapid expansion of our understanding of physical and biological phenomena. As a result of these successes, it became only a matter of time before the methods of natural science would be employed to understand psychological events. The implication of this bit of history is that the conception of psychology as a natural science has its roots in naturalism, a philosophical position that was born in ancient times.

Not only are methods of modern psychology linked to the past, but so are its major ideas. A theme that pervades modern psychology is that humans seek pleasure. As stated, this assumption says much less than is apparent. For the assumption to be completely meaningful, *pleasure* must be defined. Aristippus (ca. 435–356 B.C.), a philosopher who was a student of Socrates, defined pleasure as the complete gratification of all one's desires. Epicurus (341–270 B.C.) offered a different view: Pleasure is essentially the absence of pain and can only be attained by the rational control of one's desires. Numerous hedonistic theories (i.e., formulations that assume humans are driven to seek pleasure) have been formulated since ancient times. One's understanding of modern versions of such theories can be improved by comprehending their historical roots.

Although historical information from the distant past is often interesting and frequently valuable, authors of books on the history of psychology are confronted with a practical problem. Time is limited! Some history courses last only one quarter or one semester. Either historical material from the period before psychology became an independent discipline in 1879 or after that date must be omitted.

This book is based on the assumption that when studying the history of their discipline, psychology students should pay primary attention to the efforts of psychologists. This does not mean that the historical background of the major psychological ideas will be totally ignored. It means only that the background will be limited to the bare essentials in order to acquaint the reader with those historical influences that *directly* shaped modern psychology. For those readers whose interests extend to the more distant past, suggested readings will be offered to assist them in satisfying their curiosity.

A FRAMEWORK FOR HISTORICAL ANALYSIS

The first hundred years of psychology as an independent discipline has been marked by continuing debates about the nature of psychology, its subject matter and its methods of investigation. These debates have never really been resolved and, as a consequence, there are many different kinds of psychology: Wundtian psychology, structuralism, functionalism, psychoanalysis, behaviorism, cognitive psychology, humanistic psychology, and others.

Comprehending these different systems of psychology requires more than just knowing the distinctive characteristics of each. One must also know the historical forces that led to the development of each system and understand how each orientation differs from others. To achieve this kind of historical perspective requires a common frame of reference with which to judge all psychological systems. The framework that will be employed emphasizes three features of all systems of psychology: *methodology, strategy,* and *theory.* We will briefly examine each concept, while realizing that a fuller appreciation of their meanings will be gained as we proceed through the book.

Methodology

Methodology refers to the general methods psychologists have employed to investigate and interpret psychological events. A variety of methods have been, and are still being, used in psychology. This plurality has resulted from psychologists offering different answers to four basic methodological questions: What is the nature of science? What is the subject matter of psychology? What are the proper methods for investigating psychological events? What is the criterion of psychological truth?

The Nature of Science. Most people think of *science* as a general method to discover truth but are unclear about the method itself. One basic question about which philosophers and scientists disagree is whether the scientific method consists of a single basic method or a collection of different methods, each specially designed to reveal valid knowledge in different disciplines. The single-science point of view considers the scientific method, which has been successfully employed in the natural sciences of physics and chemistry, to be a systematic mode for arriving at warranted empirical conclusions that transcend the borders of various scientific disciplines. Regardless of the particular investigatory procedures used, the criteria of empirical truth remains the same. This single-science view has been adopted by natural science psychologists who believe the methods that have been used by physics and chemistry can be employed in psychology.

Scientific method can also be conceived as a set of methods, each designed to meet the special needs of specific disciplines such as psychology. One such view of science dates back over 200 years to Giambattista Vico (1668–1744), a Neopolitan philosopher who denied that the scientific method used to investigate the physical sciences was the only valid mode of scientific inquiry. History, Vico argued, requires a different method than physics because physical events must be observed from the outside while human events can be observed from the inside, within conscious experience. Vico was careful to point out that the method for understanding human events is not inferior to the method of physical science. In fact, he suggested the opposite; the historian, a human studying human events, is capable of empathizing, sharing experiences, with those who made history and thus the historian can achieve an *intimate* acquaintance with his or her subject matter that is denied the physicist. Numerous variations of this human science approach have been proposed and some psychologists have found them to be more congenial than the natural science approach.

The Subject Matter of Psychology.   One of the basic methodological controversies that has occupied center stage in the history of psychology is whether psychology should be conceived as the science of the mind or the science of behavior. In other words, should psychologists study private mental events (e.g., feelings, thought, images) or overt behavior (e.g., reactions under the influence of alcohol, aggressive behavior). More specifically, should psychologists study feelings of depression or depressed behavior? Some psychologists have insisted that only one of these two subject matters, private experience or overt behavior, is the legitimate subject matter of psychology, while others maintain that both must be studied.

The Methods of Investigation.   How does one investigate psychological phenomena? There is more than one way. This should not be surprising considering that psychology has two different kinds of subject matter: mind and behavior. The methods used to investigate each can be strikingly different.

The early psychologists who considered psychology a mental science employed the method of self-observation; they observed their own conscious experience. Although early psychologists agreed that self-observation was a basic psychological method, they disagreed about the way it should be conducted. Some insisted that rigorous training was needed if an accurate picture of the mind was to be obtained. These psychologists employed the method known as *introspection*. Others argued that a faithful description of the mind could only be obtained by those who observed their inner experience in a naive fashion in the absence of any training. Their method became known as *phenomenology*. The description of conscious experience was determined by the method—introspection or phenomenology—employed to observe consciousness.

Some psychologists, known as behaviorists, argued that a mentalistic psychology could not be scientific. The mind is private. It can only be observed by one person, the experiencing individual. If science depends upon information that is objective, based upon the observations of more than one individual, while a mentalistic psychology is limited to subjective data, then it follows that a mentalistic psychology cannot be a science in the same way that physics, chemistry, and biology are. To demonstrate that psychology could be a science without investigating the mind, behaviorists studied the behavior (i.e., public actions that are observable by all) of lower animals and infants, organisms that are incapable of self-observation. If psychologists could understand and predict their behavior, the behaviorists' argument went, then psychology need not study the mind. However, behaviorists themselves were not in complete agreement about the proper methods to study adult human behavior. Some insisted that self-observation had no relevance to a behavioral psychology, while others suggested that it could perform a useful function.

Psychologists who were committed to study both the mind and behavior were confronted with a special problem. Can you use a common method to study mental and behavioral events, or must distinctive procedures be used for each? If you adopt the latter position, how can you have an integrated science of psychology? Psychologists who opted for a science of the mind and behavior failed to agree on how these questions should be answered.

The Criterion of Psychological Truth. Truth is the object of scientific inquiry. But how does one know whether a statement is true or false? Baruch Spinoza (1632–1677), the great Dutch philosopher, suggested that "He who would distinguish the true from the false must have an adequate idea of what is true and false." But what is an "adequate idea" of truth and falseness?

The history of science tells us that philosophers and scientists have not been able to formulate a universally acceptable set of rules by which to judge the truth of a statement. Thus, it should not be surprising that different criteria to judge the truth of psychological observations and conceptions have been employed. What is judged true for one psychological system will not necessarily be judged true by another system. Thus, to understand a particular system of psychology demands knowledge of its criterion of truth.

It will prove useful at this point to briefly sketch in the outlines of four major criteria of understanding that have been employed in the history of psychology.

Deductive explanation—understanding an event by deducing it from one or more general propositions—is the form of comprehension commonly associated with natural science methodology. A simple example of this kind of explanation is given in the dramatic story of the discovery of the planet Neptune in 1843. It had been noted that the planet Uranus followed a peculiar and variable path around the sun. Astronomers deduced from the theory of gravitation that some unknown celestial body of a given size must be exerting gravitational pull on Uranus. As a result, the location of a heretofore unknown planetary body, later to be named Neptune, was predicted, and subsequently discovered. The hypothesis was judged to be true because it led *logically* to a prediction that was in agreement with empirical data.

Behavioral control—understanding a psychological phenomenon by controlling it—is a form of understanding that has been adopted by psychologists who pride themselves on being tough-minded. They reject the notion that theories are necessary; only facts are important. Thus, if one can control behavior—train a dog to catch a flying frisbee or eliminate the fear of high places among acrophobics—then one understands that form of behavior.

Interpretive consistency achieves understanding by interpreting phenomena within a coherent and meaningful conception even though the formulation appears impossible to prove or disprove by objective evidence. In spite of this, the system appears to be essentially valid because it seems to work in treating psychological disorders as well as proposing a compelling picture of human psychology. Psychoanalysis, in the form presented by Freud, Adler, and Jung, is considered by some to illustrate this form of understanding.

Intuitive knowing is a subjective conviction of understanding that does not require any independent evidence to justify it. *Humans are basically good* is a compelling truth for some philosophers and psychologists.

Strategy

Many people share a naive conception of science. They believe that if a scientist is persistent and rigorous, he or she will discover important data and formulate significant theories. The history of science denies this. The contributions of many dedicated scientists have not been influential and have long been forgotten.

Unfortunately, no simple recipe can be employed for a scientist to guarantee the fruitfulness of his efforts. Science, in some ways, is like a game of chess, backgammon, or bridge. A clever strategy is needed to "win." Scientists must devise clever plans to ensure the success of their research and theorizing.

Strategy plays an important role in two related scientific enterprises, collecting data and formulating theories. A scientist who merely gathers data, much like a child who picks up shells at the beach, has as much chance of being successful as a chess player who moves his pieces in a haphazard manner. Collecting data must be guided by a rational plan. Darwin carefully collected samples of different species to throw light upon the question of how and why species differ.

Psychologists are not always in agreement about what is the best strategy to pursue when gathering data. Some social psychologists believe that social phenomena should be investigated in the laboratory. They rationalize this tactic by arguing that the advancement of any science is highly correlated with the ability to investigate phenomena in a controlled experimental situation. Other social psychologists employ a different tactic. They suggest that social reality cannot be replicated in an artificial experimental situation. To understand terrorism, mob violence, and voting behavior requires that they be studied in their natural settings.

Psychologists also disagree about the best tactic for theorizing. Some argue that theories should be expressed in mathematical terms, while others suggest that it would be more strategic for psychologists to avoid emulating physics and just describe the variables that are responsible for the occurrence of important phenomena. The data of psychology, they imply, cannot be expressed by high-powered mathematical formulas. Still others believe that the best strategy is to be relaxed about theory construction; be as precise as possible, but at the same time tolerate ambiguities. Time and additional research will inevitably lead to better and more exact theories.

It must be understood that strategies cannot be evaluated as true or false, right or wrong. They are essentially gambles that either pay off or do not. They are like a recipe, where "the proof of the pudding is in the eating." All the important systematic orientations in psychology have used distinctive strategies.

Theory

Psychologists, like all scientists, strive to offer coherent interpretations of empirical evidence. A theory is a statement, or a group of statements, meant to interpret a group of events. A variety of theoretical systems have been offered throughout the history of psychology, varying from descriptions of the structure of the mind to formulations of the basic principles of behavior, from hypothesis about the function of consciousness to biochemical explanations of depression. Psychological theories assume a variety of forms, mainly because different kinds of understanding are sought. Without a discussion of important theories, the history of psychology would be not only incomplete, but also much less interesting.

SUMMARY

The history of psychology will be analyzed in terms of the significant ideas that have directly shaped modern psychology.

A historical analysis demands a common framework to evaluate as well as compare and contrast the different systematic orientations in psychology. The framework that will be employed emphasizes *methodology, strategy,* and *theory.*

Four basic methodological questions will be carefully examined when the important systematic orientations in the history of psychology are analyzed. What is the nature of the scientific method employed? What is the subject matter of psychology? What empirical methods are appropriate for investigating psychological events? What criteria—*deductive explanation, behavioral control, interpretive consistency, intuitive knowing*—should be employed to judge the truth of psychological statements?

Psychologists have employed different strategies in collecting data and formulating theories. Strategic decisions can be evaluated only in terms of their fruitfulness.

A central feature of all psychological orientations has been the theoretical assumptions that have been proposed to interpret psychological phenomena.

SUGGESTED READINGS

The philosophically inclined student who is interested in the history of psychological ideas from ancient and medieval times will find Daniel N.

Robinson's *An Intellectual History of Psychology* (1981) to be both informative and challenging. On a much simpler level Robert I. Watson in his *The Great Psychologists* (1978) describes the influences on psychology of Plato, Aristotle, and other Greek philosophers, as well as medieval philosophers such as St. Augustine and Thomas Aquinas. Edna Heidbreder's *Seven Psychologies* (1933) contains a highly readable chapter entitled "Prescientific Psychology," which describes and analyzes significant psychological notions from the time of the sixth century B.C. to the period immediately preceding the founding of the first psychological laboratory at the university of Leipzig in 1879. Richard A. Littman's chapter entitled "Social and Intellectual Origins of Experimental Psychology," which appears in *The First Century of Experimental Psychology,* edited by Eliot Hearst (1979), is highly recommended.

Numerous books have been published that contain excerpts from classical papers in the history of psychology. One of these that students find interesting is *A Source Book in the History of Psychology,* edited by Richard J. Herrnstein and Edwin G. Boring (1966). William S. Sahakian sprinkles the first chapter of the *History and Systems of Psychology* (1975) with important quotations from a variety of philosophers who influenced the development of psychology. Howard H. Kendler's *Psychology: A Science in Conflict* (1981) presents an extended discussion of the different conceptions of science and modes of understanding employed in psychology.

2

Wundtian Psychology

Imagine yourself living about a hundred years ago and given the task of starting a science of psychology. What would you do? Where would you begin? What problems would you investigate? What research techniques would you use? Without any guidance from other psychologists the task would appear overwhelming. Wilhelm Wundt (1832–1920), however, did not have to start from scratch. Historical forces influenced Wundt to establish an independent science of psychology and to shape its character in the way he did.

HISTORICAL ROOTS

Four different influences on Wundt can be identified. A complete historical background to the beginning of psychology cannot be limited to these influences nor to the time frame in which they occurred. But these influences were powerful in directly molding an independent science of psychology.

René Descartes

René Descartes (1596–1650), a great philosopher and a great mathematician, was one of the most original and creative intellects of all times. He shaped psychology by his dualistic thesis that a human being represents a union between a psychological mind and a mechanical body. The mind is a thinking substance, conscious of itself and capable of being studied by self-observation. Study of the body requires the methods of natural science, those methods that have been successfully employed in physics,

FIGURE 2.1 René Descartes

National Library of Medicine

chemistry, and biology. While the mind is free, the body is constrained by principles of physics. To overcome the separation between the mind and body, Descartes postulated a mechanism for their interaction, the pineal body. The pineal body, a small gland the size of a pea that lies in the brain, is controlled by the mind and in turn controls the body.

Descartes's dualism touches upon fundamental methodological problems that have continuously remained at center stage in the history of psychology. First, by postulating two worlds, one of the mind, the other of matter (body), Descartes raised the question whether knowledge about each derives from different sources. He answered by suggesting that different procedures are needed to investigate mind and body. Self-observation, examination from inside, is needed to study the mind, while observations from the outside, the procedure of the natural sciences, is needed to examine the body. When you imagine a friend's face, you are observing from the inside; when you are actually observing your friend's face you are observing it from the outside. The image is within, the face is outside. Second, Descartes anticipated the distinction between private conscious experience and publicly observed behavior as the subject matter for psychology. Should psychology study feelings of anger (e.g., a sense of rage) or angry behavior (e.g., a temper tantrum), or both? Third, Descartes recognized the significance of the problem of the relationship between mind (conscious experience) and body (behavior). Although his proposed solution, based upon the activities of the pineal gland, has only historical interest, the problem itself is still significant and still a source of controversy.

Johann Friedrich Herbart

To become an independent science, psychology first had to be conceived as one. Credit for this notion is usually given to Johann Friedrich Herbart (1776–1841), a German philosopher, who encouraged the view that psychology is a science independent of philosophy and physiology. Two of his books, A Textbook of Psychology (1816–1891) and Psychology as a Science (1824–1825) were instrumental in getting his views accepted. Problems of psychology had been discussed and analyzed long before Herbart appeared on the scene, but it was Herbart who vigorously and persuasively argued for the separation of psychology from other disciplines.[1]

Herbart was designated the "father of psychology" but few modern psychologists would award him such a title. Although acknowledging Herbart's influence on establishing an independent science of psychology, most psychologists would now question his paternity; he never did anything to make psychology a science except to suggest that it could be one. Although endorsing an empirical approach to psychology, Herbart himself failed to do any research. His psychology was a product of armchair speculation, not of empirical investigations. At best, Herbart deserves the title, "grandfather of psychology." He fathered the thought that fathered the action of creating an independent science of psychology.

In spite of the lack of an empirical foundation to his system, Herbart influenced subsequent psychologists in four ways. First, he conceptualized psychology as the science of consciousness, thus steering psychology in the direction of a mental science. Second, he thought of mental events as being analogous to forces that interact with each other. Sometimes these interactions between mental events, such as feelings and desires, force an idea below or above the threshold of consciousness. That is, an idea could be pushed into the unconscious or released from the unconscious to appear in consciousness. Those familiar with Freudian theory will recognize Herbart's anticipation of this fundamental psychoanalytic notion. Herbart's third influence on scientific psychology

---

[1]Johann Nicolaus Tetens (1736–1805), a German philosopher, also argued for the independence of psychology. He had less influence on the early psychologists than Herbart did. Consequently Herbart is usually given the credit for advancing the idea of an independent discipline of psychology.

FIGURE 2.2 Johann Friedrich Herbart

Dan McIntosh

emerged from his effort to mathematize the interaction of ideas in consciousness. Although his mathematical interpretation has no value because it lacked an empirical foundation, the notion that mental events, like physical phenomena, could be represented mathematically encouraged a quantitative orientation among many subsequent psychologists. Herbart's fourth and final contribution was accomplished indirectly. He denied that psychology could be an experimental science. Once this idea was asserted, it was bound to be challenged.

Psychophysics

Psychophysics is an excellent term because it defines itself. *Psycho*, mental; *physics*, physical: psychophysics is the study of the relations between mental and physical processes. Two German scholars—one a physiologist, the other an odd and versatile intellectual—were responsible for guaranteeing psychophysics an important place in the science of psychology.

Ernst Weber. Ernst Weber (1795–1878) discovered the first quantitative psychological law based on experimental results. By so doing, Weber

FIGURE 2.3   Ernst H. Weber

Dan McIntosh

produced a verdict on two of Herbart's claims: Psychology could be quantitative but not experimental. Weber's verdict supported the first claim while denying the second.

Weber was interested in discovering how sensitive humans are to differences between physical stimuli. In one experiment, a subject was required to lift successively two different weights and judge whether they felt equal or not. For example, a *standard* weight of 40 grams would be contrasted with a *comparison* weight. If the comparison weight is 40.001 grams, the subject will judge them to be the same. The difference between one thousandths of a gram is too fine for humans to detect. When the comparison weight is gradually increased a point will be reached, known as the difference threshold, at which the subject, more often than not, judges the comparison weight to be heavier. For most persons, this difference threshold would be reached when the comparison stimulus is approximately 41 grams.

Would you conclude from these data that you are sensitive to any weight difference of 1 gram? Upon reflection you would not; although you can discriminate between weights of 40 and 41 grams, you would not

be able to tell the difference between a sack of potatoes weighing 23 kilograms (approximately 50 pounds) and one weighing 23 kilograms and 1
gram. This example suggests that difference thresholds are relative, not
absolute values. Weber expressed this idea by formulating a law that
bears his name: *A stimulus must be increased by a constant fraction of its value
to be just noticeably different.*

According to Weber's law, if one gram is a sufficient addition to 40
grams to produce a just noticeable difference (j.n.d.), then 2 grams must
be added to 80 grams to produce a j.n.d., 3 grams must be added to 120
grams, 4 grams to 160 grams, and so forth. In all these cases, the difference threshold, the amount required to produce a sensation of a difference, is a constant fraction of the weight being judged:

$$1/40 \ = \ 2/80 \ = \ 3/120 \ = \ 4/160 \ = \ 5/200 \ = \ .025.$$

The above relationship can be summarized in the following simple
formula:

$$\frac{\Delta S}{S} = K$$

Where S represents the intensity of the stimulus (weight in the above
example), ΔS is the increment sufficient to produce a just noticeable difference, and K a constant. Table 2.1 reports a series of Weber's constants
for various sense modalities. The smaller the fraction, the greater the
sensitivity.

Weber's law suffers from a limitation. Although fairly valid for middle
ranges, the law tends to break down in the extremes when the intensity
of the stimulus is exceedingly high or low. Weber's constant is much
greater for exceptionally dim or bright lights than for lights of moderate
intensity. In other words, we are more sensitive to differences in light
intensities in the middle range than at the extremes.

Imperfections of Weber's law should not hide its tremendous historical importance. It demonstrated, beyond dispute, that psychology could
be both experimental and mathematical. The only question remaining after Weber's law was whether a combined experimental mathematical ap-

TABLE 2.1   Approximate Weber's Constants for Different Sense Modalities

Modality	Weber's Constant
Pitch of tone	1/333
Visual brightness	1/70
Loudness of a tone	1/11
Smell of rubber	1/10
Skin pressure	1/7
Taste of saline solution	1/5

FIGURE 2.4 Gustav Theodor Fechner

National Library of Medicine

proach could be applied successfully to all psychological problems or whether it was limited to a few special domains.

Gustav Theodor Fechner. At one time or another during his life-time, Gustav Theodor Fechner (1801–1887) was a physicist, physiologist, satirist, philosopher, mathematician, poet, and esthetician. Although he achieved prominence in his early thirties as a physicist, his intellectual curiosity led him away from physics to other fields of inquiry. As he approached forty he experienced a mid-life crisis brought on by an eye injury suffered while doing research on after-images. He had gazed at the sun through colored lenses to discover the visual sensations he would experience after turning away. (After-images can safely be observed by gazing at a lit bulb for several seconds and then glancing at a blank wall. An image of the bulb will be perceived in the absence of any direct stimulation.) Soon after his accident, Fechner became depressed and resigned his professorship.

Fechner's inquiring mind was redirected by his illness to broad philosophical and religious issues. He became convinced that the entire universe is fundamentally spiritual in nature. The physical world is a manifestation of this spiritual reality. The mind and body are not different from each other but instead are different aspects of a common unity, just as the inside and the outside of a circle represent different aspects of the same geometric form.

Fechner sought to validate these mystical speculations by scientific means. The validation could be accomplished, he thought, by formulating a mathematical statement of the relationship between mind and body. Basing his effort on psychophysical research similar to that reported by Weber, Fechner concluded that the relationship between the mind and body was like the mathematical relationship between the arithmetic series 1,2,3,4,5,6 . . . and the geometric series 1,2,4,8,16,32 . . . . Each number in the arithmetic series increases by one while the successive numbers of the geometric series double. Fechner assumed that mental intensities increase arithmetically while corresponding physical intensities increase geometrically. For example, as the physical intensity increases from 2 to 4 and from 4 to 8, the corresponding mental intensities change by only 1, from 2 to 3 and from 3 to 4.

Fechner's theory was expressed in his book *Elements of Psychophysics* which appeared in 1860 and was described as the "exact science of the functional . . . [relationship] . . . between body and mind" (Fechner 1860/1966). His conception of the mind-body relationship is summarized in the formula

$$S = K \log R$$

where S = sensation, K = a constant, and R = stimulus intensity (*Reiz* is German for stimulus). This formula states that sensation is proportional to the logarithm of the fundamental stimulus value. In essence, this means that mental sensations increase at a much slower rate than do corresponding physical intensities.

When judged in terms of his stated goal, Fechner's efforts must be considered a failure. He erred in believing that the empirical methods of science could confirm, or deny, the mystical view that the entire universe is an expression of a spiritual unity. Such a view can only be adopted on the basis of faith; it cannot be validated by empirical evidence. Subsequent generations of philosophers and psychologists realized this and exhibited no enthusiasm for, or even much interest in, Fechner's conception of the mind-body relationship.

Viewed within the context of the history of psychology, Fechner's efforts must be considered a success. One historian suggests that the publication of Fechner's *Elements of Psychophysics* in 1860 should mark the official birth of the science of psychology (Boring, 1950). After stripping the mystical notions from this book, the argument goes, a brilliant demonstration remains of a combined experimental quantitative approach to the functioning of human sensory systems. With imaginative research and sophisticated mathematics, Fechner described the relationship between human sensations and physical stimulation. The key to his success was based on the realization that a human being can be conceived as a measuring instrument just as a scale of weight can. After hefting two weights a person tells which is heavier. After weighing two weights a scale tells which is heavier. These two kinds of measurement—psychic measurement and physical measurement—provided the essential ingredients for a new science of psychometrics, that is, the measurement of mental events. The methods used in this new science later proved useful in the construction of a variety of psychological tests such as those that measured social attitudes and intellectual ability. Fechner's failure, however, to recognize the necessity of establishing an independent science of psychology deprived him of being acknowledged the "father of psychology."

Experimental Physiology

Experimental psychology emerged from experimental physiology. Wundt trained with Johannes Müeller (1801–1858), "the father of experimental physiology," and later worked in the laboratory of one of the greatest nineteenth century scientists, Hermann L. F. von Helmholtz (1821–1894), who made brilliant contributions to both physiology and physics.

The importance of experimental physiology is illustrated in the name Wundt coined, *physiological psychology,* to represent the new science of experimental psychology. Wundt used the term physiological psychology primarily to designate a psychology that employed the experimental methods of physiology, believing that "psychology was a science only to the degree that it employed methods and approaches like those a physiologist would use" (Hearst, 1979). The early work in sensory psychology resembled, in many ways, the research of Helmholtz when studying the experimental physiology of seeing and hearing. The term *physiological psychology* is also consistent with Wundt's view that a complete psychology had to relate mental events to physiological processes.

WUNDTIAN PSYCHOLOGY

Wilhelm Wundt, the founder of the independent science of psychology, has become one of its most controversial figures. According to one historian, Wundt "is the most misunderstood of all important psychologists" (Leahey, 1980).

The blame for this confusion is not entirely the fault of those historians who misrepresent Wundt's position. Unfortunately, Wundt himself contributed to the misunderstanding by an ambiguous writing style, compounded by a penchant for changing theoretical positions.

Wundt, even before the days of "publish or perish," was a prodigious writer; his bibliography contains approximately 500 publications spanning a variety of fields (e.g., experimental psychology, social psychology, physiology, anthropology, ethics, language, mathematics, philosophy, and law). Wundt's shifting positions and range of interests makes it difficult, if not impossible, to simply describe Wundtian psychology.

An added source of difficulty stems from the conflict between American culture and the intellectual climate of nineteenth century Germany from which Wundt emerged. The American tradition is to simplify scientific issues and to search for practical applications. In contrast, the German Zeitgeist, at the time of Wundt, was to deliberately ignore, if not reject, practical considerations while simultaneously viewing all scientific problems within a broad, complex, philosophical framework, covering such topics as the meaning and purpose of human existence.

Listing these difficulties is not intended to discourage or frighten, but instead to indicate the problems ahead. The history of psychology might have been easier to comprehend if it began with a simple coherent conception of psychology, but it did not. Discussing Wundt initially does have the advantage of introducing many complex issues that will be repeatedly met in the history of psychology.

Wilhelm Wundt (1832–1920)

Wilhelm Wundt, a child of a Lutheran pastor, was born in 1832 in Neckarau, a suburb of Mannheim, located in the southwest part of Germany. His childhood was supervised by his father's vicar with whom he established a much closer relationship than with his parents. Education, plus much daydreaming, not friendships or play, dominated his early years. At thirteen he attended a Gymnasium, a German secondary school, that rigorously prepared a student for a university education. By the time he was nineteen, Wundt was not only ready for a university education but also for the life of a scholar. He read extensively and began to develop an independence of mind that characterized his entire professional life.

Wundt decided to become a physician partly because of the need to earn a living. In addition to studying anatomy, physiology, physics, chemistry, and some clinical medicine, Wundt, at the age of twenty-one, published his first research project in the field of human physiology. He received his M.D. from the University of Heidelberg in 1855, summa cum laude. Nevertheless, a strong aversion to the practice of medicine led him to go to the University of Berlin to study

---

FIGURE 2.5 Wilhelm Wundt

National Library of Medicine

physiology. When he was twenty-four, Wundt suffered a severe illness that kept him close to death for several weeks. In this time of crisis he developed his views about philosophy, religion, and the mind. In 1857, he received an appointment to teach physiology at the University of Heidelberg where he remained for seventeen years, during which time he published numerous research papers and books and shifted his interest from physiology to the psychological problems of sensation and perception.

During his early years at Heidelberg, Wundt established his own private psychological laboratory. His first experiment, with his wife Sophie serving as subject, was designed to test whether it was possible to attend simultaneously to two different events (p. 28). During his final years at Heidelberg, Wundt's *Principles of Physiological Psychology* was published, and it proved to be a popular and influential book. It went through six editions (1873–1911) and contributed to establishing psychology as an independent science.

Wundt left Heidelberg in 1874 for Zürich but stayed there only a year. The following year he accepted an invitation to a chair of philosophy at the University of Leipzig. Here he stopped teaching physiology and divided his lecturing between psychology and philosophy, with the latter subject being taught with a psychological slant. His psychological courses ranged from *general psychology* to the special topics of *cultural psychology, language,* and the *psychological interpretations of the cortex.*

After arriving in Leipzig in 1875, Wundt was assigned an old, unused auditorium for laboratory space. The first experiment, by one of his students, to be published from this laboratory was begun in 1879, and therefore Wundt chose this date as the founding of his psychological laboratory. In 1897, the University of Leipzig, in recognition of Wundt's accomplishment and his international reputation, opened a spacious psychological laboratory in a specially designed new building.

Wundt's involvement in the laboratory gradually declined in the 1880s, leaving the actual supervision to his leading students. One reason was that his extensive writing, including his attempts to systematize psychology, required an enormous amount of time. Another reason was his conviction that not all psychological questions could be answered by experimental investigations. The human mind, he believed, is an outgrowth of historical forces, particularly those that result from cultural influences. Therefore, a complete psychology should depend as much on historical and social analyses as on experimental methods. This view was expanded in a ten-volume work entitled *Völkerpsychologie,* roughly translated as *ethnic* or *cultural* psychology.

Although Wundt retired from teaching in 1917 at the age of eighty-five, he continued to work on his *Völkerpsychologie* and his autobiography. In 1920 the last volume of *Völkerpsychologie* was published and on August 23 of that year Wundt completed his autobiography. He died eight days later.

METHODOLOGICAL ASSUMPTIONS

Because Wundt was the first representative of the young science of psychology, his methodological position automatically became the standard for the new discipline. Students from all over the world flocked to Leipzig to learn about the new psychology. Many of them returned to their home countries to establish their own psychological laboratories. How they perceived and evaluated Wundt's conception of psychology determined how psychology would be taught and practiced in its new environment. Thus, the methodological foundation of Wundtian psychology is not only important in its own right but also as a point of departure for the changes in psychology that would inevitably take place.

The Subject Matter of Psychology

Although controversy is rife about Wundt's conception of psychology, one fundamental point is clear. For him, psychology was a science of the *mind*, of *conscious experience*. Unfortunately, this simple definition is insufficient. *Mind* or *conscious experience* can be interpreted in a number of ways and therefore it becomes necessary to understand what Wundt meant.

Wundt assumed that consciousness at a given moment can be experienced in two different ways, directly and indirectly. Consider looking at the moon in the sky. When experienced directly, the moon produces a *subjective* pattern of sensations and feelings. One might directly sense a flat, yellowish surface, while feeling relaxed. An indirect experience of the moon is achieved by eliminating all subjective factors from consciousness; the moon is experienced *objectively* by its shape, position in the sky, and the intensity of the light reflected.

The difference between direct and indirect experience was expressed in Wundt's distinction between *immediate* and *mediate experience*. The former is, in Wundt's words, "the content of psychological experience in its immediate nature, unmodified by abstraction and reflection" (Wundt, 1897). The immediate experience of looking at a table is a pattern of sensations uninfluenced by the knowledge that it is a piece of furniture with a particular function. The mediate experience of a table would be influenced by the conception of tables, including their physical and social properties.

It is important to recognize that Wundt does not deny the assumption that all sciences, physics as well as psychology, have their roots in observation, the "facts of experience." Instead, he claims, mental experience can be sensed in two different ways: It can be observed directly (immediate experience) or indirectly (mediate experience). The former, immediate experience, is the object of inquiry in psychology, while the latter, mediate experience, is the observational base of physics and other natural sciences.

Preconceptions about Immediate Experience. A scientist is commonly believed to have a completely open mind about the subject of his inquiry. If one seeks to understand the nature of immediate experience, then one merely investigates it. But it is impossible to investigate a problem without some guiding notions. Without them, a scientist would not know where to begin or what to do.

Wundt's research and theorizing were guided by four beliefs about the nature of consciousness. First, consciousness is not a stable substance that could be carefully and precisely examined. Instead, "conscious contents are at the opposite pole from permanent objects; they are processes, fleeting occurrences, in continual flux and change" (Wundt, 1910). Second, the mind is not a single homogenous whole but instead is divided into different psychical processes (e.g., sensing, feeling, thinking, language). Third, mental events cannot be reduced to physiological events, even though there is a physiological substrate to conscious experience. A feeling of depression is different from the biochemical conditions to which the feeling is correlated. Fourth, mental events occur in a lawful fashion and consequently it should be possible to formulate general principles that govern their occurrence.

Methods of Investigation

No major psychologist in the history of psychology used as many diverse methods to investigate psychological phenomena as did Wundt. His three major methods were introspection, experimentation, and historical analysis.

Introspection. Introspection, the observation and reporting of conscious experience, can be done in many different ways (Danzinger, 1980a). The early psychologists disagreed strongly among themselves about the proper method for introspection. Wundt, of all the psychologists, argued for the most stringent requirements. If they were not met, he argued, a distorted picture of the consciousness would inevitably result.

The key to understanding Wundt's views about introspection is contained in his insistence that the observation of consciousness in the psychological laboratory should strive to be as accurate as the observation of physical events in the physics laboratory. Observations of inner life, "inner perceptions," he thought, could, in principle, be as valid as perceptions of the outer world, if they took place under analogous conditions, when the observer is properly trained and the experimental situation is repeatable.

Proper training to ensure that a valid description of consciousness is obtained requires that the introspector be capable of distinguishing immediate experience from mediate experience. That is, the "fleeting occurrences" of consciousness must be observed from the psychological perspective, not from a physical orientation. In addition, the mental event must be reported as it is experienced, not as it is remembered. When a physicist records the position of a pointer on a gauge he does not trust his memory. He records the reading while the gauge is in front of him. Similarly, the introspector must be trained to report observations of mental events that are presently in consciousness instead of those that have gone into memory.

Wundt insisted that valid observations could take place only under rigorously controlled conditions. The logic of Wundt's position was that a person's mental content could be controlled by exposing the person to a constant source of physical stimulation. For example, if an introspector was repeatedly stimulated by a particular physical stimulus (e.g., a 2,000 cycle tone, a metronome beating thirty times per minute) then the mental events produced by the physical stimulus could be repeatedly observed. The significant question is whether Wundt was justified in assuming that a constant source of physical stimulation would always produce the same mental event.

Experimentation and historical analysis. In spite of Wundt's conviction that accurate introspection is possible, he rejected the notion that the only data that psychology required was introspective evidence. By insisting that valid introspective evidence could be obtained only in an experimental situation in which the introspector was exposed to a specific *physical* stimulus, Wundt effectively eliminated from self-observation those mental processes, like thinking and language, that are not directly controlled by physical stimulation. Wundt's position about introspection led to two possible alternatives: Either psychology was limited to the investigation of those mental processes that could be studied by introspection or other methods had to be employed. Wundt chose the latter alternative.

To study mental processes outside the scope of introspection, Wundt suggested that laboratory experiments and historical analysis could be used even though they did not provide the same kind of information as did introspection. Introspection *directly* revealed mental processes while laboratory experiments and historical analyses provided information from which the nature of mental events could be *inferred*. For example, the question of how voluntary actions take place (e.g., moving your finger) cannot be fully answered by observing "fleeting occurrences" in consciousness. Instead, objective evidence in the form of the time it takes for a person to initiate action can be used as the basis for inferring the nature of mental processes involved in voluntary actions. Similarly, the development of language or religion cannot be studied by introspection, or even experimentation, but instead must be considered from the viewpoint of cultural history which is capable of revealing the responsible psychic structures.

Criterion of Truth

Scientific truth has two distinct facets, observational truth and theoretical truth. Are the observations accurate? Are the theoretical interpretations valid? The problem of observational accuracy does not present the physical or biological scientists with any great difficulty. The reason is that physical or biological events (e.g., the amount of air pressure, electrical activity in the brain) can be observed by many scientists. Consensual agreement among scientists about the accuracy of an observation (e.g., the location of the pointer in the pressure gauge, the electroencephalogram record) is usually easy to achieve. Observational accuracy presents a special problem for psychology when it is conceived as the science of the mind. Mental events can only be observed by one person, the individual who is experiencing them. How do you know that the introspective reports are accurate? As just noted, Wundt assumed that a veridical (true) description of consciousness was possible *if* introspection was carried on by a trained observer in an experimental situation in which physical stimulation could be repeatedly presented.

Wundt never directly addressed himself to the complex problem of defining the criterion of theoretical truth. From his writings, one can infer that the criterion of truth employed for experimental psychology differed from that used in cultural history. The interpretation of experimental results was to be judged by the deductive model of explanation. A theoretical hypothesis was considered valid if it generated logical predictions that agreed with obtained results.

Wundt's interpretation of cultural phenomena, such as the development of language and religion, did not lead to any clear-cut empirical predictions that could be precisely evaluated. Therefore, the validity of his conjectures could not be judged by the deductive model of explanation. What, then, encouraged Wundt to believe his hypothesis to be true? First, Wundt considered his interpretation to be an intuitively convincing description of mental processes involved in cultural phenomena. Second, his social psychological theory was consistent with his earlier conception of the mind that was based upon the results of introspection and experimentation. In sum, intuitive knowing and interpretive consistency, standards frequently employed in human science, were used as criteria by Wundt to evaluate his cultural psychology.

STRATEGY

As the leader of the new science of psychology, Wundt suffered from the disadvantage of being unable to plan a strategy in the light of the successes and failures of his predecessors. In addition, unlike most of his successors, he did not restrict his strategy to one particular field of psychology. Wundt's concerns were broad, ranging from the psychology of sensation to social psychology. He responded to his self-imposed challenge by borrowing strategic orientations that were popular in the natural sciences while simultaneously adopting other tactics that served the special needs of a human science. It should be noted that when Wundt described psychology as "a new domain of science" he did not mean that psychology was just another natural science comparable to physics, chemistry, and biology. Instead he meant that psychology was a new kind of science possessing features that were shared with the natural sciences but having other characteristics that set psychology apart.

Wundt borrowed from the natural sciences a combined analytic-synthetic strategy and a strong commitment to formulate a general theory.

He was interested in both analytical and synthetic questions about the mind: what the basic components of the mind are and what principles govern their combination.

Gathering facts from introspection, experimentation, and cultural history represented only the first step for Wundt in his scientific effort. Facts had to be organized into a coherent theory of the mind. A debate raged during the time of Wundt, as it does today, about the content of a satisfactory theory of the mind. Many psychologically oriented scientists of Wundt's day assumed a materialist position, that the workings of the mind could only be understood by identifying the underlying neurophysiological causes of mental events. Psychological phenomena, for them, must be reduced to material events, specifically to changes in matter. Wundt rejected this materialist and reductionist position. He believed in "psychic causality," finding the causes of mental events in previous mental events.

Consider the simple case of a word association task. You are instructed to respond to a word with the first word that comes to your mind. If the stimulus word is *chair*, you are likely to respond with the word *table*. The two mental events—*chair* and *table*—have a dependent relationship. Wundt was essentially arguing that the mind is an organized system that could be studied independently of neurophysiology. Wundt was not saying that mental events are unrelated to neurophysiological processes but rather that they could be studied independently of material events. Mental events, by themselves, are lawful.

Perhaps the dominant feature of Wundt's strategy was its intrinsic diversity. It supported a natural science approach while recognizing its limitations in the field of social psychology. While emphasizing the significance of experimentation for psychology, Wundt acknowledged that it was inadequate for the task of revealing all aspects of mental phenomena such as language. He was essentially arguing that an appropriate strategy for psychologists to pursue should be based on the recognition that psychology is a hybrid discipline, representing a combination of a natural science and a human science.

WUNDTIAN THEORY

Wundt's theory of psychology cannot be described in any simple integrated fashion. The main reason is that the formulation was exceedingly complex and the relationship between hypothesis and data was, at times, unclear. The secondary reason, already noted, is that Wundt's theory was continually being modified, sometimes making it difficult to identify its basic principles.

Although Wundt expounded the view that psychological theory must be based upon a foundation of facts, he sometimes ignored his own advice by indulging in pure armchair speculation in the absence of any guiding empirical evidence. Titchener (1921a) attributed Wundt's lack of concern with data to his "imperative need to systematize the unripe."

Wundt continually changed his theoretical position, which is, in itself not a fault. Modifications of a theory are demanded by empirical and rational considerations. Wundt, however, constantly modified his theory without justifying the changes, so much so, that William James (Chapter 4), an early admirer, finally expressed exasperation about the inability to pin down Wundt's conception. James finally concluded that Wundtian theory contained many parts, without a central core. He likened it to a worm that had been cut into several fragments each of which crawled by itself, thus making it impossible to deal with Wundt's theory "all at once."

Therefore, several parts of Wundtian theory will be described as they each relate to a specific research area: reaction time and the measurement of mental processes, the content of consciousness, and social psychology. When this exposition is completed, an attempt will be made to describe the major principles of Wundtian theory.

Reaction Time and the Measurement of Mental Processes

The reaction time method which originated in physiology has had an immense impact on psychology. Hermann von Helmholtz (p. 19) developed a method to test the prevailing notion that nerve conduction occurred too rapidly to be measured. He tested this conjecture by investigating neural transmission in a motor nerve of the frog, a nerve that transmits neural impulses from the central nervous system to a muscle. The motor nerve was electrically stimulated at two different distances from the muscle. The time interval between the stimulation and the muscular contraction was measured. This time interval, the reaction time, was slightly longer when the nerve was stimulated from a greater distance. Knowledge of the distance between two points of stimulation and the difference in reaction times of the muscles enables the computation of the speed of neural transmission which, in this particular case, was 26 meters per second.

If reaction time could be employed to measure the speed of neural events, Wundt reasoned that it could also be used to measure the speed of mental events. He experimented on *the fastest thought* at Heidelberg several years before he established the first psychological laboratory at Leipzig. The study was labeled a *complication experiment* because it complicated the simple reaction time procedure in which the time intervening between stimulus presentation (e.g., a sound of a bell) and a response (e.g., releasing a telegraph key) is measured. In Wundt's study the subject, instead of responding to a single stimulus, had to respond to two. The subject was required to judge the position of a pointer moving at a constant rate across a calibrated scale at the exact time a bell sounded. If it were possible to think of these two ideas simultaneously then the subject should be able to see the position of the pointer at the exact time the bell sounded. The task is analogous to that of a baseball umpire at first base who has to decide whether the foot of the batter touched the base before or after the ball reached the fielder's glove.

Wundt reported that one cannot attend to two different events simultaneously. The subject initially attended to the bell and then shifted attention to the pointer. During this brief period of shifting attention the pointer moved a short distance. The time taken for a pointer to move from its position at the time the bell sounded, to the position at which it was detected, was one-eighth of a second. Wundt proudly announced to the word that *the fastest thought* occurred in one-eighth of a second. He also concluded that his findings could answer an age-old question that interested Aristotle: "Is it possible to think of two thoughts at once?" Wundt wrote that "consciousness holds only a single thought, a single perception. When it appears as if we have several percepts simultaneously, we are deceived by their quick succession" (Diamond, 1980a).

Wundt overstated his case. He demonstrated only that a subject, under certain conditions, could not respond to two percepts simultaneously. All thoughts need not operate as do percepts of a moving pointer and a sound of the bell. Research done later at Leipzig with a different experimental design suggested that humans could attend to several thoughts simultaneously (Leahey, 1980). The historical significance of Wundt's early complication experiment, however, does not stem from the result obtained but instead from the demonstration that an objective experimental analysis of mental processes is possible.

Franciscus Cornelius Donders (1818–1889), a Dutch physiologist, developed superior procedures for complication experiments that were subsequently adopted in Wundt's laboratory in Leipzig. Donders's research methods, known as mental chronometry, were based on three assumptions: mental acts, like physiological acts (e.g., heart beat) take time; complicated reaction times are the sum of the times of individual mental acts that are involved; and by the method of subtraction, it becomes possible to estimate the time required for any individual mental act.

Mental chronometry can be illustrated by the following example: A subject is presented with a *simple* reaction-time problem in which a telegraph key must be released as soon as a red light appears. The average reaction time in this situation is 200 milliseconds (a millisecond, abbreviated as ms, is one thousandth of a second). The subject is then confronted with a *choice* reaction problem in which one telegraph key must be released with the left hand when a red light goes on and another key must be released with the right hand when a green light appears. The average reaction time now is 288 ms. In the simple reaction time the subjects only respond to the stimulus while in the choice reaction time two additional mental acts are added: stimulus categorization (Is the light red or green?) and response selection (Should I respond with my right or left hand?). By subtracting the simple reaction time (200 ms) from the choice reaction time (288 ms) an estimate can be made (88 ms) of the time required for stimulus categorization plus response selection. By additional complications of the reaction time method, plus the subtractive procedure, stimulus categorization was estimated to be 46 ms, while response selection required 42 ms (Woodworth, 1938).

Wundt planned to systematically extend Donders's method of mental chronometry to the entire gamut of mental processes. The simple reaction time was to serve as a baseline. The procedure was to be complicated a step at a time so that the time required for each successive mental act could be ascertained.

Reporting the results of Wundt's research program on mental chronometry must be delayed for a brief excursion into two core conceptions of his theoretical position: apperception and voluntarism. The significance of Wundt's research program in mental chronometry can then be fully appreciated.

Apprehension, Apperception, and Voluntary Behavior. Wundt did not conceive of simple reaction time as consisting of only one mental act. Three successively occurring mental processes are involved: admitting the sensory impression (e.g., a red light) into consciousness (apprehension), focusing attention on the sensory impression (apperception), and voluntarily releasing the reaction (voluntary behavior). When a sensory impression is admitted into consciousness, known as *apprehension*, the impression is sensed but not clearly perceived. When attention is focused on the impression, known as *apperception*, the clarity of the mental impression is enhanced. Thus, according to Wundt, there are two zones of consciousness: a background zone where mental events are sensed or registered (apprehended) and a zone of focal consciousness where events are apperceived, that is, clearly perceived.

You can demonstrate to yourself the difference between apprehension and apperception. Focus on the letter c in apperception. The zone that immediately surrounds the letter c is apperceived; the letters within this zone can be identified. They are in the zone of focal clarity. The adjacent zone contains letters that are apprehended; they can be seen but not identified. You see black markings which you know are letters but not which ones. Events that fall outside of both zones are below the threshold of consciousness; the observer is unconscious of them.

A key assumption in Wundt's system is that apperception, in contrast to apprehension, is not a passive registration of stimulation. Apperception requires an *act of will*, an intent to pay attention. If you return to the task of focusing on the letter c in apperception and persist in attending to the letter c, you will experience some strain in keeping your attention from shifting elsewhere. Wundt's position was essentially that the focal clarity in consciousness that results from apperception can be achieved only by the active participation of the observer.

Wundt's third assumption in his analysis of a simple reaction time, namely, that the reaction is voluntarily released, stresses the importance of conscious control of behavior. Whereas involuntary behavior, such as withdrawing a finger from a hot surface, does not involve conscious intent, voluntary behavior always does.

A philosopher friend of Wundt thought that Wundt's emphasis on conscious intent in apperception and in the control of behavior was so predominant that he suggested *Voluntarism* as a name for Wundtian psychology. *Voluntarism* is a philosophical term that stresses the importance of will, the transformation of an idea into action. It is an appropriate name for Wundtian psychology because Wundt repeatedly acknowledged the significance of wishes and desires—what some would call motives—in human experience.

Wundt's research program in mental chronometry. Soon after the Leipzig laboratory opened in 1879, a research program involving both experimentation and introspection was initiated to measure the speed with which different mental acts were executed (e.g., discriminating between two stimuli, the moment when an idea made its appearance in consciousness). Evidence was soon obtained that cast suspicion on two of Wundt's fundamental assumptions: (1) A subject in a simple reaction time experiment apperceives the sensory impression from the signal and voluntarily releases the reaction, and (2) During complicated reaction time problems the mind operates with an invariant order of mental acts each of which requires a specific time.

In a simple reaction time problem, James McKeen Cattell, Wundt's first American student, frequently found it impossible to detect any experience of apperceiving the signal or willing the reaction. A reaction to a stimulus in a simple reaction time study appeared to him to be no different from a response in a sensory-motor reflex (e.g., withdrawing a finger from a hot surface). In both cases the input (the stimulus) triggers the output (the response) with no intervening conscious activity. Both appear automatic.

According to Wundt's interpretation of complicated reaction time problems, adding an additional mental act to a set of existing ones should increase the reaction time. However, the opposite sometimes occurred; an added complication produced a faster reaction time suggesting that the subject did not attach a new mental act to a chain of existing ones but instead reacted in an entirely new way. These data support the notion that the human mind can operate flexibly to complicated reaction time problems rather than in rigid step-by-step fashion. If true, this would prevent the identification of a fixed sequence of mental acts and the estimation of the duration of each.

Perhaps Cattell's failure to detect mental events that corresponded to Wundt's analysis of a simple reaction was a consequence of introspection being too insensitive to the "fleeting occurrences" in consciousness. If experimental procedures superior to introspection were used, support might be gained for Wundt's contention that the subject apperceives the stimulus and wills the response in a simple reaction time problem. This possibility gained credence from studies that compared simple reaction times of subjects who were either paying attention to the impending stimulus or to the intended response.

Imagine yourself a subject in a simple reaction time problem in which you have to release your finger from a telegraph key as soon as you hear a tone. Should you focus your attention on the tone or on the reaction? An analogous problem is faced by a sprinter on the starting block. Should the sprinter fixate on the starter's gun or on getting off the block as fast as possible? Paying attention to the impending stimulus is called the *sensorial attitude*, while focusing on the response is the *muscular attitude*. A muscular attitude in Wundt's laboratory resulted in reaction times being about 100 ms faster than the sensorial attitude.

Wundt explained these results by suggesting that the sensorial attitude gave a complete reaction because the stimulus (tone) was apperceived, while during the muscular attitude the stimulus was only apprehended. That is, the mental act of consciously attending (apperceiving) to the stimulus was essentially bypassed when the subject assumed a muscular attitude. The subject with the muscular attitude only had to will his response. Because the sensorial attitude produced a reaction time 100 ms slower than the muscular attitude, Wundt concluded that apperception occurred in about 100 ms.

Believing now that the simple reaction was fully understood, Wundt proceeded with the mental chronometry research program. Results from the sensorial attitude were to serve as a baseline for more complicated reactions. It soon became apparent, however, that this plan was not going to work. Many subjects could not maintain a sensorial attitude. Others who thought they could found themselves unsure as to whether they were only sensing the tone (apprehending) or fully recognizing (apperceiving) it. Some subjects who tried to maintain the sensorial attitude found that with continuing practice they uncontrollably shifted to a muscular attitude. Questions were raised, even in the Leipzig laboratory, whether a pure sensorial or muscular attitude must both sense the stimulus and react to it. The controversy surrounding the psychological reality of the sensorial attitude exacted a toll in the reaction times obtained. They varied tremendously, and it soon became apparent that they were too unstable to serve as the baseline for the mental chronometry research program. In addition, evidence continued to be collected questioning the major assumption of mental chronometry that, in complicated reaction time problems, the human mind operates in a rigid step-by-step fashion. Because of these difficulties, Wundt's research program in mental chronometry ultimately failed. Wundt never discovered a set of distinct mental acts each of which required a particular time span.

Failures in science are never complete; some positive contributions always result. Wundt's mental chronometry research program demonstrated that mental processes could be analyzed by experimental techniques even though an adequate theory was not forthcoming; mental processes could be inferred from two sources, introspective evidence and behavior; and data from introspective reports and from the behavior of the subjects does not always agree about underlying mental processes. This discrepancy challenged subsequent psychologists to discover the relative merits of each kind of evidence in revealing the nature of mental processes.

The Content of Consciousness

Of what does consciousness consist? Global experiences that cannot be analyzed? Or is immediate experience capable of being reduced to a set of elementary events? Not surprisingly, Wundt, with a background in physiology, a discipline that had demonstrated that complex systems can be analyzed into elementary processes, concluded that within immediate experience were the irreducible "elements of the mental life." These basic psychical processes were of two kinds, *sensations* and *feelings*.

Basic Processes of Mental Life. Sensations were raw, elementary sensory experiences devoid of any meaning. They were termed "objective elements of the mental life" because they could be initiated by events in the physical world. A light wave of 555 nanometers (a nanometer is a billionth of a meter) produces a sensation of yellow-green, while an ice cube results in a sensation of cold. Feelings accompanied sensations "as their subjective complements, and are referred not to external things but to the state of consciousness itself" (Wundt, 1910).

Two problems are immediately generated by a theory that analyzes a complex state, like consciousness, into elementary events. How is the analysis executed? How do the elementary events combine to form the complex state? In response to the first question Wundt noted that irreducible psychical events, such as basic sensations and feelings, do not appear in consciousness in an "uncompounded state." Instead, they must be abstracted by skilled introspectors in an experimental situation.

For the time being, the concern with problems of synthesis, that is, how the elementary mental events are combined into complex psychical states, will be limited only to examples. According to Wundt, an idea represents a combination of sensations, that is, sensations are the "ultimate and irreducible elements of ideas." The idea of a chair is some combination of sensations of lines, color, hardness, and so forth. Similarly we experience "complex feelings" or "emotions" as combinations of elementary feelings.

Sensations. Although Wundt considered sensations as "objective" mental events because they are triggered by sensory stimulation, he did not believe that their occurrence in consciousness depended exclusively upon physical stimulation. A memory image of blue for example, "is, oftentimes, weaker and more transient than the image of direct perception. But this difference is by no means constant; we may sense in dreams, or in the state of hallucination, as intensively as we sense under the operation of actual sensory stimuli" (Wundt, 1910). Note that Wundt is denying any psychical distinction between a sensation from a physical stimulus (e.g., a light wave of 480 nm) and a memory image of having experienced that sensation. He was interested only in describing mental events and for that task the manner in which the event got into consciousness is irrelevant.

Although sensations are not necessarily dependent on physical stimulation, as just noted, sensory experience could most easily be investigated by relating it to physical stimulation. The most common type of research conducted in Wundt's laboratory at Leipzig was psychophysical in nature; relating psychical events with physical events. A list of the major psychophysical research topics investigated in the Leipzig laboratory includes the psychophysics of vision and audition (how visual and auditory experiences are related to physical properties of light and sound), color contrast (discovering the laws that govern the tendency for hues to induce their complementary color in neighboring areas; e.g., a gray patch surrounded by blue will look yellowish while the same gray enveloped by yellow will appear bluish), time sense (the experience of passage of time as a function of different time periods and events within the interval, e.g., a filled versus empty interval, auditory versus visual stimulation, rhythmic versus nonrhythmic events) (Boring, 1942).

Concluding that sensations are one of the two irreducible processes of the mind leaves one question unanswered. Do different sensations, such as tone and color, share any common properties? That is, are there any common dimensions of experience that all sensations have? Wundt concluded that all sensations could be described in terms of two attributes of experience, quality and intensity. Quality refers to the nature of the experience (e.g., color, pitch), while intensity denotes its strength. Sensations of a particular tone and a color would differ in their quality but nevertheless could have a similar intensity. Sensations of different blues would have the same quality but not necessarily the same intensity.

Feelings.   Sensations always occur within a context of feelings. "Sensations and feelings are, always and everywhere, complementary constituents of our mental experiences." Like sensations, feelings also have attributes. Wundt postulated a tridimensional theory of feeling which held that all feelings could, in an experimental situation, be introspectively analyzed and classified on three dimensions: *pleasantness-unpleasantness, excitement-calm,* and *strain-relaxation.* Just as an object (e.g., a bulb in a floor lamp) can be located by specifying its position in relation to the length, width, and height of a room so could any feeling be described in terms of its position on the three dimensions of pleasantness-unpleasantness, excitement-calm, and strain-relaxation. To be specific, a feeling of affection could be described as moderately pleasant, mildly relaxing, and halfway between the extremes of excitement and calm.

The tridimensional theory could be, and has been, perceived in two different ways: as a direct description of affective experiences in consciousness or as an abstract theory of how affective processes operate in the mind. The evidence collected by introspective analyses of feelings failed to consistently support Wundt's tridimensional theory or any other formulation (Woodworth, 1938). Some introspectors denied the existence of feelings as an elementary mental event; for them the feelings of pleasantness, strain, and so on were complexes of sensations. Others insisted that feelings only ranged over one dimension from pleasantness to unpleasantness. The other two dimensions in Wundt's theory for these introspectors were not truly dimensions of feelings but instead were patterns of organic and kinesthetic sensations. In contrast, other introspective studies, mainly from Wundt's laboratory and those of some of his students, provided data consistent with the tridimensional theory of feeling.

Theoretical differences are common in science. However, empirical methods should be available to resolve the differences; to determine which if any of the competing formulations has truth value, evidence consistent with the theory. The argument as to whether the earth was round or flat was decided by a large amount of empirical evidence including, in recent years, photographs from satellites. Were the differences in theories of feelings amenable to empirical resolution? Is a valid picture of feelings in consciousness as obtainable as an accurate picture of the shape of the earth? Different cameras in different positions can take pictures of the earth, and if for some reason they provide different information about the shape of the earth, the cameras can be independently checked to determine whether they produce distorted images. What independent evidence can be obtained to decide whether feelings are basically complex sensations, or whether all feelings can be represented along a single dimension or require three dimensions? How can the psychologist decide among three groups of observers each of which report different observations of their own feelings? Because these observations are available only to the experiencing observer they cannot be checked by others. Consequently, no independent means are available to determine which set of observations are valid. When theories of conscious experience depend exclusively on self reports, proponents of competing viewpoints can accuse their opponents of employing defective methods of introspection, in which they are not accurately observing the contents of consciousness. Such criticisms could not help resolve the disagreement for the simple reason that no one could prove that their own observations of mental events are more accurate than others.

Introspective reports apparently depended upon the laboratory in which they were obtained. Self-observation conducted in Wundt's laboratory tended to yield findings consistent with the tridimensional theory of feeling while introspective evidence from other laboratories tended to be consistent with the theoretical views that prevailed there. Such findings suggest that what is observed in consciousness is not independent of the observer, even though Wundt maintained that it was. So when theories of feeling, such as Wundt's tridimensional formulation, were viewed solely in terms of introspective evidence, they could not be objectively evaluated and hence the controversy could not be resolved.

The argument can be advanced that Wundt's tridimensional theory was more of an abstract theory designed to make objective predictions than a description of mental events. The introspective evidences served as a source of suggestive ideas for a theory that would be capable of being objectively tested. Wundt used his tridimensional formulation to predict that three patterns of physiological conditions would be discovered that corresponded to his three dimensions of feelings. Again, the evidence failed to support his theoretical expectations.

The major contributions of the tridimensional theory of feeling were the problems it raised. Most important were the methodological questions about how the mind can and should be investigated. How can mental events be best understood—by a descriptive theory of the mind or by an abstract theory that generates deductions that can be objectively evaluated? Of secondary importance, the tridimensional theory directed attention to the psychological problem of emotion. What are the psychological characteristics of emotion, and how do affective processes interact with other processes such as cognition and volition (motivation)? These questions proved to be major ones in the history of psychology.

One legacy of the tridimensional theory is both suggestive and instructive. A striking parallel appeared between Wundt's formulation and the results of factor analytic studies of emotions (Schlosberg, 1954) and connotative meaning of words (Osgood, Suci & Tannenbaum, 1957). Factor analysis is a sophisticated statistical technique, developed in the 1920s and thus unavailable to Wundt, that analyzes complex phenomena into basic components. Facial expressions, presumably reflecting different emotions, were factor analyzed into three dimensions: *pleasantness-unpleasantness, high-low activations,* and *attention-rejection.* The connotative meaning of words, that is, their suggestive significance aside from their explicit meaning (e.g., the word *danger* denotes a threat and connotes something that is bad; *kitchen* denotes a room that is used for cooking and connotes something that is good), were analyzed into three basic dimensions: *good-bad, active-passive,* and *strong-weak.*

The similarity of the basic dimensions resulting from factor analysis of emotional reactions expressed through facial expressions and of connotative meaning of words to Wundt's three dimensions of feeling is striking. The three common dimensions of all three studies are *evaluative* (degree of pleasantness or goodness), *activity* (degree of action), and *potency* (level of concentration).

Do these results from studies occurring over fifty years after the tridimensional theory was initially proposed represent a historical coincidence or a delayed confirmation? At present we can only speculate. Perhaps future research and theorizing will be able to offer a definitive answer.

Social Psychology

Wundt's concern for social phenomena did not express a peripheral interest that was aroused late in life. Instead, from early life on he believed that the most important problem in both psychology and philosophy was to understand the relationship between individuals and society. He, himself, was actively engaged in politics, and at one time served as a representative to the legislature of the independent German state, Baden.

Wundt spent twenty years in writing the ten volumes of *Völkerpsychologie: Eine Untersuchung der Entwicklungsgesetz von Sprache, Mythus, und Sitte*, which can be translated as *Cultural Psychology: An Investigation of the Developmental Laws of Language, Myth, and Morality* (Blumenthal, 1975). The series "contains two books on language, three on myth and religion, one on art, two on society, one on law, and one on culture and history." *Völkerpsychologie* has been translated as *ethnic* or *cultural psychology*; if written today it might have been entitled *social psychology*.

The Relationship between Experimental and Ethnic Psychology. Wundt stated that the phenomena of ethnic psychology include "those mental products which are created by a community of human life and are, therefore, inexplicable in terms merely of individual consciousness" (1916). In spite of this, he readily acknowledged a close and intimate relationship between experimental and ethnic psychology:

> By its use of objective techniques, experimental psychology enters into close relationship with another important branch of psychological research, ethnic psychology. While the task of the former is the exact investigation of individual consciousness, the latter seeks to learn the psychological laws that govern the products of collective mental life—in particular, language, myth, and custom. However, not only do these two areas of objective psychology supplement each other, but in many ways, they are also dependent on each other. For the collective mental life of a people points everywhere to the individual energies that have entered into it, and individual consciousness, in its higher forms of development, is supported by the mental life of the collectivity to which it belongs (Wundt, 1980, p. 63).

The relationship between experimental and ethnic psychology must be viewed from two different perspectives, the theoretical and the methodological. In regards to psychological theory the two areas, as Wundt notes, "not only . . . supplement each other, but . . . are . . . dependent on each other." An understanding of individual psychology will contribute to a comprehension of social (ethnic) psychology. Similarly, social psychology can clarify our understanding of individual psychology.

The tie-in between individual and ethnic psychology is mediated by Wundt's conception of levels of mental processes. He assumed that mental processes can be divided into two major levels, lower and higher. Lower mental processes were *sensing, perceiving, feeling,* and *willing,* while higher mental processes were *language, memory,* and *thinking.* Sensing and perceiving could be observed directly by introspection in an experimental situation, while feeling and willing could be inferred from experimental results. The higher mental processes were beyond experimental investigation; they must be studied historically.

Wundt's treatment of the interaction between lower and higher mental processes was based on the holistic principle—widely accepted in the German culture of his day—that human systems, like consciousness and society, cannot be treated atomistically, as mere aggregates of component parts. Holists argue that these systems are irreducible to their constituent elements; the action of the elements is insufficient to explain the operation of the whole system. When applied to the distinction between lower and higher mental processes, holism, expressed through Wundt's concept of *creative synthesis,* postulated that the lower mental processes played a role in the higher processes but the higher mental processes were not simply an additive combination of the lower processes. When you *perceive* four successive letters—page—you do not just see four letters but instead a word whose meaning is not contained in the individual letters. The display $\frac{7}{3}$ offers another example of creative synthesis. The two numbers are not perceived as independent events but are *creatively synthesized* into a sum (10), or difference (4), or product (21). Thus, a theory of sensation, perception, affect, and will, based on evidence from experimental psychology, would contribute to an understanding of cultural psychology. But it could not tell the whole story.

Whereas harmony characterizes the theoretical relationship between experimental and ethnic psychology, the two branches are discordant in regards to their methodology; experimental psychology operates as a natural science while ethnic psychology functions as a human science. Experimental psychology employed controlled observations in the laboratory, a method of data collection that, Wundt insisted, could not be used in social psychology. Social psychology was a historical discipline; "ethnic psychology . . . seeks to derive general psychological laws of development from the objective products of the collective mental life: language, myth, and custom" (Wundt, 1980). By examining these cultural products—language, myth, custom—it was possible by historical analysis to discover their psychological causes.

As already noted, Wundt never offered any clear statement about the criteria that should be employed to judge the truth of psychological principles. The manner in which he justified his hypotheses suggests that he used different criteria of theoretical truth for experimental and ethnic psychology. Introspective data were considered a valid reflection of mental events if the evidence were obtained under appropriate experimental conditions. Hypotheses about mental processes operating in experimental situations could be evaluated by testing their empirical implications as in some of Wundt's research in mental chronometry. Because ethnic psychology could not employ experimental methods, Wundt seemed to conclude that criteria of truth other than introspective validity and deductive explanation were needed. It has previously been suggested that Wundt judged the historical analysis of cultural phenomena by its intuitive validity and interpretive consistency. One historian, an admirer of Wundt, suggests that Wundt followed the German tradition prevailing at the time of his *Völkerpsychologie:* "It was generally believed that history could be used as a method for arriving at an intuitive understanding of human psychology" (Leahey, 1980). The important point to recognize is that the criterion of truth employed by Wundt, whether it be described as "intuitive understanding" or "intuitive knowing and interpretive consistency" (Kendler, 1981), was based upon a subjective judgment rather than an objective criterion.

Language. The portion of Wundt's cultural psychology that is most relevant to contemporary psychology is his view of language. Many of his ideas are surprisingly similar to modern conceptions (Blumenthal, 1970), as is illustrated by his insistence that a sentence is not simply a sequence of words, but instead an expression of an organized idea:

> A sentence does not consist of separate mental structures that emerge in consciousness, one by one, each existing as an individual word or an individual sound while all before and after sink into oblivion. It rather remains in consciousness as a totality while it is being uttered. . . . As a result, all relevant components of a sentence are already mentally given in the brief moment when one first begins to utter it. (Wundt, quoted by Gleitman, 1985, p. 421).

Wundt distinguished between outer and inner linguistic phenomena. The outer phenomena are what can be directly observed, as is the case for written or spoken statements we produce or perceive. The inner phenomena refer to the internal cognitive principles that are assumed to be responsible for the outer phenomena. This distinction between observable (outer) phenomena and underlying theoretical processes (inner phenomena) reappears throughout the history of psychology. A vast majority of psychologists, but not all, believes that in order to account for observable psychological phenomena, internal psychological processes must be postulated as did Wundt.

Wundt assumed that thought was basic to language. Producing a sentence, for example, originated in a unified idea. Consider the case of a grandfather communicating his observation of his granddaughter, Jenny, hitting his grandson, Seth. Wundt created a tree diagram to represent the transformation of an organized idea, consisting of three distinct ideas (Jenny, hitting, and Seth), into a sequence of words:

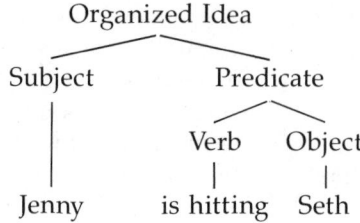

The unified idea can be transformed into a different sentence: *Seth is being hit by Jenny.* This variation of linguistic expression from the same cognitive base demonstrates the Wundtian distinction between the inner cognitive processes and outer linguistic utterances. The two sentences, *Jenny is hitting Seth* and *Seth is being hit by Jenny,* are not psychologically distinct but rather are an expression of a common inner phenomenon.

Whereas a linguistic utterance results from the transformation of an organized idea into a sentence, linguistic comprehension occurs in the reverse order: A sentence is comprehended when converted into the idea that generated it. To support this interpretation, Wundt suggested that we do not remember the exact words of a sentence that are heard or read (the outer phenomenon), but instead its underlying idea (inner phenomenon). Subsequent research has repeatedly demonstrated that general ideas are remembered instead of the specific set of words with which they are expressed.

Wundt's theory of psycholinguistics, of which only a small segment is presented here, is based on two primary assumptions, that cognitive processes are basic to language, and that principles of psycholinguistics govern linguistic utterances and comprehension. The reader who is familiar with modern psycholinguistics will recognize the contemporary quality of Wundt's ideas.

The Group Mind. Wundt believed that different ethnic groups had different collective *minds;* a country like Germany, for example, possessed a distinctive mental outlook. He arrived at this position by applying the concept of *creative synthesis* to social groups. Just as a person's mind is creatively synthesized from individual psychic experiences, so is the group mind created from the individual minds of the common culture.

Wundt's strategy for dealing with social phenomena like the group mind was to work backwards in time from the present (historical retrogression). His analysis of historical events led him to conclude that evolutionary principles governed cultural development. Cultures evolved in a sequence of stages from primitive tribal organization in early times to the highly structured national states of the present. Wundt's specific views were simplistic in that they assumed that the complexity of cultural change could be represented along a single dimension of the development of social organization. It soon became apparent that cultural change was much more complicated and, as a consequence, Wundt's ideas never received much attention after they were proposed.

Wundt's use of the concept of the group mind did raise an interesting problem that is still important. During World War I, Wundt wrote nationalistic tracts in which he argued that the group mind in Germany was superior to those of her enemies. Germany, he believed, had achieved a truly organic society in which the needs of the state and individuals were properly balanced to produce a superior culture that emphasized heroism, duty, and spiritual ideals. In contrast, British and American societies were weighted toward the individual with excessive concern with materialism, pragmatism, and commercialism.

It can be suggested that Wundt's patriotic outbursts during the war represented an understandable aberration that should not be considered part of his psychology. This view can be countered by noting that within his ethnic psychology is the idea that cultures develop through stages that lead to higher goals and ideals. Within this framework, Wundt essentially argues, *as a psychologist,* that certain types of cultures are superior to and better than others. His ethnic psychology, it can be argued, was not limited to describing cultural development; it also *prescribed* the values that societies should seek. For him, Germany had achieved a higher, and therefore better, level of ethical development than either Great Britain or the United States.

Wundt's nationalistic interpretation of group minds accents a persistent problem in social psychology. Should the discipline be descriptive or prescriptive? Should social psychologists offer a detached analysis of cultural phenomena without evaluating their social impact? Or, is it the responsibility of the social psychologist to prescribe what is socially good or bad? There is no simple answer to these queries (Kendler, 1981), and psychologists have taken opposite positions in regard to their social responsibilities. Some have insisted that psychologists can best serve society by enlarging our understanding of psychological phenomena without advocating any public policy (e.g., capital punishment, TV violence). Others insist that because of their special insights, psychologists have a responsibility to advise society as to which policy best serves its interest.

Quotations of Wilhelm Wundt

Each chapter will present a series of quotations of the psychologist whose ideas are being reviewed. The purpose of these quotations is twofold: to provide first-hand evidence of the psychologist's thinking and writing style and review some of his major ideas.

   1. Psychology . . . seeks to give account of the interconnection of processes which are evidenced by our own consciousness, or which we infer from such manifestations of the bodily life in other creatures as indicate the presence of consciousness similar to our own (Wundt, 1910, p. 1).

2. The assertion that the mental life lacks all causal connection, and that the real and primary object of psychology is, therefore, not the mental life itself but the physical substrate of that life—this assertion stands self-condemned (Wundt, 1910, p. 10).

3. Objectively, we can regard the individual mental processes only as inseparable elements of interconnected wholes (Wundt, 1910, p. 20).

4. The supreme advantage of the experimental method lies in the fact that it and it alone renders a reliable introspection possible (Wundt, 1910, p. 8).

5. All accurate observation implies that the object of observation (in this case, the psychical process) can be held fast by the attention, and any changes that it undergoes attentively followed. And this fixation by the attention implies . . . that the observed object is independent of the observer (Wundt, 1910, p. 5).

6. There are other sources of objective psychological knowledge, which become accessible at the very point where the experimental method fails us. These are certain products of common mental life, in which we trace the operation of determinate psychical motives: chief among them are language, myth, and custom (Wundt, 1910, p. 5).

Wundt's Theory: A Systematic View

One of Wundt's current admirers acknowledges the "notorious slipperiness" of his theoretical ideas; they cannot be described precisely (Danziger, 1980b). In addition, Wundt's theory, by modern standards, falls far short of being integrated. Nevertheless, an attempt to systematize Wundt's conception will be made in order to highlight both its main features and striking similarities to some current notions.

A Theory of the Mind. Wundt's major focus was on mental processes. Although his interests extended to both physiology and behavior, the point of reference was always the mind. Physiological correlates of the mental events were investigated, not to explain them, but, instead, to merely describe the relationship between the two. In some cases, as with the tridimensional theory of feeling, physiological correlates of the mental events were sought in order to provide objective evidence of their occurrence. Behavior was also studied, but not as an end in itself, as was the case for a subsequent group of psychologists known as behaviorists. Behavior (e.g., reaction time) was investigated to reflect the operation of mental processes, a methodological tactic that is employed by many modern cognitive psychologists.

Voluntarism.   Wundt's emphasis on voluntarism—that all psychic activity is influenced by the will—anticipated the central role that motivation would play in many subsequent psychological theories. At the same time, this concern with volition distinguished his psychology from some modern forms of cognitive psychology that seek an understanding of the mind. Cognitive processes for Wundt never occurred in a vacuum. The activities of the mind are always shaped by a person's motives, such as desires, purposes, and goals. Humans are not simply rational organisms, but rather organisms that use rational means to satisfy their desires. To underline this position, Wundt insisted that cognitive activities are not conducted in an atmosphere of pure reason, but are always accompanied by an affective (emotional) state.

Apperception.   Wundt's voluntaristic orientation was expressed in his concept of *apperception,* the forerunner of the construct *attention.* Apperception referred to the process by which a mental event enters the focal area of consciousness, the area of greatest clarity. Wundt did not assume that apperception results from the attention-getting quality of external or internal stimulation (e.g., a bright color in our visual field, kinesthetic cues from a tennis stroke). Humans are *not* passive recipients of sensations. Our senses are *not* windows to our outer or inner world. Instead, apperception is a manifestation of volition. Focal clarity in consciousness is achieved as an expression of a person's will.

Creative Synthesis.   Wundt assumed that the fundamental psychological processes were operating in the mind, not as independent entities, but rather as components in a highly complex system. This holistic notion was expressed in his basic *principle of creative synthesis,* which postulated that mental constructions from component processes always produce novel consequences.

Any scientific theory, whether it be of the mind or behavior, of psychology or chemistry, must postulate principles that specify how relevant component events (processes, principles, variables) interact to produce a phenomenon. The principle of creative synthesis was Wundt's first attempt to deal with the synthetic problem of science, that is, the combination of parts to form a whole. Although holistic principles, such as creative synthesis, can be very appealing, they can also be annoyingly vague. For instance, the principle of creative synthesis merely states that the whole is different from the sum of its parts, but leaves unspecified how and why this occurs. Wundt attempted to remedy this omission by formulating subsidiary principles that would explain creative synthesis.

Principle of psychological relations.   Wundt assumed that an innate level of organization operated in the human mind that prevented psychical phenomena from being reduced to a level that would destroy the organization. Our mental impressions of a musical note are not separable from the chord within which it is embedded, nor is a word independent of the sentence of which it is a part. A natural (innate) order apparently governs our mental activity to guarantee that the elementary processes of the mind occur in an organized fashion rather than in a series of discrete events.

Principle of psychological contrasts. This principle states that opposing mental experiences intensify each other. Candy tastes much sweeter after drinking lemonade than after consuming a chocolate soda. This means that mental activity resulting from stimulation (e.g., sweetness) is altered by recent experiences (e.g., sourness). Experiences, therefore, are relative, not absolute. To accomplish the integration of experiences, the mind must be capable of synthesizing discrete experiences (successive sensations of sweet and sour) into an interrelated pattern. Wundt's principle of psychological contrasts anticipated the influential notion of adaptation level (Helson, 1964), that assumed that our experiences are influenced by the standards we adopt. A child who experiences much sadness, and therefore expects it, will experience more pleasure from a happy occasion than will a fortunate child who has learned to be optimistic.

Principle of heterogeneity of ends. This awkwardly phrased principle refers to developmental changes that occur in individuals and social groups. The principle postulates a discrepancy between psychological cause and effect; emergent unanticipated results, not originally planned for, will inevitably result. The graduating medical student views a medical career in a different light than when, as an undergraduate, he or she was struggling to gain admission into medical school. New and unforeseen consequences occur when the goal of being a physician is attained. This produces a shift in the purposes that originally motivated the student to become a physician. The numerous unexpected side effects resulting from the Vietnam War illustrate the principle of heterogeneity of ends. Radical changes in social values and attitudes within the United States were the unanticipated result of President Johnson's effort to prevent a Communist takeover of South Vietnam.

Principle of mental growth. This principle, like the preceding one, is concerned with the mental development of individuals and social groups. Mental development for Wundt occurs in a manner similar to embryological development. The union of the sperm with the egg in the human initiates a series of cell divisions that ultimately result in the embryo being differentiated into a variety of organs (e.g., stomach, brain) and systems (e.g., nervous, circulatory). In a similar way, Wundt assumed, mental processes differentiated from an inchoate mass to an interrelated organization of different cognitive processes. Languages, cultural products, also undergo developmental differentiation within the course of history. Latin differentiated into several Romance languages (e.g., Spanish, Italian). In all cases of differentiation, whether of the individual or society, the final product contains remnants of the initial form (e.g., Spanish contains Latin structures, adult thought can reflect childish thought).

Principle of development toward opposites. Cyclical patterns of development characterize both individual and society. Activities tend to fluctuate between two opposite extremes. Individuals seek social stimulation and then get bored and retreat into isolation. Gaiety is followed by depression and vice versa. Cool jazz gives way to raucous rock and roll. The Great Depression, which occurred when an individualistic philosophy dominated, was followed by a turn to a liberal welfare state conception during the presidency of Franklin D. Roosevelt and subsequent Democratic leaders. President Reagan shifted to the conservative views that prevailed prior to the Great Depression. Wundt was suggesting with this principle that one type of mental experience or activity increases the tension to operate in the opposite manner.

CONTRIBUTIONS OF WILHELM WUNDT

Wundt's foremost contribution to psychology was his success in creating an independent science of psychology. Not only did he establish the first psychology laboratory, but he also trained a large number of students and started a new journal entitled *Philosophische Studien (Philosophical Studies)*, that was primarily devoted to the publication of articles in experimental psychology. All in all, he created experimental psychology and the conditions necessary for its survival.

Many students from all over the world—Germany, United States, Great Britain, Russia, Italy, India, Japan—flocked to Wundt's laboratory in Leipzig, where the exciting new science was being taught. Wundt's success as a teacher is testified to by the large number of psychology laboratories that his students established throughout the world. By 1900, there were forty-three psychology laboratories in the United States, and twelve of them were begun by students of Wundt. Wundt could take partial credit for the remaining thirty-one, because they were based on his conception of psychology as a laboratory science.

Wundt's students did not slavishly establish laboratories in the image of the one that was begun by their professor. Some of them followed their own views as to how psychology was to develop. As a consequence, many new research techniques were designed that effectively enlarged the empirical range of psychology. Emil Kraepelin, a young physician who studied with Wundt, extended Wundt's methods to the field of psychopathology. The abnormalities of the mind were studied experimentally, and some were interpreted within Wundtian theory. Schizophrenia, for example, was thought to be a disorder of apperception; a schizophrenic was unable to maintain a focal clarity in consciousness which was expressed in a lack of continuity in speech. Charles Spearman returned to his native England and developed an influential theory of intelligence that concluded that a basic component of all intellectual efforts was a general intelligence factor in addition to specific intelligences (e.g., mechanical, mathematical). Vladimir Bekhterev, after returning to his native Russia, did research on reflexes that led to important work in conditioning, which was considered a basic and important form of learning. Edward B. Titchener, whose work will be described in the next chapter, reformulated Wundtian psychology and played a leading role in establishing psychology in America. These four students of Wundt represent only a small sample of the large influence Wundt had on the growth of psychology and related fields.

Although Wundt's impact on the development of the science of psychology is clear, the influence of his ideas is obscure. Factors beyond his control intervened to drastically diminish the impact of his conceptions. As Blumenthal explains:

> In view of such recognition, the precipitous decline of Wundtian psychology between the World Wars was breathtaking. The massive body of Wundtian research and writings all but disappeared in the English-speaking world, apparently confirming Wundt's own principle of the development toward opposites (Blumenthal, 1985, p. 44).

The major reason was the social and cultural upheaval that followed World War I. Germany suffered a terrible economic calamity that led to the loss of its premier position in the world of science. That position gradually shifted to the United States where a radical modification of Wundtian psychology was presented by Titchener. This version met with great resistance and was soon to be eclipsed by strikingly different approaches to psychology. In Europe, the intellectual ferment in psychology was expressed in a variety of new approaches, most notably psychoanalysis, which had the effect of relegating Wundtian psychology to the past.

One of the ironies in the history of psychology is that some of the basic ideas of Wundtian psychology reemerged in the current orientation known as *cognitive psychology* (Chapter 11), but that Wundt's ideas apparently had no recognized influence on its development. Neisser's *Cognitive Psychology* (1967), a book that was instrumental in initiating the cognitive revolution, does not reference any of Wundt's writings. Lachman, Lachman, and Butterfield (1979), offer a perceptive historical analysis of cognitive psychology and one of its major offshoots, the information processing paradigm, but fail to list Wundt as one of the historical contributors. Wundt was ignored even though he, like the cognitive psychologists of today, emphasized the significance of cognitive processes, attention, and the organizational principles that govern linguistic utterances and comprehension. This oversight was a combined result of a prevailing lack of interest in the history of psychology and an inaccessibility of an accurate description of Wundtian psychology.

If Wundt is judged, not in terms of the specific influences he exerted on contemporary psychology, but instead, within the historical context in which he lived, then a truly impressive picture of his efforts emerges. He anticipated many themes—methodological, empirical, theoretical—that subsequent history proved to be important: the limitations of introspection in revealing mental processes, the need for objective measures when investigating the mind, the significance of motivation, emotion and attention in psychological theories, the possible limits of experimentation in social psychology and, most of all, the need to make psychology an empirical science.

Wundt is bound to remain a controversial figure in the history of psychology. His efforts have so many facets that it becomes difficult not to agree with some of his views while disagreeing with others. Ultimately, his place in the history of psychology will be determined as much by the direction psychology takes in the future as by his efforts in the past. For the present, the following hypothetical debate between two psychologists who take opposing viewpoints should provide some perspective on the value of Wundtian psychology.

A Debate about Wundtian Psychology

Moderator: The rules of this debate are simple. Initially, a positive view (pro) of Wundtian psychology will be offered, followed by a critical interpretation (con). The points of disagreement will then be argued.

Pro: Wundt's role in establishing psychology as an independent science is acknowledged as his major achievement. It had a broad cultural impact that affected not only higher education, but also encouraged men and women to examine human beings within a scientific perspective. To limit Wundt's contributions to the creation of the science of psychology, however, would encourage a historical omission. Wundt not only began psychology, he became one of the greatest of all psychologists. He developed methods—introspection, experimentation, historical analysis—to make psychology a thriving empirical science. His theoretical notions were rich in implications for future psychologists to pursue: motivation, emotion, cognitive processes, language, and so forth. In sum, he built a foundation for the new science of psychology and designed a blueprint for its development.

Con: I'll accept the notion that Wundt was, literally speaking, the father of psychology, but my combative nature can't avoid mentioning that a case can be made for assigning the title to Fechner, who did brilliant experimental and theoretical work in sensory psychology, or Galton who initiated the scientific analysis of individual differences. But, I'm willing to accept Wundt as the father of psychology, as long as we reject the sentimental notion that fathers always do good. Wundt behaved like a father who couldn't make up his mind, encouraging his child to behave in one way at one time, while criticizing the child for the same behavior at another time. With such parental guidance, the child is doomed to be confused. Wundt encouraged confusion with four important distinctions that are impossible to justify. First, experience is experience and one cannot consistently or reliably distinguish between immediate and mediate experience. Second, the attempt to draw a sharp line between valid and invalid introspection is doomed to failure. If the notion is accepted that consciousness can be observed, what is the difference between observing it when a tone is sounded or when a mathematical problem is presented? Third, the division between experimental and social psychology is artificial and inconsistent. We now know beyond dispute that experimental analysis of social phenomena is possible. One does not have to pit experimentation against historical analysis. Both are legitimate enterprises that can beneficially supplement each other. Fourth, the notion of psychology as a hybrid science, part natural science, part human science, inevitably will lead to inconsistencies and contradictions. It is like playing one game with two sets of rules. Imagine playing bridge and poker simultaneously with the same deck of cards. It can't be done! Neither is it possible to collect data and formulate theoretical assumptions under two different sets of methodological rules. It is not surprising, therefore, that we cannot point to any permanent contribution of Wundt in regard to either significant empirical laws or theoretical hypothesis.

Pro: Your evaluation of Wundt is excessively harsh because you are insensitive to the realities of science. Important distinctions rarely, if ever, have sharply defined boundaries. A clear line does not divide day from night or life from death, yet these distinctions are meaningful and useful. So are Wundt's distinctions to which you object. We can respond to the world in a subjective or objective fashion. We are all aware of the Müller-Lyer illusions in which the length of two lines are psychologically different but physically equal. Introspection, as you will admit, can be useful, and Wundt should be commended for predicting that it would be most useful in psychophysical relationships, as is the case when a description of experience is correlated with specific physical characteristics of light or sound waves. If Wundt was so far off base in insisting that social psychology should be a historical discipline, why is it that some highly respected modern social psychologists favor such a position? The significant phenomena of social psychology *cannot* be replicated in the laboratory. Finally, your objection to psychology's status as a hybrid science again reflects your insensitivity to reality. Many modern psychologists believe that psychology cannot be forced into the mold of other sciences. Why do you choose to ignore Wundtian ideas that are so basic to psychology, like the importance of motivation, emotion, and attention?

Con: You are a worthy defender of Wundt. You carry on his tradition of ambiguity. I, frankly, don't see how the Müller-Lyer illusion validates the distinction between immediate and mediate experience. They represent two ways of interpreting experience, not two kinds of experiences. Furthermore, I reject the relevance of the argument that some modern psychologists agree with Wundt's historical views of social psychology and conception of psychology as hybrid science. A scientific position is not necessarily supported by somebody agreeing with it. I'm sure, at least I hope, that you are not persuaded by the fact that some people still believe that the earth is flat. Finally, I do not ignore Wundt's recognition of the significance of motivation, emotion, and attention, but it should be noted that science is more than the mere recognition of important factors. Recognizing the importance of the sun in human life was not much of an achievement. Discovering how it generated heat and how it aided plant growth were important scientific achievements. Wundt's findings in the areas of motivation, emotion, and attention, and his theories to explain them did little to advance our scientific understanding of these concepts.

Pro: Wundt should not be considered in the framework of polished theories of psychology. He was an innovator, a beginner, and within this framework he was a great psychologist. Knowledge of cognitive psychology reveals Wundt's amazing perceptiveness of significant psychological issues.

Con: I'll agree that Wundt served an important function in the history of psychology by helping to create it and by encouraging its growth with his efforts as a researcher and theorist. But, he was not a great psychologist if he is judged within the rigorous standards of promoting significant theories.

Moderator: We will end the present debate now that a slight agreement is being achieved.

SUMMARY

Wilhelm Wundt's conception of psychology was directly influenced by the philosophical writings of René Descartes and Johann Herbart and the experimental efforts of Ernst Weber and Gustav Fechner. Descartes was a dualist who assumed the mind was a thinking substance capable of being studied by self-observation, while the body, governed by mechanical principles, could be studied by the methods of natural science. Herbart insisted that psychology should be a science independent of philosophy and physiology. Both Weber and Fechner demonstrated in their psychophysical research that experimental investigation of sensory experience is possible. These influences encouraged Wundt to establish an independent science of psychology that studied mental events.

Wundt assumed that consciousness could be experienced in two different ways: Immediate experience is raw subjective experience unmodified by interpretation, while mediate experience is objective experience shaped by preconceptions and interpretations. Psychology studies immediate experience; physics studies mediate experience.

Wundt did not assume immediate experience to be a stable substance but instead groups of processes (e.g., sensing, feeling, thinking, linguistic) that continually interact. Although Wundt recognized that physiological events are correlated to immediate experience, he insisted that they are not equivalent (e.g., a feeling of elation is different from physiological events to which it is correlated). Wundt accepted the notion of psychic causality; mental events occur in a lawful fashion and, consequently, psychologists can formulate psychological principles to explain them.

Wundt employed three methods to investigate psychological phenomena: introspection, experimentation, and historical analysis. He argued that introspection, the observation of one's own immediate experience, could only be effective in an experimental situation in which the introspector was trained and was exposed to physical stimulation. Experimentation, without introspection, could produce objective evidence (e.g., reaction times) that could serve as the basis for inferring mental processes. Historical analysis, the method of social psychology, also provided information about cultural phenomena that could be used to infer a valid picture of the mind.

Wundt judged the truth value of his different methods of investigation by different criteria. Introspective evidence was considered to be valid if it was obtained in an experimental situation in which a properly trained introspector was exposed to physical stimulation. Theories of mental processes were judged by their capacity to generate deductions in agreement with experimental results. The truth of historical conclusions was evaluated by their intuitive validity and consistency with Wundt's theory of the mind.

Wundt's strategy in constructing a theory of the mind was as diverse as his methods of investigation. He believed that psychology was a hybrid science in the sense that the methods of the natural sciences could be used for experimental results but not for historical analysis. He did not believe that a theory of psychology could be formulated on the basis of results obtained from one particular research situation. As a consequence, he formulated a piecemeal theory from evidence from a variety of research areas.

Wundt's efforts to discover a discrete set of mental processes in reaction time studies failed, but, nevertheless, called attention to the problem of how the mind works and the influence of attentional processes in its functioning. Wundt's experimental research on the content of consciousness revealed two fundamental mental processes, *sensations*, and *feelings*, which operated simultaneously. He concluded that feelings could be analyzed and classified on three dimensions: pleasantness-unpleasantness, excitement-calm, and strain-relaxation. His theory of the content of consciousness did not gain wide acceptance because of the absence of any clear-cut criteria to evaluate the validity of introspective reports and the failure of the theory to be supported by objective evidence. Wundt's most important work in social psychology was his analysis of language. He assumed thought was basic to language. A thought in the mind transformed into language during the communication process. When comprehending the language, a listener or reader transforms language into the idea that generated it.

The core concepts of Wundt's psychological theory were *voluntarism, apperception,* and *creative synthesis.* Voluntarism represents the view that the activities of the mind are always controlled by a person's desires and goals. Apperception refers to the process by which a mental event enters the focal area of consciousness, the area of greatest mental clarity. This process is controlled by motivational factors. The principle of creative synthesis postulates that all mental constructions resulting from the interaction of component mental processes produced novel consequences.

Wundt formulated a set of principles to describe these novel events: *psychological relations, psychological contrasts, heterogeneity of ends, mental growth,* and *development toward opposites.*

Wundt's major contributions to psychology were (1) the central role he played in establishing psychology as an independent science, (2) the development of methods to investigate psychological phenomena, and (3) the theoretical notions he proposed. His ideas served as points of reference for subsequent developments in psychology.

SUGGESTED READINGS

The most influential interpretation of Wundtian psychology until recent years was contained in Boring's *A History of Experimental Psychology* (1950). This view has been challenged in a number of recent books and articles. An especially informative book, edited by R. W. Rieber, is *Wilhelm Wundt and the Making of a Scientific Psychology* (1980). Wundt's own *Principles of Physiological Psychology* (1910) has been translated and is well worth reading even though its translator, E. B. Titchener, has been criticized for distorting some of Wundt's ideas.

Individual articles which are illuminating are Arthur Blumenthal's "A Reappraisal of Wilhelm Wundt" (1975), Kurt Danziger's "The Positivist Repudiation of Wundt" (1979), and Thomas H. Leahey's "Something Old, Something New: Attention in Wundt and Modern Cognitive Psychology" (1979). A number of interesting articles are contained in *Wundt Studies: A Centennial Collection,* which is edited by W. Bringmann and R. D. Tweney (1980).

3

Structuralism

If Wilhelm Wundt had not lived, you might not now be reading about structuralism and its founder, Edward Bradford Titchener (1867–1927). Titchener's claim to fame rests on his special relationship to Wundt. He was Wundt's student and pursued Wundt's goal of providing an accurate picture of the mind. Although Titchener aspired to further the cause of Wundtian psychology, he contributed, despite his intent, to its demise.

Titchener was an Englishman who studied in Germany with Wundt and then emigrated to the United States, where he became an eminent psychologist. Although he was perceived as an exponent of Wundtian psychology, Titchener was actually espousing a psychology that was distinctively his own. Titchener was a lesser psychologist than Wundt, but a more influential one. He lacked Wundt's originality and breadth, but he had the good fortune of residing in America where historical forces dictated the major center of psychology would be. In addition, his impact on psychology was enhanced by a writing style that was both lucid and stimulating. Unlike Wundtian psychology, Titchener's conceptions were so clearly stated that they served as a convenient reference point in the continuing debate about the nature of psychology.

HISTORICAL ROOTS

Wundt's influence on Titchener was obvious, but not as complete as has been commonly believed. Although Titchener himself conveyed the impression that he was Wundt's apostle in America, such a view is somewhat of a distortion. Before taking his Ph.D. with Wundt at Leipzig,

53

FIGURE 3.1 Edward B. Titchener

Archives of The History of American Psychology

Titchener studied at Oxford, where he acquired a marked preference for tough-minded English philosophy over the romantic, idealistic version that influenced Wundt. Near the end of his career, in a letter to a psychologist, Titchener wrote, "I am myself very decidedly an English psychologist, if the adjective means nationality; and I hope I am the same thing if it means type of thinking" (Roback, 1964).

Two intellectual traditions were particularly important in influencing Titchener: associationism and positivism.

Associationism

Mental events tend to be related; they do not occur in a random sequence. Plato offered the following example of the association of mental events: "What is the feeling of lovers when they recognize a lyre or a garment or anything else which the beloved has been in the habit of using? Do not they from knowing the lyre form in the mind's eye an image of the youth to whom the lyre belongs?" (Warren, 1921) Plato was suggesting that the act of recollection was controlled by the associationistic principle of contiguity. Events that occur together in time tend to be associated in the mind. Seeing the lyre triggers the image of its owner.

Aristotle believed mental phenomena could be studied as carefully as physical events. By examining his own recollections, he concluded that three principles of association governed the succession of thought: similarity, contrast, and contiguity. The image of an apple may bring forth an image of a pear (similarity), a gnawing pang of hunger may remind one of the satisfying sensation of satiety (contrast), and the thought of a steak may produce an image of french fried potatoes (contiguity).

Associationism became a dominant concept in the philosophical treatment of the mind through the efforts of a group of brilliant British philosophers who spanned a period of about 200 years beginning in the middle of the seventeenth century. The fundamental notion of the school of British Associationism is that mental events are controlled by principles of association; what occurs in consciousness is determined by the linkages mental events have with each other.

Three key questions were raised by an associationistic outlook to psychology: What mental events (e.g., sensations, ideas) are associated? What principles (e.g., similarity, contiguity) govern the formation of associations? Are mental events modified through associations? British Associationists offered a variety of answers to these questions, some of which resemble the answers subsequent psychologists proposed to interpret psychological phenomena.

Positivism

Positivism is a complex philosophical position that insists valid knowledge about the world is based exclusively on the methods of the natural sciences; conceptions such as religious convictions or philosophical speculations that go beyond objective scientific facts cannot be accepted as valid. Wundt, a philosophical idealist (a position that views mind (ideas) as fundamental), opposed positivism with his subjective view of psychic causality (Chapter 2) and with his belief that the methods of natural science could not be applied to ethnic psychology. Titchener was attracted to positivism which, during their days at Leipzig, was achieving a dominant position in philosophy. Titchener was predisposed to a positivist view of psychology because of his exposure at Oxford to the writings of the British Associationistic philosophers who believed that the human mind is a natural phenomenon and is understandable by the methods of natural science. His conversion to positivism was encouraged by Oswald Külpe (1862–1915), who was one of the intellectual leaders among Wundt's students, and who, during his early career, had strong positivist commitments.

Edward Bradford Titchener (1867–1927)

Edward Bradford Titchener was born in 1867 in Chichester, England, of a distinguished family with little money. The lack of money did not hamper his education. His exceptional academic ability brought him early recognition in the form of a scholarship to Malvern College. His performance there was so outstanding that the American ambassador, the noted poet James Russell Lowell, who was distributing prizes one year, was led to comment, "I am tired of seeing 'you, Mr. Titchener," when Titchener appeared for one prize after another.

In 1885, Titchener was awarded another scholarship that brought him to Brasenose College of Oxford University, where he received his A.B. in philosophy in 1889, and subsequently studied experimental physiology for a year. These interests encouraged him to translate Wundt's third edition of *Principles of Physiological Psychology*. When finished with the task, Titchener discovered that Wundt was completing his fourth edition, thus making Titchener's translation out of date. This was not to be the last time Titchener's efforts to translate Wundt's works were to be frustrated by Wundt's frequent revisions.

Not unexpectedly, Titchener decided to travel to Leipzig to study physiological psychology with Wundt. In 1892, after only two years of research, he received his Ph.D. These two years at Leipzig shaped Titchener's entire career. Although he was not close to Wundt, he nevertheless adopted Wundt's conception that psychology was the science of the mind and that experimental psychology should be pursued in the absence of practical considerations. Even when his own views diverged from those of Wundt, Titchener never relinquished the ideals and values of his professor concerning the role of psychology in the university.

While at Leipzig, Titchener was friendly with a fellow student, Frank Angell, an American, who became responsible for Titchener's emigration to the United States. Titchener, after completing his doctorate, would have liked to return to Oxford, but his alma mater was not interested in the new psychology from Leipzig, perhaps because of the prevailing conviction that all that need be said about psychology had been said by the British Associationists. Angell, who was leaving for a position at the newly founded Stanford University, encouraged Titchener to accept a position at Cornell University, where he had established a psychology laboratory a year earlier.

Titchener arrived at Cornell in 1892 and, three years later at twenty-eight years of age, became a full professor. He stayed at Cornell for his entire academic career which lasted thirty-five years. At Cornell, he succeeded in two important missions: providing a firm foundation for the new science of psychology in America and contributing to the development of a psychology that emerged from the conception he had learned at Leipzig.

At Cornell, Titchener succeeded in separating psychology from the philosophy department, a success that assisted many other psychology departments to win their battles for independence. He translated important works of Wundt and Külpe to acquaint American psychologists and their students with the current thoughts of those leading German scholars. In 1896, before reaching the age of thirty, he published his own book, *An Outline of Psychology,* which was succeeded in two years by his *Primer of Psychology,* and then by his classic four-volume *Experimental Psychology,* finished in 1905.

Titchener shaped American psychology not only by his writings but also by his inspirational teaching that attracted crowds of students. He lectured in his Oxford master's gown because "It confers the right to be dogmatic." The staff of the psychology department attended his undergraduate lectures and were frequently rewarded by hearing about a new discovery or a theoretical insight. His graduate courses were dominated by his erudition and brilliance. He exerted a strong impact on graduate students, fifty-four of whom earned doctorates with Titchener. Many of them became leading figures in psychology.

In spite of his successes, his American audience gradually slipped away. His brand of psychology, which restricted Wundtian psychology to introspective analysis of consciousness, was considered inadequate to psychology's potential. Although he constantly warned his audiences to beware of false prophets, most American psychologists assigned such a role to him.

Titchener promised a final statement about his systematic views in psychology, but after his untimely death from a brain tumor at age sixty, it was discovered that the book he was writing entitled *Systematic Psychology: Prolegomena* (1929/1972) contained only four completed chapters. It did nothing to stem the tide away from Titchener's psychology. E. G. Boring, Titchener's best-known student, described it as:

> a little book, not at all an *opus,* and did not take even Titchener's world by the ears. Somehow Titchenerianism in America had been sustained by his brilliant personality. With his death it suddenly collapsed, dwindling rapidly from the staus of a vital faith in the importance of consciousness to the equally essential but wholly inglorious state of having been an unavoidable phase of historical development (Boring, 1950, p. 420).

Boring's verdict was not universally shared. Evans and MacLeod, in preparing the preface for the reissuance of *Systematic Psychology: Prolegomena* in 1972, note that "Titchener's *Prolegomena* was not understood in his time, but he expected that. His hope was that students of the future would be better grounded in science, history, and logic and so be in a better position to understand." In a letter to another psychologist, Titchener expressed the hope for a just verdict of the *Prolegomena:*

> Sad experience has taught me that my own training and that of many of my contemporaries did not insist on clear thinking. So I am trying to be so far clear so that those who read me later on will be able to accept or reject with full understanding of what it is that they are accepting or rejecting (Titchener, 1929/1972, p. xvi).

Your decision "to accept or reject" should be easier to make at the end of this chapter.

METHODOLOGICAL ASSUMPTIONS

The history of psychology is dominated by methodological disagreements. These disagreements are rarely complete. While rejecting certain methodological positions of their predecessors, psychologists accept many others, as in Titchener's reaction to Wundt. The significance that is assigned to rejected and accepted assumptions determines whether the newer position is perceived as a revolutionary or an evolutionary change. The concern with labeling a new position as a revolutionary or evolutionary change is relatively unimportant when compared to the task of identifying *both* continuities and discontinuities between historically related conceptions.

The Subject Matter of Psychology

Titchener agreed with Wundt that psychology was the science of the *mind,* of *conscious experience.* According to Titchener, *mind* refers to the sum total of mental processes occurring during the lifetime of the individual, while *consciousness* refers to the sum total of mental processes occurring at any given present time.

Although agreeing about the subject matter of psychology, Wundt and Titchener disagreed about the meaning of experience. Wundt, you recall, distinguished between *immediate experience* and *mediate experience.* Psychology studied immediate experience, experience that was direct and "unmodified by abstraction and reflection." The natural sciences, like physics and biology, studied mediate experience, the experience from which all subjective factors had been removed.

Titchener's positivism encouraged him to reject Wundt's distinction between immediate and mediate experience. If valid knowledge can only emerge from a natural science methodology, as Titchener assumed, how can psychology offer a veridical account of the human mind if it studies immediate experience, a kind of experience that does not properly belong to the methods of natural science?

Psychology, for Wundt, was a hybrid science combining features of a natural science with those of a human science. Psychology, for Titchener, was a completely natural science: "all the sciences have the same sort of subject matter; they all deal with some phase or aspect of the world of human experience" (Titchener, 1923, p. 2).

Titchener, nevertheless, shared Wundt's belief that experience for the psychologist was somewhat different from the experience of the physicist. He resolved this conflict between his Wundtian background and his positivist commitment by concluding:

> human experience . . . may be considered from different points of view. . . . First, we will regard experience as altogether independent of any particular person; we will assume that it goes on whether or not anyone is there to have it. Second we will regard experience as altogether as dependent upon the particular person; we will assume that it goes on only when someone is there to have it (Titchener, 1923, p. 6).

This distinction can be illustrated with the Müller-Lyer illusion (see p. 60). When the observation is dependent on a person, the line attached to the oblique lines that extend outward is experienced as longer than the one with the inward-pointing oblique lines. When experienced "altogether independent of any particular person," as measured by a ruler, the lines are equal in length. In other words, when experienced within a psychological perspective, the lines are judged unequal; when viewed from within a physical frame of reference, the lines are experienced as equal. This example illustrates an important concept in Titchenerian psychology: *stimulus error.* A stimulus error is committed when the introspector attends to the physical properties of the stimulus instead of the psychological sensations. In the case of the Müller-Lyer illusion, a stimulus error would result if the introspector tried to perceive the actual length of the lines instead of how they appeared; the observation would be made independent of the observer.

At first glance, Titchener's distinction between dependent and independent experience appears to be essentially the same as Wundt's distinction between immediate and mediate experience. The lines of the Müller-Lyer illusion are unequal in immediate (dependent on the observer) experience and equal in mediate (independent of the observer) experience. Nevertheless, the two analyses diverge in a significant way. Wundt postulated two kinds of experience (immediate and mediate), while Titchener insisted on only one kind that could be viewed in two different ways (dependent or independent of a particular person). As a consequence of distinguishing between two kinds of experience, Wundt was led to conclude that psychology was a hybrid science; it was not completely a natural science. Because Titchener thought psychology dealt with the same experience as did physics, he was encouraged to conclude

FIGURE 3.2 The Müller-Lyer Illusion

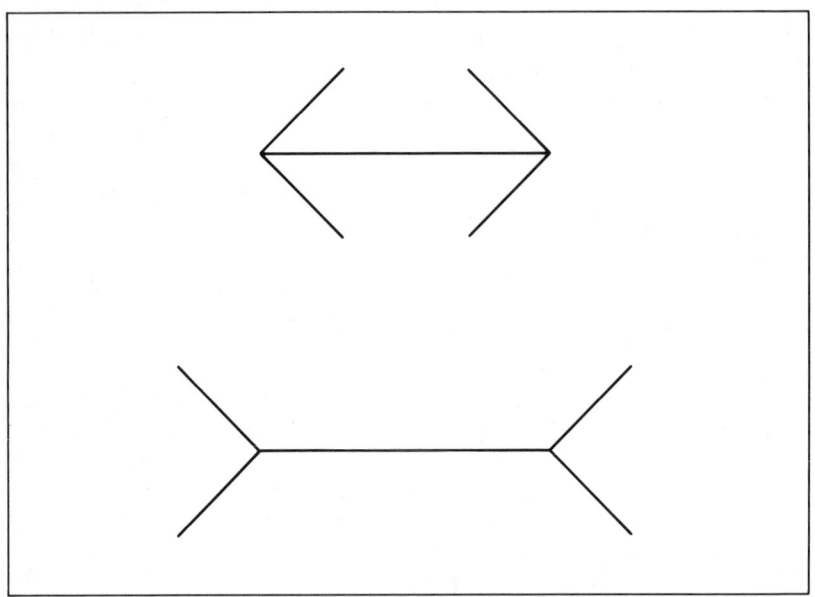

The lengths of the lines are physically equal but psychologically unequal.

that psychology was, in total, a natural science. This difference in the methodological conclusions of Wundt and Titchener represents an important bifurcation in the history of psychology; one path leads to a psychology that is distinct from the natural sciences, while the other path leads to a psychology that is methodologically similar to the natural sciences. Two questions have now emerged: Should psychology be considered a natural science or a science that is distinctly different from the biological and physical sciences? Is Titchener correct in his argument that psychology can be a natural science when its goal is to describe human consciousness? These are two of the most important methodological questions in the history of psychology.

Preconceptions about Conscious Experience. Titchener's ideas about consciousness emerged from two major sources, Wundtian psychology and British Associationism. This latter influence predisposed Titchener to adopt a position that differed from Wundt's in regards to both the observational clarity and the structure of consciousness. Although Titchener acknowledged that consciousness was everchanging, he did not believe, as did Wundt, that it was in such a state of flux that it was beyond direct examination except under special experimental conditions. Consciousness could be clearly observed in a much wider range of situations than Wundt thought possible.

Titchener's views of consciousness were shaped by the atomistic approach of many British Associationists. Two particular influences were those of James Mill (1773–1836) and his son, John Stuart Mill (1806–1873). James Mill adopted the position of *mental mechanics* that assumed that complex mental events are simple additive sums of simple events. The complex idea of *fruit* is a simple sum of all lesser ideas of individual fruits (e.,g., *apple, pear, peach,* etc.). John Stuart Mill promoted the position of *mental chemistry:* ideas coalesce and lose their identity when associated together as hydrogen and oxygen do when they combine to form the liquid water. Both of the Mills accepted the idea, as Titchener put it, that the "mind is built up from its elements." The Mills differed as to the principles that controlled the synthesis of the basic elements. Titchener's view of mental synthesis was more in line with the atomistic views of the British Associationists, falling somewhere between those of James and John Stuart Mill, than with the holistic view of creative synthesis adopted by Wundt.

Wundt concluded that introspection was of limited use in studying consciousness. It could only be trusted when self-observation occurred in an experimental situation in which the introspector was exposed to a specific physical stimulus. His position led to two possible alternatives about the methodology of psychology: either limit psychology to introspective evidence or use other methods to investigate the mind. Wundt chose the latter alternative when he employed both experimental evidence in the absence of introspective reports and historical analysis of social phenomena. When confronted with the same choices, Titchener chose the alternative rejected by Wundt: Introspection is the sole method of investigating conscious experience. Titchener, however, expanded the role of introspection when he rejected Wundt's requirement that the introspector be exposed to physical stimulation:

> The experimenter of the early nineties [when Titchener was a student at Leipzig] trusted, first of all, in his instruments. . . . it is hardly an exaggeration to say . . . [that they were] of more importance than the observer. . . . Now twenty years after we have changed all that. The movement toward qualitative analysis has culminated in what is called, with a certain redundancy of expression, the method of 'systematic experimental introspection' (Titchener, 1912, p. 427).

Essentially, Titchener was arguing against Wundt's position that the only way to accurately and reliably observe consciousness is to control incoming stimulation. Special training, Titchener argued, could enhance the ability of introspectors to observe mental events. When combined with appropriate conditions, introspection could be made to be as precise and accurate as observations of physical events:

> To secure reliable results, we must be strictly impartial and unprejudiced, facing the facts as they come, ready to accept them as they are, not trying to fit them into any preconceived theory; and we must work only when our

general disposition is favorable, when we are fresh and in good health, at ease in our surroundings, free from outside worry and anxiety. If these rules are not followed, no amount of experimentation will help us (Titchener, 1923, p. 25).

Although he maintained that "the method of psychology is much the same as the method of physics," Titchener acknowledged some difficulties. For example, when observing the effect of a word on consciousness, introspection could modify the experience itself; the act of observation could distort the mental event under surveillance. To overcome this difficulty, Titchener suggested that the introspector should suspend his introspective analysis and permit the mental sequence to run its course and then offer a retrospective report; "introspection becomes retrospection, introspective examination becomes *post mortem* examination." Self-observation in such cases need not be limited to *post mortem* examination. The entire experience can be repeated, especially if, "the practiced observer gets into an introspective habit, has the introspective attitude ingrained in his system; so that it is possible for him, not only to take mental notes while the observation is in progress, but even to jot down written notes." (Titchener, 1923).

The following is an introspective report of a repeated experience of recognizing a musical excerpt from the opera *Il Trovatore:*

> The first note seemed to draw my body over toward it. I experienced a motor tendency to keep time, an innervation of the throat as in humming, and kinaesthetic imagery of swaying with the rhythm. Then I went back in memory, to my first sitting here for a name—this in visual imagery of the situation here. A momentary search, attitude of listening, and 'Trovatore' came to mind in auditory imagery (Woods, 1915, p. 340).

Criterion of Truth

The relationship between Titchener's and Wundt's criterion of truth reflected in form their different views about the appropriate methodology for investigating psychological events. Titchener adopted one of Wundt's three criteria of truth but modified it. Wundt considered psychological truth to arise from three sources: accurate introspective description, valid theoretical deductions, and consistent historical analyses. Titchener rejected the latter two criteria because he concluded that the legitimate subject matter of psychology, mental events, could only be revealed by the direct introspective examination of consciousness. He was encouraged to adopt this view because of his rejection of both the general concept of causality and Wundt's particular construct of psychic causality: "I don't *explain* or *causally relate* at all, at all! In science all the 'explanation' there is for me is the correlation of a dependent with . . . [an] independent variable. . . . Causality I regard as mythological, if you mean by it anything more than correlation" (Titchener, 1929/1972, p. 273). Consistent with this position is Titchener's conclusion that, "The problem of science may be summed up in the single word, 'description'."

Titchener was expressing the idea that the task of science is not the formulation of theories to explain phenomena (i.e., identify their causes), but instead is the economical description of such phenomena (i.e., the sequence of observations correlated with their occurrence). Consider the case of focal clarity in consciousness. Titchener rejected the notion implicit in Wundt's concept of apperception that focal clarity is caused by the effort of our will. Some events are clear in consciousness, others are not. We merely have to describe, thought Titchener, the conditions under which each occur. By restricting our interpretation to description, twin evils could be avoided: postulating processes such as apperception, which cannot be observed, and becoming entrapped in the impossible task of identifying the "real" agents responsible for psychological phenomena such as focal clarity.

STRATEGY

Titchener offered a simple strategy for psychologists:

> The aim of the psychologist is threefold. He seeks (1) to analyze concrete (actual) mental experience into its simplest components, (2) to discover how these elements combine, what are the laws that cover their combination, and, (3) to bring them into connection with their physiological (bodily) conditions (1896/1921, p. 15).

At first glance, this research strategy appears eminently reasonable and simple to execute. It did not turn out that way.

STRUCTURALISM

The term *structuralism* was used to describe Titchener's systematic position to contrast it with functionalism, the orientation that will be discussed in the next chapter. The difference is analogous to the one between anatomy and physiology. Anatomy studies the structure of an organism and all its parts, while physiology examines the functions of an organism and all of its components. The aim of structural psychology, according to Titchener, is "to analyze the structure of the mind; to ravel out the elemental processes from the tangle of consciousness, or . . . to isolate the constituents in the given conscious formation" (Titchener, 1898).

To be in the best position to understand Titchener's conception of the mind, it will help to retrace his steps in arriving at his formulation. According to Titchener, science begins with observation, and observation in the science of psychology is introspection, the observation of one's own conscious experience. Introspection is a special kind of observation and is not be be confused with the philosophical speculations about the nature of the mind that date back to the early philosophers and persist to this date. Nor is introspection to be identified with the informal, everyday, natural examination of consciousness which you, no doubt, indulge in. Introspection is a rigorous and precise kind of observation for which training is required. Training is especially important because we do not find simple processes in consciousness but, instead, complex blends of mental elements. A naive observer, like an untrained chemist, would be incapable of isolating the elements (e.g., sodium, chloride) from the compounds (e.g., salt) of which they are a part. Thus, for Titchener, the observation of the sophisticated chemist is qualitatively identical to the introspection of the propertly trained psychologist.

Content of Consciousness

Once the well-trained observers are available, thought Titchener, the project of accurately describing the structure of the mind can be implemented. The first step is to identify the elements of consciousness, those mental events that cannot be dissected into more basic parts. Introspection revealed three major classes of conscious experience: *sensations, images,* and *affections. Sensations,* the most prevalent elements of consciousness, are the basic components of patterns of sights and sounds, tastes and smells, and tactual and muscular "feels." *Images,* the elements of ideas, occur in mental processes that represent events that are not present, as is the case of a memory of a person's face or the anticipation of a graduation ceremony that has yet to take place. *Affections* are the elements of emotion that combine to form such experiences of happiness and sorrow, love and hate.

Titchener (1896/1921) listed more than 44,000 different kinds of sensory elements, the majority of which were visual (32,820) and auditory (11,600). Both sensations and images have four common attributes: quality, intensity, duration, and clarity. For example, a visual sensation could be bluish, strong, lasting, and very clear. Affections had the first three attributes but not clarity.

Titchener rejected Wundt's tridimensional theory of feeling. Feelings, when analyzed introspectively in the Cornell laboratory, varied along only one dimension, *pleasantness* to *unpleasantness.* Wundt's other two dimensions—*excitement-calm* and *strain-relaxation*—were reduced by introspective analysis to sensations and images, especially kinesthetic.

Titchener believed he had enhanced the powers of the introspective method and, consequently, the results obtained in his laboratory were automatically superior to those data from laboratories that failed to employ his methods.

> We must remember always that, within the sphere of psychology, introspection is the final and only court of appeal, that psychological evidence cannot be other than introspective evidence (Titchener, 1896/1921, p. 358).

He did not deny that improvement could take place in introspective descriptions of mental events but insisted that any revisions would have to be consistent with his procedures and goals. Although he recognized individual differences in mental processes, such as variations in the capacity to have rich visual imagery, he nevertheless insisted that the major task of psychology was to describe the general adult human mind, those basic psychic elements that constitute human consciousness.

Titchener's insistence that the proper concern of psychology was the general adult human mind automaticaly eliminated from consideration the mental events of those organisms, like children, the psychologically disturbed, and animals, who were incapable of correctly looking into their own consciousness.

Principles of Synthesis

The descriptive analysis of consciousness was only the first task for psychologists. The next step was to discover the principles that governed the integration of the elementary processes into mental compounds. The problem of analysis was of dominant concern to Titchener and occupied the largest part of his professional effort. He did, however, try to cope with the task of synthesis but, for the most part, it was of secondary importance. In fact, he argued that valid principles of synthesis emerged from correct analysis:

> Analysis needs to be tested in two ways. We must always ask with regard to it: Has it gone as far as it can go? and: Has it taken account of all the elements which are contained in the experience? To answer the first question, the analysis must be repeated: analysis is its own test. When one psychologist says that a process is elemental, other psychologists repeat his analysis for themselves, trying to carry it further than he could do. If they stop short where he did, he was right; if they find his 'simple' process to be complex, he was wrong. As regards the second question, on the other hand, the test of analysis is *synthesis*. When we have analyzed a complex into the elements a, b, c, we test our analysis by trying to put it together again, to get it back from a, b, and c. If the complex can thus be restored, the analysis is correct; but if the combination of a, b, and c does not give us back the original complex, the analyst has failed to discover some one or more of its ingredients. Hence, the psychologist, when he has analyzed consciousness, must put together the results of his analysis, must synthetise, and compare his reconstruction of mental experience with the experience as originally given. If the two tally, his work on the mental experience is done, and he can pass on to another; if not, he must repeat his analysis, watching constantly for the factors which he had previously missed (Titchener, 1896/1921, pp. 16–17).

Titchener realized that the implementation of these procedures for synthesis would be more difficult than is implied by the above quotation:

> If the conscious elements were "things," the task of reconstruction of an experience would not be difficult. We should put the simple bits of mind

together, as the bits of wood are put together in a child's puzzle map or kindergarten cube. But the conscious elements are 'processes': they do not fit together, side by side and angle to angle; they flow together, mix together, overlapping, reinforcing, modifying or arresting one another, in obedience to certain psychological laws. The psychologist must therefore . . . seek to ascertain the *laws which govern the connection of the mental elements*. Knowledge of these laws renders the synthesis of elements into concrete experience possible, and is of assistance also in subsequent analysis (Titchener, 1896/1921, pp. 17–18).

Unlike Wundt, Titchener never composed a set of principles of synthesis. But his commentaries on the problem of synthesis reveal clearly that he did not share Wundt's commitment to an extreme holism that postulated emergent properties from the combination of elementary parts. Titchener acknowledged that certain elements of a complex experience could be obscured by the presence of others. For example, when initially analyzing the experience of anger, "the mass of sensations accompanying the flush of anger," could be hidden by other mental processes. They could, however, be revealed in repeated introspective sessions.

An important example of Titchener's treatment of synthesis comes from his context theory of meaning. Elementary mental events, such as sensations, images, and feelings, are devoid of meaning. These elements, on the most basic level, are simply experienced. Yet, our perceptions of the world have meaning. We perceive apples, trees, people, have stomach aches, and feel sad. That is, meaningless sensations combine to form meaningful perceptions. How? Meaning, Titchener tells us, results from the constellation of mental elements. A sensation of red by itself has no meaning, but when that same red is associated[1] in consciousness with a round shape and a distinctive sweet odor, we perceive a red apple. The context generates a meaning that does not reside in the individual mental elements.

On which side of the perennial debate in psychology between atomism and holism would Titchener's context theory of meaning fall? Does this formulation suggest that the whole is predictable from its parts or does it argue in favor of the uniqueness of the whole relative to its parts? The reason that this conflict between atomism and holism has been unceasing is that many more issues than one are involved. Two important factors in the debate are (1) the degree of interaction among parts of the compound and (2) the similarity between the properties of the whole and those of the parts. Interaction effects obviously operate in Titchener's context theory because of the meaning that accrues to the elements as a consequence of their combination. By acknowledging interaction effects, Titchener rejected an extreme atomistic position that denies that the ele-

---

[1]Although influenced by British Associationists, Titchener's form of association stressed, not the linking of meaning, but instead sensory content.

ments of a compound influence each other. At the same time, the property of the whole (appleness), in the context theory, appears to be the sum of the individual mental elements (roundness, distinctive odors, redness). However, the holistic property of appleness does not necessarily depend on all the mental elements that make up appleness. Appleness can suddenly emerge from an incomplete set of characteristic elements, as it would with a wax model of an apple or a green apple.

We are forced to conclude that Titchener's context theory of meaning has both atomistic and holistic properties. Although an exact measure of his atomistic and holistic orientation cannot be offered, a relative comparison can be suggested. Titchener was much less holistic than was Wundt. Nothing in Titchener's system is comparable to Wundt's thesis of creative synthesis which assumes that consciousness is irreducible to its constituent elements, that is, the elements of consciousness combine to produce unanticipated consequences (Chapter 2).

The difference between Wundt's and Titchener's views on synthesis reflect their different conceptions of psychology. Wundt argued that creative synthesis characterized the mental (human) sciences, whereas an atomistic approach that treated phenomena as mere aggregates of their component parts described the natural sciences. Titchener, as noted, conceptualized psychology as a natural science, and, therefore, in comparison to Wundt, should be more sympathetic to an analytic approach.

Psychophysiology

The third task of psychology for Titchener was to relate conscious experience with physiological conditions. The term *psychophysiology* describes this task of defining the relationship between the mind and the body. Titchener's views on psychophysiology can be easily misunderstood if not considered within the context of his entire approach to psychology. Titchener contributed to a possible misunderstanding of his views on psychophysiology by his use of the term *explanation* in the following quotation: "Bodily processes . . . are the conditions of mental processes; and the statement of them furnishes us with scientific explanation of the mental processes" (Titchener, 1913, p. 18). Titchener did not use *explanation* in this passage either in a causal or deductive sense. Titchener adopted psychophysical parallelism, a philosophical position that assumes that mental and physical processes occur in a parallel fashion like two roads that run along side by side. The implication of psychophysical parallelism for psychology is that mental and physiological events occur together, but one is not the cause of the other. For example, the sensation of blue is not caused by neurochemical events in the visual cortex or vice versa. However, changes in visual experience are always accompanied by changes in neurochemical events in the visual cortex.

Titchener was not deeply involved in the philosophical issue of psychophysical parallelism; he viewed this assumption about the mind-body problem as a convenient way of organizing psychological knowledge. He believed that the mind could be studied independently of physiological processes but, at the same time, a complete study of psychology would have to include the physiological correlates of the mind.

Titchener used the analogy of the map to interpret the relationship between body and mind; the nervous system explains consciousness as a map of a country explains the roads and towns of a countryside. Remember that Titchener regarded the notion of *causality* as mythological. Because of this, he concluded that *description* was the goal of science. The map analogy employed by Titchener essentially implies a parallel relationship between mental and physiological events. The designation of a road that connects two towns on the map essentially describes the parallel relationship between the two towns and road in the countryside.

Little was accomplished during Titchener's tenure at Cornell in uncovering the physiological correlates of conscious experience. Two major reasons are responsible for this lack of progress. First, the primary concern with discovering basic mental processes did not leave much time for psychophysiological research. Second, the technology to investigate physiological processes was exceedingly primitive by contemporary standards. The major effort during Titchener's lifetime in understanding psychophysiological relationships was to relate sensory experience to receptor activity. In some cases the search for receptors for certain experiences proved unsuccessful:

> the evidence is that . . . [sexual needs and processes] . . . are perceptions . . . perhaps with pleasant pain more involved in the male process than has usually been supposed. The histological search for lust receptors has not led to certain results (Boring, 1942, p. 564).

Quotations from Edward B. Titchener

1. Wundt is . . . too dogmatic and too ready to change his views (Titchener, 1929/1972, p. 19).

2. But in general, the method of psychology is much the same as the method of physics (Titchener, 1910, p. 17).

3. It cannot be too strongly urged that our introspection must be absolutely impartial, and extremely careful (Titchener, 1896/1921, p. 133).

4. There is no psychological evidence of a mind which lies behind mental processes. Introspection reveals no trace of it: whenever we look inward, we find nothing but processes of varying degrees of complexity (Titchener, 1896/1921, p. 358).

5. We have laid it down as rule without exception that every mental process has as its condition a bodily process, some change in the central nervous system and more particularly, in the cerebral cortex (Titchener, 1896/1921, p. 360).

6. Description is precisely what we have found the business of science to be: an analysis undertaken with the view to a later synthesis (Titchener, 1929/1972, p. 62).

7. Of all . . . possible forms . . . [of meaning] . . . two appear to be of special importance: kinaesthesis and verbal images. We are locomotor organisms, and change of bodily attitude is of constant occurrence in our experience; so that typical kinaesthetic patterns become . . . ingrained in our consciousness . . . all sorts of sensory and imaginal complexes receive their meaning from some mode of verbal representation: we understand a thing, place a thing, as soon as we have named it (Titchener, 1910, pp. 367–371).

8. We cannot undo our past; but we can prevent the evils which flow from the ignoring of it (Titchener, 1929/1972, p. 83).

CONTRIBUTIONS OF STRUCTURALISM

Titchener shares with Wundt an important role in creating an independent science of psychology. Although Wundt's role was primary, it was Titchener's efforts in the United States and Canada that contributed to the rapid growth of the science of psychology in that part of the world where it was to flourish most. He trained many important students who assumed leading roles in American psychology: Edwin G. Boring (1886–1968) became the leading American historian, Margaret F. Washburn (1871–1939) played an instrumental role in the development of the popular field of animal psychology, and Joy P. Guilford (born 1897) did important work in the psychology of measurement and individual differences. Titchener also was responsible for establishing an elite organization of researchers known as the Society of Experimental Psychologists, as well as a Cornell series of publications which disseminated important research findings and theoretical speculations to an eagerly awaiting audience in the new field of psychology. Scientific progress depends on the exchange of information and ideas, and Titchener served this need by establishing important communication channels among psychologists and transmitting important notions through them.

In addition to his professional contributions, Titchener offered a clear-cut conception of psychology. Because it was ultimately rejected by most psychologists, his contribution can easily be underestimated. He stated a clear set of goals for psychology and specified the means by which they could be achieved. He and his followers collected a vast amount of information and offered interesting interpretations. A systematic position, such as structuralism, with a clear research program, inevitably makes a significant contribution to psychology, regardless of whether it is ultimately adopted. It provides the necessary information upon which judgments about its potential can be made. An ambiguous conception with skimpy evidence, in contrast, fails to generate the information necessary to judge its future worth. In the new science of psychology, it was particularly important to judge the implications of the competing conceptions of psychology. Titchener offered the necessary evidence on which to base sound and considered judgments about the potential of structuralism.

Although structuralism emerged from Wundtian psychology, it assumed an entirely different character that demands separate treatment. Essentially, Titchener selected one segment of Wundtian psychology and made it the whole of psychology. The secondary tasks of describing the manner in which mental processes are synthesized and are correlated with physiological processes both depended on the success of the initial task of introspective analysis.

The fundamental questions that structuralism raised were: (1) Should psychology be considered the science of the mind? (2) Should its method be limited to introspection? (3) Should its major goal be the description of mental elements?

No major objection to conceptualizing psychology as the science of the mind occurred during the early years of psychology. Philosophical psychologists had looked upon their area of interest as the mind and, therefore, when Wundt, Titchener, and their contemporaries enunciated an empirical approach to psychology, it appeared natural that the effort should be directed to the study of the mind.

Titchener's insistence that systematic introspection was the sole method of psychological research had the following three important influences on psychology.

The Scope of Psychology

The scope of psychology was drastically reduced; any mental process, incapable of being observed by a trained introspector, was automatically considered, at best, of peripheral interest to psychology. Child psychology, abnormal psychology, and animal psychology were therefore excluded from the mainstream of psychology.

Although in his later years Titchener acknowledged the legitimacy of other approaches to psychology that did not depend exclusively on introspection, he nevertheless insisted that the description of mental events was psychology's first and most important task.

Applied Psychology

Problems of applying psychological knowledge were overlooked. The central role of introspection in structuralism guaranteed that this brand of psychology would remain a pure science; introspective evidence of elementary mental events had no striking practical uses and consequently the task of applying psychology was largely ignored. This attitude was consistent with Titchener's lack of sympathy for the efforts of applied psychologists who sought to employ psychological techniques (e.g., aptitude tests) to solve practical problems. Titchener believed that applied psychology would corrupt the study of the mind. An approach that sought to use information about mental events for practical purposes would inevitably distort the science of psychology.

Titchener was emotionally committed to ivory-tower science. He probably shared Sir W. R. Grove's view, which Titchener cited (1929/1972): "For my own part, I must say that science to me generally ceases to be interesting as it becomes useful." On a more basic level, Titchener strongly believed the scientist as a scientist must be disinterested and unbiased. Applied scientists, Titchener thought, are incapable of maintaining such attitudes because they strive to attain practical goals. In his search to understand the mind, Titchener concluded: "The name 'description,' . . . suggests not only fidelity to fact but also restriction to fact, it bids us abstain from application as well as from interpretation" (1929/1972, p. 72).

Although Titchener did not deny that cooperation could occur between the pure psychologist and the applied psychologist, the immediate and essential task for psychology was to describe the structure of the mind. Any effort that failed to serve this purpose would retard progress. Titchener was instrumental in America in encouraging pure research independent of practical considerations. There is some reason to believe that this tradition, which he helped establish in American universities, was responsible both for the United States achieving preeminence in the world of psychology and for the successful development of applied psychology. This latter contribution was indirect; many of the leading American applied psychologists were trained as pure researchers, thus acquiring those rigorous scientific skills that facilitated the development of applied psychology.

Introspection

Perhaps the most important consequence of Titchener's commitment to systematic introspection as the sole tool of psychological research was the attention it focused on this method. Titchener's position, at first glance, appears eminently reasonable. Science begins with observation and, therefore, if psychology was to be a natural science, its observational techniques must be as precise as those of the physical and natural sciences. To attain this goal, introspectors must be properly trained.

Implicit in Titchener's analysis of the task of observing consciousness was the assumption that the observation of physical events is equivalent to the observation of mental events. Historical evidence questions this assumption. For the most part, physical scientists have no difficulty in agreeing about basic observations. The time required for a ball to roll down an inclined plane, the color of a chemical compound, the electrical changes in the brain are all events that yield agreement among scientific observers. If disagreements do occur, repeated observations usually generate consensual agreement.

The distinctive feature of observations of natural sciences is that the event that is to be inspected is available to all who wish to perceive it. This is not true for mental events. They can only be observed by the experiencing individual. What happens when two introspectors, observing the same event, report different mental experiences? Who would be judged correct? For example, there was a historical debate as to whether green is a unique color sensation or experientially a mixture of blue and yellow (Boring, 1942). That is, if you look at a patch of pure green will you sense a unique green or a combination of blue and yellow? Psychologists committed to the introspective method could not agree, with some arguing that there are three basic color sensations, blue, yellow, and red, while others insisted that there are four.

The inability to resolve disagreements about the content of consciousness proved to the the Achilles' heel of Titchener's introspective psychology. Titchener did not deny that his description of consciousness could not be improved. In fact, his recipe for introspection (p. 65) encouraged psychologists to repeat the introspective analyses of others to determine whether the basic mental processes reported could not be analyzed still further. Nafe (1924), a student of Titchener, finally concluded that feelings are not basic elements but complexes of sensations. A pleasant feeling contains sensations of a "bright pressure" while unpleasantness involves sensations of a "dull pressure." In tracking down the physiological correlates of these complex sensations, which previously had been judged to be elementary feelings, Nafe concluded that vascular changes were occurring in a parallel fashion with the sensations.

In a similar vein, an experiment by Perky (1910) at Cornell questioned the distinction between sensations and images. Subjects were told to project an apple on a blank screen while, unknown to them, a faint picture of an apple was physically projected. The subjects were usually unaware that a "real picture had been added; some of them made the comment that their imagery was especially good that day." In another series of experiments, the subjects were instructed to observe a faint picture on the screen. Unknown to them the illumination was reduced to zero. Nevertheless, most subjects continued to see the picture. If sensations cannot be distinguished from images, why conclude that they are different?

Titchener was convinced that repeated introspective analyses of consciousness would ultimately reveal whether feelings and images were basic mental elements or complex sensations. He had complete confidence in the method of introspection to offer an accurate description of consciousness. He failed, however, to fully appreciate the ambiguity within the notion of an "accurate description of consciousness." No method was available to determine which of two conflicting introspective reports (e.g., green is a unique color experience versus green is a combination of blue and yellow experiences) was valid. Titchener argued that the introspective reports from his laboratories, and those supervised by his students, were accurate because the introspectors were properly trained. Was it not beyond the realm of possibility that other methods of introspection were more valid than those employed by Titchener? Thus, a deadlock was created by the conflicting descriptions of consciousness generated by introspective evidence. These conflicts appeared unresolvable and as a consequence a disenchantment began to grow about a psychology that had as its goal a veridical account of consciousness. This disenchantment became overpowering as the consequences of the failure to resolve the controversy about imageless thought.

The Imageless Thought Controversy

Wundt had rejected the notion that thought could be introspectively analyzed in an experimental situation. He was convinced that mental processes could be properly examined only when directly controlled by physical stimulation. Many of his students, including both Titchener and Külpe, considered this view much too rigid and therefore began to introspectively observe a much broader range of psychological events. Although Külpe was not convinced that thought could be introspectively examined he did believe that an attempt was worthwhile. He initiated such an attempt after leaving Leipzig, at the age of thirty-two, for a professorship at the University of Würzburg.

Külpe's plan to investigate thinking was to confront an introspector with a problem and then have him describe his experience from the time the problem was presented to the time it was solved. One of the first problems used to study thought (Mayer & Orth, 1901) was a word-association task. The selection of this task was based on the assumption, prevalent at the time, that thought consisted of a series of associations. Observing a specific association would presumably reveal the mental content of thought. Most subjects at Würzburg reported definite images or feelings in consciousness during the association test. But some did not. Thought for these subjects was *unanalyzable*. The word associated (e.g., table-chair) popped into consciousness without any trace of images or other conscious content.

A similar finding was obtained in another kind of thought experiment. Subjects were asked whether they agreed with some of Nietzche's aphorisms (e.g., Distrust all in whom the impulse to punish is powerful; One must separate from anything that forces one to repeat no again and again). Some introspectors reported that they were able to reach a decision without having any image in consciousness.

Why was the evidence of imageless thought considered to be so important? Both Wundtian psychology and structuralism, although not fully agreeing about the content of consciousness, nevertheless assumed that thinking depended on mental images. If thinking could occur in their absence, then this basic assumption was incorrect.

Neither Wundt nor Titchener was willing to accept the conclusion that the Würzburg studies were damaging to their respective positions. Wundt rejected the results because they were due to a faulty methodology; one cannot observe thought while thinking. In addition, thinking cannot be studied by rigorous experimental methods because an introspector cannot repeatedly observe the mental processes associated with the original presentation of a problem. Once the problem is solved, as when a specific response word is given to a stimulus word or when a subject decides whether he agrees with an aphorism, the original mental processes can never recur.

Titchener rejected the results of the Würzburgers, not because thought could not be introspectively observed but, instead, because their observations were faulty. When thought was analyzed at Cornell, images were always reported. This encouraged Titchener to conclude that the unanalyzable imageless-thought experiences reported by the Würzburgers were really unanalyzed. When observed at Cornell, imageless thought was revealed to be complexes of kinesthetic sensations and images.

Several attempts were made to resolve this three-corner debate among Külpe, Wundt, and Titchener, but to no avail. One obvious solution was to attribute the different results to individual differences; some people think with images, others do not. But this kind of explanation was rejected for two reasons. First, at the time of the controversy the aim of psychology was the description of the general adult mind, not the differences among individual minds. Just as the anatomy of the heart or brain could be described without reference to individual variations, so could the structure of the mind be so described. Second, individual differences could not reasonably explain the inconsistency between the introspective evidence obtained in the Würzburg and Cornell laboratories; why should all the imageless thought individuals be located in Würzburg, and none at Cornell?

The major effect of the imageless thought controversy was to destroy confidence in introspection. It appeared to be too fragile and unreliable to serve as the basic method of collecting psychological data. Psychology, if it were to continue its development as a science, needed new methods that were more reliable.

The failure of introspection to generate an unequivocal picture of the mind does not mean that the analysis of conscious experience was a waste of time. Throughout the history of psychology, introspective evidence proved useful, especially when it served as the beginning for further exploration instead of an end in itself. The psychology of sensation is a case in point. Once a sensory experience such as visual brightness or auditory pitch was identified by introspection, it became possible to search for the characteristics of the physical stimuli (e.g., the intensity of light, the frequency of the sound wave) to which the experience was related. After the psychophysical relationship was discovered (e.g., pitch as a function of sound frequency) the next step became the discovery of the psychophysiological relationship underlying the conscious experience (e.g., how the sensation of pitch was influenced by the activity of the organ of Corti on the basilar membrane of the inner ear). In sum, the development of the field of sensory psychology was aided by a methodological strategy of investigating three successive problems: introspective analysis of conscious experience, psychophysical relationships, and psychophysiological relationships.

A Final Comment

One way of judging the contributions of scientists is to identify their impact on modern conceptions. Although the name of Titchener is rarely mentioned today, his contributions to the fields of sensation, perception, emotion, and psychological measurement are readily acknowledged. He failed to retain the eminent position that he achieved during his lifetime, but his role in the development of psychology cannot be forgotten.

A HISTORICAL NOTE

Some historians suggest that Titchener, near the end of his career, entertained second thoughts about both introspection and the analysis of consciousness into basic processes (Evans, 1972).

Consciousness can be observed in many ways. Structuralism was built upon the premise that only trained introspectors could accurately observe consciousness. But, as noted, no independent criterion was available to determine what constituted "proper training." Inevitably, this ambiguity encouraged different perspectives in observing conscious experience. Even Wundt and Titchener disagreed about the exact training an introspector should receive.

Another approach to the observation of consciousness, known as phenomenology, attempts to get at the essence of conscious experience independent of any training that might slant the observer to perceive mental events consistent with any preconceptions (e.g., consciousness consists of basic mental events). Titchener described phenomenology as follows:

I mean by a phenomenological account of mind, an account which purports to take mental phenomena at their face value, which records them as they are "given" in everyday experience; the account furnished by a naive, commonsense, nonscientific observer, who has not yet adopted the special attitude of the psychologist, but who from his neutral standpoint aims to be as full and accurate as the psychologist himself (Titchener, 1912, p. 489).

When the above quotation was written Titchener was not sure that a phenomenological analysis was possible. But he did not completely reject the method. In one of his final talks about the state of psychology, he stated:

Phenomenology is not yet a safe and sure mode of approach to the analysis of our psychological subject-matter; and our recourse to it, our realization of its promise may be taken as a sign of adolescence. (Titchener, 1925, p. 323).

One of the last doctoral theses that Titchener edited was a phenomenological study done at Cornell under Titchener's colleague and former student, Harry P. Weld. Titchener was obviously sympathetic to his phenomenological study and phenomenology in general. It would seem that Titchener, in the latter part of his career, was once again facing the conflict that confronts all psychologists who base their conceptions on the direct observations of consciousness: What method permits one to observe consciousness without bias? Perhaps consciousness cannot be observed in any unbiased fashion for the simple reason that the attitude or language, whatever it may be, of the introspector, naive or sophisticated, will determine what is observed; the observer and what is observed are not independent (Kendler, 1981). Titchener did not entertain this last possibility because of his conviction that the first task of psychology is to describe conscious experience.

Combined with his reconsideration of phenomenology was Titchener's entertainment of the notion that consciousness should not be analyzed into elements but instead into dimensional attributes of experience: quality, intensity, protensity (duration), extensity, and attensity (clearness). In a letter to a graduate student, Titchener wrote:

You must give up thinking in terms of sensations and affections. That was all right ten years ago; but now, as I have told you, it is wholly out of date . . . You must learn to think in terms of dimensions rather than in terms of systematic constructs like sensation (Evans, 1972, p. 174).

The historical significance of these two redirections in Titchener's thinking is trifling in one sense and important in another. Titchener's contribution to psychology is his structuralist conception of the mind that was based on systematic experimental introspection and on the idea that consciousness consisted of basic mental processes (elements). Structuralism was the system Titchener developed, and was one that had a major impact on psychology. It stands as an entity in itself, independent of second thoughts or ad hoc speculations. Yet the strong suggestion that Titchener, near the end of his career, was raising questions about some basic assumptions of structuralism reinforced the belief that structuralism was not a satisfactory conception of psychology. It will be interesting to consider or evaluate subsequent developments in psychology in light of Titchener's later views about phenomenology and dimensions of experience.

A Debate about the Early Psychologists

Moderator: Two issues will be debated. The first will concern the general contributions of the early psychologists Wundt and Titchener to the advancement of the science of psychology. The second will be a discussion of the differences between the views of Wundt and those of Titchener with attention focused on the question of whether Titchener's contributions represent a step forward from those of Wundt. As is the custom, the positive view (pro) is entitled to the opening remarks.

Pro: In anticipation of the attitude that my opponent will no doubt assume, I wish to emphasize that the only reasonable way of evaluating Wundt and Titchener is to judge them within a historical context. We must assess their contributions within the intellectual climate that prevailed in Germany during the end of the nineteenth and the beginning of the twentieth century. Judged within this context, they each deserve, to varying degrees, our accolades. Wundt created a science of psychology by providing a solid base of data that not only converted psychology from a speculative discipline to an empirical science but also gave guidance to the research efforts of subsequent psychologists. Titchener, with a commitment to develop psychology as a natural science, refined Wundt's approach and helped develop psychology as a laboratory science. Although his description of mental processes failed to gain unanimous acceptance, his research techniques proved invaluable to the young science of psychology particularly in the areas of sensation and perception. All in all, these two psychologists started psychology and helped it grow. What more can you demand?

Con: That is a good question. I'll try to answer it. I would have liked the early psychologists to create a thriving science that would not be in a constant state of wrangling about the proper methods of investigation. I would have liked the early psychologists to discover some basic psychological principles that had some permanence, at least to the extent of surviving for more than several decades.

Your emphasis on judging the efforts of the early psychologists "within a historical context" seems to imply that their shortcomings were an expression of the Zeitgeist of their times rather than to their own misconceptions. In spite of their talent and dedication, the efforts of Wundt and Titchener seemed to suffer from basic misdirection. Their science of the mind failed to produce the kind of progress they argued was possible. Nor did it set a clear course for future generations of psychologists to take. In a very fundamental sense the verdict of history is clear; they were failures, not in spirit or dedication, but in achievement.

Pro: The problem with your criticism is that it is based on naive conceptions of science and psychology. Science doesn't progress in a nice, neat series of steps. Science has always progressed in a zigzag path. Redirections and misdirections are essential ingredients of scientific progress. Admittedly the early psychologists zigged and zagged but they were nevertheless moving forward. Your naive conception of psychology also needs to be rebutted. There are many different approaches to, and conceptions of, psychology as history demonstrates. It is naive to diagnose any of them as basically invalid. They must be judged in terms of fruitfulness, not validity. Furthermore . . .

Moderator: This is a good place to interrupt. Both of you have made your points. Let us shift attention to the question of whether Titchener improved upon Wundt's conceptions. The defender of the early psychologists will discuss this issue first.

Pro: The answer to the question posed depends upon the frame of reference that is adopted. If you look upon psychology as a broad discipline that ranges from sensory to social phenomena, then I believe the efforts of Titchener represent a step backwards. If you consider systematic integration a significant aspect of scientific conceptions, then I would be forced to conclude that Titchener's position represented a step forward.

Con: As a matter of principle, I dislike agreeing with my opponent but I must admit that I share some of his views. However, my bias is definitely in favor of highly integrated, systematic formulations. They have a great advantage over vague formulations like Wundt's principles of creative synthesis. A precise formulation is capable of being evaluated because its views are sufficiently explicit to be proven wrong. Equivocal conceptions survive indefinitely because their inexactness protects them from being tested and their ambiguity generates a false sense of understanding. Consequently, I favor Titchener's conception over that of Wundt's.

Moderator: Let us end this discussion on that partial note of agreement.

SUMMARY

Titchener was a student of Wundt and his conception of psychology can be considered a modification of his professor's systematic position. Titchener was also influenced by two philosophical conceptions, associationism and positivism. Associationism, which dates back to Greek philosophy, postulates that mental events are connected by associationistic principles. Three questions are generated by associationism: What mental events (e.g., sensations, images) are associated? What principles (contiguity, similarity) govern the associative process? Are mental events modified when associated? Positivism is a philosophical position that insists that valid knowledge about the world can only be obtained by the methods of the natural sciences.

Titchener believed that mental events are the subject matter of psychology. Unlike Wundt, Titchener believed that psychology was completely a natural science. All sciences, for Titchener, had their origins in human experience. He did, however, distinguish between the experience of the psychological scientist from that of the physical scientist. Psychologists deal with conscious experience that is dependent on the human observers while physicists deal with experience that is independent of human observers.

Titchener argued that consciousness could be clearly observed in a much wider range of situations than Wundt thought possible *if* the introspector were properly trained. Titchener also assumed that consciousness was a combination of basic mental events. Along with positivists of his day, Titchener insisted that an explanation of psychological events is achieved when the phenomena are described. He rejected the concept of causality if it meant "anything more than correlation."

Titchener's strategy in his research program was to first analyze consciousness into its simplest components, then discover the principles that govern their combination, and finally to relate the mental elements to their physiological conditions. The first step, the analysis of consciousness into its basic processes, dominated Titchener's career. Introspection revealed three major classes of mental elements: *sensations, images,* and *affections.* Both sensations and images possess four attributes: quality, intensity, duration, and clearness. Affection possessed the first three attributes but not clearness. Contrary to Wundt's tridimensional theory of feeling, feelings (affections) varied along a single dimension of pleasantness-unpleasantness according to Titchener.

The problem of synthesis of mental elements, for Titchener, was of secondary importance to that of analysis. Although not explicitly stating any general principles of synthesis, Titchener was much less holistic in his views than was Wundt. In his context theory of meaning, which has both atomistic and holistic properties, Titchener postulated that basic mental elements were devoid of meaning, but when they combine during the perception of an object (e.g., book) meaning results. Thus, the meaning is created by the interaction among mental elements. At the same time the meaning, the property of the whole (e.g., a book), is the sum of the individual mental elements (e.g., size, shape, color).

Titchener adopted a philosophical position known as psychophysical parallelism in dealing with the relationship between mental and bodily events: mental and physical processes occur in parallel fashion but one is not the cause of the other. The major effort, during Titchener's career, was to relate sensory experience to receptor activity.

Titchener's two major contributions were the central roles he played in the development of psychology in the United States and Canada and in the formulation of structuralism. Structuralism was not, however, embraced by all American psychologists mainly because of its affirmative response to three fundamental questions: Should psychology select consciousness as its subject matter? Should psychology's methods be limited to introspection? Should psychology's major goal be the description of basic mental processes? The second question initially posed the greatest conflict because introspection proved to be unreliable; introspective analyses of the same mental event did not always agree. The unreliability of the introspective method was highlighted by the imageless-thought controversy that was generated by Külpe and his colleagues at Würzburg. Evidence of imageless thought was reported in Külpe's laboratory but was later denied by introspective reports obtained in Titchener's laboratory at Cornell. Wundt rejected both kinds of evidence because of his conviction that thought could not be subjected to introspective analysis. Confidence in introspection was undermined because of the inability to resolve this dispute about imageless thought. If psychology was a natural science, as Titchener argued, then its basic method of investigation, introspection, should be capable of yielding reliable data about psychological phenomena.

SUGGESTED READINGS

An excellent source of Titchener's views is the writings of Titchener himself. Some recommended books are: *An Outline of Psychology* (1896/1921), *Lectures on the Elementary Psychology of Feeling and Attention* (1908/1973), and *Lectures on the Experimental Psychology of the Thought-Processes* (1909). Good secondary sources are E. G. Boring's *A History of Experimental Psychology* (1950) and E. Heidbreder's *Seven Psychologies* (1933).

Külpe's systematic position is covered in Boring's history and also in G. Murphy's *Historical Introduction to Modern Psychology* (1949). Excellent reviews of the imageless-thought controversy are reported in R. S. Woodworth's *Experimental Psychology* (1938) and G. Humphrey's *Thinking: An Introduction to Its Experimental Psychology* (1951).

4

William James

William James (1842–1910) occupies a paradoxical position in American psychology. He was, and still is, regarded with reverence and considered by many to be the greatest of all American psychologists. In spite of his exalted position, he was at best ambivalent about psychology. After completing his classic *The Principles of Psychology* (1890), which required twelve years to write and on which his fame as a psychologist mainly rests, he wrote that the book proved "that there is no such thing as a science of psychology." On another occasion, he characterized psychology as "a nasty little subject."

One can guess that the major reason for James's ambivalence toward psychology is that temperamentally he was a philosopher primarily interested in those issues of the human condition that were more amenable to philosophical analysis than to empirical investigation. He disliked research, once confessing, "I hate experimental work."

In spite of James's ambivalence toward psychology and distaste for doing research, he made important contributions to the discipline in which he could not feel at home. His contributions were exceptionally varied, and their total impact on psychology is still a source of controversy.

William James is commonly considered the precursor of functionalism, the systematic position that emphasizes the function of consciousness instead of its structure. This historical characterization of James is valid but incomplete. Although his major impact was on the development of functionalism in America, James's ideas extended to other important orientations. Within his writings are ideas that anticipated behaviorism, Gestalt psychology, psychoanalysis, and humanistic psychology. The most appropriate way to characterize William James's influence on psychology is as a crossroads or junction in the history of psychology; his various methodological and theoretical notions led to strikingly different psychological systems. Within all modern views of psychology can be found ideas that were expressed earlier by James.

HISTORICAL ROOTS

The simplest way to describe James's intellectual ancestry is to state that he emerged from the totality of Western civilization. He was knowledgeable about philosophy, science, art, and comparative religion. These various traditions merged within James's conception of psychology. Two specific influences, however, deserve special attention. One was the realization that Darwin's theory of evolution implied that consciousness and behavior should be considered within the context of an organism's adaptation to its environment. James's recognition of the relationship between evolution and psychology anticipated the central roles that evolutionary theory would later be assigned in functionalism and behaviorism. The second influence was clinical research on the disorder known as hysteria, which James learned about on a visit to Paris. This research influenced James's views on the psychology of personality, which, in turn, stimulated the development of abnormal and clinical psychology in America.

Charles R. Darwin

As a young man, Charles Darwin studied for the ministry at Cambridge University. At that time, he believed in the creationist theory of the origin of species: The variety of animal and plant species represents the unalterable work of God. He lost interest in the ministry and turned to the study of nature (e.g., zoology, botany, geology), and then accepted the position of naturalist aboard the *Beagle*, which set forth on a five-year cruise in 1831 to survey the coasts of South America. He spent the major part of the rest of his life attempting to explain the variety of animal and plant life he had observed on that trip. The problem was illuminated for him by reading Thomas Malthus's *An Essay of the Principle of Population* (1872/1976). Malthus contended that poverty and famine were unavoidable because the human population increases much more rapidly than does the means of subsistence (e.g., food supply, material for housing). Having concluded from his observations during his *Beagle* voyage that a struggle for existence occurred among animals and plants, Malthus's theory triggered the thought, as Darwin wrote in his notebook, "that under these circumstances [struggle for existence] favourable variations would tend to be preserved, and unfavourable ones would be destroyed. The result of this would be the formation of new species. Here, then, I had a theory by which to work" (Darwin, 1877).

FIGURE 4.1 Charles R. Darwin

National Library of Medicine

Darwin's theory of evolution, sometimes referred to as Darwinism, essentially states that members of species *vary*, and those members with variations which prove helpful in the struggle to survive will more likely procreate. This is the *principle of natural selection*. In essence, Darwin postulated a reproductive competition among members of the same species. Those that were best adapted to *a given environment* had a reproductive advantage. One example is the effect of a recent drought on Darwin's finches, so named because Darwin had discovered them in the Galápagos Islands during the voyage of the *Beagle:* "Large birds . . . with large [stout] beaks, survived best because they were able to crack large and hard seeds that predominated in the drought" (Boag & Grant, 1981). Evolutionary pressures, in this case, favor the reproduction of large birds with large beaks, because these anatomical features favor survival and reproduction.

Darwinism influenced James in three major ways:

First, Darwinism encouraged a functional orientation in psychology. The large, stout beak of a finch was functional during a period of drought because it served the purpose of adaptation to the environment, thus increasing the probability of species survival. If psychology is considered to be the science of the mind, then according to Darwinism the significant question becomes, "How does consciousness help humans adapt to their environment?" For James, function superseded description as the central problem in psychology.

Second, Darwinism encouraged James to view psychology as a biological science. The anatomy of an organism and its physiological functioning determines an organism's ability to adapt to its environment. Consciousness functions within a physiological system; it is an expression of underlying neurochemical changes of the brain. Understanding consciousness requires understanding brain processes. James assumed that every particular mental event is a result of a particular brain event, and in principle, psychological events are reducible to physiological processes. This position, sometimes referred to as the identity hypothesis in regard to the mind-body problem, is obviously at odds with Titchener's parallelism, which assumed that mental and physiological events occur in parallel fashion without one being responsible for the other.

Third, Darwinism made *adaptation* a key concept in psychology. In order for the gene pool of a species to survive, its members must adapt to their environment. James borrowed this notion by suggesting that the mind helps humans adapt to both their physical environment and their social environment.

Psychopathology

While German psychologists were concerned with understanding normal mental events in the laboratory, French psychiatrists and psychologists were trying to unravel the mysteries of abnormal mental processes (psychopathology) in the clinic. Psychology and psychiatry were always closely related in France, because they shared a common interest in psychopathology. William James was particularly influenced by the research of Jean Martin Charcot (1825–1893) and his student, Pierre Janet (1859–1947).

The organic view of psychopathology prevailed in France; mental disorders were regarded as disorders of the brain. Thus, Charcot, a specialist in neurology, and therefore automatically a psychiatrist, conceptualized *hysteria* as a neurological disease. Patients suffering from *hysteria* exhibit such symptoms as paralysis of some part of the body (e.g., hand) and/or sensory defects (e.g., blindness). The notion that hysteria was simply a neurological disease was challenged by two kinds of evidence in the days of Charcot.

First, the hysterical symptoms frequently did not coincide with the anatomical distribution of nerves. In glove anesthesia, a common hysterical symptom, the patient has a pattern of insensitivity in the form of a

---

FIGURE 4.2 A Lithograph of a Painting of Charcot Demonstrating Hypnosis in a Hysterical Patient

---

The patient would exhibit a variety of physical states and imaginary sensations.

The National Library of Medicine

glove. Any pinprick within the area "covered" by the glove is not felt. This distribution of insensitivity fails to make anatomical sense because the nerves in the hand are distributed in an entirely different pattern.

The second reason for questioning the idea that hysteria is a neurological disease was Charcot's dramatic demonstration that hysterical symptoms could be eliminated by hypnosis; the glove anesthesia disappeared when the patient was placed under hypnosis.

How was hysteria to be explained? One answer was that hysterical patients were malingering, faking their symptoms. Charcot dismissed this interpretation because of his conviction that hysterical patients were truly and severely distressed about their disability. Instead, he proposed that hysteria resulted from a hereditary degenerative disease of the nervous system even though he was unsuccessful in discovering evidence of neural deterioration. In order to explain the fact that hysterical symptoms could be removed during hypnosis, Charcot hypothesized that only persons with a hereditary hysterical degenerative disease of the nervous system could be hypnotized. These ad hoc attempts to salvage his neurological theory of hysteria collapsed in the face of the evidence that normal individuals could be hypnotized and made to exhibit hysterical symptoms indistinguishable from those of hysterical patients.

Janet, a psychologist and physician, shifted attention, to some degree, from the hysteric's neurophysiology to his mental processes. He concluded, after observing many hysterics, that they suffer from *mental dissociation:* certain ideas and emotions become detached from the rest of the mental life of an individual, thus generating hysterical symptoms. When it came to explaining the cause of this dissociation, Janet reverted back to the ideas of his teacher. Mental dissociation was due to some hereditary degeneration of the nervous system which lowered a person's mental energy to unify consciousness into a single organized system. This notion of dissociation was picked up by James and employed in his theory of the self, which anticipated modern conceptions of personality organization.

Another theory of hysteria was to be developed by a young Viennese physician after he studied with Charcot. He abjured the neurological basis of hysteria and postulated that hysterical symptoms were an expression of underlying psychological conflict. Sigmund Freud was the name of that physician and his story will come later.

William James (1842–1910)

William James was born in New York City of wealthy parents in a household committed to an intellectual lifestyle. His father, Henry James, Sr., who was to exert a profound influence on William, had quit divinity school as a young man because of his aversion to the stern Presbyterian doctrines. His yearning for some theological guidance, however, persisted. At thirty-three years of age, he suffered a full-blown anxiety attack:

> In a lightening flash, as it were—"fear came upon me, and trembling, which made all my bones to shake." To all appearances it was a perfectly insane and abject terror, without ostensible cause, and only to be accounted for to my perplexed imagination, by some damned shape squatting invisible to me within the precincts of the room, and raying out from his fetid personality influences fatal to life. I felt myself a wreck; that is, reduced from a state of firm, vigorous, joyful manhood to one of almost helpless infancy (quoted from a letter by Henry James, Sr., contained in Matthiessen, 1961, p. 161).

A chronic state of anxiety followed which could not be relieved by the advice of physicians who prescribed vacations to encourage relaxation. Two years after the anxiety attack, Henry James, Sr., became acquainted with the writings of Emanuel Swedenborg

FIGURE 4.3 William James

Courtesy of Harvard University

(1688–1772), a Swedish mystic who apparently had also experienced a severe anxiety attack. Reading Swedenborg's obscure theological system helped Henry James, Sr., gain control over his anxiety neurosis. As a consequence, he felt obligated to spread Swedenborg's message. His books and lectures about Swedenborg failed, however, to convert many followers mainly because James's message was as opaque as Swedenborg's. It was said that Henry James, Sr., not only discovered Swedenborg's secret, but also kept it.

Henry James, Sr., was, however, successful in providing his children, particularly his two older sons, William and Henry, with an unusually stimulating education. Their formal education consisted of irregular attendance in private schools in England, France, Switzerland, and Germany. Of greater impact was the informal education at home, where spirited discussions of philosophy, religion, science, and art frequently took place, sometimes in the presence of distinguished visitors such as Ralph Waldo Emerson. The impressive achievements of both sons seem to have some root in their unique educational experience. As a novelist, Henry achieved a fame equal to William

James's. It has been said that William James wrote about psychology in the style of a novelist, while Henry James wrote novels in the style of a psychologist.

William James's intellectual life was filled with conflicts between art and science, psychology and philosophy, and empiricism and mysticism. His broad interests and immense talents trapped him into seeking goals that were incompatible. He suffered bouts of depression at times when he was unsure about which direction his life should take; he appears to have been a victim of the indecision that he warned others against: "There is no more miserable human being than one in whom nothing is habitual but indecision" (James, 1890).

At age eighteen, William James decided to become a painter, but six months in an art institute convinced him that his talents fell short of his aspirations. In 1861, he entered Harvard to study chemistry, but because of his dislike for laboratory research he shifted to medical training, partly because of his fascination with recent breakthroughs in the science of physiology. He interrupted his medical education at Harvard Medical School several times, due in part to a lack of enthusiasm for his chosen profession. During that period he suffered several bouts of illness involving both severe physical symptoms and depression that bordered on the suicidal. He finally obtained his M.D. at twenty-seven, but soon thereafter suffered an attack of intense insecurity. In a book entitled *The Varieties of Religious Experience* (1902/1928), which he wrote many years later, James described his own experience in the guise of a case history of a fictional "Frenchman":

> suddenly there fell upon me without warning, just as if it came out of the darkness, a horrible fear of my own existence. Simultaneously, there arose in my mind the image of an epileptic patient whom I had seen in the asylum, a black-haired youth with greenish skin, entirely idiotic, who used to sit all day on one of the benches, or rather shelves against the wall, with his knees drawn up against his chin, and the coarse gray undershirt, which was his only garment, drawn over them inclosing his entire figure. He sat there like a sort of sculptured Egyptian cat or Peruvian mummy, moving nothing but his black eyes and looking absolutely non-human. This image and my fear entered into a species of combination with each other. *That shape am I,* I felt, potentially . . . After this the universe was changed for me altogether. I awoke morning after morning with a horrible dread at the pit of my stomach, and with a sense of insecurity of life that I never knew before, and that I have never felt since (James, 1902/1928, p. 160).

Like his father, his condition improved after a chance reading, in William's case, an essay on free will by a French philosopher. The following day, he wrote in his diary:

> I think that yesterday was a crisis in my life. I finished the first part of Renouvier's second "Essais" and see no reason why his definition of free will—"the sustaining of a thought *because I choose to* when I might

have other thoughts"—need be the definition of an illusion. At any rate, I will assume for the present—until next year—that it is no illusion. My first act of free will shall be to believe in free will . . . Hitherto, when I have felt like taking a free initiative, like daring to act originally, without carefully waiting for contemplation of the external world to determine all for me, suicide seemed the most manly form to put my daring into; now, I will go a step further with my will, not only act with it, but believe as well; believe in my individual reality and creative power (Henry James, 1920, I, pp. 147–148).

When he was thirty, William James accepted a position at Harvard to teach physiology. He proved to be a great teacher because of his enthusiasm and ability to lecture as he wrote. Physiology failed to satisfy his broad intellectual needs and as a consequence his interests began to shift to psychology. He started a laboratory where he could demonstrate psychological phenomena and, in 1878, signed a contract to write *The Principles of Psychology* which he thought he could complete in two years. While teaching physiology and writing on psychology, James became interested in numerous philosphical issues—free will versus scientific determinism, the meaning of truth, the nature of morality—that influenced his psychological views. Although James reported many of the psychological facts of his day, *The Principles of Psychology* can be described as a psychological autobiography by a master of self-observation. The book was based more upon James's conscious experience than upon systematic psychological investigations.

James's philosophical bent became so apparent that, in 1880, two years after he began *The Principles* and ten years before he finished it, he was appointed assistant professor of philosophy at Harvard, and five years later he became a full professor. In anticipation of the publication of *The Principles of Psychology* in 1890, James's academic title shifted to professor of psychology, but in 1897 he once again became a professor of philosophy and remained in that niche for the remainder of his academic life.

The Principles of Psychology (1890) was an instant success not only because of its ideas, but also because of the brilliant prose in which they were expressed. Who could fail to be persuaded by the following "truth?":

The hell to be endured hereafter, of which theology tells, is not worse than the hell we make for ourselves in this world by habitually fashioning our characters in the wrong way (James, 1890, vol. I, p. 127).

During the last twenty years of his life, James completed the transition from psychology to philosophy, although never fully acknowledging the independence of the two disciplines. *The Principles of Psychology*, which exceeded 1300 pages, was condensed into a 478-page volume, known as "The Briefer Course" (1892a), in order to serve as an undergraduate textbook. Following this he wrote *Talks to Teachers* (1899), a book based on a series of lectures designed to apply psychological principles to classroom teaching, and the aforementioned *The Varieties of Religious Experience* (1902/1928), the title of which aptly describes its content. Its underlying theme is that religious experiences should not be judged by their so-called normality. Unusual mystical experiences can be adaptive: They can serve to conquer despair and reveal the entire universe as intrinsically unified and good.

James's interest in mystical experience was a combined expression of his open-minded attitude about all psychological events, both normal and abnormal, and a fascination with the occult, which he expressed in his assistance in founding an American organization dedicated to psychical research. Telepathy, thought transference from one person to another without the mediation of the senses, was a reality to James, and he also thought that communicating with the dead was a real possibility.

William James resigned from Harvard in 1907 because of his failing health. Three important philosophical books—*Pragmatism* (1907), *The Meaning of Truth* (1909a), and *A Pluralistic Universe* (1909b)—were published soon thereafter. In the spring of 1910, he traveled with his wife to a health resort in Germany that specialized in heart diseases. His condition did not improve, and he and his wife returned home in the company of James's brother, Henry. William James died a few days after his return home.

METHODOLOGICAL ASSUMPTIONS

In contrast to Wundt, who was known as the *systematic psychologist*, James was called the *unsystematic psychologist*, a position he defended. He felt that the provisional nature of psychology should not be ignored, and that a rigid systematic methodological position during the infancy of the new science could prove self-defeating: "At a certain stage in the development of every science, a degree of vagueness is what best consists with fertility."

The Subject Matter of Psychology

In the tradition of Wundt, James considered psychology a science of the mind: "Psychology is the Science of Mental Life, both of its phenomena and their conditions" (James, 1890, I). The qualifications relating to mental "phenomena and their conditions" are important because they reflect preconceptions about mental life that are at odds with those of Wundt.

Preconceptions about the Mind

James said that the fundamental phenomena of mental life were not basic processes such as sensations, images, and affects, as Wundt and Titchener thought, but were instead "such things as we call feelings, desires, cognitions, reasoning, decisions, and the like." Activities, not states, of consciousness, were the mental events to be observed. In addition to observing these activities, psychologists must also identify the conditions under which they occur. For example, when discussing memory, James asks why we can

> retain so much better the events of yesterday than those of last year, and best of all, those of an hour ago? Why, again, in old age should its grasp of childhood's events seem firmest? Why should illness and exhaustion enfeeble it? Why should drugs, fevers, asphyxia, and excitement resuscitate things long since forgotten? (James, 1890, I, pp. 2–3)

The quest for conditions under which these mental phenomena operate "becomes the psychologist's most interesting task." Intertwined with this task is the understanding of the functional value of mental activities.

> Mental life is primarily teleological; that is to say, that our various ways of feeling and thinking have grown to be what they are because of their utility in shaping our *reactions* on the outer world (James, 1892a, p. 4).

Thus, James's preconceptions about mental life encouraged the observation of the activities of the mind, the conditions under which they occurred, and the purposes they served.

Methods of Investigation

Introspection. James considered the observation of one's own consciousness the basic psychological method:

> *Introspective Observation is what we have to rely on first and foremost and always.* The word introspection need hardly be defined—it means, of course, the looking into our own minds and reporting what we there discover (1890, I, p. 185).

When James looked into his mind he found that

> Consciousness . . . does not appear to itself chopped up in bits. Such words as 'chain' or 'train' do not describe it fitly as it presents itself in the first instance. It is nothing jointed; it flows. A 'river' or 'stream' are the metaphors by which it is most naturally described. *In talking of it hereafter, let us call it the stream of thought, of consciousness, or of subjective life* (James, 1890, I, p. 239).

This passage, except for its greater eloquence, appears to be consistent with Wundt's (1910) characterization: "conscious contents are at the opposite pole from permanent objects; they are processes, fleeting occurrences, in a continual flux and change." In spite of the similarity, Wundt and James disagreed about the nature of consciousness partly because of their differing views about introspection. Wundt believed that introspectors must be trained to accurately observe consciousness. James questioned this assumption and coined the term *the psychologist's fallacy* to refer to the *"confusion of the* [psychologist's] *own standpoint with that of the mental fact."* The discovery of discrete mental processes or elements in Wundt's laboratory did not persuade James that these basic mental events were in the mind originally. Instead, he suggested that the introspectors reported them in consciousness because they anticipated their presence. Employing an orientation similar to phenomenology that assumed consciousness could be accurately observed naturally in the absence of training and preconceptions, James failed to discover that his mental content contained assemblages of basic mental elements (processes). Instead, his stream of consciousness consisted of integrated events: The thought of "the-pack-of-cards-is-on-the-table" was of a *unitary undivided* object, not a combination of separate ideas such as a table top with legs and a pack of fifty-two separate cards. This holistic view anticipated Gestalt psychology.

Experimentation. James acknowledged the importance of experimentation in psychology but did not view it within the narrow confines of Wundt's Leipzig laboratory. He expressed little enthusiasm for Wundt's research program (e.g., mental chronometry, psychophysics), saying that "the results have as yet borne little theoretic fruit commensurate with the great labor expended in their acquisition. But facts are facts, and if we only get enough of them they are sure to combine" (James, 1890, I).

Many of James's ideas encouraged novel experimental methods unheard of in European laboratories. One example is his personal support of Edward L. Thorndike's investigation of animal learning. Stimulated by his reading of James's *The Principles of Psychology* (1890), which described "living creatures from an outward point of view . . . [as] bundles of habits," Thorndike went to Harvard for his graduate work in order to study habits. He decided to use chicks as his subjects, believing he could incubate them and hatch them in his bedroom. His landlady rejected this plan and Thorndike then sought the assistance of James. James was unsuccessful in getting space for the project at Harvard. Rather than permit it to die, James offered Thorndike the use of the basement at his home, much to the delight of James's children. Here, Thorndike began his experimental approach to the psychology of learning which later was to become a classic and propel him to the forefront of the ranks of learning theorists. Although James disliked doing experimental research, his fertile mind encouraged it in others.

Comparative Method. James coined the term the *comparative method* to denote a mode of investigation designed to supplement introspective knowledge of the normal human mind by inferring mental activities in the minds of others:

> instincts of animals are ransacked to throw light on our own; and . . . the reasoning faculties of bees and ants, the minds of savages, infants,

madmen, idiots, the deaf and blind, criminals, and eccentrics, are all invoked in support of this or that special theory about some part of our own mental life. The history of sciences, moral and political institutions, and languages, as types of mental products, are pressed into the same services (James, 1890, I, p. 194).

James realized that "there are great sources of error in [his] comparative method. The interpretation of the 'psychoses' of animals, savages, and infants is necessarily wild work" because subjective factors will influence the interpretation of the mental events of other organisms: "A savage will be reported to have no moral or religious feelings if his actions shock the observer unduly." James acknowledges that he could offer no rules to make the comparative method valid. The only recommendation was, "to test some pre-existing hypothesis; and the only thing then is to use as much sagacity as you possess, and to be as candid as you can."

Over the years, the meaning of the *Comparative Method* changed from James's original usage. Now it usually refers to the comparison of behavior of different species. But, it should be noted that the seed of the contemporary meaning is contained in James's belief that psychological knowledge of different kinds of organisms could be enhanced by comparisons, a view that is consistent with Darwinism.

Criterion of Truth

When it came to observational validity of mental events, James disagreed with Wundt. Wundt thought that an introspector could observe the same mental event on different occasions. A trained introspector who is repeatedly exposed to the same physical stimulus in an experimental situation would have the same sensory experiences and, consequently, reliable and accurate observations were possible. James denied this possibility by insisting that consciousness is ever changing, thus precluding repeated observations of the same mental event: "No state once gone can recur and be identical to what was before." Our minds are cumulative products of our past experiences, never to become what has been.

James also insisted that introspective validity cannot be guaranteed regardless of what experimental controls are employed: "*Introspection is difficult and fallible; and that the difficulty is simply that of all observations of whatever kind*" (James, 1890, I). Just as we can err in observing the external world, so can we make mistakes when examining our internal world.

Believing that introspection (i.e., phenomenology) is the major method of investigating consciousness while simultaneously assuming that consciousness is everchanging and introspection is fallible posed a difficult problem for James. How is one to judge the observational validity of introspective evidence? His solution was borrowed from the traditions of the natural sciences: "The only safeguard [against introspective errors] is in the final *consensus* of our . . . knowledge about the thing in question, later views correcting earlier ones, until at last the harmony of a consistent system is reached" (James, 1890, I). James was essentially making a historical prediction that psychologists would ultimately agree about the nature of mental events. This agreement, however, has yet to be achieved. Why? A common explanation is that the observation of consciousness is always influenced by the preconceptions of the introspector. James was right when he leveled the criticism of *the psychologist's fallacy* against Wundt and his associates. What he failed to realize is that all introspection suffers from observational bias, including his own. As long as consciousness can only be observed by one individual, the argument goes, it will be impossible to separate the influence of the observer from what is observed.

James's view of theoretical truth reflects the conflict between his admiration for natural science and his involvement with broad philosophical issues. He conceptualized psychology as a natural science, although admitting that psychology had yet to meet the standards achieved by physics and biology. Nevertheless, he thought that psychology would "become worthy of the name of natural science at no very distant date . . . I wished, by treating Psychology *like* a natural science, to help her become one" (James, 1892b).

James believed that prediction and control were the hallmarks of natural science, and essentially treated them as equivalent. Sometimes they are. For example, physical theory was able to deduce (predict) the amount of thrust that was required for a space craft to escape from the earth's gravitational field and the trajectory needed to land on the moon. These theoretical predictions enabled American space scientists in 1969 to control the flight of the spacecraft, U.S. Apollo, in order that it would land on a designated area on the surface of the moon.

On other occasions, prediction and control are not synonymous; one can occur in the absence of the other. Eclipses can be deductively explained, but obviously cannot be controlled. In contrast, control is sometimes possible in the absence of understanding (deductive explanation). Witch doctors, who believe that illnesses result from the invasion of evil spirits into the victim's body, can sometimes eliminate the symptoms by prescribing supposed magical herbs to expel the spirits. The spirit theory is irrelevant to the treatment's success; the herbs contain drugs that effectively counteract the illness. But the treatment, regardless of theoretical inadequacies, controls the illness.

James went out of his way to emphasize the importance of control in psychology because, unlike Wundt, he was convinced that psychology must be a practical science:

> We live surrounded by an enormous body of persons who are most definitely interested in the control of states of mind, and incessantly craving for a sort of psychological science which will teach them how to *act*. What every educator, every jail warden, every doctor, every clergyman, every asylum superintendent, asks of psychology is practical rules (James, 1892a, p. 148).

As a philosopher, James formulated a pragmatic theory of truth that reflected this concern for utility. James thought that scientific ideas are practical because empirically demonstrated knowledge can be put to use in serving the needs of individuals and society. At the same time, he realized that some important ideas cannot be evaluated by the methods of science; the existence of God, for example, cannot be verified by the scientific method. Why not, James thought, evaluate such extrascientific notions by their usefulness: "On pragmatic principles, if the hypothesis of God works satisfactorily in the widest sense of the word, it is true." In essence, truth, for James, became utility. In a phrase that shocked many philosophers, James equated the truth of ideas with their "cash value."

James's critics argued that he was committing a philosophical sin by substituting a subjective criterion of truth for an objective one. A scientific hypothesis is true, that is, it works, when it can deduce consequences in agreement with empirical evidence. James was suggesting that a hypothesis works, is true, when beneficial effects result from believing in it. Believing in the healing effect of some undemonstrated cure for cancer can improve the quality of life of a cancer victim, but that fact, the argument against James's position would go, does not contribute one iota of truth to the hypothesis that the cure works. In sum, James's critics insisted that truth is independent of utility.

The question can be raised as to why James, committed to a natural science approach to psychology, was willing to adopt such an elastic concept of truth as that proposed in his pragmatic theory. Perhaps the answer lies in his broad psychological interests that extended well beyond the confines of a natural science psychology. He was concerned with all aspects of the human condition: the meaning and significance of life, the moral principles that should guide behavior, the reality of mystical experiences such as communicating with the dead. It would appear that his broad interests conflicted with his conception of psychology as a natural science. Either he had to resist the problems that fascinated him or abandon the notion that psychology can be limited to natural science methodology based upon publicly verified empirical evidence. James never directly faced up to this conflict. But, in his concluding sentence to the brief version of his *Principles* (1892a) he wrote: "The best way we can facilitate [the future advent of geniuses in psychology] is to understand how great is the darkness in which we grope, and never to forget that the natural science assumptions with which we started are provisional and revisable things." His pragmatic theory of truth enabled James to escape the restrictions of natural science psychology without directly renouncing it. The flexible conception of truth gave him the freedom (James 1912) to conclude that "Everything real must be experienceable somewhere, and every kind of thing experienced must somewhere be real" (1912). The rigors of the verification procedures of natural science were essentially abandoned, thereby permitting James's creative imagination and artistic inclination full freedom to range over the entire landscape of the human experience.

STRATEGY

James did not have to be concerned with strategic issues associated with research, such as what phenomena to investigate and what hypotheses to test. The absence of any research involvement permitted James's imagination free rein to speculate about any topic that interested him. In truth, James was a throwback to the rational psychologists of previous eras who operated as armchair philosophers. But there was one important difference. His speculations occurred in an age in which psychology had become a research science. Thus, James's ideas were influenced by his knowledge of empirical facts both from psychology and physiology.

THEORY

An unsystematic psychologist would not be expected to formulate a systematic psychological theory. James did, however, offer many independent hypotheses, some of which are still stimulating research.

James-Lange Theory of Emotion

James's most original contribution to research psychology is his theory of emotion. He was led to this conception by a case of a lady who was bedridden from a riding accident in which she broke her neck. She failed, in spite of her tragedy, to exhibit much emotion when visited by friends and relatives. Perhaps, thought James, the patient's inability to experience bodily changes resulting from the neck injury was responsible for her lack of emotion. Emotional experience, James speculated, depended on awareness of bodily change.

James, in formalizing his view, argued that emotional experience is the consequence, not the cause, of bodily changes.

> Common sense says, we lose our fortune, are sorry and weep; we meet a bear, are frightened and run; we are insulted by a rival, are angry and strike. The hypothesis here to be defended says that this order of sequence is incorrect, that . . . the more rational statement is that we feel sorry because we cry, angry because we strike, afraid because we tremble (James, 1890, II, pp. 449–450).

The notion that experience of bodily changes is emotion[1] met with much resistance. The most influential criticisms were offered by Walter Cannon (1871–1945), a physiologist, who argued that the James-Lange theory was deficient in several respects. Cannon noted that if James were correct that emotional experience is the perception of bodily activities,

---

[1] Carl Lange (1834–1900), a Danish physiologist independently proposed a theory of emotion similar to James's. To acknowledge the contributions of both, the formulation became known as the James-Lange theory of emotion.

then distinctive bodily patterns should be associated with different kinds of emotion, such as happiness, fear, aggression, and so forth. Otherwise, how could we experience different emotions? But distinctive bodily patterns of emotions were never discovered. In addition, Cannon argued that surgically separating the viscera (the internal organs such as the heart and the stomach) from the central nervous system should eliminate emotional states. But, such separations failed to shut off emotional reactions, thus suggesting that perceptions of bodily changes could not be the sole cause of emotion. These and other cogent criticisms, however, did not rule out the possibility that the James-Lange formulation contained a kernel of truth. Theories are rarely born complete. They have to be refined in reaction to data that are not available at the time of their formulation.

The James-Lange theory, many decades after it was proposed, returned to center stage of the psychology of emotions as part of a two-factor theory that postulated that bodily reactions were a necessary, but not a sufficient, cause of emotional states (Schachter, 1971). According to this theory, two components were necessary for emotional reactions, physiological arousal and a person's cognitive interpretation of the situation. By independently controlling each factor, it was demonstrated that both were required for emotional reactions. A person who was physiologically aroused (e.g., elevated heart rate and blood pressure) by taking the drug epinephrine without knowing it would experience an emotion appropriate to the situation: In an anger inducing situation the subject would become angry, and in a euphoria inducing situation the subject would become euphoric. The physiological arousal was the same in each situation, but the subject experienced different emotions because he interpreted his situation differently. If, however, subjects knew that their physiological arousal was due to epinephrine, they tended not to get angry or euphoric because they understood that their bodily sensations stemmed from the drug, not from their environment.

In actual fact, James's original theory was a two-factor theory, although he emphasized only the importance of bodily reactions. In an early description of his theory, James (1884) wrote, "*My thesis is . . . that the bodily changes follow directly the PERCEPTION of the exciting fact, and that our feeling of the same changes as they occur IS the emotion.*" Note the emphasis on *perception*. One perceives the bear, runs, and then experiences fear. What would happen if one were ignorant of the danger of bears? Running and fear would not ensue. Consequently, a careful reading of James's theory, actually more careful than his, suggests that a cognitive interpretation of the *emotional situation* is as essential as are the bodily changes, a position similar to Schachter's.

Regardless of future developments, the James-Lange theory has earned an honored place in the history of the psychology of emotions (Mandler, 1979). It shaped the course of history by offering an imaginative conception that generated much significant research and theoretical ideas. James, however, was not satisfied just to offer a theory of emotion without suggesting its possible utility. If emotional experience is a function of bodily changes, then emotions can be modified by changes in bodily reactions:

> if we wish to conquer undesirable emotional tendencies in ourselves we must assiduously, and in the first instance cold-bloodedly, go through the *outward movements* of those contrary dispositions which we prefer to cultivate. The reward of persistency will infallibly come, in the fading out of the sullenness or depression, and the advent of real cheerfulness and kindliness in their stead (James, 1892a, p. 383).

If you are depressed, stop *acting* depressed! Stop moping! Become active and engage in pleasurable activities. The pleasurable bodily sensations will eliminate the depression. From the perspective of our contemporary knowledge of psychotherapy, James's recommendation is an oversimplification. But it has merit for some patients, and it identified an important strategy for modifying behavior that formed the basis for many subsequent educational and therapeutic practices; substitute a desirable form of behavior for an undesirable one.

In addition to its specific contributions, James's theory of emotion had a general influence on psychology. Although James considered the subject matter of psychology to be consciousness, his theory of emotion shifted attention to bodily activity, that is, to behavior. Emotional experience is an expression of behavior. To eliminate an undesirable emotion, one should modify behavior. This slight reorientation from consciousness to behavior contributed to a trend in American psychology that finally led to the behaviorist revolution (Chapter 6) that substituted *behavior* for *consciousness* as the subject matter of psychology.

Habit

James assigned *habit* a central role in psychology: "When we look at living creatures from an outward point of view, one of the first things that strike us is that they are bundles of habits (James, 1890, I). James failed to offer a precise definition of habit, but his numerous examples—habit of playing the violin, habits of thought, habits of being a soldier—suggest its meaning. Habits are consistent modes of conduct.

James's treatment of habit emphasized two important methodological positions. By perceiving habit "from an outward point of view," James encouraged a trend in psychology to observe public behavior. In addition, James, with his treatment of habit, encouraged the view that psychology is a biological science. He assumed that "*the phenomena of habit in living beings are due to the plasticity of the organic materials of which their bodies are composed*" (James, 1890, I). Habits are basically neurophysiological mechanisms. They can be thought of as paths through the nervous system which become more easy to traverse the more frequently the habit is practiced.

James pointed out the functional values of habits. First, *"Habit simplifies the movements required to achieve a given result, makes them more accurate and diminishes fatigue"* (James, 1890, I). Practicing playing the piano can improve the pianist's performance by strengthening the appropriate habits.

Second, *"Habit diminishes the conscious attention with which our acts are performed"* (James, 1890, I). When we learn a habit, such as driving a car, we have to interrupt ourselves frequently to ensure that we will make the correct movement. However, once we become sufficiently proficient, the "chain" of successive acts fuse "into a continuous stream." The fusing results, not by conscious thought, but by "the sensation occasioned by the muscular contraction just finished." The successive movements of the bow of a violin player are controlled by the kinesthetic cues resulting from previous movements. While recognizing the improved efficiency that results from habitual actions in the absence of conscious control, James did not ignore the undesirable consequences that habits might produce. Habitual errors in playing tennis or typing can interfere with establishing a high level of skill.

James could not discuss psychological principles without considering their social and personal implications. In his most famous passage, he comments about the social values of habit in a manner that would not endear him to liberals:

> Habit is thus the enormous fly-wheel of society, its most precious conservative agent. It alone is what keeps us all within the bounds of ordinance, and saves the children of fortune from the envious uprisings of the poor. It alone prevents the hardest and most repulsive walks of life from being deserted by those brought up to tread therein. It keeps the fisherman and the deck-hand at sea through the winter; it holds the miner in his darkness, and nails the countryman to his log-cabin and his lonely farm through all the months of snow; it protects us from invasion by the natives of the desert and the frozen zone. It dooms us all to fight out the battle of life upon the lines of our nurture or our early choice, and to make the best of a pursuit that disagrees, because there is no other for which we are fitted, and it is too late to begin again. It keeps different social strata from mixing. Already at the age of twenty-five you see the professional mannerism settling down on the young commercial traveller, on the young doctor, on the young minister, on the young counsellor-at-law. You see the little lines of cleavage running through the character, the tricks of thought, the prejudices, the way of the 'shop,' in a word, from which the man can by-and-by no more escape than his coat-sleeve can suddenly fall into a new set of folds. On the whole, it is best he should not escape. It is well for the world that in most of us, by the age of thirty, the character has set like plaster, and will never soften again (James, 1890, I, p. 121).

When discussing the applications of laws of habit for personal use, James (1890, I) offered four maxims:

1. *"We must make automatic and habitual, as early as possible, as many useful actions as we can,* and guard against the growing into ways that are

likely to be disadvantageous to us, as we should guard against the plague."

2. *"Never suffer an exception to occur till the new habit is securely rooted in your life."*

3. *"Seize the very first possible opportunity to act on every resolution you make, and on every emotional prompting you may experience in the direction of habits you aspire to gain."*

4. *"Keep the faculty of effort alive in you by a little gratuitous exercise every day."*

Although these four maxims are more elegantly than precisely stated, and lack supporting evidence, they are nevertheless historically significant because they anticipated, in general, the central role of the concept of habit in subsequent learning theories, and specifically, the importance of practice and of competition between desirable and undesirable habits in the adjustment of individuals to their environment.

The Self

James recognized the psychological importance of our view of ourselves. We acquire ideas about ourselves, and these ideas profoundly influence our sense of well-being and our adjustment to our world. Alerting psychologists to deal with the problem of *the self* proved to be an important contribution. James's efforts, however, extended well beyond the recognition of the problem. In addition, he offered interesting hypotheses about *the self* which were important in the development of the fields of personality and what was to be called "abnormal psychology" (psychopathology).

The self, for James, was not a single entity. We do not have one self but many selves. His analysis of the self, largely a result of phenomenological self-examination, was directed at identifying its various components and suggesting their psychological implications. James's major distinction was between *me* and *I*. *Me* is the self as known, the object of self-observation and self-evaluation. One woman might perceive herself as competent and attractive, while another judges herself as inadequate and clumsy. The act of self-observation is the same, but the results are different.

Me, the observed self, has numerous components. We have bodily selves (e.g., healthy, attractive), social selves (student, lover, son or daughter), and spiritual selves (immoral, religious). These selves can contain both motives and goals; a person's professional self can seek prestige, and thus steer her toward the medical profession.

To observe oneself requires an observing agent. *I*, "the self as knower," is that agent. *I* is conscious of *me*. The *me* changes from time to time, as when a person shifts from the role of student in class to daughter at home. The *I* remains constant in that transition; the knower knows that behind the two roles is one person. The *I* usually remains constant throughout life. The old man knows that he is the same *I* as when he was the young child. The constancy of *I* can sometimes be destroyed, as happens in cases of multiple personalities. The same person exhibits two or more independent personalities; each personality, to use Janet's description, is dissociated from the other. In the language of James, these individual personalities in the same person have different *I*'s. A famous case of multiple personality illustrates how one personality of an individual treats the other as independent: "When I go out and get drunk, *she* wakes up with a hangover" (Thigpen & Cleckly, 1957).

James's treatment of *the self* led him to realize that different *me*'s could be the source of conflict. James, a handsome man, speculated about the consequences of perceiving oneself both as a "lady-killer" and philosopher:

> The philosopher and the lady-killer could not well keep house in the same tenement of clay. Such different characters may conceivably at the outset of life be . . . *possible* . . . But to make . . . one of them actual, the [other] must more or less be suppressed. So the seeker of his truest, strongest, deepest self must review the list carefully, and pick out the one on which to stake his salvation. All other selves thereupon become unreal, but the fortunes of this self are real. Its failures are real failures, its triumphs real triumphs, carrying shame and gladness with them (James, 1890, I, pp. 309–310).

Although some modern philosophers would not share James's sense of incompatibility between the roles of philosopher and lady-killer, the example nevertheless suggests the importance of rivalry among different *me*'s. Life is filled with conflicts between social *me*'s: the son and husband, the wife and mother, the adolescent and adult.

James recognized that the feeling of success and failure is determined by one's view of oneself.

> I, who for the time have staked my all on being a psychologist, am mortified if others know much more psychology than I. But I am contented to wallow in the grossest ignorance of Greek. My deficiencies there give me no sense of personal humiliation at all. Had I 'pretentions' to be a linguist, it would have been just the reverse (1890, I, p. 310).

James proposed the following formula to represent the influences that *success* and *pretensions* have on self-esteem:

$$\text{Self-esteem} = \frac{\text{Success}}{\text{Pretensions}}$$

Self-esteem can be increased by one of two methods, increasing the numerator or decreasing the denominator. That is, self-esteem can be raised by becoming more successful or reducing aspirations (pretensions). The middle-aged woman whose self-esteem depends upon looking as young and slim as an adolescent is bound to meet with failure. Damage to her self-esteem can be avoided by following James's advice:

How pleasant is the day when we give up striving to be young—or slender! Thank God! we say, *those* illusions are gone. Everything added to the Self is a burden as well as a pride (James, 1890, I, p. 311).

The essence of James's advice, then, is to avoid unrealistic goals and seek successes that are within one's grasp.

Attention and Will

An overview of James's major psychological notions demands some reference to both *attention* and *will*. Both *attention* and *will*, like most of James's ideas, were treated primarily within a phenomenological framework. James, like Wundt, noted that "although we are besieged at every moment by impressions from our whole sensory surface, we notice so very small a part of them." Attention refers to "the narrowness of consciousness," the small proportion of the total sensory impressions impinging on us.

Will, for James, is a state of mind, "which everyone knows, and which no definition can make plainer." The meaning of *will* is clarified by contrasting it with *wish*. Both are desires for something, but *wish* implies that what is desired is unattainable, while *will* suggests it can be achieved. One wishes to be independently wealthy, but one wills to get to class on time. *Will* is a determination to act, and the stronger the determination, the more likely will the act be forthcoming.

James illustrates his theory of volition by discussing the indecision that occurs when one desires to get out of bed on a freezing morning:

Probably most persons have lain on certain mornings for an hour at a time unable to brace themselves to the resolve. We think how late we shall be, how the duties of the day will suffer; we say "I *must* get up, this is ignominious," etc.; but still the warm couch feels too delicious, the cold outside too cruel, and the resolution faints away and postpones itself again and again just as it seemed on the verge of bursting the resistance and passing over into the decisive act. Now how do we *ever* get up under such circumstances? If I may generalize from my own experience, we more often than not get up without any struggle or decision at all. We suddenly find that we *have* got up. A fortunate lapse of consciousness occurs; we forget both the warmth and cold; we fall into some revery connected with the day's life, in the course of which the idea flashes across us, "Hollo! I must lie here no longer"—an idea which at that lucky instant awakens no contradictory or paralyzing suggestions, and consequently produces immediately its appropriate motor effects. It was our acute consciousness of both the warmth and the cold during the period of struggle, which paralyzed our activity then and kept our idea of rising in the condition of *wish* and not of *will*. The moment these inhibitory ideas ceased, the original idea exerted its effects (James, 1890, II, pp. 524–525).

The conflict generates indecision and the resolution of the conflict comes about when one stops thinking about the conflict. The thought of the cold outside "robs" the "impulsive power" from the act of getting out of bed. The key to conflict resolution in this case is an inattention to the inhibitory thoughts of the conflict while executing the desired act. More dramatic are the "life and death" conflicts that require willful attention to reality in order to execute the desired response.

> How many excuses does the drunkard find when each new temptation comes! It is a new brand of liquor which the interests of intellectual culture in such matters oblige him to test; moreover it is poured out and it is a sin to waste it; also others are drinking and it would be churlishness to refuse. Or it is but to enable him to sleep, or just to get through this job of work; or it isn't drinking, it is because he feels so cold; or it is Christmas-day; or it is stimulating him to make a more powerful resolution in favor of abstinence than any he has hitherto made; or it is just this once, and once doesn't count, etc., etc., *ad libitum*—it is, in fact, anything you like except *being a drunkard. That* is the conception that will not stay before the soul's attention (James, 1890, II, p. 565).

The solution, when confronted with an opportunity to drink, is for the alcoholic to ignore possible excuses and attend to the fact that accepting the drink makes him a drunkard: "If through thick and thin he holds to it that this is being a drunkard and is nothing else, he is not likely to remain one long."

Attention and *will* go hand in glove in guiding behavior. A will to act has the idea of the desired response, to get out of bed, for example, or to refuse a drink. Attending to that act while ignoring inhibiting thoughts will increase the probability of the desired behavior. As was the case for *habit*, James thought it necessary to speculate about the neurological basis of *will*. He suggested that the *will* could be strengthened by practice. Practicing willpower would create neural pathways that would mediate actions that are willed.

James's Prose

To offer a list of quotations to convey the intellectual style of James here would be redundant; the discussion of James's ideas included abundant quotations. Were the large number of quotations used convenient or necessary? Can James's ideas stand alone, or do they depend to a significant extent on the elegant form in which they are expressed?

Quite obviously, some of his notions, such as his theory of emotion, did not rely on captivating prose. His theory that emotional experience is the perception of bodily changes had relatively clear deductive consequences, as history testifies. Thus, James's theory of emotion was in the tradition of natural science psychology that equated truth with the capacity of a theory to deduce (predict) empirical events.

James's views about *habit, the self, attention,* and *will* did not have as obvious deductive implications as his theory of emotion. All of these formulations contained many ideas that were subsequently modified to serve as hypotheses for research investigations. But the manner in which James expressed many of his more important ideas appealed not to direct empirical tests, but instead to intuitive understanding. For example, his phenomenological description of struggling to get out of a warm bed on a cold morning encourages readers to say: "That's exactly how I feel!" In this sense, James's prose is close to the tradition of great literature that captures the quality of human experience. But intuitive understanding is not equivalent to deductive explanation. A scientific theory can be checked against relevant objective empirical evidence, while a compelling phenomenological description can only be supported by subjective testimony. Needless to say, not everyone will agree with a phenomenological description. I sometimes extend my stay in bed on a cold morning, but then I grit my teeth and consciously get out of bed. My own experience is at odds with James's suggestion that one escapes from bed when one's mind is ignoring the conflict. Am I right or is James?

The important point is that James's ideas were not always evaluated by the same criterion of truth. At times he formulated hypotheses that appeared to have the potential of being judged by the criterion of deductive explanation. At other times his formulations took on the quality of artistic insights comparable to those of great writers, a category to which he eminently belonged.

CONTRIBUTIONS

Although James offered many specific ideas, most notably the James-Lange theory of emotion, that stimulated research and theorizing, his major historical importance stems from his general influence on shaping psychology. One historian aptly notes: "Whereas Titchener was intent chiefly on making the new psychology a science, James was more concerned that the new science be psychology" (Heidbreder, 1933). James rejected the restrictions Titchener was placing on psychology, limiting it primarily to the introspective analysis of sensation and perception. The whole gamut of human experience and behavior became, for James, not only acceptable but necessary topics for psychological investigations. Modern psychology reflects James's broad interest patterns that ranged from sensory experience to religious experience, from rational behavior to irrational behavior.

In addition to expanding the empirical base of psychology, James also stressed the importance of certain methodological orientations. He maintained the tradition of conceptualizing psychology as the science of consciousness but in a manner that encouraged new modes of observation. He suggested that being trained to observe consciousness, in the manner of Wundt and Titchener, will actually distort the observation; a veridical account of consciousness can best be achieved by perceiving conscious experience in a natural and open manner. In the struggle between the methods of trained introspection and naive phenomenology, James sided with the latter. While maintaining this mentalistic orientation to psychology, James simultaneously but unintentionally helped undermine that approach by emphasizing the importance of physiological and behavioral events, thus encouraging both the development of biopsychology and behavioral psychology.

James was particularly influential in encouraging the development of the psychology of personality and its applied field of clinical psychology. The longest chapter (110 pages) by far in *The Principles of Psychology* (1890) was dedicated to the topic of the *self*, a concept that has been central to the notion that each of us possesses a psychological unity which is called our *personality*. This unity, although stable to a degree, can nevertheless be altered by age and experience. Sometimes the alterations can be maladaptive, thus producing a psychic illness. Such sicknesses, James thought, required treatment. In both his father's and his own cases, treatment was self-initiated. Both, by their own will, were able to overcome the disabling effects of their sickness. In the discussion of the self and his own efforts to deal with his personal problems, James helped shape three important components of the field of personality: the development of personality, the structure of personality, and the treatment of the sick personality.

James felt that for the psychologist "the religious propensities of man must be at least as interesting as any other of the facts pertaining to his mental constitution." James's religious interests anticipated the concerns of humanistic psychologists with the spiritual needs of humans.

Finally, James created an atmosphere for viewing psychological events within a functional orientation. He encouraged psychology to incorporate Darwinism. Consciousness was not something to be described, but rather an activity to be understood in relation to an organism's attempt to cope with the problems of life. Consciousness for James guided behavior so that individuals could satisfy their needs and solve their problems.

James's range of influence is impressive. But, are his different views compatible? Can a natural science psychology be based upon naive phenomenology? Can human spirituality be understood within a biological orientation? Can an outward point of view be incorporated into a mental science? Can artistic sensibilities be substituted for scientific explanations? In sum, was not James's impressive versatility purchased at the price of inconsistency?

A Debate about William James

Moderator: In view of the numerous facets of William James's psychology, it becomes essential, in order to avoid confusion, to agree about the topics to be debated. The affirmative side will initiate the debate by first specifying the significant issue for discussion.

Pro: We are dealing with the contributions of a man of tremendous talent, a true genius who is universally recognized as a great psychologist and a great philosopher. His specific contributions have already been cited and, therefore, I would like to turn to the central issue of judging James's role in the history of psychology, namely, were his basic contributions fatally compromised by his inconsistent methodological stance? One way of responding to the charge is to quote Walt Whitman in James's defense:

> Do I contradict myself?
> Very well then I contradict myself,
> (I am large, I contain multitudes).

Psychology is large; it contains multitudes. It cannot be squeezed into a form that is inappropriate to its subject matter. James exhibited great wisdom when he decided to approach psychology initially by the methods of natural science and then to employ other methods of knowing when necessary. I fail to see why James should be criticized for trying to understand all aspects of psychology—consciousness, behavior, physiology—and to deal with the basic problems of the human condition—the self, spiritual needs, morality.

Con: Your defense is romantically appealing but logically wanting. Let us avoid confusing issues. I am not questioning James's talent. He was a genius, and perhaps his greatest talent was that of a writer. His psychological notions were expressed in expository prose that is unmatched in quality. But being a great writer does not make James a great psychologist. He was essentially a throwback to the armchair philosopher who speculated about psychological phenomena in the absence of any hard evidence.

Although I agree with the notion that James represented the crossroads of psychology, it must be noted that James failed to offer signposts to indicate the different destinations to which his various orienting ideas led. He implied that they all led to a common destination of a scientific psychology. But his naive phenomenology, exquisitely expressed, led to a literary psychology that offered an intuitive understanding in the absence of any predictive power. His biological explanations, like his pathway interpretation of habit, gave the impression that he was offering biological explanations of psychological processes. But was he? His physiological speculations were practically free of empirical content. They only stated that changes in behavior were due to changes in the central nervous system. Big deal! Where else could they be located? Some of James's hypotheses, like the James-Lange hypothesis, led to empirical tests because of its deductive implications. In contrast, his flirtation with the mystical side of life encouraged the view that intuitive conviction was a sufficient basis for adopting a psychological hypothesis. By employing incompatible standards of proof, James set the stage for the current confusion that surrounds the nature of psychological explanation. To suggest that psychology can allow complete leniency when it comes to adopting a criterion of truth is tantamount to admitting that psychology cannot be scientific.

Pro: I find your criticism unnecessarily rigid. We are trying to evaluate a brilliant man who offered many important theoretical notions and methodological stances that were subsequently adopted. His foresight appears to be the target of your criticism.

Con: Yes! James did anticipate functionalism, behaviorism, Gestalt psychology, personality theory, including some psychoanalytic notions, and humanistic psychology, and implied that all these orientations could be fruitfully combined. This would be equivalent to playing bridge, poker, gin rummy, and casino with the same deck of cards at the same time. It can't be done. And by implying it can, James encouraged a confused approach to psychology that compromised its natural scientific status.

Moderator: You both agree that William James is an influential historical figure in psychology but disagree about the value of his contributions.

SUMMARY

William James exerted an important influence on the history of psychology by modifying its methods, expanding its empirical realm, and encouraging its practical usefulness.

Although he shared Wundt's conception of psychology as the science of consciousness, James's approach differed in three important ways: First, he insisted that trained introspectors who sought to describe consciousness as assemblages of elementary processes would inevitably offer a fallacious description of mental life. James's introspection, conducted in a naive, natural manner, revealed that consciousness contained integrated mental events that could not be further analyzed into basic elements as both Wundt and Titchener postulated. Second, James, influenced by Darwin, believed that the fundamental phenomena of mental life were activities (e.g., cognitions, desires) that served the function of shaping reactions to the demands of the outer world. Third, James encouraged psychological research on a variety of human and animal subjects.

James's criterion of truth was influenced by his assumption that psychology is a natural science. Observational truth, which included introspective evidence, was determined by consensual agreement. Theoretical truth was measured by the capacity of a hypothesis to predict and control psychological events. Simultaneously, James was influenced by his pragmatic conception of truth, that if a hypothesis works satisfactorily, it is true. James's conflation of truth and utility enabled him to deal with two of his major concerns: the practical usefulness of psychological principles in assisting humans to adapt to their environment and certain psychological beliefs (e.g., the validity of moral beliefs, mystical processes), the truth of which could not be determined by natural science methodology.

James was never an active researcher. He speculated about various psychological phenomena and, in many cases, offered penetrating insights that stimulated both research and theory.

James's theory of emotion, which was independently formulated by the Danish physiologist Lange, postulated that emotional experience is the perception of bodily changes; we feel "afraid because we tremble." The James-Lange formulation anticipated in important respects the current two-factor theory of emotion that postulates both physiological arousal and cognitive interpretation as necessary for emotion (Schachter, 1971).

James considered habit, a consistent mode of conduct, to be a core concept in psychology; organisms are basically "bundles of habits." Habits are functional because they can facilitate an organism's adaptation to its environment. James realized that maladaptive habits could be acquired that would interfere with an organism's adjustment. He offered a set of maxims designed to promote a person's adjustment. These maxims emphasized the importance of practicing desirable habits while preventing the development of undesirable habits.

James's self-examination of conscious experience revealed an awareness of oneself. Selfhood contained many independent entities. A major division is between *I*, the observer, and *me*, the object of the self-observation. *I* is the observer of *me*. *Me*, the observed self, has numerous components, among which are the bodily self, social self, and spiritual self. The *me* tends to change from one social situation to another, while the *I* usually remains constant throughout life, with the exception of patients who suffer from what Janet termed *mental dissociation*, the splitting apart of an individual personality (one *I*) into multiple personalities (several *I*'s). Different *me*'s can be a source of conflict because of the incompatible goals they generate. In addition, a person's *me* will determine how success and failure will influence self-esteem; self-esteem $= \dfrac{\text{success}}{\text{pretensions}}$.

The concepts of *attention* and *will* were considered by James to be core concepts in psychology: Attention refers to the narrowing of consciousness, while will is a determination to act to achieve an attainable goal. Attention to a willed act can facilitate conflict resolution.

James was one of the greatest expository writers of all times. His compelling phenomenological descriptions frequently created a sense of intuitive understanding that was not matched by deductive clarity. James, as a psychologist, failed to employ a consistent criterion of truth, varying mainly between deductive explanation and intuitive understanding.

James's major contribution to psychology was to enlarge its empirical realm; to encourage naive phenomenology in place of trained introspection; to emphasize the importance of the biological foundations of psychology; to introduce an "outward (behavioral) point of view"; to help develop the fields of personality, abnormal psychology, and clinical psychology; to raise interest in the spiritual needs of humans; and to encourage a functional orientation in psychology. He anticipated many ideas that resurfaced later in such psychological orientations as functionalism, behaviorism, Gestalt psychology, psychoanalysis, and humanistic psychology. The ultimate evaluation of James's contributions depends on the importance one attaches to a consistent criterion of truth.

SUGGESTED READINGS

The best and most enjoyable way to learn about James's psychology is to read him. His major contributions are contained in his two-volume *The Principles of Psychology* (1890), its abridgement, entitled *Psychology: Briefer Course* (1892a), and *The Varieties of Religious Experience* (1902/1928).

Insights into William James's personality can be gleaned from a collection of his letters, edited by his son, Henry James (1920) and two biographies: *William James: A Biography* by G. W. Allen (1967), and *Becoming William James* by H. M. Feinstein (1984). Two excellent secondary sources of James's psychology are Heidbreder (1933) and Fancher (1979).

5

Functionalism

Functionalism can be called the most reasonable orientation in the history of psychology or the most trivial one. The first judgment can be justified by the functionalists' decision to study both consciousness and behavior within a framework that emphasizes an organism's adjustment. The second point of view can be defended by arguing that functionalism is merely a transitional position between structuralism and behaviorism and consequently has no importance in its own right.

Functionalism is not a highly integrated position. It lacks a dominant spokesman, like Wundt, whose methodological stance and theoretical position was essentially embraced by his followers. Functionalism does not even have a clear historical beginning and certainly no ending, because many contemporary psychologists would proudly accept the designation of *functionalist* while admitting that the name represents more of an attitude than an organized system. Functionalism is essentially an eclectic position that combines ideas from different sources in the fields of biology, philosophy, and psychology.

HISTORICAL ROOTS

While Titchener was espousing his psychological views, several ideas from entirely different traditions began to merge in the United States. A general dissatisfaction with Wundtian psychology and structuralism served as an impetus for the creation of a psychology that would be more in tune with American practical orientation. The observation of the content of consciousness seemed to many Americans to be much too tame an enterprise for a subject matter as exciting as psychology. Rather than being an ivory tower discipline, detached from the realities of life, psychology should serve the needs of individuals and society. Functionalism redirected psychology toward these goals mainly through the influences of William James and Charles Darwin. An additional influence came from research in the psychology of individual differences. This research owed its impact to the efforts of an English gentleman intellectual, Sir Francis Galton (1822–1911), an influential American psychologist, James McKeen Cattell (1860–1944), and the versatile and inventive French psychologist, Alfred Binet (1857–1911).

William James

James is frequently referred to as the precursor of functionalism because he believed that the function of mental activities is to assist humans to solve life's problems. But in spirit and deed, James's psychology differed in important ways from mainstream functionalism. His penchant for armchair speculation, especially about spiritual and mystical phenomena, placed him at odds with the strong empirical orientation that developed in functionalism, and although he shared a pragmatic approach with the functionalists, his meaning differed radically from theirs. Because of these differences and James's unique pattern of beliefs, a distinction between James's psychology and functionalism is appropriate in spite of the intimate historical relationship between them.

Charles Darwin

Functionalism essentially transposed the basic core of Darwinism to psychology. Thanks to Darwinism, James became interested in the function of consciousness, began to view psychological phenomena within a neurophysiological framework, and became concerned with the adaptive effects of psychological activities. These same Darwinian notions were equally important, if not more so, for the functionalists.

The notion of evolutionary adaptation was particularly influential in functionalism because it emphasized the importance of the process of psychological adjustment, encouraged the adoption of a selection-by-consequence model of behavior, and stimulated the development of the psychology of individual differences.

Psychological Adjustment. The fact that species survival depends on the adaptation of its members to the environment suggested to functionalists that an analogous mechanism was operating in psychology. To survive, humans have to adjust to their environment. Thus, the idea behind biological adaptation of a species was transferred to the psychological adjustment of the individual. As a consequence, functionalists, with their concern for the practical, directed attention to the psychological processes that enable humans to cope with problems of life, with the struggle to adjust.

A Selection Model of Behavior. For the principle of natural selection to be effective, members of a species must vary. Those variations that are effective in adapting to the environment are selected. Functionalists hypothesized that a similar selection-by-consequence model can be applied to behavior. When confronted with a problem such as the need for food or the requirements to solve a puzzle, an organism emits in succession a variety of responses. Those responses which are unsuccessful tend to be eliminated, while successful acts tend to persist.

Psychology of Individual Differences. Although the early functionalists were not the original investigators in the field of individual differences, they rapidly perceived its importance and encouraged its development.

Sir Francis Galton. Galton (1822–1911), an Englishman of enormous talent himself, was particularly interested in the inheritance of talent. He learned to read at the age of two and a half and could read some French and Latin at the ripe age of five (Pearson, 1914–1930). At age seven, he was reading Shakespeare for pleasure. It is estimated from modern intelligence tests that the minimal IQ that could reasonably account for Galton's accomplishments during childhood was 200 (Cox, 1926).

Galton, like many of his contemporaries, was influenced by Darwin, who happened to be his cousin. The major impact of this influence was to interest Galton in problems of human evolution. When forty-seven, Galton published *Hereditary Genius: An Inquiry Into Its Laws and Consequences:*

> I propose to show in this book that a man's natural abilities are derived by inheritance, under exactly the same limitations as are the form and physical features of the whole organic world. Consequently, as it is easy . . . to obtain by careful selection a permanent breed of dogs or horses gifted with peculiar powers of running, or of doing anything else, so it would be quite practicable to produce a highly gifted race of men by judicious marriages during several consecutive generations (Galton, 1869/1952, p. 1).

Two related ideas are contained in this statement: Human abilities are genetically determined, and the human species can be improved by controlled breeding practices. Galton sought to demonstrate the heritability of human abilities by showing that professional eminence achieved by one in 40,000 persons (such as scientists, authors, and judges) clings to families. His evidence demonstrated that the probability of a relative of an eminent person achieving fame was significantly less than one in 40,000. In addition, the probability of a relative of a distinguished person becoming eminent was a function of the closeness of the genetic relationship. A son, for example, had a greater chance of achieving fame than a grandchild. These data led Galton to conclude that intellectual eminence was determined genetically.

FIGURE 5.1 Sir Francis Galton

Archives of American Psychology

Shortly after *Hereditary Genius* was published, Charles Darwin wrote to Galton:

> I do not think I have ever in my life read anything more interesting and original . . . You have made a convert of an opponent in one sense, for I have always maintained that, excepting fools, men do not differ in intellect, only in zeal and hard work (Quoted in Galton, 1908, p. 290).

Although Galton's findings have been replicated, his interpretation is unconvincing because he failed to control for environmental influence. Relatives of eminent persons tend to have more stimulating intellectual environments than do ordinary persons. To demonstrate genetic influences requires control of environmental factors.

Galton's support of eugenics, the social program that seeks to improve a population by controlled breeding, was based upon, at best, oversimplified and optimistic notions. When he assumed that the principle of natural selection which operates in nature to produce adaptive organisms could easily be applied to human society, he failed to appreciate the complex ethical issues involved in any eugenic program. What constitutes a good psychological trait? How would society choose the trait for selective breeding? How would the selective breeding program be implemented? What would happen to individuals who possess the least amount of the preferred psychological attribute? Today, any sort of large-scale eugenic program reawakens memories of the Nazis' heinous attempts at genocide against Jews, Gypsies and retarded people to breed a master race. In fairness to Galton,

> He was always more interested . . . in raising high intelligence than in eliminating low intelligence, which he was much more willing to leave to the slow process of natural selection. . . . He always insisted that the great need was for research, to acquire a knowledge of heredity that would be a sufficient basis for wise eugenic practice (Diamond, 1980b, p. 52).

The historical impact of Galton's eugenic views was to heighten interest in genetic factors and in their interaction with environmental variables. In addition, his views encouraged the development of methods of measuring psychological abilities. To this end, Galton's contributions were immense, both in the design of tests to measure individual differences and in the development of statistical procedures to evaluate the implications of test results.

In 1884, Galton established an Anthropometric Laboratory at London's International Health Exhibition. Here, for a small fee, a person could take a series of tests whose results would be reported to him along with the average performance of previous subjects. The test measured visual and auditory acuity, judgment of visual distance, breathing power, reaction times, color discrimination, the strength of a blow, and other abilities, mostly of sensory discrimination. Scores on these tests were assumed to reflect various aspects of a person's intelligence. This view was based upon the conception that ideas were combinations of elementary sensations. Consequently, those with the most acute sensory powers would be better able to absorb ideas and become the brightest people! Again we find Galton off target when it came to the problem of intelligence, but nevertheless making an important contribution. He was measuring individual differences, and thereby launched the field of psychometrics, the measurement of the mind, that ultimately developed within functionalism as a major field of psychology.

Not only did Galton develop methods to measure psychological differences among individuals, but he also invented statistical techniques to organize the results. A score on a test is uninformative. It gains meaning when it is compared to the scores of others. Galton developed several methods of ranking so that a person's score could be judged in comparison to scores of members of a reference group. Galton's most significant contribution to statistics was his development of the concept of correlation, which was later refined by his friend and biographer, Karl Pearson, the distinguished mathematical statistician. The ability to measure how two variables co-vary proved to be a powerful tool in analyzing complex phenomena such as environmental and hereditary influences on various psychological abilities. Correlation was an especially important tool in studies of twins, which Galton originated to assist in the the unravelling of environmental and hereditary influences.

Galton's influence on functionalism, the first systematic psychology that emerged in America, can be summarized as follows:

> Galton's innovative methods for the study of human capacities were accepted as part of psychology, and they helped to give American psychology its distinctive character. It seems quite unlikely that the same development could have taken place in anything like the same time span without Galton's influence (Diamond, 1980b, p. 53).

James McKeen Cattell. James McKeen Cattell (1860–1944) was not an important psychologist because of his profound ideas; his historical significance derives from his practical contributions to the science and profession of psychology.

After graduating from college, Cattell traveled to Europe and spent a semester with Wundt at Leipzig. He returned to the United States, where he studied psychology at Johns Hopkins University and did an experiment on reaction time. Cattell was more interested in individual differences in the reaction times than in introspective reports. He returned to Leipzig, where he refused to conduct the introspective problem that Wundt assigned him. He developed more precise methods to measure reaction times and carried out his research in his own rooms because of "Wundt's refusal to admit any subject to the laboratory except a psychologist who could use the results introspectively" (Cattell, 1928). In spite of their differences, Wundt had sufficient respect for Cattell to make him his first assistant (Sokal, 1981). After receiving his doctorate at Leipzig in 1886, Cattell traveled to England, where he worked with Galton, with whom he shared a passionate interest in individual differences and statistical methods. Cattell's lifetime concern with the quantitative aspect of mental functioning clearly reflects the greater influence of Galton than Wundt.

Not only did Cattell question the empirical methods of Wundtian psychology and structuralism but also their ivory tower attitude. "We should be practical men and see to it that we have a practical psychology," he said. Cattell furthered this goal by encouraging research in applied problems at Columbia University, where he chaired the psychology department from 1891 to 1917. In his own research on reaction time, he discovered that the time required to read a short word was comparable to the time required to read a single letter. He interpreted this finding as giving support to the educational practice of teaching elementary school children to read whole words instead of individual letters.

Cattell's major practical concern was with measuring differences in human capacities. Cattell developed a *mental test*, a term he invented, and

FIGURE 5.2 James McKeen Cattell

Dan McIntosh

gave it to the undergraduate students at Columbia College. The test was Galtonian in form, consisting of a series of subtests that measured sensory and motor skills, as well as memory. They measured reaction time, strength of the squeeze of each hand, time for naming colors, accuracy of estimating ten seconds, number of letters remembered after one reading, and so on. Although the battery of tests, intended to be a test of intelligence, initially created much interest and excitement, it rapidly lost favor because the scores failed to correlate with any reasonable criteria such as academic grades. Like Galton, Cattell believed people differed in intelligence, and that such differences could be measured, but they both failed to offer any compelling evidence that their method of measuring intelligence was valid.

In 1921, Cattell founded the Psychological Corporation, which provided psychological services, mainly in the area of psychological testing, to the public, education, industry, and government. He died in 1944, leaving American psychology the legacy of an established field of individual differences, along with a group of talented students trained to carry on the traditions he established.

FIGURE 5.3 Alfred Binet

National Library of Medicine

Alfred Binet. Binet (1857–1911) developed the first successful intelligence test by finessing the problem of defining intelligence. Both Galton and Cattell shared a common hypothesis about intelligence which stemmed from the associationistic view that ideas are combinations of elementary sensations. It followed from this position that intelligence could be measured by tests of sensory ability. Tests based upon this assumption, however, failed to serve any practical use and were quickly abandoned.

Binet's early work in intelligence testing stemmed from the theoretical assumptions of faculty psychology that postulated that the mind is endowed with a number of independent powers (faculties). Binet's preconceptions encouraged him to construct individual tests for eleven faculties of the mind: imagery, memory, attention, imagination, comprehension, force of will, motor skill, judgment of visual space, moral sentiment, esthetic appreciation and suggestibility. Unlike Galton and Cattell, Binet was not willing to accept his theoretically generated tests of intelligence as automatically valid. He thought that the scores on a valid test of intelligence should increase with age and be positively correlated to academic performance.

Binet's research on tests of individual faculties produced a conflict between his theoretical preconceptions and his intuitive expectations. None of the tests were found to be closely correlated to age and school performance. What should be done—abandon the faculty theory or his intuitive conception? Binet was forced to give an answer when the French Minister of Public Instruction consulted with him about the problems raised by children who were unable to cope successfully with regular work in elementary schools. Binet and his collaborator, Theodore Simon, a physician who had worked in an institution for intellectually retarded persons, decided that a test for identifying such children had to be developed. In describing the problems of constructing such a test, Binet and Simon wrote:

> But how to conduct the examination of each child? What methods to follow? What observations to make? What questions to ask? What tests to invent? How compare the child to the normal? . . . It is necessary to guard against . . . the habit of leaving decisions to luck, based on subjective and hence uncontrollable impressions, which will be sometimes good, sometimes bad, and will give too large a part to the arbitrary, the capricious. This would indeed be unfortunate, and the interests of the children demand greater circumspection. It will never be to one's credit to have attended a special school. We should at the least spare from this mark those who do not deserve it. Mistakes are excusable, especially at the beginning. But if they become too gross they could injure the good name of these new institutions [i.e., special schools]. And finally, as a principle, we are convinced, and will not cease repeating, that one must introduce into the practical procedures [of testing] the precision and the exactitude of science every time one can, and one can almost always (quoted by Tuddenham, 1962, pp. 482–483).

The immediate need for a test of intelligence postponed Binet's theoretical concerns. The paramount issue became one of objectively diagnosing retardation. This task could be made easier if it were possible to construct a dimension of intelligence that could be used to identify the amount of intelligence a child had. Such a dimension of intelligence was contained in Binet's strategy of requiring a test of intelligence to be related to age. This strategy led to the simple but ingenious plan known as the *age-standard method:* A child's intelligence was measured in relation to the intellectual performance of children of different ages. By using a series of tests ranging from very easy to very difficult, it was possible to identify groups of tests each of which could be passed by the average individual of five different age groups: three, five, seven, nine, and eleven years.

The Binet-Simon scale of intelligence enabled psychologists to measure a child's intellectual performance in an objective and quantitative

manner and to diagnose the cause of a child's poor academic performance. The poor performance of a seven-year-old who was doing badly in
school and scored at a five-year mental age level would be attributed to
intellectual deficiency. The low academic performance of another seven-
year-old who scored at the mental age level of a seven-year-old could not
reasonably be attributed to low intelligence. In this case, a search for
some nonintellectual cause (e.g., poor motivation, hearing defect) would
be initiated.

The first Binet-Simon test of intelligence was finished in 1905 and contained thirty tests covering a wide range of difficulty: visual coordination
(tracking a lighted candle with head and eyes), identifying objects in a
picture, digit-span (recalling a series of numbers in the order of their
presentation), definitions of words, comprehension, and many others,
some of which are used in present-day tests of intelligence. Improved
revisions appeared in 1908 and 1911, and similar tests were constructed
in other countries. A year after Binet died, William Stern (1871–1938), a
German psychologist, proposed an index of intellectual brightness, the
famous intelligence quotient: $IQ = \dfrac{MA}{CA} \times 100$. Dividing a child's mental
age (MA) by his chronological age (CA), and multiplying the quotient by
100 to avoid the inconvenience of decimals, resulted in a score that permitted simple comparisons among individuals with respect to intellectual
brightness. The IQ measure was used by Lewis Terman (1887–1956) in
the American version of the Binet-Simon test known as the Stanford-
Binet, which originally appeared in 1916 and since that time has under-
gone several revisions.

Although the Binet-Simon test was considered a success and was
widely used, it has been criticized repeatedly from the very beginning. A
persistent objection to Binet's test, as well as to intelligence tests in general, is that they do not measure innate intellectual endowment. Binet
never suggested that his test did. He viewed it as a measuring instrument
similar in function to a weight scale. The scale does not indicate whether
a person's weight is due to genetic or dietary factors, or to any specific
interaction between the two. Binet did not believe that a child's intelligence, as measured by his test, was fixed beyond modification. Binet suggested that the intelligence of retarded children could be raised by proper
training or what he called *mental orthopedics.* Improving the child's memory, judgment, and attention would help the child become literally more
intelligent than before.

Another objection to Binet's test is how Binet knew that it was really
testing intelligence. The implication of the question is that intelligence is
a real entity like a tree or a car, the existence of which can be independently confirmed. Such is not the case. Modern methodological analysis
suggests that intelligence, as measured by Binet's test, and other tests of
intelligence, refers to an attribute of behavior. The attribute of behavior
that is chosen to define intelligence is based, in Binet's case, upon his
intuition that a test of intelligence should be related to chronological age

and academic performance. Scores on the Binet-Simon scale met these requirements and, therefore, the test was accepted as a measure of intelligence. Cattell's test, you may recall, was rejected because it failed to predict academic achievement.

One cannot deny the circularity of this argument: Intelligence is related to academic performance and, therefore, a test that can predict academic performance is a test of intelligence. Such circularity cannot be avoided. It can, however, be overcome by demonstrating the usefulness of the test in a variety of situations. Several tests of intelligence which have their origins in Binet's test have demonstrated a versatility that justifies their use; their predictive powers of academic success are not limited to the early years of elementary school but to the entire range of education, including college, professional schools, and graduate school. In addition, they have proved effective in selecting individuals for special jobs in government, industry, and the military and in diagnosing psychologically disturbed patients.

The correlation between scores on intelligence tests and school grades is not perfect. We know that variables other than academic talent are involved in school performance. If it were possible to eliminate the influence of these nonintellectual factors, the correlation between intelligence test scores and academic performance would be greater. This expectation is supported by the fact that IQ scores correlate better with objective educational test scores than with subjective school grades. Furthermore, the degree to which intelligence tests are related to academic success depends on the subject matter in which the grades are received. Intelligence test scores are more highly correlated, as might be expected, with science and English grades than with grades in home economics and shop work (Thorndike & Hagen, 1961).

The success of Binet's test set the stage for the construction of other psychological tests that were successful in predicting subsequent performance. Being able to predict behavior has practical value because it increases the probability that a person selected for a specific type of training or job will be successful. Once it was demonstrated that psychological tests could be effective, the demand for them increased. Schools, industry, the military, and the medical profession all saw the advantages that psychological tests would bring to the efficiency of their operation. Psychological testing (psychometrics), partly as the result of Binet's achievements, established itself as one of the major fields of psychology in America. One reason for its rapid growth was the utilitarian atmosphere that functionalism created in American psychology.

FUNCTIONALISM: A SYSTEMATIC ANALYSIS

Functionalism does not have an official birthdate. It did not emerge suddenly with the publication of a book or paper that proposed a new system of psychology. It developed gradually as a set of orienting attitudes that was shared by many American and some European psychologists. Titch-ener decided to call this nameless orientation functionalism in order to contrast it with his own system, which William James had previously named structuralism. As Titchener (1899) noted, "introspection, from the structural standpoint, is observation of an is; introspection, from the functional standpoint, is observation of an is-for." Structuralism sought to describe what consciousness *is;* functionalism aspired to reveal what consciousness *is-for.*

The ambiguity associated with the origins of functionalism creates a problem. Many psychologists qualify for membership in this movement, some of whom never even described themselves as functionalists. Whose efforts best represent the core beliefs of functionalism? Popular candi-dates for this niche are three psychologists who came to the University of Chicago soon after it was founded in 1891, John Dewey, James R. An-gell, and Harvey A. Carr.[1]

John Dewey, James R. Angell, and Harvey Carr

Although sharing an American pragmatic heritage and a functionalist orientation, Dewey, Angell, and Carr were surprisingly different kinds of individuals and scholars. Dewey was fundamentally a phi-losopher, who was concerned with setting guidelines for dealing with practical matters in such realms as individual adjustment, educational policy, and moral values. Angell was an urbane scholar destined by natural talent and family tradition to become a high-level university administrator. Carr was a tough-minded empiricist who felt most comfortable dealing with empirical evidence.

John Dewey (1859–1952) was born in Burlington, Vermont, and ex-hibited throughout his life the traditional New Englander's passion for fairness and righteousness. He was a shy youth and a good, but not brilliant, student. He attended the University of Vermont, where in his junior year, his intellectual curiosity and independence began to assert itself. Unsure about the career he should choose, he decided to teach high school for a few years, where he began to think about the problems of pedagogy and the purpose of education, topics that concerned him for his entire life. His interest in philosophy, encour-aged by independent study, finally led him to attend graduate school at Johns Hopkins University, where he received his doctorate in phi-

---

[1]The Columbia School of Functionalism, which Cattell helped develop, could also serve as a model of the functionalist movement. Both schools of functionalism, Chicago and Columbia, share many methodological and theoretical ideas.

FIGURE 5.4 John Dewey

University of Chicago Archives

losophy in 1884. There he studied with Charles Sanders Pierce (1839–1914), the founder of pragmatism, the original meaning of which was drastically modified by both James (Chapter 4) and Dewey. Dewey also became acquainted with G. Stanley Hall, who had established one of the earliest psychological laboratories at Hopkins. Hall had studied briefly with Wundt at Leipzig but was much more influenced by Darwinism. Hall's attempt to apply evolutionary principles to the development of the child's mind earned him the title "the Darwin of the mind," of which he was enormously proud.

Dewey taught in the philosophy department of the University of Michigan from 1884 to 1894, except for an intervening year at Minnesota (1888). In 1886, when twenty-seven years old, he wrote the first American textbook in the new scientific psychology. Dewey (1886), the philosopher, viewed psychology as an introduction to philosophy: "there is a way of raising questions, and of looking at them, which is philosophic; a way which the beginner can find more easily in psychology than elsewhere, and which, when found, is the best possible introduction to all specific philosophic questions." This attitude reflected Dewey's conviction that psychology was a tool to achieve philosophical goals such as discovering the principles on which a just and fair society could be based.

Dewey went to the University of Chicago in 1894 as professor of philosophy and chairman of the department of philosophy, psychology, and pedagogy. He was elected president of the American Psychological Association in 1899 and delivered as his presidential address a paper entitled "Psychology and Social Practice" (1900), which stressed the potential importance of psychology in the solution of social problems.

Dewey implemented his social concerns by becoming involved with projects designed to find solutions to social problems such as those created by rapid industrialization and urbanization. In addition, he helped establish a laboratory school, which became known as the Dewey School, designed to test his educational hypotheses. This was the beginning of *progressive education*, a form of pedagogy that Dewey thought to be consistent with democratic values. Rote learning was abandoned in favor of learning by doing, in expectation that intellectual curiosity would be encouraged and understanding would be enhanced.

A disagreement with the administration at the University of Chicago over the policy that would govern the activities of the laboratory school led Dewey to move to Columbia University in 1904, where, in addition to his association with the philosophy department, he also became affiliated with Columbia Teachers College. At Columbia, he became the most influential American philosopher and the world's most important educational authority. He retired from Columbia University in 1929 but continued to publish significant philosophical works and engage in political activities, especially when he believed an injustice was being committed. At seventy-eight, he served as the chairman of a commission to investigate the Moscow trials of the late 1930's that found Leon Trotsky guilty of heading a plot to overthrow the Soviet regime by organizing attempts to assassinate Stalin and collaborating with Hitler and the Japanese militarists. Dewey's commission found Trotsky innocent of the charges. At eighty-two, Dewey championed the cause of academic freedom by leading a protest against the decision of the City College of New York to deny Bertrand Russell, the great English philosopher and Dewey's philosophical adversary, permission to teach because of his unconventional views about sex and marriage.

He died at the age of ninety-one, bequeathing an enormous intellectual heritage to philosophy, education, psychology, political science, jurisprudence, and society. His conviction that psychological knowledge could contribute to the solution of social problems has served as a continuing challenge and goal to many psychologists.

FIGURE 5.5 James Rowland Angell

University of Chicago Archives

James Rowland Angell (1869–1949) was destined for an academic
life. When he was born, his father was president of the University of
Vermont. His maternal grandfather, an eminent mathematician and
astronomer, had been president of Brown University. At three years
of age, Angell moved to Ann Arbor, Michigan, where his father assumed the presidency of the University of Michigan. As a child, Angell came into contact with many distinguished academic and
political leaders from whom he acquired a graciousness that served
him well in his later career.

In college, Angell became interested in psychology; it "instantly
opened up a new world, which it seemed to me, I had been waiting
for, and for the first time I felt a deep and pervasive sense of the
intellectual importance of the material I was facing" (Angell, 1932).
He studied with John Dewey at Michigan for a year following his
graduation and then spent a year at Harvard where he received his
master's degree with William James. Studying with Wundt seemed to
be the next step in rounding out his education, but when Angell

arrived in Leipzig, he discovered to his dismay that the laboratory was so overcrowded he could not be admitted. He therefore studied at German universities in Halle and Berlin and was completing his doctorate at the latter institution when he received an invitation from the University of Minnesota to become an instructor in psychology and to set up a psychology laboratory. Either the offer was too good to refuse or Angell was desperate to get home to be married, for he returned to America without a Ph.D., a loss that never seemed to interfere with his subsequent career. The following year, John Dewey invited Angell to go with him to the University of Chicago and take charge of both the psychology courses and laboratory.

At Chicago, Angell's career blossomed. He and a colleague (Angell & Moore, 1896) published a paper on reaction time that demonstrated that practice was an important variable; unpracticed subjects with a sensorial attitude responded more rapidly than unpracticed subjects with a muscular attitude. The opposite relationship prevailed for practiced subjects. This paper gained immediate fame for Angell because, at that time, an acrimonious controversy was taking place about which attitude, attending to the stimulus or to the response, produced faster reaction times. Angell and Moore demonstrated that it depended on the conditions. More importantly, the results revealed the limitations of the structuralist's research strategy to employ only highly practiced subjects. Such a strategy overlooked important changes produced by practice even in such simple phenomena as reaction times.

Angell published a successful introductory psychology textbook in 1904 which went through four editions plus a brief version (1920). In his mid-thirties he was elected president of the American Psychological Association, and gave as his presidential address a paper intended to clarify the meaning of functionalism, *The Province of Functional Psychology* (1907). Not to be overlooked is Angell's sponsorship of many Ph.D. students. Two of his most famous students were John B. Watson, who founded behaviorism, and Harvey Carr, who became Angell's successor at Chicago.

After Dewey went to Columbia, Angell assumed the chairmanship at Chicago. Under his leadership, the department became one of the most influential departments in the world and graduated many of the future leaders of American psychology. Angell's administrative talents were quickly recognized and the remainder of his career was spent in academic administration and public service. Beginning in 1911, he assumed, in succession, the following administrative positions: dean of the faculties of the University of Chicago, acting president of the University of Chicago, chairman of the National Research Council, president of the Carnegie Corporation, and president of Yale University. Under his administration, from 1921 to 1937, Yale

University's reputation as an educational and research institution was enhanced. One achievement particularly important for psychology was the establishment of the Institute of Human Relations, an interdisciplinary research center. Angell believed that one of the primary goals of a university was to study all aspects of human behavior.

After retiring from Yale at the mandatory age of sixty-eight, Angell became an educational consultant to the National Broadcasting System. He was instrumental in establishing, both in the United States and in parts of Europe, the principle that private and public organizations of mass communication had the responsibility for what Angell called *public service programming,* that is, to air educational, social, scientific and cultural programs that serve the needs of a democratic society. Thus, to the end of his life, Angell continued to be a functionalist both in conviction and practice. He had been instrumental in developing an orientation in psychology that focused on the adaptive functions of both consciousness and behavior. As an administrator, both in academia and in the scientific and commercial worlds, he instituted programs that enabled organizations to adapt to their own needs and those of society.

Harvey Carr (1873–1954) could be considered a minor figure compared to Dewey the philosopher or Angell the administrator, but, as a functionalist, he can be considered more important because he provided empirical and theoretical substance that was previously lacking.

Unlike Angell, Carr traveled a thorny road to success. Born in Indiana, he lived an ordinary life without any sign to indicate his future achievement. After two years at college at De Paul University, Carr became ill and was forced to interrupt his education in order to recover his health and finances. He taught public school and then acquired a bachelor's degree at the University of Colorado with mathematics as his major. At the age of twenty-nine, Carr entered the graduate department of psychology at the University of Chicago. He received his doctorate in 1905, but no job offer was forthcoming. He taught in a high school in Texas and then accepted a position at Pratt Institute in Brooklyn, New York. His break came when John Watson left Chicago for Johns Hopkins and Carr was chosen as his replacement. Eleven years later, Carr replaced Angell as chairman at Chicago. For a period of two years, his status was that of an acting chairman, but then he was given the official appointment. During Carr's tenure at Chicago, from 1918 to 1938, 150 doctoral degrees were awarded, thus spreading the influence of Chicago's functionalism. In 1925, Carr published his introductory text which, when compared to Dewey's effort in 1886, indicates the progress functionalism had made both in research findings and theoretical clarity.

FIGURE 5.6 Harvey Carr

University of Chicago Archives

METHODOLOGICAL ASSUMPTIONS

Functionalists were not self-conscious methodologists. Unlike Wundt and Titchener, they espoused no particular methodology. Instead, they went about their task of investigating psychological phenomena without being concerned about what was proper. Carr actually expressed hostility toward the notion that psychologists should be deeply concerned with their distinctive methodological assumptions. When he was approached to prepare a chapter on functionalism for a distinguished series of books designed to compare various methodological approaches in psychology, Carr told the editor, "I don't like your damned book!" (Hearst, 1979). All psychologists, thought Carr, regardless of their persuasion, were trying to find a common solution to their problems, and it did not help matters to create artificial barriers that would impede progress.

In spite of Carr's position, functionalism did employ a methodological orientation which stressed practical goals in research, theorizing, and application. To appreciate their stand, a brief description of John Dewey's philosophical notions will prove helpful.

The goal of philosophy for Dewey was not the resolution of ivory tower issues such as the nature of eternal reality, but instead the development of effective methods to solve life's problems. To achieve this aim, Dewey applied the Darwinian selection by consequence framework to his own pragmatic conception of moral principles and social policy. Values and policy were not to be judged by their intrinsic righteousness or truth but, instead, should be evaluated in terms of their consequences.

In the current debate about abortion, Dewey's pragmatic position would be to reject the notion that abortion is either an absolute moral sin or an absolute moral right. The key issue would be the consequences for society of laws that permitted or prevented abortion. These consequences could be ascertained by the analysis of past history and by social research.

Dewey's pragmatism should not be confused with James's version. James had a pragmatic conception of truth (Chapter 4) which Dewey rejected. For Dewey, a true statement must be objective, socially determined, a position that is consistent with the tradition of the natural sciences. Dewey's pragmatism was concerned with social values; social principles are pragmatically justified when they are valuable, when they serve the practical needs of society.

Indirectly, Dewey's pragmatism encouraged a modest approach to theorizing among functionalists. He strongly rejected the notion that a complete blueprint of a good society could be prepared all at once, because he believed that those social policies that would work best could only be discovered gradually by empirical means. An analogous strategy was adopted by functionalists in formulating psychological theories. Theories should be gradually developed by the careful monitoring of interactions between hypotheses and data. Sweeping theoretical generalizations were avoided in preference to specific hypotheses.

During the early part of his career, Dewey wrote a methodological paper, "The Reflex Arc Concept in Psychology," (1896) which had an important impact. At that time, Dewey was still under the influence of German philosophers (e.g., Hegel), who encouraged a holistic orientation in preference to an analytical approach, a position from which Dewey later drew away. In this paper, he argued that the sensory stimulus, central neural connections, and motor responses of the reflex arc should *not* be viewed as "separate and complete entities in themselves, but as . . . functioning factors, within the single concrete whole, now designated the reflex arc." Considered within the context of the time this paper was published, it had two major implications. One was that the *experience* of the sensory stimulus and motor response do not have distinct psychical existence but, instead, a coordinated experience fused together, a position consistent with James's view. The second implication is that a reflex arc must be understood in terms of its utilitarian character, not simply in terms of experiential qualities. Thus, Dewey's paper was written in opposition to psychological systems that would reduce conscious experience to atomic elements while ignoring its purpose. The utilitarian emphasis was enthusiastically incorporated into functionalism, but the holistic orientation tended to be minimized if not ignored.

The Subject Matter of Psychology

Functionalism continued the tradition of conceptualizing psychology as the study of the mind. However, its view of consciousness, as already noted, was different from that of Wundt and Titchener who were mainly interested in the experiential qualities of consciousness. James shifted away from that orientation when he viewed consciousness more as an activity with adaptive functions. Carr represents the terminal point in James's redirection with his description of psychology as "primarily concerned with the study of mental activity" (1925).

Conceptions of Mental Activity

To acknowledge the importance of mental activity falls short of offering a clear conception of psychology. James Angell recognized functionalism's lack of a definitive position in his most famous paper entitled, *The Province of Functional Psychology* (1907). At the time he delivered the paper, Angell admitted that "Functional psychology . . . [was] little more than a point of view, a program, an ambition." In order to provide more substance to functionalism, Angell offered three different meanings without expressing a preference for one.

The first meaning that Angell assigned to functionalism was designed to distinguish it from structuralism. He identified functional psychology "with the effort to discern and portray the typical *operations* of consciousness under actual life conditions, as over against the attempt to analyze and describe its elementary and complex *contents*." Mental operations, not mental content, was the subject matter of functionalism.

The second meaning of functionalism, according to Angell, is that it is interested in the utilities of consciousness; how consciousness mediates between the demands of the environment and the needs of the organism. Angell was careful to point out that in this pragmatic view of consciousness, the "accommodatory activities of the organism always sooner or later" expressed themselves in "a muscular movement." The utility of consciousness was intimately tied to adjustive behavior.

The third meaning that Angell assigned to functionalism is that it represents "a form of psychophysics." By this, he did not mean that functionalism was a variation of the combined experimental quantitative analysis of the relationship between sensation and physical stimulation that had been initiated by Weber and Fechner. Angell employed the term *psy-*

chophysics to refer to the general relationship between mind and body. Functionalism "finds its major interest in determining the relations to one another of the physical and mental portions of the organism." The "physical portion" is equivalent to physiological processes and, consequently, functionalism is a branch of biology that studies "the translation of mental process into physiological process and conversely."

These three different meanings of functionalism are not mutually exclusive but they do offer markedly different conceptions of psychology. The first view, the study of mental operations, makes psychology a mental science that focuses on the functional mechanisms of consciousness, such as thought and memory, for example. The second meaning, the utilities of consciousness, emphasizes the adaptive features of consciousness as revealed in an organism's behavior. The third meaning makes psychology a biological science that studies the relation between mental events and bodily processes.

Methods of Investigation

Angell shared with his teacher James the view that the "fundamental psychological method is introspection" (Angell, 1904). Carr (1925) backed away from this position by noting that "mental acts may be subjectively or objectively observed" without suggesting the superiority of one method over the other. Each has advantages and disadvantages, he said. Introspection (subjective observation) can provide "intimate . . . knowledge of mental events" that is not reflected in behavior (objective observation). For example, one cannot discern whether a person is employing words or images when trying to solve a puzzle. Only introspection provides such information. But introspective evidence is suspect: "Any verification or disproof of [introspection] is practically impossible inasmuch as [the] particular mental event can be observed only by [one] individual." Only behavioral data can meet the standards of objective evidence. For functionalism, the solution to this quandary was to use both kinds of data. "Psychology like the other sciences utilizes any fact that is significant for its purposes irrespective of how or where or by whom it was obtained" (Carr, 1925).

The tolerance for both subjective and objective data encouraged a variety of research methods. The experimental method was the method of choice only because it was the most effective procedure for controlling the influence of psychological variables. But functionalists readily accepted the notion that all psychological events could not be examined in the laboratory. Empirical procedures were therefore developed to make naturalistic observations more precise. One example of this effort was the development of numerous kinds of psychological tests (e.g., attitude, achievement) to investigate psychological phenomena occurring in schools, clinics, industry, business, and the military. The concern for making psychology practical tended to discourage the view, upheld by

Titchener (Chapter 3), that a sharp division existed between the experimental method and naturalistic observation as well as between pure and applied research. In the pursuit of knowledge, functionalists felt free to employ any method they thought would prove useful.

Criterion of Truth

Carr's reservations about the observational validity of introspection was at odds with James's optimism that consensual agreement about mental events would ultimately be achieved. By backing off from James's position, Carr essentially removed himself from the controversy that continually raged about introspection. Functionalists, at the time of Carr, tended to avoid getting deeply involved in this debate leaving it to the structuralists and behaviorists to defend the extreme positions that introspection was the cardinal method of psychology or that it was fundamentally invalid.

The functionalists' view of theoretical validity was never spelled out in detail partly because it tended to be overshadowed by strategic considerations. Carr thought of theories as instruments of research:

> A theory develops from some problematic situation and it represents what its author believes to be the best and most feasible solution to the problem that is possible for the present. All science resorts to theory in so far as a final conclusion cannot be obtained. Theories have their value. A tentative and provisional formulation of the factual data is usually better than none at all. Theories represent partial solutions of scientific problems and thus constitute a point of departure for further investigations (Carr, 1925, p. 204).

Theories, according to this instrumental conception, were means, not ends; they helped guide research and provide a systematic framework for the data collected. Whether a "tentative and provisional formulation" was pursued was determined by whether its implications were consistent with empirical evidence. In this sense, functionalists adopted the natural science standard of deductive explanation.

STRATEGY

Functionalism did not have any grand strategic design. It was essentially a problem oriented approach. Problems that were considered important, such as learning and perception, were conceptualized in provisional fashion. A constant interaction occurred between hypotheses and data, and produced usually modest theoretical formulations that interpreted specific empirical phenomena.

THEORY

A general theory, accepted by all functionalists, cannot be described because there is none. But it is possible to sketch a "tentative and provisional formulation" that evolved at the University of Chicago as expressed by Harvey Carr. This informal formulation is historically important because it contained many ideas that were subsequently adopted, after some modification, by the behaviorists and then later by cognitive psychologists.

Carr's Theory

Carr's psychological theory emerged from the functionalists' view that consciousness was an activity:

> Every mental act is thus more or less directly concerned with the manipulation of experience as a means of attaining a more effective adjustment to the world. Every mental act can thus be studied from three aspects—its adaptive significance, its dependence upon previous experience, and its potential influence upon the future activity of the organism. For example, perception is a constituent part of a larger act; it is a process of cognizing objects on the basis of what we are doing, or in terms of their relation to some contemplated mode of behavior. Perception also involves the use of past experience, for the significance of any object can be appreciated only in terms of our previous experiences connected with that object. Likewise, every experience with an object is likely to exert some effect upon the way in which that object is apprehended on subsequent occasions (Carr, 1925, p. 2).

In a similar manner, other activities of the mind—attention, memory, volition, emotion—were conceptualized within this tripartite framework that viewed mental events in terms of their past history, adaptive value, and future consequences.

The Adaptive Act.   A special kind of mental act was the *adaptive act* which served as a key concept in Carr's theory. An adaptive act is essentially a successful mental act.

The concept of the adaptive act is related to Darwin's evolutionary mechanism of selection by consequences: Those psychological acts that lead to adaptive consequences will persist; those that do not will be abandoned. To make this concept more concrete, consider the behavior of a rat in a modern instrumental conditioning apparatus, sometimes referred to as a Skinner box (Figure 5.7). When placed in this apparatus for the first time, a hungry rat will typically wander around, sniffing in the corners, standing up on its hind legs, and making other apparently exploratory responses. Sooner or later, by chance, it will lean on the bar or press it

---

FIGURE 5.7 An Instrumental Conditioning Apparatus

Pressing the bar is an instrumental act that obtains food for the rat.

Courtesy of B. F. Skinner

and, as a result, a small pellet of food will be delivered to the food cup which the rat will consume. If the rat is repeatedly confronted with the same problem, it will learn to press the bar more quickly until a point is reached when it presses the bar immediately.

Pressing the bar is an adaptive act because, as Carr (1925) says, it "alters the situation in a way that satisfies the motivating conditions." Standing on the hind legs is not an adaptive act in this situation because it fails to produce food and thereby reduce hunger.

Carr was very careful to point out that his concept of the adaptive act was not teleological. "The performance of an [adaptive] act cannot be legitimately explained in terms of its subsequent effects," he said. The food delivered by the bar-press did *not* cause the rat to depress the lever. To support his contention, Carr analyzed the adaptive act of certain larvae that hatch at the base of trees and crawl up to feed upon the leaves. Carr notes that if the leaves are removed, the larvae will still ascend. Climbing the tree is caused by the neurological organization of the larvae that results in their crawling toward the source of light. Crawling upward "incidentally [brings] them into sensory contact with the leaves, and this stimulus [evokes] the food response." The explanation of the adaptive acts of both the rat and the larvae lies in their past and the present but not in the future.

Carr thought of the adaptive act as the basic unit of behavior. All of our behavior, whether it is reading a book, going to a party, depressing the brake at a stop sign or solving a problem, are attempts at adjustment. Although Carr did not work out all the details of an adaptive act, he suggested that there were six basic factors: a *motive*, a *motivating stimulus*, a *sensory situation*, a *response*, an *incentive*, and an *association*.

FIGURE 5.8   A Schematic Representation of an Adaptive Act, the Basic Unit of Behavior for Carr

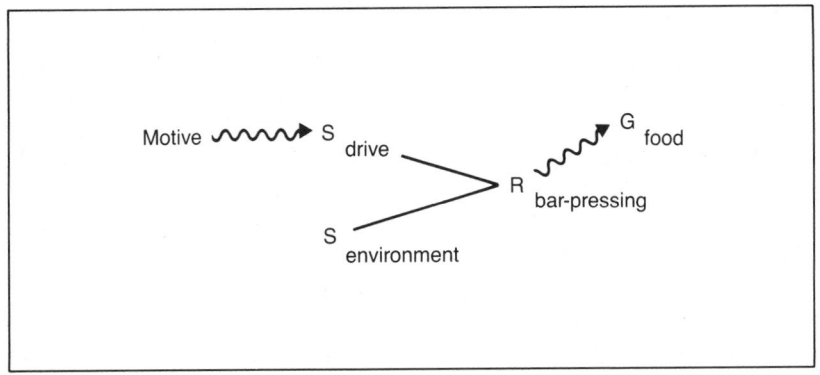

Depriving the experimental animal of food results in a hunger motive that produces ($\rightsquigarrow$) a drive stimulus (S_{drive}) which along with environmental cues, including the lever ($S_{environment}$) become associated (———) with the bar-pressing response ($R_{bar-pressing}$) that produces ($\rightsquigarrow$) the goal object, food (G_{food}).

An adaptive act begins with a *motive*, a condition within the organism that initiates behavior directed toward reducing or eliminating the motive. Fundamental motives, like hunger and escape from pain, are usually referred to as organic needs because their satisfaction is required for the continued welfare of the organism. Other motives, such as the need to pass an examination, are not directly related to an organic need. Motives produce a *motivating stimulus* which "is a relatively persistent stimulus" (e.g., hunger pang) that "arouses and energizes" the adaptive act. The adaptive act is a *response* to a particular *sensory situation* that frees the individual from the dominance of the drive stimulus. Any commodity (e.g., water) or event (e.g., termination of a pain-inducing stimulus) that produces motivational satisfaction functions as an *incentive*.

The concept of an adaptive act reflected the strong associationistic traditions in psychology (p. 54). Instead of employing the old conception of an association between mental events, Carr substituted an *association* between a stimulus and response; in the case of the Skinner box example, an association between a pattern of stimuli consisting of the hunger drive stimulus and the lever, and the bar-pressing response. This association, which can also be described as a habit, varies in strength. The more frequently an association or habit is performed, the stronger it will be, and the stronger it is, "the greater is the ease and facility and accuracy with which it is performed." Figure 5.8 schematically represents the essential features of the adaptive act.

The Emergency Theory of Consciousness.   Carr suggested that adaptive acts can operate at two levels of consciousness: automatic and unconscious (involuntary), and cognitive and conscious (voluntary). An automatic habit is an association in which the stimulus triggers the response with no intervening conscious thought. The stimulus is sensed and the response spontaneously occurs. It is involuntary. In contrast, the cognitive act involves the active voluntary choice among competing forms of behavior.

The distinction between the two forms of adaptive acts is illustrated in a hair-raising episode experienced when driving down one of the steepest hills in San Francisco. My car was picking up speed and I automatically depressed the brake pedal. The brakes, however, did not hold. What happens under such conditions? According to Carr, conscious processes take over from the automatic habits that are now ineffective. I started to think of possible solutions: Should I steer toward the curb, downshift, use the parking brake? The emergency encouraged me to behave in a cognitive rational manner.

Carr would interpret both the automatic depression of the brake and the cognitive attempt to solve the emergency as expressions of habits previously learned. In the former case, the habit was an involuntary one in which the sensation directly elicited the response. In the latter case, cognitive habits of problem solving, such as specifying the nature of the problem, listing alternative solutions, and selecting the best one were being used.

Reactions to the sensory situation differ in involuntary and voluntary habits. The stimulus of an automatic (involuntary) habit is sensed. The stimulus of a cognitive (voluntary) habit is perceived. Perception, for Carr, "is a process of cognitively evaluating any aspect of a behavior situation as a means of effecting an adequate adjustment." Perception begins with "an act of attention" which enhances perceptual clarity by eliminating "irrelevant and distractive stimuli," while simultaneously promoting "a more effective cognition of the stimulus pattern." When my brakes went out, I began to perceive the environment in relation to possible solutions to my predicament. I could not get to the curb because of the cars parked against it. I downshifted and gradually applied the parking brake. I survived!

Meaning.   For Carr, the perception of meaning is also an associative process. Meaning depends on the "indirect and partial arousal of some . . . previous experiences associated with an event or object." Learning to read depends on "a process of establishing associations, or as a process of endowing specific symbols with meaning." The word *cat* becomes associated with a specific cat, a picture of a cat, an image of a cat, or some other symbol of a cat. With age and experience, the associations enlarge so that the word *cat* becomes associated with all kinds of cats, even lions and tigers, as well as numerous characteristics of cats (e.g., "graceful as a cat").

A Final Comment.   By modern standards, Carr's theorizing suffers from imprecision. He failed to answer basic questions that his tentative formulation raised: Are all motives (e.g., curiosity, esthetic) linked in some manner to organic needs such as hunger and sex? Is motivational satisfaction necessary to form and strengthen associations? What characteristics of perceptual cognitions make them effective for solving problems? Is motivational satisfaction a suitable criterion of adjustment? Such questions would not have been raised if Carr had not systematically analyzed his concept of the adaptive act. Before a basic theoretical question can be answered it first must be raised in a significant context. Carr and the functionalist tradition should be given credit for identifying many issues that subsequent generations of psychologists considered to be of basic importance.

A methodological issue of profound importance raised by Carr's model, one that will be discussed in the next chapter, is whether it is productive to formulate a theory that combines experiential and behavioral events. For the most part, Carr's model was concerned with publicly observable behavior (e.g., recalling a series of words, solving a problem). But the important concepts of *motivational satisfaction* and *perceptual cognitions* cannot be publicly observed because they are directly observed only by the organism that experiences them. Functionalists believed that the combination of experiential and behavioral events would enhance the explanatory powers of a theory, but behaviorists concluded that the use of experiential constructs would destroy the natural science status of psychology.

Delayed Reaction

Most of the research projects conducted in the laboratories of the functionalists were designed to investigate a specific problem rather than to test a hypothesis from a general theory. A representative example of a problem-oriented approach is Walter S. Hunter's doctoral thesis, *Delayed Reaction in Animals and Children* (1913). The thesis was directed by Harvey Carr, whom Hunter "credited with instilling in him a love of careful experimentation" (Riggs, 1968).

Hunter developed the delayed reaction technique to study symbolic behavior in human and infrahuman animals. When a delayed reaction box is used with a laboratory rat, the subject is initially trained to choose the compartment with a light at the entrance by rewarding a correct choice with food (see Figure 5.9). The compartment that is lit varies from trial to trial to ensure that the animal is responding to the light and not just a particular position. After the animal has learned to select the lighted compartment, the delayed reaction feature is introduced. The light over one compartment is turned on and then turned off *before* the animal is released from a wire mesh enclosure (delay chamber). Hunter reported that rats and dogs were capable of correctly choosing the compartment that had been lit if they oriented themselves toward the light and maintained that orientation during the delay period. This suggested that kinesthetic cues from their bodily orientation were responsible for their correct choices. In contrast, raccoons and children would respond

---

FIGURE 5.9 A Delayed Reaction Apparatus

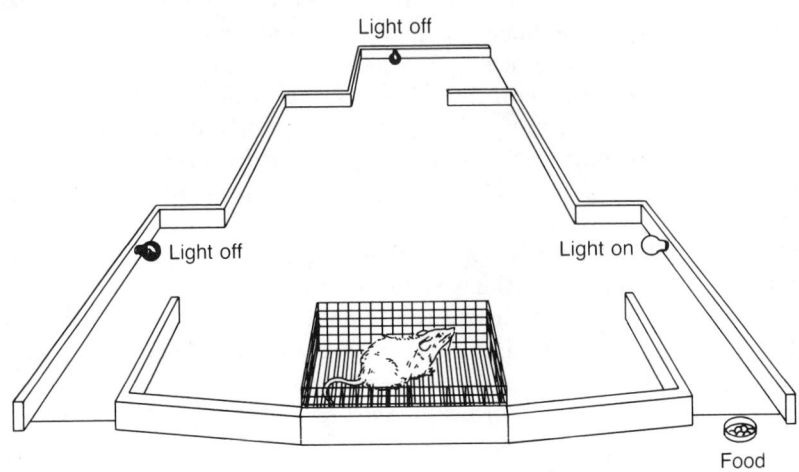

The subject is placed in a wire mesh enclosure that serves as a starting box. After learning to choose the lighted compartment, the animal must learn to choose the compartment which had been lighted but is dark at the time the subject makes the choice (After Hunter, 1913.)

correctly after long delay periods in which their bodily orientation was disrupted. This suggested to Hunter that *symbolic processes* were operating in raccoons and children. (Later research suggested that symbolic processes could occur in lower mammals.)

The historical significance of Hunter's efforts is that he developed an experimental technique that served to compare the symbolic capacity of animals at different stages of individual and evolutionary development. This research technique, along with others that were designed to investigate intellectual functioning, demonstrated the increased complexity and effectiveness of symbolic processes as children mature and as organisms ascend the evolutionary scale.

Mental Measurement and Psychological Tests

Although functionalism encouraged the growth of psychological testing, Dewey, Angell, and Carr had little direct involvement with this increasingly important field. They did, however, create an atmosphere at Chicago which contributed to its development both by training future leaders and by fashioning a realistic orientation about the interpretation of individual differences.

Carr recognized wide individual differences in human abilities ranging from specific skills such as typing to general faculties such as intelligence. He believed properly constructed psychological tests were useful, effective, and economical instruments for measuring individual differences in abilities. When it came to interpreting the cause of these differences, Carr was exceptionally cautious. He denied that any general answer was possible about the relative influence of environmental and hereditary factors on such human abilities as intelligence. Carr insisted that one is forced to limit conclusions to *specific* comparisons in *specific* situations. For example, in one case of two siblings, one brain injured at the time of birth and the other normally delivered, the cause of the difference in intelligence is mainly environmental. In the other case of siblings, one of whom suffers from mental retardation resulting from phenylketonuria (PKU), a metabolic disorder which is transmitted as a single gene recessive hereditary characteristic, while the other sibling does not, the difference is primarily due to heredity.

Carr did not accept the position that a person's IQ was set for life. He shared Binet's view that "mental orthopedics" could elevate intelligence by appropriate training techniques. Physiological intervention could also be helpful. Phenylketonuria, for example, can be simply diagnosed in infants by a chemical analysis of their urine, and the condition can be alleviated by diet.

While refusing to accept a rigid ceiling to an individual's intelligence, Carr did not believe that any person could be trained to achieve any level of intelligence. In essence, Carr's analysis of the nature-nurture controversy helped structure the problem for future researchers so that their efforts would be directed at issues that could be resolved by empirical investigations. He was convinced that only rigorous research could unravel the complicated interaction between environmental and hereditary influences on human abilities.

Louis L. Thurstone.   One of the major contributions to mental measurement by the functionalists at the University of Chicago was the graduate training they gave to Louis L. Thurstone (1887–1955), who received his doctorate in 1917. With a background in engineering and work experience with Thomas A. Edison, Thurstone readily adopted the pragmatic orientation of functionalism. With his talent for mathematics, Thurstone gravitated toward the problem of measuring mental events. After he returned to the University of Chicago in 1924 as an associate professor, he was responsible for teaching psychophysics. He soon admitted that he was becoming bored with the traditional psychophysical tasks such as measuring the sensations resulting from lifting cylinders of different weights. Why not employ the same precise psychophysical methods to measure something important such as social attitudes (Thurstone, 1959)? By developing quantitative methods for measuring attitudes (e.g., toward ethical values or different nationalities), Thurstone provided researchers with a powerful tool to investigate numerous social phenomena associated with attitudinal change.

Thurstone also made important contributions to the theoretical analysis of intelligence. He was one of the leaders in developing factor analysis, a statistical technique that analyzes mental test scores into their basic components. Charles Spearman (1863–1945), an eminent English psychologist, had concluded that there is a general intellectual factor common to all intelligence, which became widely referred to as *g*. According to Spearman's theory, the apparently different abilities required for spelling, mathematical reasoning, remembering, and other skills are in part determined by this basic *g* factor. In addition to the *g* factor, there are specific factors, or *s*'s. Thus, a person's performance in a mathematics test is the combined result of the amount of *g* factor combined with some specific mathematical ability.

Thurstone (Thurstone & Thurstone, 1941), employing his newly developed mathematical procedures of factor analysis, inferred from his analyses of sixty different kinds of intelligence tests that human intelligence consisted of seven independent *primary factors: number ability, word fluency, memory, reasoning, spatial relations,* and *perceptual speed.* To understand fully a person's intellectual capabilities, therefore, a single global measure of intelligence such as IQ is insufficient. A battery of tests that provides a measure of each primary factor is more informative. Thurstone (1948) did, however, acknowledge that, in addition to primary factors, a second-order general factor operates. One can conclude that Spearman and Thurstone were not disagreeing about the existence of a general factor of intelligence, but instead about its importance.

Although different methods of factor analysis did not always reach the same conclusions, the method itself had a salutary effect on psychological testing. It encouraged a more analytic approach to the study of aptitudes and abilities. Frequently, tests based on factor analyses had a greater predictive power than did general tests for performance in numerous kinds of professions (e.g., engineering) and jobs (e.g., automobile mechanic). By measuring mental activities more precisely, Thurstone contributed to a fuller understanding of their adaptive functions.

Quotations from John Dewey, James Angell, and Harvey Carr

1. Consciousness can neither be defined nor described. We can define or describe anything only by the employment of consciousness . . . all attempts to define [consciousness] must move in a circle (Dewey, 1896, p. 2).

2. The conventional type of education which trains children to docility and obedience, to the careful performance of imposed tasks because they are imposed, regardless of where they lead, is suited to an autocratic society (J. Dewey & E. Dewey, 1915, p. 303).

3. Psychology will never provide ready-made materials and prescriptions for the ethical life, any more than physics dictates off-hand the steam-engine and the dynamo. But science, both physical and psychological, makes known the condition upon which certain results depend, and therefore puts at the disposal of life a method for controlling them. Psychology will never tell us just what to do ethically, nor just how to do it. But it will afford us insight into the conditions which control the formation and execution of aims, and thus enable human effort to expend itself sanely, rationally, and with assurance (Dewey, 1900, p. 124).

4. All life is built upon physical and physiological foundations. It is quite impossible to understand human nature, even in a common-sense way, without a knowledge of the bodily structure of the human being (Angell, 1920, p. 2).

5. [When introspection is] carried out carefully and systematically by many individuals, it has resulted in the accumulation of a very respectable body of knowledge entirely worthy of the term scientific (Angell, 1920, p. 4).

6. An organism represents, among other things, a device for executing movements in response to the stimulations and demands of the environment. In the main these movements are of an organically beneficial character, otherwise the creature would perish (Angell, 1904, p. 8).

7. Irrespective of definitions, psychology has been concerned with an ultimate comprehension of those operations by which an organism in virtue of its previous experience is enabled to adapt itself to a complex and variable environment (Carr, 1917a, p. 182).

8. The psychophysical conception of mental process . . . permits the widest latitude as to methods of approach; it permits mental processes to be studied from the standpoint of immediate experience, of objective observation, or of clinical data (Carr, 1917a, p. 185).

9. Psychology as a young and growing science must . . . produce its miracles in order to secure popular acclaim to its worth and greatness, and what can be more wonderful and miraculous than the discovery and labored empirical demonstration of a truth which directly contradicts the common sense opinion of mankind? (Carr, 1917b, p. 374).

CONTRIBUTIONS OF FUNCTIONALISM

In 1962, George Miller, an important figure in the development of cognitive psychology, was led to conclude that, "In the U.S. today functional psychology *is* psychology." If nothing else, this statement indicates the profound influence functionalism had upon the course of the history of psychology. It represented a revolutionary shift away from a psychology that sought to reveal the structure of conscious experience. And by dominating American psychology, functionalism's influence automatically spread to other nations.

Viewing psychology within Angell's tripartite conception of mental activity (p. 130) enlarged functionalism's appeal by offering a variety of approaches to the study of psychology, including mentalistic, behavioristic, and physiological. The rigidity of structuralism proved to be no match for the flexibility of functionalism in the American intellectual market place. Functionalism's flexible orientation gave a new look to psychology. Structuralism in America had limited the major concern of psychologists to sensation and perception. Now other research areas—learning, memory, motivation, cognitive processes, personality, social psychology—were opened for investigation. In addition, psychology freed itself from laboratory restraints and began to develop techniques and collect information that could be used in the solution of personal and social problems.

John Dewey's pragmatic theory of values expressed the optimistic view that applied psychology could combine moral purpose with utilitarian goals. *Progressive Education* was a case in point. "Learning by doing," not only resulted in improved learning, he argued, but also helped students become worthy and productive members of a democratic society. But Dewey's idealistic efforts failed:

> Dewey wanted to instill in children the best of American ideals. Unfortunately, the American ideal of the good mixer somehow became dominant over the American ideal of individualism: intellectual excellence became second in importance to life adjustment. In Dewey's own lifetime "Learning by doing" had degenerated into an empty slogan and progressive education passed into scornful disrepute (Miller, 1962, p. 64–65).

One could argue that Dewey was partly to blame for progressive education's loss of popularity. He was too willing to recommend educational policies without having sound empirical evidence about their possible consequences. Perceiving *learning by drill* in opposition to *learning by doing* oversimplified a complex educational problem. Each procedure has merit for different kinds of tasks. In addition, their effectiveness varies for different kinds of students. By insisting that science could be a useful servant of a democracy, Dewey was obligated to offer compelling scientific evidence in support of his educational reforms.

Functionalism's central concern with the process of adjustment exerted several profound influences on the history of psychology. By raising the question of the utility of consciousness, functionalism, as noted, shifted attention away from the content of consciousness to mental acts. This in turn led to the expansion of the meaning of mind to include "nonconscious components of mental life" (Carr, 1917a). Many psychological activities, Carr suggested, occur in absence of any conscious awareness:

memory, problem solving, habit, and "the wealth of subterranean activities brought to notice by the investigations of abnormal psychology." Although such phenomena would be ignored by psychologists who focused exclusively on *conscious* experience, Carr (1917a) insisted on revising the "definition of the nature of mental process in such a way to include such data." This shift of interest to mental acts even when they lacked conscious correlates inevitably led to greater reliance on behavioral measures in psychological investigations.

Assigning central importance to the concept of adjustment yielded an additional spinoff that still encourages much debate. For the most part, functionalists assumed that the concept of psychological adjustment was equivalent to the evolutionary concept of adaptation, which is debatable. Evolutionary adaptation has a fairly clear empirical meaning: Anatomical structures are adaptive when they increase the probability of individual survival and reproduction. In contrast, the meaning of psychological adjustment is ambiguous. It is certainly not equivalent to adaptation with its emphasis on reproduction. If it were, a homosexual or a person who practiced celibacy for religious or other reasons would automatically be maladjusted. A common conception, consistent with the pragmatic outlook of the functionalists, is that adjustment refers to one's ability to meet the demands of society and satisfy one's own drive. Does this mean that nonconformists are maladjusted or that all who are socially successful are well adjusted? The important point which many functionalists failed to realize is that adjustment, unlike adaptation, is not solely an empirical concept, but instead involves value judgments (Kendler, 1981). As a result, psychologists, especially those who treat patients, are not always in agreement about the goals of therapy. Functionalism identified the important problem of psychological adjustment but ignored its ethical complexity.

In listing the contributions of functionalism, the development of many new research techniques (e.g., delayed reaction) and the formulation of numerous hypotheses (e.g., adaptive act) cannot be overlooked. A testimony to their importance is the difficulty in discovering a contemporary problem that does not have roots in functionalism.

A Debate about Functionalism

Moderator: Although some might disagree with George Miller's (1962) judgment that "functional psychology *is* psychology" in America, no one will deny its powerful influence on contemporary psychology. Thus, this debate should be focused on the historical effects of its influence. Good or bad?

Pro: I must confess that I find it difficult to believe that a reasonable debate can take place about whether functionalism exerted a beneficial effect on psychology. Judging functionalism is practically equivalent to judging modern psychology. Modern psychology reflects so many features of functionalism, admittedly in a more sophisticated form, that a criticism of functionalism automatically becomes a condemnation of contemporary psychology.

Con: I share, to some extent, your opinion. But you should recognize that there is much more to modern psychology than a functionalist heritage. If we limit our discussion to the influence of functionalism, we will recognize some unfortunate consequences. First, and perhaps foremost, functionalism attempted to become a natural science by offering a confused and inconsistent methodology that used incompatible kinds of data—privately observed mental events and publicly observed occurrences. Second, functionalism, mainly in the writings and actions of John Dewey, offered a confused picture of the proper role a scientist should assume in a democracy. Should he be a detached scientist or a political activist? History has demonstrated, in my opinion, that psychologists will never be successful in contributing to the solution of social problems if they function as political activists instead of detached scientists (Atkinson, 1977). Third, functionalists, by their cautious approach to theorizing, failed to offer a general psychological theory capable of interpreting humans and animals in their full complexity.

Pro: Your comments amaze me. You refuse to evaluate functionalism within the historical context in which it developed. Instead, you are judging it by modern standards, and, it must be noted, by standards that are questionable. Functionalism was instrumental in employing behavioral measures, but you criticize it for not employing them exclusively, as if mental events should be excluded from psychology. Functionalism encouraged the application of psychological knowledge to the solution of social problems, but you quibble that such use was contaminated by advocacy, as if it is possible for any scientist to be completely detached from moral principles. And finally, you condemn functionalism for formulating modest theories, while seemingly ignoring the fact that the available evidence did not provide the empirical foundation for broad theories. Would you prefer theoretical fantasies to realistic theories?

Con: You are distorting my views. You fail to distinguish between functionalism as a revolution against structuralism and functionalism as a positive orientation in its own right. As a revolution against a narrow sterile approach, functionalism deserves the highest compliments. But, as a positive contribution it lacked cohesiveness and generality. It is interesting to note that the name functionalism gradually disappeared from usage. Carr practically never mentioned it simply because it really does not express a clear positive conception of psychology.

Moderator: There does not appear to be much agreement between you two except that functionalism was a noble revolution that was successful in reorienting psychology along more productive paths. The disagreement revolves about the positive contributions of functionalism and there is an implication that an understanding of behaviorism will illustrate the shortcomings of functionalism. We shall see.

SUMMARY

Functionalism, an eclectic position opposed to structuralism, combined ideas from many different sources, most notably Charles Darwin and William James. Darwinism (1) encouraged the study of the adaptive aspects of consciousness and behavior, (2) conceptualized psychology as a biological science, (3) suggested a selection-by-consequence model of behavior, (4) focused attention on the problem of individual differences, and (5) suggested the importance of the concept of psychological adjustment.

James's special influence was his conception of psychology as a mental science that viewed experience in terms of acts, not content. Also, James's own brand of pragmatism encouraged the position that psychology should serve a practical purpose for individuals and society. Functionalism, because of its Darwinian heritage, was receptive to the study of individual differences. Consequently, the efforts of Alfred Binet, who developed the successful age-standard method of measuring intelligence after attempts by Galton and Cattell failed, were readily incorporated within functionalism.

Functionalism developed gradually as a set of orienting attitudes that eventually were combined under the rubric of functionalism. According to Titchener, his own brand of psychology, structuralism, sought to describe what consciousness *is*, while functionalism aspired to reveal what consciousness *is-for.*

John Dewey, James Angell, and Harvey Carr, all from the University of Chicago, launched functionalism as a major systematic position in psychology. John Dewey, primarily a philosopher, encouraged the idea that psychology could and should contribute to the public welfare. Dewey implemented his own pragmatic views as the leader of the progressive education movement, a pedagogical approach that prescribed that students should discover truth and achieve understanding by their own efforts.

James Angell clarified the meaning of functionalism by distinguishing among three different areas of study: mental operations, the utilities of consciousness, and psychophysics (the relationship between mental and physiological processes). This tripartite view encouraged mentalistic, behavioristic, and physiological approaches to the study of psychology.

According to Harvey Carr, the subject matter of functional psychology was mental activity. He saw mental activities, such as thinking, perceiving, and learning, as modes of adjustment that could be analyzed in terms of their past, adaptive function, and future consequence. Mental activity was assumed to be an expression of neurophysiological activities and, consequently, empirical investigations of one of these two activities could reveal important information about the other.

Psychological theory, for functionalists, was an instrument to guide research. This orientation encouraged tentative formulations usually with limited generality. The nearest approximation to a general theory was Carr's treatment of the adaptive act which was based on the assumption that acts will persist if they have adaptive consequences. The six components of this unit of behavior are: *motive, motivating stimulus, sensory situation, response, incentive,* and *association.*

According to the emergency theory of consciousness, automatic habits govern behavior until a novel situation arises which makes them ineffective. In order to adapt to this emergency, consciousness begins to operate, thereby encouraging attempts at rational problem solving. Carr assumed that habits operated at two levels of consciousness, unconscious automatic associations and conscious cognitive associations. Meaning, which resides in cognitive habits, is a result of the experiences previously associated with a given word, situation, or event.

The delayed reaction technique which was designed to study symbolic behavior in human and infrahuman subjects illustrates the research style of many functionalists; a psychological issue is translated into an experimental procedure that allows for answers to specific questions.

Functionalists tended to be cautious in interpreting psychological tests, particularly in regard to the relative contributions of heredity and environment on IQ. Only rigorous research, it was argued, could unravel these influences, and the resulting answers would be relevant only to particular patterns of interaction. Louis Thurstone, who received his doctorate at the University of Chicago during the time of Angell and Carr, made fundamental contributions to psychometrics with his research on attitude testing and his factor analytic approach to intelligence.

Functionalism redirected psychology away from the task of analyzing the structure of conscious experience. In its place it offered a provisional orientation that was primarily designed to study mental activity in regard to the adaptive function of consciousness. This approach focused attention on mental operations such as memory and thinking, the adaptive features of consciousness as revealed in an organism's behavior, and the relationship between mental events and physiological processes. This varied orientation expanded the empirical realm of psychology while breaking down the barriers between pure and applied research.

SUGGESTED READINGS

Leading psychologists during the early years of psychology tended to write introductory psychology texts. Texts by Dewey (1886), Angell (1904, 1920), and Carr (1925) provide an excellent original source for studying functionalism as well as its historical development. Angell's (1907) classic *The Province of Functional Psychology* offers important ideas about functionalism, while Dewey's *Psychology and Social Practice* (1900) discusses issues associated with applying psychological knowledge to education. Good secondary sources for the study of functionalism are Heidbreder (1933), and Marx and Hillix (1979).

An excellent and readable account of Galton's contributions to the psychology of individual differences is contained in Fancher's *Pioneers of Psychology* (1979). Tuddenham's chapter (1962) on "The nature and measurement of intelligence" is highly recommended.

6

Behaviorism

"Scientific psychology denies man his soul and now behaviorism is forcing him to lose his mind." This witticism reflects the resentment and antagonism many felt toward the advent of behaviorism—the systematic position that psychology is the science of behavior, not of the mind. By conceptualizing humans as analogous to machines, behaviorism proposed an image of man that was interpreted in some quarters as demeaning and insulting. While behaviorism was disparaged by some, others received the new movement with enthusiasm and high expectations. Behaviorism, its proponents argued, did more than just pay lip service to the idea that psychology is a natural science; it *made* psychology a natural science like physics and biology. The *New York Times* judged John B. Watson's *Behaviorism* (1924) to mark "an epoch in the intellectual history of man," while the *New York Herald-Tribune* declared that "perhaps this is the most important book ever written."

Time has not resolved the controversy that surrounded behaviorism during its early years. The reason is that like most important ideas in the history of mankind, behaviorism contains several components. Which component is emphasized influences how behaviorism is judged.

HISTORICAL ROOTS

Although John B. Watson (1878–1958) officially founded behaviorism and invented its name, the ideas behind this orientation have deep roots in history. These ideas were expressed in philosophical interpretations of the nature of man, in explanations of animal psychology, and in behavioristic research programs that were conducted during the era when psychology was conceptualized as the science of the mind. Finally the development of behaviorism was nourished by Ivan P. Pavlov's brilliant research in conditioning, which provided an empirical base and an experimental technique on which Watson would erect his theoretical conceptions.

Philosophical Behaviorists

Behaviorism argues that psychology is the science of behavior, not of the mind. This idea was anticipated by two French philosophers more than two centuries ago in a strikingly different context from the one that prevailed at the time Watson attempted to redirect the young science of psychology away from its mental moorings.

Julian Offray de La Mettrie. La Mettrie (1709–1751), throughout his brief life, was successful in making enemies. He particularly enjoyed directing his intellectual barbs at pious members of the middle class and at the medical profession, to which he belonged. He is best known for his book *L'Homme Machine (Man a Machine)* (1748/1960) in which he enunciated a mechanistic interpretation of the mind. Two very different meanings have been assigned to the man-machine doctrine throughout history. One, the man-machine identity, is that man *is* a machine no different in quality than a mechanical slot machine or electronic computer. The second, the man-machine analogy, is that humans can be thought of as a kind of machine without assuming that all machines are qualitatively equivalent. Those who espouse a man-machine doctrine have mainly been attacked for upholding the position of man-machine identity, that humans are nothing more than machines. The sophisticated defense of the man-machine doctrine is that the most effective method to analyze human psychology is to view humans in a detached manner, as some sort of a machine the characteristics of which must be discovered.

La Mettrie was a materialist, atheist, and hedonist, all of which are relevant to his view of the man-machine doctrine. As a materialist, he believed that psychic activity has no independent reality; it is a consequence of the actions of the brain and other parts of the central nervous system. Translated into modern doctrine, La Mettrie was arguing that mental events could only be understood in terms of material processes within the nervous system.

As an athiest, La Mettrie believed that the explanation of human actions does not require the assumption of a divine Creator. This position also lends itself to two possible interpretations: denying the existence of God or refusing to consider His influence in explaining human psychology. La Mettrie accepted both positions, but it should be noted that it would be possible to believe in God without considering His actions as a necessary part of psychological explanations.

As a hedonist, La Mettrie considered life to be a farce, with nothing, soul or spirit, surviving death. Pleasure, therefore, was the only justification for existence. Happiness, the optimal state of pleasure, was, therefore, a basic ethical value that everybody should accept. La Mettrie

FIGURE 6.1 Julian Offray de La Mettrie

Dan McIntosh

followed his own prescription, perhaps too earnestly. His death in his early forties was attributed to overeating, which according to his enemies demonstrated the dangers of both hedonism and atheism.

La Mettrie did not suggest that the hedonism he preached had a counterpart in the world of machines; a lubricant, like oil, did not provide pleasure to a machine as food did to himself. Thus it would seem that La Mettrie rejected the notion that machines were *identical* to humans, and instead believed it would be profitable to adopt a man-machine analogy in the attempt to understand human psychology.

It is interesting to note, in light of reactions to behaviorism, that La Mettrie's writings were received in France with such hostility that he was forced to exile himself to the more liberal Holland. But even there, he met with such resentment and criticism following the publication of *L'Homme Machine* that he was forced to flee. Fortunately for La Mettrie, Frederick the Great (1712–1786) offered him refuge in Berlin where he had the opportunity to continue the development of his unorthodox and unpopular views.

FIGURE 6.2 Auguste Comte

Dan McIntosh

Auguste Comte. Auguste Comte (1798–1857) is generally acknowledged to be the founder of a philosophical school of positivism, a systematic position that holds that valid facts and knowledge can only be ascertained by the methods of science. He formulated the *law of three stages* which purportedly describes the development of the mode of understanding humans employ in interpreting natural phenomena, including their own history and behavior. In the initial *theological* stage, natural events are attributed to the direct actions of supernatural forces. In the *metaphysical* stage, natural phenomena result from the operation of abstract forces, such as *human destiny*, while in the final *positive* phase, events are explained by observation, hypotheses, and experimentation, that is, by the scientific method.

Comte claimed that the knowledge of the various sciences can be organized in the form of a triangle. Mathematics is at the base and then come astronomy, physics, chemistry, biology, and sociology in ascending order. Each science depends in part on the science below it. Thus, the most basic science, sometimes referred to as the *mother science,* is mathematics. At the apex, is the science of sociology, a name that Comte coined, which is based upon all the sciences below it.

Why was psychology omitted from this unified conception of science? Comte had reservations about the scientific status of observing mental events, which was generally considered to be the major method of psychology, even before the establishment of Wundt's laboratory in 1879. Sociology, in contrast, did not depend on examining consciousness, but rather on observing objective social events.

One can easily get the impression that Comte's positivism was created by a cold, detached scholar. Nothing could be further from the truth! He was an ideological social reformer who passionately believed that social harmony could prevail if government policy were based on the scientific principles of sociology. If people agree about the scientific laws of astronomy, his argument went, they would also agree about the scientific laws of sociology. If a government were designed on the basis of the scientific principles of sociology, the citizens would automatically abide by the laws of the land. A common criticism of Comte's idealistic position is that it overlooks the point that applications of scientific laws involve value judgments and therefore universal acceptance of any particular social policy (e.g., capital punishment) will not automatically be forthcoming. Even if the laws of sociology were as precise as those of astronomy, arguments would inevitably occur about the social policies society should adopt.

Comte preached a religion of humanism which presumably was shorn of metaphysics, and in which a cult of reason would prevail. He thought his positivist religion would encourage everybody "to live for others." Positivism could provide "the means to avoid violent revolutions, arising from misunderstandings" and "reduce them to a simple moral movement in the march of mankind" (Quoted in Samelson, 1974).

Animal Psychology

Darwin's evolutionary theory affirmed a continuity between humans and animals. Like many naturalists of his day, Darwin offered anecdotes to suggest that dogs, cats, and other animals shared human mental processes, such as reasoning.

C. Lloyd Morgan (1852–1936), a British psychologist, expressed strong reservations about the usefulness of the anecdotal method for interpreting the mental processes of animals. His observations denied that dogs reasoned like humans. From watching his own dog learn to open the latch on the front gate, he concluded that the achievement derived neither from reasoning nor imitation. The first successful response made by his fox terrier occurred when the dog inserted its head between the iron bars of the fence and accidentally raised the latch.

> He withdrew his head, and began to look out elsewhere, when he found that the gate was swinging open, and out he bolted. After that, whenever

I took him out, I shut the gate in his face, and waited till he opened it for himself and joined me. I did not give him any assistance in any way, but just waited and watched, sometimes putting him back and making him open it again. Gradually he went, after a few pokings of his head out in the wrong place, to the one opening at which the latch was lifted. But it was nearly three weeks from my first noticing his actions from the window before he went at once and with precision to the right place (Morgan, 1894, p. 288).

Morgan concluded that "we need . . . careful investigation in place of anecdotal reporting." He also added a proviso, which became known as *Lloyd Morgan's Canon:* "In no case may we interpret an action as the outcome of the exercise of a higher psychical activity, if it can be interpreted as the outcome of the exercise of one which stands lower in the psychological scale."

Other investigators suggested that some kinds of animal behavior did not require any explanation in terms of conscious processes. Jacques Loeb (1859–1924), was a German physiologist and zoologist who in his later years taught at the University of Chicago where Watson came under his influence. Loeb developed a theory of animal behavior based upon the concept of *tropism*, which is an involuntary movement in response to a stimulus. A plant reacts in a tropistic fashion when its leaves turn to the sun. Loeb concluded that many forms of animal behavior were purely a direct reaction to stimuli in the complete absence of any conscious processes. Although Loeb did not exclude conscious processes in higher forms of animal life, he denied the necessity of invoking consciousness to explain the behavior of animals. This position encouraged an idea that proved attractive to behaviorists: If the actions of lower organisms can be explained without reference to mental events, why cannot human behavior be explained in the same way?

Behavioristic Research

Before Watson's vigorous rejection of a mentalistic psychology in favor of a science of behavior, many psychologists, without explicitly denying a mentalistic outlook, conducted research in a behavioristic manner; they investigated how *behavior* changes as a function of experimental conditions. When Cattell was chairman of the Department of Psychology at Columbia University, he boasted "that most of the research work that has been done by me or in my laboratory is nearly as independent of introspection as work in physics or zoology." If Cattell had omitted the word "nearly" he would have qualified as a strict behaviorist.

Three psychologists were particularly influential in demonstrating that important behavioral research could be conducted without the direct examination of consciousness.

FIGURE 6.3 Hermann Ebbinghaus and His Curve of Memory

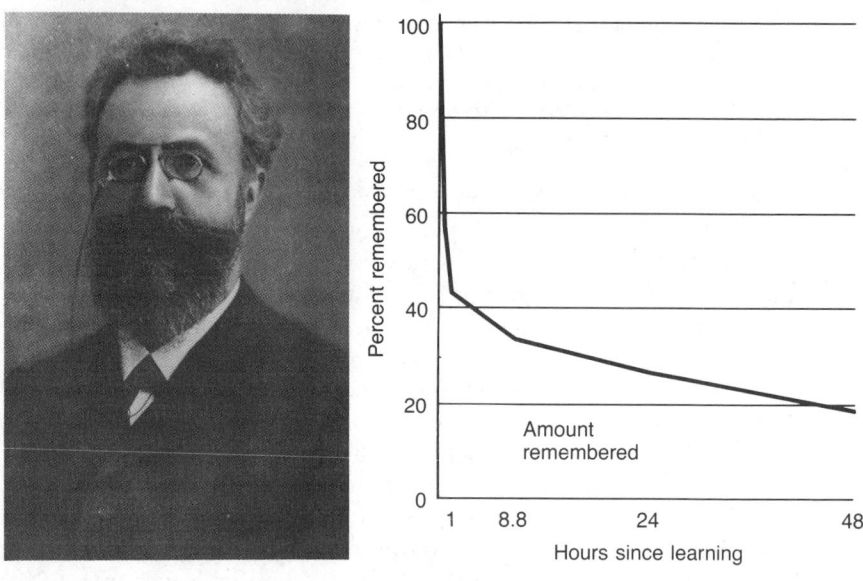

The curve indicates that the amount remembered decreases with time.

Photo courtesy of the National Library of Medicine

Hermann Ebbinghaus. Hermann Ebbinghaus (1850–1909), after receiving his doctorate in philosophy at age twenty-three, decided to pursue independent study instead of a career in philosophy. He became interested in science and by chance came across a copy of Fechner's *Elements of Psychophysics* (1860/1966) in a Parisian secondhand bookstore. The book stimulated the thought that if experimental methods could be used to study sensations, they also could be employed to investigate higher mental processes such as memory. In an amazing display of ingenuity and dedication, Ebbinghaus, in the absence of any university affiliation or support, demonstrated that an experimental analysis of memory is possible. Using himself as a subject, he systematically examined how his ability to remember a list of nonsense syllables (e.g., *vur*) was a function of a number of variables (e.g., the length of time between learning and recall). Since he was interested in studying the laws of associative learning and memory in their pure form, Ebbinghaus thought that the retention of nonsense syllables would be less influenced by special associations than would real words.

Figure 6.3 shows Ebbinghaus's famous retention curve that illustrates the amount retained after various time intervals between learning and

FIGURE 6.4   Edward L. Thorndike and His Curve of Learning

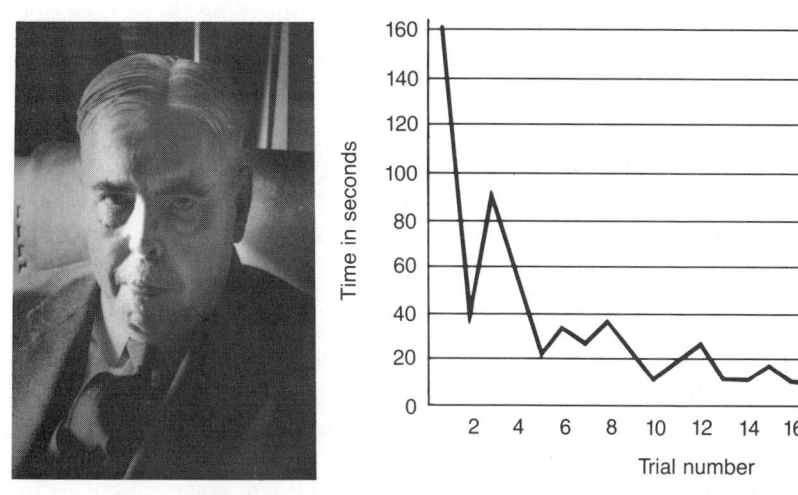

The curve indicates the time that was required for the animal to escape from the puzzle box on successive trials. (Adapted from Thorndike, 1898.)

Photo courtesy of Robert L. Thorndike

recall. The important methodological point is that Ebbinghaus was not interested in the subjective experience of remembering but with the objective evidence of how much he could recall.

Edward L. Thorndike.   Edward L. Thorndike (1874–1949) took his master's degree with William James at Harvard where he studied how chicks learned to escape from a puzzle box. He continued these investigations with a greater variety of animals at Columbia University, where he received his doctorate with Cattell. His first major series of experiments was published in 1898 under the title, *Animal Intelligence: An Experimental Study of the Associative Processes in Animals.* These studies, which were primarily concerned with the influence of reward and punishment on learning, served as the foundation of a research career that lasted half a century and led to a major theory of learning that frequently served as a reference point for subsequent formulations.

Thorndike, along with the many behaviorists he influenced, believed that the basic laws of learning could be applied with equal validity to animals and men alike. The core of Thorndike's theory is contained in his description of the behavior of his animals in the puzzle box; the doctrine of "learning by trial and error with accidental success" (Thorndike, 1898). Unsuccessful acts in the puzzle box "will be stamped out" while the "successful act will be stamped in by the resulting pleasure."

Thorndike's theory was labeled as *connectionism* because of the assumption that an automatic bond was established between the situation and the response it evoked. The major factor influencing the connection is the effect of the response; if the response led to a reward, the connection would be strengthened; if not, the association was weakened. A secondary *law of exercise* supplemented the primary law of effect: "Any response to a situation will, other things being equal, be more strongly connected with the situation in proportion to the number of times it has been connected to that situation" (Thorndike, 1898). That is, if two associations are both rewarded, the one that is rewarded more frequently will be stronger.[1]

Thorndike rejected behaviorism as too confining and restrictive. He was not willing to eliminate mental processes from psychological discourse as evidenced by his use of such mentalistic terms as *pleasing, satisfying,* and *annoying.* Watson insisted that all mentalistic terms be expunged from psychology. The question raised later was whether mentalistic terms were intrinsically at odds with behavioristic doctrine or whether the manner in which the terms were defined was the key issue. After Watson, behaviorists agreed that mentalistic terms, if undefined or defined subjectively, would corrupt psychology. But if a mentalistic term were defined objectively, that is, publicly, it would meet the methodological demands of behaviorism for at least some of them. Thorndike actually defined the mentalistic terms he employed in an objective behavioral fashion:

> By a satisfying state of affairs is meant one which the animal does nothing to avoid, often doing such things as attain and preserve it. By a discomforting or annoying state of affairs is meant one which the animal commonly avoids and abandons (Thorndike, 1911, p. 245).

Henri Piéron. Many European psychologists think of their American colleagues as being excessively ethnocentric. American psychologists, the accusation goes, largely ignore the efforts of foreign psychologists. A case has been made that Henri Piéron (1881–1964) formulated the idea of behaviorism prior to Watson and in a more sophisticated manner (Fraisse, 1970). An examination of this claim reveals an important difference in the attitude toward the philosophical underpinnings of psychology in America and in Europe. Americans, for the most part, attempted to detach themselves from their philosophical moorings while Europeans insisted that such a separation could only be achieved at the expense of oversim-

---

[1]The similarity between Thorndike's learning theory and Carr's conception of the adaptive act (p. 133) is not coincidental. Thorndike's theory was known to Carr at the time he was formulating his conception. Carr, however, unlike Thorndike, postulated two kinds of associations: one involuntary, similar to Thorndike's connections, in which the stimulus triggered the response; and the other voluntary, in which cognitive processes intervened between the stimulus and the response.

FIGURE 6.5 Henri Piéron

Courtesy of Paul Fraisse

plification. Boring expressed the American position in his widely respected history of psychology (1929) when he concluded that psychology was too involved with philosophy: "Psychology ought to fare better when it completely surrenders its philosophical heritage."

Piéron, like many Europeans, received a broad education that combined general training with specific experiences. He received advanced training in psychology, physiology, pathology, and philosophy. He worked with Pierre Janet and in Alfred Binet's laboratory conducting research projects in the experimental analysis of memory, the physiology of sleep, and animal behavior. Such varied experiences made it difficult to accept the popular notion of his day that introspection was the major method of psychological research. Pathological behavior, such as hysteria, strongly suggested that mental processes were at work that were inaccessible to direct examination. The physiological correlates of sleep and the biological and ethological aspects of animal behavior did not require introspection or mentalistic interpretations. Several years before the advent of Watsonian behaviorism, when Piéron was only twenty-six years of age, he declared that psychology is the science of an *organism's activity*, a concept that is synonymous to behavior. In contrast to Watson, Piéron did not express his conviction with revolutionary fervor and extreme statements:

> In a general manner, psychology, after being the study of the soul, became the study of the phenomena of . . . consciousness. But since the phenomena of consciousness can only be understood by each person individually, psychology from that time on was destined to become nothing more than one of the diversified aspects of philosophical reflection, contained in the subjective domain in which systematic exploration is far from contemptible, but which, by its individual character, does not fulfill the requirements of science, because as the Greeks even knew, "all science is general" . . . we must adopt a purely objective conception . . . which will permit psychology to take its due place among the biological sciences. But what else besides consciousness can this research bear upon that hasn't already been taken up by physiology? It is the study of the activity of beings and their sensory-motor relationship with the environment (translated from Piéron and quoted by Fraisse, 1970, p. 114).

Piéron's basic point was a simple one. Consciousness exists but cannot serve as the foundation of a science of psychology. There is no litmus test to determine who is endowed with consciousness and who is not. To attain the status of a natural science psychology must deal with public events. Behavior of organisms, not consciousness, meets this requirement.

In spite of Piéron's commitment to a science of behavior, he did not feel it necessary to expunge introspective reports from psychological research. He only insisted that introspective evidence be viewed in a different light from those psychologists who assumed that such data directly and accurately reflect mental events. Introspective reports are forms of behavior and should be treated as such. A subject who reports that one of two lights appears brighter is behaving in the same way as an animal who presses the lever in a Skinner box only when the brighter of two lights appears. By their actions both the human and the animal are indicating in a publicly observable manner that they can detect a difference between the two lights. "It is better to establish contact between objective phenomena studied by experimental means and introspective verifications than to claim to cut out an impassable ditch between both of them," Piéron said. Fraisse (1970) concludes that Piéron enunciated a sophisticated form of behaviorism that was adopted by neobehaviorism (a new form of behaviorism) thirty years after Watson's revolutionary position was initially formulated.

Ivan P. Pavlov and Russian Physiology

Without the contributions of Ivan P. Pavlov (1849–1936), Watsonian behaviorism would never have achieved the success it did. Pavlov provided empirical substance to the methodological recipe that Watson offered psychology. Pavlov was a physiologist, not a psychologist. He entertained strong reservations about psychology: "It is still open to discussion whether psychology is a natural science, or whether it can be regarded as a science at all" (Pavlov, 1927). Psychology, for Pavlov, was the study of the mind. He was expressing a common opinion among Russian physiologists that a pure mentalistic psychology and the scientific method were incompatible.

Ivan Sechenov. The emphasis on objective methods in Russian physiology owes much to the influence of Ivan Sechenov (1829–1905), who argued that psychology should be studied by the objective methods of physiology. A key concept in Sechenov's system was the reflex, the *connection* between stimulation and a response. A *simple* example of a reflex occurs when you accidentally prick your finger, and automatically withdraw your hand from the source of painful stimulation.

Sechenov, in his *Reflexes of the Brain* (1863/1935) regarded conscious phenomena as instances of neural reflexes. Such mental processes as learning, memory, and thought were essentially complex chains of reflex action. In the case of thought, the motor or action portion of the complex chain of reflexes was inhibited until the thought led to the solution of the problem.

Sechenov expressed the essence of behaviorism in the following comment:

> Be it a child laughing at the sight of toys . . . a girl trembling at the first thought of love, or Newton enunciating universal laws and writing them on paper,—everywhere the final manifestation is muscular movement (Sechenov, 1863; quoted in Herrnstein & Boring, 1966, p. 309).

Sechenov's point was that even though the actions of others are usually described in terms of underlying subjective mental processes, the only events that are observed are objective behavioral phenomena. Arguing that natural science is based on public observations, Sechenov insisted that psychology must employ the same objective procedures.

Ivan P. Pavlov. Pavlov continued Sechenov's commitment to reflexology and objectivism in his classical work on conditioned reflexes. He conducted these experiments relatively late in his career after he achieved international recognition with his research on digestive processes for which he was awarded a Nobel prize in 1904.

Pavlov's interest in digestion dated back to his student days when, after reading about digestion in a standard text on physiology, he asked

FIGURE 6.6   Ivan P. Pavlov with His Conditioning Apparatus and Curve of Conditioning

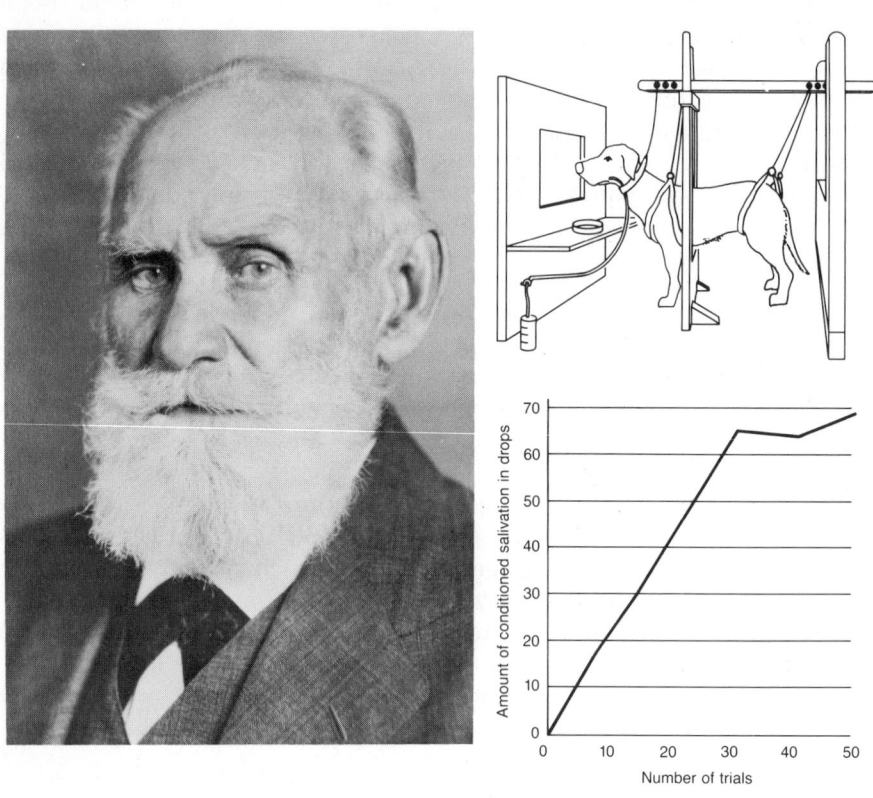

National Library of Medicine

himself how such a complicated system works (Babkin, 1949). To answer this question, Pavlov revolutionized methods of research. The conventional method was to observe the digestive process by surgically exposing a particular organ. These *acute preparations* tended to produce a state of shock which interfered with the digestive process. *Chronic preparations* were needed to observe normal digestive processes over long periods of time. Pavlov knew about the dramatic case of a man who had suffered a severe gunshot wound to his stomach and unexpectedly survived. The wound never completely healed leaving a window in his abdomen through which the activities of the stomach could be monitored by the removal of gastric substances. Why not, thought Pavlov, create a window, or what is technically known as a fistula, at various parts of the digestive systems of experimental dogs? This would permit the collection of digestive substances from different organs thus revealing the workings of the entire system. His investigations of the digestive processes ultimately led to his research on conditioning.

The experimental operations required for conditioning are simple. A hungry dog with a salivary fistula that empties into a graduated glass cylinder is exposed to a tone (conditioned stimulus) and food (unconditioned stimulus). Initially the conditioned stimulus (tone) is presented alone and fails to evoke any salivation. In contrast, when the dog is exposed to the unconditioned stimulus (food), salivation occurs. After these initial tests are completed, a series of training trials begin in which the tone is sounded, followed by food a fraction of a second later. If the paired presentations of the tone and food are repeated from ten to twenty times, the presentation of the tone (conditioned stimulus) *alone* will evoke salivation (conditioned response). The tone, which initially lacked the power to evoke salivation, has the power to elicit the reaction after being paired with food. The course of the acquisition of a conditioned response by a dog in Pavlov's laboratory is graphically illustrated in Figure 6.6. Note that the amount, or amplitude, of salivation gradually increases with successive paired presentations of the conditioned and unconditioned stimuli.

Vladimir M. Bekhterev. Another Russian physiologist, Vladimir M. Bekhterev (1857–1927), who also gained fame as a psychiatrist, developed a method of motor conditioning in which the conditioned response was muscular, as contrasted with the glandular reaction employed by Pavlov. For example, a tone (conditioned stimulus) which preceded a shock (unconditioned stimulus) to the finger, would, after paired presentations, elicit finger withdrawal by itself (conditioned response). In addition to extending the empirical range of conditioning to include muscular responses, motor conditioning provided a more convenient method because difficult surgical techniques were unnecessary. Bekhterev also encouraged a behavioristic orientation by denying that mentalistic interpretations of psychological events were necessary. Conditioned finger withdrawal, for example, does not result from mental associations (e.g., between a tone and shock) but instead from neural connections formed during the course of conditioning (e.g., between the neural activity aroused by the conditioned stimulus and the sensory-motor reflex triggered by the unconditioned stimulus). Bekhterev suggested, as had Sechenov, that such high level psychological processes as thinking consist of compounds of lower level sensory-motor reflexes.

Although Bekhterev encouraged research in motor conditioning, supported theoretical interpretation based on reflexology, and advocated an objective psychology, he had less influence on American psychology than Pavlov. Pavlov was one of those rare scientists who was both a brilliant researcher and a brilliant theorist; his total effort served as a model for theoretically oriented behaviorists to emulate.

FIGURE 6.7 Vladimir M. Bekhterev

Dan McIntosh

Association, Habit, and Objectivity. Conditioning is neither a dramatic nor a surprising phenomenon. Why did it prove to be so important? The reason is that conditioning embodied in a concrete fashion the confluence of three important ideas in the history of psychology: association, habit, and objectivity (Hilgard & Marquis, 1940).

Association. Modern psychology has been strongly influenced by the concept of association, which philosophers from the time of Plato and Aristotle have advanced as the basic process that governs mental activity. The British Empiricists were particularly influential because they suggested a number of specific associationistic principles, such as contiguity and frequency, which governed the linkage of one mental event to another. Conditioning represented a tangible expression of the associative process; a conditioned stimulus becomes associated with a response it did not originally evoke. In place of speculative principles that govern mental associations, conditioning substituted an experimental analysis of factors responsible for forming and strengthening an association between a conditioned stimulus and a conditioned response, both publicly observable events.

Habit. Habit is an important evolutionary mechanism which facilitates an organism's adaptation to its environment. James and the functionalists acknowledged the psychological significance of habits and assigned a major role to it in their theorizing. In spite of its importance, no clear method was available to systematically investigate forming and strengthening habits. Conditioning filled that void.

Objectivity. As functionalism matured, the tendency to redirect psychology from a subjective mentalistic science to an objective behaviorial discipline became more apparent. Although many objective methods of investigating psychological phenomena were available, none was as important as introspection in studying consciousness. Conditioning, for the early behaviorists, became the objective method par excellence. All the basic components—the conditioned and unconditioned stimuli, the conditioned and unconditioned responses—could be measured precisely. In addition, conditioning was considered to be such a highly controlled and flexible methodology that it would only be a matter of time before systematic research would reveal the basic principles governing the two related concepts of association and habit.

BEHAVIORISM

History tells us that successful political revolutionaries (e.g., Danton, Mao Zedong) have greater talent for gaining power than for constructive achievements. John B. Watson, the founder of behaviorism, fits this mold in that his polemics were more successful in establishing a dominant position for behaviorism in American psychology than in formulating a compelling behavioristic theory. It was left to his successors to refine his methodological notions so that the potentials of behaviorism could be realized.

John B. Watson (1878–1958)

John Watson's life was dominated by controversy even as a child. His teachers in his native South Carolina described him as troublesome and argumentative, and he himself acknowledged that he was lazy

FIGURE 6.8 John B. Watson

Archives of The History of American Psychology

and rebellious. His early adolescence was marred by fights and even two arrests, one for firing a gun within the city limits of Greenville, South Carolina (Bakan, 1966). In spite of his abrasive personality and unpromising beginning, Watson entered Furman University with the intention of becoming a minister, presumably to please his mother, a devout Baptist. His mother's death apparently changed his plans and instead of entering a theological seminary upon graduation he stayed at Furman to earn an M.A. Watson then went to the University of Chicago to pursue graduate work in philosophy with John Dewey but found him to be "incomprehensible . . . I never knew what he was talking about then, and unfortunately for me, I still don't know" (Watson, 1936).

Angell, in contrast to Dewey, was a clear speaker, and he encouraged Watson to take a doctorate in psychology. He did, along with minors in neurology and philosophy. He also studied physiology and biology with Jacques Loeb, an experience that heightened his interest in animal psychology. In describing his research career as an instructor in psychology at the University of Chicago from 1903, the year he received his Ph.D., to 1908, Watson wrote,

> I never wanted to use human subjects. I hated to serve as a subject. I didn't like the stuffy, artificial instructions given to subjects. I was always uncomfortable and acted unnaturally. With animals I was at home. I felt that, in studying them, I was keeping close to biology with my feet on the ground. More and more the thought presented itself: Can't I find out by watching their behavior everything that the other students are finding out by using [introspectors]? (Watson, 1936, p. 276).

Watson responded to his own question with a series of animal studies that offered behavioral evidence to answer such questions as what sensory modalities rats employ when learning a maze (Watson, 1907) and how terns (a gull-like bird) return to their home nests (Watson, 1908). His reputation as an ingenious researcher and original thinker rapidly spread throughout America and in 1908, when Watson became eligible for an assistant professorship at the University of Chicago, he was offered a full professorship at Johns Hopkins University, an offer he could not refuse even though he would have liked to remain at Chicago. He stayed at Hopkins for twelve years and published the major works on which his reputation as a dominant figure in the history of psychology rests.

While a graduate student, Watson began thinking about a purely objective approach to psychology which would abolish all references to subjective mental events. Watson's notions about behaviorism were fully formed by 1912, when he gave a talk at Yale University and a series of lectures at Columbia University at the invitation of Cattell. The next year, Watson's paper entitled *Psychology as a Behaviorist Views It* (1913) was published, followed shortly by his first book, *Behavior: An Introduction to Comparative Psychology* (1914), which supported the thesis that behavioral analysis is sufficient for the science of psychology.

His revolutionary methodology was rapidly accepted by many psychologists, particularly the younger ones, and he was elected to the presidency of the American Psychological Association in 1915 at the age of thirty-seven. One of his graduate students described the impact of Watson's conception of psychology on younger psychologists:

> It shook the foundations of traditional European-bred psychology, and we welcomed it. . . . it pointed the way from armchair psychology to action and reform and was therefore hailed as a panacea (Jones, 1974, p. 582).

After a year in the service during World War I, Watson returned to Hopkins and published his most important book, *Psychology from the Standpoint of a Behaviorist* (1919). His success as a scientist was matched by his popularity as a teacher. In his second year at Hopkins the students dedicated their yearbook to him and several years later he was voted the most handsome professor. His looks and charm probably contributed to a scandal that ultimately led to his banishment from university life. After returning to Hopkins following World War I, he embarked on a research program in infant behavior with the assistance of several graduate students, including an attractive and bright young lady named Rosalie Rayner. An indirect consequence of this research project was a highly publicized divorce suit initiated by Watson's wife, Mary Ickes Watson (a sister of Harold Ickes, who was to become the Secretary of the Interior in the cabinet of President Franklin D. Roosevelt) in which Rosalie Rayner was named as a corespondent.

Watson was forced to resign from Johns Hopkins and soon thereafter married Rayner. It seems odd now that adultery and divorce could exile a distinguished professor from academic life. But the moral conventions of those days were much closer to Victorian standards than to the more tolerant views of today.

Although he regretted leaving academia when only forty-two years old, Watson did not abandon his mission to convert others to behaviorism. After becoming an advertising executive, he found time to argue the case of behaviorism, but now his message was directed, not to scholars, but to the general public. Articles in popular magazines, lectures, radio talks, and two books, *Behaviorism* (1924) and *Psychological Care of the Infant and Child* (1928), all expressed in the language of the advertising executive, carried the message that Watsonian behaviorism could solve human problems ranging from child rearing to social planning. Not surprisingly, he oversimplified his views in search for popular approval. He attracted the attention he sought but his exaggerated claims encountered as much opposition as support. He later expressed regret over some of his extreme statements, particularly those associated with his views of parenting. One of his two sons (J. R. Watson, 1950) also expressed regrets by attributing his unhappy childhood to his behavioristic upbringing.

Watson's propagandistic efforts to persuade society to adopt his psychological principles confuses the task of describing and evaluating behaviorism. Should Watsonian behaviorism be judged by the dogmatic assertions of his public career or the more cautious arguments offered during his early academic career? Proponents and critics of behaviorism never fully agreed about the basic tenets of behaviorism and their debates frequently generated more confusion than clarification. With time, however, it became apparent that behaviorism was not a single cohesive view. Behaviorism splintered into several different orientations, each based on a different set of assumptions (Chapters 9 and 10).

A few years before he reached sixty, his second wife died. "In a way the light seemed to go out of Watson's life. He ceased to be a man-about-town and more and more spent time on his estate with his two boys" (Larson, 1979). John Watson died in 1958 at the age of eighty. Psychologists agreed that his influence was both tremendous and profound but disagreed whether the total sum of his impact was positive or negative.

METHODOLOGICAL ASSUMPTIONS

Of all his contributions to psychology, Watson's methodological position is generally considered to be the most important. Recognizing that his success in redirecting psychology from the study of the mind to that of behavior depended upon the logic and clarity of his methodological argument, Watson tried to formulate his methodological position in a clear and precise fashion. To a large extent he was successful in his early writings.

The Subject Matter of Psychology

Behaviorism was officially born with Watson's 1913 article entitled *Psychology as the Behaviorist Views It*:

> Psychology as the behaviorist views it is a purely objective experimental branch of natural science. Its theoretical goal is the prediction and control of behavior. Introspection forms no essential part of its methods, nor is the scientific value of its data dependent upon the readiness with which they lend themselves to interpretation in terms of consciousness. The behaviorist, in his efforts to get a unitary scheme of animal response, recognizes no dividing line between man and brute. The behavior of man, with all of its refinement and complexity, forms only a part of the behaviorist's total scheme of investigation (Watson, 1913, p. 158).

First and foremost, this statement asserts that the subject matter of psychology is behavior, the actions of organisms that can be publicly observed. Second, it states that this subject matter, behavior, is completely independent of its relationship to consciousness. Whereas functionalists studied behavior because it reflects mental activity, Watson insisted that behavior could and should be studied in its own right. Third, contrary to Alexander Pope's maxim, "The proper study of mankind is man," Watson argued that human psychology is neither unique nor necessarily of primary concern. Behavior, of animals and humans, is the subject matter of psychology.

Conception of Consciousness

Watson's rejection of consciousness as the subject matter of psychology raises the issue of the role of consciousness in behaviorism. A common criticism was that behaviorism denied consciousness to humans. This accusation is false when applied to his early writings. In one of his initial papers, Watson (1913) wrote that psychology "needs introspection as little as do the sciences of chemistry and physics." He did not, however, deny the existence of consciousness per se.

> If you will grant the behaviorist the right to use consciousness in the same way that other natural sciences employ it—that is, without making consciousness a special object of observation—you have granted all that my thesis requires. . . . In this sense consciousness may be said to be the instrument or tool with which all scientists work (Watson, 1913, pp. 175–176).

Watson's thesis is that all natural sciences are based on the conscious experience of the observing scientist. There is no qualitative difference between a physicist observing the speed of a ball rolling down an inclined plane, the chemist observing the consequence of mixing two chemicals, and the psychologist observing the amount of a dog's salivation. All three scientists report what they experience and therefore employ consciousness in exactly the same way.

Critics thought the Watson's position suffered from a fatal flaw; he acknowledged the existence of consciousness but suggested it could not be studied scientifically. Rather than admit that the scientific method could not be applied to the study of consciousness, Watson, eleven years after stating that consciousness was a "tool with which all scientists work," shifted to the radical methodological stance of denying the very existence of human consciousness:

> It has never been seen, touched, smelled, tasted, or moved. It is a plain assumption just as unprovable as the old concept of the soul. . . . The Behaviorist cannot find consciousness in the test tube of his science. He finds no evidence anywhere for a stream of consciousness, not even for one so convincing as that described by William James (Watson & McDougall, 1929, pp. 14–26).

These two views of consciousness have been labeled *methodological behaviorism* and *metaphysical behaviorism* (Bergmann, 1956). Methodological behaviorism, Watson's original conception, emerged from his conviction that the *direct examination* of consciousness could not serve as a method of psychological investigation because it had not, and could not, yield reliable knowledge of the type found in natural science. Because of this failure, behavior, which can be objectively observed, should become the subject matter of psychology, and conscious experience should be considered only a tool, not the object, of scientific inquiry.

The shift from methodological behaviorism to metaphysical behaviorism, the position that consciousness does not exist, had the effect of enlarging the ranks of antibehaviorists. The major objection to methodological behaviorism was that a psychology that ignored mental processes would inevitably be incomplete and distorted. But even those who expressed these reservations recognized that the study of behavior had merit.

Metaphysical behaviorism was another matter. Psychologists did not take kindly to the suggestion that conscious experience is an illusion. To suggest that behavior should be the subject matter of psychology did not require the assumption that humans are mindless. In time, the verdict on metaphysical behaviorism was expressed by a noted philospher of science and a great admirer of Watson; metaphysical behaviorism was "silly" (Bergmann, 1956). Its historical impact was to confuse the picture for those who sought to understand and evaluate behaviorism.

Preconceptions about Behavior

Although Watson repudiated structuralism he did not reject all of its features. Structuralism was analytical; it sought to analyze the mind into its basic elements. Watson sought to analyze behavior into its basic components. To accomplish this goal he conceptualized behavior as being analogous to a reflex in which a stimulus elicits a response:

> The rule, or measuring rod, which the behaviorist puts in front of him always is: Can I describe this bit of behavior I see in terms of "stimulus and response"? By stimulus we mean any object in the general environment or any change in the tissues themselves due to the physiological condition of the animal, such as the change we get when we keep an animal from sex activity, when we keep it from feeding, when we keep it from building a nest. By response, we mean anything an animal does—such as turning towards or away from a light, jumping at a sound, and more highly organized activities such as building a skyscraper, drawing plans, having babies, writing books, and the like (Watson, 1924, pp. 6–7).

Watson linked his stimulus-response associationism to conditioning in a manner suggested by Pavlov:

> It is obvious that the different kinds of habits based on training, education and discipline of any sort are nothing but a long chain of conditioned reflexes (Pavlov, 1927, p. 395).

A conditioned response is a unit of habit and all complex behavior consists of a chain of conditioned responses.

Methods of Investigation

The only demand that Watson made of psychological research is that it employ objective methods of measurement. The criterion of objectivity was that the events, in principle, be publicly observed, that is, perceived by more than one person. This automatically eliminated the introspective analysis of the mind because private mental events are perceived by only one person, the experiencing individual. This requirement of objectivity did not prove restrictive; a great variety of research methods easily met its standards. In addition to Watson's favorite research method, conditioning, other procedures were encouraged, such as psychological testing, psychophysiological studies in which changes in behavior were related to physiological processes, human memory, psychophysics, naturalistic observations. Verbal reports were not outlawed by behaviorism but instead were viewed in a different light. They were considered as publicly observed responses and not as valid reflections of conscious experience.

Criterion of Truth

Watson never grappled with the complex problem of defining truth. By acknowledging that psychology was a natural science he accepted the notion that the test of a theoretical hypothesis is its capacity to deductively predict empirical events. He was more interested in applying psychological knowledge to problems of personal adjustment and social improvement than in formulating precise theories of behavior. Consequently the importance of predicting and controlling behavior came to be emphasized in preference to the construction of an integrated theory with clear deductive consequences. In his effort to predict and control behavior, Watson employed the stimulus-response conception of behavior as a tool. Discovering and subsequently controlling the stimulus to which a form of behavior is connected allows for control of that behavior.

STRATEGY

Watson had two major goals: First, to convert the discipline of psychology to a behavioral science and second, to formulate psychological principles that would be effective in planning a better society.

The strategy Watson adopted for his methodological goal was to demonstrate that psychological phenomena (e.g., sensation, perception, learning, and memory) could be systematically investigated without employing introspection. To prove his point, he showed how the basic problems of human psychology could be investigated with lower animals.

Watson's strategy for formulating psychological principles to serve practical needs was based on the assumption that conditioning held the key to an effective program for modifying behavior. While in academic life, he attempted to demonstrate how laboratory research supported this assumption. Later on, without access to laboratory facilities, Watson tended to offer dogmatic assertions in lieu of tentative hypotheses.

THEORY

In place of a highly integrated theory, Watson offered some specific hypotheses and supporting evidence. Some of his more important research projects will be described first and then an overall review of Watsonian behaviorism will follow.

Conditioned Emotional Responses

Watson was critical of James's notion that experience of bodily changes is emotion. Conscious experience was not an essential component of emotional behavior, Watson argued. To Watson, emotions were simply bodily reactions to specific stimuli. To understand emotions one had only to identify the bodily reactions and the stimuli that elicited them.

Watson was encouraged to develop his ideas about emotions when a noted psychiatrist, Adolf Meyer, invited him to do research with human infants at the Phipps Clinic of Johns Hopkins. His research was interrupted by a stint in the United States Army that provided him with the time needed to develop his views about conditioning. When he returned to Johns Hopkins following the end of World War I he was ready to implement his hypothesis that emotions could be associated with a neutral stimulus in the same way that Pavlov had demonstrated that salivation could be conditioned to a tone (Watson & Morgan, 1917).

With the assistance of his future wife, Rosalie Rayner, Watson began to condition an eleven-month old child, Albert B., to fear a white rat. The unconditioned stimulus was a sudden, loud sound that elicited fearful behavior (unconditioned response). When a steel bar was suddenly struck by a hammer behind Albert,

> The child started violently, his breathing was checked and the arms were raised in a characteristic manner. On the second stimulation the same thing occurred, and in addition the lips began to pucker and tremble. On the third stimulation the child broke into a sudden crying fit. This is the first time an emotional situation in the laboratory has produced any fear or even crying in Albert (Watson & Rayner, 1920, p. 2).

The conditioned stimulus was a white rat to which Albert initially responded positively. In the laboratory notes, the first two conditioning trials were described:

1. White rat suddenly taken from the basket and presented to Albert. He began to reach for rat with left hand. Just as his hand touched the animal the bar was struck immediately behind his head. The infant jumped violently and fell forward, burying his face in the mattress. He did not cry, however.

2. Just as the right hand touched the rat the bar was again struck. Again the infant jumped violently, fell forward and began to whimper (Watson & Rayner, 1920, p. 4).

After seven paired presentations of the rat and the loud sound over a period of two days, the reaction to the conditioned stimulus (rat) alone was:

The instant the rat was shown the baby began to cry. Almost instantly he turned sharply to the left, fell over on left side, raised himself on all fours and began to crawl away so rapidly that he was caught with difficulty before reaching the edge of the table (Watson & Rayner, 1920, p. 5).

Once the conditioned emotional response was established, Watson and Rayner sought to discover whether stimulus generalization would occur, that is, would stimuli similar to the rat evoke fearful reactions? Yes, furry stimuli such as a rabbit and a dog evoked fear five days later, but not to the extent that the rat did. About two months later a seal skin fur coat and a Santa Claus mask elicited mild fear.

According to Watson, infants have three innate emotional responses: fear, rage, and love, each of which is evoked by distinctive stimuli. Fear results from a sudden, loud noise or loss of support; rage from physical restraint that prevents movement; and love from stroking and manipulation of the erogenous zones. When evoked, these instinctive associations allow neutral stimuli to become connected to the emotional reaction, as occurred when the white rat (stimulus) became connected to fear (response). Adult emotions can also be conditioned; "as every lover knows, vision, audition and olfaction soon become conditioned" to erotic reactions (Watson & Rayner, 1920).

An obvious question raised by the case of Albert is whether learned emotional reactions to previously neutral stimuli can be unlearned, that is, replaced by less traumatic responses. Watson and Rayner suggested several methods but surprisingly, in light of apparent ethical responsibilities, they never attempted to rid Albert of the fear of furry objects which they created. Their excuse was that Albert was taken from the hospital before he could be treated, an unconvincing apology in light of the fact that they knew a month in advance when Albert would be leaving (Harris, 1979).

Mary Cover Jones (1924), a student of Watson, demonstrated later how a counterconditioning technique could rid a child of fear. An infant, Peter, feared white rabbits. While Peter was eating, a white rabbit was brought into the room but at a considerable distance from the child. Eating continued, suggesting that consuming the food was a stronger association than the fear reaction to the rabbit at a distance. On successive days the rabbit was brought closer until a point was reached where Peter ate while handling the rabbit without fear. This treatment can be described as counterconditioning because a new incompatible response, relaxation that accompanied eating, is substituted for the old response, fear.

Psychologists have faulted Watson and Rayner's classic experiment on conditioned fear reactions. To argue in favor of the conditioning model of emotions on the basis of evidence from one subject in one restricted condition is poor science. Perhaps the positive results reported were due primarily to unusual characteristics of Albert, such as his phlegmatic personality; perhaps the circumstance was unusual. In addition, the experiment was conducted in a shoddy manner (Samelson, 1980). The original report of the research differs in important details from subsequent descriptions offered by Watson, making it impossible to know the exact procedure used and results obtained. In spite of its limitations Watson and Rayner's experiment proved to be a landmark study in the history of the conditioning model of disordered behavior, a model that recently reached its maturity in the behavior modification approach. The study illustrates how a disordered reaction (e.g., excessive fear of a relatively safe stimulus) could be conditioned and by implication how the disordered reaction could be eliminated.

Habits

The basic unit of behavior for Watson was the sensory-motor reflex, commonly referred to as a stimulus-response association. Such associations, according to Watson, could be innate or acquired. An innate reflex, like fear of a sudden loud noise, is a consequence of genetic organization of the nervous system. An acquired stimulus-response association, like Albert's fear of a white rat, results from learning.

Stimulus-response associations could be a single-unit connection or a chain of such connections. An example of a single-unit reflex, innately determined, is the patella reflex; a blow on the knee elicits a knee jerk. An acquired chain of associations, like playing the piano, illustrates a habit: "We can define habit . . . as a complex system of reflexes which functions in a serial order" (Watson, 1919).

A habit could be explicit or implicit. An explicit habit is clearly observable as in the case of tennis and violin playing. A habit could be implicit, hidden from direct examination but nevertheless made observable by technical procedures. Pavlovian conditioning illustrates an implicit salivary habit that is brought out in the open by surgical techniques. Watson considered that "a great many of the activities involved in thinking are really implicit bodily movements" in the hands, tongue, larynx, throat, etc.

The significance and pervasiveness of habits directed attention to the principles that govern their actions. Watson (1919) admitted that he could only speculate about a theory of stimulus-response associations. But he suggested that several different principles operated, among them *recency, frequency,* and *context.* According to the *principle of recency,* the last response made in a situation is the most likely to occur on the next occasion. The last response a cat makes in Thorndike's puzzle box (e.g., pulling a string) is successful in allowing the subject to escape and get food and thus becomes the most probable act that will be evoked on the next trial. What would happen on the first trial if the cat never had the experience of pulling a string? Then the *law of frequency* would take over: "The act which has been most frequently connected with the object is the one most likely to be called out" (Watson, 1919). If the cat had been placed in a wooden box previously, the response he practiced most frequently, like pushing against the walls, would be the one most likely to occur. The *principle of context* suggests that:

> The act called out is likely to be one which is most closely connected with the general setting of the situation as a whole . . . We are expected to display churchly behavior, funeral behavior, and wedding behavior under certain circumstances. The situation as a whole envelops us and each object in that situation can call out for the time being only a narrowly appropriate and conventional type of act (Watson, 1919, p. 299).

Watson's theorizing about habits never extended beyond the simple speculations just described. A research program designed to develop a systematic theory was never attempted. In addition, Watson sometimes failed to examine critically the implications of his hypotheses. How could his first principle of recency explain the facts of *experimental extinction? Experimental extinction* occurs, following conditioning, when the conditioned stimulus is presented without the unconditioned stimulus. Pavlov found that when the tone (conditioned stimulus) is repeatedly presented alone, the conditioned salivary response gradually decreases in amount until finally it disappears. The principle of recency states, however, that an organism responds to a stimulus with the last response it made. If this be true then experimental extinction should never occur; at the beginning of extinction the animal salivates to the tone and should continue thereafter regardless of whether the tone is followed by food (unconditioned stimulus). The principle of recency was subsequently modified to explain experimental extinction (Guthrie, 1935), but Watson appeared insensitive to the problem experimental extinction raised for his principle of recency.

Watson's conception of habit formation and strengthening has only historical interest today. But the theory nevertheless exerted an important influence by directing attention to the basic problem of discovering principles that govern habitual behavior.

The Peripheral Theory of Thinking

Watson proposed a counterintuitive theory of thinking that reduced thought to implicit motor behavior in contrast to the common sense view that it occurs in the brain. Language habits, involving movements in the throat and tongue, were assigned a central role in his theory. Watson offered developmental evidence to support his peripheral theory. Children at early ages talk aloud when thinking. Later when thinking, the children reduce their overt speech to a whisper and finally the speech becomes inaudible. Even when inaudible, Watson insisted that muscular responses were occurring in the speech mechanism. He coined the phrase *subvocal talking* to describe thinking but acknowledged that kinesthetic and emotional cues were also involved:

> We . . . think and plan with the whole body. But since . . . word organization is, when present, probably usually dominant over visceral and manual organization, we can say that *'thinking'* is largely *subvocal talking—* provided we hasten to explain that it can occur without words (Watson, 1924, p. 215).

Watson acknowledged that the empirical evidence supporting his peripheral theory of thinking was limited. The best he could offer was some naturalistic observations of young children and deaf mutes. Companions of deaf mutes report that mutes frequently exhibit hand movements associated with sign language when reading and thinking. These observations later encouraged Max (1937) to use electronic methods to record muscular activity too slight to see. Deaf mutes and subjects who were not hearing impaired were instructed to multiply and divide numbers in their heads. Seventy percent of the deaf mutes exhibited muscular activity in their hands as compared to only thirty percent of those who heard normally. In addition, the amplitude of such activity was four times greater for the deaf mutes. Numerous other studies (e.g., Jacobsen, 1932) also demonstrated that muscular activity, particularly those associated with speech, accompanies thinking.

Watson's peripheral theory of thinking, at the time it was proposed, suffered not only from insufficient evidence but also an intrinsic ambiguity. Peripheral events were emphasized to such a degree that the theory was interpreted to imply that the central nervous system, including the brain, plays a nonessential role in thinking. Watson actually denied such a position:

> A simple eye-hand coordination, the picking up of a pin from the ground, brings about a well-ordered and integrated response of the organism as a whole. Such a well-ordered response will not take place without a central nervous system, but it must be said with equal truth that it will not take place without a heart, without bones, and without glands and muscles (Watson, 1919, p. 154).

Watson was essentially arguing not to overlook the importance of peripheral factors in thinking. In so doing he overstated his case by interpreting too literally the statement that thinking is a response of "the organism as a whole." Because the heart, bones, glands, muscles, and brain are operating in a thinking organism, it does not follow that they are of equal importance. Damage to the heart, bones, glands and muscles will not have as devastating effect on thinking as will injury to certain portions of the brain.

In the final analysis, Watson's peripheral theory of thinking encouraged interesting research on motor involvement in thinking. But the theory itself proved to be both superficial and incomplete.

Watsonian Behaviorism: A Historical Perspective

Watsonian behaviorism, sometimes referred to as classical behaviorism, emphasized four major viewpoints: *objectivism, stimulus-response associationism, peripheralism,* and *environmentalism* (Koch, 1964). Later on (Chapters 9 and 10) you will study new forms of behaviorism that emerged from Watsonian behaviorism—neobehaviorisms—and learn how each of these four core beliefs fared over time.

Objectivism. Some psychologists (e.g., Kendler, 1985) argue that Watson's most important contribution by far was his endorsement of an objective approach to psychology. By insisting that psychologists study publicly observable behavior instead of privately observable consciousness, Watson provided the means by which psychology could attain the status of a natural science.

Stimulus-Response Associationism. Watson assumed that the goal of a natural-science psychology would be assisted by adapting the concept of sensory-motor reflex to psychological events. He proposed that psychological phenomena could be described in terms of three basic components: *stimulus, response,* and the *association* between them. A stimulus is an environmental event such as the presentation of a tone, a response is a measurable behavioral event such as the amount of salivation, and the association between them is represented by the tendency for the stimulus to evoke the response. The stimulus-response association was considered to be a unit of behavior. All complex behavior, in principle, could be analyzed into basic stimulus-response associations.

Peripheralism. Peripheralism is best explained in relation to its antonym, *centralism.* Centralism postulates that the root causes of behavior are to be found in the central nervous system, the brain and spinal cord. Peripheralism argues that peripheral events, external to the central nervous system, play a major role in behavior. Watson's peripheralism was expressed in his theory of thinking, which argued that laryngeal movements, subvocal talking, represented thinking.

The question has been raised as to whether Watson's peripheralism stemmed solely from empirical considerations or whether this view was contaminated by his methodological orientation (Kendler, 1985). According to this latter view, Watson's penchant for objectivity made him suspicious of any explanation based on events that are hidden from view, whether they be in the mind or in the brain. Consequently, he was predisposed to accept hypotheses that postulated the importance of readily observed peripheral events such as muscular movements.

Environmentalism. Watson's environmentalism is captured in his famous boast:

> Give me a dozen healthy infants, well formed, and my own specified world to bring them up in, and I'll guarantee to take any one at random and train him to become any type of specialist I might select—a doctor, lawyer, artist, merchant chief, and yes, even begger-man and thief, regardless of his talents, penchants, tendencies, abilities, vocations and race of his ancestors (Watson, 1926, p. 10).

Watson's concluding qualification to his widely quoted statement is customarily omitted, "I'm going beyond my facts and I admit it, but so have the advocates to the contrary, but they have been doing it for many thousands of years." Watson was essentially taking the extreme environmentalist position to contrast it with the extreme hereditarian position that human behavior is genetically preset and therefore unmodifiable. In actual fact, Watson acknowledged the influences of hereditary factors:

> The behaviorist would *not* say: "He inherits his father's capacity or talent for being a fine swordsman." He would say: "This child certainly has his father's slender build of body. . . . He, too, has the build of a swordsman." And he would go on to say: "—and his father is very fond of him. He put a tiny sword into his hand when he was a year of age, and . . . he talks sword play, attack and defense, the code of duelling and the like." A certain type of structure, plus early training—*slanting*—accounts for adult performance (Watson, 1924, p. 75).

These quotations suggest that Watson was an interactionist in regard to the nature-nurture controversy. Both heredity and environment played a role in behavior, but training was more important. One reason that Watson emphasized nurture over nature was his interest in social planning. He was convinced that psychological knowledge could be employed in planning a better society. The techniques available for that task were limited to educational methods. Genetic influences were beyond any simple direct control. It is interesting to speculate whether Watson would have maintained his strong environmentalist position if he were alive today when methods of controlling genetic influences (e.g., chemical intervention) are being developed.

Quotations from John B. Watson

1. The young student of behavioristic psychology has to endure no holy vigil before beginning to use psychological materials and methods, nor does he at any time have to pass through secret initiation ceremonies before beginning research work. The key which will unlock the door of any other scientific structure will unlock the door of psychology. The differences among the various sciences now are only those necessitated by the division of labor. Until psychology recognizes this and discards everything which cannot be stated in the universal terms of science, she does not deserve her place in the sun (Watson, 1919, p. vii).

2. Many psychologists have misunderstood the behaviorist's position. They insist that he is only observing the individual movements of the muscles and *glands. . . . The behaviorist is interested in integrations and total activities of the individual. . . .* objective psychology can study brick-laying, house building, playing games, marriage or emotional activity without being accused of reducing everything to muscle twitch or the secretion of a gland. . . . we can describe a man's behavior in selecting and marrying a wife. We can show how that event has influenced his whole life after marriage (Watson, 1919, pp. 39–40).

3. Instinct and habit are undoubtedly composed of the same elementary reflexes. They differ so far as concerns the origin of the pattern (number and localization of the simple reflex arcs involved) and the order (temporal relation) of the unfolding of the elements composing the pattern. In instinct the pattern and order are inherited, in habit both are acquired during the life time of the individual (Watson, 1919, p. 272–273).

4. When we study implicit bodily processes we are studying *thought;* just as when we study the way a golfer stands in addressing his ball and swinging his club we are studying *golf* (Watson, 1919, p. 326).

5. It seems to be a human failing to stop improving at the lowest economic level that enables an individual to get along in his group. People are lazy. Few want to work. . . . The formation of early work habits in youth, of working longer hours than others, of practicing more intensively than others, is probably the most reasonable explanation we have today not only for success in any line, but even for genius. The only geniuses I have ever met have been thoroughly hard working fellows (Watson, 1924, p. 171).

6. I have attempted to show that while there is a science of psychology independent, interesting, worth while in itself, nevertheless to have a right to existence it must serve in some measure as a foundation for reaching out into human life. I think behaviorism does lay a foundation for saner living. It ought to be a science that prepares men and women for understanding the first principles of their own

behavior. It ought to make men and women eager to rearrange their own lives, and especially eager to prepare themselves to bring up their own children in a healthy way. . . . Will not these children in turn, with their better ways of living and thinking, replace us as society and in turn bring up their children in a still more scientific way, until the world finally becomes a place fit for human habitation? (Watson, 1924, pp. 247–248).

CONTRIBUTIONS

John Watson's most important contribution to psychology was the behaviorist revolution he initiated. Regardless of one's evaluation of its merits, no one denies that the revolution profoundly affected the course of psychology. Watson's research and theoretical contributions are controversial, even among behaviorists. Perhaps his most unqualified success was his application of conditioning principles to the analysis and treatment of behavior disorders. In spite of the numerous limitations of his research program, he nevertheless anticipated behavior modification techniques of treating disordered reactions, a form of therapy currently used by psychologists, psychiatrists, and other practitioners in the health sciences.

John Watson, like his functionalist predecessors, was convinced that psychological knowledge could be used to benefit individuals and society. If nothing else, his efforts revealed the complexities and potential pitfalls of such attempts. His book, *Psychological Care of the Infant and Child* (1928), which he later publicly regretted (Skinner, 1959), recommended the proper method for bringing up children:

> Never hug and kiss them, never let them sit on your lap. If you must, kiss them once on the forehead when they say good night. Shake hands with them in the morning. Give them a pat on the head if they have made an extraordinarily good job of a difficult task. Try it out. In a week's time you will find how easy it is to be perfectly objective with your child and at the same time kindly. You will be utterly ashamed at the mawkish, sentimental way you have been handling it (Watson, 1928, pp. 81–82).

What evidence justified this stern advice? Watson's research on conditioning of emotions encouraged him to believe that the personalities of infants and children were completely malleable. With proper training, they could be molded into highly controlled, unsentimental individuals, a personality type that Watson obviously admired. Watson's recommendation to raise children as miniature adults suffered from three major defects. First, evidence was not available to support the contention that personalities could be shaped into any form desired. Second, Watson ignored the possibility, which present evidence supports (e.g., Harlow & Harlow, 1962), that human infants and other mammals are genetically preprogrammed to profit from emotional contacts with their parents or their surrogates. Third, Watson took his personal preference of a desirable personality type to be everyone's psychological ideal. Do unsentimental, controlled individuals suffer fewer psychological disturbances than other type personalities? Are they more successful? In sum, what justification could he offer for his advice?

Watson's attempt to formulate principles of child rearing, in spite of its limitations, encouraged the idea that psychological knowledge could be useful. Although many subsequent books on child rearing suffered from similar defects—lack of evidence to support recommendations and confusion of the author's personal likes with psychological ideals—many current books do contain information based on research that is helpful in raising children.

Watson's other major contributions contain positive and negative features. His stimulus-response associationism and peripheralism served to upgrade standards of objectivity in psychological research and contributed to the discovery of important principles of conditioning and learning, but at the same time encouraged superficial answers to complex problems. All in all, John B. Watson's contributions to psychology are neatly summarized in the citation he received from the American Psychological Association in 1957:

> To Dr. John B. Watson whose work has been one of the vital determinants of the form and substance of modern psychology. He initiated a revolution in psychological thought, and his writings have been the point of departure for continuing lines of fruitful research.

A Debate about Watsonian Behaviorism

Moderator: B. F. Skinner (1959), an intellectual offspring of John B. Watson, wrote that "Watson's taste for, and skill in, polemics led him into extreme positions from which he never escaped." Let us not succumb to similar exaggerations when assessing his contributions. In the light of history try to evaluate Watsonian behaviorism in a sensitive and fair manner.

Pro: Watson's greatness can only be appreciated if his faults are recognized. If everything he wrote is given equal weight his genius can be overlooked. His one great contribution was his clear recognition that only by studying behavior could psychology achieve the status of a natural science. Although others hinted at this idea, none perceived the problem as clearly as did Watson when he insisted that the direct examination of mental events be eliminated from psychology. Whereas Descartes encouraged self observation of mental events—the idea which ultimately led mentalistic psychologists to embrace the method of introspection or naive phenomenology— Watson realized that the subjective quality of self-observation prevented psychology from becoming a scientific discipline. In sum, the key idea of behaviorism, a natural-science psychology, represents a profound methodological contribution, the importance of which cannot and should not be diminished by any of the shortcomings of Watson's theoretical and experimental efforts. I hasten to add that acknowledging these shortcomings does not imply an absence of solid and theoretical contributions. Although not matching the importance of his methodological revolution, Watson's efforts in behavior modification, learning theory, and environmental controls of behavior, served as springboards for his successors to realize goals in research and application to which Watson aspired.

Con: You make the best possible case for John Watson. By acknowledging his shortcomings you try to disarm his critics. But that tactic is unsuccessful. While you are willing to accept methodological behaviorism, I reject it as an impossible orientation for psychology. I'll even admit that the direct examination of consciousness fails to produce reliable knowledge, but such an admission does not imply that information about consciousness is without value. By his strong aversion to self observation of mental processes, Watson denied psychologists an important source of information for discovering basic facts and principles. My point is simple, although obviously not simple enough for behaviorists to understand: We do have minds and how our minds function determines how we behave. Our behavior—ranging from solving an arithmetic problem to falling in love—cannot be detached from our mental processes. By being obsessively concerned with the natural science status of psychology, Watson destroyed an indispensable part of psychology—the mind.

Moderator: Your comments are direct and to the point and therefore raise fundamental questions about behaviorism that each member of the audience must answer.

SUMMARY

The basic idea of behaviorism, that psychology is the science of behavior, not of the mind, was anticipated by philosophers (La Mettrie, Comte) who argued that mental events need not be invoked in order to explain human conduct. Animal psychology also contributed to the development of behaviorism by demonstrating that the action of lower organisms can be explained in the absence of introspective evidence. Behaviorism was also anticipated by the efforts of a number of important psychologists (e.g., Ebbinghaus, Thorndike, Piéron) who investigated human behavior in the absence of introspective evidence. Of particular importance in the development of behaviorism was the work of Russian physiologists—Sechenov, Pavlov, Bekhterev—who emphasized objective methods of research while suggesting that the simple sensory-motor reflex is the basic unit of behavior. Pavlov brought this orientation to fruition with his discovery of the conditioned reflex, an empirical phenomenon that reflected three important traditions in the history of psychology: association, habit, and objectivity.

The basic methodological assumption of Watsonian behaviorism is that "psychology . . . is a purely objective experimental branch of natural science . . . with its . . . goal . . . the prediction and control of behavior" (Watson, 1913). Initially Watson acknowledged that consciousness was a tool of natural science, but its analysis was not the task of psychology. Later this position, known as methodological behaviorism, shifted to that of metaphysical behaviorism which denies consciousness exists.

Watson conceptualized behavior as consisting of basic stimulus-response associations. Individual associations could be chained together by response-produced cues to form lengthy sequences of behavior. The basic method of psychological investigation, for behaviorists, was objective; behavioral events must be, in principle, publicly observable. Introspective analysis of the mind was prohibited because mental events are private, observable only by the experiencing individual. Watson never discussed in any detail his criterion of truth. Although he tested the deductive implications of his hypotheses, he was more interested in predicting and controlling behavior than in constructing an integrated theory. In predicting and controlling behavior, Watson employed the stimulus-response model of behavior as a tool; discover the stimulus to which a desired response is associated and then control that response by controlling the stimulus.

Watson had two major goals: to convert psychology into a science of behavior and to formulate a model of behavior that could be used to enhance the adjustment of individuals and to improve society. The strategy Watson employed to demonstrate that psychology did not need introspection was to show that animal behavior could be investigated by the methods of natural science. If animal behavior could be objectively investigated, Watson argued, so could human behavior. The strategy behind his goal of improving individual and social behavior was to demonstrate how methods of conditioning could be used to achieve those ends.

Watson's theoretical efforts were restricted to specific empirical problems. He demonstrated by conditioning techniques that a child could be conditioned to fear an object (e.g., white rat) which initially did not evoke any fright. This study anticipated the modern method of behavior modification. Watson conceptualized habits, innate or acquired, as chains of stimulus-response connections. Watson postulated three major principles that governed the action of habits: *recency, frequency,* and *context.* His peripheral theory of thinking proposed that language habits involving muscular movements in the tongue and throat were basic to thinking.

A historical perspective of Watsonian behaviorism identifies four major features: *objectivity, stimulus-response associationism, peripheralism,* and *environmentalism.* The evaluation of behaviorism depends on whether all four characteristics are considered essential or whether the core assumption of behaviorism is objectivity with the other three characteristics not being basic to the behaviorist view of psychology.

History suggests that the major contribution of John B. Watson is his redefinition of psychology from the science of the mind to the science of behavior. He also served as a important influence in encouraging the application of psychological knowledge for the public good. His efforts in this direction backfired because he failed to distinguish his own personal concept of good from that of society's. Watson initiated many lines of research that proved important in subsequent years.

SUGGESTED READINGS

John B. Watson was a vigorous writer and the student who reads his words will gain an additional insight into his successful launching of behaviorism. His early efforts, the paper *Psychology as a Behaviorist Views It* (1913) and his classic book *Psychology from the Standpoint of a Behaviorist* (1919) are his best. The popular book *Behaviorism* (1924) conveys Watson's style in his postacademic career when he was trying to persuade society that behaviorism held the key to the solution of individual and social problems.

Interesting insights into Watson as a person and psychologist can be gleaned from his autobiography in a *History of Psychology in Autobiography* (Volume 3) edited by C. Murchison (1936). The obituaries by B. F. Skinner (1959) and R. S. Woodworth (1959) will also prove revealing. G. Bergmann's article *The Contributions of John B. Watson* (1956) represents a carefully reasoned analysis of Watsonian behaviorism by a philosopher of science. A lively debate about behaviorism is contained in a slender volume *The Battle of Behaviorism* which is co-authored by the two participants: J. B. Watson and W. McDougall (1929).

To appreciate the important role conditioning played in Watsonian behaviorism one should read I. Pavlov's brilliant book *Conditioned Reflexes* (1927).

7

Gestalt Psychology

FIGURE 7.1   What Do You See?

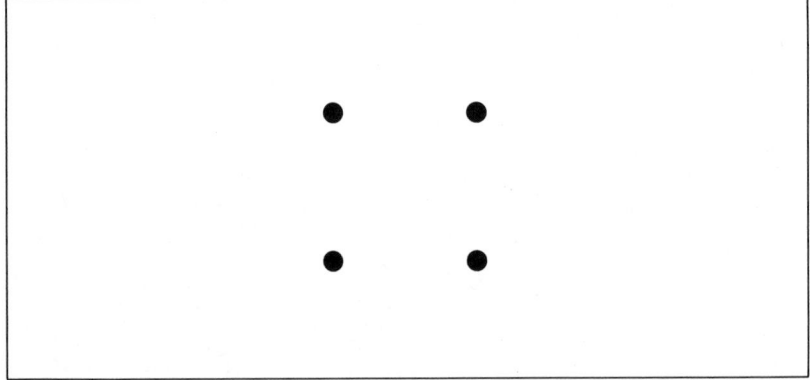

Look at the above figure. What do you see? Not just four dots. You see a square. You have just had a *Gestalt experience*. Instead of a mere assemblage of parts, you perceived an integrated whole. This demonstration captures the essence of Gestalt psychology's appealing slogan: "The whole is greater than the sum of its parts." The square you perceive is a unique property not present in the dots themselves.

Gestalt is a German word that can be loosely translated into the English equivalents of *configuration* or *form*. Gestalt psychology, with its emphasis on configurational properties of psychological phenomena, initiated two revolutions: the first in Germany against Wundt's attempt to analyze consciousness into basic mental processes, the second in America against behaviorism's effort to reduce behavior to stimulus-response associations. Although Gestalt psychology was not victorious in its battle against atomistic approaches in psychology, it nevertheless altered the course of the history of psychology.

HISTORICAL ROOTS

Gestalt psychology represents a unique combination of three important philosophical ideas that achieved popularity among German intellectuals, *holism, phenomenology,* and *nativism.*

Holism

One legend from ancient Rome is that a plebeian revolt, an uprising of the common people, was quelled by a state official who persuaded the mob that the state is like a living organism with each part dependent on all other parts. It would be self-defeating, the official argued, for one segment of society to fight against another; it would be like fighting against oneself. Whether the legend is true or not, the fact remains that the appeal to holistic principles frequently finds a receptive audience. The holistic dentist attracts customers by advertising that successful treatment demands that a patient be treated as a whole human being instead of someone who suffers from a defective part.

Holism is more complex than the declarations of the Roman statesman and the holistic dentist suggest. It represents a protest against the atomistic conception that assumes a simple continuity between parts and a whole. But, in many cases, this atomistic conception is correct. The money you have in your billfold is, unfortunately, no more than the sum of its parts. So is a mechanical clock; its operating characteristics can be understood by dismantling the clock and then reassembling its parts. While not denying that certain systems can be accurately described as the sum of their parts, a sophisticated holist argues that the relationship between the whole and its parts that prevails for money and mechanical clocks is not characteristic of all systems, particularly those involving psychological processes.

A driving force behind the popularity of holism in Germany was the complex philosophical system of George W. F. Hegel (1770–1831), so complicated that Hegel, himself, reputedly confessed, "One man has understood me, and even he has not." Hegel proposed a *theory of organicism* to account for human history that assumed that the basic unit of history is the nation state and not individuals. For Hegel, a nation is more than the sum of its citizens; its culture, traditions, and spirit have independent existence apart from its members. History cannot be reduced to the actions of individuals, even great individuals such as Napoleon, because their behavior is not understandable outside of the context of the nation in which they lived. In the language of holism, the Hegelian notion is that the nation is *prior* to its citizens; the whole is *prior* to its parts.

In addition to describing the part-whole relationship between citizens and their nation, Hegel added an important psychological assumption, that a person's adjustment is determined by his or her role in the state. Happiness is achieved by those who participate in the larger purpose of the state. Unhappiness is a consequence of the alienation of the individual from the ideals of the state. In sum, Hegelian holism postulated that the whole (the state) has a purpose with which the parts (the citizens) can identify. This purposiveness of the holistic doctrine has become a source of much controversy.

Holism was brought to the forefront of psychology by attempts to explain the perception of geometrical forms and musical melodies. Consider the perception of a square. Is the perception simply a product of sensing four lines? Christian von Ehrenfels (1859–1932), a forebear of Gestalt psychology, denied that squareness can be reduced to a combination of elementary sensations of lines. In a similar vein, he argued that a melody is not perceived as an assemblage of individual tones. To explain perceptions of integrated patterns of stimulation requires the assumption, Ehrenfels thought, of a new element, the element of form quality (*Gestaltqualität*). Squareness was perceived as a combination of four lines *plus* the *element* of form-quality; a melody is perceived as a combination of the notes *plus* the *element* of form-quality. Although anticipating Gestalt psychology, Ehrenfels differed in a fundamental way from the Gestalt position. For Ehrenfels, form quality was another element which, in combination with other elements of experience, produced an integrated perception of form. Gestalt psychologists assumed that the perception of form is not mediated by an additional element, but instead emerges from the intrinsic configuration of the parts. This difference, extremely subtle, is that for Ehrenfels the parts were *prior* to the whole while for Gestalt psychologists, the whole was *prior* to the parts.

Phenomenology

Phenomenology has been described as the "unbiased scrutiny of experience" (MacLeod, 1968) and "disciplined naiveté" (Katz, 1935). Late in his career, Titchener suggested that naive phenomenology might have some advantage over trained introspection in describing conscious experience (Chapter 3). Although observing consciousness in a naive manner (phenomenology) is a different method than introspection by trained observers, both methods, in contrast to the behaviorist view, share the assumption that a veridical description of conscious experience is possible.

FIGURE 7.2 Newton's Demonstration that a White Light (Sunlight) Is Composed of Many Different Colors

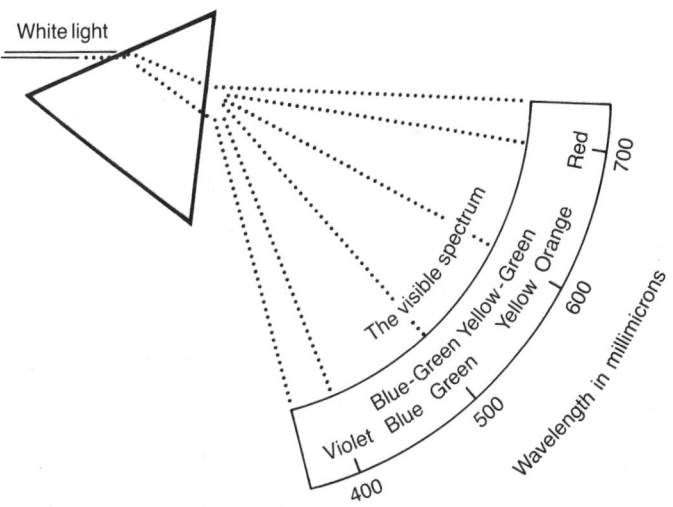

By passing a beam of white light through a prism, the various components are separated to produce the visible spectrum from red at one end through the various hues to violet at the other end.

Johann Wolfgang Goethe (1749–1832), the great German poet whose talents extended into the realm of science, considered phenomenology the natural method for studying perception. In a book on color experience, Goethe (1810/1840) described many important phenomena, including the negative afterimage which occurs when, after viewing a patch of one color (e.g., blue), an observer perceives an image of its complementary color (e.g., yellow).

Goethe's faith in phenomenology produced a ludicrous episode in the annals of science. Goethe bluntly rejected Isaac Newton's (1642–1727) discovery that white light (sunlight) is a mixture of colored lights. Newton had demonstrated this principle by passing a beam of white light through a prism, thus separating the various wavelengths into a spectrum of hues (Figure 7.2). The phenomenological examination of white light—"the unbiased scrutiny of experience"—convinced Goethe that it is not composed of varicolored hues and, therefore, Newton must be incorrect. Even though a prism was available to Goethe, he never attempted to test Newton's findings.

Goethe's absurd rejection of Newton's discovery need not be blamed on phenomenology. Phenomenology's aim is to describe conscious experience and not its physical basis. The mistake Goethe made was to commit the inverse of the *stimulus error.* Titchener criticized introspectors who contaminated their observations of consciousness with their knowledge of the physical properties of the stimulus. Goethe rejected Newton's physical description of light because it failed to agree with his own phenomenological experience of white light being "pure," incapable of being reduced to a spectrum of color lights. In essence, Goethe failed to distinguish between the phenomenology of white light and the physics of white light.

The efforts of two physiologists, the Czech, Johannes E. Purkinje (1787–1869) and the German Ewald Hering (1834–1918), demonstrate that phenomenology can serve as a fruitful first step in psychological research. By careful phenomenological analyses of visual experience, both reported observations that gave direction to psychological and physiological research. Purkinje described the *twilight shift* in the relative brightness of colors which raised the question of why colors at the red end of the spectrum lose brightness more rapidly in low illumination than those at the violet end. A red rose, for example, loses brightness faster than the surrounding green leaves. The answer came seventy years later when the discovery was made that the retina contains two kinds of receptors, rods and cones. The shift from cone vision during daytime to rod vision at twilight is responsible for the shift in the relative brightness of different colors. In a similar fashion, Hering analyzed color experience and noted that certain pairs of colors like red and green operate in an opposing manner; a gray patch will appear greenish when surrounded by red and reddish when enveloped by green. Hering postulated the operation of three opponent pairs of visual mechanisms (red-green, yellow-blue, white-black) that has served as the basis of a modern color theory (Hurvich & Jameson, 1957).

Franz Brentano (1838–1917), a philosopher-psychologist-priest born in Germany of an ancient Italian family, encouraged a phenomenological approach that anticipated Gestalt psychology. Brentano's major psychological work, *Psychology from the Empirical Standpoint* (1874/1925), viewed psychology as an independent science of the mind based on an observational approach not necessarily dependent upon experimental techniques. Stressing experimentation to the exclusion of phenomenological analysis, he argued, could blind one to significant issues. Directly observing conscious experience could prove to be a more important strategy than obtaining quantitative experimental results, a view that Gestalt psychologists were to enthusiastically adopt.

Brentano is best known for his elusive and controversial thesis that all mental phenomena but no physical phenomena exhibit intentionality. For example, I *intend* to descend a staircase, while a ball rolls down an inclined plane *without any intention*. At first glance, this distinction appears reasonable. The important issue is not so much the distinction, but rather its implications. For Brentano, one major implication was that if intentionality characterizes mental life, then a description of consciousness in terms of its content alone is both incomplete and misleading. It is necessary to distinguish between the color seen and the seeing of a color. Seeing a color is an act; the color seen is its content. The act is the basic psychological process in experience. Mental life can best be described with verbs like seeing, hearing, remembering, and perceiving, not with nouns like sensations, images, and affections, as Wundt suggested. Thus, Brentano's view is known as act psychology to distinguish it from the content psychology of Wundt. An important feature of Brentano's act psychology is its view of consciousness as an activity *directed toward some goal*, for example, seeing red, remembering a face, or solving a problem. This view is shared by functionalism (Chapter 4), and also anticipates the Gestalt view.

Nativism

Psychology has inherited from philosophy the age-old controversy between *empiricism* and *nativism*, one facet of which is focused on the importance of learned and innate factors in psychological activities. John Locke (1632–1704), an early British associationist, enunciated the empiricist doctrine that at birth the mind is blank, a *tabula rasa* (a blank tablet), upon which experiences of the world gained through the senses are written. David Hume (1711–1776) gave substance to this assumption with his interpretation of causality. The concept of causality is learned as a result of experience; certain events, like one billiard ball hitting another, are invariably contiguous in space and time. From this kind of experience we learn that one event can cause another; one billiard ball hitting another causes the second ball to move at a certain speed in a certain direction. Immanuel Kant (1724–1804), the great German philosopher, rejected Hume's analysis. The concept of causality is not simply learned; in order for causality to be understood, the mind must be endowed with the capacity to understand causality. "There can be no doubt that all our knowledge begins with experience . . . but it does not follow that it all arises out of experience" (Kant 1781/1950). The psychological issue that this philosophical controversy raises concerns the relative influences of genetic preprogramming and learning upon psychological events. Behaviorism, emerging from the traditions of British Associationism, emphasized the importance of learning, while Gestalt psychology, arising from a German philosophical orientation, stressed nativistic factors. Learning (empiricism) and nativism (genetic preprogramming) are not necessarily antithetical; the task of psychology is to discover the influence of each factor and the interactions between them.

Max Wertheimer, Wolfgang Köhler, and Kurt Koffka

Three young men met in 1910 and launched Gestalt psychology. The meeting was not premeditated; it occurred almost by chance. While traveling on a train during his vacation, Max Wertheimer (1880–1943), who had a doctorate in psychology, attempted to solve a problem that obsessed him: how to transform his holistic notion of psychology into a concrete experimental design. He decided this could be accomplished by studying the phenomenon of apparent movement, the perception of movement from a series of still images. He disembarked from the train at Frankfurt and purchased a toy stroboscope, an instrument that produces apparent movement of still pictures by periodically interrupting light. In the hotel room, he set up his experiment by substituting a series of lines for the pictures in the toy and demonstrating to his own satisfaction the apparent movement effect, later to be known as the phi phenomenon; *phi* representing the temporal relationship between the two successive stimuli. Wertheimer then contacted a former teacher who was at the Frankfurt Psychological Institute and requested experimental facilities and the cooperation of some subjects. Two postdoctoral assistants, Wolfgang Köhler (1887–1967) and Kurt Koffka (1886–1941) volunteered, and the three demonstrated the phi phenomenon together, in essence founding Gestalt psychology. The friendly relationship that was established in the laboratory in Frankfurt was to persist throughout their lives; they became a closely knit triumvirate in their common commitment to Gestalt psychology. Their personalities and intellectual styles differed though, and as a consequence their contributions were distinctive. Wertheimer, who had difficulty getting his ideas down on paper, served as a prophet and catalyst. He generated many ideas that served as a starting point for the research of others. In addition, as his original contacts with Koffka and Köhler illustrated, he was most effective in unleashing the creative forces of others. In the early days of Gestalt psychology, Koffka served as its leading organizer and promoter, being most responsible for bringing the movement to America, where he emigrated in 1927. Köhler became the most productive researcher and systematic theorist of the original three Gestalt psychologists.

Max Wertheimer was born in Prague and grew up in an intellectual and artistic household. His father, an educator, became financially successful with his novel and effective methods for teaching shorthand and bookkeeping. Not only did his father's success stimulate in Max a lifelong interest in methods of education, but it also provided him with the financial independence to pursue his intellectual interests. As a child, Max exhibited talent in mathematics, philosophy, literature, and most of all, music. He learned to play the violin and the piano and composed symphonies and chamber music. Later on, as a psychologist, Wertheimer illustrated many of his ideas with musical examples.

During adolescence, Wertheimer's interests were directed toward literature; he wrote poetry and formed friendships with members of the local literary circle. At the same time, he became fascinated with

FIGURE 7.3 Max Wertheimer

Archives of The History of American Psychology

Baruch Spinoza (1632–1677), the philosopher who was born of a Spanish-Portuguese-Jewish family in Amsterdam. Spinoza believed that nature could not be understood without comprehending its basic structure; in the words of holism, the whole of nature was prior to its parts. God and nature are one and the human mind reflects this unity. Truth and goodness can be understood if we can understand the human mind. Spinoza preached an optimistic view of mankind that Wertheimer, as well as Köhler (1938) and Koffka (1935), were to incorporate into Gestalt psychology.

With so many talents—artistic, scientific, and philosophical—Wertheimer was hard put to decide on a career. He started law school but soon discovered that he was more interested in the philosophy of law than in the more mundane practice of law. He then became interested in the truth of legal testimony and this interest directed him toward psychology. Initially he studied at the University of Berlin but then shifted to the University of Wurzburg, where he studied with

Külpe and received a Ph.D. with the highest honors. While at Würzburg, Wertheimer devised the word-association test which he employed to evaluate the truth of legal testimony.

After receiving his doctorate, Wertheimer visited several intellectual centers of Europe, where his inquiring intellect involved him in different problems: the perceptual ability of children suffering from reading disorders, the psychology of music, and the thinking patterns of primitive people as revealed by anthropological evidence. All of these efforts strengthened his conviction that a holistic approach to the study of psychology is essential. Finally, the study of the phi phenomenon at Frankfurt with the assistance of Köhler and Koffka led to the birth of Gestalt psychology.

During World War I Wertheimer was a captain in the German Army and conducted research on the problem of locating the source of sounds. After the war, from 1916 to 1929, Wertheimer served as *Privatdozent* at the University of Berlin, where his popular lectures attracted many scholars from various fields. Along with Koffka, Köhler, and Kurt Goldstein, a neurologist, Wertheimer founded the *Psychologische Forschung* and served as editor for the first twenty volumes. In spite of his great intellectual impact, he was not offered a professorship of psychology until 1929, when he was forty-nine. At that time the University of Frankfurt appointed him to such a post. The delay was due in part to Wertheimer's reluctance to publish; his perfectionistic tendencies encouraged him to try to improve everything he wrote.

Wertheimer, who was Jewish, was destined to stay at Frankfurt for only a few years. Listening to Hitler on the radio convinced him that the future of his family and of the cultural values which he embraced was bleak. The Wertheimer family ultimately found their way to the United States where Wertheimer accepted a professorship of psychology at the New School for Social Research in New York, an institution that had been established for refugee scholars from Nazism. In New York his influence was great; many young psychologists were stimulated by Wertheimer's gestalt views.

In 1943, he died suddenly of a coronary embolism. Among his papers was discovered a manuscript which was posthumously published as *Productive Thinking* (1945), a slender volume that reflects Wertheimer's distinctive style. The influence of Wertheimer cannot be judged only by his written contributions. His ideas blossomed through the efforts of the colleagues and students whom he inspired.

Kurt Koffka was born in Berlin to a distinguished family of lawyers. His education at the University of Berlin was interrupted with a year at the University of Edinburgh, where he perfected his English. That prepared him to become the first apostle to bring the message of Gestalt psychology to America.

FIGURE 7.4 Kurt Koffka

Archives of The History of American Psychology

Koffka took his doctorate with Carl Stumpf (1848–1936) at the University of Berlin in 1908 where he wrote a thesis entitled "Experimental Investigation of Rhythm." Stumpf's influence on Koffka and on Köhler, who became his student later, was indirect but important. Stumpf's passion in life was music; he began to compose at age ten and played six different instruments during his adolescence. A career in music was sidetracked into philosophy but his first love finally gained ascendancy when Stumpf conducted experimental investigations of music and tones. This ultimately led to an acrimonious debate with Wundt:

> The clash seems to have arisen because Stumpf leaned heavily upon his own musical sophistication, while Wundt relied on the laboratory results with apparatus and the psycho-physical methods. Whatever is obtained under unprejudiced, carefully controlled experimental conditions must be right, Wundt virtually said. If the laboratory yields

results that are obviously contrary to expert musical experience, they must be wrong, was Stumpf's rejoinder (Boring, 1950, p. 365).

Thus, the problem of discovering the most accurate method of observing conscious experience was brought to the forefront for Koffka. He was prepared for, and ultimately receptive to, Wertheimer's conclusion that naive phenomenology was the best method to observe consciousness and that integrated wholes were the basic units of experience.

During World War I, Koffka was involved in military research and afterwards taught at the University of Giessen. During the 1924–1925 academic year, he was a visiting professor at Cornell University, and two years later he taught at the University of Wisconsin. In 1927 he was appointed to a newly established chair at Smith College where he remained until his sudden death in 1941.

Through his lectures and articles, Koffka served as the major spokesman for Gestalt psychology in America. He applied gestalt principles to mental development in his book *The Growth of the Mind* (1924). His major thesis was that a child's experience is not chaotic but instead consists of organized wholes. In *Principles of Gestalt Psychology* (1935), his major work (dedicated to Köhler and Wertheimer "in gratitude for their friendship and inspiration"), Koffka undertook the ambitious task of integrating phenomena from a variety of research areas—perception, memory, learning, social psychology, and personality—within gestalt theory. It proved to be a difficult book to read, but nevertheless alerted American academic psychologists to a viable alternative to functionalism and behaviorism.

Wolfgang Köhler, of the three founders of Gestalt psychology, achieved the greatest fame, both in Germany and America. Köhler was born in Estonia but was raised in northern Germany. His formal education, which was terminated in a doctorate with Stumpf at the University of Berlin in 1909, also included training with the eminent physicist, Max Planck.

After receiving his doctorate, Köhler became associated with the psychology laboratory at the University of Frankfurt. In 1913, he was appointed Director of the Anthropoid Station of the Prussian Academy of Science on Tenerife Island of the Canary chain in the Atlantic Ocean. Because of World War I, he was unable to return to Germany and was forced to remain on the island until the war was over. The war did not serve as an excuse to stop research, and during his tenure on Tenerife Köhler was extremely productive, his best-known work being insight learning experiments with apes. He became the director of the psychological laboratory at the University of Berlin in 1921 and upon the retirement of his teacher, Stumpf, Köhler assumed the most prestigious professorship in Germany.

FIGURE 7.5 Wolfgang Köhler

Dan McIntosh

The rise of Nazism in Germany confronted intellectuals with a moral challenge that a large majority chose to ignore. The Nazis fired Jewish professors and those opposed to Nazism. Years later Köhler remarked,

> Nothing astonished the Nazis so much as the cowardice of whole university faculties, which did not consist of Nazis. Naturally this corroborated the Nazis' contempt for the intellectual life (Henle, 1978, p. 940).

In contrast, Köhler responded to the challenge with high moral purpose. During the early days of Nazism, after Jews and anti-Nazis had been dismissed from the universities, Köhler wrote the last anti-Nazi article to be published in a German newspaper, an act that appeared to guarantee his arrest. On the evening he expected to be arrested, he prepared by playing chamber music with his colleagues. Köhler later wrote about the dismissal of James Franck, the great experimental physicist:

> The greatest German experimental physicist of the present time is Franck; many believe that he is the greatest experimental physicist of our age. Franck is a Jew, an unusually kind human being. Until a few days ago, he was professor at Göttingen, an honor to Germany and the envy of the international scientific community . . . [Franck's dismissal] shows the deepest reason why all these people are not joining [the Nazi party]; they feel a moral imposition. They believe that only the quality of a human being should determine his worth, that intellectual achievement, character, and obvious contributions to German culture retain their significance, whether a person is Jewish or not (Henle, 1978, p. 940).

Köhler persisted in his efforts to stem the tide of Nazism and defend the freedom of science and of his colleagues and students. Finally, when no hope remained, he emigrated to the United States where he became a professor of psychology at Swarthmore College in 1935. He remained in that position until his retirement in 1955. He was then appointed research professor at Dartmouth College in Hanover, New Hampshire, an area of America that reminded Köhler of his native Germany.

Köhler's first book in English was *Gestalt Psychology* (1929) which was dedicated to Max Wertheimer:

> I should like to dedicate something of which I could be prouder than these ten chapters. I hope he will accept them, however, as a testimony of my good will and of our friendship (Köhler, 1929, pp. ix–x).

Köhler was the William James Lecturer at Harvard during the 1934–1935 academic year and later published his lectures under the title *The Place of Value in a World of Facts* (1938). This complex book assumed that our phenomenological experience could reveal important information about human values. He was elected to the National Academy of Sciences in the United States and to the Presidency of the American Psychological Association in 1959. He also received the Distinguished Scientific Contribution Award from that organization. He died in 1967, leaving a legacy of important contributions to psychology and the memory of a scientist who, in a time of crisis, did not abandon his ethical responsibilities to his profession and colleagues.

METHODOLOGICAL ASSUMPTIONS

Gestalt psychology emerged from a German background but was modified by its American experience. It was shaped initially by its opposition to Wundtian psychology but later, in its confrontation with behaviorism,

Gestalt psychology was encouraged to change its methodological orientation. As with many psychological systems, a methodological analysis of Gestalt psychology demands consideration of evolutionary changes occurring within the orientation as it matured.

Subject Matter

Although Gestalt psychology opposed Wundtian psychology in Germany, they both shared the common belief that the subject matter of their discipline is mental life. As a result of its exposure to behaviorism in America, Gestalt psychology shifted its emphasis more in the direction of behavior:

> Although psychology was reared as the science of consciousness or mind, we shall use behaviour as our keystone. This does not mean that I regard the old definition as completely wrong . . . but it means that if we start with behaviour it is easier to find a place for consciousness and mind than it is to find a place for behaviour if we start with mind or consciousness (Koffka, 1935, p. 25).

Whereas Watsonian behaviorism insisted that behavior must be divorced from mental events, Gestalt psychology argued that behavior could only be properly studied within a mentalistic framework.

Preconceptions about Consciousness

Köhler (1929) acknowledged that two different attitudes can be adopted in observing one's own consciousness, naive phenomenology or trained introspection. Köhler illustrated the difference between the two with the phenomenon of brightness constancy. If a naive observer compares the brightness of gray paper in sunlight with white paper in deep shadow the observer will report that the white paper is brighter even though it reflects less light. For the trained introspector, operating within the traditions of Wundt and Titchener, the results would be different. When observing white and gray paper in different illuminations, the trained introspector seeks to analyze experience into basic sensory elements. This requires isolating the experience of sensing the gray and white patches from the surrounding illumination. By ignoring contextual factors, the experience of the trained introspectionist would be correlated with the intensity of light falling upon the retina. Since the gray paper reflects more light, the trained introspector reports, contrary to the naive phenomenologist, that the gray is brighter than the white patch.

Although acknowledging that these two attitudes are possible, Köhler (1929) argues that trained introspectionism generates a distorted view of consciousness. A true picture of consciousness contains integrated wholes not assemblages of parts. We observe the white paper in a shadow as being brighter than the gray paper in sunlight because we do not *naturally* divorce the papers from their context. White paper reflects about 90 percent of the light shining on it regardless of whether the surroundings are bright or dull. Gray paper reflects a lower percentage. Consequently, white paper always reflects a higher percentage of the available light than does gray paper and, therefore, is naturally perceived as brighter. The *relationship* of the paper to the surroundings is the important variable in perceived brightness, not the *absolute* amount of light reflected.

Gestalt psychologists, it should be noted, were essentially agreeing with the criticism of the *psychologists's fallacy* (page 93) that William James leveled against trained introspectionism; the isolated elements of experience that were reported in consciousness were not there originally but were actually projected into consciousness by the preconception that conscious experience consists of combinations of basic elements.

Methods of Investigation

Gestalt psychology combined the methods of naive phenomenology and experimentation. Initially, gestalt principles could be most conveniently revealed by phenomenological reports in simple laboratory demonstrations. Sometimes these principles could be sharpened when used in combination with more elaborate experimental procedures. As Gestalt psychology matured and extended its principles to the fields of learning, thinking, memory, and social psychology, it began to rely more on systematic experimental investigations that employed behavior as the dependent variable. But, unlike behaviorism, gestalt psychologists always combined phenomenological reports or inferences about conscious experience with their experimental approach.

Criterion of Truth

In his presidential address to the American Psychological Association, Köhler frankly confessed that:

> Almost from its beginnings, American psychology has given more attention to questions of method and strict proof than gestalt psychology did in [its early] years. In this respect American psychology was clearly superior. Secondly, sometimes the gestalt psychologist did make mistakes. Not in all cases was the reliability of their findings up to American standards, and some concepts which they used were not immediately clear (Köhler, 1959, p. 729).

By "American psychology," Köhler was referring to behaviorism. Although he explicitly rejected the behaviorist doctrine that the study of conscious experience fell outside of the boundaries of natural science (Köhler, 1925), Köhler nevertheless recognized the inherent difficulties in proving theoretical claims with phenomenological evidence alone. In spite of this awareness, many gestalt hypotheses were, during the early days, supported by the intuitive conviction generated by phenomenological reports. This kind of evidence failed, however, to convince the majority of their American audience. Challenged by the criticism of subjectivity, Gestalt psychologists tried to formulate their explanations of publicly observable experimental evidence in a deductive mold. They made some progress in this direction, but not enough to dissuade their critics that their holistic theory suffered from an inherent vagueness.

STRATEGY

No group of psychologists was more concerned with questions of strategy than were Gestalt psychologists. They strongly believed that scientific efforts must be planned ahead in order to avoid misdirection. The tactics that Gestalt psychologists adopted were to:

1. *Guide psychological research by phenomenology.* Why do things look as they do? Why do we regularly perceive a dinner plate as round even though it rarely projects a perfectly circular image on the retina? Why does a white paper appear white and not reddish even when a red light shines on it? The tendency to perceive objects as relatively unchanged under widely different conditions of stimulation—technically known as *perceptual constancy*—was considered to be a significant research and theoretical problem for Gestalt psychologists simply because of their commitment to the strategy of interpreting everyday experience:

> Direct experience is at the root of our knowledge. The phenomenal is the scene that humans inhabit, and it is the sole starting point for psychology, as for science generally (Asch, 1968a, p. 116).

2. *Demonstrate the inadequacy of an atomistic approach in psychology.* Gestalt psychologists were convinced that Wundt started psychology off in the wrong direction with his attempt to identify basic elements of consciousness, and that Watson was repeating this mistake with his effort to reduce complex behavior to a chain of stimulus-response associations. The most effective tactic to adopt in redirecting psychology to an appropriate holistic approach would be to demonstrate that psychological atomism is incapable of explaining basic psychological phenomena.

3. *Study perception to reveal basic psychological principles of organization.* Gestalt psychologists believed that their holistic principles were applicable to all areas of psychology (e.g., learning, thinking, social interaction) but could be most efficiently investigated and revealed in studying perception. The research area of perception had developed rigorous research procedures which could yield definitive results in relatively brief periods of time, unlike the extensive time commitments required in research on learning.

4. *Don't rush quantification of psychological phenomena; first demonstrate qualitative differences.* Quantification for the sake of quantification serves no purpose in science. Only when an important phenomenon is identified and understood is quantification justified. Premature quantification can actually be misleading. The laws of memory that Ebbinghaus proposed suggested that learning nonsense syllables is a gradual process of associative strengthening when, in fact, the opposite may be true. The sudden transformation of a meaningless trigram into a meaningful one, as when RMN is recognized as the initials of a former president, Richard M. Nixon, can result in learning the syllable. The first step in science is understanding; quantification follows.

5. *Extend holistic principles that govern psychological processes and events to other fields of inquiry.* Michael Wertheimer, the psychologist, son of Max Wertheimer, stated that the idea of *gestalt* was for his father

> not only a theory of psychology, or even an entire philosophy; it was rather a weltanschauung [world view], indeed an all encompassing religion. The core of this religion is that the world is a sensible coherent whole, that reality is organized into meaningful parts, that natural units have their own structure (Michael Wertheimer, 1978, p. 1).

The doctrine of isomorphism—identical (iso), form or shape (morphism)—emerged from Wertheimer's global view and essentially prejudged the relationship between psychology and neurology. More specifically, the doctrine of isomorphism assumed that *holistic principles* that governed experiential events, like the phi phenomenon, also govern brain activity. The thrust of this assumption is that the phenomenal and the neurological are more than simply lawfully correlated; they both share a common structure. For example, the brain, according to the Gestalt psychologists, could not be designed like a telephone switchboard because perceptual events are not experienced as connected parts, but instead as integrated wholes. A better analogy for the design of the brain would be an electrical field of charged particles in which all points within the field are interdependent.

Isomorphism, which emerges from the holistic orientation that views the world as "a sensible coherent whole," is essentially a theoretical strategy; principles discovered in one area (e.g., phenomenology) should be applied to other areas (e.g., behavior, neurophysiology). Köhler (1920/ 1950), who had been trained in physics, extended the range of isomorphism by suggesting that psychologists should be alert to holistic principles in physics that could guide their own theoretical efforts.

GESTALT THEORY

The fundamental "formula" of Gestalt theory might be expressed in this way: There are wholes, the behavior of which is not determined by that of their individual elements, but where the part-processes are themselves determined by the intrinsic nature of the whole. It is the hope of Gestalt theory to determine the nature of such wholes (Wertheimer, 1950, p. 2).

A program of research is contained in this formula. The first step is to demonstrate that analyzing a phenomenon into component parts without considering the nature of the whole will lead to erroneous conclusions. The second step is to discover the principles that govern the organization of psychological wholes.

The Phi Phenomenon: A Case against Atomism

Wertheimer wished to illustrate the poverty of an atomistic theory which assumes that perception involves only a combination of individual sensations. He chose the phenomenon of apparent motion to argue his case. Two short lines, one vertical, the other horizontal, both on the same plane, were successively shown for a brief period of time. If the time interval between the two is neither too brief nor too long, one perceives the vertical line *move* to the horizontal position.

The phenomenon of apparent movement has long been known; motion pictures are based on it. Why did Wertheimer consider it important? Because the phi phenomenon, thought Wertheimer, contradicted an atomistic theory of perception. If the observer senses two static lines, how could he perceive motion if perception is a mere *summative* combination of individual sensations? Wertheimer reasoned that another factor must be operating in addition to the sensations of two static lines. That factor, he concluded, must be the temporal relation between the lights, which he named *phi*. He concluded that brain processes organize the two sensations to produce apparent motion; the whole—apparent motion—is greater than the sum of its parts—two static sensations.

Wertheimer essentially convinced himself that a holistic interpretation was *demanded* because he was unable to offer any satisfactory atomistic explanation. He systematically tested available atomistic interpretations and found them all wanting. For example, one possible atomistic explanation was that sensations of successive static lines were experienced but kinesthetic cues from eye movements from one line to the other gave a sense of movement. If this were so, reasoned Wertheimer, then it would be impossible to experience apparent movement simultaneously in two opposite directions. Wertheimer neatly ruled out this explanation by using two pairs of flashing lines in opposite directions and demonstrating that the observer under such conditions perceives movement in both directions.

Perceptual Organization

Gestalt psychologists offered a variety of perceptual phenomena to demonstrate that we integrate incoming stimulation into organized percepts.

FIGURE 7.6 An Inkspot that Evokes a Figure-Ground Perception

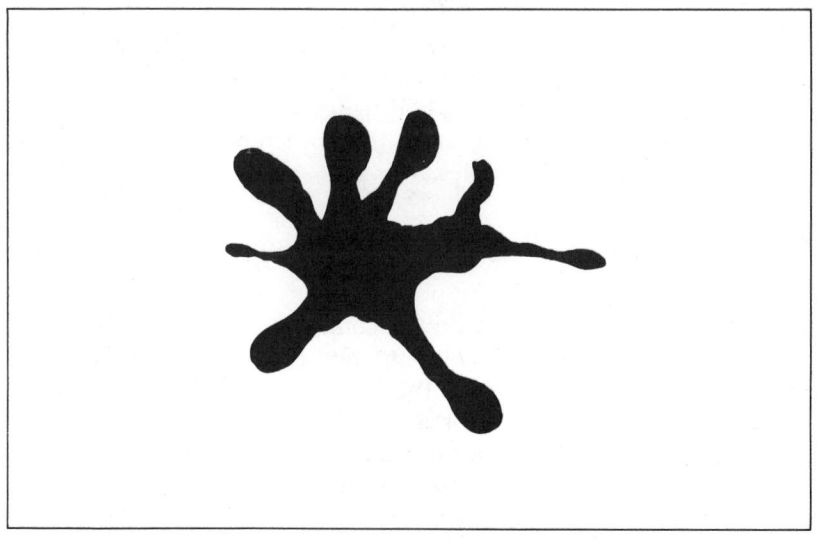

Figure and Ground.   Edgar Rubin (1886–1951), a Danish psychologist who favored the phenomenological method, began to study the figure-ground phenomenon a few months before Wertheimer initiated his research on the phi phenomenon. Although they were not aware of each other's efforts, it became apparent that they shared a common theoretical orientation. Although Rubin was not officially a member of the gestalt group, his work on the figure-ground phenomenon expresses the gestalt orientation.

Figure 7.6 is an inkspot. You do not perceive the entire visual field as an assemblage of two parts: inkspot and non-inkspot. Instead you instantly perceive the inkspot as a definite cohesive figure standing out against a formless background. A phenomenological description reveals that the figure-ground perception has three major characteristics: (1) the figure is perceived as a form while the ground appears formless; (2) the contour line, the line that divides the inkspot from the background, belongs to the figure, not to the ground; and (3) the figure appears to be located in the foreground with the ground behind.

These characteristics of a figure-ground perception are clearly demonstrated by the reversible figure-ground design that appears in Figure 7.7, which can be perceived as either a vase or two profiles. When perceived as a vase, the white portion has form and comes forward while the black portion appears formless and recedes. The reverse is true when the figure is perceived as two profiles; the white loses its contour line and recedes into the background, while the black profiles take on form and come forward.

FIGURE 7.7 Is It a Vase or Two Faces in Profile?

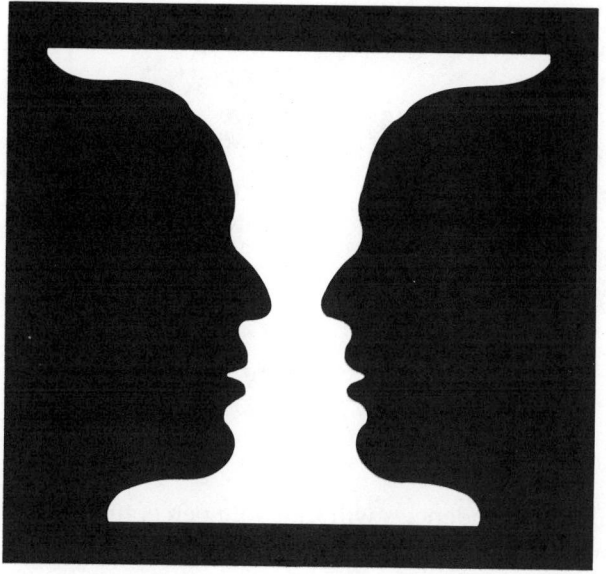

Gestalt psychologists consider the figure-ground perception to be important for three reasons: First, it illustrates the fact that incoming stimulation is perceived in an organized fashion. Second, the figure-ground perception appears to be fundamental in the sense that it is the first distinction to emerge when you look at a stimulus pattern. With a tachistoscope, experimental subjects can be shown stimulus patterns just long enough for a quick look—shorter than one-thousandth of a second. Under such circumstances the subject reports perceiving some kind of figure against a background even though the form of the figure is not identifiable (Flavell & Draguns, 1957). When the exposure time is lengthened, other perceptual features, such as form, emerge. Third, the figure-ground perception is unlearned; it is not acquired as a function of practice, but instead occurs spontaneously. Gestalt psychologists hypothesize that the mind is endowed with the capacity to organize patterns of stimulation into a figure-ground perception in essentially the same fashion that a vessel is endowed with the capacity to force a liquid to assume its shape. In other words, simple patterns of stimulation are organized by the innate structure of the nervous system. An argument in favor of innateness is that Figure 7.7 cannot be perceived as two figures simultaneously— vase and profiles—without a ground.

Laws of Perceptual Grouping. Closely related to the spontaneous figure-ground perception are perceptual-grouping tendencies. Simple constellations of stimuli are organized according to a few basic principles

FIGURE 7.8   A Stimulus Pattern Illustrating the Principle of Nearness

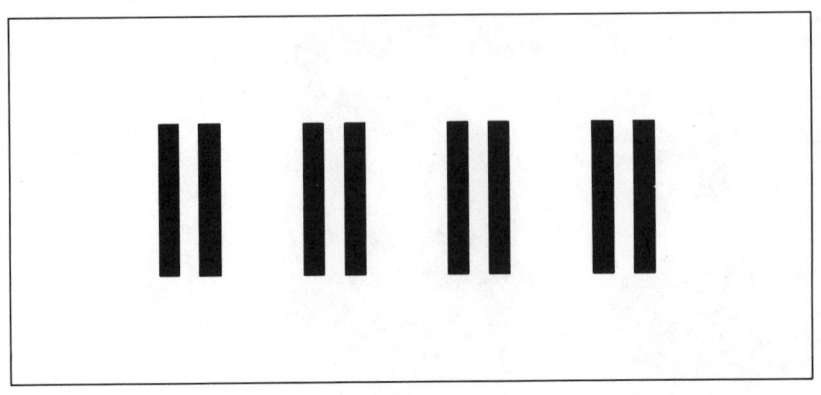

You organize the lines in groups of two.

of perceptual grouping. Three tendencies will illustrate perceptual grouping. Three principles will be illustrated.

Principle of nearness.   Stimulus elements that are close together tend to be perceived as belonging together. The eight vertical lines in Figure 7.8 are usually perceived in four groups of two. The first and second, the third and fourth, the fifth and sixth, and the seventh and eighth lines are grouped together. It is practically impossible to perceive the second and third or the fourth and fifth as being members of the same perceptual pair.

Principle of similarity.   The principle of nearness does not hold for all patterns. In some situations, other factors operate to override its influence. In Figure 7.9, each square is nearer to a circle than it is to another square, yet the squares are perceived as being grouped with other squares instead of with neighboring circles. Similar stimuli tend to be perceived as part of a common group.

Principle of good form.   Stimulus elements that compose a *good* or *simple* form, or what Gestalt psychologists originally called *prägnanz*, are grouped together. The pattern in Figure 7.10 is perceived in two parts, the straight section and the curved section of Figure 7.10A. Given only the principles of nearness and similarity, you should just as readily perceive the two other components that are illustrated in Figure 7.10B. But you do not because, as Gestalt psychologists suggest, perceptions tend to be organized into good (simple) forms. The *A* components are better than the *B* components because the dots continue in the initially established direction.

We also perceive good form when our perceptions fill in gaps. Instead of perceiving a curved line and two broken straight lines in Figure 7.11,

FIGURE 7.9 A Stimulus Pattern Illustrating the Principle of Similarity

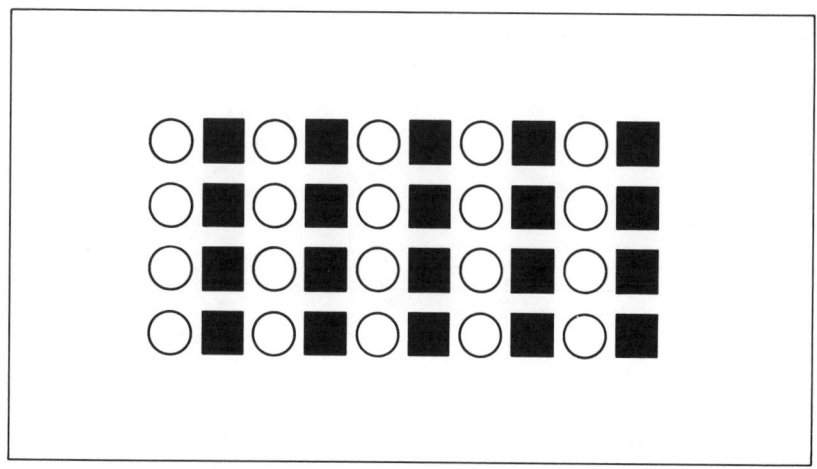

You perceive the pattern as a group of columns, not rows.

(p. 207), we see a circle and rectangle; thus the tendency to perceive good form encourages the perception of closed figures.

Concluding Comments on the Gestalt Theory of Perception. Gestalt psychologists argued that the phi phenomenon, perception of figure-ground, and perceptual grouping demonstrated the validity of their fundamental formula. Again, the formula states: "There are wholes, the behavior of which is not determined by that of their individual elements, but where the part processes are themselves determined by the intrinsic nature of the whole" (Wertheimer, 1950). Two separate issues are conflated in their argument: the falsity of an atomistic interpretation and the validity of a holistic explanation. It does not follow that the lack of an adequate atomistic interpretation automatically validates a holistic explanation. A holistic interpretation must stand on its own feet; it should be clearly formulated so that its truth value can be ascertained. In addition, it should be recognized that the failure to formulate a satisfactory atomistic explanation does not rule out the possibility that one might be discovered in the future.

Within this context two questions can be raised: How effectively did Gestalt psychologists invalidate an atomistic approach to perceptual experience? How well did they demonstrate the validity of their holistic interpretation of perception?

In response to the first question, the evidence strongly suggests that Gestalt psychologists demolished available atomistic or piecemeal accounts of perceptual experience. They illustrated with numerous examples that the relationship among the parts of a perceptual display—the context—plays a powerful role. The four dots in Figure 7.1 (p. 184) cannot

FIGURE 7.10 A Stimulus Pattern Illustrating the Principle of Good Form
(Prägnanz)

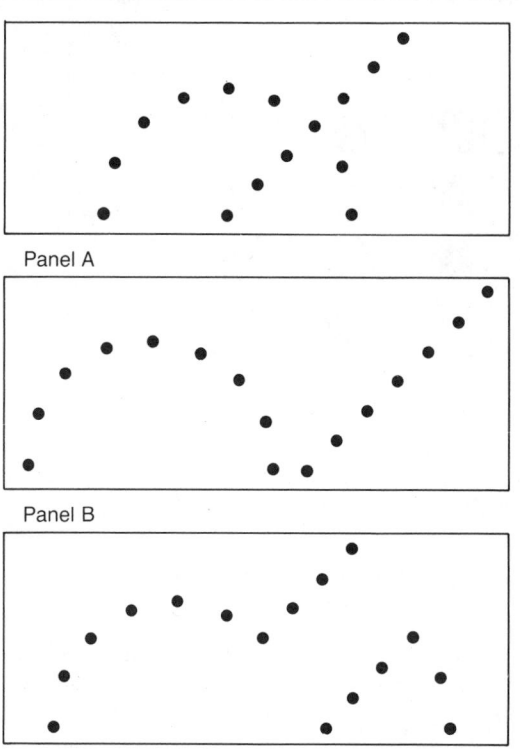

Panel A

Panel B

You tend to perceive the top pattern as being composed of the components in Panel A,
not those in Panel B.

be said to add up to a square because if the locations of the dots are changed the perception of squareness is destroyed.

The answer to the second question, the validity of gestalt holistic principles, is unclear. At best, Gestalt psychology offered limited explanations. Simple principles, such as *good form*, were identified and illustrated. No effort was made to go beyond these simple qualitative descriptions by attempting to formulate the principles in greater detail. For example, Koffka (1935) readily admitted that the principle of *good form* is "vague." But the confidence placed in the capacity of phenomenological analysis to reveal ultimate theoretical truths seemed to discourage attempts to search for a deeper understanding.

American psychologists were not as easily persuaded by phenomenological evidence as were Gestalt psychologists. They believed that the principle of *good form* had to be evaluated in a more objective and detailed manner. Two American psychologists (Attneave, 1954; Garner, 1962), after conducting systematic experimental research, reformulated the principle

FIGURE 7.11 Illustrations of the Principle of Good Form (Prägnanz)

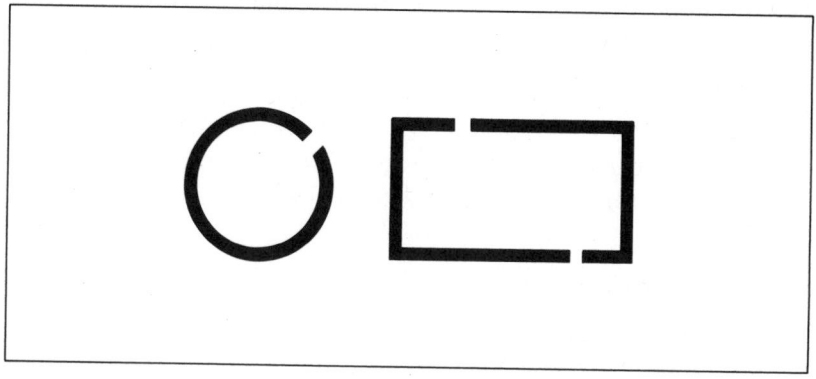

You tend to perceive a completed figure where none exists.

FIGURE 7.12 Which Form Has a Greater Amount of Goodness?

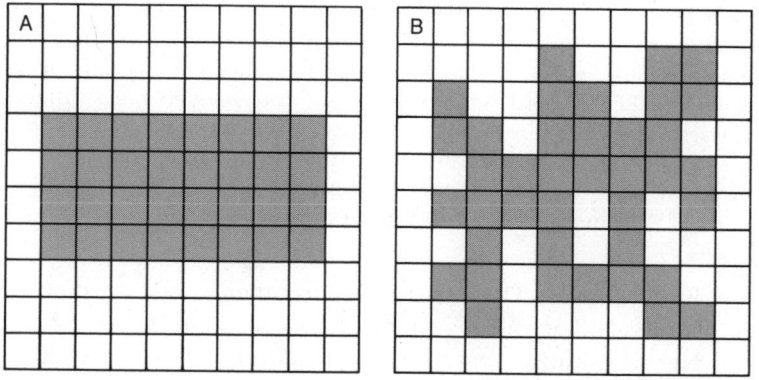

As the text explains, the figure in Panel A is more redundant and hence is a "better" figure.

of good form into the objective statement that perceptual patterns with good forms are redundant; they contain surplus information.

Figure 7.12 illustrates the relationship between redundancy and form quality. Both patterns have been drawn on graph paper within an area of 100 small squares, ten rows by ten columns. Predicting the shape of the form by knowlege of its parts is an easier task for pattern A than for pattern B. This can be demonstrated by instructing subjects, prior to their perceiving the entire figure, to move square by square across the page beginning with the upper left-hand corner, guessing before the next square is uncovered whether it is black or white. Subjects have a higher percentage of correct hits with pattern A than with pattern B. Guessing is required at the beginning for both patterns, but the subject very rapidly learns to guess correctly for the upper three rows of A because they are all white. The upper left black square of the rectangle is guessed incorrectly, but soon the errors disappear as the subject perceives the entire pattern. Pattern B would generate significantly more errors because of its irregular contours and unsymmetrical shape. Figure A is redundant; if you know the upper half you can predict the lower half. In essence, *good forms* are redundant because the whole can be predicted from a few parts while *poor forms* are unpredictable (Kendler, 1981).

Learning and Thinking

The key to understanding learning and thinking according to Gestalt psychology, lies in the phenomenological experience of the learner and thinker. The importance of phenomenological experience in understanding behavior is illustrated in a dramatic German legend that Koffka offered to distinguish between two different environments which organisms inhabit, the physical (geographical) and psychological (behavioral):

> On a winter evening amidst a driving snowstorm a man on horseback arrived at an inn, happy to have reached a shelter after hours of riding over the wind-swept plain on which the blanket of snow had covered all paths and landmarks. The landlord who came to the door viewed the stranger with surprise and asked him whence he came. The man pointed in the direction straight away from the inn, whereupon the landlord, in a tone of awe and wonder, said: "Do you know that you have ridden across the Lake of Constance?" At which the rider dropped stone dead at his feet (Koffka, 1935, pp. 27–28).

Koffka's point is simple. The physical environment must be distinguished from the psychological environment as it appears to the organism. The traveler physically crossed a frozen lake but psychologically crossed a plain. After realizing that he had just traversed a sheet of ice which could have been shattered by the weight of the horse and himself and plunged them both to a watery grave, the traveler dropped dead of fright. The lesson of this legend is clear: psychologists must understand the psychological environment, the environment as it appears to the organism. The following descriptions of gestalt research will illustrate the role the concept of the psychological environment plays in understanding the psychology of learning and thinking.

Transposition. Köhler (1918/1950) trained chickens, in a simple discrimination-learning task, to choose the darker of two gray stimuli represented by the numbers 1 and 2, with 2 being the darker. After learning to select 2, the chickens were tested with a choice between 2 and 3, with 3 being darker. Which one would they choose? This experimental design, according to Köhler, represented a critical test between stimulus-response conditioning theory and gestalt theory. Köhler argued that stimulus-response theory would predict the choice of stimulus 2. An association had been formed during the initial training between stimulus 2 and the response of choosing it so "it would be quite incomprehensible" for the animals to choose 3, the darker stimulus. Gestalt theory, in contrast, predicts the choice of stimulus 3. The reason for this prediction is that the chickens do not perceive stimuli 1 and 2 as independent events but instead as related cues. That is, the psychological environment is not that stimulus 1 is incorrect and 2 correct, but instead that the darker one is correct. Consequently 3 should, according to gestalt theory, be chosen.

The results suggested that the subjects transposed a relational response from the training to the test situation. Sixty-eight percent of the chickens chose stimulus 3, the darker of the two stimuli in the test situation. Such evidence appeared intuitively convincing to Köhler that his relational theory was correct while a stimulus-response conception must be false.

Subsequent history indicates that Köhler's treatment of transposition as a critical test between gestalt and stimulus-response theories was oversimplified. He was too eager to accept a holistic interpretation without expending some effort to analyze the problem. Why were 32 percent of the responses in the test trials to the absolute stimulus, 2, instead of the relational stimulus, 3? Would the same amount of transposition occur if the three stimuli, 1, 2, and 3, were very similar (like three shades of light gray) or very different (like a very light gray, a medium gray, and a very dark gray)? Is it really true that a stimulus-response conditioning theory could not, under any circumstances, predict the selection of the relational stimulus in the test situation? In actual fact, a few years after Köhler declared that "it would be quite incomprehensible" for a stimulus-response conception to predict relational responding, Spence (1937) offered a quantitative conditioning theory that predicted a relational responding when the differences among the three stimuli were small, and an absolute response when the differences were large. Much research was generated by the competing formulations of Köhler and Spence, but it gradually became apparent that the problem of transposition is more complicated than either formulation suggests. But the controversy did indicate beyond dispute that Köhler was incorrect in prejudging the potential of atomistic theories.

Insight. Köhler rejected the prevailing behaviorist view that trial and error learning situations accurately reflect basic laws of learning. He argued that Thorndike's famous puzzle-box task was not a meaningful problem to the subject in the sense that rational principles could be employed in solving the problem. Pulling a string to escape from the puzzle box is no more sensible than inserting a paw through the slats or lying down or jumping up. Learning depends upon understanding a problem, not accidentally solving it as Thorndike (1898) suggested. To investigate learning requires a meaningful problem in which a rational relationship prevails between the problem and its solution. Köhler designed such a problem with his insight-learning task. A banana was suspended from the top of a cage out of a chimpanzee's reach. Several boxes were scattered around the floor. Köhler (1925) reported that the animal repeatedly jumped for the fruit without success. Eventually these futile leaps ceased, giving way to restless pacing. Then the pacing stopped, and after some apparent contemplation, the animal stacked the boxes below the banana, permitting it to climb to the top and grab the fruit.

Köhler used the term *insight* to describe the problem-solving behavior of his chimpanzees. He assumed that *insight* was a consequence of a sudden change in the psychological field of the subjects. Initially the boxes and banana were perceived as isolated objects, but then they became related parts of a common problem. This perceptual reorganization, insight, enabled the chimpanzees to solve the problem. A qualitative difference exists, according to Gestalt psychology, between learning based upon arbitrary associations (e.g., pulling a string to escape from a box) and learning that comes from understanding rational relationships (e.g., stacking boxes to get a banana out of reach). If this distinction were correct, then a theory of learning based upon arbitrary associative tasks such as puzzle boxes and conditioning would be inadequate for explaining learning by understanding.

Wertheimer (1945) later illustrated the distinction in a classroom where children were learning to compute the area of a rectangle. With the *associative method* children were *blindly* taught to obtain the areas of different rectangles by simply multiplying the length by the width without understanding the rationale of the formula, that area equals height times width. With the *method of understanding,* the children learned the identical arithmetical operation but were taught the reasons for its use. They learned that the length is multiplied by the width because area refers to the amount of surface enclosed within the boundaries of a geometric figure. They learned that if one divides the surface within a rectangle into small squares that represent the length and width of adjacent sides, one can compute the area by simply counting the number of squares. They were taught further that a shortcut to counting all the enclosed squares is to multiply the number of squares on one side (length) by the number of squares of the adjacent side (width). In sum, they were taught the structural organization of a rectangle.

Why is it important to understand the reasons for using a formula? The important thing is to obtain the correct answer! True, both methods do lead to the same answer when the areas of rectangles are computed. But the two methods do not necessarily lead to the same consequence when similar but slightly different problems are presented. The manner in which the child learns to compute the area of a rectangle, Wertheimer argued, will determine the success he or she has in computing the area of a parallelogram.

FIGURE 7.13 The Associative Method versus the Method of Understanding in Teaching Children to Compute the Area of a Rectangle

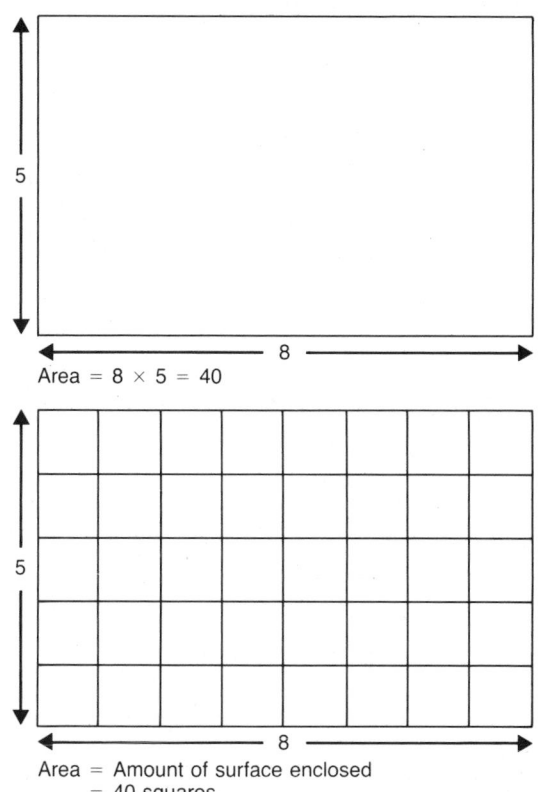

Area = 8 × 5 = 40

Area = Amount of surface enclosed
= 40 squares

According to Wertheimer a child can learn to compute the area of a rectangle either by "blindly" applying the rule of multiplying the length of one side by the length of its adjacent side, or by understanding the principle underlying this rule. The principle can be taught by encouraging the child to comprehend that area refers to the amount of surface enclosed, and that it can be computed by counting the number of squares, or more simply by obtaining the product of the lengths of adjacent sides.

The child who has memorized by rote the rule that the area of a rectangle equals the product of the lengths of two adjacent sides tends to apply the same rule to compute the area of a parallelogram and gets an incorrect answer. On the other hand, the child who has learned the reasons for multiplying the length of two adjacent sides of a rectangle to obtain its area will attempt to understand the structural relationship between a rectangle and parallelogram, the relationship between the regular ends of the rectangle and the lopsided ends of the parallelogram. By perceiving that one lopsided end can be removed from the parallelogram and attached to the other end (Figure 7.14, next p.), the child will understand that the parallelogram is a rectangle in disguise and, as a result,

---

FIGURE 7.14 The Relationship between a Parallelogram and a Rectangle

---

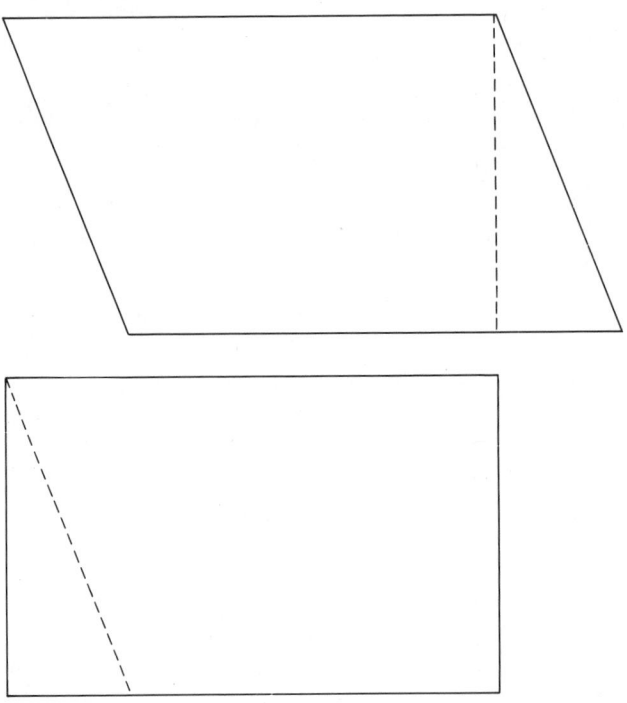

To find the area of a parallelogram, the student must understand that it is a rectangle in disguise.

conclude that the formula for the area of a rectangle applies to the parallelogram. To compute the area of a parallelogram requires knowing the altitude (height) of the parallelogram and then multiplying it by the length of the base. Wertheimer summarizes:

> In short, the role of past experience is of high importance, but what matters is *what* one has gained from experience—blind, un-understood connections, or insight into structural inner relatedness. What matters is how and what one recalls, how one applies what is recalled, whether blindly, in a piecemeal way, or in accordance with the structural requirements of the situation (Wertheimer, 1945, p. 62).

In the gestalt interpretation of insightful behavior of both apes and children the emphasis is on the appropriate organization of the psychological environment so that the subject perceives an integrated whole that reflects the structural "requirements of the situation."

Two major criticisms have been directed at the gestalt interpretation of insightful behavior:

First, the explanatory power of the concept of psychological environment can be misleading. A noted philosopher of science raised the following objection:

> But even so, what is the predictive value of the suggestive metaphor "psychological environment?" Is it not the business of science to ascertain which objective factors in the past and present states of the organism and its environment account for the differences in response, so that we can actually predict it instead of attributing it, merely descriptively and after it has happened, to the differences in the psychological environment? (Bergmann, 1943, p. 133).

Bergmann is arguing that in order for the concept of *psychological environment* to serve a useful function it must be defined independently of the behavior it seeks to explain. In light of this criticism, reconsider the German legend that Koffka reported (p. 208). The traveler's death was attributed to fright triggered by the change in his psychological environment when he learned that he had crossed a lake and not a plain. What evidence, aside from his dropping dead, supports this interpretation? Perhaps his heart attack resulted from some cardiac dysfunction that would have occurred regardless of his crossing Lake Constance. Although intuitively persuasive, the explanation that he died of fright lacks independent supporting evidence.

In order for the concept of *psychological environment* to be useful, it must be able to *predict* future behavior. To state that insight will occur when the subject perceives the problem "in accordance with the structural requirements of the situation" has utility only when conditions responsible for an insightful solution are specified. Wertheimer went beyond a simple post hoc explanation by describing the educational method, learning by understanding, that would increase the probability of insightful behavior. But for the most part, Gestalt psychologists did not fully face up to the important task of specifying clearly how the psychological environments of organisms could be controlled so that their behavior could be predicted "instead of attributing, merely descriptively and after it has happened, to differences in the psychological environment."

Second, the sharp qualitative distinction that Gestalt psychologists made between insightful learning and learning by arbitrary associations may be unjustified. In one insight problem (Birch, 1945), young chimpanzees were confronted with food just beyond their reach outside their cages. Within reach was a hoe they could use to gather in the food. One animal who had extensive experience playing with sticks and using them as tools (e.g., reaching out of the cage with the stick to turn the electric switch on and off) easily solved the problem. Four animals who could not solve the hoe problem were then given sticks to play with for a three-day period. During this time, they were never observed using the sticks as rakes; they used them to poke the other chimpanzees or the experimenter; the stick was used "as a functional extension of the arm." Yet, when these four animals were retested, they solved the problem with ease. The experience with sticks enabled them to use the sticks as rakes in solving the problem. This evidence suggests that for insight to occur, certain component skills must have been acquired. The question can be raised whether principles of associative learning that are involved in conditioning and trial and error learning may not have played an important role. Rather than treat insightful learning and associative learning as distinctly different processes, it may be more productive to search for similarities as well as dissimilarities between the two.

Personality and Social Psychology

A holistic orientation has a tendency to feed upon itself; the basic whole tends to absorb more and more. A temptation prevails for the holist to argue that one cannot limit the study of psychology to specific processes such as perception, learning, and thinking. The personality of the individual who perceives, learns, and thinks must be considered. But that is not sufficient; the social situation must also be included.

Kurt Lewin (1890–1947), a psychologist who had received his Ph.D. in 1914 at the University of Berlin where he was associated with both Köhler and Wertheimer, was most responsible for extending gestalt notions to the fields of personality and social psychology. Lewin's work can be considered more of an outgrowth of Gestalt psychology than a continuation. He adopted the holistic orientation of the Gestalt psychologists but ignored their concern for biological processes as expressed by their assumption of isomorphism. Psychology for Lewin was strictly a social science.

During his early career, Lewin was interested in cognitive processes, learning, motivation, and conflict. Later he became involved with the psychology of personality (Lewin, 1935). One of his core concepts, possessing both phenomenological and holistic properties, was that of *psychological life space*. The life space of the individual is conceived to be the total environment as it exists for the individual. It is characterized as a field, presumably because of similarities to the field concept in physics (e.g., electric field). One of the major properties of the life space is the degree of integration among the various components of one's life.

Lewin's interest in personality theory gradually expanded to a social psychology. He attempted to describe *social space* by representing the interaction of many factors including political, economic, cultural, and physical events. This led to the study of *group dynamics*, the interaction among social groups. Realizing that such problems have practical implications, Lewin initiated the movement known as *action research*, which was designed to effectuate social change. One of its earlier efforts was to improve the relationships between blacks and whites in interracial housing projects that were built after World War II.

Another spin-off of action research was *sensitivity training,* a group training technique in which the participants uninhibitedly express themselves. This procedure was applied in industry and education to reduce both intragroup and intergroup conflict and to unleash individual potential. Sensitivity training, and many variations that sprang from it, was enthusiastically adopted by humanistic psychologists as a basic therapeutic technique.

Unlike many psychologists' interest in solving practical problems, Lewin did not minimize the importance of general psychological theories. In fact, he took the opposite view; he said there is "nothing as practical as a good theory." But history judged his theoretical efforts to be less important than the empirical problems that he investigated, the research techniques he developed, and the applied orientation he encouraged.

Quotations of Gestalt Psychologists

1. Science is rooted in the will to truth . . . the responsibility of the scientist increases with his difficulties, the demand grows for unswerving determination in the search for truth . . . and wills the truth untainted by wish or commands (Wertheimer, 1934, reprinted in Henle, 1961, p. 28).

2. A science . . . gains in value and significance not by the number of individual facts it collects but by the generality and power of its theories (Koffka, 1935, p. 9).

3. Never, I believe, shall we be able to solve any problems of ultimate principle until we go back to the sources of our concepts,—in other words, until we use the phenomenological method, the qualitative analysis of experience (Köhler, 1938, p. VII).

4. The privacy of direct experience does not disturb anybody—in physics . . . each individual physicist . . . tacitly assumes that his fellow workers have objective experiences highly similar to his own, and he does not hesitate to take the words of his colleagues as statements about these experiences. According to the behaviorist this means, of course, that the physicist allows private affairs to play a part in exact science (Köhler, 1947/1964, p. 21).

5. Two processes A and B happen to occur together and, whatever the nature of A and B may be, a bond is formed between them! I do not know a single law in physics or chemistry which could in this respect be compared with the law of contiguity . . . there are no examples of interaction in which the nature of the interacting factors plays no part. And yet, in the classical law of association by contiguity, the nature of the things which become associated is tacitly ignored (Köhler, 1947/1964, p. 153).

6. "Knowing" is an ambiguous term. To know a blind connection, such as the connection between the switch and the light, is very different from realizing or discovering the inner relatedness between means and ends, their structural fitting (Wertheimer, 1945, p. 44).

7. A psychology which has no place for the concepts of meaning and value cannot be a complete psychology. At best it can give a sort of understanding, treating of the animal side of man, on which the main building, harbouring his cultural side, must be erected (Koffka, 1935, p. 9).

CONTRIBUTIONS OF GESTALT PSYCHOLOGY

Few contemporary psychologists would describe themselves as Gestalt psychologists. This does not mean that Gestalt psychology has been abandoned. Instead, Gestalt psychology has been absorbed but not in its original form. Certain selected core assumptions and findings have been integrated into various modern conceptions.

Holism

It is ironic to note that the disintegration of the gestalt view into component parts was mainly brought about by its passionate devotion to holism. Two major criticisms have been directed against holism. First, the doctrine of holism is fatally vague. Second, the doctrine suggests a sharp division between *holism* and *atomism* which in reality may not exist.

Although the slogan, "The whole is greater than the sum of its parts" is intuitively appealing, it suffers from a basic ambiguity. What is a whole and how can it be identified? Consider the task of explaining the behavior of a specific woman. Can you explain her behavior without considering the activities of her husband? And should not the behavior of her children be considered? Her own parents? The extended family? Society as a whole? Neighboring societies? The international situation? This line of reasoning leads to the conclusion that the world, or perhaps the entire universe, determines the behavior of one woman. The point is that every whole is embedded in a larger whole and holism fails to offer any clear-cut rule about how to select the appropriate whole that is required to understand a given phenomenon. This problem led William James to conclude that holism is an impossible orientation because "everything would have to be known before anything is known!"

In supporting the gestalt thesis, Köhler (1920/1950) employed examples from the physical world which he thought illustrated the important distinction between gestalt (holistic) and summative (atomistic) phenomena. A soap bubble is an example of the former; an alteration in one part of the system causes a change in all other parts. The other extreme, a summative system, is exemplified by "Three stones, one in Australia, another in Africa, and the third in the United States." Because the "displacement of one has no effect on the others, nor upon their mutual relation," the system is considered summative (atomistic). In actual fact, Köhler was not quite correct in drawing this conclusion. Ernest Nagel (1961), a distinguished philosopher of science, responded to Köhler's example by noting that "if current theories of physics are accepted, such displacement is not without *some* effects on the other stones, even if the effects are so minute that they cannot be detected with present experimental techniques." The thrust of Nagel's analysis raises doubts about the presumed dichotomous relationship between gestalt and summative phenomena. Instead of adopting this sharp distinction, it would be more strategic to accept the fact that phenomena vary along a dimension of interactive complexity, where at one extreme the component parts are inextricably interdependent while at the other end they are completely independent. This general orientation discourages the scientist from getting embroiled in the irresolvable atomistic versus holistic controversy while simultaneously encouraging him or her to discover both the basic components of a phenomenon and the principles that govern their interrelationships.

While Gestalt psychologists were proclaiming their ambiguous holistic doctrine, they were frequently operating in a manner consistent with a combined analytic-synthetic approach. The discovery of the figure-ground perception, for example, was a consequence of analyzing a perceptual phenomenon into two major, mutually interdependent components. At other times, their obsessive concern with holistic properties functioned as an obstacle to necessary analysis, as in their treatment of the principle of good form and the phenomenon of transposition.

Partly as a result of the gestalt influence, modern psychologists recognize the importance of interaction and contextual factors in psychological phenomena. But the extreme holism of Gestalt psychology has been rejected for a more balanced view toward analysis and synthesis; both are essential and neither should be emphasized to the exclusion of the other.

One can speculate that the unbalanced gestalt view in favor of holism reflected the German passion for holism which was previously expressed by Hegel. This passion seemed to increase in Germany soon after Gestalt psychology was launched. The defeat in World War I created a painful past and bleak future that generated a sense of despair among Germans. The holism that Wertheimer espoused served to counteract this demoralization by providing meaning to life; it says that "the world is a sensible coherent whole, reality is organized into meaningful parts."

This world view inevitably led Gestalt psychology to deal with ethical issues; "a psychology which nowhere refers to . . . value is hardly worth its name" (Köhler, 1938). The conviction that the world is a meaningful whole encouraged the view that facts and values are intimately related, and therefore it should be possible to discover a valid set of moral principles capable of guiding human conduct. Köhler (1938, 1944) suggested that this goal could be achieved by phenomenological research.

The conventional view of philosophers and scientists is that facts and values are logically dissociated and therefore psychologists cannot properly prescribe a set of ethical imperatives (e.g., capital punishment is morally wrong). Although the relationship between facts and values never became a dominant issue in the controversy between Gestalt psychologists and their critics, the gestalt view had an important influence on the subsequent development of humanistic psychology (Chapter 12). In sum, the extreme holism that Gestalt psychologists initially enunciated was rejected by most of the experimental psychologists to whom the message was directed but, at the same time, the holistic orientation was adopted by a receptive audience, mainly clinical and personality psychologists, who were destined to launch humanistic psychology.

The Influences of Gestalt Psychology on Cognitive Psychology

Although Gestalt psychology cannot be detached from its holistic moorings, some of its individual research programs and strategies can. Three important influences on modern cognitive psychology then emerge.

Associative versus Cognitive Learning. Gestalt psychologists reversed the relationship between simple associative learning and rational (cognitive) behavior that was proposed by Watson. Watson considered simple associative learning as revealed by conditioning and trial and error learning to be the basic component of complex rational behavior. Gestalt psychologists rejected the notion that cognitive behavior, such as the insightful behavior of animals and true understanding achieved by children in the classroom, could be explained by principles of association. In fact, they suggested that associative learning is frequently mediated by rational understanding instead of being a function of arbitrary associative linkage.

One byproduct of Gestalt psychology's distinction between associative and cognitive learning was to encourage a shift to a transfer criterion of learning from the criterion of measuring learning by changes in the response that is being acquired. Progress in acquiring a conditioned response or solving a trial and error problem is measured by increases in the efficiency of making the learned response, for example, an increase in the probability of salivating to a conditioned stimulus or a reduction in errors when traversing a maze. Gestalt psychologists argued that the ability to repeat a response does not automatically reflect what is being learned. This point was driven home by Köhler's research on transposition and Wertheimer's efforts to teach children the area of a rectangle. As a consequence of their efforts, psychologists, particularly those interested in cognitive behavior such as concept learning, reasoning, and problem solving, found it necessary to employ transfer measures in order to reveal what was being learned.

The Influence of Genetic Factors. Influenced by the Kantian notion that human skills are in part a function of an innate capacity to acquire them, Gestalt psychologists sought to demonstrate the influence of genetic factors on psychological processes (e.g., basic principles of perceptual organization). Their efforts alerted psychologists to the notion that genetic factors cannot be minimized, and certainly not ignored, when seeking to understand psychological events.

The Importance of Consciousness in a Science of Psychology. While acknowledging the importance of behavioral measures in psychology, Gestalt psychologists believed that it is essential to employ phenomenological methods to understand behavior. Without considering consciousness, they warned, any attempt to understand behavior will fail.

Biopsychology

Gestalt psychology, with its assumption of an isomorphic relation among neurophysiology, conscious experience, and behavior, encouraged the view that psychology cannot, and should not, ignore biological processes. Although the assumption of isomorphism, with its holistic rejection of associationism, was at odds with the simpler biological approach of Watsonian behaviorism which aspired only to relate neurophysiological events to behavior, both orientations encouraged the development of biopsychology, a discipline that approaches psychology as a biological science.

A Debate about Gestalt Psychology

Moderator: The discussion of Gestalt psychology raises special problems. Although Gestalt psychology originated in the laboratory, it was always concerned with large philosophical issues about psychology and life. So, it becomes exceedingly important when evaluating the system to isolate the general philosophical content from the specific psychological contributions.

Pro: I disagree! Isolating the philosophical from the psychological in Gestalt psychology will distort the position and minimize its importance. Gestalt psychologists did not offer a dried-out psychology that was irrelevant to life or a set of vague philosophical generalities that were unrelated to empirical evidence. Instead, Gestalt psychology represents a coherent melding of psychological and philosophical ideas that produced a relevant science of psychology.

Con: Your argument against the reasonable request of the Moderator illustrates the unnecessary anti-analytic bias of Gestalt psychology. Not only can the philosophical orientation of Gestalt psychology be separated from its psychological content; it must be if the historical role of Gestalt psychology is to be properly understood. I consider the philosophical orientation of Gestalt psychology to be badly misdirected. In spite of this, the important empirical and theoretical contributions of Gestalt psychologists must be acknowledged. First, gestalt research in perception not only identified interesting principles of perception but also argued convincingly that they could be attributed to innate factors. The efforts of Gestalt psychologists served as a useful antidote to the unrealistic and misleading notion that human beings are infinitely malleable. Second, their research in learning and thinking discovered important phenomena (e.g., transposition, insight) that broadened the perspective of psychologists who had for the most part limited their attention to simple conditioning and trial and error learning. Third, the transfer criterion of learning employed by Gestalt psychology proved to be a more sensitive measure of learning for many tasks than the simpler behavioristic method of measuring changes in the response that is being learned. Important theoretical and practical educational issues were highlighted by the transfer criterion of learning, such as what kind of learning produces the deepest kind of understanding. Fourth, the Gestalt psychologists' assumption about the psychological environment, how the perceiving organism interprets the world, highlighted an important question, the significance of which is becoming ever more apparent. How does stimulation from external sources, ranging from physical stimulation (e.g., light waves) to social stimulation (e.g., language), get transformed by the perceiving organism? The study of psychophysics initiated the effort to answer this question and Gestalt psychology extended it to all areas of psychology. Now that the positive comments have been offered, let me briefly refer to the misdirection and confusion that was generated by Gestalt psychology's extreme holistic bias. Some holistic explanations in fact did not explain and actually obstructed attempts at understanding. In addition, the holistic bias got Gestalt psychology entrapped in issues of human purpose and ethical values which belong more properly to the philosophy of religion than to the science of psychology. Actually, the holistic commitments of Gestalt psychology were excess baggage which interfered with the efforts of Gestalt psychologists to offer a systematic explanation of the phenomena they investigated.

Pro: Your argument is inconsistent. You acknowledge the important contributions of Gestalt psychology and then criticize a basic component. Did it ever occur to you that the specific contributions of Gestalt psychologists were inextricably linked to their general philosophical views? Without their holistic view, combined with their phenomenological orientation, they never would have made their important contributions that you have acknowledged.

Con: The history of psychology has answered the question you raise. Two important orientations in psychology—cognitive psychology and humanistic psychology—have their roots in Gestalt psychology. One, cognitive psychology is influenced by the research and theory of Gestalt psychology; the other, humanistic psychology, has been shaped by the holistic philosophy of Gestalt psychology. This historical fact justifies my contention that the holistic philosophy should be detached from Gestalt psychology.

Moderator: You agree about your disagreement! We can decide later whether Gestalt psychology can be neatly divided into two separate entities, one based on the philosophical orientation and the other an expression of the psychological views.

SUMMARY

Gestalt psychology was born in Germany in 1910 with an experiment conducted by Max Wertheimer, in collaboration with Wolfgang Köhler and Kurt Koffka, on the phi phenomenon, the perception of movement from a sequence of still images. Gestalt psychologists considered the phenomenon of apparent motion inconsistent with the Wundtian notion that consciousness consisted of a combination of basic mental processes. Instead they argued that the experience of apparent motion emerged from the configurational properties of the total pattern of stimulation, thus supporting a view that consciousness consists of integrated wholes, not basic elements.

Gestalt psychology was influenced by three intellectual traditions that were popular in German culture: holism (the whole is greater than the sum of its parts), phenomenology (the naive examination of consciousness), and nativism (psychological skills are partly a function of the innate capacity of the organism).

Although Gestalt psychology developed in Germany where psychology was considered to be the science of the mind, the importance of behavior as a dependent variable was acknowledged after Koffka, Wertheimer, and Köhler emigrated to the United States. Unlike the behaviorists, Gestalt psychologists insisted that a psychology that ignored conscious processes would be incomplete and that an adequate theory of psychology must be based on mental processes. Gestalt psychology accepted naive phenomenology as the most appropriate method to directly investigate consciousness, sharing with William James the belief that trained introspection, of the sort that Wundt encouraged, gave a distorted picture of the mind.

Initially Gestalt psychologists sought to demonstrate theoretical principles with simple laboratory demonstrations combined with phenomenological reports. Later on, particularly after Gestalt psychology relocated in America, more systematic experimental procedures were employed. The criterion of understanding that the Gestalt psychologists used varied from intuitive understanding to deductive explanation.

Gestalt psychologists stressed the importance of strategy in scientific work, believing that the simple desire to be scientific could backfire. Their principle tactics were to: (1) *guide psychological research by phenomenology,* (2) *demonstrate the inadequacy of an atomistic approach,* (3) *study perception to reveal basic psychological principles of organization,* (4) *don't rush quantification of psychological phenomena; first demonstrate qualitative differences,* and (5) *extend holistic principles that govern psychological processes to other fields of inquiry (e.g., neurophysiology).*

The fundamental thesis espoused by Gestalt psychology is that the whole determines the functioning of its parts. The phi phenomenon, the argument went, exemplified this principle while simultaneously invalidating atomistic assumptions that postulate that a configuration consists merely of the sum of its parts. Gestalt psychologists, after demonstrating to their own satisfaction that a holistic approach was demanded, sought to formulate principles of perceptual organization that would account for various phenomena such as figure-ground and perceptual grouping.

The gestalt view of learning and thinking stressed the importance of the psychological environment—how the problem appeared to the subject. This orientation was illustrated in Köhler's work on transposition and insight. Transposition demonstrates, according to Köhler, that organisms in a discrimination-learning task do not learn specific stimulus-response associations, but instead acquire a relational conception of the discriminative stimuli. Insight learning, which requires the subject to perceive the rational relationship between the structure of the task and the behavior required to solve it, is qualitatively different from the learning that occurs in conditioning and trial and error learning tasks. Wertheimer illustrated this distinction by demonstrating the difference in transfer occurring from rote learning and learning by understanding.

An outgrowth of Gestalt psychology was Kurt Lewin's efforts in the fields of personality and social psychology, which combined a holistic and phenomenological orientation with a practical concern for implementing desirable changes in social groups and society.

Although the holistic orientation of Gestalt psychology has been criticized for being vague and creating a false dichotomy between atomistic and holistic approaches, it nevertheless has had salutary effects in alerting psychologists to the importance of contextual factors in psychological phenomena. In addition, the commitment to a holistic philosophy has encouraged Gestalt psychologists to argue that a valid set of ethics can be scientifically determined.

Gestalt psychology has influenced modern cognitive psychology by (1) emphasizing the distinction between rote associative learning and cognitive understanding, (2) acknowledging the importance of innate factors in behavior, and (3) demonstrating the relevance of consciousness to a science of behavior. Gestalt psychology, with its assumption of isomorphism, encouraged the development of biopsychology.

SUGGESTED READINGS

Both Koffka's *Principles of Gestalt Psychology* (1935) and Köhler's *Gestalt Psychology* (1929) seek to explain the basic notions of Gestalt psychology. Neither one is easy to read, but Köhler's book would be a better first choice. Max Wertheimers' posthumously published *Productive Thinking* (1945) accurately reflects his intellectual style. Two interesting collections of important papers in Gestalt psychology are W. D. Ellis's *A Source Book of Gestalt Psychology* (1950), and Henle's *Documents of Gestalt Psychology* (1961). Kurt Lewin's *Resolving Social Conflicts* (1948) and *Field Theory in Social Science* (1951) represent good summaries of his work in social psychology.

A good secondary source which was written at the time American psychologists were being introduced to Gestalt psychology is Heidbreder's chapter in her book *Seven Psychologies* (1933). An excellent treatment of Gestalt psychology from the viewpoint of an adherent is Asch's article (1968b), *Gestalt Theory*, in the *International Encyclopedia of the Social Sciences*.

8

Psychoanalysis

Sigmund Freud (1856–1939), the founder of psychoanalysis, was a genius of such proportion that his ideas ultimately permeated all of Western culture. His impact on psychology, psychiatry, literature, painting, social philosophy, drama, cinema, anthropology, sociology, religion, and even the common sense view of the nature of man, was so profound that discussing Freudian ideas within the confines of the history of psychology presents a special problem. Can an appropriate assessment of psychoanalysis be achieved by treating it solely as a psychological system? Yes and no. Without denying the broad cultural impact of Freud's innovative ideas, it is possible to describe and evaluate his psychological notions within the same methodological frame of reference that has been employed for other important psychological systems. At the same time, it should be understood that such an analysis fails to treat the full range of Freud's genius.

HISTORICAL ROOTS

Freud's historical roots are as varied as his cultural influences. He shares with William James a broad background in the arts and sciences. But these two psychologists differed not only in their national origin but also in their professional affiliation. James was basically a philosopher, aware of psychological evidence, but nevertheless freed from the daily responsibilities of coping with experimental data or clinical evidence. Freud, in contrast, was a physician, initially a neurologist, who was confronted with the daily task of interpreting clinical symptoms of mentally ill patients. His efforts to deal with this task were shaped by his clinical experience with hysteria and hypnosis which, in turn, encouraged him to

FIGURE 8.1 Sigmund Freud

National Library of Medicine

emphasize the importance of unconscious processes in mental illness. In addition, the *Zeitgeist* of Vienna predisposed Freud to recognize the importance of human sexuality and to be influenced by the psychological insights of the philosopher, Friedrich Nietzsche.

Hypnosis, Hysteria, and the Unconscious

Psychoanalysis was a direct outgrowth of the confluence of hypnosis, hysteria, and the unconscious. Each gained in importance as their relationship to the other two was clarified.

Hypnosis has had a checkered career. Although the term *hypnosis* was invented in the nineteenth century, the phenomenon of hypersuggestibility which occurs in a hypnotic trance began to achieve notoriety in 1775 during the trial of a popular country priest, Johann Gassner (1727–1779), who practiced exorcism, a ritual act of driving demons from a person's body. Gassner selected for exorcism persons with symptoms such as pains, convulsions, and paralysis that could be shifted from one part of the body to another. By today's standards Gassner's ability to transfer the symptoms would indicate a hysterical disorder. Having demonstrated his control of the symptoms, Gassner would force the demons to leave the body by command and thus relieve the symptoms. Although the Church accepted the controversial practice of exorcism because of its biblical roots, the desire to control its practice led to an investigation of Father Gassner.

One of the witnesses who testified was a flamboyant Viennese trained physician, Franz Mesmer (1733–1815), who in his doctoral thesis had postulated that planets affect the health of people by influencing the gravitational force within their bodies. After he started medical practice, he forgot this idea for a while, but an acquaintance with a Jesuit priest with the unlikely name of Father Hell revived Mesmer's interest in a gravitational bodily force. Father Hell's hobby was studying magnets, which encouraged Mesmer to employ them in the treatment of a twenty-seven-year-old woman with a mystifying pattern of symptoms that resisted conventional treatment. Encouraged by Father Hell, Mesmer applied magnets to the patient's body. Lo and behold, the patient entered what Mesmer described as a crisis state, twitching, trembling, and experiencing pain at each site of her symptoms. The crisis state gradually subsided and the patient's condition improved. Repetition of the magnetic treatment produced successive crises and improvements until finally the symptoms all disappeared.

Mesmer tried the magnetic treatment on other patients, *always informing them beforehand* that they would suffer a crisis state that would lead to the disappearance of their symptoms. In search for an explanation of the success of his new cure Mesmer simply substituted a magnetic field for his previous conception of a gravitational force; within every person's body was a magnetic field force which could become misaligned and produce symptoms at the locus of the misalignment. The application of magnets helped realign the magnetic field and thus restore the health of the patient.

Mesmer accidentally discovered that passing his hands near the site of the symptoms produced results similar to those obtained with magnets. This discovery convinced him that his own body was magnetized! His explanation of Gassner's success was that Gassner was a highly magnetized person like himself. The commission was thus persuaded that Gassner was not truly practicing exorcism and therefore should desist from such treatment. Gassner was exiled to a country parish, soon to be forgotten, in contrast to Mesmer who was on his way to international fame.

In 1777, Mesmer fled to Paris after being accused by his medical colleagues in Vienna of fraudulent practice. The move benefitted his career because, a decade before the French Revolution, Paris was ripe for Mesmer's dramatic ideas and lavish style. His concept of *animal magnetism* became so popular that he soon had so many patients he instituted group treatment. The groups met in a dimly lit room, through which soft music wafted. At the appropriate moment, Mesmer, wearing a flowing robe, would make a dramatic entry. One at a time, he would point to individual patients and tell them to grasp a specific iron rod projecting from a tub filled with iron filings. Those patients who showed signs of entering a crisis state were carried by Mesmer and his assistants to an adjacent room to receive individual treatment. Most of the patients reported an alleviation of their symptoms and, consequently, the popularity of what became known as mesmerism increased.

Commercial success was not enough for Mesmer; he also wanted professional recognition. This desire ultimately led to his undoing. His powerful aristocratic friends and clients persuaded the King of France to appoint a special commission to investigate Mesmer's scientific claims. Among the commissioners were Benjamin Franklin (1706–1790), the American Ambassador to France, and Antoine Lavoisier (1743–1794), the founder of modern chemistry. This commission unanimously concluded that the evidence failed to support the existence of animal magnetism and suggested that the curative power of Mesmer's treatment was probably due to the patients' imaginations. The Parisian medical society was elated. Antagonized by Mesmer's flamboyance, they forced him to leave Paris. He emigrated to Switzerland where he became a semirecluse, quietly practicing medicine for the remainder of his life.

In spite of this setback, mesmerism persisted and ultimately evolved into the scientific study of hypnosis, partly through the efforts of a nobleman, Amand-Marie Jacques de Chastent, the Marquis de Puységur (1751–1825). One day Puységur mesmerized a male servant who unexpectedly entered a sleeplike state instead of the usual crisis state. Although apparently asleep, the young man responded to commands to move parts of his body. When awake, he recalled nothing about events during the trance state but did recall them later when the trance state was reinduced.

Puységur decided to induce this sleeplike state in his patients, a method which became known as *artificial somnambulism* because of its resemblance to ordinary somnambulism in which walking, talking, and other acts are performed while a person is asleep. Puységur recognized that the dominant factor in artificial somnambulism is the person's degree of suggestibility; the more suggestible a patient is, the more likely the person will comply with the instructions (e.g., become insensitive to a pinprick). Puységur also discovered what is currently known as the posthypnotic suggestion—the execution, during the wakeful state, of a command previously given during the trance state. The significance of this phenomenon is that the posthypnotic suggestion (e.g., pulling the ear lobe in reaction to a light being turned on) is performed without the person knowing the cause of the action.

The attitude of the scientific establishment toward the phenomena of mesmerism and artificial somnambulism improved as a consequence of the efforts of a highly respected Scottish physician, James Braid (1795–1860). Braid, who was suspicious of mesmerism, carefully examined a subject of a stage mesmerist and concluded that the trance state was real and deserved rigorous scientific inspection. His own research, published in a prestigious medical journal, conferred a badge of scientific respectability on the phenomenon. This respectability was further enhanced when Braid discarded the term *mesmerism* and replaced it with the scientific name *neuro-hypnology* (nervous sleep), which over the years was transformed into *hypnotism*. Braid supported Puységur's claim that the important factor in hypnosis is the susceptibility of the patient, not the power of the hypnotist (magnetizer), as Mesmer had argued.

A French country doctor, August Liébeault (1823–1904), who practiced in a village near Nancy, incorporated hypnotic techniques into his medical procedures. He induced hypnosis by instructing a patient to attend to feelings in the eyelids while repeatedly suggesting that the patient was getting tired and falling asleep. While the patient was in a trance, Liébeault would tell him that his symptoms would disappear (posthypnotic suggestion). This procedure was successful enough to attract the attention of many young physicians who formed what became known as the *Nancy school*. One member of this group, Hippolyte Bernheim (1840–1919), a professor of internal medicine, was sufficiently impressed with Liébeault's therapy to conduct clinical research on hundreds of patients. Bernheim discovered that, with skillful questioning, a person in the waking state could recall events in the trance state, a finding that conflicted with Puységur's conclusion that the normal and hypnotic states were completely dissociated. Bernheim became so impressed with the powers of suggestion that he began to use persuasion in the awake state for some patients instead of posthypnotic suggestions. By convincing patients that they could be cured, Bernheim concluded, they would be cured.

At the time that Bernheim was investigating hypnosis, a leading neurologist, Jean Charcot, who had influenced William James (Chapter 4), observed that hysterical patients would frequently imitate the convulsive behavior of epileptics with whom they shared a hospital ward. This suggested to Charcot the idea for a dramatic clinical demonstration that eventually became notorious. He would produce, on demand, a hysterical patient who went into convulsions at a prearranged signal (e.g., tap on the shoulder) because of a previous posthypnotic suggestion. Charcot concluded that the ability to be hypnotized is a symptom of hysteria, and that hysteria is a product of a hereditary disorder of the central nervous system. This interpretation set the stage for a controversy between the Nancy school, which argued that all persons can in principle be hypnotized and Charcot, who maintained that only persons with a hereditary degenerative disease of the nervous system could be hypnotized. The controversy, ultimately decided in favor of the Nancy school, focused attention on the intimate psychological relationship between hypnosis and hysteria.

One of Charcot's students, Pierre Janet (1859–1947), formulated a theory that shared similarities with psychoanalysis. Janet's ideas were triggered by a patient who exhibited different personality characteristics at different levels of the hypnotic trance. This patient's behavior suggested to Janet that certain desires and memories could become dissociated from the rest of mental life. He labeled these dissociated mental events *subconscious fixed ideas,* and argued that they could cause hysterical symptoms. Janet's treatment for these hysterics was psychological analysis; the subconscious ideas responsible for the hysterical symptoms would be revealed and presumably the symptoms would then disappear.

Other Views of the Unconscious. The concept of the unconscious, or what Janet referred to as the subconscious, has origins that are unrelated to either hypnosis or hysteria. Arthur Schopenhauer (1786–1860), a philospher who emphasized the darker side of life, rejected the popular notion that a rationally governed will controls human action. Schopenhauer argued that the rational intellect is not the will's master, but only its servant. The will is controlled by unconscious, irrational forces without plan or purpose. The intellect only rationalizes human behavior without understanding its unconscious origins.

You may recall that Johann Friedrich Herbart postulated the existence of an unconscious, a region of the mind in which mental events are inaccessible to recall (Chapter 2). He also speculated that mental events could function as forces; ideas could be pushed into, or released from, the unconscious.

Gustav Fechner, whom Freud greatly admired, estimated from his experimental analysis of the mind-body problem that some sensory experiences had negative values; they fell below the sensory threshold, suggesting an unconscious status. Negative values were not only a consequence of intensity of the stimulus but also of whether the observer is awake or asleep. Fechner offered a metaphor to describe a plus or minus value of a particular mental activity: *The mental event could be displayed on different theater stages.* This notion suggested to Freud a topographical conception of a mind composed of different regions.

Hermann von Helmholtz was the giant of nineteenth century science. He made basic contributions to physics, physiology, mathematics, and psychology. Temperamentally he was a physicist and his philosphy of science encouraged rigorous theoretical formulations. This goal did not prevent him from postulating unconscious processes in his explanation of perceptual phenomena such as depth perception. For example, when throwing a ball you essentially compute your distance from the target from a variety of cues (e.g., size of the target). This computation, according to Helmholtz, is not accomplished by rational conscious processes; it is an *unconscious inference,* the product of the unconscious learning of depth perception cues. Psychologists who investigated thought processes also concluded that unconscious mental processes operate in solving intellectual tasks.

Finally, reference to the German philosopher Eduard von Hartmann (1842–1906) completes the brief account of pre-Freudian notions of the unconscious. While in his twenties, Hartmann wrote *The Philosophy of the Unconscious* (1878/1931), which achieved such popularity that it went through eleven editions. Essentially Hartmann postulated unconscious mental forces, blind impulses of the will, that were constantly in conflict with the conscious forces of reason, a conception that anticipates the Freudian view.

The Importance of Sexuality

Freud was not, as is sometimes thought, the revolutionary innovator of the view that sex is of prime psychological importance. Numerous cultures, from the Greeks on, acknowledged the importance of sex and its intimate relationship with mental illness. Aristotle believed that the enthusiasm achieved by the participants in highly emotional rituals was essentially "a state of temporary madness related to sexuality" (Freedman, Kaplan, & Sadock, 1972). Phillippus Aureolus Paracelsus (1493–1541) postulated that hysteria and other disorders could have sexual origins. Before Freud advanced his ideas on sexuality, Richard von Krafft-Ebing (1840–1902), an Austrian psychiatrist, published an enormously popular book, *Psychopathia Sexualis* (1886), that contained a large number of case histories of patients who exhibited unusual sexual behavior. Although Krafft-Ebing emphasized the importance of constitutional factors in sexual deviation, other investigators soon challenged this position with numerous articles and case histories that sought to demonstrate the importance of early sexual experiences on later aberrant sexual behavior. A popular hypothesis, advanced at this time, was that sexual pathology resulted from unconscious forces that had their origins in childhood experiences (Ellenberger, 1970).

The influence of sexuality was not limited to the pathological. Instead, sexuality was widely thought to be a central component of human existence influencing all aspects of living, from personality development to concepts of beauty. The belief that the Vienna of Freud's time adhered to the Victorian idea that sex was an unimportant factor in human life fails to square with the facts. Popular books on sex were published and sold openly. A new science of sexology was developing. Hypotheses were offered that sexual feelings were experienced by children and parents toward each other. In sum, Freud did not have to be a wild revolutionary to argue that sex was a basic motive in human psychology and a possible source of maladjustment. But he did require considerable strength of character to resist the social criticism directed at his presumed exaggeration of the importance of sex.

Friedrich Nietzsche

Freud frankly admitted that in his desire to maintain an intellectual independence, he avoided reading Friedrich Nietzsche (1844–1900), the great German philosopher. According to Freud, Nietzsche's "guesses and intuitions often agree in the most astonishing way with laborious findings of psychoanalysis" (quoted in Ellenberger, 1970).

Friederich Nietzsche's ideas permeated German and Austrian culture when Freud was a young man; they appeared with such frequency in newspapers, magazines, and journals that it was impossible to avoid them and their implications for psychology and social philosophy.

Nietzsche anticipated six important Freudian notions:

1. *Psychic energy operates in a manner analogous to physical energy.* According to the principle of conservation of energy, physical energy can be changed in form, but it can neither be created nor destroyed. In a similar fashion, Nietzsche postulated that the mind is endowed with a certain amount of psychic energy that activates drives and instincts. Psychic energy can be transformed into action in a variety of ways. For example, it can be dammed up and subsequently released in explosive force, it can be voluntarily stored to be used later, or it can be transferred from one motive to another. The idea of psychic energy was incorporated into Freudian psychology with the concept of *libido,* a predetermined amount of psychic energy each person is born with and which is directed toward the attainment of pleasure.

2. *Humans are driven by unconscious motives.* Because humans are presumably rational animals, they need to explain their behavior to themselves and others. But they are driven by motives about which they are unaware. Consequently, they are forced to deceive themselves and others when justifying their own behavior. As an example, Nietzsche warns, "Distrust all in whom the impulse to punish is powerful" (Nietzsche, 1878/1984). Why? Because they are incapable of identifying their true motive: "To see another suffer is pleasant; to make another suffer is still more pleasant." (Nietzsche, 1886/1955).

3. *Disturbing memories are forced out of consciousness.* Nietzsche anticipated Freud's basic concept of repression, a mechanism that protects a person's ego from anxiety by forcing unpleasant memories into the unconscious. Nietzsche exemplified the process in the following way: "'I did this,' says my memory. 'I cannot have done this,' says my pride, remaining inexorable. Eventually my memory yields" (Nietzsche, 1886/1955).

4. *Dreams are psychologically significant.* Dreams are not accidental events but are an expression of unconscious processes. The disorder and obscurity in dreams reflect the turmoil in the unconscious. Implied in Nietzsche's view is the potential dreams have for revealing what goes on in the unconscious, an assumption that was adopted by psychoanalysis.

5. *Sexual and aggressive instincts can be redirected to socially accepted ends.* Nietzsche (Ellenberger, 1970) argued that "Good actions are sublimated evil ones," meaning that the energy of socially inhibited drives can be diverted into socially esteemed channels such as art and literature. Freud assigned the term *sublimation* to refer to this psychological mechanism.

6. *Understanding and resolving conflicts between conventional morality and animalistic urges is therapeutic.* One of Nietzsche's core ideas was that of the *Superman,* the highest level of human development. By Superman, Nietzsche definitely did not mean those qualities of physical power and unselfish nobility of the comic strip character of the same name. Nor did he mean by Superman what the Nazis erroneously interpreted him to mean—the superiority of the "pure" Aryan race over members of other racial groups. Actually, Nietzsche was neither anti-Semitic nor pro-German. In fact, he rejected German culture, saying that "wherever Germany extends her sway, she ruins culture." What Nietzsche meant is that man has to conquer the debilitating conflict between his false social morality and his deep-seated animalistic aggressive urges. If the conflict is conquered, man can then establish his own scale of values and abide by them. "This man, the superman, is now strong, even hard, but kind to the weak, and follows the highest possible moral rule" (Ellenberger, 1970).

Nietzsche was suggesting, with his concept of the Superman, the essence of Freudian psychoanalytic treatment: make the unconscious conscious and then creatively resolve the conflict between the demands of society and a person's animalistic urges.

PSYCHOANALYSIS

In a certain sense, knowledge about a scientist's life is irrelevant to the task of understanding and evaluating his or her theory. The scientific theories of Darwin, Newton, and Einstein would be interpreted and judged the same way regardless of their background and personalities. But Freud's life has a special relevance to his theory. Disputes have arisen about the methodological assumptions that guided Freud's efforts as well as the meaning of some of his hypotheses. Biographical evidence helps to clarify these issues. In addition, Freud was a psychological determinist who believed that everything a person does, including formulating a theory of personality, is a function of his background. This orientation encourages an interest in the question of how Freud's life influenced his theory of psychoanalysis.

Sigmund Freud (1856–1939)

Sigmund Freud, originally named Sigismund, was born in 1856 in Freiburg, Moravia (now Pribor, Czeckoslovakia) within the Austria-Hungary empire. When he was four, his family moved to Vienna where he lived the remainder of his life, except for the final fifteen months spent in London.

Sigmund Freud was a Jew, and it has been suggested that his Jewish heritage played *the major* role in the development of his psychological theory (Bakan, 1958). Others have argued that the significant influence on Freud was Germanic culture transmitted through the intellectual life of Vienna (Wittels, 1924). A more reasonable position would be that both shaped the development of psychoanalysis.

Jakob Freud, Sigmund's father, is an enigmatic figure because of lack of hard evidence about his background and religious commitments. An adolescent experience which he related to Sigmund suggests that he encountered anti-Semitism. He had been forced off the road by a Christian youth who threw Jakob's hat into the mud and ordered, "Jew, get off the sidewalk." Sigmund, who was then eleven, was shocked and angry to learn that his father meekly recovered his hat and refused to fight back. Sigmund Freud was never meek when anti-Semitic attitudes and actions, real or imagined, were directed at him.

Jakob Freud came from Galicia, a region in southeastern Europe that contained a sizable Jewish minority. He conducted his business as a wool merchant in a town where Jews could not settle on a permanent basis, but could obtain successive residency permits for six-month periods. A few years before the birth of Sigmund, a liberal policy toward Jews began which ultimately led to the Emancipation of Jews in 1867 that officially granted them equal political rights. In the absence of marked anti-Semitism, many Jews became successful in science, the arts, law, and business.

Before the emancipation, most Jewish families maintained their ethnic traditions, lived within the Jewish community, and spoke Yiddish, a German dialect interspersed with Hebrew words. Emancipation created a conflict between isolated Jewish communal life and the Viennese lifestyle. The common view is that Jakob Freud achieved a reasonable compromise by assimilating Viennese social values without rejecting his Jewish identity. One minority view (Bakan, 1958) is that Jakob Freud was a closet Hassid who was committed to the mystical tradition of the Kabbala. The basic premise of the Kabbala is that the full meaning of the scriptures is not contained in its literal statements. Profound religious intuitions can be gained by decoding biblical texts with secret and mystical letter and number codes, thus revealing their deep, hidden meanings. In essence, Kabbala assumes that appearance is not reality; the deep meaning of the scriptures must be excavated by methods that penetrate below its surface meaning. Bakan argues that this method was adopted by Freudian psychoanalysis; outward behavior can only be explained by revealing its inner unconscious causes.

Sigmund Freud's mother, Amalia Nathanson, also from Galicia, was nineteen when she became the second wife of Jakob Freud. Two of Jakob's sons from his first marriage were approximately the same age as Amalia. Sigmund was the firstborn of eight children Amalia had with Jakob within the space of ten years. She was known to be an attractive woman, an authoritarian personality, and a great admirer of her firstborn.

It is unclear whether Sigmund Freud grew up in a secure middle class household or one that suffered from repeated economic crises. What is clear is that Sigmund was an excellent student which earned him a privileged status in a family that valued scholarship. Freud attended a secondary school with high standards and led his class, in part due to his retentive visual memory and exceptional writing style. Although undecided about the career he would pursue, he became predisposed to biology by an early interest in Darwin's evolutionary theory. This interest was magnified when he listened to a lecture by a distinguished zoologist who quoted from a poem ascribed to Goethe entitled *Nature:* "Nature['s] . . . laws are unchangeable—she has few springs of action but they never wear out; they are always operative, always manifold . . . even the most unnatural things are natural." From early youth, Freud was preoccupied with cultural matters and thought of art and science as being intimately related.

He entered the medical school of the University of Vienna in 1873 and completed his studies eight years later, taking three years more than were required. Because medical students needed to pass only three examinations, they were free to do anything they desired— enroll in any class in or out of medical school, attend or not attend classes, do research, and so forth. This educational format encouraged Freud to satisfy his broad intellectual interests and thus delay his graduation.

His research in zoology and comparative anatomy began during his third year of medical school. He dissected more than 400 eels in an attempt to identify the exact structure of the testes. His interest shifted to neuroanatomy in order to do research in the laboratory of Ernst Brücke (1819–1892), whose views about science Freud adopted. Brücke was a positivist who believed that psychological principles could be reduced to physiological laws which in turn could be explained by principles of physics and chemistry. Freud's first publication reported a neuroanatomical analysis of the spinal cord of fish interpreted within an evolutionary framework.

During his stay in Brücke's laboratory, Freud gained a fatherly friend in a postdoctoral fellow, Dr. Josef Breuer, who told him about his interesting case, Anna O. Anna O. was a young, attractive lady who exhibited a variety of bizarre hysterical symptoms including a strong aversion to drinking water. When placed under hypnosis she recalled an event that apparently precipitated the symptom—as a child she had witnessed a dog she disliked drinking water from a glass. The recollection and its accompanying emotional reaction eliminated the symptom. This kind of treatment became known as the cathartic method; the symptom was relieved by recalling its origin.

In 1879 Freud served in the military for a year. He used this time to translate a book by John Stuart Mill, which argued that all knowledge is based on empirical evidence. He returned to Brücke's laboratory in 1880, passed his first two medical school examinations and his final in 1881, and then became a teaching assistant with a small stipend. Freud suddenly decided to leave Brücke's laboratory, probably because he had fallen in love with and become engaged to Martha Bernays, an attractive and strong-willed young lady from a distinguished Jewish family. In those days marriages were expected to take place only after a man was financially secure. Freud decided that the most promising road to travel was to practice some medical specialization. It was a career that he did not relish, but one that would lead to financial security while providing some opportunity for scientific research and a chance for a scientific discovery that would satisfy his intense yearning for fame.

In order to select a medical specialization, Freud obtained a poorly paid position in the highly prestigious Viennese General Hospital where, after training in various departments, he finally decided to specialize in clinical neurology. During this period, he got involved with studying the effects of cocaine after reading an article extolling its medical benefits. Thinking it harmless, he took it himself and recommended it to others, particularly for fatigue, irritability, and inability to concentrate. He published a paper in 1884 praising cocaine's properties as a stimulant, an aphrodisiac, and a cure for morphine addiction. Freud tried treating a friend with cocaine, who had become addicted to morphine while coping with severe pain. The morphine addiction was eliminated only to be replaced by cocaine addiction. Freud's espousal of cocaine earned him much criticism when its addictive properties became known. He also became annoyed with himself when he overlooked a promising lead that cocaine usage provided. He had mentioned in a casual conversation with colleagues that cocaine usage numbed the tongue. One of the listeners pounced on the idea that cocaine could be used as an anesthetic for eye operations, did the necessary research and clinical application and soon achieved the recognition that Freud would have dearly loved to earn.

Freud passed an examination for *privatdozent* in neuropathology and, after a trial lecture, received an official appointment. More importantly, he was awarded a traveling grant to study with Charcot in Paris, where he was exposed to two important ideas that shaped his future thinking. First, by dramatically demonstrating that nonhysterical patients could be trained under hypnosis to exhibit hysterical symptoms (e.g., paralysis, tremors), Charcot showed that physical symptoms could result from the workings of the mind. Second, Charcot directed Freud to the importance of sex by casually remarking that sexual problems were frequently the root cause of hysteria. Freud had gone to Paris as a practicing neurologist but returned to Vienna with the interests of a psychiatrist.

Building a practice proved difficult, but Freud was helped by his fatherly friend, Josef Breuer, now a highly successful neurologist, who referred to Freud patients suffering from nervous disorders. The publication in 1895 of *Studies in Hysteria*, co-authored by Breuer and Freud, marks the beginning of psychoanalysis. The book contained a chapter on hysteria by Breuer and one on psychotherapy by Freud, in addition to several case histories, including that of Anna O. The basic message of the book was that hysteria is due to psychic trauma in early life and that successful treatment requires the recall of the forgotten traumatic experience. In spite of their shared views, Freud's thinking was beginning to diverge from Breuer's, particularly in regard to the essential role Freud assigned to sex in the etiology of all neuroses, a position that the more timid Breuer was reluctant to adopt, or at least to express publicly. The collaboration between Freud and Breuer ultimately dissolved because of Breuer's failure to follow Freud's leads.

The estrangement from Breuer was followed by the closest professional relationship of Freud's entire life, expressed mainly through an exchange of letters, with William Fliess (1858–1929), an ear, nose, and throat surgeon who resided in Berlin. On the surface, this relationship appears baffling because the strong-minded Freud assumed a dependent relationship to Fliess, who was two years his junior and the author of two bizarre theories. One of these theories was that all humans are bisexual, and behavior is completely governed by the interaction between a female cycle of twenty-eight days and male cycle of twenty-three days. By appropriate arithmetical manipulation of these two numbers it becomes possible, according to this theory, to gain deep insights into a person's psyche. The other conception was that because of a physiological correspondence between the tissue of the female genitalia and the nose mucosa, certain gynecological disturbances could be cured by cauterizing appropriate sections of the nasal passage.

The relationship between Freud and Fliess becomes comprehensible when it is recognized that at the height of their correspondence, Freud was going through a neurotic episode while making giant strides in the development of his psychoanalytic theory. Freud suffered from a cardiac disturbance, shortness of breath, gastrointestinal problems, severe distress from repeated attempts to stop smoking, and an obsession with the date of his death which, according to Fliess's biological numerology, would occur at age sixty-one or sixty-two (he died when he was eighty-three). During this hectic, creative period Fliess functioned as an emotional support and as an intellectual sounding board, both of which Freud needed to bring his ideas to fruition.

An important foundation of psychoanalytic theory was Freud's self-analysis. He believed his own unconscious could be revealed by interpreting his dreams. The belief in the importance of dream interpretation was reinforced by the death of his father in 1886, which generated an emotional reaction far greater than anticipated. An interpretation of a dream led Freud to realize how much his father meant to him, in spite of the resentment he had harbored toward him. On the basis of insights he was gaining from the analyses of patients and of himself, Freud developed a psychosexual theory of personality development. Describing the theory in a letter to Fliess, he said, "I cannot give you an idea of the intellectual beauty of the work" (Ellenberger, 1970).

The publication of *The Interpretation of Dreams* in 1900, generally regarded as his most brilliant book, hypothesized that dreams are heavily disguised forms of infantile wishes and thought processes, the meanings of which can be revealed during psychoanalysis. The publication of this book seemed to coincide with the end of his neurosis, although not the termination of his self-analysis which he continued for the rest of his life. Freud's dependency on Fliess ended at this time with the dissolution of their close friendship, which later was replaced by enmity. Freud now was emancipated from all the relationships in which he was intellectually dependent: with Brücke, Charcot, Breuer, and Fliess. He had reached a point in his career in which he served as the final judge of his own theories.

Freudian theory incurred much criticism as it became better known but, at the same time, a small group of medical men, mostly neurologists, were attracted to his ideas. Freud offered them both an interpretation of the little understood nervous disorders and a method of treatment. Among his early followers were Karl Abraham (1877–1925) of Germany, Carl Jung (1875–1961) of Switzerland, Ernest Jones (1879–1958) of Great Britain, and Alfred Adler (1870–1938) and Otto Rank (1884–1939) of Austria. The first International Congress of Psychoanalysis was held in 1908 and in the following year a journal was published.

G. Stanley Hall who openly described his life as a psychologist as "a series of fads or crazes" (Clark, 1980), invited Freud to participate in a series of lectures on psychology to commemorate the twentieth anniversary of the founding of Clark University in Worcester, Massachusetts. Freud did not prepare his allotted five lectures even though he was aware of their importance to the psychoanalytic movement. Nevertheless, the improvised lectures were brilliant, persuasive and, in general, well received in spite of their radical notions. Upon his return to Vienna, Freud prepared the lectures from memory for publication, which he did with amazing accuracy according to those who had heard the original delivery.

Shortly before World War I, the psychoanalytic movement was rocked by basic disagreements that led to the resignation of some important members. Alfred Adler defected when his views became clearly incompatible with the orthodox Freudian conception. Freud regretted the subsequent defection of Carl Jung more, since Freud had planned that he would assume leadership of the psychoanalytic movement upon his own retirement. Both Adler and Jung rejected the all-important role that Freud assigned to sex and each substituted a different basic motivation—a striving-for-mastery for Adler and a general psychic energy for Jung.

The remainder of Freud's life was spent in promoting and refining his psychoanalytic formulation. In order to satisfy the general interest in his ideas, he wrote such works as *The Psychopathology of Everyday Life* (1901) *Introductory Lectures on Psycho-analysis* (1916–1917), and *New Introductory Lectures on Psycho-analysis* (1933). In spite of the great demands on his time, Freud never stopped treating patients. This was, he maintained, the source of the evidence that served as the foundation of his theories.

In his later writings, Freud became more speculative and more concerned with the social implications of his theory. In *Civilization and Its Discontent* (1930), Freud offers pessimistic answers to questions about the human condition. The best that we can hope for are reasonable compromises between the inevitable and irreconcilable demands that dominate our existence. To make matters worse, these reasonable compromises are beyond the reach of those who inhabit a society that encourages aggression and destruction while denying opportunities for close emotional attachments.

Freud's last years were spent in illness and pain, both of which he bore with stoicism and an unwavering dedication to the cause of psychoanalysis. At sixty-six years of age, Freud discovered a cancer in his mouth, most likely brought on by his lifelong addiction to cigars. His immediate reaction was to express concerns for his own dignified exit from the world and the unfortunate consequence such an event would have on his aged mother. He was subsequently to suffer through more than thirty operations, including a drastic removal of the entire roof of his mouth which was replaced with a metal prosthesis. The prosthesis caused constant pain and interfered with his talking and eating, but not with his cigar smoking. During the sixteen years he spent with this device, which he named "the monster," Freud persisted with his psychoanalytic practice, professional responsibilities, and theoretical efforts.

While the first cause to which Freud was most dedicated—psychoanalysis—was beginning to be widely accepted, his second cause—Jewish ethnicity—was threatened by the rise of Nazism.

Freud was not religious; in fact he thought the belief in God was analogous to a neurotic crutch required by some to adjust to life's problems. Nevertheless, when asked about what was Jewish about him, he responded, "Not very much, but probably the main thing" (Ellenberger, 1970). By this he meant the Jewish intellectual and ethical traditions which dominated his own life and of which he was most proud.

Hitler incorporated Austria into the German Reich in 1938. Freud's life was now threatened; Jewish psychoanalysis was as much of an anathema to Nazi culture as was the Jewish physics of Einstein. Freud's friends persuaded him that he must leave in order to save himself and his immediate family. Through the intervention of the governments of the United States and Great Britain, Freud and his wife and younger daughter, Anna, were permitted to emigrate to London, after a stock of Freud's books were publicly burned and financial blackmail was paid. Freud's attempt to take four younger sisters, now old women, with him failed; they were subsequently murdered in concentration camps.

In the remaining fifteen months of his life, which were spent in London, Freud kept busy with his writing and patients. But the cancer was relentlessly conquering his body and causing him unbearable pain, so much so that his wife wrote that "in the end he suffered terribly, so that even those who would most like to keep him forever had to wish for his release!" (Clark, 1980). He died on September 23, 1939. Obituaries and tributes acknowledged the force of his ideas and their permanent place in Western civilization. He had achieved the fame that he so much desired by offering a dramatic theory of psychology and a mode of treatment which he thought would reduce human suffering. To critics who rejected his theory, he responded simply, "They may abuse my doctrines by day, but I am sure they dream of them by night" (Clark, 1980).

METHODOLOGICAL ASSUMPTIONS

The key to understanding Freudian psychoanalysis is to comprehend the methodological principles that guided its formulation. This is not an easy task because, unlike Wundt, Titchener, and Watson, Freud was not a systematic methodologist who clearly and consistently articulated the methodological foundation upon which he erected his psychological theory. In fact, Freud delivered a mixed message to his audience about his methodological stance, thus creating confusion about the kind of theory he was offering and disagreement as to how it should be judged. So it is important to discover not only Freud's opinions about methodological issues, but also his actual methodological practices.

The Subject Matter of Psychoanalysis

In the tradition of the majority of the psychologists already studied—Wundt, Titchener, James, Angell, Wertheimer—Freud investigated mental life. But Freud's view of mental life appears so startlingly different from those of academic psychologists that their shared interests are frequently overlooked. Academic psychologists were primarily concerned with the nature of conscious experience of which the observer was momentarily aware either in relation to its structural or functional properties. Momentary conscious experience had interest for Freud primarily in the relation it bore to the unconscious. Although some academic psychologists, particularly those interested in thinking (e.g., Külpe with his research on imageless thought), realized that a full understanding of mental functioning could not be gleaned only from observations of consciousness, they nevertheless failed to face up to the task of describing the organization of the mind, particularly the relationship between conscious and unconscious processes. Freud, in contrast, offered a specific description of the organization of the mind. He likened a mind to an iceberg, the great bulk of which is concealed. The mind consists of three compartments: the conscious, preconscious, and unconscious. The conscious is analogous to the small part of the iceberg above water, the preconscious is like the segment of the iceberg that rises above and falls below the waterline with the sea's motion, and the unconscious is the large mass hidden below the waterline. The conscious content of the mind is what the person is momentarily aware of. The preconscious contains those mental events that are not in a person's consciousness at the moment but which can be retrieved without difficulty (e.g., what did you do last Saturday night?). The unconscious portion of the mind contains mental events of which the person is unaware and which can influence behavior.

Methods of Investigation

Freud was an empiricist by training and conviction; observations were basic to all scientific knowledge. As a research biologist he sought to identify physiological structures within the endocrine and nervous systems of lower animals. As a clinical neurologist he observed patients' reactions in order to understand the structure and functioning of their nervous systems. As a psychotherapist, Freud observed his patients' reactions in order to gain insights into their unconscious mental processes. Initially, this was accomplished by hypnotizing the patient to retrieve forgotten memories. Later on, other techniques were developed to serve the same purpose.

Freud believed that all of the methods he employed, as a research physiologist, clinical neurologist, and medical psychologist, were essentially similar in that they were all based on systematically observing empirical events and interpreting them. Fundamental to his point of view was the assumption that laboratory and clinical observations are not qualitatively different. They both provide empirical evidence that could serve as the foundation of a scientific theory.

In addition to his empirical orientation, Freud assumed that the content of the mind could be examined directly and accurately, a methodological position that places him alongside Wundt, Titchener, James, and the Gestalt psychologists. But Freud diverged sharply from their positions in regards to both the technique of self-observation and mental events to be observed. Academic psychologists, who thought of their discipline as a mental science, considered their major task to be the observation of consciousness but disagreed about the appropriate method, trained introspection or naive phenomenology. Freud's orientation was entirely different; the observation of the unconscious, not the conscious, was the major task of psychology. For this effort a new method of self-observation was required, a method that was capable of penetrating the veil that surrounds the unconscious.

Criterion of Truth

One of the most controversial problems in judging psychoanalysis revolves about the issue of selecting a relevant criterion of truth. This controversy still rages because Freud and his followers failed to come to grips with this fundamental methodological issue. As a consequence the historian is left with the task of selecting a criterion of truth appropriate for psychoanalysis.

In terms of his training and apparent convictions, Freud was a positivist. This orientation, which equates truth with the outcome of natural science methodology, was the philosophical view of Brücke, whose laboratory attracted Freud during the early stages of his career. Throughout his life, Freud chose to think of psychoanalysis as a natural science, a science that ultimately would be reduced to biochemical principles. Freud expressed this attitude in his prediction that psychoanalytic therapy would finally be replaced by biochemical treatment. Since Freud offered psychoanalytic theory as a natural science, it should be judged by its ability to generate deductions in agreement with empirical evidence.

The conception of psychoanalysis as a natural science has been refuted by those who argue that Freud's actions belie his professed positivism. Freud, the argument goes, failed to support his theory by objective empirical evidence. Instead, he offered a coherent interpretation of personality that many found intuitively compelling, in spite of a lack of empirical support. Other intuitively compelling interpretations, however, are possible as demonstrated by the acceptance of competing psychoanalytic interpretations offered by Adler, Jung, and others. Psychoanalysts have yet to offer empirical procedures that can objectively resolve the theoretical differences among these competing theories. As a consequence, the suggestion has been offered by many, including psychoanalysts, that psychoanalytic formulations are more appropriately evaluated within the framework of human science than of natural science. That is, psychoanalysis should not be judged by its capacity to logically interpret the objective facts of personality development but, instead, should be evaluated by its ability to offer an interpretation of personality that is intuitively valid, a criterion that is obviously subjective.

This controversy about the selection of a natural science or human science framework to judge the truth value of psychoanalysis raises the problem of identifying the guidelines that Freud himself was employing when he formulated his theory. Although arguments have been advanced to suggest that he was either operating within a natural science or human science framework, a third alternative has tended to be overlooked. Perhaps Freud's broad cultural preoccupations, which became stronger as he grew older, blunted the distinction between the truth requirements of these two methodological frameworks to such an extent that he himself failed to distinguish between the demands of each orientation, thus complicating the task of judging psychoanalysis.

STRATEGY

Freud's conception of the mind and clinical responsibilities forced him to devise a research strategy that differed markedly from those of traditional academic psychologists. He was confronted with three related tasks: First, a method had to be developed to observe unconscious events and processes. Second, the unconscious bases of psychological disorders had to be discovered. Third, a theory of normal personality development had to be formulated in order to fully understand the etiology of mental illness; as Freud explained, "A satisfactory general theory of [psychological] disturbances is impossible if it cannot be brought into association with clear assumptions about normal mental processes" (Freud, 1893–1895).

Another feature of Freud's strategy sets him apart from most academic psychologists except for Wundt. Freud believed that the forces that shaped personality development cannot be duplicated in the laboratory, a position analogous to Wundt's view that social psychology cannot be an experimental science. Both Freud and Wundt shared the view that personality and ethnic (social) psychology must be investigated from a historical perspective. Essentially their methodology parallels that employed in archaeology; the past is reconstructed from available historical evidence. For example, the culture of the Incas has been inferred from their relics, monuments, and other artifacts that have been recovered. Freud's specific strategy was to reconstruct the past life of a patient by retrieving historical evidence from the patient's unconscious.

PSYCHOANALYTIC THEORY

Theories are designed to interpret data. Understanding psychoanalytic theory requires understanding both the techniques employed to obtain evidence and the nature of the evidence.

Clinical Techniques

When Freud began his clinical practice, the most effective technique available for treating hysterics was to remove symptoms by posthypnotic suggestions. Because the symptoms often reappeared or new ones took their place, a better treatment was sought. The case of Anna O. not only suggested a superior therapy to Freud but, of even greater importance, offered an insight into the origins of psychological disorders. The essence of Breuer's cathartic method was that recalling the unpleasant memory that precipitated the hysterical symptom under hypnosis would help eliminate the symptom. Two fundamental psychoanalytic principles were suggested by the case of Anna O.: (1) Symptoms of mental illnesses have their origins in early unpleasant experiences which are forced into the unconscious, and (2) Retrieval of unpleasant memories, along with their accompanying emotionality, is therapeutic.

Freud soon sensed that the cathartic method suffered from four limitations. First, the cathartic method ignored the resistance of the patient to explore unconscious memories and to fully accept them when recalled. Although their symptoms were unpleasant, the patient acted as if the identification of their causes would be even more unpleasant. Second, the cathartic method ignored the patient-therapist relationship, the importance of which was dramatically suggested by the case of Anna O. Anna's treatment was terminated because of an attack of jealousy by Breuer's wife, who had become suspicious of the amount of time her husband was spending with Anna. Breuer decided to stop the treatment in order to preserve his marriage. After informing Anna of his decision, she exhibited symptoms of "phantom birth" within a few hours, in which she was delivering Breuer's child. This surprising turn of events frightened Breuer so much that he turned the case over to a colleague and left town with his wife. When a female patient threw her arms around Freud, he, unlike Breuer, did not feel threatened by the emotional outburst. Instead, he sought to understand the psychological basis of the patient's affection instead of simply attributing it to his own irresistible attraction. He finally concluded that the patient was transferring feelings to the therapist from a person such as her father, with whom she had a strong emotional relationship. Later, Freud was to recognize the mechanism of *transference* as an essential component of successful psychotherapy. The third limitation of the cathartic method was that it was not as successful as Breuer believed. Anna O. required much psychiatric treatment after having been treated by Breuer. Fourth, and finally, the cathartic method employed hypnosis to excavate unconscious memories. Some patients could not be hypnotized either because of their resistance to succumbing to the trance state or because of Freud's ineffectiveness as a hypnotist. Whatever the reason, Freud decided that a psychotherapeutic method that could be used with all patients was required.

Freud's recollection of a technique employed by Bernheim at the Nancy Clinic led to the free association method that replaced hypnosis as the psychoanalytic tool to penetrate the unconscious. Unable to get a patient to recall events occurring during a hypnotic trance, Bernheim insisted she would remember everything when he placed his hand on her head. To Freud's surprise, she did!

Freud adapted Bernheim's method of retrieving unconscious memories with the procedure that became known as the *pressure technique:*

> I decided to start from the assumption that my patients knew everything that was of any pathogenic significance and that it was only a question of obliging them to communicate it. Thus, when I reached a point at which, after asking a patient some questions such as: 'How long have you had this symptom?' or: 'What was its origin?' I was met with the answer: 'I really don't know', I proceeded as follows. I placed my hand on the patient's forehead or took her head between my hands and said, 'You will think of it under the pressure of my hand. At the moment at which I relax my pressure, you will see something in front of you or something will come into your head. Catch hold of it. It will be what we are looking for—well, what have you seen or what has occurred to you?' (Freud, 1893–1895, p. 110).

Although the pressure technique seemed to work for some patients, others could recall nothing or responded with apparently irrelevant remarks. When Freud tried to redirect the inappropriate comments of one patient, she criticized him for interrupting her thoughts. Freud recognized the possibility that an uninhibited and uninterrupted stream of thought—the free association method—might produce material that would ultimately yield memories responsible for the psychological disorder.

The effectiveness of the free association method was further enhanced when it was applied to dream interpretation, which Freud believed to be the "royal road to a knowledge of the unconscious activities of the mind." A prolific dreamer, Freud became convinced that essential clues to his own psychological development occurred in his own dreams.

Clinical Evidence

While developing clinical techniques designed to reveal unconscious content, Freud stumbled on startling evidence that confirmed his suspicion that sexual difficulties were responsible for neurotic conditions. A majority of Freud's patients reported that as children they had been sexually abused by a grown person. The seducer of a female patient "was almost always" her father, while the culprit for a boy was mainly a nursemaid, servant, governess, or teacher.

The evidence of childhood seduction encouraged Freud to distinguish between two kinds of neuroses, *actual neuroses* initiated by current sexual problems (e.g., excessive masturbation, anxiety due to frustrated sexual desires) and *psychoneuroses* resulting from childhood seduction. After Freud presented a paper to the Society of Psychiatry and Neurology in Vienna which described both his clinical procedures for constructing a patient's past and his seduction theory of psychoneuroses, Krafft-Ebing, the organization's president said that, "It sounds like a scientific fairy tale."

Several years later, Freud was forced to agree with Krafft-Ebing's verdict. He concluded that the remembered scenes of seduction never happened. They were fantasies. The seduction theory for Freud proved not to be a gross error, but, instead, a wrong step in the right direction. Instead of dismissing the seduction theory out of hand, Freud asked the question as to why such seduction fantasies were so prevalent. The answer was that instead of adults having sexual desires for children, children had sexual desires for adults.[1]

Psychosexual Theory of Development

After recognizing the sexual motivation of children, the next task for Freud was to understand its impact on personality development. To account for his clinical evidence, Freud offered a theory of psychosexual development which, in combination with his topographical conception of the mind and theory of the structure of personality, provides the essence of psychoanalysis.

Personality, according to Freud, is made up of three major systems: *id, ego,* and *superego.* The id is entirely unconscious, while the ego and superego during adulthood have both conscious and unconscious components. Essentially the id consists of animal (biological) drives, whereas the superego is the monitor of conduct that is guided by moral principles. The ego, guided by reason and profiting from experience, functions as the executor of personality that seeks a reasonable compromise between the conflicting forces of the id and superego.

---

[1]Recently, Freud's abandonment of the seduction theory in favor of the fantasy hypothesis has been judged to be unwarranted (Masson, 1984). The resulting controversy has generated much discussion and even more heat because the issues have extended beyond the realm of psychology and science into questions about personal honesty (Malcolm, 1984). With increased attention being directed toward child sexual abuse, some psychoanalysts are reexamining the seduction theory (Efron, 1985). The important historical point, however, is that the fantasy hypothesis is a core assumption in Freudian theory and that abandoning it would completely change Freudian psychoanalysis.

Freud assumed that everybody is born with a predetermined amount of mental energy, the *libido*, that drives a person to seek pleasure, especially erotic pleasure. Psychosexual development occurs as a succession of stages, each characterized by a dominant mode of achieving libidinal gratification.

The first stage of psychosexual development is the *oral erotic*, especially characteristic of the first year of life. During this period, the individual is bent upon securing libidinal satisfaction through sucking, nursing, and other oral activities. The *anal erotic* is the next stage, which lasts until two or three years of age. The eliminative functions become the main focus of the child's libidinal activities, and pleasure is achieved from the expulsion and retention of waste products. Next comes the *phallic stage*, which lasts until about five. During this stage, the child discovers the pleasure-giving qualities of the sexual organs by indulging in self-stimulating play.

Up to and including the early portions of the phallic stage, the child's libido is directed inwards, that is, the pleasures are autoerotic. At the end of the phallic stage, an important change takes place; the libido is directed to external love objects. Freud hypothesized that the libido of the male child is first pointed toward the mother, resulting in what he called the *Oedipus complex*, named after the young man in the Greek myth who unknowingly slew his father and married his mother. According to Freud, the son's incestuous desires are totally unconscious. Although they guide his behavior, he is unaware of them. As the desire becomes stronger, the boy unconsciously competes with his father for the affection of the mother and becomes hostile toward his competitor. This brings on another complex—the *castration complex*—in which the boy fears that his father will retaliate by injuring him, particularly by harming his genitals. This imagined threat helps the boy resolve his Oedipus complex; because of his fear of being harmed by his father, who is physically more powerful, the child renounces his libidinal desire for his mother and escapes the castration threat. At the same time the boy *identifies* with his father, whose pleasures and accomplishments he now regards as his own, thus indirectly satisfying his libidinal desires for his mother.

The personality development of a girl follows a similar course. She, too, develops an Oedipus complex (sometimes called an *Electra complex*). Her hostility is directed toward the mother because she is being perceived responsible for the little girl's "inferior" sex organ. *Penis envy* encourages the little girl to develop libidinal desires toward the father in order to compensate for her missing penis. Fear of the mother's disapproval as well as the failure of the father to satisfy the little girl's desire encourages the girl to gradually identify with her mother and *sublimate* (make socially acceptable) her feelings toward her father.

Following the Oedipal period, the child, about five years of age, enters the *latency period*, a stage during which the sexual drive remains in a quiescent state. Then, with puberty, the *genital stage* begins. Libidinal urges intensify as a consequence of the increased activity of the genital glands. If the Oedipus complex has been satisfactorily resolved, libidinal energy is transferred to a person of the opposite sex outside the family and the individual proceeds to a mature heterosexual adjustment.

One of the major consequences of psychosexual development is the change that occurs in the structure of personality. At birth the id completely dominates the infant's mental life. The id operates according to the principle of *primary process;* an automatic and irrational kind of mental activity that is designed to achieve immediate drive satisfaction. Having no capacity to delay or control its overwhelming biological urges, the infant is incapable of coping with the inevitable frustrations of living. To adjust to these frustrations a personality agent is needed to compromise the insistent needs of the id and the demands of physical and social reality. The ego that grows out of the id at the time when the infant learns to differentiate its own body from the rest of the world serves this need. The ego gains strength through the experience of controlling the id during the time that the child is weaned and toilet trained. The effectiveness of the ego is also enhanced when the child becomes capable of the *secondary process* mode of mental activity. In contrast to the automatic, irrational quality of the primary process, secondary process mental activity is capable of rational thought and prudent judgment. The ego continues to grow stronger as the child successfully passes through the successive stages of psychosexual development.

The ego has both a conscious and unconscious component. The conscious ego controls the child's perception of the world and bodily activity, so that the individual can practically and effectively satisfy motivational needs. The unconscious ego serves the individual by acting as a censor to prevent anxiety-inducing thoughts from entering consciousness.

In the task of controlling the id's passions, the ego has the assistance of the superego. Freud assumed that the infant inherits an unconscious sense of morality, albeit a weak one. In addition, conscious moral principles are acquired from experience; one important event being the child's identification with the parent of the same sex that not only resolves the Oedipus complex but also provides the child with that parent's moral code.

The alliance between the superego and the ego does not always run smoothly; the ego must curb the superego as well as the id. If the psychological development of an individual progresses through its normal course, the ego becomes sufficiently strong to reconcile the demands of the conflicting id and superego. If, however, the id dominates, the individual has difficulty in conforming to the demands of society because of the ego's inability to check and inhibit the id's antisocial impulses. If the superego becomes hypermoral, too strong for the ego to control, the individual becomes too fearful to satisfy pleasure-giving urges.

Psychoanalytic Therapy

Psychoanalytic theory of personality development has two direct implications for personality disorders. It suggests the cause of the disorder: the failure to progress through the successive stages of psychosexual development. For example, inability to resolve the Oedipus complex could result in a boy identifying with his mother and later seeking love objects like himself—one cause of homosexuality according to Freud. Psychoanalytic theory also suggests a treatment; by remedying the psychological damage done during inadequate psychosexual development, the psychological condition of the patient can be improved.

A basic assumption of psychoanalytic therapy is that the symptoms displayed by disordered personalities are expressions of deeply buried conflicts which must be uncovered in order to reveal the etiology of the disorder. During psychoanalytical sessions, which usually take place several times a week for approximately 50 minutes a meeting, the patient lies on a couch with the analyst sitting behind and out of sight. This arrangement helps the patient relax and minimizes the distractions that looking at the analyst might produce. The patient is encouraged to express personal thoughts or feelings without fear of embarrassment or criticism.

Various methods are used for laying bare the unconscious, the most common being the method of free association. The patient is instructed to say aloud everything that comes to mind without any attempt to edit, no matter how foolish, absurd, irrelevant, or indecent the thoughts may seem. Since people are trained to censor what they are about to say, the task of free associating is difficult. But the permissive, nonjudgmental ambience of the psychoanalytic sessions enables the patient to gradually react freely.

In the psychoanalyst's watchful attempt to observe unconscious material, so called *parapraxis*—faulty acts of the mind such as making slips of the tongue, losing or mislaying objects, or forgetting names—are considered important clues:

> In the psychotherapeutic procedure which I employ in the solution and removal of neurotic symptoms, I am often confronted with the task of discovering from the accidental utterances . . . of the patient the thought contents, which, though striving for concealment, nevertheless unintentionally betray themselves. In doing this, the mistakes often perform the most valuable service . . . For example, patients speak of an aunt and later, without noting the mistake, call her "my mother," or designate a husband as a "brother." In this way, they attract my attention to the fact that they have "identified" these persons with each other (Freud in Brill, 1938, p. 78).

Insights into a person's unconscious can also be gained from dreams. Dreams, according to Freud, are primary-process mechanisms that reflect unconscious desires. Because these unconscious urges are threatening, the dream censor, an unconscious component of the ego, transforms the *latent content*—the unconscious wishes that are unacceptable to the ego and superego—into the *manifest content* of the dream—the image sequence that the dreamer reports experiencing. To reveal these unconscious desires, the patient, with the help of the analyst, has to penetrate the manifest content to lay bare the latent content.

Freud, while struggling with his own self-analysis, remembered a vivid dream that he had when eight or nine years of age, in which "my beloved mother, with a peculiar calm, sleeping countenance, was carried into the room and laid on the bed by two (or three) persons with bird beaks" (Freud in Brill, 1938). Freud awoke from the dream terrified and screaming, thus awakening his parents. The analysis of the dream by free association generated thoughts of both death and sex. The beaked figures reminded Freud of the funeral gods that he had seen in his family Bible. The appearance of his mother's face in the dream was similar to the way his grandfather looked while in a coma a few days before his death. *Vogel,* the German word for bird, was associated with the German slang word for sexual intercourse, *vögeln,* which Freud had learned in his childhood.

Freud recalled that after waking up frightened, he suddenly became calm when he saw his mother. Presumably he needed the assurance that she was not dead. But in a deeper interpretation, the anxiety was not triggered by dreaming that his mother was dying. Instead the anxiety "could be traced, through the repression to a dark, plainly sexual craving, which had found appropriate expression in the visual content of the dream." Freud's dream revealed to him the libidinal attachment a son has for his mother.

For several reasons, psychoanalysis is a long, drawn-out form of treatment, usually lasting two to five years. First, as noted, the patient must learn the difficult technique of free association. Second, the patient has a built-in resistance to the process of retrieving unconscious material because the recall of repressed memories and feelings evokes anxiety. Third, the patient must establish a close and intimate relationship with the analyst, known as *transference,* that replicates the relationship the patient had with an important figure, like a father or mother. Transference is a core process in psychoanalysis because it provides patients with opportunities to reexperience the traumas of their psychosexual development and to meliorate the psychological damage the trauma caused.

Defense Mechanisms

In attempting to achieve the goals of psychoanalysis—"to make the unconscious conscious" and "where Id was Ego shall be"—the patient must learn the defense mechanisms that he or she employed to divert feelings of anxiety from consciousness. Two defense mechanisms, identification and sublimation, have already been mentioned. Identification reduces the anxiety that is aroused by the negative feelings one has toward another (e.g., a son toward the father) by mentally equating oneself with the other person. Sublimation occurs when the energies of libidinal urges are channeled into a socially acceptable creation, as, for example, when an artist redirects his sexual and aggressive drives into a work of art. Defense mechanisms occur in many forms.

Repression is the principal defense mechanism. It operates in two ways, by forcing unacceptable wishes and ideas out of consciousness into the unconscious mind and by preventing an unconscious mental event from becoming conscious. A child who feels both love and hate toward a mother would repress the hostility and thus escape the retaliatory punishment that overt aggression would bring and the guilt that hostile feelings would generate. Urges from the id, such as incestuous desires, are kept bottled up in the unconscious by the mechanism of repression.

Displacement is the redirection of a mental impulse toward a safer object. A man who marries a woman like his mother is displacing his Oedipal desires onto a person who does not arouse the anxiety that the original target would evoke. *Projection* attributes to others the objectionable impulses one harbors; the wife perceives her husband to be overly aggressive in order to justify her own aggression toward him. *Reaction formation* conceals an anxiety-inducing impulse by converting it into its opposite; the vehement crusader against vice can be expressing his powerful, repressed sexual urges. *Rationalization* is the technique by which a person interprets his own behavior in an acceptable manner; a shoplifter justifies his theft because he feels the store has previously stolen from him. *Denial* changes an unpleasant and disturbing reality into an unthreatening situation. The sibling of a boy who is fatally ill refuses to acknowledge the illness because of the overwhelming pain that would result. *Intellectualization* is designed to reduce the anxiety that an emotionally threatening situation generates. Adolescents try to cope with their sexual feelings by treating sex as an object of study that requires a detached intellectual attitude.

Termination of Psychoanalytic Treatment. According to psychoanalytic doctrine, an analysis is concluded when a decline in transference takes place. At that time the patient presumably has gained insight into the origins of his or her psychological difficulties; symptoms are supposed to be reduced or eliminated and the patient should feel more comfortable and competent to deal with the problems of life.

EVALUATION AND CONTRIBUTIONS OF PSYCHOANALYSIS

To evaluate psychoanalysis requires distinguishing between the two domains it straddles. One can evaluate it as a theory of personality or as a method of psychological treatment. The theory could be valid but psychoanalytic treatment might be ineffective. Conversely, it is possible that psychoanalytic theory is invalid but the treatment is effective. For example, the patient may improve, not because control was transferred from the id or superego to the ego or because repressed material from the Oedipus complex was brought to consciousness, but because the patient was able to discuss personality problems with a nonjudgmental, supportive therapist.

Complicating the problem of evaluating psychoanalysis both as a theory of personality and as a method of therapy is the recognition that the ensuing verdict will be influenced by the methodological frame of reference employed for judgment. Different standards for evaluating psychoanalysis as a theory and as a therapy can and have been used.

Psychoanalytic Theory as a Natural Science Conception of Personality

Freud considered his efforts as a medical psychologist to be consistent with the methods of natural science. He said that "Psycho-analysis is a part of the mental science of psychology [which is] . . . a natural science. What else can it be?" (Freud, 1940). Freud regarded the psychoanalytic revolution as analogous to the scientific revolutions initiated by Copernicus and Darwin. Copernicus demonstrated that the earth was not the center of the universe, Darwin proved that man was not a unique creature, while Freud showed that man was not the rational master of his own fate.

How should psychoanalysis be evaluated as a natural science theory? Nagel (1959), an important philosopher of science, offered the following judgment of Freudian theory: "as a body of doctrine for which factual validity can be reasonably claimed, I can only echo the Scottish verdict: Not proven." According to Nagel, Freudian theory is so vaguely stated that almost any kind of psychological evidence can be interpreted to be compatible.

Natural science theories should be so stated that their implications are capable, in principle, of being shown to be false as well as true. A widely held opinion is that psychoanalytic theory fails to meet the methodological standard of falsifiability; its intrinsic vagueness and ambiguity prevents it from being refuted. This inability to meet the standard of falsifiability is due in part to Freud's penchant for postulating opposed psychic forces. This predilection was revealed when he was confronted with the task of accounting for the tendency of World War I soldiers suffering from war neuroses to repeatedly recall and relive their traumatic combat experiences in their dreams. Children were also noted to exhibit this *repetition compulsion* to recall unpleasant events. How can such acts be reconciled with the pleasure principle which assumes that mental events are automatically controlled by the urge to seek desirable goals? Freud responded to this question by postulating a competing death wish, a drive to return to an inanimate state. In Freud's words (1920), "The aim of all life is death." As a consequence of his theoretical modifications,

Freud could explain all kinds of thoughts and actions that ranged from pleasure seeking to death dealing by simply assuming that one of the competing drives—life or death—gained dominance over the other. In a similar fashion, the range of psychological events from unbridled hedonism to extreme self-denial could be interpreted as a particular kind of resolution of the conflict the ego has with both the id and superego. Psychoanalytic theory combined with the variety of defense mechanisms was capable of explaining any psychological event; a man's unresolved Oedipus complex can be expressed in such widely diverse behaviors as homosexuality, marrying a woman who resembles his mother, marrying a woman who is totally unlike his mother, not marrying, avoiding all sexual contacts, and ignoring or being obsessed with sex.

Postulating opposed processes does not necessarily result in theoretical ambiguity. If the relative strength of the competing processes, like the life and death urges, can be specified beforehand, future behavior then can be explained. But the strength of these antagonistic psychic processes in psychoanalytic theory cannot be precisely estimated, and consequently a Freudian theorist with a modicum of ingenuity has license to offer a consistent psychoanalytic interpretation of any kind of behavior occurring under any set of conditions.

When judged as a natural science formulation, Freudian theory has been criticized for two additional failings: (1) The self-observations by psychoanalytic patients of mental events are tainted, and (2) The requirements that psychoanalytic theorists demand for judging Freudian theory are unjustified.

Recall that James accused structuralists of being the victims of the *psychologist's fallacy*; basic elements of experience were not observed in consciousness but instead were projected there by introspectors who had been trained to believe that consciousness was composed of basic psychic elements. Psychoanalysts, similarly, have been criticized for projecting psychoanalytic ideas into their patient's minds. To be specific, the argument is that memories of Oedipal desires are not a consequence of a patient's unbiased self-observations but instead reflect ideas that have been planted in the patient's mind. Freud admitted to the possibility of committing an error analogous to the psychologist's fallacy when offering reasons for abandoning the seduction theory: "I was at last obliged to recognize that these scenes of seduction had never taken place, and that they were only phantasies which my patients had made up or which I myself had perhaps forced on them" (Freud, 1925, p. 34).

Even though Freud recognized the danger of the analyst suggesting ideas to the patient, he nevertheless concluded that explicit psychoanalytic interpretations by an analyst were necessary to overcome resistance. In regards to sexual etiology of psychological disorders, Freud argued that psychoanalysts should be willing to

> boldy demand confirmation of our suspicions from the patient. We must not be led astray by initial denials. If we keep firmly to what we have

inferred, we shall in the end conquer every resistance by emphasizing the unshakeable nature of our convictions (Freud, 1898, p. 269).

For Freud the dangers of committing the psychologist's fallacy were far less than ignoring the power of the patient's resistance.

Freud also believed that resistance could encourage criticism of his theory. For example, the accusation that psychoanalytic theory fails to meet the demands of natural science methodology could be an expression of the critic's unconscious resistance to psychoanalytic ideas. The implication of this position is that only a properly psychoanalyzed person is capable of judging Freudian theory because only such a person has successfully overcome the resistance that everybody experiences to Freud's view of psychosexual development. This attitude, not surprisingly, reinforces the conviction of critics who have concluded that psychoanalytic theory falls outside the boundaries of natural science. A basic tenet of natural science methodology is that the validity of theoretical statements can be judged in a detached, objective manner. Limiting judgment to those who have been analyzed essentially restricts criticism to those who have been converted to psychoanalysis. Freud's position is equivalent to having a minister judge Christianity and a rabbi evaluate Judaism.

For many observers of the psychological scene, the criticisms of unfalsifiability, tainted observations, and biased evaluations, seem sufficient to reject Freud's contention that his theory qualifies for natural science status. Such an unqualified rejection, however, can be rebutted. Scientific theories do not emerge full-blown; they require corrections and revisions. Freud acknowledged the tentativeness of his theory. He believed that with time and additional clinical evidence the formulation would become more precise and complete. Has it? The answer is debatable. The worst thing that has happened to psychoanalytic theory, some would argue, are psychoanalysts. For the most part, they have banded together in psychoanalytic associations that have reinforced their unswerving commitment to psychoanalytic methodology and theory while simultaneously isolating themselves from other segments of the psychological and psychiatric community, the efforts of which could contribute to the development of psychoanalytic formulation that would approach the standards of natural science.

In contrast to the closed-minded, party line psychoanalysts are a minority of psychologists (e.g., Meehl, 1970; Silverman, 1976) and psychoanalysts who recognize the methodological deficiencies of Freudian theory but nevertheless believe that with new research techniques, including laboratory experiments and naturalistic studies (Grünbaum, 1984), Freudian theory could be revised in a way that would meet the standards of falsifiability. Such a possibility cannot be ruled out, but for the most part psychologists who are sympathetic to many Freudian ideas are pessimistic about remolding Freudian theory into a scientific formulation with a clear-cut deductive capacity. One survey of objective studies of psychoanalytic hypotheses drew the following conclusion:

Other social and psychological sciences must gain as many hypotheses and intuitions as possible from psychoanalysis but . . . further analysis of psychoanalytic concepts . . . may be relatively fruitless so long as those concepts rest in the theoretical framework of psychoanalysis (Sears, 1943, p. 143).

What are those Freudian ideas that should be incorporated into a natural science theory of personality? Although such a list would vary from one psychologist to another, the following notions represent a fair sampling of Freudian ideas that are generally acknowledged to be important and influential:

Psychological determinism. Freud was not the first psychologist to argue for a psychological determinism. The notion of determinism is a core assumption in natural sciences; variables responsible for the occurrence of phenomena can, in principle, be identified. Wundt, who assumed that psychology in part was a natural science, adopted the position of psychic determinism; mental events are causally related. Freud, who acknowledged the influence of Wundt, also adopted a psychic determinism but extended it to phenomena that were largely ignored, including dreams and mental mistakes (parapraxes) such as slips of the tongue and failures of memory. Freud's deterministic outlook expanded the vision of psychologists in the search for psychological causes for everyday behavior.

Unconscious determinants of personality. The emphasis on the psychology of consciousness by early psychologists reinforced the prevailing belief in Europe and America that humans are basically rational animals, a view that Freud considered to be an illusion. Many historians and psychologists assert that Freud's emphasis on unconscious and irrational determinants of behavior was his greatest single contribution to psychology and contemporary thought. His assumption about unconscious processes encouraged subsequent researchers in a wide variety of experimental and psychological test situations to demonstrate the influence of unconscious motives.

The prevalence of psychological conflicts. Along with the rational conception of the human organism went the belief that humans harbor consistent positive or negative feelings toward others. Freud questioned whether such unequivocal attitudes validly describe interpersonal relationships, particularly close ones. Ambivalence characterizes close relationships. The child, for example, feels both affection and hostility toward parents and vice versa. Freud suggested that human love requires ambivalence; one does not love a dog as much as a person because one is not usually ambivalent about a dog! The significance of the topic of psychological conflict in contemporary psychology, is due in great part to the theoretical efforts of Freud.

Defense mechanisms. Freud suggested that people employ a variety of mental acts, defense mechanisms, to control anxiety. Psychologists who completely reject Freudian theory nevertheless recognize that defense mechanisms like identification, denial, and so forth have a significance that transcends Freudian theory. Defense mechanisms can be conceptualized as adaptive acts which are widely used in coping with frustration, conflicts, and anxiety. Defense mechanisms proposed by Freud, as well as those suggested by others (e.g., compensation), have been incorporated into numerous theories of psychological adjustment and mental health.

The importance of motivation in human behavior. The significance of motivation was elevated by Freud to a level of importance beyond that of any previous theoretical psychologists. Although others had acknowledged the importance of motivation, no one had offered such a systematic interpretation. In addition to identifying sex as the core motive, Freud suggested how this basic drive interacted with a variety of influences to determine personality development. While conceding that the influence of sex might have been exaggerated and acknowledging the vagueness of the psychosexual theory of personality, one can still argue that the psychoanalytic formulation serves as a useful model for psychologists. Any theory that aspires to interpret human psychology must deal with the conceptions Freud viewed as basic—the general role of motivation and the specific influence of the sexual drive. In this sense future theories of personality will inevitably bear the imprint of Sigmund Freud.

To sum up, when viewed within the framework of a natural science theory of psychology, two contrasting evaluations are possible. Psychoanalytic theory, as formulated by Freud, falls far short of the demands of natural science methodology. The theory is so loosely organized and vaguely stated that it is incapable of generating unequivocal empirical interpretations and predictions; it is easy to confirm but impossible to refute. The other evaluation is that Freudian theory suffers from fatal inadequacies as a natural science psychological theory but nevertheless suggests profoundly significant orienting attitudes and keen empirical insights that ultimately must be incorporated into some more successful theory of personality.

Psychoanalytic Theory as a Human Science Conception of Personality

Two influential psychologists, both of whom were psychoanalyzed and both of whom operated within the traditions of natural science psychology, offered this interesting and suggestive view of psychoanalytic theory:

> What does psychoanalytic theory have to offer? Some people like the picturesque language which Freud uses to project his ideas. They are attracted by the skillful way in which he employs literary and mythological

allusions to put across fairly abstruse notions and his talent for turning a phrase or creating a figure of speech in order to illuminate a difficult point for the reader. His writing has an exciting literary quality which is rare among scientists. The style is matched by the excitement of the ideas. Many people find Freud's concepts fascinating and sensational. Of course, sex is an alluring topic and has a sensation value even when it is discussed in scientific works. . . . Aggression and destructiveness are almost as absorbing as sex. It is only natural, then, that people are attracted by Freud's writings.

But a fine literary style and an exciting subject matter are not the main reasons for the great esteem in which Freud is held. Rather it is because his ideas are challenging, because his conception of man is both broad and deep, and because his theory has relevance for our times. Freud may not have been a rigorous scientist nor a first-rate theoretician, but he was a patient, meticulous, penetrating observer and a tenacious, disciplined, courageous, original thinker. Over and above all of the other virtues of his theory stands this one—it tries to envisage a full-bodied individual living partly in a world of reality and partly in a world of make-believe, beset by conflicts and inner contradictions, yet capable of rational thought and action, moved by forces of which he has little knowledge and by aspirations which are beyond his reach, by turn confused and clearheaded, frustrated and satisfied, hopeful and despairing, selfish and altruistic; in short, a complex human being. For many people, this picture of man has an essential validity (Hall & Lindzey, 1957, p. 72).

One possible interpretation of Hall and Lindzey's conclusion is that psychoanalytic theory may be judged more appropriately within the context of a human science than a natural science. Natural science can be conceptualized as a method of investigating phenomena *from the outside* with the intent of objectively identifying their causes. Human science, in contrast, seeks to understand human events *from the inside* by an intuitively valid and consistent account of human experience. That is, natural science seeks objective truth while human science aims for subjective meaning.

Although Freud considered his theoretical efforts to be within the traditions of natural science and thought his theory would ultimately be reduced to neurological processes, he and his followers often gave the impression that psychoanalytic theory was accepted, not because of its capacity to logically interpret objective data, but because of the intuitively compelling picture of human experience it offered. Freud himself, struggling with his own personal problems after his father died, suddenly gained a meaningful understanding of his own past with his psychoanalytic theory of personality development. He finally understood! In the same sense and in the same way, Freud understood the character of Hamlet that Shakespeare created; Hamlet's reluctance to avenge his father's murder at the hands of his uncle stemmed from guilt generated by his unconscious desire to kill his father because of his incestuous desire for his mother.

This style of intuitive understanding was later extended to illuminate the life of the great Renaissance genius, Leonardo da Vinci, who achieved fame as a painter, sculptor, architect, engineer, and scientist. According to Freud:

> The accident of [Leonardo's] illegitimate birth and the pampering [by] his mother exerted the most decisive influence on his character formation, and on his later fate, through the fact that the sexual repression following this infantile phase caused him to sublimate his libido into a thirst for knowledge, which conditioned his sexual inactivity for his entire life (Freud, 1947, p. 119).

In spite of Freud's convictions that he was a natural scientist, the argument is being advanced that he was operating as a human scientist offering an interpretation of human experience *from the inside*. Some have argued that such an interpretation should not be conceived as falling short of natural science requirements, but instead, of going beyond them in offering an integrated and intuitively compelling picture of human existence.

Quotations of Sigmund Freud

1. A man like me cannot live without a hobby-horse, a consuming passion—in Schiller's words a tyrant. I have found my tyrant, and in his service I know no limits. My tyrant is psychology. (Freud, 1895/1954, p. 119)

2. Complete theories do not fall ready-made from the sky. (Freud, 1910a, p. 20)

3. Every single hysteric and neurotic . . . remember[s] painful experiences of the remote past . . . [and] still cling[s] to them emotionally; they cannot get free of the past and for its sake they neglect what is real and immediate. (Ibid, p. 17)

4. Psychoanalysis, which has taught us the intimate connection between the father complex and the belief in God, has shown us that the personal God is psychologically nothing but an exalted father, and daily demonstrates to us how youthful persons lose their religious belief as soon as the authority of the father breaks down. (Freud, 1947, p. 103)

5. (Freud, in a letter to Jung, comments on the difficulty of preparing an important case history for publication): I am finding it very difficult . . . it is almost beyond my powers of presentation; the paper will probably be intelligible to no one outside our immediate circle.

How bungled our reproductions are, how wretchedly we dissect the great art works of psychic nature! (McGuire, 1974, p. 238)

6. It is a long superseded idea, and one derived from superficial appearances, that the patient suffers from a sort of ignorance, and that if one removes this ignorance by giving him information (about the causal connection of his illness with his life, about his experiences in childhood and so on) he is bound to recover. The pathological factor is not his ignorance in itself, but the root of this ignorance in his *inner resistances*; it was they that first called this ignorance into being, and they still maintain it now. The task of the treatment lies in combating these resistances. Informing the patient of what he does not know because he has repressed it is only one of the necessary preliminaries to the treatment. If knowledge about the unconscious were as important for the patient as people inexperienced in psychoanalysis imagine, listening to lectures or reading books would be enough to cure him. Such measures, however, have as much influence on the symptoms of nervous illness as a distribution of menu-cards in a time of famine has upon hunger. (Freud, 1910b, p. 225)

PSYCHOANALYTIC THERAPY

Attempts to evaluate psychoanalytic therapy, or any form of psychotherapy, are notoriously difficult. Unlike specific physiological disorders, like a toothache or bone fracture, clear-cut and accepted criteria to judge the treatment are not available.

Many psychoanalysts believe that their professional expertise combined with their intimate acquaintance with their patients qualifies them as the most competent judges of psychoanalytic treatment. Psychoanalysts are in general agreement, not surprisingly, that their treatment is effective. They do not, however, believe that psychoanalysis is always helpful or that it is appropriate for all disturbed patients. Even Freud expressed reservations about psychoanalysis by acknowledging that its methods were sometimes inadequate to the task of curbing the powerful psychic forces of the unconscious. But he was convinced that, in spite of its shortcomings, psychoanalysis could be a successful method of treatment for patients who are intelligent and strongly desirous of gaining relief from psychic distress. In support of this position, Freud (1905) was proud to note, "Psychoanalytic therapy was created through and for the treatment of patients permanently unfit for existence, and its triumph has been that it has made a satisfactorily large number of these permanently *fit* for existence."

The positive attitude of Freud and other psychoanalysts toward psychoanalytic therapy is dismissed by psychologists who insist that psychological treatment must be evaluated by controlled studies that yield objective data. Some early studies which attempted to meet these standards compared groups of psychoanalytic patients before and after therapy; if their conditions improved the beneficial effects were attributed to the treatment. The logic of such a research design is faulty. Persons who are psychologically disturbed sometimes improve spontaneously. Obviously, then, all improvement which occurs during psychoanalysis cannot necessarily be attributed to the treatment itself. The question, "What would have happened if the patient had not received psychoanalytic treatment?" is always present.

In order to judge the effectiveness of psychoanalysis, or any other type of therapy, changes in a group of patients who receive treatment must be compared with a similar control group who do not. Controlled studies of this sort offer mixed results; some report findings favoring psychoanalysis while others fail to observe any difference between the treatment and control groups. Numerous possibilities could be responsible for the ambiguous results, including vast differences in the psychological measures employed to judge therapeutic effectiveness, differences in therapists and patients, overwhelming difficulties in equating the treatment group with the control group, sampling error, and so on.

Because different forms of psychotherapy share common procedures, many psychologists argue that theoretical differences between major methods of treatment should be ignored while attention should be focused on the effects of specific procedures in psychotherapy. One implementation of this practical suggestion is an analysis of 166 studies that evaluated psychotherapy (Luborsky, Chandler, Auerbach, Cohen, & Bachrach, 1971). This report concluded that certain characteristics of patients (e.g., adequacy of personality functioning prior to treatment, high anxiety, higher levels of intelligence) and therapists (e.g., amount of experience, ability to empathize, compatibility between therapist and patient) were correlated with therapeutic success. The specific kind of treatment did not seem to make much difference. In sum, when objective measures and controlled designs are employed, psychoanalytic treatment does not fare well in comparisons to other forms of psychotherapy or even no treatment at all.

There is another way of evaluating psychoanalytic treatment that is simple and does not require objective measurements. Ask psychoanalyzed patients whether they feel better, whether they have profited from the treatment. A large majority say "yes" (e.g., Jersild & Lazar, 1962). They feel happier and believe that they are more effective in their work, two goals toward which Freud thought psychoanalytic treatment should be directed. A typical response of a patient after psychoanalysis is "I feel more comfortable; I think I have a better grasp of life."

These testimonials fail to meet the requirements of objective evidence but the question can be raised as to whether they should therefore be ignored. If the goal of psychotherapy is to provide the patient with a meaningful interpretation of life, then personal testimonies are needed. The argument can be advanced that patients who seek psychoanalytic treatment do so because their lives do not have meaning to them. Psychoanalysis provides that meaning; it enables them to understand their own psychological development and the psychological forces that govern their lives.

Essentially this emphasis on meaning, which reflects a major concern of human science, implies that the history of a person's life that is brought to consciousness with the assistance of the psychoanalyst is not discovered, but instead created. In other words, the psychoanalytic interpretation can only be subjectively confirmed, not objectively validated.

This admission immediately raises the question as to whether other psychological theories, some opposed to Freudian ideas, cannot also offer a meaningful interpretation for a patient whose own life appears incomprehensible. The answer would have to be yes. For some people, other conceptions of psychological development and the nature of personality are intuitively more believable and/or more attractive than is the Freudian view. But for some patients, the Freudian theory is the most compelling, and therefore becomes the most effective therapy for that person.

Freudian psychoanalysis also has an appeal to some patients that is not shared by other forms of psychotherapy; it does not preach. Freud admitted, when dealing with patients, "I do not break my head very much about good or evil" (Clark, 1980). Freud insisted that psychoanalysis should not try to convert patients to any particular moral code or political view. Psychoanalysis was designed to help patients become more comfortable with their own lives, to enjoy the pleasures of life and to work more effectively. The personal views of the therapist on morality or politics were not to be imposed on the patient in the guise of treatment.

COMPETING INTERPRETATIONS

Freud's radical and imaginative notions, based on his own life and clinical evidence gleaned from patients, inspired the development of the psychoanalytic movement. Considering the selective quality of the evidence, it should come as no surprise that other psychoanalytic interpretations would be offered in competition to the one proposed by Freud. Two early followers initiated rebellions against Freudian theory.

Alfred Adler's Individual Psychology

Alfred Adler (1870–1937), a Viennese physician and one of Freud's earliest followers, came to the conclusion that Freud's emphasis on infantile sexuality as a powerful determiner of adult personality was exaggerated and distorted. Two personal reasons, perhaps related, have been offered for Adler's rejection of Freudian theory. As a child, Adler was frequently ill.

FIGURE 8.2 Alfred Adler

Courtesy of H. L. Ansbacher

He was unable to walk until he was four because of a case of rickets. His accomplishments as a boy and adolescent fell far behind those of his older brother, producing a sense of inadequacy. Later, Adler became a member of the Marxist oriented Social Democrat party that blamed capitalism for human suffering and psychological disorders. These early experiences and political attitudes presumably encouraged Adler to stress social factors at the expense of the biological variables that Freud emphasized. Adler, for example, rejected Freud's idea that women felt inadequate because of a lack of a penis; *penis envy* was a symbolic resentment of male social dominance.

According to Adler, the fundamental psychological driving force is a self-assertive drive, an urge to seek mastery and perfection. Adler perceived infants as being constantly frustrated because of their weakness and inadequacy. Seeking ways to overcome their sense of inferiority, children learn methods of controlling and dominating their parents. They accomplish this goal by employing the defense mechanism of *compensation;* they counterbalanced their limitations in one area (e.g., weakness) by gaining strength in another (e.g., cuteness). Adler postulated that individual personalities are shaped by the particular feelings of inadequacy, real or imagined, that a person experiences, along with the methods used to overcome them and how effective they are. The famous Greek orator, Demosthenes, had a weak voice and poor delivery as a child; his efforts to *over*compensate, excel where he was weakest, made him an eloquent speaker. Sometimes an effort to compensate can backfire; the shy and isolated person becomes so aggressively and offensively gregarious in an effort to gain admission into a group that he alienates those whose friendship he seeks. Mental illness, for Adler, resulted from inappropriate and ineffective modes of compensating when striving for mastery.

Adler rejected the Freudian notion of motivation as a drive reduction or tension relief mechanism. Human motivation, for him, was directed toward self-improvement and perfection, with the ultimate goal being the achievement of harmony between the individual and society.

Adler's theory, like Freud's, suffered from a questionable empirical base and a lack of theoretical precision. In addition, it fell far short of the detailed description of psychological development that Freudian theory offered. Although it never gained the support or popularity that Freudian theory achieved, it was influential in the development of a number of psychoanalytic formulations (e.g., Horney, Fromm) that emphasized the social and creative forces in human experience.

Carl Jung's Analytic Psychology

Carl Jung (1875–1961) was born in Kesswil, Switzerland, the son of a pastor and a housewife, neither one of whom established a close relationship with their son (Ellenberger, 1970). During his adolescence, he was deeply involved with problems of religion but found no clarification in the lengthy discussions he had with his father. Like Freud, he was greatly impressed by the writings of Goethe, Schopenhauer, and Nietszche. He was also fascinated with the topic of spiritualism and actively engaged in experiments with mediums.

Jung received a medical degree from the University of Basel in 1901 with his major interest being in psychiatry. Freud's *The Interpretation of Dreams* (1900) inspired him and he became a dedicated disciple. His admiration and respect for Freud was reciprocated; Freud perceived Jung as a disciple worthy of being his successor in the psychoanalytic movement. They misjudged each other. Freud wanted disciples who were completely dedicated to the major tenets of his theory. Jung desired an opportunity to develop his own ideas about unconscious processes. In later years, Jung recalled Freud's statement made to him during their early days: "My dear Jung, promise me never to abandon the sexual theory. That is the most essential thing of all. You see, we must make a dogma of it, an unshakeable bulwark!" (Jung, 1963). Freud obviously did not know that Jung, although committed to the power of unconscious mental processes and the

FIGURE 8.3 Carl G. Jung

National Library of Medicine

mental processes and the importance of balancing conscious and unconscious forces for achieving mental health, could not accept the Freudian emphasis on sex.

According to Jung, libidinal energy emerges from the opposition of introversion and extroversion; introversion directs attention to inner life, to conscious experience, while extroversion orients attention to outer life, to other people and society. These conflicting forces must achieve a reasonable balance for healthy psychological functioning. Dreams, instead of being wish fulfilling mechanisms as Freud thought, are designed to attain such an equilibrium.

As the person matures, libidinal energy flows toward different ends. In infancy, the libido is directed toward nourishment; in childhood, toward play; after puberty, toward heterosexual relationships; and still later, toward spiritual values. The emphasis on spirituality, both in the mystical and religious senses, distinguishes Jung's views from the combined biological-social orientation of Freud and the strong social stress of Adler.

Jung expanded the realm of the unconscious to include two different systems. The *personal unconscious,* resembling Freud's conception, contains complexes, an integrated set of feelings and attitudes about some subject. For example, a girl with repressed hostilities toward her father would have a father complex that would interfere with establishing a satisfactory relationship with her husband. The task for the Jungian analyst, like that of the Freudian analyst, is to extirpate these debilitating unconscious memories and reduce or eliminate their destructive influences. In addition, Jung postulated a *collective unconscious* containing archetypes, primitive patterns of ancestral images associated with birth, death, power, God, and other significant cultural ideas. The collective unconscious predisposes persons to feel and think and act as have countless generations of humanity before them. An individual's psyche, for Jung, has its roots in the history of mankind and strives for self-realization, a selfhood in which opposed psychical forces, such as introversion and extroversion, are reconciled.

As Jung grew older, his writings became more mystical, more concerned with philosophical than empirical issues. He did emphasize positive goals toward which humans strive, as did Adler, and as a result, influenced subsequent humanistic theories of personality (Chapter 12).

Psychoanalysis: Competing Theories or a Unified Approach?

There are many other theoretical offshoots—so many as to make it difficult to state the number precisely—that have emerged from Freud's original psychoanalytic conception. It must be recognized that the various psychoanalytic theories share a common methodology that unites them in spite of theoretical differences. The are all based on clinical evidence and they all employ a *talking cure* to improve the mental health of their patients. Although adherents of one approach (orthodox Freudianism) have claimed superiority for their own systematic position, no acceptable method has been developed to support such claims either in terms of the validity of the theory or the effectiveness of therapy. One segment of the psychoanalytic community has argued that different theoretical narratives (e.g., Freudian, Adlerian) can be used effectively with the same patient and that psychoanalysts would benefit from "getting be yond fruitless, naively objectivist . . . arguments over the so-called 'facts of the case' " (Schafer, 1984). This is an admission that during psychoanalysis the facts of a person's life history are not simply being *discovered,* as Freud suggested, but to some extent, are being *created.* This admission essentially removes the theoretical differences within psychoanalysis from the realm of empirical evaluation and assigns them to the domain of therapeutic usefulness. As long as a patient is helped by a particular story line of his life's history, it does not matter whether it is empirically true.

A Debate about Psychoanalysis

Moderator: We all recognize the controversial nature of psychoanalysis and the tendency to exaggerate its merits or liabilities by its proponents or critics. It therefore becomes incumbent upon both of you, in order to fulfill your responsibilities to your audience, to avoid polemics by focusing upon the real issues that divide you.

Pro: Your request appears reasonable and I will try to comply. My strong support of Freudian theory stems simply from its intrinsic validity. The theory reflects the essence of the human condition. We are driven by motivational urges of which the sex drive is the most powerful. In addition, we are frequently unaware of our urges and the influence they exert on our behavior. Although Freud's psychosexual theory of development is difficult to accept at first, its reasonableness becomes apparent after some reflection. Anybody who has observed children will recognize the importance of the feeding experience, toilet training, and sexual play in their psychological development. Freudian theory also offers an intuitive understanding of everyday psychological events—the ambivalent nature of interpersonal relationships, especially close ones, the numerous psychic tricks (defense mechanisms) we all employ to ward off anxieties, and the constant conflict between our powerful passions and the relentless demands of society. Finally, allow me to buttress my argument by evidence from everyday life, phenomena that academic psychologists are too eager to ignore. Have you ever thought about the amazing frequency of bizarre sexual behavior, sometimes of a criminal nature? The prevalence of sheer violence? What explains these acts? Although Freudian theory is admittedly incomplete, as Freud himself acknowledged, it nevertheless offers insights into sexual pathology and violence that are far more perceptive than any other formulation, especially those with distinguished scientific credentials. In sum, of all our psychological theories, Freudian theory comes closest to the realities of human life and experience.

Con: I cannot deny your emotional commitment to the Freudian view of life. But you should recognize that a devotion equal to yours can be, and has been, directed to other psychoanalytic formulations, different religions, and I might add to make my argument more forceful, to astrology. We do not accept the Copernican view of astronomy or the Darwinian theory of evolution because we intuitively believe it to be true, but instead because they fit the facts. Freud's argument that his theory is comparable in importance to the Copernican and Darwinian views can only be justified when it meets the same methodological standards of scientific truth. When initially formulated, Freudian theory fell far short of those standards; it still falls far short, almost 100 years later.

Pro: Your argument has a hollow ring! It substitutes ivory tower methodological concerns for the psychological problems of everyday life. I am reminded that Einstein acknowledged the fact that before he could rationally justify his theory, he intuitively knew that he was on the right track. Human psychology is even more complex than is the science of physics and therefore more time is required for a theory to achieve the methodological status of the physical theory of relativity. But Freudian theory, with its wide acceptance in art and literature, is constantly progressing toward that day when it will be acknowledged as a valid theory of psychology.

Con: You have not answered my criticism. You merely persist in supporting Freudian theory by your subjective judgments. I am forced to interpret your defense of Freudian theory in terms of some vaguely defined discipline of human science. Freudian theory offers an appealing and meaningful description of personality development and functioning but not a valid causal analysis. In a very fundamental sense, Freudian theory of personality is an artistic creation, not a scientific discovery.

Pro: Why are you so convinced that art and science are separated by an unbridgeable chasm? Many scientific theories—Darwin's, Einstein's, and Freud's too—have been described as beautiful, and they are beautiful because they offer an integrated and elegant interpretation of important segments of our experience in the same way Cezanne interprets a countryside. Isn't it possible that with more information and improved technology that Freudian theory will reach a level of explanation that will even satisfy doubting Thomases like yourself? Meanwhile, we, and there are many, who are convinced that Freudian psychology is valid, will continue to profit from Freud's profound insight into the human condition.

Con: Your defenses are impenetrable. By equating art with science you homogenize two distinctly different human endeavors and thus destroy the uniqueness of each.

Moderator: That ends this debate.

SUMMARY

Freudian psychoanalysis is a psychological system that offers a theory of personality as well as a method of psychotherapy. Its historical roots are within the confluence of the study of hypnosis, the treatment of hysteria, and the concept of the unconscious; and the *Zeitgeist* of Vienna in the latter half of the nineteenth century that emphasized the psychological importance of sexuality and the philosophy of Nietzsche.

The subject matter of Freudian psychoanalysis is the mind. Freud postulated a topographical structure of the mind consisting of three compartments: the conscious, preconscious, and the unconscious, with the latter being the largest and the most influential. Freud was an empiricist who relied on clinical observations to serve as the empirical bases of his theory. Although Freud assumed he was operating as a natural scientist, controversy still reigns as to whether he was *discovering* the causes of personality development (natural science), or *creating* an intuitively compelling interpretation of personality (human science).

Freud's strategic concerns were with three related tasks: the development of a method for accurately observing the unconscious, the discovery of the unconscious origins of mental illness, and the formulation of a theory of normal personality development.

He finally adopted the free association technique combined with the interpretation of dreams and faulty acts of the mind (parapraxes) as a method for observing unconscious processes responsible for patients' psychological disorders.

According to Freudian theory, personality is the product of three major psychological systems: *id, ego, superego*. The id, completely unconscious, consists of biological urges directed at immediate gratification, and operates in an automatic, irrational manner (primary process). Both the ego and superego have conscious and unconscious components. The superego, representing ethical and legal demands of society, operates essentially as a person's conscience. The ego, representing reason, attempts to reconcile the conflicting forces of the id and the superego.

Initially, Freud thought that many adult neuroses were a consequence of sexual abuse during childhood, but he concluded later that reports of childhood seductions of patients were fantasies representing their incestuous desires. This led him to formulate his theory of psychosexual development. The theory, along with his topographical conception of the mind and structure of personality, postulated that personality develops during a predetermined sequence of stages, each of which is characterized by a dominant mode of achieving libidinal satisfaction: the oral erotic, anal erotic, and phallic stages. Up to and including the early portion of the phallic stage, the child's libido is directed toward achieving libidinal satisfaction by autoerotic means. An important change occurs when the child's libido is directed outwards toward the parent of the opposite sex. If the Oedipal complex is resolved by the child identifying with the parent of the same sex, thereby indirectly satisfying the incestuous desire, then the child can progress toward mature heterosexual relations. Successful psychosexual development produces a stronger and more effective ego that relies on the secondary process of mental activity involving both rational thought and prudent judgment.

The aim of the psychoanalytic treatment is for the patient, with the help of the analyst, to become aware of the unconscious memories and motives responsible for the psychological illness. Psychoanalysis tends to be a lengthy treatment, covering many years, because of the time required to learn the free association technique, overcome resistance, and establish transference between the patient and analyst. In attempting "to make the unconscious conscious" during psychoanalysis, the patient learns about the defense mechanisms (e.g., identification, projection, denial) that had been acquired to divert feelings of anxiety from consciousness.

In judging psychoanalysis, it is important to distinguish between psychoanalysis as a theory of personality and as a method of psychotherapy. The major shortcoming of Freud's theory of personality, from a natural science viewpoint, is that it fails to meet the methodological standards of falsifiability; it is so ambiguously formulated that any kind of evidence can be interpreted as being consistent with it. In addition, the clinical evidence cited in favor of the psychoanalytic theory has been criticized as being contaminated by the psychologist's fallacy; the analyst encourages patients to observe mental events consistent with Freudian theory which may not have been in the mind originally. Finally, the insistence of Freud and his followers that only persons who have been psychoanalysed can properly judge the validity of psychoanalytic theory confirms the suspicion of many critics that psychoanalysis fails to meet the basic requirement of objectivity, a cornerstone of natural science methodology.

In spite of criticisms directed at the inadequacies of psychoanalysis as a natural science formulation, there are those psychologists who accept the criticisms but nevertheless maintain that Freudian theory has contributed basic ideas that must ultimately be incorporated into a natural science interpretation of personality—psychological determinism, unconscious determinants of psychology, the prevalence of psychological conflict, defense mechanisms, and the importance of motivation in human behavior.

An interpretation of psychoanalysis that has been gaining in popularity is that it should be judged as a human science, an attempt to interpret human psychology from the inside, by offering an intuitively appealing and consistent account of human experience.

The evaluation of psychoanalytic therapy depends upon the criterion selected. In terms of objective measures (e.g., elimination of symptoms; more effective work habits), psychoanalysis does not appear to be strikingly more effective than another treatment or measurably better than other forms of psychotherapy. When judged in terms of the patient's reactions to psychoanalytic treatment, the verdict is positive; psychoanalytical patients feel, for the most part, that their psychoanalysis has contributed to a better understanding of life and a more effective mode of adjustment.

Two prominent followers of Freud who ultimately proposed competing psychoanalytic formulations were Alfred Adler and Carl Jung. The methodological structures of their theories are similar to that of Freud's but neither were developed in as integrated or detailed a manner. For Adler, the fundamental psychological driving force was a self-assertive drive seeking the goal of self-improvement, mastery, and harmony with society. According to Jung, libidinal energy results from the opposition of introversion (attention to inner life) and extroversion (concern with an outer social life). Healthy psychological functioning depends on achieving a reasonable balance between these two psychological forces. Jung also postulated that libidinal energy is directed toward different goals as a person matures.

SUGGESTED READINGS

Sigmund Freud was one of the great literary stylists of the German language and his skill is captured in most English translations. Freud was always eager to acquaint the public with the tenets of psychoanalysis and frequently gave lectures and wrote books for that purpose. His first extended treatment of psychoanalysis consisted of five lectures he delivered at Clark University in 1909, which later were written from memory (Freud, 1910a). This book, *Five Lectures on Psycho-Analysis,* still serves as an admirable introduction to Freud. Collections of Freud's writings, such as A. A. Brill's edited book entitled *The Basic Writings of Sigmund Freud* (1938), and Freud's *A General Introduction to Psychoanalysis* (1938), also provide excellent introductions to psychoanalysis. The former is particularly good since it includes *The Interpretation of Dreams* and *Psychopathology of Everyday Life.* The complete writings of Sigmund Freud are contained in a twenty-four volume series that was translated from the German under the general editorship of James Strachey, in collaboration with Anna Freud.

Thousands of books have been written about Sigmund Freud and psychoanalysis. One of the best and most informative is Henri F. Ellenberger's *The Discovery of the Unconscious* (1970), which discusses the psychoanalytic movement, including the efforts of Adler and Jung. An excellent biography of Freud, including his intellectual efforts, is Ronald W. Clark's *Freud: The Man and the Cause* (1980). A good secondary source is Raymond E. Fancher's *Psychoanalytic Psychology: The Development of Freud's Thought* (1973).

Sidney Hook's (Ed.) *Psychoanalysis, Scientific Method, and Philosophy* (1959) reports the proceedings of a symposium, the participants of which were leading psychoanalysts and philosophers of science. Adolpf Grünbaum (1984), a philosopher, has offered a careful and exhaustive treatment of psychoanalysis in *The Foundations of Psychoanalysis: A Philosophical Critique*. In an interesting but difficult article, James G. Blight (1981) argues that human science is not clearly distinguishable from natural science and, therefore, psychoanalysis should be treated and understood within the traditions of natural science. Roy Schafer (1984), a practicing analyst, has summarized some case histories in an article entitled "The pursuit of failure and the idealization of unhappiness," which illustrates a human science approach to psychoanalysis. A fascinating and revealing book on the practice of psychoanalysis is Janet Malcolm's *Psychoanalysis: The Impossible Profession* (1982).

A good introduction to Adler is his brief article "Individual psychology" (1930). Carl Jung's *The Psychology of the Unconscious* (1912) illustrates his approach.

For those students whose interest in psychoanalysis has been whetted, a perusal of books on psychoanalysis in the campus library would prove to be both informative and entertaining.

9

Neobehaviorism I: Tolman versus Hull

John B. Watson, the self-styled "Behaviorist," convinced many psychologists that behaviorism was the only road to travel to reach the goal of a natural science psychology. Among his converts were Edward C. Tolman (1886–1959) and Clark L. Hull (1884–1952), both of whom achieved great distinction as behaviorists while sharply differing between themselves, and with Watson, about strategy and theory.

Tolman and Hull are described as *neo*behaviorists because each created a novel form of behaviorism while retaining Watson's major belief that behavior, not consciousness, was the subject matter of psychology. Tolman formulated a cognitive theory of animal learning, and soon thereafter Hull began to construct a stimulus-response reinforcement theory. The two theories, although committed to methodological behaviorism and constructed according to a common methodological blueprint, appeared to be in complete opposition and thus generated a lively theoretical controversy that influenced the subsequent course of psychology.

HISTORICAL ROOTS OF NEOBEHAVIORISM

The theories of Tolman and Hull emerged from Watsonian behaviorism, the philosophical position known as *logical positivism*, and the psychology of animal learning.

Watsonian Behaviorism

Watson's behaviorism was a reaction to the prevailing mentalism of his day, as expressed in both structuralism and functionalism. Watson justified his revolutionary thesis that behavior is the object of psychological

FIGURE 9.1 Edward C. Tolman and Clark L. Hull

Courtesy of University of California, Berkeley   Painting courtesy of Yale University

inquiry by both enunciating methodological principles of behaviorism and by formulating a theoretical conception of behavior. For the most part, his audience failed to distinguish his methodology from his theory, believing that, in combination, they represented what behaviorism truly is. Tolman and Hull both demonstrated that this global interpretation of behaviorism as both a general methodology and a specific theory is misleading. Tolman and Hull each formulated an interpretation of behavior that was based on a behaviorist methodology while simultaneously being at odds with Watsonian theory. They demonstrated that methodological behaviorism (Chapter 6) was capable of supporting a variety of theories, some of which could be strikingly different from Watson's conception.

Logical Positivism

Logical positivism, a school of philosophy that developed in Vienna during the early part of the twentieth century, sought to redirect philosophy from a purely speculative discipline to one that analyzes scientific thought and practices. Its goal was to identify the major features of natural science methodology and scientific knowledge.

Logical positivism held that the meaning of statements is equated with the empirical operations designed to investigate them. Thus, the metaphysical question, "How many angels can dance on a pinpoint?" is nonsensical because it is unanswerable by objective methods. In a similar vein, the meaningfulness of the question, "Can thought occur in the absence of images?" is problematic because the introspective methods designed to answer the question are based upon private observations that are beyond public scrutiny, and therefore cannot yield reliable knowledge.

In contrast, questions about publicly observed behavior are clearly meaningful. For example, the question, "Will highly motivated rats emit more responses during experimental extinction than those with a weak motivation?" can be easily answered. Logical positivism's analysis of the methods of science endorsed the behaviorist view that a natural science of psychology requires the objective study of behavior instead of the subjective examination of consciousness.

Logical positivism equated the empirical meaning of a statement with its observational base. Thus, for any question to have empirical meaning, it must refer to variables that can be publicly observed now or in the future. This position led to the idea of operationism; concepts should be defined operationally, that is, by the operations a scientist uses when he employs the term. Thus, one possible definition of strength of motivation would be the number of hours of deprivation from previous satiation; an animal deprived of food for twenty-two hours would, by definition, have a stronger drive (motivation) than one deprived for three hours.

The significance of operational definitions is twofold. First, they facilitate communication by reducing vagueness. Knowing how a particular intelligence test was constructed and is administered makes it possible to understand the meaning of IQ scores. Secondly, operational definitions discourage scientifically confused questions. If we ask, "Can you change human nature?" we must be able to describe the techniques by which we measure human nature. We must know how changes can be detected. That is, we need an operational definition if we choose to discuss human nature within a scientific framework. In the history of all fields of science, certain questions, considered important at one time, were later discovered to lack operational meaning and thus to be scientifically meaningless.

Animal Learning

John Watson believed that the goal of modifying behavior, whether it be the aim of the parent, educator, or society, could only be achieved by understanding the principles of learning. He also assumed that the principles of learning could be most effectively investigated with animal subjects.

Neobehaviorism converted Watson's views about animal psychology and the psychology of learning into a strategy that held the promise for a truly mature scientific interpretation of the learning process. The strategy was simple in conception: Study learning in its purest form with a simple, convenient organism such as the laboratory rat. From the evidence obtained, formulate principles of behavior that would be relevant to all learning tasks. Underlying this general strategy were two basic tenets: (1) Studying a phenomenon in its simplest form is the most effective method of discovering basic theoretical principles. Principles governing the movement of celestial bodies have been revealed from observations of pendulums and balls rolling down inclined planes. Principles that govern human heredity have been suggested by studying genetic transmission in fruit flies. Tolman and Hull believed that the bare essentials of the learning process can be studied with rats in a simple laboratory situation. (2) Although acknowledging that human behavior is more complex than that of the laboratory rat, Tolman and Hull believed that understanding rat behavior would represent a giant step toward understanding human action.

TOLMAN'S COGNITIVE BEHAVIORISM

Tolman was an unusual theoretical psychologist. He was dedicated to the task of formulating a theory of learning without feeling compelled to vigorously defend his efforts or deny their limitations. He was convinced that psychology was at a stage in its development that required serious attempts at formulating general theories of behavior while recognizing that such attempts must inevitably be incomplete and ambiguous. The only reasonable approach was to get on with this basic task and do the best one could.

Historical Roots

In addition to being influenced by Watsonian behaviorism, logical positivism, and animal learning, Tolman's conception of psychology was also markedly affected by the ideas of William McDougall (1871–1938) and Gestalt psychology (Chapter 7).

William McDougall. William McDougall was a psychologist of broad training and wide experience who emphasized the importance of studying behavior from a mentalistic outlook. In addition, he stressed that the key problem, especially in human psychology, is purpose.

McDougall was born and educated in England where he studied biology, medicine, and the humanities. After completing his medical training in 1897, he went first to Germany to study physiology and psychology and later to Borneo and New Guinea where he did anthropological field work. Upon returning to England, he first joined the psychological faculty at the University of London, and then spent sixteen years at Oxford University. During World War I, he was a medical officer in the British Army with the responsibility of treating cases of war neurosis.

In 1920, Harvard University, desirous of elevating the prestige of its department of psychology offered a position to McDougall, who by then had a worldwide reputation due in part to his popular *Introduction to Social Psychology* (1908). This book ultimately went through twenty-three editions and helped establish social psychology as one of the major areas of psychology. McDougall, who never seemed to receive the admiration from his colleagues that he thought he deserved, gladly left Oxford for Harvard. Harvard, however, proved to be less congenial than McDougall had anticipated; many of his colleagues reacted negatively to McDougall's belief in free will, the reality of the soul, and parapsychology. He left Harvard for Duke University in 1927, where he chaired a department more in tune with his views.

The general psychological orientation that McDougall enunciated, although admittedly vague, heralded ideas that were to gain acceptance later on. He was the first psychologist to define his discipline as the science of behavior: "Psychologists must cease to be content with the sterile and narrow conception of their science as the science of consciousness, and must boldly assert its claim to be the positive science . . . of conduct or behaviour" (McDougall, 1905). Nevertheless, he later objected so vigorously to Watsonian behaviorism that he reverted back to the definition of psychology as "the science of the mind." To explain his difference with Watson, he wrote, "The two principle alternative routes are (1) that of mechanistic science, which interprets all its processes as mechanical sequences of cause and effect, and (2) that of the sciences of the mind, for which purposive striving is a fundamental category, which regard the process of purposive striving as radically different from mechanical sequence" (McDougall, 1923).

His formulation differed from Watson's in four fundamental ways:

1. Watson conceptualized behavior as a linear sequence or chain of stimulus-response associations in which each successive response is triggered by a preceding stimulus. According to McDougall, the entire sequence of behavior is controlled by some superordinate idea or principle that guides the entire sequence of behavior. To be specific, each individual muscular movement in a tennis stroke is not controlled by a preceding stimulus (e.g., kinesthetic cue), but, instead, the entire stroke is guided by a mental plan as to how the tennis stroke should be executed.

2. Watson viewed behavior as analogous to the actions of a machine that runs automatically, without plan or purpose. For McDougall, behavior is purposive, striving to achieve some goal in the future, whether it be a full stomach or an advanced degree.

3. Although Watson did not completely ignore innate factors in the analysis of behavior, he minimized their influence. In contrast, McDougall considered them all-important. Purposive behavior was an expression of innate drives seeking fulfillment. Initially, McDougall labeled these innate desires *instincts,* but he soon learned to his dismay that the term encouraged misunderstanding. By instincts McDougall did not mean inherited, stereotyped, unmodifiable patterns of behavior but rather genetically prewired desires striving toward a satisfying goal. These *propensities,* a term he later substituted for instinct, consisted of two components, an urge and a response pattern. The urge was innate but the pattern of behavior that was effective in gratifying the urge could vary. The basic urges for food and sexual satisfaction, for example, persist throughout life, but the modes of behavior that are utilized vary both within the same individual and among different individuals.

Initially, McDougall (1908) listed twelve major propensities, but later he (McDougall, 1923) extended the list to eighteen. In addition to the biological propensities of hunger and sex, he included such social urges and actions as the propensity to acquire attractive objects and the propensity to laugh at the inadequacies of other humans.

4. While Watson insisted that the mind be expunged from psychology, McDougall, who described himself as a "sane behaviorist," in opposition to the antimentalistic Watsonian behaviorist, thought behavior should be interpreted within a mentalistic framework that emphasized purpose, a position that Tolman was to adopt.

Gestalt Psychology. Tolman's views can be described as falling between behaviorism and Gestalt psychology; methodologically, he was a behaviorist, while theoretically he was a Gestalt psychologist. Two related ideas from Gestalt psychology influenced Tolman's cognitive behaviorism, the psychological environment and psychological field theory.

Learning, for Gestalt psychology, does not consist of the formation and strengthening of stimulus-response associations, as Watson proposed. Instead, learning depends upon the psychological environment becoming appropriately organized. For example, Köhler's chimpanzees solved the insight problem (p. 210) by perceiving the boxes and bananas as parts of an integrated whole rather than as unrelated elements. Insight (perceptual reorganization) could not, therefore, be adequately represented by associative processes; for example, associating the boxes with the stacking response, connecting the stacked boxes to climbing, and the top of the stack eliciting the response of grabbing the bananas. Instead, the psychological environment must be interpreted as a psychological field analogous to a magnetic field in which all parts of the region are interrelated. In other words, perceptual reorganization is not a result of new associations being formed, but, instead, of parts of a psychological field being fused together. Whether the difference between association theory and field theory is one of substance or semantics has been a topic of continual debate over the years. But for Tolman, the difference was real, and he opted to formulate his theory of learning in terms of a psychological field instead of a network of associations.

Edward C. Tolman (1886–1959)

Edward C. Tolman was born in Newton, Massachusetts, in 1886 to a well-to-do family that stressed New England democratic values including "equal rights for Negroes, women's rights, Unitarianism, and humanitarianism" (Tolman, 1952). Edward Tolman entered the Massachusetts Institute of Technology not because of any desire to become an engineer, but because his natural talents in mathematics and science led him there. His brother, who was similarly endowed, became a renowned theoretical chemist and physicist. Edward received a B.S. in electrochemistry from MIT in 1911, but when he was a senior he read William James and decided to become a philosopher. After entering Harvard summer school, Tolman discovered that he was not cut out to be a philosopher and his interests soon shifted to psychology.

At Harvard, in the joint department of philosophy and psychology, Tolman was greatly influenced by a course in ethics taught by the philosopher, Ralph Barton Perry (1876–1957). Reading McDougall's *Social Psychology* and other texts, including some by Titchener and Watson, laid the basis for Tolman's later interest in motivation and theoretical problems.

In order to prepare for the required Ph.D. examination in German, Tolman traveled to Germany, learned the language, and spent a month with Koffka, who successfully interested him in gestalt notions.

After receiving his doctorate at Harvard, he became an instructor at Northwestern University for three years, during which time he experienced "a compulsive drive . . . to do research and write." He also acknowledged being "self-conscious and inarticulate" and "afraid of my classes." The entrance of the United States into World War I brought retrenchment to Northwestern, and Tolman was dismissed, due most likely to the combined effects of his poor teaching and expressed pacifism. Fortunately, he was offered an instructorship at the University of California:

> From the very first, California symbolized for me some sort of final freeing from my overwhelmingly too Puritanical and too Bostonian upbringing . . . there are features about the climate and landscape which

seem to me better as a steady diet than those provided by any other place in the world. . . . Whatever my early psychological instabilities, they have all but disappeared. Whatever my increasing psychological maturity—and there has been some—I like to credit most of it to social, intellectual, and physical virtues of Berkeley plus an extraordinarily happy marriage (Tolman, 1952, p. 328).

Teaching a course in comparative psychology "finally launched [Tolman] down the behavioristic slope." He acquired some rats from the anatomy department and, along with both graduate and undergraduate students, conducted some maze learning experiments, the results of which nourished his theoretical ideas.

In 1932, he published his most important book, *Purposive Behavior in Animals and Men,* and two decades later, when judging its contributions in historical perspective, Tolman perceived virtue in its behavioristic stance: "Today we are practically all behaviorists. In some loose sense we practically subscribe to the doctrine that the only psychological statements that can be scientifically validated are statements about the organism's behavior, about stimulus situations or about inferred, but objectively definable . . . variables" (Tolman, 1952).

The advent of World War II drove Tolman "to discuss the psychology of war and its possible abolition." In a slender volume entitled *Drives toward War,* he offered a combination of hypotheses from his own conception of learning and motivation and those of Freudian theory. He identified the motives that lead to wars and suggested the social controls that were required to keep warlike drives in check. His previous pacifism did not inhibit him from helping the war effort during World War II by serving for two years (1944–1945) in the Office of Strategic Services. Several years after the end of World War II, Tolman became the faculty leader of the protest against the state loyalty oath that each faculty member at the University of California was required to sign. Tolman refused to sign the oath, believing it violated his civil liberties and academic freedom, a position that the courts finally supported. For taking this stance, he was suspended from his duties in California, but was invited to teach at the University of Chicago and Harvard University. Tolman is still remembered as the person most responsible for saving academic freedom at the University of California. In 1959, the Regents of the University of California essentially admitted that Tolman was morally correct in his opposition to the oath by awarding him an honorary doctorate.

Although Tolman was basically a shy and gentle man, he was an intellectual and moral leader because he was compulsively honest about expressing his own views, regardless of what others thought. All those whose paths he crossed developed a deep affection and great admiration for Edward C. Tolman.

Methodological Assumptions

Tolman refuted, as did Watson, the idea that psychology is a mental science:

> The definition of psychology as the examination and analysis of private conscious contents has been something of a logical sticker. For how *can* one build up a science upon elements which, by very definition, are said to be private and noncommunicable? (Tolman, 1922, p. 44).

The only solution to this difficulty, Tolman insisted, was to make psychology the science of behavior.

The Subject Matter of Psychology. While sharing Watson's view that psychologists should study behavior, Tolman concluded that Watson failed to distinguish between two different forms of behavior, molecular and molar. Molecular behavior refers to physiological reactions such as glandular secretions or muscular contractions, while molar behavior is defined by the functional consequences of a given act. Pavlovian conditioning equates behavior with a molecular response, the amount of salivation. Köhler's research on insight employed a molar response; the chimpanzees stacked the boxes which enabled them to obtain the banana. The specific pattern of muscular responses was totally ignored; attention was only directed to those acts bearing on the solution of the problem.

In discussing behaviorism, Watson employed both molecular and molar definitions of behavior. When describing behaviorism in a general way, Watson tended to offer as examples of molar behavior "anything an animal does—such as turning towards or away from a light, jumping at a sound, and more highly organized activities such as building a skyscraper, drawing plans, having babies, writing books." When proposing theoretical interpretations, Watson tended to suggest a molecular explanation in terms of muscular responses and the kinesthetic cues they produce. One example of his molecular theorizing is Watson's peripheral theory of thinking (Chapter 6). Another is his theory that maze learning occurs when an integrated chain of stimulus-response associations is formed with each link of the chain being connected to the preceding and succeeding link by response produced (kinesthetic) cues. To be specific, the choice of the correct response in a maze is a combined product of the kinesthetic cues from the previous response and the stimuli at the choice point. These response produced cues ultimately enable the rat to acquire a smooth-flowing sequence of muscular responses that leads directly, without error, to the goal box.

Tolman faulted this kind of molecular "muscle-twitch" interpretation of thinking, maze learning, and other phenomena for two reasons. First, it really did not represent a psychological explanation, "an account [of behavior] in terms of muscle contraction and gland secretion, as such, would not be behaviorism at all but a mere physiology." Second, learning could not be reduced to a linear chain of stimulus-response associations. Along with Gestalt psychology, Tolman believed that what was learned was more like a percept or idea that guides an organism's behavior.

Methods of Investigation. Tolman was a committed experimentalist who believed that systematic research could serve as the foundation of a broad theory of behavior. At the same time that he espoused the merits of experimentation, Tolman acknowledged that significant psychological problems associated with individual adjustment and social progress could not simply be solved by laboratory research. When confronted with these issues, Tolman made valiant attempts to extrapolate judicious applications to childrearing and international peace from available evidence and theory.

Criterion of Truth. Tolman considered a theory to be valid if it were capable of generating deductions in line with empirical data. By adopting this methodological principle, Tolman was expressing his conviction that psychology was a natural science.

Strategy

Five clearly expressed strategies governed Tolman's research and theoretical efforts.

1. *Behavioral Determinism.* Tolman believed that not only was it possible, but also desirable, to erect a purely behavioral theory of conduct that ignores underlying neurophysiological processes (Tolman, 1922). His position was analogous to that of Wundt's assumption of psychic determinism in conceptualizing mental processes. Behavior for Tolman, like the mind for Wundt, was considered a self-contained entity, a closed system, which could be explained by processes within the system. Tolman's behaviorial determinism did not deny the influence of neurophysiological processes on behavior; it merely considered them unnecessary when formulating a theory of behavior.

2. *Common Sense Phenomenology.* In spite of Tolman's commitment to *methodological behaviorism,* he believed that fruitful theoretical notions could be generated by empathizing with his rodent subjects: "I, in my future work, intend to go ahead imagining how, *if I were a rat,* I would behave" (Tolman, 1938). As a result of this tactic, Tolman's theoretical concepts assumed phenomenological characteristics and names such as "demand," "hypotheses," and "expectations," mentalistic terms that Watsonian behaviorism considered an abomination.

3. *Choice Behavior.* Tolman considered choice behavior to be the fundamental psychological act. Unlike Watson, Tolman was not enamored with the idea that conditioning was the basic research area for the psychology of learning. When investigating conditioning, the psychologist's attention is focused exclusively on a single behavioral tendency, for example, the tendency for a tone (conditioned stimulus) to elicit salivation (conditioned response). In all learning situations, Tolman argued, different behavior tendencies compete with each other, whether it is to hit a forehand or backhand, or to get a job or go to graduate school. A choice point in a maze, Tolman suggested, represents real life situations more accurately than does conditioning, because information is provided about how one form of behavior gains ascendancy over a competing one.

4. *Transfer Criterion of Learning.* Tolman's cognitive view of psychology encouraged him to adopt the transfer criterion of learning that Gestalt psychologists had previously proposed. Only a test of transfer, Tolman believed, could reveal what an organism had learned. Having a subject merely repeat a response, as occurs in conditioning, may not be a valid indication of what the organism has learned.

5. *Intervening Variables.* Tolman noted that the psychological theorist who desires to interpret the maze behavior of the rodent is confronted with an impossibly complex task if he or she seeks to discover the relationships between all possible independent (environmental and organismic) variables with the variety of possible dependent (behavioral) measures. The number of environmental variables such as the size and kind of goal object, the number of choice points in the maze, the distance between choice points, the illumination, the cues at the choice points, and so on, are essentially infinite. So are the number of organismic variables (e.g., the strength of the subject's motivation, its age, the genetic strain), as well as the response measures (e.g., the number of trials required to reach the criterion of learning, the time required to reach the goal box on successive trials, the number of errors on each trial, the location of errors). Tolman suggested a short cut; instead of dealing with an infinite number of independent variables, formulate a finite number of *intervening variables* to bridge the gap between the independent and dependent variables. Each of the intervening variables would be a function of a set of independent variables that exert a common effect on behavior.

Intervening variables was a new term for an old idea; they were essentially theoretical constructs, predispositions to behave in a certain way. Theoretical constructs—Carr's *adaptive act,* Köhler's *insight,* Freud's *superego*—are all abstract constructs designed to explain behavior. The difference between these theoretical concepts and an intervening variable is Tolman's emphasis on the requirement that intervening variables be operationally defined, that is, connected to both independent and dependent variables. When so connected, the meaning of an intervening variable is relatively clear, thus facilitating research designed to investigate its influences.

Cognitive Behaviorism

By stressing the importance of theoretical clarity and objective evidence, Tolman automatically highlighted the interdependence between theory

---

FIGURE 9.2 The Floor Plan of the Maze Employed by Tolman and Honzik (1930) in Their Study of Latent Learning

---

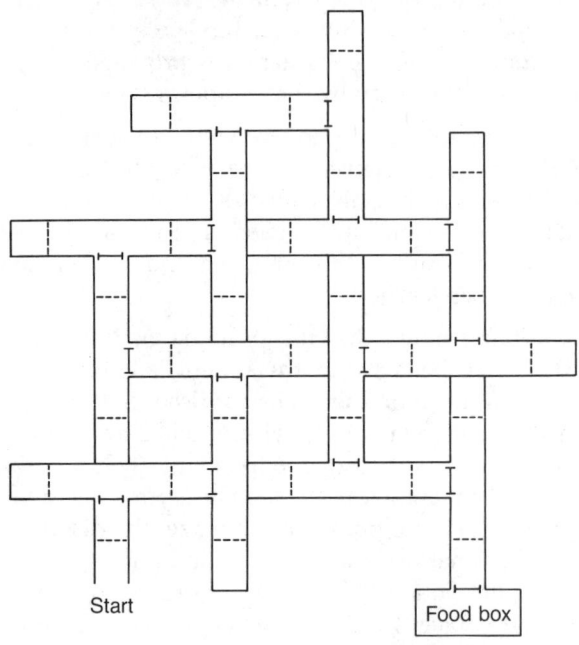

The broken line (----) represents a curtain while the solid line (|———|) indicates a door that prevents retracing.

---

and facts. The test of any soundly constructed theory is its capacity to explain facts. Theory by itself, no matter how intuitively compelling, requires empirical evidence to support it. Two sets of facts illustrate some core ideas of Tolman's (1932) cognitive theory of animal behavior.

Latent Learning and the Learning-Performance Distinction. Tolman's cognitive view of maze learning, which was proposed in opposition to the stimulus-response conception, is most clearly revealed in the California latent learning studies. The conventional S-R associationistic interpretation of maze learning, such as the fourteen-unit maze depicted in Figure 9.2, is that at each choice point, competition occurs between the correct and incorrect habit, between the choice that leads to the direct path to the end box and the one that enters the blind alley. Maze learning, according to this conception, occurs when the correct response at each choice point gains ascendancy over the incorrect response, thus resulting in errorless performance.

In the most famous latent-learning study (Tolman & Honzik, 1930), three groups of hungry rats were run in the maze represented in Figure 9.2. Group R (rewarded) received food on every trial after entering the

FIGURE 9.3 The Results of the Latent Learning Experiment

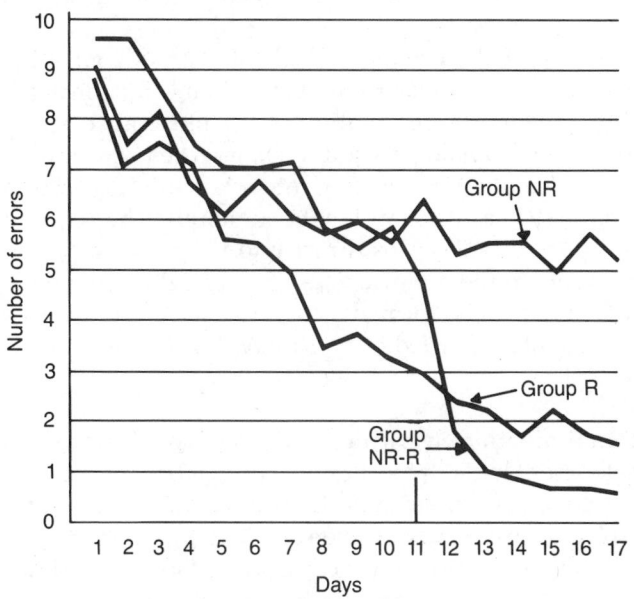

The graph reveals the error curves for Groups NR, R, and NR-R. Note that the day after food was introduced, Day 11, the performance of Group NR-R approximates that of Group R. (Adapted from Tolman and Honzik, 1930.)

end box, while for Group NR (nonrewarded) the end box was empty. Group NR-R (nonrewarded-rewarded) received a combination of these two procedures; for the first ten days, the end box was empty, but on day eleven and thereafter, food was present. As Figure 9.3 shows, Group R outperformed (fewer errors) the nonrewarded (NR) animals. In the language of stimulus-response psychology, the R subjects were being reinforced more for their correct responses than were the NR subjects. The principle of reinforcement postulates that certain events, like food for a hungry animal, strengthen stimulus-response associations. The superiority of the R subjects over the NR animals, therefore, was attributed to a difference in reinforcement.

From Tolman's viewpoint, such an explanation could be challenged. The difference between Groups R and NR represents a difference in performance, not necessarily learning. Perhaps the obtained difference in performance between R and NR subjects is a consequence of motivational factors; rats have a greater *demand* for food than for an empty end box. If this were so, then equating the motivational conditions of the R and the NR groups should result in equal performance. This prediction was tested and confirmed by the performance of Group NR-R. After receiving food on the eleventh day, thus equating the demand quality of the end box with the R subjects, the two groups, R and NR-R, then performed at essentially the same level on the twelfth day (test trial). This suggested that in spite of differences in reinforcement during training, equal amounts of learning had taken place.

These data were interpreted as being consistent with Tolman's hypothesis that rats do not learn *stimulus-response associations* but, instead, acquire a *cognitive map*, a mental representation of the physical structure of the maze. Tolman's theory is analogous to the experiences of a traveler who arrives in a new town and, after checking into a hotel, walks around the central square. She passes a restaurant, a book store, a theater, and so on. Later on, when hungry, she walks directly to the restaurant, and afterwards, when she wants to see a movie, she goes straight to the theater. In the words of Tolman, she had formed a cognitive map of the town's square and then utilized her knowledge to satisfy her immediate demands.

Hypotheses in Discrimination Learning. Tolman's cognitive theory encouraged the development of a hypothesis-testing model in animal learning in opposition to an associationistic theory. Thorndike had proposed that animals solve a puzzle box problem by "trial and error with accidental success." This view of problem solving was adopted by stimulus-response associationists when interpreting a discrimination-learning task such as the one that is illustrated in Figure 9.4.

The problem confronting the subject is to learn which one of four cues—right, left, black, white—is the correct one, that is, the one that will be consistently followed by a food reward. According to the S-R associationistic view, the subject responds in a trial-and-error manner and sooner or later selects the black stimulus. Every time the black cue is chosen, the subject is rewarded, thus increasing the strength of the habit to choose black. Since the habit is the only one that is consistently rewarded (the right- and left-turning habits are intermittently rewarded because the position of black is randomly shifted from side to side), the choice of black gradually gains ascendancy over the three other competing habits (left, right, and white).

This interpretation was questioned by Karl S. Lashley (1890–1958), an early co-worker of John B. Watson, who noted in his research on the discriminative capacities of animals (Lashley, 1929), that some subjects consistently chose one of the two spatial responses from the beginning, right or left. He conceived of these systematic responses as *attempted solutions*, rather than chance behavior as Thorndike had suggested. In effect, he proposed that in a discrimination-learning task, animals test a sequence of hypotheses until the correct one is discovered. For example, the rat may initially choose the right side consistently, and then the left side, before adopting the correct hypothesis that "black is correct."

I. Krechevsky, who had taken a postdoctoral fellowship with Lashley after a doctorate with Tolman, developed the hypothesis-testing model.

FIGURE 9.4 A Discrimination Learning Apparatus

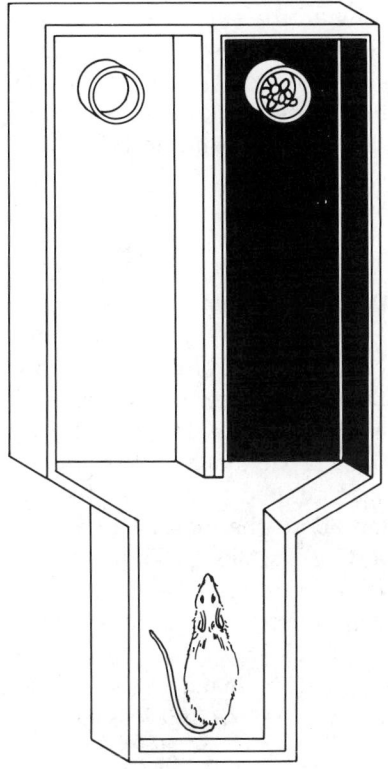

The subject, a rat motivated by hunger, chooses one of the two alleys. The apparatus is arranged so that the position of the two alleys vary from trial to trial. In this particular arrangement the choice of the black alley is reinforced as is indicated by the location of the food pellets.

In one of his early studies, he analyzed the learning curves of rats solving a discrimination-learning problem and concluded that "in light of all the evidence presented here, it is suggested that helter-skelter unorganized trial and error response as a description of the early part of the learning process is invalid, and that we must change our description of the learning process so as to recognize the existence of organized and systematic responses at *all* stages of the process" (Krechevsky, 1932).

An important feature of the hypothesis-testing model is that discrimination learning is assumed to be a *noncontinuous* process. Learning entails testing a series of distinct hypotheses during which time the information gained is relevant *only* to the hypothesis being tested. For example, if the *right-is-correct* hypothesis is being tested when black, as the correct cue, is on that side, the reward received confirms only the hypothesis under consideration and has no effect upon the ultimate adoption of the *black-is-correct* hypothesis. In contrast, the S-R model assumes that discrimination learning is a *continuous* process with the correct association gradually gaining dominance. Even when the subject consistently chooses the right side, the strength of the habit to choose black increases when black is located on the right side. The tendency to respond to the right is gradually overcome by the habit to choose black because *black* is rewarded consistently while *right* is rewarded only intermittently.

Tolman's Cognitive Theory

Now that the flavor and some of the details of Tolman's theory have been conveyed, a brief critique is in order. At the core of Tolman's theory are the intervening variables that bridge the gap between the experimental and behavioral variables. The explanatory capacity of this intervening variable theory depends on the precision with which these theoretical constructs are defined and related to behavior. For several reasons, Tolman's cognitive theory did not reach a level of rigor capable of yielding unambiguous predictions. Tolman and his associates failed to conduct the extensive research needed to gain information about the manner in which experimental operations influence intervening variables, for example, how the clarity of a cognitive map increases as a function of the amount of practice or the intensity of a drive. Another source of the ambiguity lay within Tolman himself: "I don't enjoy trying to use my mind in too analytical a way . . . I have an inveterate tendency to make my ideas too complicated and too high flown so that they become less and less susceptible to empirical tests" (Tolman, 1959).

The historical importance of Tolman's efforts is not contained in the precision of his theory but instead in its general approach and core ideas. Learning was a process, the end result of which was the acquisition of a cognitive map representing a subject's environment. In the latent-learning studies, the major variable determining the clarity of the cognitive map was the number of trials; the more training an animal had in a maze, the clearer was the "mental" representation of the maze.

A basic question every learning theorist faces, and the one that has proven to be the most troublesome, is, "What is the relationship between motivation and learning?" More specifically, how do the two major components of motivation, drives (e.g., hunger) and incentives (e.g., food), affect learning? A major implication of the latent-learning studies was that maze learning was independent of the incentive; animals that received food did not learn any more than those who did not. The influence of drives on learning was left unanswered. A hypothesis that gained popularity, consistent both with Tolman's common sense approach as well as the perceptual orientation he adopted from Gestalt psychology, is that strong drives narrow the perceptual field of the organism to events relevant to the drive. Thus, the different portions of a cognitive map acquired under a strong hunger drive would vary in its degree of clarity. But the precise nature of the relationship between the intensity of the drive and the clarity of the cognitive map was never spelled out in detail.

Learning could be facilitated, Tolman proposed, by environmental features that perceptually highlighted relevant cues. For example, having a light over the end box in the multiunit maze depicted in Figure 9.2 would accelerate learning by offering a distinctive cue that could be employed by the rat from all parts of the maze. Similarly, learning to discriminate between black and white instead of two mid-grays would be easier because the perceptual distinctiveness between correct and incorrect cues would be greater.

Tolman acknowledged the importance of hereditary factors by noting that the ability to learn a task was dependent on the innate capacity of the animal. This point had been previously demonstrated by functionalists who showed that the solution of a delayed reaction problem is species related. A colleague of Tolman also demonstrated the importance of genetic factors; Robert Tryon (1940) had selectively bred two strains of rats, one of which learned a maze much more rapidly than did the other. It was also discovered that these maze-bright and maze-dull rats differed in the kinds of hypotheses they employed in a discrimination learning task (Krechevsky, 1933).

In sum, Tolman's cognitive theory of animal behavior postulated two interacting theoretical constructs, cognitive map and motive, with behavior determined by their interaction. The hypothesis-testing assumption suggested another difference between cognitive and stimulus-response theories that was to be stressed in the development of cognitive psychology (Chapter 11). According to the hypothesis-testing model, animals actively select hypotheses which encourage them to attend to certain features of the maze (e.g., black alley) while ignoring others (e.g., right alley). In contrast, the stimulus-response conception suggests that the animal passively and nonselectively receives all incoming stimulation. In other words, the cognitive model conceptualizes an organism as an agent that actively transforms environmental inputs while the stimulus-response model suggests that animals are passive recipients of environmental stimulation.

Late in his career (1949), Tolman suggested a radical departure from his original position. In place of the assumption that there is one basic kind of learning, Tolman proposed a list of six distinctive forms of learning, some of which require rewards. Although this effort had limited influence, it nevertheless raised the important question about whether a general theory of learning could be based on a single form of learning.

HULL'S STIMULUS-RESPONSE REINFORCEMENT THEORY

Although Tolman and Hull shared the common goal of formulating a deductive theory of learning, they differed widely in the style in which they sought to achieve their aim. Hull did not suffer from any doubts about his own ability to construct an objective theory of behavior or exhibit any indecision as to how this goal was to be achieved. His confidence was rewarded by his theory becoming the most dominant one in psychology during the fifteen-year period that followed the publication of his major work, *Principles of Behavior* (1943).

Historical Roots

Hullian theory was shaped by the ideas of both Pavlov and Thorndike. Hull saw conditioning as the simplest form of learning and therefore an excellent source of theoretical hypotheses. Thorndike's *Law of Effect* appeared to Hull to be an essential behavioral mechanism which was consistent with Darwin's evolutionary theory in that it led to the acquisition of behavior that enhanced survival.

Clark L. Hull (1884–1952)

Hull had a harsh life. He was born in a log house near Akron, New York, the son of an unschooled, powerful father with a violent temper and a quiet, shy mother, who was wed at fifteen and later helped her husband learn to read.

Hull attended a one-room rural school but was forced to miss school when the farm work became heavy. Before his teens, he was converted to an evangelical church, but after some thought became "very doubtful regarding the whole religious hypothesis" and finally in an open meeting "withdrew my affiliation."

He passed a teacher's examination when he was seventeen and later taught for a year in a one-room rural school. His desire to be educated encouraged him to return to school, where he found mathematics and science to his liking, but languages "extremely difficult." At school, he and a number of other students contracted typhoid fever from contaminated food. Several students died; Hull barely survived a week of intensely high temperatures which left him, he believed, with a defective memory. He was forced to take a year off to recuperate and then went to Alma college where he prepared to become a mining engineer. At twenty-four years of age, he secured a job in Minnesota where his task was to determine the manganese content of iron ore. After being on his new job for only two months, he contracted poliomyelitis which left him with one leg so badly paralyzed he could not walk without crutches. He returned home to convalesce and replan his life. One alternative was to become a minister of the Unitarian faith, "a form of free godless religion." But he realized that he really wanted an occupation in a field allied to philosophy in the sense of involving theory: one which was new enough to permit rapid growth so that a young man would not need to wait for his predecessors to die before his work could find recognition, and one which would provide an opportunity to design and work with automatic apparatus. Psychology seemed to satisfy this unique set of requirements (Hull, 1952a, p. 145).

Hull read James's *Principles of Psychology* to prepare himself for his chosen field and also designed a steel brace for his paralyzed leg to facilitate getting about. He secured a job teaching in the elementary school to which he had gone as a child, now expanded to two rooms. To help teach his eighth- to twelfth-grade students, he set up a small biological laboratory. After two years in this job, he had enough savings to continue his education. He entered the University of Michigan as a junior, where he had a course in experimental psychology that he called "outstanding." He also completed a small research project in learning. In connection with a course in logic, Hull constructed a logic machine, mainly composed of concentric sheet metal plates, that could simulate syllogistic reasoning.

After graduation, his savings exhausted, Hull accepted a position in a school of education in Kentucky, where his teaching load was twenty hours of classes per week. He nevertheless found time to study concept learning and plan his doctoral dissertation. Applications for a graduate fellowship to Cornell and Yale were rejected, but he was able to get a part-time teaching assistantship at the University of Wisconsin. Joseph Jastrow, whom Hull served as a teaching assistant, "had remarkable linguistic fluency. He would sometimes lecture for five minutes at a time in perfectly good sentences, yet hardly say a thing."

Four years were required to complete his dissertation on concept learning (Hull, 1920), during which time his status changed from a part-time assistant to a full-time instructor. After completing his dissertation, he accepted a research grant to investigate the influence of tobacco smoking on mental and motor efficiency, a task he accomplished with the use of a clever research design (Hull, 1924). He was then asked to teach a course in psychological tests and measurement, which he did with enthusiasm because of his interest in mathematics. In his efforts to develop a scientific basis for vocational guidance, he authored *Aptitude Testing* (Hull, 1928), a book that helped elevate the standards of research in the psychology of tests and measurements. A by-product of this enterprise was Hull's invention of an ingenious machine to compute correlation coefficients.

Hull was then assigned an introductory course for premedical students. Believing that the psychology of suggestion and hypnosis would be a useful topic for these students, Hull learned hypnotic techniques and "instituted an experimental program which utilized fully the quantitative methodology customary in experimental psychology." This research program was finally published in a book entitled, *Hypnosis and Suggestibility* (Hull, 1933), which twenty-eight years later was praised by an expert in hypnosis as a "model of clarity and objectivity" (Hilgard, 1961).

Hull was then assigned to teach experimental psychology: "This was the one course above all others that I desired to give, because . . . it constitutes the foundation of a truly scientific psychology." Hull, at this time, was "sympathetic with Watson's views concerning the futility of introspection and the general virtues of objectivity . . . [but nevertheless] felt very uncertain about many of his dogmatic claims." Hull became interested in Gestalt psychology and was instrumental in inviting Kurt Koffka to the University of Wisconsin to lecture for a year.

> While I found myself in general agreement with his criticisms of behaviorism, I came to the conclusion not that the Gestalt view was sound but rather that Watson had not made out as clear a case for behaviorism as the facts warranted. Instead of converting me to *Gestalttheorie,* the result was a belated conversion to a kind of neobehaviorism—a behaviorism mainly concerned with the determination of the quantitative laws of behavior and their deductive systemization (Hull, 1952a, p. 154).

In 1929, Hull was invited to become a Research Professor at Yale University, where he previously was denied a graduate fellowship. He became the central figure in the Institute of Human Relations, a research organization that James R. Angell, among others, helped organize to integrate the theoretical efforts of behavioral scientists from different disciplines, including psychologists, sociologists, and cultural anthropologists. One project led Hull, in association with Neal E. Miller, John Dollard, and O. H. Mowrer, to identify the essential similarities between Freudian and Hullian theories in the hope that an integrated social science theory could be formulated.

Between 1929 and 1950, Hull wrote a series of twenty-one theoretical articles in the *Psychological Review* (Amsel & Rashotte, 1984). A major work, *Mathematico-Deductive Theory of Rote Learning* (1940) was a combined product of the efforts of Hull, some of his students, logicians, philosophers, and mathematicians. It was based upon the assumption that rote learning phenomena were an expression of underlying conditioning principles. Hull judged the work to "At the very least . . . represent in a clear manner the form which the more scientific works on the behavior theory of the future should take."

In 1943, Hull published his major work, *Principles of Behavior,* which presented a formal theory of conditioning that Hull assumed would serve as the core of a general theory of behavior. After completing that manuscript, Hull embarked on another book, later published as *A Behavior System* (1952b), which interpreted more complex phenomena in terms of assumptions related to those initially expressed in *Principles of Behavior.*

In 1948, Hull suffered a massive coronary attack that made him an invalid for the remainder of his life. He died in 1952 after a final heart attack. In spite of declining health, he mustered all the energy he could to continue his research program and complete the manuscript of *A Behavior System,* which he finished four months before he died. Near the end of his life, he expressed profound regrets that he could not complete the third book which would have been "by far the most important portion of the system" because of its major concern with "the strictly social relationships among human subjects."

Hull's career illustrates the virtues of dedication and persistence. In spite of humble origins, personal illnesses, and numerous social obstacles, Hull achieved a doctorate in psychology at the relatively late age of thirty-four. When assigned to work in fields such as aptitude testing and hypnosis that did not correspond with his basic interests, he nevertheless became sufficiently absorbed in them to make fundamental contributions. Although he only spent a little more than twenty years on the topic of behavior theory with the final years as an invalid, he nevertheless profoundly influenced the course of the history of psychology, particularly in regard to elevating standards of theory construction.

Methodological Assumptions

Hull did not entertain any doubts that psychology was a natural science. He believed that only by using the rigorous and objective methods employed by physics could psychology achieve a deep understanding of behavior that, in turn, could be employed for the betterment of human society.

The Subject Matter of Psychology. The dependent variable in Hull's theorizing was behavior. He described it as molar behavior but employed the molecular-molar distinction differently than had Tolman. Tolman used the distinction to refer to behavior, Hull to theory. For Tolman, molecular behavior was a physiological response such as a muscular contraction or glandular secretion, while molar behavior represented an act that was defined in terms of its functional consequences. For Hull, the molecular-molar distinction referred to the nature of the behavior theory: a molecular theory is a neurophysiological interpretation of behavior while a molar conception is a behavior theory that employs purely abstract theoretical constructs (intervening variables). He admitted that the molar-molecular distinction is "relative rather than absolute" and therefore employed both physiological (e.g., glandular secretion) and functional (e.g., lever pressing) responses.

Methods of Investigation. As his research on concept learning, tobacco smoking, aptitude testing, and hypnosis indicate, Hull placed no limits on behavioral research. Any kind of phenomena could be productively investigated as long as the research adhered to the canons of natural science.

Criterion of Truth. Hull insisted that explanations of psychological phenomena must be shaped in a deductive mold. Logic and mathematics are essential components of an explanatory theory because common language is not sufficiently rigorous to generate unambiguous deductions. Thus, a theory is capable of explaining phenomenon when its occurrence can be deduced from theoretical principles.

While stressing the importance of deductive explanation, Hull also was careful to point out that pseudoexplanations, "explanations" that cannot be evaluated, were more common in psychology than psychologists were willing to admit. The litmus test for a scientific hypothesis was whether it, in principle, could be tested; *"Science has no use for unverifiable hypotheses."*

Strategy

Hull had strong convictions about the appropriate method for formulating basic principles of behavior and the theoretical organization of these principles. A fivefold strategy flowed from his beliefs:

1. *The Stimulus-Response Conception of Behavior.* Hull's decision to employ a stimulus-response conception of behavior was as much a function of tradition as a deliberate choice. The popularity of reflexology and classical conditioning encouraged the attitude that psychological events could best be represented in terms of stimulus-response language. A sensory-motor reflex, such as a patellar reflex, could be simply and objectively described in terms of a stimulus (e.g., blow to kneecap) evoking a response (e.g., kneejerk). Conditioning, likewise, could be represented clearly in terms of stimulus-response language; the stimulus, *tone*, becomes connected to the response, *salivation*, and thereafter elicits the salivary response.

Hull's use of stimulus-response language differed in one important respect from that of Watson. Whereas Watson believed that all behavior could be interpreted solely in terms of stimuli, responses, and the association between them, Hull concluded that other factors (e.g., drive) must be considered. For Hull, stimulus-response language was useful but not sufficient for a satisfactory representation of psychological events.

2. *Conditioning as a Source of Theoretical Principles.* Conditioning became a popular experimental paradigm in America because it represented the confluence of three popular ideas: association, habit, and objectivity. At that time it was not fully appreciated that the role of conditioning in behavior could be conceptualized differently. Both Pavlov and Watson considered conditioned responses to be the unit of habit. Hull, in contrast, viewed conditioning as a source of theoretical principles. By studying conditioning it would be possible to abstract principles of behavior that would apply to all areas of psychology. This idea is expressed in the preface of Hull's major book, *Principles of Behavior:*

> As suggested by the title, this book attempts to present in an objective systematic manner the primary, or fundamental, molar principles of behavior. It has been written on the assumption that all behavior, individual and social, moral and immoral, normal and psychopathic, is generated from the same primary laws; that the differences in the objective behavioral manifestations are due to the differing conditions under which habits are set up and function. Consequently, the present work may be regarded as a general introduction to the theory of all the behavioral (social) sciences (Hull, 1943, p. v).

3. *A Mechanistic View of Behavior.* Behaviorism was a rebellion against the effort to understand the mind by the direct examination of consciousness. Because no agreement could be obtained about consciousness, Watson argued that psychologists should study public behavior instead of private experience. Animal psychology, Watson thought, was an ideal illustration of what psychological research should be; the observation of behavior in the absence of any introspective reports. Hull went one step further. Even when the behavior of a subhuman organism is being interpreted, the psychological theorist "begins thinking what he would do if he were a rat, a cat, or a chimpanzee; when that happens all his knowledge of his own behavior, born of years of self-observation, at once begins to function in place of the objectively stated general rules or principles which are the proper substance of science." In order to prevent such subjective interpretations, Hull suggested the strategy of viewing a behaving organism, human or subhuman, "as a completely self-maintaining robot, constructed of materials as unlike ourselves as may be." Thus, Hull was suggesting, in opposition to both Thorndike and Tolman, that the use of mentalistic terms and ideas, even though operationally defined, was misleading because of the false sense of understanding it encouraged. Only by viewing the behaving organism as a machine could one properly guard against pseudoexplanations that employed mental processes instead of logical explanations. Hull was a modern exponent of La Mettrie's view that humans could be best understood when conceptualized as machines in which the principles of functioning have to be discovered.

4. *Hypothetico-Deductive Theorizing.* Hull was passionately devoted to the hypothetico-deductive mode of reasoning. He admitted that, when he was a student,

the study of geometry proved to be the most important event of my intellectual life; it opened to me an entirely new world—the fact that thought
itself could generate and really prove new relationships from previously
possessed elements (Hull, 1952a, p. 144).

For Hull, the essence of science was contained in Euclidean geometry
and the Newtonian theory of motion and mechanics:

a theory is a systematic deductive derivation of the secondary principles
of observed phenomena from a relatively small number of primary principles or postulates, much as the secondary principles or theorems of geometry are all ultimately derived as a logical hierarchy from a few original
definitions and primary principles called axioms. In science, an observed
event is said to be explained when the proposition expressing it has been
logically derived from a set of definitions and postulates (Hull, 1943,
p. 2–3).

Hull did not only consider a hypothetico-deductive theory as a goal,
but also as a means to achieve a truly scientific theory of psychology.
From the very beginning of theorizing, Hull thought it necessary to formulate his ideas in a hypothetico-deductive fashion: "a clear formulation,
even if later found incorrect, will ultimately lead more quickly and easily
to a correct formulation than will a pussyfooting statement which might
be more difficult to convict of falsity" (Hull, 1943).

5. *Intervening Variables and Hypothetical Entities.* Only after Hull began
formulating a hypothetico-deductive theory of behavior did he realize its
similarity to the intervening variable plan of Tolman. Instead of trying to
discover the relationship between each independent variable with each
dependent variable, Hull attempted, as Tolman prescribed, to identify
those independent variables that exerted a common influence on behavior. Hull stressed the importance of having intervening variables "securely anchored" to both independent and dependent variables. If they
remained unanchored their meaning would be vague and, hence, they
could not generate testable predictions.

Unlike Tolman, Hull thought that it would be strategic to offer physiological analogues to his intervening variables, for example, changes in
the nervous system or blood chemistry that are associated with the concepts of habit and drive. Such suggestions, he hoped, would guide physiological research so that ultimately his behavior theory could be reduced
to a neurophysiological interpretation.

Stimulus-Response Reinforcement Theory

Hull's theorizing progressed through two stages. First, he published a
series of articles in the *Psychological Review* (Amsel & Rashotte, 1984) that
proposed miniature theories designed to account for a relatively narrow
range of phenomena. Later he formulated a general theory of behavior.

FIGURE 9.5   Two T-mazes with Blind Alleys of Different Lengths

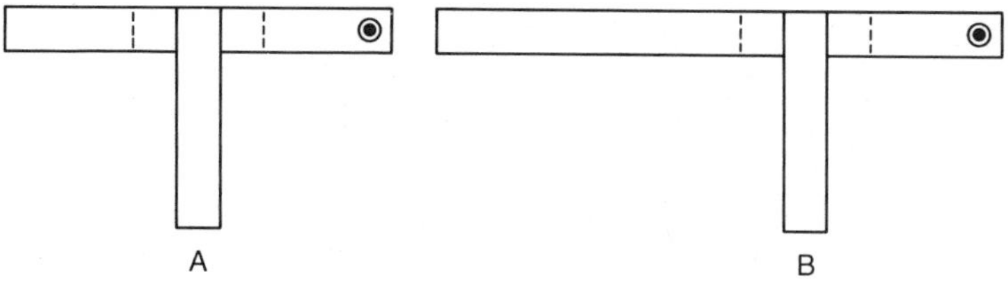

A   B

Maze B is easier to learn according to Hull's goal gradient hypothesis. Broken lines represent curtains while a solid line indicates the location of a door that prevents retracing.

Goal Gradient Hypothesis.   One example of this theorizing is his attempt (Hull, 1932) to derive certain maze phenomena from the goal gradient hypothesis which assumed that the nearer a response is to a reinforcement, the greater is the increment of habit strength that is acquired. For example, in a simple T-maze in which food is located in the right arm, the prediction is that the animal would finally learn to choose the right side because the right-turning habit will gradually become stronger than the left-turning habit. Each time the animal enters the right side, the increment of habit strength is greater than when it turns left, because the time between the right turn and consumption of food (reinforcement) is less than between the left turn and food consumption. When turning left, the animal has to retrace back past the choice point to the end of the right alley where food is located.

Predicting the elimination of blind alley entrances does not seem to qualify as a profound theoretical achievement. It isn't! But two aspects of this prediction have to be appreciated to realize its significance. First, Hull's prediction is objective. Its logic is completely open to public scrutiny. It is based upon a simple mathematical analysis of the relative strengths of competing habits that lead to reinforcement following different delay periods. The common sense view is that a rat selects the shorter path to the goal because it *knows* it to be shorter. But how does one know that the rat knows that the right path is shorter? How many trials will be required for a group of rats to perceive the right path to be shorter than the left path? These questions cannot be answered by the common sense "knowing" hypothesis.

Second, Hull's goal gradient hypothesis says more than that an animal will choose the shorter of two paths to a goal. It generates deductions about a variety of phenomena. For example, examine the two mazes in Figure 9.5. They differ only in the length of the blind alley; in maze A the blind alley is two feet, while in maze B it is four feet. Which maze would be easier to learn? A or B? Hull's goal gradient hypothesis predicts B is an easier problem to learn and experimental evidence supports this prediction (Hull, 1932). The reason is that the end of the left alley in maze B is further away from the reinforcement than it is in maze A and, therefore, a weaker incorrect habit would be acquired in maze B than in maze A. Maze B presents an easier problem because the correct response has less competition from the incorrect response.

Another example of the predictive power of Hull's goal gradient hypothesis relates to the order of elimination of blind alleys in a multiunit maze (Figure 9.2). When learning such a maze, all the correct choices throughout the maze could be learned at approximately the same rate or the blind alleys in different parts of the maze—beginning, middle, or end—could prove to be more difficult than at other parts. By assuming a mathematically exact gradient of delay, Hull was able to predict that errors (blind alley entrances) would be eliminated in a backward order; the last errors eliminated prior to learning were those blind alley entrances at the beginning of the maze.

A General Theory of Behavior. After completing a series of *Psychological Review* articles designed to interpret specific learning phenomena, Hull decided he was ready to formulate a general theory of behavior based on conditioning principles (Hull, 1943). Although the theory is complex, an understanding of its structure and some of its core ideas can be gleaned from the following simplified formula which expresses the relationship between the theoretical estimate of behavior, known as reaction potential ($S^E R$), and two intervening variables:

$$S^E R = (S^H R \times D)$$

where $S^E R$ is *reaction potential*, $S^H R$ is *habit strength*, and D is *drive*. To estimate the value of $S^E R$ first requires the determination of the values of $S^H R$ and D.

Habit. Habit refers to the tendency for a given stimulus to evoke the same response on successive occasions. Hull assumed, as had Thorndike, that the formation and strengthening of habits depended on their consequences. For the consequence of satisfaction, which Thorndike proposed, Hull substituted motivational reduction, a consequence which facilitates individual and species survival. Survival of an organism demands "optimal conditions of air, water, food, temperature, intactness of bodily tissue, and so forth; for species survival among the higher vertebrates there is required at least the occasional presence and specialized reciprocal behavior of a mate" (Hull, 1943). Hull labeled the process of need (drive) reduction, *reinforcement*, and assumed that the acquisition and strengthening of a habit depended on it being followed by a reinforcing state of affairs.

Hull recognized that all conditioning phenomena did not depend directly on drive (need) reduction. Higher-order conditioning was a notable exception (Pavlov, 1927), which demonstrates that a stimulus that has no reinforcing properties can acquire some. In one example, a first-order conditioned response was established by pairing the sound of a metronome (conditioned stimulus) with food (unconditioned stimulus), thus producing a conditioned response in which the metronome elicits salivation. Then, a second-order conditioned response was established by pairing a black square with a metronome. Since the metronome had acquired the capacity to evoke salivation, it was possible to use it as a reinforcer in place of drive-reducing unconditioned stimulus (food). Pavlov found that after a series of pairing the black squares with the metronome, the black square by itself elicited a salivary response. This finding demonstrated to Hull that a neutral stimulus can acquire reinforcing properties and thereby function as a reinforcement in the formation of a new stimulus-response association. Thus, Hull distinguished between two kinds of reinforcers; primary reinforcers (e.g., food) that result in drive (need) reduction, and secondary reinforcers (e.g., metronome), stimuli that acquire reinforcing properties as a function of their close temporal relationship with primary reinforcers.

On the basis of experimental evidence Hull hypothesized that habit strength was a function of four independent variables: the number of reinforced trials, the quality and amount of reinforcement, the delay of reinforcement, and the temporal relationship between a conditioned stimulus and the conditioned response. Hull expressed the relationship between each of these independent variables and the intervening variable of habit in a mathematical fashion so that it was possible in given experimental situations to infer a quantitative estimate of habit strength between a stimulus and response.

Drive. Behavior is not determined by habits alone. Habits, which are acquired response readinesses, must be activated to be transformed into behavior. At this moment, most of your habits are inactive. You can play checkers and you can whistle, but you are probably doing neither. Your reading habits are activated.

Hull's ideas about the activation of habits were revealed in a study (Perin, 1942) that related the amount of reinforced training with the degree of hunger during experimental extinction when pressing a bar no longer yielded a food pellet. Separate groups of rats, each deprived of food for twenty-three hours, received a different number of reinforced trials varying from five to ninety. Later, each group was subdivided during experimental extinction into two groups, each having different amounts of food deprivation, either three or twenty-two hours. The results are revealed in Figure 9.6. The two curves, designating the degree of hunger, show that the longer the deprivation period, the greater the persistence in pressing the bar during extinction.

According to Hull's theory, the number of reinforcements would determine the strength of the bar-pressing habit. To be specific, the subjects who had thirty reinforcements during reinforced training would acquire the *same* habit strength, but as Figure 9.6 reveals, they would exhibit different behavior during extinction; the twenty-two-hour hunger group emits many more responses during extinction than does the three-hour group. To predict such results, Hull had postulated that behavior (reaction potential), which can be measured by the number of responses to

FIGURE 9.6 A Test of Hull's Theoretical Assumption that Behavior Is a Multiplicative Function of Habit and Drive

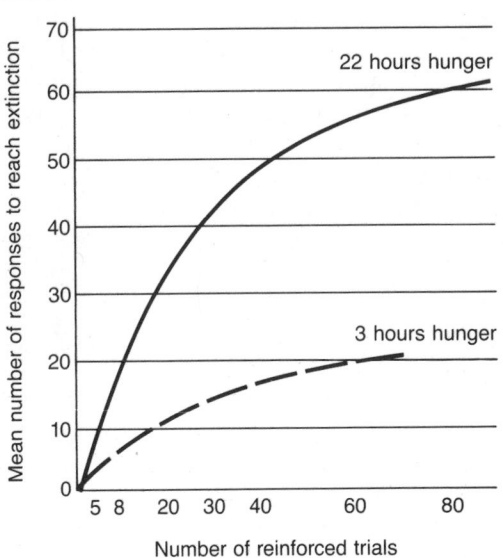

The graph reveals the relationship between the number of reinforced trails during acquisition of the instrumental response and the number of responses made during experimental extinction under two levels of hunger. See text for fuller explanation. (After Perin, 1942.)

reach extinction, is a joint function of *habit* and *drive*. This assumption is similar to Tolman's postulate that performance is a combined function of a cognitive map and demand. Both Tolman and Hull agreed that behavior is a joint function of a learning (cognitive map or habit) and a motivation (demand or drive). Hull went one step further. He specified that the relationship between learning and motivation, or in his terms, between habit and drive, is multiplicative. Drive energizes habits in a multiplicative manner. Assume that the strength of the bar-pressing habit after eight food-reinforcements is 5, that the strength of the hunger drive after three hours is 1, and that after twenty-two hours, the value of the hunger drive is 4. Now multiply the habit value by the drive values. The product, the reaction potential, of eight reinforcements and three hours of hunger (5 × 1) is 5, whereas the reaction potential of the same number of reinforcements and the greater twenty-two-hour drive (5 × 4) is 20. This theoretical assumption that a response is a function of habit multiplied by drive, explains the findings reported in Figure 9.6. A strong, as compared to a weak, drive energizes a specific habit into more persistent behavior. In addition, the notion of a multiplicative relationship between habit and drive predicts that, as the value of habit strength increases, the divergence between reaction potential produced by a weak and strong drive increases.

Although in the experiment reported in Figure 9.6 drive strength was defined in terms of the hours of food deprivation, Hull assumed that drive represented a general motivation, or, the sum of all drives operating at a given time. For example, the value of drive (D) would be greater if, in addition to a food deprivation,the subject had also been deprived of sex. Like Freud with his concept of libido, Hull postulated a general drive that energized all forms of behavior.

A final note. Soon after the publication of *Principles of Behavior* in 1943, major modifications of the theory were required. Several important empirical tests of the theory produced unanticipated results. One illustrative example was Hull's assumption that the magnitude of a goal object influenced habit strength as evidenced by the fact that as the size of a food reinforcement increased, so did the speed with which rats traversed a runway. In other words, the larger the reinforcement, the stronger the habit. If this assumption were correct, then the substitution of a large food reinforcement for a small one, and vice versa, should produce a *gradual* change in running speed in both groups. When, however, the switch was implemented, a sudden and sharp change in running speed occurred; the small-to-large group ran much faster while the large-to-small group slowed down markedly, with both groups quickly matching the performance of subjects who consistently received large or small rewards (Crespi, 1942; Zeaman, 1949). To account for these inconsistent findings, Hull postulated that magnitude of reinforcement was not a component of habit but instead influenced the motivation of the animal. More specifically, the size of the goal object was postulated to influence incentive motivation (K) which, in combination with drive (D), energized habits to produce behavior.

The discovery of disconfirming evidence that revealed fundamental inadequacies in Hull's original theory (1943) was not perceived as a failure but instead as a success. It revealed that the theory was capable of generating clear, testable implications. When the findings were at odds with the theory, it was possible to modify the formulation to account for the previously inconsistent evidence. That is, the theory was responsive to the evidence. This encouraged Hull and his associates to believe that their efforts were heralding a new period in the history of psychology in which behavior theories would match the rigor of biological and physical formulations. Whether this optimism was justified is revealed in a brief review of two theoretical controversies between Hull's stimulus-response reinforcement theory and Tolman's cognitive behaviorism.

TWO THEORETICAL CONTROVERSIES

A common misconception about science is that theoretical controversies can be resolved by critical experiments. The Hollywood version of this idealistic notion is that two theorists who hold conflicting views agree about an experimental design that will be capable of determining which theory is correct. They then retire to the laboratory in white coats where they conduct the experiment and later, in the spirit of true science, announce smilingly which of the two theories is valid. No scenario could be further from the truth. A theory challenged by inconsistent findings can usually be defended in two major ways. One is by showing that the presumed critical test falls short of being a satisfactory test of the theory. The second possible defense is to offer ad hoc modifications of theory in order to accommodate the previously embarrassing evidence.

Latent Learning

Tolman's cognitive theory, you will recall, conflicted with Hull's formulation by assuming that reinforcement is not necessary for learning and that cognitive maps, not stimulus-response associations, are learned. These two differences appeared striking, leading psychologists to believe that with time and research the controversies would be clearly resolved in favor of one of the two competing theories. That outcome never materialized because as the controversy progressed, the theoretical differences that initially appeared so clear became more and more murky. It gradually became apparent that the theories of Tolman and Hull, even with much ad hoc theorizing, were not sufficiently detailed and rigorous to integrate all the data the controversy generated. The community of psychologists finally expressed a negative verdict about the controversy by discontinuing research in latent learning. Nevertheless, the controversy is historically significant because it dramatically revealed the shortcomings of the general theories of that era.

1. *The Operational Meaning of Reinforcement.* The Tolman and Honzik experiment (1930) was offered as evidence against a stimulus-response reinforcement theory because the group without the food reward (reinforcement) learned as much as the consistently rewarded group. According to the cognitive view, the subjects, during the nonreward period, were learning a cognitive representation that was utilized when they were motivated to get food in the goal box.

The results reported by Tolman and Honzik in Figure 9.2 have one disturbing feature. Note that during the nonreward period when food was not in the goal box, the number of errors, entrances into blind alleys, gradually decreased. Why? If the so-called nonrewarded subjects were not reinforced for getting to the end box, should not the number of entrances into blind alleys remain essentially unchanged? Numerous experiments (e.g., Kanner, 1954) demonstrated that being removed from the empty end box is apparently reinforcing for the rat, as evidenced by the reduction in errors on successive trials. In one summary of the latent-learning findings, the conclusion was that "it is impossible to rule out the possibility that reward was present in some form in any experiment on latent learning" (Kimble, 1961). Such a conclusion raises doubts about the interpretation that the Tolman-Honzik experiment demonstrated that learning can occur in the absence of reinforcement. At best, the study shows that a relatively weak reinforcement (escape from the maze) can be as effective as a stronger reinforcement (food).

Attempts to pinpoint the relationship between learning and reinforcement generated numerous experiments. In one such study (Kendler, 1947), a T-maze was employed in which food was in one end box and water in the other. The *motivated* group was both hungry and thirsty, while the other group was *satiated* for both food and water. During training, both groups entered into each end box the same number of times, but only the motivated animals consumed the food or water. The subjects were then given a series of test trials in which they were either hungry or thirsty. According to Tolman's original formulation, the satiated animals, even though they did not eat and drink during the training trials, would form a cognitive map of the maze, including the location of the food and water. When hungry or thirsty, they should choose the path to the appropriate incentive (food when hungry, water when thirsty). The performance of the satiated animals should therefore match that of the motivated subjects during the test series. According to Hull's original conception, the satiated animals did not consume the food or water and, hence, were not reinforced. Consequently, they should exhibit chance performance on the test trials while the motivated subjects should evidence definite signs of learning. The results were inconsistent with both theories. The motivated subjects had a much higher percentage of correct responses, thus contradicting Tolman, and the satiated animals manifested some signs of having learned the positions of the food and water, thus contradicting Hull.

Both theories could offer reasonable ad hoc interpretations of these results; but neither could be revised in a manner that could satisfactorily interpret *all* the latent learning data.

2. *Unreliable Knowledge.* The latent learning phenomenon, as reported by Tolman and Honzik (1932), proved to be somewhat unreliable. Attempts to replicate the phenomenon sometimes failed and the exact set of conditions required to obtain latent learning has never been fully identified. To make matters more complicated, Kanner (1954), who essentially replicated Tolman and Honzik's procedures, found that with their test of latent learning, the nonrewarded animals learned as much as the rewarded rats; but with a more stringent test, the rewarded subjects learned much more. In other words, according to one measure of behavior latent learning occurred, but according to another it did not.

3. *Cognitive Maps versus Stimulus-Response Associations.* Although the differences between the views of Tolman and Hull as to what was being learned, cognitive maps or stimulus-response associations, seemed clear, the differences between the two gradually began to fade. A cognitive map is essentially a set of expectancies; the animal expects that a left turn will lead to one consequence (e.g., water), while a right turn will lead to another (e.g., food). A Pavlovian (classical) conditioned response can also be conceptualized as an expectancy; the tone elicits salivation in *anticipation* of the forthcoming food. Hull postulated a mechanism, based upon principles of conditioning, that became known as *anticipatory goal response*. It operated in a manner analogous to Tolman's expectancy. As a result, the theoretical difference between the conceptions of Tolman and Hull were blunted, thus making it impossible to design an experiment in which the two theories clearly generated opposed predictions.

Continuity Theory versus Noncontinuity Theory

The continuity-noncontinuity controversy described previously generated numerous experiments designed to evaluate the relative merits of each theory. One reviewer (Riley, 1968) drew the following conclusion about studies that employed animal subjects such as rats: "The evidence predominantly supported the continuity position." This comment would suggest that the continuity position achieved supremacy over the noncontinuity formulation. This proved not to be the case for several reasons. First, continuity theory could not pinpoint the reasons why some studies favored the noncontinuity position, thus suggesting that certain relevant variables, particularly perceptual processes, were overlooked by the continuity theory. Second, the hypothesis-testing model did not depend on retaining the assumption that only one hypothesis could be entertained at a time. By assuming that more than one hypothesis could be tested simultaneously, the model could explain findings that were initially inconsistent. Third, and most importantly, the hypothesis-testing assumption seemed to fit the facts of the behavior of human adults when solving simple concept-learning tasks. Although the stimulus-response reinforcement (continuity) formulation had only been formulated to explain the behavior of inarticulate organisms such as the laboratory rat (Spence, 1936), many psychologists began to challenge the notion that a theory of human behavior should await the completion of a theory of behavior of lower animals. For them, a theory that could explain human behavior was more interesting and important than one that could explain only animal behavior.

Several researchers within the Hullian camp (e.g., Kuenne, 1946) proposed a supplementary mechanism, *mediation*, to Spence's continuity theory in order to account for human concept behavior. Discrimination learning, according to Spence's continuity theory, hypothesized that the responses of animals were directly linked (associated) to stimuli (e.g., black, white), whereas the mediational model proposed that incoming stimulation was transformed into some internal conceptual representation (e.g., brightness) that guides subsequent behavior. A series of studies

(Kendler & Kendler, 1962; 1975) demonstrated that the discrimination learning behavior of rats could be accounted for by Spence's single unit continuity model, while human adults behaved in a manner consistent with the mediational S-R hypothesis. A developmental study with children varying from three to twelve years of age reported that the probability that a child's behavior will fit the continuity or mediational model depends on the age of the child; the younger the child, the more likely the child will behave according to the single unit theory, whereas the older the child, the more likely the child's performance will be consonant with the mediational model. This research program highlighted three important points: First, the stimulus-response theory, initially proposed by Hull, can be extended by additional assumptions to interpret developmental changes in conceptual behavior. Second, it is incorrect to distinguish sharply between animal and human behavior. Second, it is incorrect to distinguish sharply between animal and human behavior. When it comes to discrimination learning, we find that young children behave in a manner similar to that of lower animals, but the older they become, the more likely that their behavior will be consistent with that of human adults. Third, although the continuity and noncontinuity theories of discrimination learning were initially in opposition, they tended to complement each other within a comparative and human developmental framework.

A restrospective analysis.   At the beginning of the latent-learning and continuity-noncontinuity controversies, hopes reigned high that the force of empirical data would resolve the theoretical disputes. This hope was not realized because, in spite of much ad hoc theorizing and enormous amounts of data, key concepts such as *cognitive map, demand, hypothesis, reinforcement, drive, anticipatory goal response*, as well as others, retained a degree of ambiguity that prevented any definitive verdict in favor of either Tolman's or Hull's theory.

The failure to reach a clear-cut decision was much less damaging to Tolman's theory than to Hull's. Tolman frankly admitted the tentative nature of his cognitive formulation, believing that his major task was to offer theoretical notions and empirical evidence that challenged what appeared to him to be an oversimplified stimulus-response conception. In this effort, he was successful because he helped raise some doubts about Hullian psychology and other stimulus-response associationistic conceptions. Hull, in contrast, had a more ambitious plan: the formulation of primary principles of behavior that would serve as a foundation of a conception that could "be regarded as a general introduction to the theory of all the behavioral (social) science." He explicitly stated that his formulation would ultimately extend to social behavior of human beings. The fact that his formulation failed to incorporate all the facts of animal learning in a rigorous manner, raised grave doubts about his entire research and theoretical program. Even one of his disciples was forced to admit that "Hull tended to oversell the program, to offer more than could be delivered" (Logan, 1968).

Doubts began to be expressed about whether psychology was at that stage of historical development required for a successful general theory of behavior. Some argued that before a general theory of behavior could be successful, a more solid foundation of reliable evidence was required. Others suggested that the basic assumptions of any psychological theory must be based upon knowledge of neurophysiological functioning. Still others questioned whether the goal of a general psychological theory was reasonable because contemporary physics and other natural sciences have split, in recent decades, into separate fields, each requiring distinctive methods of investigation that produced limited theories.

History offers the verdict that the efforts of Tolman and Hull were constructive failures. They both fell far short of achieving their goals but, nevertheless, made important positive contributions to the scientific development of psychology.

CONTRIBUTIONS OF TOLMAN AND HULL

The contributions of neobehaviorism, in the forms expressed by Tolman and Hull, are difficult to sort out because of the complex interrelationships that prevail among their methodological, strategic, and theoretical views. The historical importance of Tolman and Hull can perhaps be best revealed by first discussing the major achievements of each, followed by an analysis of their shared contributions. Finally, the historical developments of each formulation will be reviewed.

Tolman's Cognitive Approach

Tolman's major historical contribution is the cognitive model he proposed in opposition to the dominant stimulus-response orientation that had prevailed since the time of Watson. Tolman's theoretical concepts of *cognitive maps, expectancies,* and *hypotheses* proved appealing to many psychologists, particularly those interested in human psychology. Stimulus-response language, for them, seemed to be too restrictive to represent the intellectual functioning of adult human beings. Tolman's freewheeling use of mentalistic processes encouraged a reconsideration of the antimentalistic stand that Watson had imposed on psychology.

While rejecting stimulus-response psychology in favor of a cognitive position, Tolman, it must be repeated, did *not* reject behaviorism:

> I wish now, once and for all, to put myself on record as feeling a distaste for most of the terms . . . I have introduced. I especially dislike the terms *purpose* and *cognition* and the title *Purposive Behavior.* I have, I believe a

strong anti-theological and anti-introspectionistic bias; and yet here my words and my title seem to be lending support of an ultimately teleological and ultimately mentalistic interpretation of animal and human behavior. Actually, I have used these terms, *purpose* and *cognition,* and the various derivatives and synonyms I have coined, in a purely neutral and objective [operational] sense (Tolman, 1932, p. xi–xii).

Tolman was essentially adopting the strategy that a mentalistic and purposive outlook could serve as a fruitful source of theoretical hypotheses. The justification for this orientation was not that it reflected conscious experience, but instead that it helped formulate fruitful hypotheses that could be evaluated by behavioral evidence.

Hull's Theoretical Standards

In 1945, Hull was awarded the prestigious Warren Medal by the Society of Experimental Psychologists with the inscription:

To Clark L. Hull: For his careful development of a systematic theory of behavior. This theory has stimulated much research and it has been developed in a precise and quantitative form so as to permit predictions which can be tested empirically. The theory thus contains within itself the seeds of its own ultimate verification and of its own possible final disproof. A truly unique achievement in the history of psychology to date.

The years following this award justified the inscription. Within the ten-year period following the publication of *Principles of Behavior* in 1943, 40 percent of all experimental studies reported in the highly regarded *Journal of Experimental Psychology* and *Journal of Comparative and Physiological Psychology* referred to Hull's works. The figure was 70 percent when articles limited to the fields of learning and motivation are considered. Hull's impact extended well beyond these two research areas; during the period between 1949 and 1952, there were 105 references to the *Principles of Behavior* in *The Journal of Abnormal and Social Psychology,* compared to twenty-five for the next most popular work (Ruja, 1956).

Hull's profound influence did not stem solely from his particular stimulus-response theory. The deductive capacity of his theory—the clear relationship between hypotheses and experimentation—appealed to many psychologists, who tried to emulate Hull in formulating a natural-science type theory, even when rejecting his theoretical assumptions and strategic orientation.

Shared Contributions of Tolman and Hull

Although their theories were markedly different in content, Tolman and Hull shared important methodological commitments, theoretical assumptions, and general strategies.

Intervening Variable Mode of Theory Construction. The intervening variable method of constructing a psychological theory which was originally proposed by Tolman, and later implemented by Hull, encouraged theorizing by proposing a recipe for theory construction. The recipe proved not to be as simple or distinctive as Tolman suggested and, as a consequence, the term intervening variable is rarely used today. Nevertheless, Tolman's proposed method did exert a salutary effect on psychological theories by stressing the importance of anchoring theoretical constructs (intervening variables) to observable independent and dependent variables, thus enhancing the clarity of theoretical predictions.

Learning and Motivation. Both Tolman and Hull were convinced that experimental evidence dictated that a general theory of behavior must assign a central role to learning and motivational processes. Although they viewed behavior within contrasting frameworks, cognitive versus stimulus-response, they both concluded that training, deprivation of biological needs, and size of incentives had potent effects on behavior. Many subsequent theoretical psychologists were to share their views.

Strategies for Theory Construction. The Tolman-Hull controversies alerted psychologists to the fact that successful theorizing cannot be reduced to a set of specific rules. To some extent, psychologists misread the signals from the philosophy of logical positivism, believing that it offered an accurate blueprint for theorizing. The truth of the matter is that theorizing is an experiment in itself with no guarantee that success will be forthcoming. The difference between the two strategic orientations of Tolman and Hull illustrates this point.

When should rigorous theorizing begin? Hull argued that the goal of a general behavior theory could be best served by rigorous theorizing from the very beginning. If a theory is vaguely stated in its initial stage, as most theories in psychology have been, then Hull argued the theory would never become precise. Tolman believed that during the early stages of theoretical development, attention should be directed at identifying major psychological processes. Unlike other behaviorists who, from the time of Watson, adopted an extreme environmentalism, Tolman encouraged the study of behavior genetics because he questioned the prevalent notion that genetic determination could be assigned a minor role in a general theory of behavior. Precise theorizing, for Tolman, should only begin after the theorist is confident that major behavioral processes have not been overlooked. Neither strategy—precise quantification or qualitative analysis—succeeded. Hull's failure has frequently been attributed to his premature theoretical quantification. But Tolman and Gestalt psychology, with their strategy of qualitative analysis, never formulated rigorous theories. Is it possible to select a strategy that is guaranteed to be fruitful?

How is a basic experimental paradigm identified? Hull took the strong position that conditioning could provide information about principles of behavior that extend from simple learning to social behavior. Tolman was much less optimistic about the potential of a specific experimental paradigm to reflect the core assumptions of a general theory of behavior, although he did assume that in the field of learning, experimental designs involving choice behavior were particularly suited for yielding information on which principles of animal learning could be based. Although the strategy of identifying a pure case of learning seemed reasonable, it gradually became apparent that the selection of a basic experimental paradigm for erecting a theory was, at best, a guess that was not guaranteed to succeed. Hull, because he viewed behavior within a stimulus-response associative framework, was predisposed to consider conditioning as an ideal task to investigate association formation and strengthening. Tolman, in contrast, perceived maze learning as an excellent method for discovering the principles that governed the formation of cognitive maps. The ultimate test of a basic experimental paradigm for theory constructing, however, is not whether the paradigm agrees with intuitive preconceptions, but instead whether it yields empirical information that can be exploited successfully in a general theory of behavior. In retrospect, Hull appeared much too optimistic about the possibilities of reducing complex behavior, especially human cognition and motivation, to principles of conditioning. Nor was animal maze learning, as Tolman had surmised, able to bear all the weight of a general theory of learning. Tolman admitted this shortcoming later when he advanced the idea that there was more than one kind of learning.

Although the efforts of Tolman and Hull did not yield any firm guidelines for the selection of a basic experimental paradigm for theory construction, they did nevertheless alert theoretical psychologists to the possible pitfalls of a premature commitment to any one experimental task.

The Historical Development of the Theories of Tolman and Hull

Tolman's cognitive theory never achieved its full potential for a variety of reasons. Tolman, himself, avoided formalizing his theory partly because he always felt that some new phenomena had to be explored before rigorous theorizing could begin. Also, he considered himself to be temperamentally unsuited for such a task. In addition, his doctoral students, although converted to Tolman's cause, failed to compensate for their professor's reluctance to embark on a course of rigorous theory construction. Interestingly, two psychologists who were not particularly sympathetic to Tolman's cognitive position, MacCorquodale and Meehl (1953, 1954), undertook the task of formalizing Tolman's notions in order to render their implications more explicit with the intention of clarifying the difference between his theory and Hull's. Although their efforts were illuminating, they failed to have much impact because psychologists were beginning to shift their attention away from the Tolman-Hull controversy to other issues and problems. Later, some of the basic ideas of Tolman's theory were absorbed into modern cognitive theory (Chapter 11).

This historical development of Hullian theory from its inception is much more complex, and its legacy more difficult to assess than that of Tolman. A major reason for this is that Hullian theory was not as monolithic as is commonly believed. One should distinguish between Hull's initial modest efforts to formulate models appropriate to specific research areas such as delay of reinforcement and his later grandiose plan to construct a general theory that he thought could be extended to the full range of animal and human behavior. Moreover, Hull's legacy was not limited to his own formulations. He was blessed with two productive and creative disciples, Kenneth W. Spence (1907–1967) and Neal E. Miller (born 1909); both carried on the traditions of Hullian psychology while simultaneously compensating for some of Hull's shortcomings. Hull was always working against time, having started his general theory building relatively late in life. As a consequence, he tended to be impatient and impulsive in his formulations and was sometimes more concerned with the formal deductive properties of his theoretical postulates than with supporting evidence. Because his theorizing was often premature, ad hoc modifications were frequently required to interpret new evidence. The ultimate consequence of these changes was to make the empirical implications of the general theory more opaque. Some experimental operations had so many different theoretical consequences, that it became impossible to predict their influence on behavior. Thus, the appeal of theoretical clarity that was seen initially as the virtue of Hullian theory finally became one of its major liabilities.

Both Spence and Miller, operating within the Hullian orientation, employed different strategies to avoid the theoretical ambiguity that finally strangled Hull's general formulation. Spence suggested that Hull's difficulties resulted from his inflexible need to barge ahead with his theorizing before essential evidence became available. In contrast to Hull's ebullient declaration that his *Principles of Behavior* (1943) could be "regarded as a general introduction to all the behavioral (social) sciences," Spence noted more than ten years later, in the preface of his major work, *Behavior Theory and Conditioning* (1956) that "psychology is at present very much lacking [comprehensive theories] . . . . Indeed, it is as yet in a very primitive state of development, one in which the primary concern is the formulation of empirical laws encompassing fairly circumscribed areas of behavior." Although in the tradition of Hull's *Principles of Behavior,* Spence's book was much less formal and much more in tune with the complexities of available evidence. In addition, Spence (1950) thought Hull was too wedded to the belief that conditioning principles could bear the full weight of a general behavior theory. A general theory, Spence thought, would only be developed gradually, in a time frame that extended well beyond the life of a single individual.

FIGURE 9.7   Kenneth W. Spence and Neal E. Miller

Courtesy of Janet T. Spence   Courtesy of Neil E. Miller

Neal Miller's style of theorizing differed in style and substance from Hull's. Miller practically ignored the problem of developing a detailed and general theory of behavior. He was more interested in extending some basic ideas from conditioning and motivation to various research areas. The problem of formulating a general theory of behavior, Miller believed, could be set aside until success was achieved in interpreting a variety of research problems that spanned the entire spectrum of psychological phenomena.

Miller was particularly successful, sometimes with the collaboration of John Dollard, an anthropologist, in formulating theoretical models of psychological conflict (Miller, 1944), displacement of aggression (Miller, 1948), learnable drives (Miller, 1951), social learning and imitation (Miller & Dollard, 1941), and personality and psychotherapy (Dollard & Miller, 1950). He later came to believe, however, that a purely behavioral analysis of psychological phenomena was not going to be as productive as Hull and Spence anticipated. Developments in neurophysiology and biotechnology convinced Miller that psychological theory must be based on biopsychological research. Miller retooled his research skills and initiated an important series of studies in visceral learning, learning to control physiological reactions that are regulated by the autonomic nervous system, such as heart rate, blood pressure, vasodilation and vasoconstriction, intestinal contractions, galvanic skin responses, and so forth. His aim was to develop biofeedback techniques that would enable one to manage one's own visceral reactions, as in the case of reducing high blood pressure. Miller's efforts, along with those of others, helped create the multidisciplinary field of *behavioral medicine* that sought to integrate biological and behavioral knowledge for research into and treatment of diseases stemming from emotional stress brought on by a person's inability to cope with life's problems.

History suggests that the strategies of Spence and Miller were more realistic that those of Hull. The task of developing a general theory of behavior from conditioning principles that Hull initiated was abandoned after his death. Only specific models that interpreted phenomena from circumscribed research areas survived. Many of these models were based upon ideas that originated with Hull, Spence, and Miller, while others were proposed by their disciples who adopted their methodological orientation while adapting their theoretical notions. The number of such models is too numerous to mention, but they covered a wide range of phenomena, including frustrative effects of nonreward (Amsel, 1962), discrimination learning and cognitive development (Kendler & Kendler, 1975), and psychological stress and coping (Weiss, 1972). Although none of these specific theories has been universally adopted, they have all generated fruitful research that, in turn, has served to identify important empirical variables and pinpoint significant theoretical issues. All in all, the efforts of Hull, Spence, Miller and their followers forced psychologists to face up to the difficulties and complexities of formulating natural science theories and by so doing have left a legacy of interesting data and fruitful hypotheses.

Quotations from Tolman, Hull, Spence, and Miller

1. I have always been obsessed by a need for a single comprehensive theory or scheme for the whole of psychology (Tolman, 1952, p. 336).

2. Although I was sold on objectivism and behaviorism as *the* method in psychology, the only categorizing rubrics which I had at hand were mentalistic ones. So when I began to try to develop a be-

havioristic system of my own, what I really was doing was trying to rewrite a commonsense mentalistic psychology . . . in operational behavioristic terms (Tolman, 1959, p. 94).

3. I do not hold, as do most behaviorists, that all learning is, as such, the attachment of responses to stimuli. Cathexes, equivalence beliefs, field expectancies, field-cognition modes and drive discriminations are not, as I define them, stimulus-response connections. They are central phenomena, each of which may be expressed by a variety of responses (Tolman, 1949, p. 146).

4. Only when man's total psychology is understood and all his absolutely necessary psychological needs are allowed balanced satisfaction will a society permitting relatively universal individual satisfaction and welfare be achieved and war be abolished (Tolman, 1942, p. 5).

5. Unfortunately, the knowledge of neurophysiology has not yet advanced to a point where it is of much assistance in telling us how the nervous system operates in the determination of important forms of behavior. This means that our theory of behavior must be at bottom almost entirely molar; i.e., it must be presented in terms of stimuli and responses together with a statement of the conditions under which these have occurred in the past and are about to occur in the present (Hull, 1951, pp. 5–6).

6. Is pure science's methodological capacity to mediate the *prediction* . . . of the occurrence of an event under given conditions of behavior of whatever nature—whether moral, immoral, or unmoral—the same thing as the capacity to make a moral judgment, i.e., to *characterize* certain behavior absolutely as ethically good or bad? . . . this difference between ethical theory and the theory of moral behavior indicates that ethical principles can never have the type of validity that the scientific theory of moral behavior may have (Hull, 1952b, p. 339).

7. Unlike the [cognitive] theorist, the *S-R* psychologist does not usually talk very much about such things as perception, meaning, knowledge, cognitive processes, etc. I suspect, however, that he deals with pretty much the same thing that the cognitive theorists do under different terms (Spence, 1950, p. 169).

8. My general strategy has been to use animal experiments to formulate and verify principles applicable to neurotic behavior rather than to attempt to duplicate in animals the spectacular aspects of neurotic symptoms (Miller, 1959, p. 234).

9. Some of the earlier writers who treated thinking as mere symbolic trial and error missed its most important attribute. Its ability to be guided by the goal (the definition of the problem), so that the dice are loaded in favor of the combination of habits likely to succeed, is one of the key characteristics of creative thinking (Miller, 1959, p. 246).

A Debate about Neobehaviorism

Moderator: This debate has an unusual feature. The debaters have to simultaneously support or criticize conflicting systems: cognitive behaviorism (Tolman) and stimulus-response reinforcement theory (Hull). Is this impossible?

Pro: Not for me! To appreciate fully the historical significance of Tolman and Hull, one must recognize their fundamental similarity. They were both behaviorists who were committed to the goal of an objective psychology but, unlike Watson, they were emancipated from his extreme and unnecessary views. Both Tolman and Hull operated as natural science psychologists but with different strategies. Tolman approached his theoretical task from the inside; first constructing a model of the mind and then anchoring this model, in an objective manner, to independent and dependent variables. Hull started from the outside of the organism; empirical relationships beween stimuli and responses guided his theoretical efforts to bridge the gap between independent and dependent variables. Although their strategy and conceptions differed, the common epistemological structure of their formulations served as a standard for subsequent theorizing.

Con: I have more difficulty lumping Tolman and Hull together than does my opponent. Although I agree they employed the same methodological orientation and shared the strategy of erecting a general psychological theory on the behavioral evidence of rodents, I consider the difference between Tolman's mentalistic orientation as contrasted with Hull's mechanistic outlook to be more important. A mindless psychology of the sort that Hull and his disciples espoused can never succeed because mental processes cannot be ignored.

Pro: That's rubbish! Behaviorists are interested in behavior and there is no way of knowing now whether it will prove necessary to formulate theoretical hypotheses from hunches about mentalistic processes, machines, computers, neurophysiological laws, etc. The proof of the pudding is in the eating; the proof of a psychological theory is in its ability to integrate and predict behavioral phenomena. A simple recipe for constructing an adequate theory of behavior is not, and never will be, available and, consequently, restrictions cannot be placed on the general strategy that can be employed.

Con: You behaviorists seem to entertain the quaint notion that developing a psychological theory is purely a random process; some strategies will work and others will not and no amount of intuition and rational thought can help identify the best approach. Well, I believe that being human, having a mind, offers insights about psychological events, and psychologists should not ignore such help when constructing theories.

Pro: I'll admit that some strategies will work better than others but we don't have any litmus test to identify the best procedure. So why argue? The basic point is that the Tolmanian and Hullian orientations, operating within a Darwinian framework, provided a considerable degree of understanding animal behavior, which, I would argue, also provides information about basic behavioral processes in humans. Neal Miller and other disciples of Hull demonstrated how principles of behavior resulting from animal behavior can be extended to human behavior. Although falling short of their goal of producing a compelling general theory of behavior, Tolman and Hull made fundamental methodological, theoretical, and empirical contributions to psychology that history will always remember.

Con: You are overoptimistic. History will demonstrate that for the most part, except for Tolman's return to mentalism, the neobehaviorisms of Hull and Tolman will prove to be an irrelevant episode in the history of psychology. In support of my contention I need only remind you that during the past decade references to either Tolman or Hull have been practically absent from professional journals. I'm convinced that such references will completely disappear in the future.

Moderator: Your historical predictions are interesting. We'll wait 100 years and discover which one of you is correct.

SUMMARY

One legacy of Watsonian behaviorism is neobehaviorism, a systematic position in line with methodological behaviorism but at odds with Watsonian theory. Two forms of neobehaviorism are Tolman's cognitive behaviorism and Hull's stimulus-response reinforcement theory. Tolman and Hull were both influenced by logical positivism, a philosophical school that sought to identify the basic structure of natural science methodology including the manner in which scientific concepts are defined. In addition, Tolman and Hull favored the methodology of animal psychology and shared the common view that learning and motivation were basic psychological processes.

Tolman's cognitive behaviorism was influenced by both William McDougall and Gestalt psychology. McDougall described himself as a "sane behaviorist" because he believed that defining psychology as the science of behavior, which he favored, did not exclude from consideration, as Watson suggested, conscious purposive strivings. McDougall also rejected Watson's extreme environmentalism, arguing that the behavior of organisms was dominated by innate motivational strivings which he labeled *propensities*. The gestalt concepts of psychological environment and field theory also played a central role in Tolman's cognitive behaviorism.

Tolman's behaviorism distinguished between molecular and molar behavior. The former referred to glandular secretions and muscular contractions, while the latter was defined in terms of the consequences of acts. Tolman rejected the notion of a muscle-twitch molecular type of theory, believing that the dependent variable of a behavioral theory should be acts. The criterion of understanding that Tolman espoused was deductive explanation.

Five different strategies dominated Tolman's research and theorizing: (1) *Behavioral determinism* which assumes that behavior can be explained by an abstract psychological theory that ignores underlying neurophysiological processes. (2) Fruitful theoretical ideas can be generated by *commonsense phenomenology*, (3) *Choice behavior* is the fundamental psychological act, (4) Only a *transfer criterion of learning* can reveal what an organism has learned, and (5) The *intervening variable* method is the most efficient and effective procedure for formulating a psychological theory.

Tolman's cognitive theory of animal behavior postulated two interacting intervening variables: cognitive map and motivation (demand). A cognitive map is a perceptual representation of the maze and its acquisition is assumed to be independent of rewards obtained in the maze. When the motivational conditions were appropriate (e.g., presence of hunger drive and food reward), the subject would utilize its cognitive map to guide it to the reward. Tolman's research efforts were designed to discover the independent variables that influenced the two intervening variables (*cognitive map* and *demand*) and, in turn, to discover how they influenced behavior.

Tolman's cognitive theory was later expanded to include the theoretical process of hypothesis testing which assumed that, in a discrimination-learning task, rats successively test different hypotheses (e.g., left is correct) until they hit upon the correct one. In one of his last papers, Tolman abandoned his early assumption of a single kind of learning and suggested six different forms of learning.

The specific historical influences that shaped Hull's neobehavioristic conception were Pavlovian (classical) conditioning and Thorndike's law of effect. Like all behaviorists, he considered observable behavior to be the subject matter of psychology, but, unlike Tolman, he used both molecular and molar forms of behavior as dependent variables. In addition, he supplemented his behavior theory with speculations about the underlying neurophysiological correlates of behavior. Hull insisted that explanations of psychological phenomena must be expressed in a deductive mold.

Hull's research and theoretical efforts were expressed in a fivefold strategy: (1) Employ stimulus-response language to represent psychological phenomena, (2) Use conditioning as a source of theoretical principles, (3) Avoid the possibility of subjective interpretations by conceptualizing organisms as machines (e.g., self-maintaining robots), (4) Build theories from their inception with rigorous deductive logic, and (5) Employ the Tolman method of theory construction, involving the formulation of intervening variables.

Initially, Hull formulated a set of miniature theories designed to interpret a circumscribed range of learning phenomena. Later, he formulated a general theory of behavior based on principles of conditioning that was designed ultimately to interpret psychological phenomena ranging from animal learning to human social behavior. Two core intervening variables of Hullian theory were *habit* and *drive*, and it was assumed that behavior is a multiplicative product of both. A basic assumption of Hull's theory is that, in order for habits to be formed and strengthened, the habitual response must be followed by a reinforcing state of affairs. Need (drive) reduction produces a primary reinforcement, while a stimulus closely and consistently related to a primary reinforcement acquires secondary reinforcing properties.

Two theoretical controversies, latent learning and the continuity versus noncontinuity interpretations of discrimination learning, were initially thought to be able to test the relative merits of Tolman's cognitive theory and Hull's stimulus-response reinforcements conception in explaining animal learning. As the controversies progressed, it gradually became apparent that both theories suffered from fundamental ambiguities that prevented a clearcut resolution of the theoretical differences. Interest in the latent-learning phenomenon gradually subsided and finally the topic was abandoned. The continuity-noncontinuity controversy was not directly resolved but instead was enlarged to include both animal and human subjects and developmental changes in conceptual behavior. The historical consequence of these two related controversies raised questions about whether psychology was at that stage of development in which a general theory of behavior was a reasonable goal.

Tolman's major historical contribution was cognitive behaviorism; the attempt to formulate a behavioristic theory based upon mentalistic processes. Hull's major contribution was the rigorousness of his theoretical formulations, the ability of his hypotheses to generate clear deductive consequences that could be empirically evaluated. Hull's efforts elevated the theoretical standards of psychological theory.

The combined efforts of Tolman and Hull encouraged the intervening variable mode of theory construction that stressed the importance of anchoring theoretical constructs to both independent and dependent variables, emphasized the central importance of learning and motivation in behavior theory, and suggested a variety of strategies in constructing a theory of behavior.

Tolman's cognitive theory was absorbed into a general cognitive approach to all psychological phenomena that developed about a decade following his death. One of Hull's major disciples, Kenneth W. Spence, pursued Hull's goal of a general theory of behavior based upon conditioning principles but in a more modest and realistic fashion. Another major disciple, Neal E. Miller, employed many Hullian ideas to interpret phenomena from specific research areas such as psychological conflict and personality development. Today, many such theories have historical roots in Hullian theory.

SUGGESTED READINGS

Reading the classic books of both Tolman (*Purposive Behavior in Animals and Men*) and Hull (*Principles of Behavior*) would be an illuminating task for the serious student of the history of psychology as well as for those who are interested in the psychology of learning. In addition, Amsel and Rashotte (1984) have republished Hull's *Psychological Review* articles along with interesting commentaries. Tolman's *Drives toward War* (1942), a slender volume, illustrates how Tolman, as a theorist, made the transition from laboratory research to social issues. Spence's *Behavior Theory and Conditioning* (1956) illustrates how Hullian theory was forced to retreat from its highly formal structure to a more informal organization. The student of the history of psychology will find the efforts of Neal Miller in extending Hullian theory to conflict behavior (Miller, 1944) and personality and psychotherapy (Dollard & Miller, 1950) to be both ingenious and fascinating.

Sigmund Koch edited a series of volumes in which important theoretical efforts were systematically analyzed by their originators or disciples. Volume 2 (Koch, 1959) contains three essays that should be of interest: Tolman's "Principles of Purposive Behavior," Miller's "Liberalization of Basic S-R Concepts: Extensions to Conflict Behavior, Motivation and Social Learning," and Logan's "The Hull-Spence Approach."

10

Neobehaviorism II: Skinner and Hebb

Neobehaviorism did not end with Tolman and Hull. A variety of neobehavioristic formulations was developed, influenced in part by the conceptions of Tolman and Hull.

One nagging question that attracted much attention stemmed from the failure of Hull's general theory, on which so much talent and effort was expended. Why did it fail? Two important neobehaviorists—so different as to make their pairing appear to be incongruous—offered contrasting answers. B. F. Skinner (born 1904) argued that Hull's attempt was doomed from the beginning; theories that employ abstract theoretical constructs (intervening variables) must fail. Donald O. Hebb (1904–1985) proposed that a theory of behavior must be based on neurophysiological knowledge, not simply on obtained regularities between stimuli and responses.

Not only did Skinner and Hebb offer contrasting views of general psychological theories, but their careers as psychologists differed in style and substance. B. F. Skinner acted as a messiah whose mission was to alert society to his model of behavior that could be employed in designing a blueprint for a utopian society. Skinner never seemed to entertain any doubts about his psychological conceptions or their ultimate value to society. His major task was to expose psychologists and society to his ideas, and in this task he was eminently successful. His talents as an author and lecturer propelled him to the front ranks of scientists; in one poll he was identified as the best known scientist in the world.

If Skinner occupied the center stage in psychology, Hebb was most of the time hidden in the wings. Only in midlife did he become generally recognized as offering a new approach to the task of constructing a general theory of behavior. Since Hebb felt that theory should be constructed

FIGURE 10.1 B. F. Skinner and Donald O. Hebb

Courtesy of B. F. Skinner

Courtesy of Mrs. Ellen Foley

within a neurophysiological framework, his efforts contributed substantially to the expansion of biopsychology.

SKINNER'S RADICAL BEHAVIORISM

Skinner proposed such fundamental changes in behaviorism and psychology that the name *radical behaviorism* was assigned to his position. The historical roots of his core ideas are contained in some of the contributions of John B. Watson, Ivan Pavlov, and Edward L. Thorndike. In addition, he shared methodological ideas with Ernst Mach (1838–1916), the Austrian physicist and philosopher.

Historical Roots

John B. Watson. Skinner is a modern-day Watson. They share much in style, goals, and ideas. Like Watson, Skinner is a prophet who initiated crusades designed to reform psychology and change society. Conditioning served both as a source of basic ideas.

Ivan Pavlov. Ivan Pavlov influenced most neobehaviorists with the notable exception of Tolman, but Pavlov's specific impact varied. For Watson, the conditioned response was a unit of habit. For Hull, conditioning was a source of theoretical assumptions. For Skinner, Pavlov demonstrated that behavior could be controlled by environmental manipulations (e.g., pairing of the conditioned and unconditioned stimuli), a revelation that was to shape Skinner's later research and social views.

Ernst Mach. Mach was an important physicist who became interested in the philosophical underpinnings of science. He formulated a philosophy of science that was instrumental in the development of logical positivism. Mach's aim was to rid science of metaphysical notions that were, for him, any events or concepts that could not be *directly* observed by the senses. In essence, Mach was interested in facts alone, not abstract theoretical constructs (e.g., habit, cognitive map) that cannot be directly observed. For Mach, the demonstration of functional relationships among directly observed variables represents the ultimate form of scientific explanation.

Edward L. Thorndike. Skinner is a methodological disciple of Watson, but, like Hull, was most influenced by the substantive views of Thorndike. A modified version of Thorndike's law of effect, that proposed a selection-by-consequence model of behavior, served as the core of radical behaviorism.

B. F. Skinner (born 1904)

B(urrhus) F(rederic) Skinner was born into a comfortable middle-class family in 1904 in Susquehanna, Pennsylvania. His mother was "bright and beautiful," while his father "was desperately hungry for praise" (Skinner, 1967). Family life "was warm and stable" and conventional in that Skinner was repeatedly encouraged to become a nice boy, a goal he delighted in resisting.

A brother, two-and-a-half years his junior, became a better athlete and socially more popular. At the age of sixteen, his brother suddenly died and Skinner (1967), recalling the event, readily admitted, "I was not much moved. I probably felt guilty because I was not." As a youngster, Skinner exhibited a great love of and talent for building gadgets—merry-go-rounds, a steam cannon, "a flotation system which separated ripe from green berries," and a perpetual motion machine that failed to work.

In school, Skinner was attracted more to literature than to science, in which he "was weak." Overhearing his father saying that some people believed that Francis Bacon authored Shakespeare's plays, Skinner proclaimed next day in class that Bacon had written the play that the class was then reading. When challenged by his teacher's comment, "You don't know what you're talking about," Skinner began a crusade to prove his teacher wrong and read every book available which supported his thesis.

Upon the advice of a friend, Skinner chose to go to Hamilton College where he majored in English and specialized in actions designed to upset the faculty and administration. He "never fitted into student life at Hamilton," never felt positively about the fraternity to which he belonged, barely endured filling the physical education requirements, and detested the daily chapel. "By my senior year I was in open revolt" (Skinner, 1967). With the assistance of several other students, Skinner created a hoax. Posters were printed to announce a lecture by Charlie Chaplin under the auspices of a professor of drama, whom Skinner disliked.

> As a nihilistic gesture, the hoax was only the beginning. Through the student publications we began to attack the faculty and various local sacred cows. I published a parody of the bumbling manner in which the professor of public speaking would review student performances at the end of the class. I wrote an editorial attacking Phi Beta Kappa. At commencement . . . I covered the walls with bitter caricatures of the faculty . . . and we [Skinner and three collaborators] made a shambles of the commencement ceremonies, and at intermission the President warned us sternly that we would not get our degrees if we did not settle down (Skinner, 1967, p. 393).

In response to my query about Skinner's behavior at Hamilton, a classmate of his who later became my dean, rolled his eyes and exclaimed, "Shocking, unbelievably shocking!"

Encouraged by the positive reaction of Robert Frost, the famous American poet, to three of his short stories, Skinner decided during his college years to become a writer. After graduating from Hamilton, Skinner started his literary career while living at home:

> The results were disastrous. I frittered away my time. I read aimlessly . . . listened to the newly invented radio, contributed to the humorous column of a local paper but wrote almost nothing else, and thought about seeing a psychiatrist (Skinner, 1967, p. 394).

Later, Skinner went to Greenwich Village in New York City for six months and then on to Paris for a summer. But he failed as a writer and over four decades later, in a three-volume autobiography, Skinner offered this revealing comment:

> I apparently failed as a writer but was it not possible that literature had failed me as a method? One might enjoy Proust's reminiscences and share the emotional torment of Dostoevski's characters but did Proust or Dostoevski really *understand*? (Skinner, 1976, p. 291).

Encouraged by the advice that "Science is the art of the twentieth century," Skinner, with high hopes and great ambition, enrolled in the graduate program in psychology at Harvard. In spite of his artistic leanings he had always been enchanted with behavior, animal and human. As a youngster, he even had developed a technique to control his own behavior in an effort to stop the unbearable nagging to which his mother subjected him if his pajamas were not hung up. She would order him from the breakfast table to his bedroom upstairs to correct his oversight. In order to prevent his breakfast from being disturbed, Skinner contructed a mechanical system that, if his pajamas had not been placed on the proper hook, would drop a sign reading "Hang up your pajamas" in the middle of the door frame from which he exited his bedroom.

Graduate school initiated new work habits for Skinner. For about two years he "would rise at six, study until breakfast, go to classes, laboratories, and libraries with no more than 15 minutes unscheduled during the day, study until exactly nine o'clock at night and go to bed (Skinner, 1967). During this period, Skinner rarely dated and never saw a movie or a play or read anything other than psychology and physiology. He was impressed with the intellectual level of the department and formed a close friendship with fellow graduate student Fred S. Keller, a "sophisticated behaviorist," who later became Skinner's most devoted apostle.

A professor, after listening to Skinner's thesis plan commented, "Who do you think you are? Helmholtz?" Skinner wrote a doctoral thesis proposal composed of a semihistorical essay on the concept of the reflex and a proposed research program based partly on some exploratory research. The proposal was submitted to Professor Boring, the noted historian who returned it with critical comments about the narrowness of the historical treatment with a suggestion for a more satisfactory plan. Skinner concluded that Boring failed to understand his major points and resubmitted his thesis without change. Boring appointed a thesis committee, excluding himself, which approved the plan. With the assistance of two successive fellowships, Skinner spent the next five years at Harvard where he implemented the research program in his thesis proposal that was designed to reveal lawful aspects of the behavior of individual organisms. His efforts were finally published in 1938 in a book entitled *The Behavior of Organisms,* which immediately identified Skinner as one of the intellectual leaders in the field of psychology.

At the end of his fellowship at Harvard, Skinner accepted a position at Minnesota in 1936 where his major responsibility was to teach small sections of a large introductory course. He attracted many bright students from other disciplines to psychology. One of his converts was William K. Estes (born 1919), who later became a leader in mathematical psychology by employing statistical models in his theoretical interpretation of learning (Estes, 1959). Skinner left the University of Minnesota in 1945 for the University of Indiana where he became professor and chairman of the department of psychology and, three years later, returned to Harvard as professor of psychology, where he has been since.

Because of his fertile imagination, Skinner was always involved with several projects simultaneously. In 1934 he "began to look at literature, not as a medium for portraying human behavior, but as a field of behavior to be analyzed," and thus the book *Verbal Behavior* was begun. It was published twenty-three years later (Skinner, 1957). From 1934 to 1957 he invented a *baby box* which would mechanize and simplify baby care for the first two years of life, wrote the novel *Walden Two* (1948) that described a utopian community based upon Skinnerian principles, completed *Science and Human Behavior* (1953), a text for an introductory course in radical behaviorism, developed teaching machines to improve educational instruction and, with his student Charles Ferster, published *Schedules of Reinforcement*, a large book that summarized an enormous amount of data collected in Skinner's conditioning laboratory.

From 1957 to the time of this writing, when Skinner is over eighty, he has continued to be productive. In 1971, he published his most controversial book, *Beyond Freedom and Dignity*, an assault on those humanists who fear employing psychological knowledge in the engineering of a better society. In *About Behaviorism* (1974), Skinner sought to explicate his unique brand of behaviorism. And, true to his tradition of proposing psychological solutions to problems of life, Skinner (1983a), in an article entitled, "Intellectual Self-Management in Old Age," offered a set of psychological techniques to improve the scholarly output of aged intellectuals like himself.

In retrospect, Skinner appears to have been, from early life on, a rebel searching for a cause. He found that cause in psychology to the mutual benefit of psychology and himself.

Methodological Assumptions

Skinner views his brand of behaviorism as unique, as qualitatively different from other forms of behaviorism. Contrary to Watson, Skinner argues that a behaviorist need not abandon the study of inner experience.

The Subject Matter of Psychology. In belief and deed, Skinner studied behavior. But he nevertheless insists that radical behaviorism does "consider events taking place in the private world within the skin" as evidenced by his use of such terms as *mental events* and the *inner world*. Private events, for Skinner, are qualitatively similar to overt behavior.

Therefore, laws that govern overt behavior will also govern inner behavior. If you know the laws of behavior you automatically know the laws of mental events. His position is the reverse of those psychologists (e.g., Gestalt) who insist you cannot understand behavior until you understand the phenomenology of the organisms. Skinner argues that you cannot understand phenomenology until you understand behavior.

Methods of Investigation. Skinner is a devout empiricist who believes that all scientific generalizations must be based on experimental procedures that yield highly regular and reliable patterns of behavior. He was satisfied that his conditioning techniques, which he judged to be fundamentally different from the research procedures employed by Tolman and Hull, met those standards. He sought to apply the knowledge that was gained from his conditioning laboratory to real life—education, behavior disorders, child rearing—believing that the same behavioral regularities are exhibited in both situations.

Criterion of Truth. Skinner, in contrast to Tolman and Hull, rejected the notion that truth resides in hypothetico-deductive theories. The criterion of understanding is not the agreement between a theoretical deduction and empirical data, but instead an accurate description of the conditions responsible for the occurrence of a psychological phenomenon. Skinner's conception of understanding is a throwback to Titchener's view that "The problem of science may be summed up in the single word, 'description.' "

In defense of his rejection of hypothetico-deductive theories, Skinner argues that the understanding of behavior resides in behavior itself; in search for explanation you cannot appeal " 'to events taking place somewhere else, at some other level of observation, described in different terms, and measured, if at all, in different dimensions'—events, for example, in the real nervous system, the conceptual system, or the mind" (Skinner, 1969). To be specific, you do not have to resort to abstract intervening variables such as *demand* and *habit* to explain behavior; you simply have to describe accurately the relationships between independent and dependent variables. But how do you know that your descriptions are accurate? If your descriptions help you control the behavior you describe, then they are accurate. Behavioral control becomes the litmus test of understanding.

Strategy

The development of radical behaviorism was shaped by Skinner's individualistic views. Again, you must be cautioned against considering a scientist's strategy as necessarily a product of much premeditated planning. Skinner (1956) admits that in his own research program, accidental occurrences and unanticipated findings shaped his efforts. His ability to exploit these fortuitous events can, however, be attributed to a general strategy involving three interrelated tactics.

1. *Environmental Control of Behavior.* In Pavlov's *Conditioned Reflexes* (1927), the behavior—amount of salivation—is reported for each individual animal on a trial-by-trial basis. The behavioral regularities exhibited by Pavlov's dogs in their highly controlled environment led Skinner to conclude, "Control the environment and you will see order in behavior" (Skinner, 1967). This conclusion has two components: (1) Individual behavior, in principle, is lawful, and (2) lawful behavior can be achieved by controlling an organism's environment.

2. *Nonstatistical Analysis of Behavior.* Skinner, unlike most psychologists, especially in the field of the psychology of learning, concluded that the use of statistics actually retards progress toward the goal of understanding behavior for two reasons. One is that statistical analysis serves to hide behavior from view. The second is that statistics obstruct the task of controlling behavior.

Look at Figure 9.3 on page 283. The learning curves of the three groups are relatively smooth. If, however, the number of errors of individual subjects were plotted, their curves would fluctuate up and down, while revealing only a crude trend in the reduction of errors. Averaging the results, according to radical behaviorists, offers only an illusion of lawful behavior. Only by plotting the performance of individual subjects can one obtain a clear picture of the degree of control of environmental variables impose on behavior. By employing group averages as a measure of behavior, psychologists are deluded into believing that they have achieved a degree of control greater than they actually have, while simultaneously abandoning further attempts to improve the degree of behavioral management.

3. *Atheoretical Approach.* In his first book, *The Behavior of Organisms* (1938), Skinner proposed a modest theory that employed intervening variables. Soon thereafter he abandoned theorizing when he became convinced that theories were not only unnecessary, but actually harmful.

> Research designed with respect to theory is . . . likely to be wasteful. That a theory generates research does not prove its value unless the research is valuable. Much useless experimentation results from theories and much energy and skill are absorbed by them. Most theories are eventually overthrown, and the greater part of the associated research is discarded. This could be justified if it were true that productive research requires a theory—as is often claimed. It is argued that research would be aimless and disorganized without a theory to guide it. The view is supported by psychological texts which take their cue from the logicians rather than empirical science and describe thinking as necessarily involving stages of hypothesis, deduction, experimental test, and confirmation. But this is not the way most scientists actually work. It is possible to design significant experiments for other reasons, and the possibility to be examined is that such research will lead more directly to the kind of information which a science usually accumulates (Skinner, 1950, pp. 194–195).

In place of a theoretical explanation, Skinner "relies on the demonstration of functional relationships among variables as the ultimate form taken by scientific explanation" (Herrnstein, 1958). The more accurately these functional relationships are expressed the more effective is the behaviorial control.

Major Concepts of Radical Behaviorism

Operant Conditioning. When one strives to formulate a systematic account of behavior, one seeks to identify a basic form of behavior from which generalizations to other kinds of behavior can be made. Hull selected conditioning, Tolman initially opted for choice behavior, while Skinner favors a certain kind of instrumental conditioning known as operant conditioning. Up to now, the distinction between two kinds of conditioning, originally labeled *classical* and *instrumental*, has been ignored, partly because the distinction was unimportant in previous discussions. Hull, for example, assumed that both kinds of conditioning obeyed the same theoretical principles.

In the most famous example of classical conditioning, the one reported by Pavlov, the tone (conditioned stimulus) is consistently followed by food (unconditioned stimulus) during the acquisition stage. The dog learns to *anticipate* the food by salivating to the tone. In instrumental conditioning, which is analogous to the procedures employed in Thorndike's puzzle box, instead of anticipating environmental events, the subject by its behavior operates on its environment to obtain a reward. In classical conditioning, the subject gets the reward regardless of what it does; in instrumental conditioning, the animal's behavior is instrumental in getting a reward.

Skinner referred to classical conditioning as *respondent conditioning* because the response was elicited by a definite stimulus, the conditioned stimulus. Operant conditioning is a form of instrumental conditioning because the behavior of the subject *operates* on the environment. Skinner's operant conditioning differed from Thorndike's puzzle box methodology in several important respects. First, the experimental situation was much simpler. Skinner (1938) designed an instrumental conditioning apparatus that consisted of a small soundproofed box containing a lever, which, when depressed, automatically delivered a pellet of food into a tray. Second, the response measure employed by Thorndike and Skinner differed. Thorndike used the latency of the instrumental response as a measure of learning; the time-lapse between the moment the cat was placed in the box and the occurrence of the instrumental response. Learning was measured by the drop in latencies on successive trials. Operant conditioning does not employ the discrete-trial procedure; the rat remains in the box with the lever always available, thus allowing the animal to press it at any time. The response measure for the free-responding situation was the rate of responding, the number of responses for a given unit of time.

FIGURE 10.2   Different Rates of Responding as Shown by Cumulative
Records

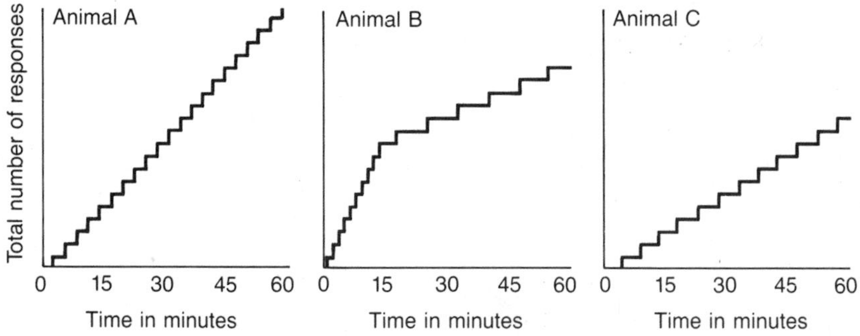

The three cumulative response curves represent the performance of three animals during a one-hour period in an operant conditioning apparatus. See text for fuller explanation.

Skinner represented the rate of responding graphically with equipment that records each bar-press on a constantly moving sheet of paper. Whenever the bar was pressed, the pen moved upward, raising the line a notch. Figure 10.2 illustrates three sample *cumulative records* that are obtained in operant conditioning. The total number of responses is shown by the height on the ordinate, while the abscissa indicates the passage of time. Each cumulative response curve records the lever pressing of an individual animal during a one-hour period. Note that at the end of the hour, the heights of the three cumulative curves differ, the curve made by Animal A reaching the highest point. The fact that the curves of Animals A and C are essentially straight for the entire time period indicates that they were both responding at an essentially constant rate, but A's rate was faster. Animal B behaved differently, responding at a higher rate during the first fifteen minutes than thereafter.

Figure 10.3 illustrates the course of operant conditioning through three phases: pretraining (operant level), conditioning, and extinction. Lever pressing was selected for experimental analysis because the response was easily repeatable, of little significance in the previous history of the subject, and possessed no built-in reinforcing properties as eating and drinking do. Because rate of responding is the dependent variable, the response of necessity has to be easily repeatable. And because one desires to study how rate of behavior changes, a response that has not been practiced in the subject's natural life history and is not intrinsically reinforcing reflects environmental influences more clearly.

When a hungry rat is placed in the Skinner box for the first time, it rarely presses the bar. If the lever presses are not rewarded, the rate of responding will remain very low. When food does reinforce bar pressing, the rate of responding increases. If food is withdrawn after a high rate of

FIGURE 10.3   A Cumulative Response Record Showing the Operant Level, Conditioning, and Extinction of an Individual Rat's Bar-Pressing Response

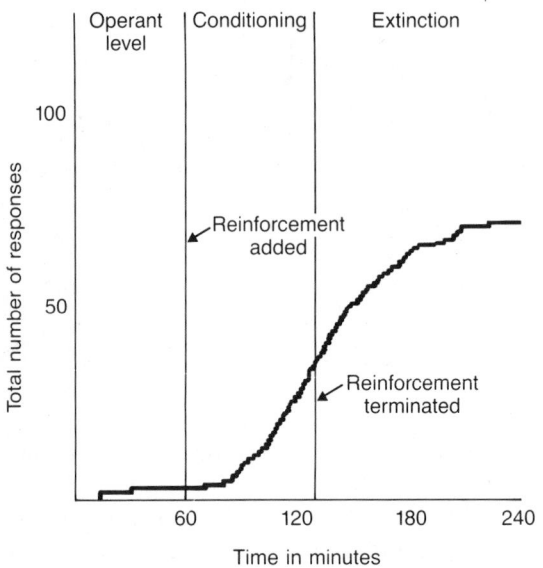

Each time the rat responds, the curve moves up a notch. Not that initially, when no reinforcement occurs, the rat responds infrequently. This rate of response represents its operant level. The introduction of reinforcement produces a marked change in the response rate. When reinforcement is withdrawn, the rate of responding gradually declines until the rat is responding at approximately its initial operant level.

responding has been reached, the response rate will return to its initial low level.

Operant conditioning has been described in this detail because Skinner's entire system rests upon ability of this experimental methodology to reveal the basic regularities of behavior. Radical behaviorists consider the Skinner box, with operant methodology, to be a simplified model of the world in which an organism's adaptive behavior can be systematically observed and manipulated. The laws revealed in operant conditioning provide the means for controlling behavior in the real world.

Reinforcement.   Both Hull and Skinner agreed that reinforcement is necessary for learning, but they disagreed about the meaning of reinforcement. For Hull, reinforcement was a covert theoretical process associated with drive reduction. For Skinner, reinforcement was a fact and nothing more; certain events, following the occurrence of a response, will alter the frequency of that response. In other words, Skinner finessed the question about what is reinforcing about reinforcement by ignoring it. In place of a theoretical answer, he defined reinforcement as an event that alters the probability of a response.

Positive and negative reinforcements. Skinner distinguished between two kinds of reinforcements. A *positive reinforcement* is a stimulus (e.g., food) that increases the probability of a response (e.g., lever pressing) above its operant level. A *negative reinforcement* is a stimulus, which when *removed*, increases the probability of a response recurring. For example, if the floor of a Skinner box delivers an electric shock to the feet of a rat and pressing a bar is instrumental in discontinuing the shock, then the termination of the aversive stimulation is reinforcing. In sum, the *presentation* of a positive reinforcement or the *removal* of the negative reinforcer increases the probability of a response.

Primary and secondary reinforcement. Radical behaviorism distinguishes between primary and secondary reinforcers. Stimuli that serve as primary reinforcers, such as food or water, are innately determined. A secondary reinforcer acquires reinforcing properties by being associated with a primary reinforcer. If pressing a bar produces a light and food for a hungry rat, the light will acquire secondary reinforcing properties. Secondary reinforcers can serve in lieu of primary reinforcers to increase the rate of responding.

Schedules of reinforcement. In their early work, radical behaviorists focused on *interval* and *ratio* schedules, each of which can be arranged in a *fixed* or *variable* mode. An interval schedule is based on a predetermined interval of time between successive reinforced responses, while a ratio schedule depends on the subject making a predetermined number of responses before being reinforced. Fixed schedules are ordered with exact intervals or number of responses. In a fixed interval schedule the subject must wait for a fixed interval, like one minute (FI 1), before its next response will be reinforced again. In a fixed ratio schedule, the subject will be reinforced after every Nth response, like 20 (FR 20). In variable schedules the interval or ratio will vary; in a variable interval five-minute schedule (VI 5), the response is reinforced once every five minues *on the average* with the interval between successive reinforcement being perhaps as long as ten minutes and as brief as a few seconds. Similarly a VR 20 can vary over a wide range while the average number is kept at 20 responses.

Figure 10.4 illustrates typical cumulative records generated by the four schedules just described. Note that the two variable schedules reveal more uniform patterns of responding. In the fixed interval schedule, especially at high rates, a low rate of responding occurs after a reinforcement because the subject learns that one reinforcement is never followed by another. This pattern of responding in a fixed interval schedule is described as *scalloping*. In a fixed ratio schedule, *a postreinforcement pause* occurs after a reinforcement. In general, the variable ratio schedule produces the highest response rates, followed by the fixed ratio schedule, then the variable interval, the fixed interval, and finally the continuous reinforcement schedule, in which every response is rewarded, with the lowest response rate.

FIGURE 10.4 Typical Cumulative Response

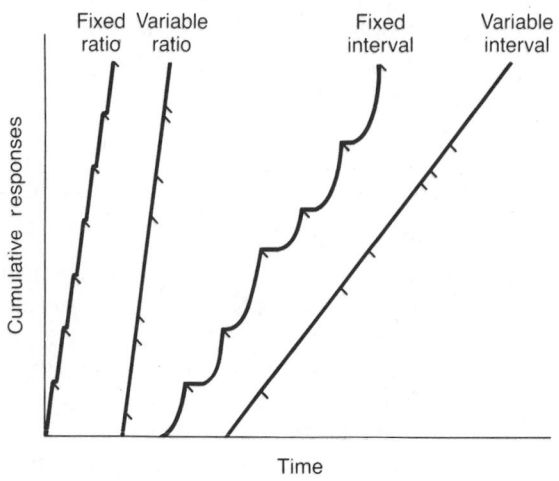

Typical cumulative response records by fixed ratio, variable ratio, fixed interval, and variable interval reinforcement schedules. (Adapted from Hergenhahn, 1976.)

SOURCE: B. R. Hergenhahn, *An Introduction to Theories of Learning,* © 1976, p. 108. Adapted by permission of Prentice-Hall, Englewood Cliffs, New Jersey.

The importance of schedules of reinforcement. Why are schedules of reinforcement considered so important by radical behaviorists? Because the performance of any act is dependent upon its reinforcement history. Thus, the study of schedules of reinforcement in the laboratory will reveal laws of performance that will govern real life behavior. A youngster who is practicing on a musical instrument and receives praise on a fixed interval schedule is likely to let down in his or her efforts shortly after each compliment. This scalloping performance can be eliminated if the fixed interval is shifted to a variable interval schedule.

Most forms of gambling are governed by a variable reinforcement schedule. Winning depends on such instrumental responses as placing a bet on the right horse or the right number of a roulette wheel. Reinforcements occur intermittently and in an unpredictable fashion, but if the gambler makes a large number of responses, he is assured of a payoff sooner or later. As a result, gambling usually generates a very high rate of responding. The chronic gambler, like the pigeon pecking five times per second for many hours, is a victim of the variable ratio schedule.

Many other more complex schedules have been investigated. Some have been especially designed to test the influence of certain variables, such as the effect of drugs, on behavior. These various schedules have been influential in the development of the field of psychopharmacology. One example illustrates the general technique.

In a *differential low rate schedule* (DLR), the subject receives a reinforcement only if a specified amount of time has elapsed since its last response. In a DLR 60, for example, a reinforcement becomes available sixty seconds after the last response. If the subject responds before the sixty seconds have elapsed, the clock is reset and another sixty seconds must pass before a response can be reinforced. When responding in this manner, the subject is essentially overestimating the passage of time; it is responding as if sixty seconds had passed when in reality they had not. A DLR schedule, as expected, produces a very low rate of responding, which accounts for its name.

In one study designed to test the influence of Δ^9-tetrahydrocannabinol (Δ^9-THC), the chemical component of marijuana presumed to be responsible for its psychological effects, a variation of the DLR schedule was employed. A reinforcement could only be obtained by the subjects, three chimpanzees, when responding in a DLR of sixty to ninety seconds. Dosage levels varied from 0.125 mg/kg to 4.0 mg/kg (the ratio between the weight of the drug and weight of subject). It was found that, as the dosage increased, so did the overestimation errors varying from approximately 17 percent at the low end of the dosage level to about 33 percent at the high end. A placebo produced slightly more than 10 percent overestimation errors, thus demonstrating that marijuana has the effect of distorting one's time sense. Interestingly, three days after ingesting Δ^9-THC, overestimating errors still persisted with as many as 30 percent occurring at the highest dosage level. In addition to the persistence of its effect, THC also depressed work output. At the higher doses, prolonged breaks in the subject's performance occurred. "The chimps appeared just to sit quietly in their cages for several hours before returning to work, if they did so at all" (Conrad, Elsmore, & Sodetz, 1972).

Shaping.   Shaping is an operant method of modifying behavior by reinforcing successive approximations of the kind of behavior desired. Suppose an animal trainer wanted to shape a pigeon to "spin like a top," a response chain that a pigeon rarely exhibits. This goal can be achieved in a matter of minutes by initially reinforcing a slight movement to turn with a secondary reinforcer like a sound of a buzzer. The tendency to turn in that direction will be increased, thus, raising the probability of a similar turning response. But the power of differential reinforcement (reinforcing only turning responses in one direction), the response chain of turning around in a circle can be made to occur over and over again at a high rate of frequency.

Superstitious Behavior.   Up to now, examples of operant conditioning have been restricted to phenomena in which the reward is *contingent* on the subject's response. In order for reinforcement to be forthcoming, the subject, rat or pigeon, is required to make an appropriate instrumental response, lever pressing or disk pecking. What would happen if reinforcements were delivered in an irregular order regardless of what the subject was doing, that is, if the reinforcement is *noncontingent*?

According to the lawful behavior observed in operant conditioning, a radical behaviorist would expect that some act would gain dominance but would be unable to specify which one. This expectation is based on the reinforcement principle. Any act that is followed by a reinforcement has an increased probability of recurring *whether or not the act is responsible for producing the reinforcement*. Consequently, when a noncontingent reinforcement occurs, the probability of recurrence of some kind of behavior will be increased. If that behavior does not occur immediately before the next noncontingent reinforcement, some other act will, and therefore the probability of *its* recurrence will be enhanced. Several noncontingent reinforcements, for example, may follow the head-raising responses of one pigeon, while the head-lowering response may be reinforced in another pigeon. As a result, the first pigeon will tend to strut around with its head high, while the second will keep its head low. This ritualistic behavior is called *superstitious* because it appears as if the pigeon believes its actions are responsible for getting the reinforcements. The behavior appears analogous to that of the gambler who pulls his ear lobe every time he places a bet at the race track; because he frequently bets, his superstitious act is inevitably reinforced on a variable ratio schedule, thus making the response resistant to extinction.

Discriminative Operant. A discriminative operant can be illustrated by procedural modification of operant conditioning after a rat has learned to depress a lever. A discrimination task is introduced so that bar pressing will only yield a reinforcement when a light is on and never when it is off. Under these conditions, the subject learns to press the bar only when the light is on. The light is referred to as a *discriminative stimulus,* an S^D, while the light off is labeled S^Δ (S delta). The discriminative operant is a form of behavior in which an operant response is made to one set of circumstances (S^D), and not to another (S^Δ).

Although simple in nature, the discriminative operant is basic to everyday behavior. Specific forms of behavior are under the control of discriminative stimuli, such as red traffic lights, internal hunger pangs, specific individuals, times of day, and so forth. In operant language, different behaviors are emitted to these S^Ds because such behaviors have previously led to reinforcements (S^Rs).

Punishment. The opposite of reinforcement is punishment, the condition that reduces the probability of the occurrence of the preceding response. The *presentation* of a negative reinforcer (e.g., electric shock) or the *removal* of a positive reinforcer (e.g., food) diminishes the response rate.

One commonsense view is that punishment weakens a response and thereby helps eliminate it. This is the principle that parents act on when punishing their children for misbehavior and that society uses to rationalize its treatment of criminals. But does punishment actually *weaken* a response tendency? This question was of basic importance to Skinner in his search for rules to control behavior. An answer to the question was offered in a doctoral thesis (Estes, 1944) that Skinner sponsored at the University of Minnesota.

Two groups of rats were trained to press a bar for food reinforcements. The response was then extinguished by withholding food. During the first portion of the extinction period, the punished rats were shocked through the floor of the apparatus after the lever was depressed. The nonpunished group received no shocks during this period. Thereafter, the instrumental responses of both the punished and nonpunished groups were extinguished without shock. If punishment (shock) does in fact weaken a response tendency, the punished subjects would be expected to make fewer bar-pressing responses than the nonpunished rats. This did not happen; the total number of responses made during extinction were the same for both groups. The punished subjects behaved differently from the nonpunished subjects only in the lower frequency with which they pressed the bar during the time they were being punished and shortly thereafter. After the punishment was terminated, their response rate increased and they eventually made as many bar-pressing responses during the entire extinction period as the nonpunished subjects. In sum, punishment *suppresses* an operant but does not weaken it.

Skinner, who reportedly experienced only one episode of punishment as a child—having his mouth washed out with soap for swearing—dismisses punishment as a method of controlling behavior. Not only is it ineffective in eliminating behavior, it produces many unfortunate side effects, such as creating fear, justifying inflicting pain, encouraging aggression, and so forth. "In the long run . . . punishment does not actually eliminate behavior from a repertoire, and its temporary achievement [suppression] is obtained at tremendous cost in reducing the overall efficiency and happiness of the group" (Skinner, 1967).

Verbal Behavior. One cannot overstress the point, when discussing Skinnerian psychology, that the laws of behavior revealed in operant conditioning are assumed to extend to the entire world of behavior—including the verbal behavior of humans. Just as a pigeon is reinforced for pecking a disk, a child is reinforced for saying, "Bread, please," at the dinner table. The Skinner box mechanism delivers the food to the pigeon; the parent delivers the bread to the child.

To demonstrate that operant principles apply to verbal behavior, college students were instructed to say a series of individual words (Greenspoon, 1955). Whenever the subjects said a plural noun, the experimenter said, "mmm-hmmm," presumably a sign of social approval. Subjects in a control group were given the identical instructions, but in their case, the experimenter remained silent when they uttered plural nouns. When the performances of the two groups were compared, it was discovered that plural nouns emitted by experimental subjects had increased in frequency. In other words, "mmm-hmmm" functioned as a reinforcer. When experimental extinction was instituted (the "mmm-hmmm" was eliminated), the plural noun responses of the experimental group dropped off to the level of those emitted by control subjects. In this manner, the experiment demonstrated that a verbal response functions as an operant; its frequency increases when it is reinforced and decreases when it is not.

Skinner (1957) distinguished among many different functions of verbal behaviors, three of which will now be noted. A *mand* de*mands* the listener give something to the speaker, usually reinforcement, as was the case for the child who requested bread at the dinner table. A *tact* makes con*tact* with the world largely by providing names for discriminative stimuli: The parent, pointing to a cat, asks the child, "What is that?" The child responds "A doggie." The child is corrected when the parent says "That is not a doggie. It is a kitty." The result of this exchange between parent and child is that appropriate tacts are acquired to describe the environment. *Autoclitic* behavior is verbal behavior that controls other verbal behavior. One example is the ordering of other behavior according to grammatical rules. The child gradually acquires the possessive noun form. After learning such relationships as the boy's glove, the man's car, and the woman's coat, the child spontaneously and without ever hearing the phrase, correctly says, "This is the girl's doll." Thus, Skinner (1957) sought to analyze verbal behavior by identifying the various behavioral functions that linguistic utterances serve in a person's adjustment to the world. The underlying assumption in his analysis is that these lawful linguistic performances are acquired and controlled by contingencies of reinforcement.

An Integrated View of Radical Behaviorism

For Skinner, the major task of psychology is to identify the experimental conditions that affect the frequency of occurrence of a specific response. A summary formula that Skinner offered to describe these conditions is: *Responses* (R) *are made to discriminative stimuli* (S^D) *as a function of contingencies of reinforcement* (S^{reinf}). If one desires to know why a rat stops bar pressing after receiving a food pellet or why a child becomes unruly when visited by his grandmother or why a student's rate of studying in a classroom is low, then it becomes necessary to uncover the reinforcement history of that particular response. In order to change the probability of the response—bar pressing, unruly behavior, studying—the reinforcement contingencies must be modified.

Basic to this description of behavior is the mechanism of selection by consequences. Skinner proposes that this mechanism operates on three levels: biological evolution, individual behavior, and the evolution of culture. For Skinner (1981), "Human behavior is the joint product of (i) the contingencies of survival responsible for the natural selection of the species and (ii) the contingencies of reinforcement responsible for the repertoires acquired by its members, including (iii) the special contingencies maintained by an evolved social environment." Just as biological entities have evolved from environmental pressures, so have individual behavior and social practices. The real cause of these evolutionary changes lies in the environment. Skinner vigorously opposes the notion that behavioral changes have to be initiated by individuals as an expression of their rationality and determination.

> The question of an initiating agent is raised in its most acute form by our own place in . . . history. Darwin . . . thought that selection would necessarily lead to perfection, but species, people, and culture all perish when they cannot cope with rapid change, and our species now appears to be threatened. Must we wait for selection to solve the problem of overpopulation, exhaustion of resources, pollution of the environment, and nuclear holocaust, or can we take explicit steps to make our future more secure? (Skinner, 1981, p. 504).

We can solve the problems confronting the human race, but probably will not. That is the gist of Skinner's reaction to the question he poses. Skinner is confident that we possess the basic core of a technology of behavior that can ultimately solve the problems that threaten our existence. By effectively employing contingencies of reinforcement, we can control population growth, conserve natural resources, decrease pollution, and reduce the threat of a nuclear holocaust. But we resist this kind of solution because, "we cling to the view that a person is an initiating doer, actor, or causer of behavior, [and therefore] we shall probably continue to neglect the conditions which must be changed if we are to solve our problems" (Skinner, 1981). Behavior change, Skinner argues, depends on modifying the environment so that appropriate contingencies of reinforcement can take control of behavior.

Skinner's message is simple. Decide what behavior is desirable. Then arrange the contingencies of reinforcement that are required to shape that behavioral outcome. He points to the successes of operant methodology to demonstrate that control of behavior is possible:

1. *Shaping.* The power of Skinner's technology for controlling behavior was initially dramatized in numerous examples of training animals to perform complex acts by the technique of shaping. By shaping behavior through a series of successive approximations, each made possible by differential reinforcement, pigeons were trained to bowl in a miniature alley with a wooden ball and toy pins, to play a modified game of ping-pong, and to peck out a tune on a toy piano. Some radical behaviorists have become so successful in shaping the behavior of animals that they have created new vocational opportunities for themselves. They are employed by famous animal shows where they teach animals ranging from porpoises to chimpanzees to perform startling stunts that have strong box office appeal (Breland & Breland, 1966).

Shaping animal behavior can have practical value. During World War II, Skinner shaped pigeons to guide airborne gliders with explosives to enemy targets. Only the conservatism of the military prevented his version of the Kamikaze fighter from being put to test (Skinner, 1960). Since that day, dogs have been trained to detect explosives in baggage at airports, porpoises to retrieve shells from spent torpedoes, monkeys to feed and help care for paraplegics, and seals to help in the rescue of drowning swimmers.

2. *Programmed Learning.* In 1953, Skinner visited his younger daughter's arithmetic class.

> Suddenly the situation seemed perfectly absurd. Here were twenty valuable organisms. Through no fault of her own, the teacher was violating almost everything we know about the learning process (Skinner, 1967).

This experience encouraged Skinner (1958) to pioneer the application of rules of shaping to the educational technique of programmed learning, self-instruction based upon a series of sentence completion questions known as a program. Five rules were emphasized: (1) Arrange the environment so that a student will emit the desired response. For example, in teaching high school physics, an effective sentence completion item to begin a program to teach electricity is: "The important parts of a flashlight are the battery and the bulb. When we 'turn on' a flashlight, we close a switch which connects the battery with the _____." (2) Once the correct response is made, immediate reinforcement should be forthcoming indicating that "bulb" is correct. (3) The third rule is to proceed by small steps. Just as the pigeon is trained gradually to make a complete turn, so the high-school physics student progresses gradually from his familiarity with a flashlight to the understanding of the relationship between heat and light. (4) The fourth rule of programmed learning is the frank recognition that individuals vary widely in their learning ability. In programmed learning, each student progresses at his own rate. (5) In programmed learning as in shaping behavior, there is continuous feedback to the educator, indicating the success or failure of the program. Individual items of the program can be modified to enhance the effectiveness of the entire program.

Over the years, numerous developments and variations (Keller & Sherman, 1974) of programmed learning have occurred. Many of Skinner's ideas, based on animal behavior, have been incorporated into computer assisted instruction, which has become an important pedagogical method in our educational systems.

3. *Behavior Modification.* Watson was the first behaviorist to advance the notion that conditioning techniques can be effective in modifying and eliminating undesirable forms of behavior such as unnecessary fear. In addition, Hull's theory served as a point of departure for behavior modification techniques in which a relaxed response is substituted for an anxiety reaction (Eyesenck, 1967; Wolpe, 1958). Although the notion of behavior modification, the substitution of desired forms of behavior for

undesirable ones, is not original with Skinner, he and his disciples have been the most influential in developing behavior modification techniques as a major form of treatment.

Some of the early efforts applied shaping techniques to institutionalized psychotics. A catatonic schizophrenic who was completely mute for nineteen years showed signs of interest in chewing gum. He was first reinforced with chewing gum when he began attending to the gum. Then the gum was withheld until the patient exhibited lip movements. When this succeeded, the patient's speech was shaped into uttering the word "gum" and gradually the shaping technique became effective in encouraging communication and social interaction (Isaacs, Thomas & Goldiamond, 1960). Similar shaping procedures have been used with autistic and retarded children (Ferster & De Myer, 1961) to increase their social competence and by so doing improve the general ward atmosphere. "Patients make fewer demands on the staff and yet display as much dignity and happiness as their pathology permits" (Skinner, 1969).

Operant methodology can be applied to one's own behavior. Skinner suggests that solving one's own problems is a mode of control that is commonly referred to as self-control; "He controls himself precisely as he would control the behavior of anyone else—through the manipulation of variables of which behavior is a function" (Skinner, 1953). For example, if a person has a tendency to turn off the alarm clock in the morning and stay in bed, she can place the alarm clock across the room, thus forcing herself to get out of bed. One can also arrange a *contingency contract* that reinforces desirable behavior. A person who is striving to lose weight can add ten dollars to her clothing budget as a reward when two pounds are dropped. One can also modify behavior by shaping mental content. Skinner assumes that private behavioral events—thought and images—operate according to the same lawful regularities that govern observable operants. Consequently, by managing one's own experience, one can modify one's own behavior. For example, a man who desires to rid himself of fear of large dogs can learn to substitute a relaxed response for the anxious one. One method of accomplishing this goal is to learn to relax, a task that requires extensive training (Jacobson, 1938). By imagining a small puppy, an image that would evoke minimal fear, the patient can learn to relax to that stimulus. By successively repeating this training to imagined cues that become more similar to the feared large dog, the patient can finally learn to relax to a real large dog.

Numerous techniques of behavior modification have been developed from operant methodology. The so-called mental illnesses are considered forms of disorderd *behavior,* not pathological events that occur in the deep recesses of the mind. The treatment of such disorders is to change behavior in the most direct and effective manner, by modifying the environmental contingencies of reinforcement.

Quotations from Skinner

1. The importance of a science of behavior derives largely from the possibility of an eventual extension to human affairs. But it is a serious, though common, mistake to allow questions of ultimate application to influence the development of a systematic science at an early stage (Skinner, 1938, p. 441).

2. Behaviorism is a formulation which makes possible an effective experimental approach to human behavior. It is a working hypothesis about the nature of a subject matter. It may need to be clarified, but it does not need to be argued. I have no doubt of the eventual triumph of the position—not that it will eventually be proved right, but that it will provide the most direct route to a successful science of man (Skinner, 1967, pp. 409–410).

3. I believe in progress, and I have always been alert to practical significance in my research (Skinner, 1967, p. 411).

4. In the behavioristic view, man can now control his own destiny because he knows what must be done and how to do it (Skinner, 1974, p. 251).

5. Those who help those who can help themselves work a sinister kind of destruction by making the good things in life no longer properly contingent on behavior (Skinner, 1983a, p. 244).

6. A reinforcing connection need not be obvious to the individual reinforced (Skinner, 1953, p. 75).

Radical Behaviorism: Contributions and Evaluation

Nobody in contemporary psychology has generated as much controversy as Skinner. Like his intellectual father, John B. Watson, Skinner is a persuasive polemicist who challenges popular psychological and philosophical beliefs of others. His talent for controversy has earned him such names as "fascist" and "dehumanizer," characterizations those who know him reject totally. These extreme views emanate from two main sources: an intrinsic ambiguity in some of Skinner's major notions and a tendency to judge radical behaviorism as a whole rather than evaluating its component parts separately.

Contributions of Radical Behaviorism.

Operant methodology. Regardless of one's views about Skinner's conception, one cannot deny the important contribution that operant methodology has made to the science of behavior. The history of science has repeatedly demonstrated that scientific advances frequently have to await technological breakthroughs that allow gathering of information that previously could not be obtained. Operant methodology is an example of such a breakthrough; one can now investigate precisely the influence of a host of experimental variables on steady-state behavior that appears under a variety of schedules of reinforcement. Operant methodology has been instrumental in the development of new fields of psychology (e.g., psychopharmacology) and clarification of old problems (e.g., localization of brain function).

Technology of behavior.   For Skinner, the litmus test for understanding behavior is the ability to control it. Such an attitude leads directly to the development of techniques, such as shaping, that are designed to train organisms to behave in a desired way. As a consequence of this concern for controlling behavior, radical behaviorists have provided technologies for education, clinical behavior modification, self-control, child rearing, social planning, animal training, and so on.

A model of behavior.   Although Skinner did not offer a theory of behavior based on abstract concepts, he did suggest a simple descriptive model that has pragmatic value. *Reponses are made to discriminative stimuli as a function of contingencies of reinforcement.* If one tries to improve one's study habits or become more assertive in social situations or toilet train one's child or improve one's tennis game or eliminate a phobia or train one's aged parents to cope with problems of memory or solve any behavioral problem, this descriptive model can be helpful. Although the degree of usefulness of such a formula is a topic of great debate among modern psychologists, radical behaviorists, while acknowledging the model's limitations, will nevertheless argue that it is the most effective model available for controlling behavior.

Philosophy of psychology.   Skinner does not perceive himself as a philosopher, but his views about psychology have important implications for psychological methodology and social philosophy.

In a period when psychological theory was considered by many leading psychologists to be the ultimate goal of research, Skinner adopted the radical position that the discovery of lawful regularities in individual behavior was the goal to be sought. Theoretical constructions and statistical analyses could only serve as obstacles to the development of effective methods for controlling behavior.

The fundamental principle of radical behaviorism is that behavior is shaped and maintained by its consequences. This principle, Skinner (1971) believes, has profound implications for a society that seeks a better life for its citizens. Let us arrange an environment based upon a science of behavior so that desirable forms of behavior will be encouraged while undesirable forms will be eliminated. Bluntly, let us control behavior in the interest of building a superior society. Such a proposal sounds threatening to those who value freedom and human dignity and fear autocratic rule. Skinner responds to such a criticism in two related ways. First, he notes that all behavior is controlled; the only difference is whether the control is planned or unplanned. The fearful child who has been overprotected by his mother has been shaped by reinforcement contingencies just as surely as the child whose mother has deliberately reinforced her for independent behavior. The issue is not whether we control behavior but how effectively we do so. Second, Skinner suggests that freedom and dignity, or what some refer to as the concept of the *autonomous man*—the human being who freely decides what to do—is an illusion. Such terms as *freedom* and *dignity* are used when we are ignorant of the underlying contingencies of reinforcement responsible for specific actions. If we stop considering behavior to be a consequence of free will and recognize its dependence on contingencies of reinforcement, we could modify the environment so that humans, for example, would not smoke, drug, and drink themselves to death. We could create a utopia.

Evaluation of Radical Behaviorism. The major criticism directed at radical behaviorism is that Skinner's claims are exaggerated. From an extremely narrow empirical base, Skinner has extrapolated his psychological conception to the entire spectrum of behavior ranging from animal training to social engineering. Is the extrapolation justified? Are the lawful regularities observed in operant conditioning applicable to the psychological realms to which operant principles have been extended? If exaggerated, should Skinner's conclusions be ignored?

Methodological notions. Radical behaviorists pride themselves on their tough-minded scientific approach to psychology. Therefore, it comes as a surprise to discover that their critics accuse them of being fuzzy minded. For example, Skinner proudly announces,

> Methodological behaviorism. . . . ruled private events out of bounds because there could be no public agreement about their validity. . . . Radical behaviorism, however, takes a different line. It does not deny the possibility of self-observation or self-knowledge or its possible usefulness (Skinner, 1974, p. 16).

While boasting that his brand of behaviorism deals with private events while other behaviorisms do not, Skinner repeatedly asserts that mental events must be considered as inferences: "In studying behavior we may have to deal with the stimulation from a tooth as an inference rather than as a directly observable fact" (Skinner, 1953), and "The radical behaviorist may . . . consider private events (inferentially, perhaps, but none the less meaningfully)" (Skinner, 1945). Skinner appears to ignore the significance of the difference between the direct examination of consciousness and inferences about the mind. Methodological behaviorism rejects the notion that the direct examination of consciousness can yield reliable knowledge. However, inferences about mental processes are quite consistent with the tenets of methodological behaviorism, as Tolman and other behaviorists have demonstrated. In sum, Skinner's suggestion that radical behaviorism offers a unique method of studying mental events within a behavioristic framework is without merit.

Skinner's antitheoretical stance suffers from a core of ambiguity. One critic suggests that his position "admits of two interpretations—one of them exciting, controversial, and practically indefensible, the other moderately interesting, rather widely accepted, and very plausible—and Skinner's views quite often appear to be stated in the first form but defended in the second" (Scriven, 1956). The importance of theories employing abstract concepts (e.g., gravity, genes) has repeatedly been demonstrated in the history of science. To suggest that they are useless is a novel argument but "practically indefensible." To suggest that the psychological theories of the sort Tolman and Hull proposed were premature and unjustified by the amount of available evidence is reasonable. Skinner assumes a radical antitheoretical stance but defends this extreme position with the modest proposal that theorizing should be initiated only after a solid foundation of empirical knowledge has been established.

Automatic effects of reinforcement. Radical behaviorists have argued that reinforcement operates in an automatic manner; the probability of a response recurring is automatically increased when followed immediately by a reinforcement. Verbal conditioning, shaping, and superstitious behavior all illustrate this principle, but in each case the automatic reinforcement hypothesis has been challenged.

Several researchers (e.g., Dulany, 1968, Spielberger & DeNike, 1966) report that verbal conditioning occurs only when the subject is aware of the reinforcement contingencies (e.g., plural nouns are reinforced). Verbal conditioning, according to this interpretation, is not a consequence of automatic reinforcement effects but instead of knowledge of results. Insurmountable difficulties were encountered by two radical behaviorists (Breland & Breland, 1961) when they tried to shape raccoons to drop coins in a piggy bank for behavioral display in a municipal zoo. The subjects tended to rub the coins together and then dip them in a container in the manner that raccoons use to wash food. That species-specific behavior, popularly known as instinctive, prevented the shaping procedure from being successful. Evidence (e.g., Staddon & Simmelhag, 1971) suggests that the ritualistic acts exhibited in so-called superstitious behavior are not a consequence of the automatic effects of reinforcements but instead are an expression of species-specific behavior associated with waiting for food. In sum, the automatic reinforcement hypothesis that radical behaviorists have employed to explain the above examples of verbal conditioning, shaping, and superstitious behavior has been seriously challenged.

Radical behaviorists have not abandoned their operant interpretation of behavior as a consequence of the above criticisms. They are not convinced that the interpretation of verbal conditioning requires an explanation based upon the vague mentalistic process known as awareness. And, as the second line of defense, they note that regardless of one's views about the role of awareness in verbal conditioning, the fact remains that the rate of verbal responses can be controlled by the contingencies of reinforcement.

Genetic influences. Radical behaviorists admit more freely than they have in the past the importance of genetic factors in behavior. But, they note, the significance of heredity does not deny the effectiveness of reinforcement for modifying behavior. Genetic factors, in most cases, cannot be changed and therefore contingencies of reinforcement represent the most direct method available for those who seek to manage behavior. In essence, they are acknowledging that Skinner's model of behavior may be incomplete but they insist that is it not necessarily wrong. This conservative view of radical behaviorism, however, is challenged by linguists and psychologists who conclude that when it comes to human language and cognitive processes, Skinner's interpretation is fundamentally flawed.

Psychology of language. In one of the most influential papers in the recent history of psychology, Noam Chomsky (1959), a linguist, attacked Skinner's (1957) interpretation of human language and offered a diametrically opposed conception. Chomsky argues that Skinner's extrapolation of operant conditioning to human language is unjustified. For example, the term *stimulus* has a clearly identifiable meaning in operant conditioning, as is the case when a discriminative stimulus controls behavior, but *stimulus* becomes a vague concept when employed in analyzing language. What is the exact stimulus that triggers a response to a confusing essay question? Memory cues, anxiety, professor's expectations, a bright thought, and so forth? Chomsky's point is that the stimulus cannot be clearly identified and that an infinite number of possible stimuli can be suggested. Similarly, *reinforcement* has a specific meaning (e.g., food) in operant conditioning but becomes a vague concept (e.g., self-reinforcement) when transferred to verbal behavior. Radical behaviorism, according to Chomsky, appears to be suggesting a scientific interpretation of verbal behavior, but actually is offering an empirically empty description.

Chomsky, whose theory of language will be discussed more fully in the next chapter, offered a conception of language that was diametrically opposed to the views of Skinner. Human verbal behavior for Skinner is continuous with animal behavior, but for Chomsky human language is a unique competence in the animal kingdom; Skinner emphasizes learning process in verbal behavior, while Chomsky stresses innate factors; Skinner expresses his views about behavior in an atheoretical fashion, while Chomsky's conception of the mind is highly theoretical.

Not surprisingly, no agreement was reached between Skinner and Chomsky about the proper psychological analysis of language. After reading a few pages of Chomsky's critique (1959), Skinner (1983b) became convinced that Chomsky did not understand him and never bothered to finish Chomsky's review. Skinner's view was not shared by most psychologists and linguists. Subsequent research in the new field of psycholinguistics was heavily influenced by Chomsky's conception of language; Skinner's view was practically ignored. Skinner reacts serenely to the turn of events, being convinced that the future will justify his own conception:

> What the psycholinguists miss is any conception of a functional analysis as opposed to a structural analysis of verbal behavior. . . . They lean very heavily on the mentalistic psychology, and they are going to be let down because there is no such psychology. But as I said earlier, now they are postulating innate ideas, and that is next to worthless, if not a little comical. But I am in no real hurry. I have had my say. I am not interested in arguing with them at all. When all their mythical machinery finally grinds to a halt and is laid aside, discarded, then we will see what is remembered fifty or a hundred years from now, when the truth will have all been brought out in the open (Skinner in an interview reported by M. H. Hall, 1967, p. 70).

Philosophical issues in radical behaviorism. Many psychologists who believe that their discipline can ultimately make solid contributions to society's betterment are reluctant to offer any recommendation in the absence of a body of reliable knowledge supporting any particular social policy (e.g., capital punishment). Not so with Skinner! He apparently does not entertain any doubt about the effectiveness of his behavioral modification techniques in implementing social change for the better. His convictions and plans have generated much angry criticism.

Many critics object to the image of man that behaviorism proposes; a mechanistic organism void of human feeling and experience. For the romantic feeling "I love you," Skinner substitutes the bland description, "I find you reinforcing." Behaviorists reject such criticism because a scientific analysis of behavior designed to predict and control behavior need not be involved in the task of describing the "experience of being human." In addition, behaviorists will note that the early history of psychology demonstrated that a veridical account of human consciousness is beyond achievement. Consequently, behaviorists dismiss the presumed antihumanistic criticism that is directed against them as being inappropriate and self-defeating because it creates an unnecessary obstacle to the development of a more efficient technology of behavior.

Other critics find the notion of society or a person *controlling* another's behavior to be intrinsically offensive and simply dismiss Skinner's rebuttal that all behavior is controlled with the only difference being whether the control is planned or unplanned.

One can be sympathetic with Skinner's goal of employing the technology of behavior to control behavior in pursuit of the goal of social improvement but still feel uneasy about the question, "Who controls the controller?" Skinner recognizes this problem:

> I think a science of behavior is just as dangerous as the atom bomb. It has the potential of being horribly misused. We must devote ourselves to a better governmental design which will have some control over all destructive instruments (Skinner in an interview reported by Evans, 1968, p. 54).

Recognizing the problem that operant methodology may be misused does not automatically ensure that it will not be misused. Skinner suggests that a society planned according to his principles will evolve into a *good* society because a reciprocal relationship will be established between the controller and controllees that will work to the benefit of all. How can he be sure? What evidence can he cite? The answers that are forthcoming have been far from reassuring. In evaluating Twin Oaks, a community patterned after the behavioral utopia that Skinner (1948) described in his novel *Walden Two,* one observer reports that "Petty jealousies, boredom and laziness have not been whipped," while another observer notes that the community, consisting of seventy-eight people, operates more in line with humanistic psychology (Chapter 12) than radical behaviorism (Cordes, 1984). Skinner's own comment about Twin Oaks as it approaches its twentieth anniversary is most revealing in illustrating the threat of authoritarian solutions to moral issues:

> [Twin Oaks] could very well be something close to Walden Two when it gets bigger. . . . If they are successful there will be no government more than simple rules to follow. They will have no religion, they will have no economic institutions. . . . The whole point is to get rid of the middle man of government, religion, and economics and design a world in which you behave well toward each other, produce what you need and enjoy yourself (Skinner, quoted by Cordes, 1984, p. 1).

The basic issue in evaluating a good society is the determination of *good.* Skinner's attempts to define good resorts to the theme of selection by consequences; a good society is one that survives. Does history justify such a notion? History is filled with examples of heroes who chose death to the abandonment of their moral principles. "Give me liberty or death!" is a philosophical statement that questions survival as the ultimate good. The adoption of survival as the sole goal of society, it can be argued, will degrade human existence because idealistic goals will inevitably be sacrificed in the struggle for survival.

A *moderate* radical behaviorist can reject the excessive claims of Skinner, but defend his position by arguing that as long as the limitations of his technology of behavior are acknowledged—hereditary limits to the powers of reinforcement and the inability of science to validate ethical goals—then operant technology can be effectively exploited in implementing individual adjustment and social welfare. All the answers to complex psychological problems have yet to be found, but radical behaviorism provides a solid foundation, based upon the reinforcement process, on which to erect a relevant and effective psychology for individuals and society.

Debate about Radical Behaviorism

Moderator: Intense controversy usually generates such emotionality that it becomes difficult to isolate and clarify the issues in a debate. Is it possible to discuss radical behaviorism in a reasonable and fair manner? I would like to encourage both of you to try.

Pro: I think it can be done, but I am not optimistic that it will be done. Skinner has challenged so many sacred cows that a large segment of his audience responds automatically with such anger that they are prevented from understanding his message, which is simple. Empirical evidence demonstrates that the probability of response recurring, human as well as animal, depends upon the consequences of that act. Thus, a technology of behavior is available by controlling contingencies of reinforcement to encourage desirable forms of behavior, while simultaneously eliminating undesirable forms. With this technology, it therefore becomes possible to modify individual behavior and improve society.

Con: I agree that Skinner's message is simple, simple as a soap commercial that repeatedly extolls its product. For several decades, Skinner has consistently advertised the power of positive reinforcement without modifying the message to account for relevant evidence that reveals its limitations. He doggedly insists, for example, that punishment only suppresses a response but fails to reduce the probability of its recurrence. That is simply not true! Strong punishment can markedly reduce a tendency for a response to be repeated (e.g., Boe & Church, 1967). No doubt, punishment can generate undesirable side effects but it may, nevertheless, be the most effective way of handling some behavioral problems. Spanking a three-year-old child for madly dashing into the road in hot pursuit of a ball may be the most effective method of preventing the child from being killed by a passing car. The point of this example is simply to illustrate that Skinner ignores a massive amount of data that limits the applicability of his model to complex forms of behavior. Perhaps the philosophical commitments that underlie his conception of a utopia blind him to evidence that is contrary to his psychological conceptions. Or, perhaps his antitheoretical bias frees him from the task of rigorously evaluating his conception of behavior in light of empirical evidence.

Pro: Tut! Tut! You are getting emotional like all of Skinner's critics. Remember you are a scientist who should be capable of offering a detached evaluation. I repeat that if you are dealing with a behavioral problem, a person who is exhibiting an undesirable form of behavior, radical behaviorism can offer the most effective techniques for modifying it. You may object to Skinner's failure to justify his behavior modification technique in alluring theoretical language but you should be satisfied that it offers the best chance for controlling significant behavioral changes.

Con: Your comment illustrates what psychologists find so annoying with Skinner's claims. Your boast is probably true when limited to teaching animals amusing tricks or ridding humans of simple phobias such as fear of snakes or heights. But the boast is flagrantly false when it comes to modifying the psychotic behavior of a schizophrenic or a manic depressive; antipsychotic drugs are far more effective. And when it comes to education, programmed learning and other operant techniques have achieved success only with simple skills such as spelling and elementary mathematics. When it comes to complex intellectual tasks—advanced physics and mathematics—operant methodology has little to offer. By his premature extrapolations during the early part of his career, Skinner created an illusion that radical behaviorism offered a broad and effective technology of behavior. That illusion is now being shattered.

Moderator: If nothing else, this debate has demonstrated that a radical behaviorism generates much emotionality. Perhaps students, in contrast to professional psychologists, are in a better position to achieve a detached evaluation?

HEBB'S NEUROPHYSIOLOGICAL THEORY

Whereas Tolman, Hull, and Skinner actively promoted behavioristic methodology, Hebb took it for granted: "All psychology has become behavioristic in the sense that it depends for its facts on the objective record" (Hebb, 1966). He also felt compelled to note:

> There are many people who are unhappy about the course of modern psychology, and, I regret to say, this includes some psychologists. The objectors do not want an objective science, but a sort of self contemplation. . . . Subjective science? There isn't such a thing. Introspectionism is a dead duck. It is theoretically impossible (Hebb, 1974, p. 73).

Sharing with Watson and other neobehaviorists the goal of an objective psychology, however, did not encourage Hebb to follow their lead in strategy, research, or theory.

Historical Roots

Psychologists throughout history have disagreed about the appropriate role of physiology in psychology. One important view, beginning with Wundt, and more recently expressed by Tolman and Skinner, is that psychological laws could and should be expressed independently of neurophysiological processes. In other words, psychological knowledge need not be reduced to neurophysiology. Wundt expressed this idea in his concept of psychic causality; the mind is a self-contained system making it possible to interpret mental events solely in terms of psychic activities. Both Tolman and Skinner assumed a similar position in regard to behavior. Their strategic orientation became known as *black-box* psychology: one can discover laws and formulate theories of behavior without any reference to internal neurophysiological events. The organism is essentially a black box, the inside of which need not be known.

Another view is that psychology is a biological science that requires ultimately that its phenomena be interpreted within a neurophysiological framework. James (1892) at times favored this position: "The immediate condition of a state of consciousness is an activity of some sort in the cerebral hemispheres." He also proposed a neurological interpretation of habit formation that anticipated Pavlovian conditioning: "When two elementary brain processes have been active together or in immediate succession, one of them, on recurring, tends to propagate its excitement into the other" (James, 1892a).

Accepting the reductionist's thesis that behavior should ultimately be explained in terms of underlying biological processes does not necessarily imply that all psychological research should involve physiology. Some behavioristic theorists (e.g., Hull) suggested the strategy of postponing neurophysiological explanations until precise empirical relationships had been established between environmental variables and behavior, and then using such information to guide research designed to discover the neurophysiological underpinnings of behavior.

Behavior and the Brain. It was once thought that the center of all psychological activities was localized in specific areas of the cortex. This conception was encouraged by an interesting medical case in the nineteenth century which led to the conclusion that language is localized in a small cortical area near the front of the brain. In 1831, a patient whose principal symptom was an inability to speak was admitted to a state institution near Paris. This patient could communicate rather effectively by means of signs. An examination by a noted surgeon, Paul Broca, suggested that the patient's vocal equipment was intact and his intelligence was normal. A localized lesion was found in the frontal lobe of the left cerebral hemisphere. Broca concluded that the lesion, the area of which became known as *Broca's Area*, was responsible for the patient's inability to talk.

Karl S. Lashley (1890–1958), an early disciple of John Watson who never abandoned methodological behaviorism, tried to answer the question, "Where are memories stored?" Lashley trained rats in complicated mazes and then surgically removed different portions of their brains in an attempt to discover where the memory engram, a neurological trace of the learning experience, was located. Following recovery from the surgery, the rats were run in the maze to discover the extent of their memory loss. Memory was found not to be localized in any specific spot or circumscribed area of the brain. Instead, the memory of the maze deteriorated with the *amounts* of brain damage. Lashley proposed the principle of *mass action:* The amount of memory loss is correlated with the amount, not the location, of brain destruction.

In marked contrast to Lashley's data are the observations of human patients by a Canadian neurosurgeon, Wilder Penfield (1975). When electrically stimulated in a specific portion of the brain, Penfield's patients reported vivid memories; for example: "Oh, a familiar memory—in an office somewhere. I could see the desks. I was there and someone was calling me—a man was leaning on the desk with a pencil in his hand."

The dramatic results that both Lashley and Penfield obtained, each supporting a conflicting hypothesis—mass action versus strict localization—were open to criticism. Maze learning for the rat is a complicated task involving a variety of skills including several sensory abilities—visual, olfactory, tactual. The destruction of the visual portion of the brain will not necessarily destroy the rat's memory of the maze if other sensory areas, such as olfactory and tactual, are left intact. But, if a learned act is exclusively dependent on visual cues, the memory of the response will be totally eliminated when the visual cortex is destroyed. Consequently, Lashley's *mass action* hypothesis that all parts of the cortex are equally important to a rat's memory was an artifact of his experimental task.

The assumption that memories are specifically localized, as the data of the surgical patients suggest, is questionable because of the failure of Penfield to employ a crucial control. How can one be sure that the episode recalled was truly a memory of an incident *that actually happened?* No independent confirmation of the recalled episode was offered. Perhaps the stimulation of a specific spot of the cortex triggered a series of images that had no counterpart in a specific episode experienced by the patient.

In general, the research area of the relationship between brain and behavior in the middle of the twentieth century appeared to consist of a set of isolated findings in search of an integrative interpretation. Hebb's major contribution was to offer such an interpretation and thereby spur the development of neuropsychology.

Donald O. Hebb (1904–1985)

Students who are convinced that their undergraduate performance fails to reflect their true talents can look to the career of Donald O. Hebb to sustain their belief. He received a B.A. from Dalhousie University in Nova Scotia, Canada, in 1925, with the lowest possible course average that would permit graduation.

Hebb, who supported himself as an undergraduate by teaching school, flirted with the idea of becoming a novelist, but was unable to complete any manuscript. He continued to teach school while halfheartedly enrolling as a part-time graduate student in psychology at McGill University. Scholarships and other forms of financial support were denied him because of his poor undergraduate record. When thirty years old he finally made a firm decision to become a psychologist and borrowed money to attend the University of Chicago, in order to study with Karl Lashley. Hebb had been intrigued with Pavlov's theorizing about the brain-behavior relationship exhibited in classical conditioning, but was quick to change his mind after Lashley attacked Pavlovian reflexology as a telephone switchboard model of the nervous system while expressing a preference for the more holistic approach favored by the Gestalt psychologists. Hebb, in describing his conversion, admitted,

> I had all the fervor of the reformed drunk at a temperance meeting; having been a fully convinced Pavlovian, I was now a fully convinced Gestalt-*cum*-Lashleyan. Though I saw that the configurational theories were not satisfactory, I thought they pointed the direction for better theorizing in the future (Hebb, 1959, p. 625).

Lashley accepted a professorship at Harvard in 1935 and arranged for Hebb to complete his doctorate there. Hebb was awarded a Ph.D. in 1936 and because of the Great Depression experienced great difficulty getting any full-time job. Fortunately, a year later he was appointed a Fellow of the Montreal Neurological Institute for two years (1937–1939), where his task was to evaluate the psychological status of Penfield's patients following brain surgery.

From 1939 to 1942 Hebb served as a Lecturer and Assistant Professor at Queen's University and then he joined Lashley, who had just been appointed Director of the Yerkes Laboratories of Primate Biology in Florida:

> I am accustomed to saying that I learned more about human beings during that time than in any other five-year period of my life, except the first. After two or three months of daily observations, I found that the thirty adult chimpanzees of the colony were as distinctive in personality as one would expect of thirty human beings assembled more or less at random (Hebb, 1980, p. 293).

The years at the Yerkes Laboratories gave Hebb time to think through his ideas about the relationships between brain activity and perception, emotion, and thought. Hebb accepted a professorship at McGill University at a time that the brain-behavior relationship interested few psychologists. The black-box conception of psychology was in style with "Hull avoiding, and Tolman and Skinner denouncing any involvement with the brain" (Hebb, 1980). Hebb finished a manuscript for a book that offered a neurophysiological theory of behavior. Two publishers rejected it, but it was finally accepted by Wiley and published in 1949 under the title of *The Organization of Behavior.* Astonishingly to Hebb, it became an immediate success. Hebb's book offered a stimulating alternative to black-box psychology, and, with the collaboration of bright neuroscientists at McGill University, neuropsychology was brought to the forefront of psychology after having been ignored for too many decades.

Methodological Assumptions

Unlike Tolman, Hull, and Skinner, Hebb did not engage in methodological discussions of specific issues such as the nature of scientific explanation or the meaning of theoretical constructs. Nevertheless, he held strong opinions about the essential nature of psychology and the best strategy to pursue in research and theorizing.

The Subject Matter of Psychology. Although committed to an objective approach, Hebb nevertheless shared with Karl Lashley the view that the key question in psychology is the mind, "the central issue, the great mystery, the toughest problem of all." This does not mean that Lashley and Hebb shared interests with mentalistic psychologists (e.g., Titchener) who believed the mind should be directly examined in order to describe its content. Instead, Hebb, like the functionalists, viewed the mind as an instrument of adjustment. In the emergency theory of consciousness, functionalists hypothesized that conscious deliberation began when habits failed (Chapter 5). In a similar fashion, Hebb (1974) considered mind to be "the capacity for thought, and thought is the integrative activity of the brain—that activity up in the control tower that, during waking hours, overrides reflex response and frees behavior from sense dominance." To understand the mind, Hebb insisted that psychologists must understand the activities of the brain.

Hebb's conception can be clarified by comparing it with Tolman's. Both employed a model of the mind in their psychological theory. Whereas Tolman sought to develop his model of the mind (e.g., cognitive map) in terms of environmental-behavioral relationships, Hebb chose to formulate his conception of the mind in terms of activities of the brain.

Methods of Investigation. Hebb naturally valued psychophysiological research designed to reveal the influence of neurological, hormonal, and other physiological variables on behavior. At the same time, he recognized that purely behavioral research, including naturalistic observations, could provide guidance to a research program that sought to relate behavior to underlying neurophysiological processes.

Criterion of Truth. Hebb, committed to a natural science view of psychology, equated understanding with the correspondence between empirical evidence and the implications of a theoretical hypothesis. But he thought a deeper understanding is achieved with a psychophysiological theory than with a black-box formulation.

Strategy

The distinctive feature of Hebb's strategy is his insistence that a theory of behavior must be conceptualized in terms of underlying neurophysiological processes. He assumed a perfect correlation between neural activity and behavior; in principle, all behavior is determined by electrochemical changes in the nervous system. Consequently, it is necessary to pose theoretical questions in psychological terms and answer them neurophysiologically.

Hebb's neurophysiological orientation encouraged him to stress the importance of genetic and developmental influences more than *black-box* neobehaviorists. Relating behavior to biological processes automatically forces one to consider how genetic influences and developmental processes determine the structure and function of the neurophysiological system, which operates as the control center of behavior.

Hebb's view of psychological theory was similar to Carr's. A theory should provide a general framework that guides research while being sufficiently flexible to absorb new empirical information. Unlike Hull, he did not believe it possible to construct a precise theory of behavior, but did feel confident that a tentative theory based upon neurophysiological evidence would ultimately mature into a satisfactory formulation.

Hebb's Theory

Hebb's theory emerged from his conviction that a telephone switchboard conception of the nervous system, which he insisted stimulus-response psychologists assumed, is fundamentally wrong. The telephone switchboard metaphor, Hebb argued, is misleading on two counts. First, it implies a direct and fixed pathway between a stimulus and response. Second, it suggests that the central nervous system operates in a passive mode, merely transmitting neural impulses without actively influencing their behavioral consequences.

Hebb cites neurological evidence opposed to the switchboard analogy. "Neural transmission is not simply linear, but apparently always involves some closed or recurrent circuits; and a single impulse cannot ordinarily cross a synapse—two or more must act simultaneously, and two or more afferent fibers must, therefore, be active in order to excite a third to which they lead" (Hebb, 1949). In other words, the connection between sensory stimulation and muscular or glandular reactions is not a one-way street. Loop circuits exist that require neural impulses to travel around a loop of neurons before proceeding toward effector mechanisms.

The assumption that the central nervous system is a passive transmitter of neural impulses is denied by the fact that external stimulation is not needed to activate the central nervous system. Cortical cells fire periodically even when a person is resting or sleeping, as evidenced by the electroencephalogram (EEG), a graphic record of the electrical activity of the brain.

Two Kinds of Behavior. Hebb's rejection of the telephone switchboard metaphor did not force him to reject the notion of a simple stimulus-response connection. Instead, he distinguished between two general kinds of behavior, *sense dominated* and *cognitive.* Pavlov's dog salivating to food (unconditioned stimulus) is an example of the former because the animal responds immediately, inasmuch as "the neural connections between receptor and effector are straight-through" (Hebb, 1972). At the other extreme is cognitive behavior, such as solving an arithmetic problem, in which complicated cortical activities mediate between the problem and its solution: "There is no opposition between two kinds of behavior but a gradation from one to the other, though at the extreme they seem quite different" (Hebb, 1972). They also can occur simultaneously. A man starts shivering (sense dominated) while playing golf in the late afternoon as the temperature begins to drop, and then decides to put on his windbreaker instead of a bulky sweater (cognitive) because the necessary warmth will be provided without interference to his golf swing. Hebb believes that theories of behavior that emphasize only one of these two kinds of behavior will be at best, incomplete, and at worst, fundamentally incorrect.

Cell Assemblies and Phase Sequences. Hebb considered the key problem of psychology to be thought, and the basic question is the nature of the neurophysiological processes that mediate between problem presentation and problem solution. To encompass thought he suggested two neurophysiological concepts—*cell assemblies* and *phase sequences*–both of which involved the organization of activities of previously unrelated neurons.

Cell assemblies. When experiencing an intricate pattern of stimulation, such as a human face, a complex bundle of neurons, called a *cell assembly*, is formed. As we examine the face, shifting our gaze from the eyes to the nose to the forehead, different neurons are stimulated. Initially, the stimulation of each facial characteristic will be independent of others. Later, the firings will coalesce so that a pattern of neurological firings will occur, with the entire configuration constituting a neurological representation of the face:

> If a neuron, A, is near enough to another, B, to have any possibility of firing it, and if it does take part in firing it on one occasion . . . the probability is increased that when A fires next B will fire as a result. In other words, "synaptic resistance" is decreased, by a microscopic growth at the synapse or the chemical change in one of the two cells. The assembly might be made up of perhaps 25, 50, or 100 neurons, and building it up in the first place would be a very slow process, requiring many repetitions of the stimulating conditions (Hebb, 1959, p. 628).

Once the face becomes familiar, the entire cell assembly can be fired, even when only a portion of the face is perceived or when a person imagines the face. The cell assembly, in essence, is the neurological basis of an image or idea.

Phase sequences. Cell assemblies themselves become organized into *phase sequences*, a sequence of cell assembly activities:

> cell assemblies that are active at the same time become interconnected. Common events in the child's environment establish assemblies, and then when these events occur together the assemblies become connected (because they are active together). When the baby hears footsteps . . . an assembly is excited; while this is still active, he sees a face and feels hands picking him up, which excites other assemblies—so that "footsteps-assembly" becomes connected with "face assembly" and the "being-picked-up assembly." After this has happened, when the baby hears footsteps only, *all three* assemblies are excited; the baby then has something like a perception of a mother's face and the contact of her hands before she has come in sight—but since the sensory stimulations have not taken place, this is ideation or imagery, not perception (Hebb, 1972, p. 67).

Theoretical significance. The concepts of *cell assemblies* and *phase sequences* offered possible solutions to age-old problems in psychology. First, in combination they offered a reasonable approach to the problem of thought within a neurophysiological orientation. As one example take the insight problem (Chapter 7) in which caged chimpanzees are confronted with food beyond their reach but have an available hoe in their vicinity. Solving the problem, raking the food in, depends on the chimps having experience with sticks. According to Hebb, separate phase sequences for getting food and using sticks as an extension of the arm are prerequisites for solution. The actual problem solving results from the appropriate temporal firing of each sequence.

Second, the two concepts illustrate a possible reconciliation between the atomistic approach of Watson and the holistic orientation of Gestalt psychology. As a result of *slow* stimulus-response learning, the neurons of a cell assembly, and the cell assemblies of a phase sequence, become organized into a neurological configuration (a *gestalt*) that functions in an integrated manner and is capable of mediating insightful behavior. Third, the suggestion that cell assemblies and phase sequences are the neurological tools of thought—concepts, ideas, images—and that they are slowly organized in early life, suggested an interesting notion about developmental changes in intelligence. Hebb speculated, as a result of some clinical and experimental evidence, that injury to an infant brain is more damaging to intelligence than a similar destruction to an adult brain. Early damage prevents the formation of potential cell assemblies and phase sequences which are required for rational behavior. Once formed, these neurological tools of thought are flexibly organized so that damage to some of their neurons can be compensated for by the activities of other neurons within the cell assembly or phase sequence. Thus, the adult, as contrasted to the young child, is more resistant to intellectual loss resulting from a similar amount of cortical damage.

Arousal Theory. Behavior can be conceptualized as varying over a dimension of arousal. At one end of this dimension is the minimal state that exists during deep sleep. At the other extreme is the maximal degree of arousal such as occurs during a disorganizing rage. In between are the moderate degrees of arousal that take place when a person is alert and responds to the demands of the task—reading and understanding a book on the history of psychology, for example.

Hebb hypothesizes that behavioral arousal is controlled by the activity of the reticular activating system (RAS), a diffuse collection of neurons, about the size of a finger, located in the middle of the brain stem (Figure 10.5). The RAS gets its name from the fact that its function is intimately tied to sleep and behavioral arousal. When a certain portion of the reticular formation is electrically stimulated, a sleeping or relaxed animal becomes activated. When a large region of the RAS is destroyed, the animal goes into a coma.

Hebb postulated a hypothetical curve that specifies the relationship between performance level and level of arousal. When arousal is too low or too high, the capacity of sensory stimulation to guide behavior is poor. When arousal is low, sensory messages are not transmitted clearly, while

FIGURE 10.5 A Schematic Representation of the Reticular Formation in Humans

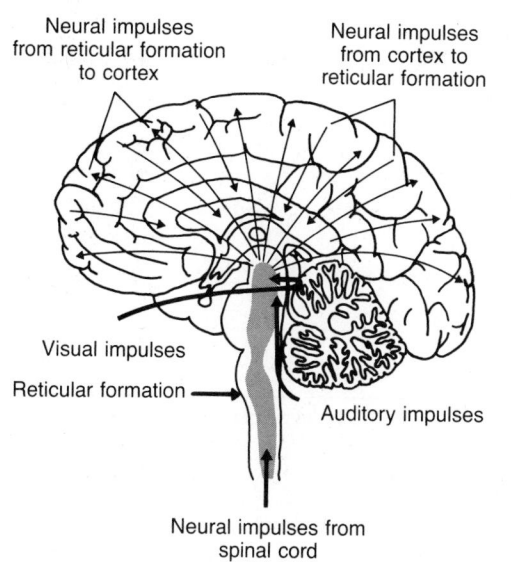

Neural impulses from reticular formation to cortex

Neural impulses from cortex to reticular formation

Visual impulses

Reticular formation

Auditory impulses

Neural impulses from spinal cord

The reticular formation is a core of nerve cells in the brain stem that influences, and is influenced by, the general activity in the brain above and in the spinal cord below.

when arousal is high too many messages get through, thus disorganizing behavior. One dramatic case of extreme arousal that Hebb (1972) cites concerns a passenger on a burning ship, who after being instructed to get on the deck immediately, was last seen ineffectually searching for his cuff link.

Optimal level of arousal depends on the task (Figure 10.7). In a simple task (a), such as buttering a piece of toast, a minimal amount of arousal is required and only intense arousal can disorganize performance. In a more complex task (b), such as solving a complex discrimination learning task, a more restricted range of arousal level is required for top-notch performance; a greater level of arousal is required to perceive the stimuli clearly and the task is more susceptible to interference from higher levels of arousal. Finally, curve (c) illustrates a relatively simple task, such as competing in a race at a track meet, that demands a relatively high arousal level for optimal performance. But even the performance of such tasks can be handicapped by excessive arousal as happens when a sprinter is immobilized at the sound of the starter's gun.

Motivational theory. Hebb postulates that certain moderate levels of arousal can be rewarding (reinforcing). When arousal is too low (e.g., boredom), an organism is motivated to raise it; when too high (e.g., anxiety), to lower it. Hebb's motivational theory is apparently at odds with

FIGURE 10.6 A Graphical Representation of Hebb's Hypothesis (A)

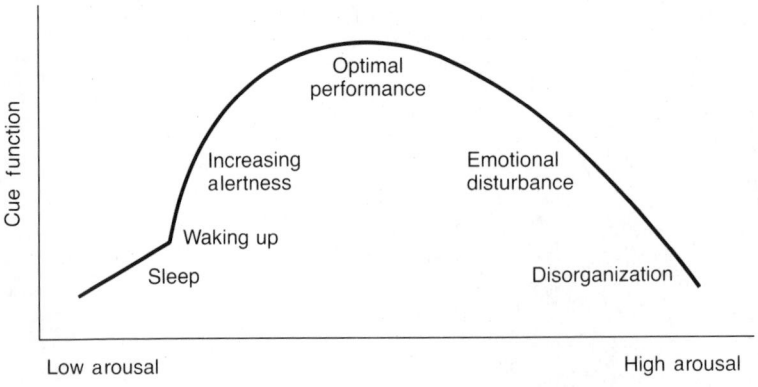

Hebb's hypothesis about the relationship between arousal level and behavior. See text for fuller explanation.

SOURCE: *Textbook of Psychology*, 3rd ed. by D. O. Hebb Copyright © 1972 by W. B. Saunders Company. Reprinted by permission of CBS College Publishing.

the Hullian formulation that equates reinforcement with drive *reduction.* For Hebb, increasing motivation, not decreasing it, can be rewarding:

> When you stop to think about it, it is nothing short of extraordinary what trouble people will go to in order to get into more trouble at the bridge table, or on a golf course; and the fascination of the murder story, or

FIGURE 10.7 A Graphical Representation of Hebb's Hypothesis (B)

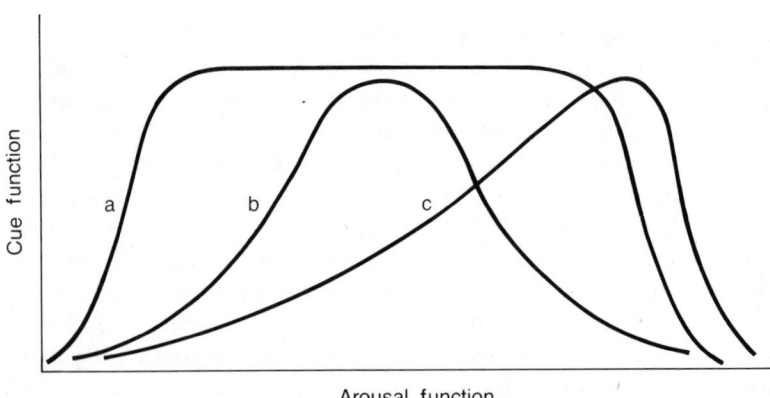

Hebb's hypothesis about the relationship between arousal level and the performance of three different kinds of tasks. See text for fuller explanation.

SOURCE: *Textbook of Psychology*, 3rd ed. by D. O. Hebb Copyright © 1972 by W. B. Saunders Company. Reprinted by permission of CBS College Publishing.

thriller . . . is no less extraordinary. This taste for excitement *must* not be forgotten when we are dealing with human motivation. It appears that, up to a certain point, threat and puzzle have positive motivating value, beyond that point negative value (Hebb, 1955, p. 250).

Reward centers in the brain. While investigating the relationship between arousal and learning, James Olds and Peter Milner (1954) who were both students of Hebb, accidentally stumbled upon *reward centers* in the brain. They implanted electrodes, connected to a light flexible wire, in rats' brains, thus enabling them to control brain stimulation while the rat was moving about. When the electrode was located in certain areas (e.g., limbic system), electrical stimulation operates as a reward. For example, a rat stimulated while in a particular location of the maze would persist in returning to that place just as if it had been fed there. This dramatic finding generated an enormous amount of research designed to locate all the reward areas within the brain as well as to discover the precise influence brain stimulation of reward areas has on behavior.

Reward centers have also been used to stimulate long-suffering psychiatric patients. One depressed patient reported that brain stimulation is "better than sex." Although the neurophysiology of brain stimulation of reward centers has yet to be fully understood, many psychologists are confident that Olds and Milner's discovery will ultimately lead to a deep understanding of the psychology of motivation and emotions.

Quotations from Donald O. Hebb

1. Psychology cannot become a branch of physiology. We cannot escape the need for large-scale units of analysis, nor the need for the special methods of behavioral study on which such analysis is based (Hebb, 1972, p. 280).

2. The problem . . . [of] the relation of qualitative to quantitative analysis . . . is . . . the problem of the hen and the egg. The two must develop hand in hand. Before one can measure profitably, one must know what one is measuring, or find the right things to measure. In this sense, qualitative analysis must precede quantitative. When the quantification is done, it is likely to react upon, and improve, the ideas that preceded it (Hebb, 1959, p. 636).

3. I am a determinist. I assume that what I am and how I think are entirely the products of my heredity and my environmental history. I have no freedom about what I *am*. But that is not what free will is about. The question is whether my behavior is entirely controlled by present circumstances. Heredity and environment shaped me, largely when I was growing up. That shaping, including how I think about things, may incline me to act in opposition to the shaping that the present environment would be likely to induce: And so I may decide to be polite to others, or to sit down to write this article when I'd rather not, or, on the other hand, decide to goof off when I should be working. If my past has shaped me to goof off, and I do goof off despite my secretary's urging, that's free will. But it's not indeterminism (Hebb, 1974, p. 75).

Historical Contributions

The major contribution of Hebb is his fairly comprehensive neurophysiological theory of psychology, which offers an alternative to the black-box orientation of most neobehaviorists. By offering a loosely knit set of ideas that had relevance to a wide variety of psychological topics—learning, attention, thought, emotion, perception, memory, developmental psychology, comparative psychology—Hebb was successful not only in stimulating significant research, but more importantly in encouraging the development of the entire field of neuropsychology. Some psychologists are convinced that their discipline can only realize its full potential as a neuroscience. If this proves to be true, Hebb will have served as an important link to the future.

It is too early to judge the ultimate impact of Hebb's major concepts, such as *arousal, cell assembly,* and *phase sequence.* All have historical importance because they directed attention to the neurophysiological processes underlying motivation, learning, and cognition. Whatever their fate may prove to be, they offered possible solutions to theoretical problems that can never be ignored.

Debate about Hebb's
Neurophysiological Approach

Moderator: My intuition suggests that the controversy that Hebb engenders will be mild compared to that generated by Skinner. Am I correct?

Pro: You are correct and the reason is that Hebb is so eminently reasonable. His self-image is not one of a messiah who was placed on the earth to lead psychology to the promised land. Hebb simply concluded that psychology, in order to achieve potential as a natural science, must investigate behavioral phenomena within a neurophysiological framework. My verdict is that the final payoff in facts and theory and future direction has justified Hebb's efforts.

Con: Although I agree with the observation that Hebb's approach to psychology appears "eminently reasonable," I question the justification for the implication that it is more reasonable than other neobehavioristic approaches. By *speculating* about neurophysiological processes he seems to escape the criticisms that were directed against Tolman and Hull, when, in fact, his approach is not distinctively different. What is the essential difference between Tolman's *cognitive map* and Hebb's *cell assembly* and *phase sequence?* They are fundamentally similar; intervening variables designed to explain behavior. Hebb, like Tolman, never measured his theoretical constructs in terms of *actual* neurophysiological changes. Similarly, the same is true for Hull and Hebb. Their actual efforts are not clearly different. Because Hebb persistently stresses the importance of a biological approach in psychology, his ideas are enveloped in the prestige of the biological sciences, in spite of the fact that neurophysiological measures are absent from much of his research. Instead of discussing intentions, let us focus on achievement. Within this framework I would argue that both Tolman and Hull have been more successful in making substantial contributions to empirical knowledge and theoretical ideas.

Pro: What you fail to understand is historical direction. Admittedly, Hebb shares with Tolman and Hull an intervening variable approach to psychological theorizing, but whenever an opportunity arose to relate behavior to available neurophysiological knowledge, as was the case for arousal theory, Hebb leaped at the opportunity. This represents a fundamental difference that favors his approach, because the future of psychology lies in biology.

Con: There is nothing so compelling as faith. Your argument encourages me to reevaluate the claims of Skinner. Perhaps the future belongs to behavioral psychology that seeks to control behavior. By being directly involved with the adjustment of individuals and the improvement of society without reference to underlying biology, psychology will be in the best state to realize its potentialities.

Moderator: Enough said!

SUMMARY

The goal of psychology, for B. F. Skinner, was not the construction of an abstract intervening-variable type theory that both Tolman and Hull sought, but was instead the collection of a body of reliable knowledge about individual behavior. Such knowledge can be productively applied to enhance individual adjustment and to plan a better society.

Many of the core ideas of Skinner's radical behaviorism emanated from Watson's behavioristic methodology and interest in conditioning, Pavlov's demonstration that environmental control of behavior is possible, Mach's proposal of equating scientific understanding with the demonstration of functional relationships among directly observed variables, and Thorndike's law of effect that postulates that the consequences of a response determine whether the response is learned.

The fundamental subject matter of radical behaviorism is behavior, but Skinner argues that his kind of behaviorism can deal with mental events. He presumably accomplishes this task by assuming that conscious acts operate in the same manner as behavioral acts. The dominant methodological assumption in radical behaviorism is that highly regular and reliable laws of individual behavior can be discovered and generalized to everyday life. The litmus test for understanding behavior is the ability to control behavior.

The strategy that governed the development of radical behaviorism was to develop experimental procedures that increased the control of individual behavior by environmental manipulations while abandoning the conventional practice of statistically analyzing group data and formulating abstract theories.

The major concepts of radical behaviorism are *operant conditioning* (free-responding instrumental conditioning), *reinforcement* (an event that increases the probability of a response, *punishment* (an event that reduces the probability of a response), *primary reinforcement* (reinforcement based on innate factors), *secondary reinforcement* (a neutral stimulus that acquires reinforcing properties), and *schedules of reinforcement* (the sequence of reinforced and nonreinforced responses in operant conditioning). Schedules of reinforcement are considered to be of basic importance because the performance of any act is dependent upon its reinforcement history. The two major kinds of schedules are interval (based on time), and ratio (based on number of responses), each of which can occur in a fixed or variable mode. *Shaping* is a method of modifying behavior by reinforcing successive approximations of the desired behavior. *Superstitious behavior* is ritualistic behavior resulting from noncontingent reinforcements. A *discriminative operant* is a cue that, if responded to, results in reinforcement, as is the case when a reinforcement occurs only in the presence of a light (S^D) in a Skinner box. According to Skinner, punishment momentarily suppresses behavior but does not eliminate it. Skinner extrapolates findings from operant conditioning to verbal behavior to illustrate how the same lawful regularities operate in both realms of behavior.

Skinner, in summarizing the research designed to reveal the experimental conditions that affect the frequency of a specific response, concludes that: *Reponses* (R) *are made to a discriminative stimulus* (S^D) *as a function of contingencies of reinforcement* (S^{reinf}). Skinner interprets this descriptive law as an expression of the mechanism of selection by consequences. In addition to operating on individual behavior, the mechanism also operates on biological evolution and the evolution of cultures. From this conceptual framework, Skinner vigorously argues that the most effective method of controlling behavior is by arranging appropriate environmental contingencies of reinforcement.

In support of his operant interpretation of behavior, Skinner points to the successes of controlling behavior by the shaping technique, programmed learning, and behavior modification. His critics suggest that Skinner's claims are often exaggerated, and argue that his basic notions are ambiguous, his model of behavior is at best incomplete, and his design of a utopian society is both confusing and value laden.

Hebb's neurobehavioristic approach in psychology is distinctively different from that of Tolman, Hull, and Skinner in that he insists that psychological theory must be based upon knowledge of neurophysiological processes. The historical roots of Hebb's theory lie in past efforts to relate behavior to brain function. Although committed to an objective approach in psychology, Hebb, nevertheless, considered the basic problem to be one of unravelling the mysteries of the mind, and especially of thought processes. To understand the mind requires an understanding of brain functioning.

Hebb, because of his conception of psychology as a biological science, considered that psychological research should have as one of its goals the discovery of the neurological, hormonal, and other physiological variables that influence behavior. He accepts the notion that deductive explanation is the ultimate form of scientific understanding, but believes that a deeper understanding is achieved with psychophysiological theories than purely black-box conceptions.

Hebb employed three strategic principles: a psychological theory must be conceptualized in terms of underlying neurophysiological processes; development and comparative investigations are particularly important in revealing basic information about the relationship between behavior and biological processes; and theories should have instrumental value in guiding research.

Two kinds of evidence—that the brain is continuously active and that neural transmission, except for sensory-motor reflexes, is not a one-way fixed pathway between stimulation and behavior—encouraged Hebb to reject the telephone switchboard metaphor for the central nervous system. Hebb postulated two kinds of behavior, sense dominated and cognitive. Cognitive behavior is mediated by two types of neurophysiological structures, each of which are learned. A *cell assembly* is an organized set of neurons that were previously unrelated. The cell asssembly is a neurological representation of some perceptual display, such as a human face. After the cell assembly is formed, one element (e.g., neurons representing the eyes) can trigger the entire pattern (e.g., the face). Cell assemblies, in the same manner, can be organized into a phase sequence that represents a progression of perceptual events, such as a baby learning to recognize the sequence of events that precedes nursing. Just as cell assemblies can be triggered by activating one cell, an entire phase sequence can be triggered by one cell assembly (e.g., footsteps) or even the imaging of the assembly.

The concepts of cell assembly and phase sequence offer a reasonable and appealing neurophysiological interpretation of thought and problem solving. In addition, these concepts suggested a possible reconciliation between associative and holistic interpretations; cell assemblies and phase sequences become integrated as a function of simple associative learning. Once formed, they operate in an organized and a flexible manner to mediate rational behavior.

Hebb's conception of motivation and emotion is expressed within his arousal theory. Behavior ranges across a dimension of arousal from the low end of deep sleep to the high end of emotional disorganization. The neurophysiological correlate of behavioral arousal is the activity of the reticular activating system (RAS). The most effective performance of a task is dependent on an optimal level of arousal. If arousal level is too low, then behavior is less responsive to the relevant cues. While under conditions of high arousal, too many cues are transmitted to the brain, thus encouraging behavioral disorganization. The optimal level of arousal is determined by the nature of the problem confronting an organism.

By assuming that emotion is closely correlated with physiological arousal, Hebb postulates that organisms are motivated to seek a moderate level of arousal, escaping from levels that are too high or low. One consequence of Hebb's arousal theory was the discovery of reward centers in an area adjacent to the RAS in the lower brain stem.

The major contribution of Hebb is the formulation of a neurophysiological theory that offers an alternative strategy to the black-box conceptions of other neobehaviorists. By his efforts, Hebb made important contributions to neuropsychology.

SUGGESTED READINGS

Skinner is prolific writer, always anxious to publicize his views. His *Science and Human Behavior* (1953) clearly and entertainingly presents his basic ideas, while *Walden Two* (1948), a novel, offers insight to Skinner's philosophy of life. *Beyond Freedom and Dignity* (1971), an extremely controversial book, proposes that society can be improved by the application of operant technology while simultaneously challenging the major tenets of humanism. *Cumulative Record* (1961) and *Contingencies of Reinforcement: A Theoretical Analysis* (1969) contain many of Skinner's most famous papers. An interesting and sympathetic analysis of Skinnerian methodology is offered in M. Sidman's *Tactics of Scientific Research* (1960).

Hilgard & Bower's (1975) *Theories of Learning* (4th edition) includes a chapter on radical behaviorism. Chomsky's review of Skinner's *Verbal Behavior* (1959) represents a complete rejection of Skinnerian psychology, while MacCorquodale (1969) offers a defense of Skinner's position. Rogers, a humanistic psychologist, engages Skinner in a debate about the relative merits of humanistic psychology versus a behavioristic conception (Rogers & Skinner, 1956).

Hebb expresses his ideas in an upfront manner without any effort to seduce his reader by overstating his case. His brief introductory textbook (1972) serves as an excellent introduction to his conception of psychology. His classic contribution, *The Organization of Behavior* (1949), is recommended for the ambitious student. His chapter "A Neuropsychological Theory" (1959) reviews his theory as well as describes its development. "What Psychology is About" (1974) is an amusingly written but serious analysis of psychology. A good secondary source of Hebb's views is Hergenhahn (1976). Lashley's classic *Brain Mechanism and Intelligence* (1929), is an important book for students who seek a deeper understanding of the history of neuropsychology.

The serious student who desires a full understanding of all aspects of behaviorism will profit from reading Zuriff's *Behaviorism: A Conceptial Reconstruction* (1985).

11

Cognitive Psychology

Cognitive psychology was never born; it gradually coalesced. A variety of orientations, within and outside of psychology, merged to produce a new force in the 1950s that achieved a clear identity in 1966 with the publication of Ulric Neisser's *Cognitive Psychology.*

Today cognitive psychology, which seeks to understand how the mind works, represents the most popular orientation in psychology, receiving a level of support among a broad range of psychologists unmatched in its history. Because cognitive psychology represents a mingling of many different ideas, it fails to have the unity of systematic positions that have been dominated by a single spokesman (e.g., Titchenerian structuralism) or by a closely knit group (e.g., Gestalt psychology). Thus, cognitive psychologists do not speak with one voice; although they share a common orientation, they frequently disagree about important methodological and theoretical issues.

HISTORICAL ROOTS

The numerous historical roots of cognitive psychology can be divided into two main classes; those that emerged within psychology and those that originated in other disciplines.

Influences within the History of Psychology

Several streams of psychological thought contributed to the development of this movement. These contributions include experimental methods for investigating the mind, theoretical interpretations of the mind, and a new field of psychology that became known as *human engineering.*

Experimental Analysis of the Mind.   Although Wundt denied that thinking could be introspectively observed he nevertheless assumed that mental activity could be inferred from both experimental and historical evidence (Chapter 2). His complication experiment (p. 28) and the application of mental chronometry (p. 31) to the analysis of reaction time illustrated the logic of inferring mental activity from empirical evidence. Wundt's efforts anticipated the strategy that was to be followed by most contemporary cognitive psychologists.

General Theoretical Notions.   While conceptualizing the mind as a general system, psychologists differed about how it is organized and functions. Wundt and Titchener distinguished between different kinds of mental content (e.g., sensations, feelings). Functionalists, who were concerned with both mental activity and adjustment, stressed the importance of mental operations. Angell (1904) expressed this interest by suggesting that the major task of the functionalist is to discover "the typical *operations* of consciousness under actual life *conditions.*" Embedded in Angell's statement is a central concern of modern cognitive psychology— how the mind operates on information in order to solve a problem, whether it be simply the recall of a person's name or the proof of a complex mathematical principle.

In contrast to the functionalists' emphasis on mental acts and their adaptive significance, structural features of the mind were stressed by both Gestalt psychology and Tolman's cognitive behaviorism. The *psychological environment* of Gestalt psychology and Tolman's *cognitive map* were mental constructions designed to represent an organism's environment.

Mental structures and cognitive processes.   Psychologists who anticipated cognitive psychology all seemed to be proposing hypotheses about the workings of the mind. As a result, the distinction between mental structures and mental processes gradually became apparent although it is often subtle and sometimes even confusing. The distinction is analogous to the difference between anatomy and physiology. For example, anatomy describes the structure of the stomach while physiology describes the processes with which that organ digests food. Sir Frederic Bartlett (1886–1969), an English psychologist, introduced this distinction when investigating memory. He rejected the conception of remembering as a reproductive process in which information is passively duplicated in memory. Bartlett (1932) proposed that memory is a reconstructivist process; when hearing a story a person transforms, or more technically, *encodes* the incoming information into a mental structure, a *schema,* that represents the interpretation of the story in line with the listener's preconceptions and attitudes. When recalling the story, the schema is *decoded,* transferred back into the remembered version. In this example the mental structure is the schema and the cognitive processes are encoding and decoding.

Jean Piaget (1896–1980), who was trained as a biologist, became interested in epistemological issues. Instead of treating epistemology as a speculative armchair discipline, Piaget decided to study it scientifically by empirically investigating the development of thought, or what he called *conceptual operations* from infancy through adolescence. In general, Piaget concluded that the growth of intelligence is not a continuous affair in which intellectual functioning gradually improves, but instead occurs in an invariant order of successive stages, each laying the foundation for the next.

Piaget hypothesizes that the structure of the mind undergoes qualitative changes just as a human embryo does during the period of gestation. The human embryo does not simply get larger; its structure changes dramatically. So do schemas, mental representations of objects, and their relations. Piaget's theory, like that of Freud's, was rich in ideas but vague in conception. His impact on modern cognitive psychology was twofold. His formulation stimulated interest in cognitive processes and thereby encouraged research and theorizing in the field of thought and intelligence. At the same time, Piaget's theory, based initially on naturalistic observations, appeared too ambiguous and therefore challenged cognitively oriented psychologists to formulate more precise theories of cognition.

George Miller (born 1920) published an influential paper entitled, "*The magical number seven, plus or minus two: Some limits on our capacity for processing information,*" in 1956. This paper sought to interpret the psychological phenomenon known as the *memory span*, the number of items an individual can recall after just one presentation. By analyzing a variety of findings, Miller concluded the magical number—seven plus or minus two—represented the storage capacity of short-term memory, a finding that was reported in 1871, but subsequently forgotten (Blumenthal, 1977). In other words, Miller suggested that the mind contains a mental structure analogous to a file with several slots with the exact number, depending on the individual, varying from five to nine.

In addition to postulating a memory structure, Miller proposed a process called *chunking*, which refers to the reorganization (encoding) of information to increase the number of items that can be packed into a single slot. For example, the task of remembering the phone number, 961-2834, can be made easier by chunking the number into five slots of information instead of seven; for example, 9-6-1-28-34 instead of 9-6-1-2-8-3-4.

Along with two collaborators, Eugene Galanter and Karl Pribram, Miller published *Plans and the Structure of Behavior* in 1960, which proposed that the *plan* should be substituted for the *stimulus-response (S-R) association* as the basic unit of behavior. A plan, in contrast to an S-R association, is a self-regulating system that uses available information to guide subsequent behavior. A thermostat is an example of a self-regulating system in which a target temperature (70°F) is maintained by the thermostat shutting down the furnace when that temperature is attained and starting the furnace when the temperature falls below that level. In an analogous manner, Miller, Galanter, and Pribram (1960) suggest that information feedback is basic to the execution of a plan. A plan has two functions: to compare the present situation with the desired goal and to activate routines of behavior that reduce the difference between the current situation and the goal state. A simple plan is illustrated in the task of hammering a nail into wood. The goal state is to have the head of the nail flush with the wood. The discrepancy between the goal state and the initial state when the point of the nail is resting against the wood is successively reduced by hammering the nail into the wood until the goal is achieved.

Another important book that encouraged the development of cognitive psychology was *A Study of Thinking* (1956) by Jerome Bruner (born 1915) and two collaborators, Jacqueline Goodnow and George Austin. They offered a mentalistic interpretation of concept learning that stressed a subject's strategy in marked opposition to the passive associationism that Hull had proposed in his interpretation of concept learning in 1920, and which had, from that time, tended to dominate this research area. Jerome Bruner felt that "the banning of 'mental' concepts from psychology was a fake seeking after the gods of the nineteenth-century physical sciences" (Bruner, 1980). Bruner and Miller helped found *The Center for Cognitive Studies* at Harvard in 1962. Establishing a physical presence as well as an active research program contributed to the launching of cognitive psychology.

Human Engineering. A new branch of psychology, human engineering, developed in response to the needs of the military during and after World War II. The dominant attitude that prevailed at the beginning of the war was that the design of weapon systems, such as airplanes, submarines, radar, and the like, was a purely physical problem. This view proved to be naive. For example, one war plane that seemed to be perfectly engineered suffered a high rate of landing accidents. The reason was discovered to be due to the close proximity between two levers the pilot had to use for braking and retracting the landing gear. Instead of braking after landing the plane, the pilot, who had to keep his eyes on the runway, sometimes accidently pulled the lever for retracting the landing gear and landed the plane on its belly. Such accidents could have been avoided had the reactions of the pilot been considered. The controls should have been designed, as psychologists would be quick to point out (Chapanis, Garner, & Morgan, 1949), so as to require entirely different arm movements for braking and retracting the landing gear. When the controls were redesigned accordingly, the source of the dangerous confusion was eliminated, and so were the accidents.

A core concept in human engineering is the *man-machine system* which stresses the principle that humans and machines operate as a single system. Thus, both psychological and engineering knowledge is essential for the effective design of machines. In addition, information processing, the flow of information through a man-machine system, was recognized as a basic variable in human engineering. If the necessary information does not reach the human, as was the case for the pilot who could not distinguish clearly between braking and retracting the landing gear, the man-machine system breaks down.

The radar operated advance warning system in Alaska is another example of a man-machine system. The radar operator's job is to detect any flying object traveling toward the United States. On his radar screen, which is similar to a TV screen, flying objects are seen as *blips*, points of light against a background of less intense light. In reacting to his scope, the radar operator must decide whether the activity observed indicates that a missile or plane is approaching. The task confronting the radar operator was conventionally conceptualized as purely a sensory problem. Did the operator see a blip or not? The analysis of this problem by signal detection theory (Green & Swets, 1966) suggested that nonsensory, as well as sensory processes are involved. When the blip is very faint, the operator is not sure he senses anything. A decision must be made to report or not to report a blip. One factor that will influence the decision is the relative cost of making one of the two mistakes: either not detecting a flying object (a miss) or reporting a blip when one is not there (a false alarm). What are the consequences of each? A miss could lead to disaster. Reporting a false alarm would waste some intercepter missiles. The relative weight of each error will influence an operator's decision. An operator who establishes a lenient criterion will produce many false alarms. A strict criterion will minimize false alarms but will risk the possibility that an incoming missile or airplane will not be reported and consequently not intercepted.

Signal detection theory provided a mathematical technique to sort out the observer's sensitivity from his decision criterion. In addition, it conceptualized humans as information processors and decision makers, basic constructs in the newly emerging cognitive orientation.

Contributions of Other Disciplines to Cognitive Psychology

A reasonable case can be made that cognitive psychology, or what some prefer to call *cognitive science*, is more a product of engineering, linguistics, and computer science than it is of psychology. These disciplines provided fundamental ideas that molded the development of cognitive psychology, particularly in the research area designated as information processing.

Communications Engineering. Modern technology demands numerous kinds of communication: telephone, television, radio, and so forth. Can all forms of communication be analyzed within a common framework? Claude Shannon (1948), a mathematician in the employ of Bell Telephone Laboratories thought so, and presented a general theory

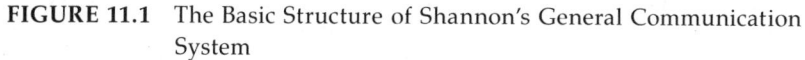

FIGURE 11.1 The Basic Structure of Shannon's General Communication System

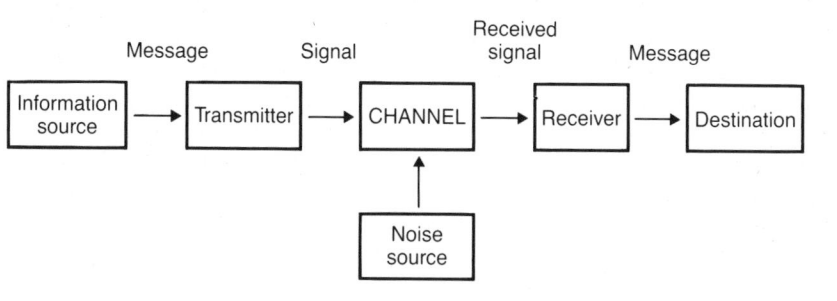

The text describes the operating characteristics of this system.

of communication for inanimate systems such as the telephone that took account of all the changes that occurred within the system from the physical input to the physical output. The basic structure of this general communication system is illustrated in Figure 11.1. Several psychologists applied to Shannon's ideas to human communication, both to the cognitive processes within an individual, and to communication between individuals.

Consider the relevance of Shannon's general communication system to the case of a student in a classroom listening to a professor's lecture. The professor is the *source* of the *message* which is *transmitted* by both auditory signals (the lecture) and visual *signals* (diagrams on blackboard) to the auditory and visual *channels*. The signals in a channel can be degraded by *noise*. For example, a neighboring conversation can prevent a student from hearing the professor clearly. The concept of noise in communication theory, however, is not simply limited to interfering sound. Noise refers to all events, outside or within a receiver, that degrade a signal. Just as static reduces the clarity of a radio signal, so do the fantasies of a student degrade the signals emitted by the professor.

The signals *received* by the student are transformed (encoded) into a message that is remembered and later decoded into information that can be utilized during an examination; test performance is determined by the quality of the message at its *destination* (examination). Numerous events throughout the general communication system can influence the quality of that message. For example, the professor's too-rapid lecturing style could overload the auditory channel and prevent the student from encoding the entire message.

Communication engineering had an important influence on the development of cognitive psychology, not because its theory could be simply superimposed on human cognition, but instead because it offered a fruitful analogy for interpreting cognitive processes. Of basic importance was the concept of *information* which, in Shannon's theory, referred to physical changes (e.g., electrical changes in a telephone line) in an inanimate communication system. Shannon offered a mathematically precise interpretation of information that proved extremely useful in designing computers and communication systems but was discovered to be inadequate for representing human knowledge. Nevertheless, the notion that information is a basic component in human cognition was encouraged, and numerous structures and processes were suggested by communication theory which provided direction, as well as hypotheses, for the experimental analysis of the mind. Examples include *encoding, decoding, information processing, communication channels, channel capacity, noise,* and so forth. Finally, communication engineering suggested the idea of a flowchart of the sort that appears in Figure 11.1. The flowchart is a diagrammatic representation of a sequence of successive events within an integrated system. Cognitive theorists found flowcharts useful for analyzing cognitive activities into their basic components.

Chomsky's Linguistic Theory. Since the time of Wundt, psychologists have sought to understand language. Skinner (1957) offered an interpretation of verbal behavior that assumed that contingencies of reinforcement govern linguistic actions. Implicit in this assumption are several important corollaries: (1) Verbal behavior is conceptualized in terms of its adaptive characteristics; (2) Human language is continuous with animal behavior; (3) Verbal behavior is primarily learned behavior; and (4) Theories, particularly mentalistic ones, are not required for understanding human language.

Noam Chomsky played a major role in stimulating the development of cognitive psychology by vigorously opposing all of Skinner's basic assumptions at the time that Skinner reigned as the dominant behaviorist. Chomsky argues that the understanding of language is not to be found in the contingencies of reinforcement but instead in the innate biological structure of human beings. Every child is born with a general notion of a universal syntax that enables her to communicate, in her native language, at an early age in a grammatically appropriate form. Even though the child cannot state the grammatical rules, and at times makes errors, linguistic usage is nevertheless guided by the innate syntactical rules, as demonstrated by the fact that she intuitively distinguishes between a correct sentence like, *Jimmy ate the apple,* and ungrammatical strings of words like, *Ate Jimmy the apple.*

Chomsky also argues that linguistic behavior is a creative enterprise; it cannot be reduced to a simple mechanical chaining conception in which a sentence is formed by each successive word triggering the next one. Two reasons are offered for rejecting this associative chaining hypothesis. One is that an enormous amount of time would be required to learn grammatically correct sentences, much too long for children to be able to speak grammatically. Second, each person is capable of uttering and understanding an *infinite* number of sentences, sentences that are different (e.g., *the unicorn jumped over the satellite*) from those previously uttered or heard. The principle of associative chaining could not possibly explain such novelty. Because of these two criticisms, Chomsky was led to the position that "rules in the head" generated sentences, not an associative network of words.

Chomsky distinguishes between *linguistic performance* and *linguistic competence*, a distinction that bears some similarity to the *learning-performance* distinction of Tolman and Hull. Linguistic performance involves sentences uttered or comprehended. Linguistic competence is the knowledge of language that enables a person to determine whether a sentence is syntactically correct.

A sentence consists of two components: *surface structure* and *deep structure*. Surface structure refers to the syntactical organization of a sentence. *The girl throws the ball* and *The ball is thrown by the girl* have two different phrase structures; the first being a simple active sentence while the second is a simple passive sentence. Both sentences express the common notion that a girl is throwing a ball, but each expresses it with a different surface structure. To account for their shared meaning, Chomsky formulates the construct *deep structure*, the crucial element of his original theory. Deep structure is a theoretical construct that represents a basic syntactical structure within the mind from which a series of sentences such as *The girl throws the ball, The ball is thrown by the girl, Is the ball thrown by the girl?* and so forth are generated into their surface form.

Supporting the distinction between deep structure and surface structure are cases of ambiguous sentences. *The shooting of the hunters was terrible* can mean either that *The hunters were poor marksmen* or *The hunters were targets.* Chomsky concludes that the ambiguity occurs when the same surface structure emerges from different deep structures. Such differences cannot be understood, Chomsky argues, if language is analyzed simply in terms of an associative chaining mechanism.

This brief description of a complicated linguistic theory stresses several of Chomsky's important attitudes and ideas that encouraged the development of cognitive psychology. First, Chomsky's concerns shifted attention away from the functional properties of verbal behavior to the organization of language, which is responsible for its endless novelty and diversity: "The central fact to which any significant theory must address itself is this: a mature speaker can produce a new sentence of his language on the appropriate occasion, and other speakers can understand it immediately, though it is equally new to them" (Chomsky, 1964). Second, Chomsky insisted that a theoretical effort was necessary to explain language, one in which postulating mental structures (e.g., deep structure) and cognitive processes (e.g., transformation of deep structure into surface structure) were demanded. Third, by emphasizing genetic factors, Chomsky alerted psychologists to theoretical distortions resulting from ignoring genetic preprogramming. Fourth, Chomsky's theory conceptualized human language behavior as species-specific, thus encouraging the view that the higher mental processes could only be understood by studying humans. By accepting this position, Chomsky was essentially bucking the Darwinian trend in American psychology which assumed that all forms of human behavior were continuous with the behavior of lower animals.

Computer Science. Computer science is a loosely organized collection of related disciplines that have emerged from the development of computers. Computers, with which most students are now familiar, are electronic machines capable of accepting, processing, and communicating information. These activities correspond to the three functional units of the typical computer: *input, information processing,* and *output* (Figure 11.2). The input unit of the computer receives the information, which is then encoded and transferred in its coded state into the information-processing unit, where the information is stored in a simple magnetic code on a disk, tape, or drum. The arithmetic-logic component performs arithmetical and logical operations on the information that is stored in memory. The control component interprets and executes the commands of the *program,* a set of instructions that is stored in memory. The computer will do exactly what it is instructed to do—nothing more, nothing less. To illustrate: at one college campus, a computer was programmed to select partners for blind dates on the basis of students' interests, attitudes, likes, and dislikes. The results were rather successful except for a brother and sister who were paired together. No one had bothered to program the instruction that siblings should not be paired.

The output unit communicates the processed information to the user of the computer in a particular form desired (e.g., printer, cathode ray oscilloscope, etc.). Computers, as you know, can be programmed to furnish immediate information about available seatings for all flights of an airline or to steer a spacecraft to a rendezvous in space. The ability of computers to *behave* intelligently has been referred to as *artificial intelligence,* a term that can be most clearly defined as "the art of creating machines that perform tasks considered to require intelligence when performed by humans" (attributed to Minsky by Kurzweil, 1985). It is important to recognize that this definition of artificial intelligence is neutral as to whether or not a particular example of artificial intelligence simulates human cognition.

While the computer, with its capacity for artificial intelligence, was revolutionizing society, two computer scientists, Alan Newell (born 1927) and Herbert Simon (born 1916), who was awarded a Nobel Prize in economics in 1978, offered an idea that revolutionized psychology, namely, that *computers can be programmed to simulate human thinking.* The justification for this strategy is that the human mind, according to Newell and Simon, can be conceptualized as a symbol manipulating system, and *so can the computer.* Both the mind and the computer are instances of the same kind of system; they both process information. This assumption led

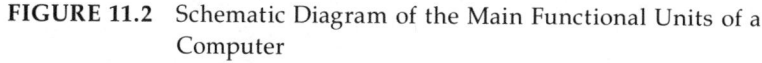

FIGURE 11.2 Schematic Diagram of the Main Functional Units of a Computer

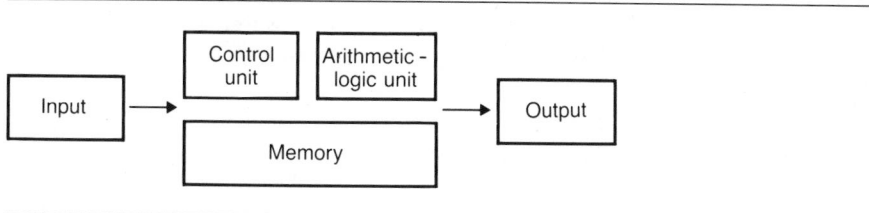

to an important research program that was designed to unravel the mysteries of the mind—the principles of human cognition—with the assistance of the digital computer.

THE EMERGENCE OF COGNITIVE PSYCHOLOGY

The historical roots of cognitive psychology all, in some way or another, are related to how the mind is functionally organized and operates. These general ideas were perceived by a large segment of the psychological community in the 1960s as being in direct opposition to the views of radical behaviorism, which had become the preeminent stimulus-response psychology. In fact, radical behaviorism's status had become so dominant that it was frequently, and erroneously, taken to be equivalent to all of behaviorism. The result of this historical error was to ignore evolutionary changes that were occurring in stimulus-response psychology from its early beginnings.

Robert S. Woodworth (1869–1962), who helped establish the Functionalist school at Columbia University, noted that:

> The objections raised to S-R formula [to describe behavior] means that it is too limited. It seems to imply that nothing important occurs between the stimulus and motor response. Or it seems to imply that the sensory stimulus is the only causative factor in the arousal of a response. These limitations can be avoided by the addition of another symbol to stand for the organism (the S-O-R formula). The O inserted between S and R makes explicit the obvious role of the living and active organism in the process; O receives the stimulus and makes the response. This formula suggests that psychologists should not limit their investigations to the input of stimuli and output of motor responses. They should ask how the input of stimuli can possibly give rise to the output; they should observe intervening processes if possible or at least hypothesize them and devise experiments for testing the hypothesis (Woodworth, 1958, p. 31).

This general S-O-R orientation was adopted by many neofunctionalists to investigate a variety of problem-solving phenomena that was later to interest cognitive psychologists. The general approach to these research problems by neofunctionalists and cognitivists differed. Influenced by the antimentalism of behaviorism, neofunctionalists minimized, if not eliminated, any mentalistic processes in their interpretation of thinking while subsequent cognitive psychologists felt no such inhibitions.

Woodworth's S-O-R conception anticipated the efforts of S-R mediational psychologists, who sought to interpret cognitive phenomena by postulating intervening processes between stimulus input and the response output within the general orientation of Hull and Spence. Osgood (1957) offered an elaborate mediational analysis of perception and language while Kuenne (1946) and Kendler and Kendler (1962) emphasized the importance of representation in developmental changes that occur in the discriminative behavior of young children. Spence (1950) acknowledged that different mechanisms were required to explain the cognitive behavior of humans than were needed to interpret animal behavior. In analyzing human cognitive behavior, Spence proposed a flowchart that anticipated later information-processing conceptions, and that radically departed from his own analysis of the discrimination learning of the rat (Spence, 1936). In his flow diagram, he employed concepts (e.g., sense reception, signification, verbal meaning) that referred to the innate organization of the brain, cognitive expectations, and linguistic meaning. These higher level processes "badly need the attention of all psychologists, cognition, S-R, or whatever else" (Spence, 1950).

Thus, the stimulus-response psychology of Hull and his disciples, which had its roots in the theoretical analysis of animal learning, was gradually expanding to the cognitive process of humans. Why did psychology have to experience a *cognitive revolution* instead of gradual evolutionary development of stimulus-response learning theories to encompass human cognition?

Four interrelated historical forces operated to encourage a cognitive revolution instead of a gradual evolutionary extension of stimulus-response psychology. First, because Hull's general theory fell far short of its stated objectives, little interest was expressed in employing the Hullian framework as a launching pad for the investigation of human cognition. Second, a disenchantment was spreading with the general strategy of basing a theory of human cognition, even partly, on the analysis of animal behavior. Many psychologists perceived human cognition as unique in the animal kingdom and, therefore, any theory of animal behavior was considered irrelevant to the task of understanding cognitive psychology, a position that S-R mediational theorists strongly rejected. Third, and probably of paramount importance, was the emerging intuition that the mind could not be ignored when interpreting human cognition. Even though the idea that the direct examination of consciousness could yield valid theoretical principles was generally rejected, the conception of a psychology free of the mind, as Hull proposed, was considered inadequate to the task of interpreting human cognition. A satisfactory theory demanded a conception of the mind, which in turn required an appropriate descriptive language. The idea that a stimulus-response language, even when enlarged by mediational mechanisms, could describe cognition seemed unrealistic. Stimulus-response language, with its antimentalistic bias, seemed too sterile and restrictive to represent the full richness of human cognition. Cognitively oriented psychologists decided it would be more strategic to start with a new language than to continue with an impoverished stimulus-response idiom. Fourth, the need for a revolution in psychology was encouraged by Thomas Kuhn's *The Structure of Scientific Revolutions* (1962), a book that described the history of physics from the time of Copernicus. Kuhn's major thesis is that scientific progress is not based on the accumulation of individual discoveries and theoretical refinements, but instead results from a repetitive historical cycle that consists of two markedly different enterprises, *normal science* and *revolution*. Normal science refers to the accumulation of knowledge within a widely adopted global orientation known as a *paradigm*, a "strong network of commitments—conceptual, theoretical, instrumental, and methodological, and quasimetaphysical" (Kuhn, 1962), that shapes the kind of research that is conducted and the type of theoretical interpretation that is offered. During this period of normal science, facts are discovered that cannot be easily incorporated into the prevailing paradigm. This initiates the second stage of historical development, during which time a prevailing paradigm is overthrown by a new one. *The Structure of Scientific Revolutions* enjoyed instant popularity and its historical conception was perceived to be applicable to psychology. Many psychologists became convinced that a paradigmatic shift from stimulus-response behaviorism to cognitive psychology was demanded. Because Kuhn's historical analysis appeared so compelling, the cognitive revolution was encouraged.

METHODOLOGICAL ASSUMPTIONS

Merging so many different historical forces to create cognitive psychology created a melange of diverse methodological assumptions that failed to cohere into a single indentifiable paradigm in the Kuhnian sense.

Subject Matter

"The functional organization of the mind" and "how the mind works" can serve as simple descriptions of the subject matter of cognitive psychology. They convey the basic idea that cognitive psychologists are interested in the organization of mind and the functioning of each component.

Preconceptions about the Mind

For the most part, cognitive psychologists avoid getting ensnared in the complicated philosophical problems that surround the mind-body problem. They accepted their own phenomenological experience that cognition involves mental processes and acknowledged the task of objectifying intellectual functioning. Cognitive psychologists generally agree that the mind functions as a system, but the nature of that system is conceptualized in different ways. Ulric Neisser, a leading theorist who helped define cognitive psychology, wrote:

> we have no direct, immediate access to the world, nor to any of its properties. The ancient theory of *eidola* which supposed that faint copies of objects can enter the mind directly, must be rejected. Whatever we know about reality has been *mediated*, not only by the organs of sense, but by complex systems which interpret and reinterpret sensory information. The activity of the cognitive systems results in—and is integrated with—the activity of muscles and glands that we call "behavior" (Neisser, 1966, p. 3).

Mediation is the term used by stimulus-response psychologists who ventured into the research area of cognitive development. Neisser shares with their mediational conception the assumption that intervening activities between stimulus input and response output must be postulated to account for cognitive behavior. For Neisser the mediational events frankly referred to mental activities. But the Hullian neobehaviorists deliberately avoided such an equation.

Whereas Neisser's conception of the mind springs from a traditional orientation in experimental psychology that employs phenomenological analysis as a first step in a research program, the conception of the human cognitive system as being analogous to a computer program or to an electronic communication system or to the human brain raises the question of whether these different metaphors would encourage divergent approaches to cognitive psychology. Or will these metaphors serve as useful analogues that will gradually lose their distinctive qualities as empirical data shape the development of cognitive theories?

Methods of Investigation

The numerous traditions that coalesced to form cognitive psychology encouraged a diversity of empirical procedures.

Verbal Learning. From the time of functionalism through Watsonian behaviorism to the variety of neobehaviorisms, the research field of verbal learning, initiated by Ebbinghaus, continued to thrive. Ebbinghaus (1885/1964) invented rigorous experimental procedures to discover how *verbal associations* are learned and remembered. Ebbinghaus made two strategic decisions that had profound effects upon research and theory. The first was his recognition that learning and remembering is strongly influenced by meaningfulness. For example, the sequence of ten letters, *psychology*, is easier to remember than the same ten letters in a random order, *sgoyohlpyc*. In order to reduce the contaminating influence of meaningfulness, Ebbinghaus invented the *nonsense syllable*, a three letter syllable composed of two consonants separated by a vowel, such as *lef* or *bup*.

Ebbinghaus's second strategic decision was to devise an experimental task that could reflect the principles of memory. He chose serial learning, a series of nonsense syllables that he repeated aloud to the rhythm of a metronome until the entire list could be repeated in order without error. He assumed serial learning and memory were products of associations being formed between each syllable and the following one; the entire list being bound together by the "invisible threads" of associations. Ebbinghaus systematically studied the influence of a number of experimental variables such as the length of the list and the time between the last reading of the list and the time of its recall.

Functionalism adopted Ebbinghaus's associative interpretation of verbal learning and later Hull, struck by its similarity to classical conditioning, attempted to explain verbal learning in terms of principles of conditioning.

Studying verbal learning as an associative process generated a great deal of research, some of which undermined a simple associative interpretation. The importance of meaningfulness was gradually recognized as a dominant variable in verbal learning of nonsense syllables. Some nonsense syllables generated more word associations than others (e.g., *tex* triggered more associates than *vox*). When the number of word associates that were generated was used as an index of meaningfulness of a nonsense syllable, it was discovered that the more meaningful lists were the easier to learn. In addition, it gradually became apparent that verbal learning could be facilitated by the subject assigning meaning to successive items; *lov, jen* could be encoded into *lov*e, *jen*ny, thereby facilitating learning.

The study of meaningfulness in verbal learning became popular. In one study (Bousfield, 1953), college students studied a random list of sixty words consisting of four fifteen item conceptual groups: *animals, vegetables, men's names*, and *professions*. Immediately thereafter, the subjects were instructed to list as many of the sixty words as they could recall. They tended to recall the words in clusters from the same conceptual grouping (e.g., *lion, tiger, fox, pig, corn, pea, carrot, Dick, Jack, Paul*). This evidence led to the conclusion that some organizing tendency, termed *clustering*, integrated the information learned into the preexisting conceptual categories that determined the order in which the words would be recalled.

The verbal learning research area, which began with Ebbinghaus and persisted to modern times, gradually underwent an evolutionary development from a narrow concern with associative processes to a broad interest in cognitive process. As a consequence, many verbal learning psychologists shifted from a stimulus-response to a cognitive orientation.

Mental Chronometry. Experimental techniques are sometimes abandoned only to be rediscovered. Such is the case for *mental chronometry*, the method that was designed about 1865 by the Dutch physiologist, Donders, to measure the speed of mental operations. Mental chronometry, in the hands of Wundt, proved to be unproductive, primarily because of the ambiguities within his theory of reaction time. But with the development of cognitive psychology, mental chronometry became a fruitful experimental method.

Consider the simple task of judging whether two simultaneously presented letters have the same name, for example AA and Aa. Errors practically never occur when pairs of the same letters are interspersed with pairs of different letters (e.g., AB, Ab). The failure to commit errors does not mean that the same mental operations are involved in an *identity match* (e.g., AA) and a *name match* (e.g., aA). An identity match is about 100 milliseconds faster, thus suggesting an additional mental operation in a name match. The explanation offered (Posner & Keele, 1967) is that an identity match is based on the perception of the same visual pattern, whereas a name match, in addition to visual perception, requires verbal encoding of each letter. Because it takes approximately 100 milliseconds to transform the upper and lower case letters into a common verbal label, the reaction time for a name match is longer. This relatively simple demonstration illustrates how mental chronometry provides a means for analyzing a cognitive task into its component mental operations.

Psycholinguistics. Psycholinguistics, a subdiscipline of both linguistics and psychology, is concerned with the psychological mechanisms of language acquisition, comprehension, and performance. Wundt, who might be called the first cognitive psychologist, postulated cognitive structures that influenced sentence production, comprehension, and memory. Psycholinguistics was elevated to a lively and productive research area as a consequence of the debate between Skinner and Chomsky. Skinner insisted that verbal behavior is susceptible to experimental analysis, like any other kind of behavior. But Chomsky, who had little enthusiasm for experimental psychology, believed purely rational analysis of human language could reveal basic truths. As one example, he *reasoned* that children could not learn language as rapidly as they do if language learning operated on principles of conditioning. Chomsky concluded that the syntactical rules of language must be genetically preprogrammed.

In spite of the fact that Skinner was an experimentalist and Chomsky was not, it was Chomsky's ideas that generated a great deal of research in the new field of psycholinguistics. His ideas of innate linguistic rules and his emphasis on infinite variety of linguistic expressions dovetailed with cognitive psychology, and therefore, were rapidly absorbed into this new orientation.

Numerous research techniques were designed to test Chomsky's sweeping generalizations. Records of spontaneous speech of children were kept as they matured (e.g.., Nelson, 1973) with the expectation that lawful changes in syntax, semantics, and other linguistic attributes would occur during language acquisition. Studies of memory were designed to determine the features of sentences, for example, syntactic or semantic, that were best remembered. Mental chronometry techniques were employed to discover how different grammatical forms of sentences (e.g., declarative, passive, questions) were processed during comprehension. Studies were initiated to test Chomsky's claim that only humans could learn a human language. This hypothesis challenged several investigators to try to teach primates, such as chimpanzees, to communicate in a human language. Research efforts in the new field of psycholinguistics literally exploded in number and variety as a function of Chomsky's views.

Computer Simulation of Cognitive Processes. The most revolutionary notion in cognitive psychology is that computers can simulate human thought. There are two aspects to artificial intelligence: The construction of programs that enable computers to behave intelligently and the formulation of programs that simulate human intelligence. To illustrate this distinction, consider computers that play chess. Many different computer programs can beat most good players, with the exception of those who have achieved master and grand master status. Some of these programs are designed to exploit the tremendous memories of computers, which greatly exceed those of humans. Such computer programs behave intelligently, but do not simulate human intelligence. Other programs are designed to imitate the cognitive processes that govern the expert human chess player. Although the artificial intelligence of computers that is not human in quality is of great importance in a technological society, the key question in psychology is whether computers can actually simulate human thought. To answer such a question requires a criterion of human thought and a determination of whether the standard is being met.

In 1950, a young, brilliant British mathematician, A. R. Turing (1912–1954), who influenced early computer theorists, suggested an apparently simple test to determine whether a computer is simulating human action. Imagine a human communicating with both another person and a computer, but the first person does not know which of the two communicants is the computer and which is the human. Let us also suppose that some game (e.g., checkers, twenty questions) is being played between the first person and his two opponents. If the first person is unable to distinguish between the performance of his two opponents, Turing suggests that the computer possesses human intelligence for that particular problem. Thus, the Turing test has encouraged a special kind of research in cognitive psychology; the information necessary to solve a common problem is entered into a computer and a human, and the psychologist determines whether the outputs are the same. If so, human cognition has been simulated for that *specific* task by a computer.

A Summary Statement. The diversity of methods of investigation in cognitive psychology raises the crucial question as to whether cognitive psychologists do, in fact, share a basic research methodology. In answering this question, the following comment of a cognitive psychologist is illuminating, but controversial:

> We [cognitive psychologists] have not returned to the methodological confused position of the late nineteenth century, which cavalierly confused introspection with theoretical processes and theoretical processes with conscious experience. Rather, many of us have become methodological behaviorists in order to become good cognitive psychologists (Mandler, 1979, p. 281).

Mandler's view is analogous to Tolman's, that self-observation cannot yield a satisfactory psychological theory. Theoretical processes, in the form of a model of the mind, can be formulated from a variety of sources—self-observations, behavioral evidence, intuition, physiological speculation, flowcharts, a computer analogy—but the ultimate test of a cognitive theory is whether its theoretical deductions coincide with behavioral evidence. While adopting the position of methodological behaviorism, Mandler is careful to offer a qualification; only "many of us" cognitive psychologists have adopted the position.

Mandler's qualification stems from two considerations. First, some of the historical foundations of cognitive psychology, as well as practicing cognitivists, are at odds with methodological behaviorism. For example, Piaget and Chomsky formulated theories that were not clearly articulated or strongly committed to a rigorous empirical analysis. In addition, Simon and Newell, in their research on artificial intelligence, have their subjects think aloud when solving cognitive tasks. They attempt to match the outputs of computer programs with self-reports of subjects engaged in thinking. Many methodological behaviorists would argue that such a procedure suffers from two fatal flaws. First, it fails to interpret thinking within an objective framework. Second, self-observation of thinking, as Wundt argued, distorts the thinking process and therefore serves as an inadequate basis for a theory of thinking. In rebuttal, Simon argues (Ericsson & Simon, 1984) that verbal reports, when properly analyzed, can meet the standards of a natural science psychology, a goal he is trying to reach.

The second reason some cognitivists have rejected methodological behaviorism stems from their conviction that cognitive psychology represents a complete revolutionary break with behaviorism. This view of history assumes that behaviorism and cognitive psychology are global paradigms that cannot be analyzed into component parts, a position that Mandler obviously rejects. The important point is that cognitive psychology, for the most part, is committed to the canons of natural science in its effort to formulate a theory of the mind.

Criterion of Truth

Unanimous agreement about any basic methodological issue is rare among cognitive psychologists. For the majority of cognitivists, who adopt a natural science framework to guide their empirical and theoretical efforts, deductive explanation serves as the litmus test for understanding psychological events. At the same time, one must recognize that mentalistic interpretations of psychological phenomena can create an intuitive sense of understanding that may far exceed the logical rigor of the deductive explanation that is offered. One should recall that Hull warned psychologists that mentalistic interpretations "born of years of self-observation . . . [begin] to function in place of the objectively stated general rules or principles which are the proper substance of science." To guard against accepting mentalistic pseudoexplanations Hull advised that an organism, human or subhuman, should be viewed "as a completely self-maintaining robot, constructed of materials as unlike ourselves as may be." Although, in principle, there is no reason that a theory formulated with mentalistic concepts cannot be organized in a rigorous logical manner, it is nevertheless important when evaluating a cognitive interpretation to distinguish between the intuitive understanding it offers and the deductive explanation it provides.

STRATEGY

The strategy adopted by cognitive psychology was strongly influenced by dissatisfaction with dominant strategic decisions of the past. Since cognitive psychology was a revolution against stimulus-response psychology, it is not surprising that the cognitive psychologists rejected many of the strategic decisions of neobehaviorism.

Leading neobehaviorists like Hull and Skinner aspired to formulate conceptions that could be generalized to all forms of behavior. In contrast, cognitive psychologists were more modest. They conceptualized the mind as a complicated system of interacting subprocesses (e.g., perception, memory, decision making). To attempt to formulate a broad general theory of cognitive psychology first would be both unrealistic and self-defeating. A more strategic plan would be to theoretically analyze individual subsystems involved in human cognition. When some understanding is reached about the various subsystems, the larger problem of formulating a general theory could be confronted. Implicit in the cognitive psychologists' rejection of the strategy of formulating a general theory of cognition was the belief that psychological theory could not be reduced to a small set of theoretical or descriptive principles as Hull and Skinner suggested. The expectation was that many different principles were required and that they all could not be excavated from a single research area, such as conditioning.

Although insisting that a variety of cognitive problems had to be investigated, many cognitive researchers opted to study memory. For them the study of memory appeared to be a convenient and effective starting point for cognitive research. The verbal learning tradition, which had been initiated by Ebbinghaus, had developed convenient research techniques that could be adapted to the study of cognitive processes. In addition, the study of memory could reveal important clues about how information is processed and transformed during storage.

One neobehavioristic strategy that cognitive psychology rejected was that animal research could serve as a source of theoretical principles. During the early days of cognitive psychology, the argument was advanced that only knowledge of human intellectual functioning could provide the evidence required to understand human cognition. Thriving animal laboratories at some universities were abandoned because interest in human cognition was considered to be isolated from animal behavior.

Cognitive psychology, for the most part, like its predecessor, neobehaviorism, emphasizes the importance of operationally clear descriptions of experimental procedures, the commitment to empiricism as the method to demonstrate the validity of theoretical hypotheses, and the view that psychology is a natural science.

COGNITIVE PSYCHOLOGY

Rumblings within cognitive psychology are currently being heard that question the strategy of ignoring general theorizing. Cognitive psychology has exploded into a large constellation of individual theories that appear unrelated to each other except for a common terminology. There is a yearning for some core conception that could help integrate cognitive psychology. Because of the absence of any systematic organization of theories within cognitive psychology, the field will be examined by describing historically significant experiments first, followed by a general discussion of cognitive psychology.

Mental Images

To illustrate the mentalistic character of cognitive psychology, a classic experiment will be briefly described. Lynn Cooper and Roger Shepard's (1973) comparison of visual perception and visual imagery demonstrates the sharp break between research problems tackled by cognitivists and stimulus-response psychologists. Subjects were shown a letter, either in a normal or in a mirror reverse orientation (R or Я). The subject's task was to press one button if the letter was normally oriented, another button if it was a mirror image. The reaction times changed in a regular fashion as a function of the angle of the tilt away from the upright. As the degree of orientation changed from 0 to 180 degrees, the reaction times increased from approximately 570 milliseconds to almost twice that amount (Figure 11.3). From 180 degrees to 360 degrees, the reaction times decreased by the same magnitude. The conclusion was that the subjects mentally rotated the letter through an internal visual space just as they would physically rotate cards with letters at various degrees of orienta-

FIGURE 11.3 The Experimental Results of a Study Designed to Compare Visual Perception with Visual Imagery

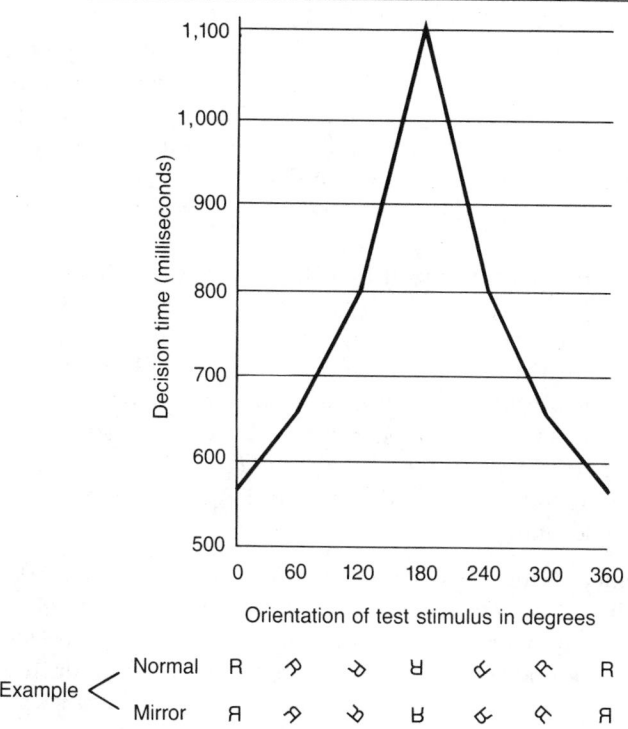

The graph indicates the time the subject needed to decide whether a letter had normal or reversed orientation as a funciton of the degree of rotation. (Adapted from Cooper & Shepard, 1973.)

tion to decide whether the letter was normally oriented or was a mirror image. The same principle governs rotation of letters in consciousness as in the real world. An important methodological point to remember is that this investigation of mental rotation was correlated with objective indexes of angles of rotation and reaction times, and it was not solely tied to introspective reports.

Memory

Memory is commonly thought to be a single unified faculty; experimental evidence suggests otherwise.

Sensory Register. We all have experienced looking at a light bulb and continuing to see its image after we turn away. This is technically called a visual *icon*. Similarly, we can also hear a sound, an *echoic* image, for a brief time after the sound source has stopped. In the language of cognitive psychology, the *sensory register* is a memory structure that stores incoming stimulation for a brief time in its original, *unprocessed* form.

In a classic experiment, George Sperling (1960) used a technique originally employed by Wundt (Blumenthal, 1977). He presented his subjects with a three by three matrix of nine letters for 50 milliseconds. When asked to recall the letters they had seen immediately after the display was terminated, the subjects, on average, reported about one half of the letters. Thus, for this exposure period, it would seem that humans are capable of storing only four or five letters in the the sensory register. Not so, said Sperling! He hypothesized that a visual icon of the *entire* display appeared in consciousness, but faded rapidly. By the time the subject reported about four or five letters, the icon had disappeared and hence no more letters could be retrieved. To prove his hypothesis, Sperling used a partial report technique. Immediately after the matrix disappeared, a distinctive tone was sounded that indicated which of the three lines of the matrix the subject should recall. When this test was employed, the subjects reported practically 100 percent of the letters, regardless of the line they were cued to report, thus supporting Sperling's contention that a visual sensory register operates to record a visual image of a display but only for a fraction of a second.

Short-Term Memory Store. The short-term memory store, or working memory, which has a limited capacity encompassed by the magical number of seven plus or minus two, holds information for immediate use. In the case of a phone number provided by the information operator, the number is transferred from the sensory store to short-term memory by rapidly rehearsing the number. If successful, the correct number will be dialed. The number, however, will soon be forgotten. The memory of the number will decay, or its recall will be interfered with by a similar number, or new information will force the phone number out of short-term memory. If, however, the decision is made that the phone number is worth remembering for further use—it is a phone number of an attractive, fascinating person, for instance,—then the number has to be rehearsed and/or chunked into a simpler form so that it can be transferred to the long-term memory store.

Long-Term Memory Store. The phone number could be rehearsed so thoroughly that it would be easily recalled like the alphabet. Or the number could be recoded to reduce the amount of information. Instead of 918-1066, it could be encoded to give it meaning; 9/18 is my sister's birthday and 1066 is the year of the Battle of Hastings. The new number is essentially transformed into old information that is already stored in long-term memory.

The capacity of the long-term memory store is large; the average college student's reading vocabulary is about 50,000 words and that probably represents only a small part of the entire long-term memory. The major problem in recalling information from the long-term memory store is to have an accessible retrieval cue.

A simple experiment demonstrates the power of retrieval cues (Tulving & Pearlstone, 1966). Students were instructed to recall a list of forty-eight words consisting of four words from each of twelve categories (e.g., *insect-ant, wasp, beetle, mosquito*). At the time of recall, the cued subjects were given a recall sheet containing the twelve category names and instructed to write down as many of the original words as possible. They were able to recall thirty words as compared to only twenty words by noncued subjects. Success in recalling the name of a new acquaintance depends on the availability of a cue that triggers the name. Success can be enhanced by associating the name of the person just met with an old friend with the same name.

Models of Memory. Only the barest skeleton of a duplex theory of memory (e.g., Atkinson & Shiffrin, 1977) has been described. In addition to data that suggest markedly different storage capacities for short- and long-term memory, the two stores differ in terms of the dominant mode of encoding and also in the ease of retrieval. Verbal material in short-term memory is encoded acoustically while information in long-term memory is primarily stored in terms of meaning. Acoustical encoding means that information is stored in terms of its sound. An example of the evidence that supports this conclusion is that the memory of the letter v, when visually presented, is more likely to be confused with b in recall because they sound alike, than with x, which it looks like (Conrad, 1964). Retrieval of information in short-term memory is relatively simple because of the small amount involved. In contrast, retrieval of information from long-term memory can be difficult because of the enormous amount of knowledge that has to be searched.

The duplex theory of memory has many forms; it is really a family of theories that share the assumption of a dual storage system but differ in regards to the structural and functional features of each store. Presumably, as more evidence is collected, one of the several competing forms or a new one, will gain ascendancy.

Such optimism can be challenged for two major reasons. The brief history of cognitive psychology has demonstrated that whenever a complicated problem such as memory has been analyzed in a rigorous manner, the problem has inevitably become more complicated. The question has been raised as to whether the duplex assumption might not itself be misleading. A *level-of-processing* approach (Craik & Lockhart, 1972) proposes that data interpreted in terms of the duplex theory can be easily handled by a theory that assumes that learning and remembering information requires a series of stages that differ along a dimension of depth of information processing. Initially, information entering memory is processed in terms of perceptual properties (e.g., acoustical characteristics). Later, the information is processed in terms of meaning and its relationship to other items in memory (e.g., the new acquaintance has the same name as an old friend). The depth of processing continues so that a particular item in memory is finally integrated within a highly organized body of knowledge (e.g., a new finding in psychology is integrated within a broad theory). Proponents of the level-of-processing approach argue that their interpretation handles the facts of rehearsal better than the duplex formulation. The duplex formulation assumes that simple rote rehearsal can transfer information from short-term memory to long-term memory, while the level-of-processing formulation assumes that the kind of processing (e.g., meaningful organization) that is associated with rehearsal is the key factor in successful remembering.

To make the problem of memory more complicated, Endel Tulving (1985), a leading memory theorist, offers a new look at "the marvelous capacity that we call by the single name of memory." According to Tulving, memory is divided into three major interrelated systems:

> Procedural memory enables organisms to retain learned connections between stimuli and responses, including those involving complex stimulus patterns and response chains, and to respond adaptively to the environment. Semantic memory is characterized by the additional capability of internally representing states of the world that are not perceptually present. It permits the organism to construct mental models of the world . . . that can be manipulated and operated on covertly, independently of any overt behavior. Episodic memory affords the additional capability of acquisition and retention of knowledge about personally experienced events and their temporal relations in subjective time and the ability to mentally "travel back" in time (Tulving, 1985, pp. 386–387).

In addition to proposing these three memory systems Tulving also postulates three interesting relationships: (1) The three systems are organized in a hierarchy with procedural memory at the base, operating independently of the other two, while semantic memory is to some extent dependent on procedural memory, and episodic memory is partially dependent on both lower systems; (2) Each system is associated with different phenomenological experiences, procedural memory with lack of awareness, semantic memory with awareness, episodic memory with awareness of oneself; and (3) The three memory systems are assumed to be correlated with different neurophysiological systems that differ in their evolutionary significance.

Tulving's conception is not the final answer; far from it! He justifies his efforts by addressing significant problems that he believes had been ignored in earlier cognitive theories of memory. It is important to note that Tulving's formulation is a more general theory of memory than prior conceptions because of its effort to encompass a wider range of empirical evidence and that it is at odds with the earlier strategy of ignoring neurophysiological processes.

Artificial Intelligence

Many modern cognitive psychologists have adopted the strategy that the most productive approach to understanding human cognition is by simulating human thought with the aid of the computer. To comprehend this approach, it will be useful to examine the early work of Newell and Simon who were most responsible for launching the idea that computer programs can simulate human cognitive processes. To prove their point, Newell and Simon (1961) constructed a computer program that generated proofs for theorems in symbolic logic similar to proofs of humans who were instructed to think aloud as they solved the very same problems. The essential assumption adopted by Newell and Simon is that matching the output of the computer program with the output of the human implies that they are both governed by the same program:

> Behavior is to be explained by specifying programs that will, in fact, produce the behavior. These programs consist of elementary information processes (Newell & Simon, 1961, p. 156).

Many programs were designed that matched human performance in a variety of tasks such as concept formation (Gregg & Simon, 1967) and verbal learning (Feigenbaum, 1970). This form of simulating human cognition was criticized as being too specific; the successful simulation represents nothing more than a set of clever programming tricks for each task. Humans do not, the argument went, solve specific problems with specific programs, but instead solve a wide variety of problems with a common set of problem solving strategies. In order to meet the objection of extreme specificity, a program known as the General Problem Solver (Simon & Newell, 1964, 1971) was designed to cope with three kinds of problems: chess playing, logical proofs, and cryptogram puzzles.

The General Problem Solver contains programmed instructions that were assumed to be equivalent to common problem-solving processes that guide human thought. The program is written not to take advantage of the capacities of the computer, but instead to simulate human cognitive processes. For example, the program is written to match the limited capacity of human memory rather than the gigantic storage capacity of computers. In addition, Newell and Simon are careful to point out:

> The adjective "general" does not imply that GPS can reason about all or most kinds of problems; or that it will simulate all or most human problem-solving activity. It simply means that the program contains no reference to the task content, and hence is usable for tasks other than the one for which it was devised (Newell & Simon, 1961, p. 166).

The General Problem Solver operates serially, coping with one major problem-solving process at a time. The most skilled chess player, the grand master, does not plan his game from beginning to end, so that a checkmate can be directly achieved. That would be impossible because of the incredible number of alternatives confronting the chess player; the number of possible alternatives of moves and counter moves in a sequence of only *eight moves* is about a million billion billion! Thus, the chess player decides on a subgoal to attain, such as the control of the four center squares or the immobilization of the opponent's queen or the safety of his own king. Because the possibilities from the beginning to the end of the game are much too large to contemplate, it becomes necessary to reformulate the problem of winning the game as a sequence of limited objectives (subgoals) which are successively achieved. A chess playing program consists of a series of algorithms, pragmatic subroutines designed to achieve desired subgoals.

Once the various subgoals are evaluated and a specific choice is made, then the means-end analysis begins to operate. This process operates to specify the difference between the existing situation (e.g., position at the end of the sixth move) and the desired situation (e.g., control of the four center squares) so that the relevant rule can be employed to reach the subgoal. The solution is not guaranteed; it may be impossible to get control of the center of the board from a particular position. If that be the case, a new subgoal is selected, and a means-end analysis of reaching that subgoal is begun.

The operation of the General Problem Solver can be represented as a decision tree. A decision tree indicates a set of alternative moves and the consequences of each. In chess, for example, a tree of possibilities would include several alternative moves that will lead to the subgoal and an analysis of possible opponent reactions and counter reactions. It is rare for a skilled player to anticipate more than seven moves ahead (de Groot, 1965). The computer, in essence, scans these decision trees and selects one alternative most consistent with the principles that have been programmed into it.

The description of the General Problem Solver illustrates several ideas that computer simulation of cognitive processes contributed to cognitive psychology. First, it conceives a human to be a symbol-manipulating system that can be represented by a computer program. Computer simulation of psychological processes does not assume that humans are computers, or that the human brain is analogous to a computer, but instead that a computer can be programmed to function like humans. Whether the program operates like a human mind is determined by the match between the outputs of the two systems; computer and human. Second, complex problem-solving tasks are broken down into a sequence of subproblems, each involving its own attempted solutions. This subsystem analysis encouraged the use of flowcharts to represent the mental structures and psychological processes involved in cognition. Third, computer simulation of human cognition, for the most part, was concerned with interpreting real life problems in preference to artificially constructed tasks. By so doing, researchers in artificial intelligence implicitly raised the issue as to whether psychological research should not be more concerned with practical problems in preference to artificial laboratory tasks which may prove to be irrelevant to everyday life.

In spite of the fact that computer programs have repeatedly demonstrated their intelligence, nagging doubts persist about whether their intelligence is similar to human intelligence. In some cases, the computer program clearly surpasses the ability of humans to solve complex mathematical problems. In other cases, human intelligence is superior; no computer can compete successfully against the grand master chess player. The basic issue is whether certain computer programs, as Simon and Newell have suggested, actually simulate human thought.

Three important criticisms have been directed against the claims made by Simon and Newell. First, the General Problem Solver does not exactly match human performance. For example, in the proof of theorems in symbolic logic (Newell & Simon, 1961) there is a discrepancy between the language of the subject, (e.g., "I'm looking at the idea of reversing these two things now") and the logical communication of the computer (e.g., Goal 6: Apply R_3). In addition, the computer sometimes provides more information than the human subject and at other times less. Second, the use of phenomenological reports of thinking as the dependent variable is suspect; the history of psychology (e.g., the imageless thought controversy) has demonstrated the pitfalls of the direct examination of consciousness as a source of reliable knowledge. The third reservation is that it is difficult if not impossible to equate a computer program, such as the General Problem Solver, with a clearly stated psychological theory. Joseph Weizenbaum (1976), a computer expert, argues that the General Problem Solver is not really a general theory but instead "is nothing more than a programming language in which it is possible to write programs for certain highly specialized tasks." Moreover, it is practically impossible to separate the theory from the mass of details in the program required to make it run (E. E. Smith, 1978).

The criticisms are not insurmountable; rather they are difficulties that have to be overcome. To some extent, computer simulation of human cognition has been harmed by the overoptimistic claims of impending success. Simon and Newell stated in 1958 that in ten years a digital computer would be the world's chess champion. Seven years later, Simon (1965) claimed that "machines will be capable within 20 years, of doing any work that a man can do." At this writing, a human is the world's chess champion and computers are incapable of translating a Russian book into English, or vice versa.

Raymond Kurzweil (1985), an inventive computer scientist, disagrees markedly with Simon and Newell. Several decades after Simon's optimistic predictions, Kurzweil answers the question of whether artificial intelligence simulates human thought with a simple "No!" Nevertheless, he remains optimistic about future successes if computer scientists adopt a less ambitious and more critical strategy than Simon:

> The fact that an algorithm works in a machine does not prove that the same technique is used in the brain, but it does prove that this is one way that the brain could work, and provides a potential theory that could be subjected to neurophysiological testing (Kurzweil, 1985, p. 263).

Note that Kurzweil suggests a neurophysiological road to follow to explain human cognition, not a path that depends initially on the phenomenological analysis of thinking.

Kurzweil believes it is important to recognize the nature of artificial intelligence at this point of time, when "we are gaining the ability to apply . . . narrowly focussed intelligence, to a wide range of problems." In the near future, artificial intelligence will function like an unimaginative expert—an idiot savant—for specific tasks (e.g., to diagnose a specific class of disease). Kurzweil (1985) claims that "Our goal . . . should not be to copy human intelligence in the next generation of computers, but rather to concentrate on the unique strengths of machine intelligence, which for the foreseeable future will be quite different from the strengths of human intelligence."

The ultimate approach to simulation of human thought, many believe, will have to await the development of a new generation of computers. Current computers process information in a serial order so that at any time only one bit of information is being processed. In parallel processing, two or more independent sequences of information can be simultaneously processed. Kurzweil believes that:

> parallel architectures [of computers] are the wave of the future, particularly, for the more complex systems which we tend to consider as artificial intelligence. The brain, as we know, more than makes up for the inherently slower speed of nerve cells as compared to silicone with almost total parallelism, and no doubt with its superior algorithms (Kurzweil, 1985, p. 262).

It is important to note that neither Simon nor Kurzweil is adopting a strategy that many cognitive psychologists would pursue when accepting the challenge of simulating human intelligence with computers. Their strategy would be to simulate experimental results in which objective behavior would be the output, an approach different from simulation of thinking aloud or modeling brain function. Thus, it would seem that computer simulation of human intelligence has three main strategies to pursue in selecting the dependent variable to model, phenomenological reports of thinking, brain functioning, and intelligent behavior. Although computer scientists disagree about the best strategy to pursue, there are obvious advantages in exercising all three options.

Psycholinguistics

Chomsky's psycholinguistic theory is a historic relic. It stimulated the development of cognitive psychology but failed to survive the onslaught of data and critical examination.

The strong empirical tradition in psychology demanded that Chomsky's (1968) pronouncement that only humans have an innate capacity for language should be challenged. Several psychologists decided to investigate the linguistic potential of anthropoid apes—chimpanzees, gorillas, orangutans—to test Chomsky's claim that language is species-specific to humans. These various projects produced fascinating information about the abilities of these apes, but also the embarrassing revelation that the criteria as to what constitutes a human language was unclear. Unless that is known, psychologists could not decide whether apes can learn a human language.

No one expected, or at least no one was willing to admit, that apes could achieve a level of performance comparable to that of adult humans but the idea was entertained that anthropoid apes might match the ability of young children. When comparison of two-word sentences of apes and children were made (Brown, 1973; Gardner & Gardner, 1971), similarities and differences were discovered. The lack of perfect match convinced some that Chomsky was correct in claiming that human language is species-specific. Others viewed the similarities as evidence of a continuity between linguistic capacities of apes and humans, thus undermining Chomsky's claim about the uniqueness of human language.

The controversy about the linguistic capacity of anthropoid apes was never clearly resolved because of the inability to specify the syntactical structure of a child's language. Psycholinguists, many of whom consider the linguistic abilities of anthropoid apes to be a side issue, recognized that their major task was to discover the principles that govern language development. Once these principles were revealed, they could then evaluate Chomsky's hypothesis that the acquisition of syntax was primarily a consequence of maturation. That is, acquiring a grammar is analogous to learning to walk; both are a product, not of training, but of physiological development governed by genetic preprogramming.

Summarizing the results of a wide variety of studies designed to abstract principles of language development suggest that the development of syntax is far more complicated than Chomsky's innate hypothesis would expect; grammatical principles do not simply appear in an orderly sequence as children mature. In contrast, the evidence suggests an absence of any general principles that govern the development of childhood grammar (Schlesinger, 1984). The more that is learned about language acquisition, the greater are the individual differences that appear both in regard to the rate of development and the sequence of the syntactical structure of sentences. This is not surprising considering that children grow up in diverse language environments, especially in regard to the amount of linguistic stimulation. In coping with these various environments, children are essentially confronted with the problem of comprehending the linguistic statements they hear. Children appear to employ different strategies in their attempted solutions to the problem of understanding language, resulting in a variety of patterns of syntactical development. The conclusion from these developmental studies is that the acquisition of syntax is markedly influenced by nonsyntactical processes.

Experimental evidence (Lachman, Lachman, & Butterfield, 1979) arrived at the same conclusion; the more research psycholinguists did, the more it became apparent that syntactic factors were interacting with other processes such as context of the sentence and semantic memory:

It is fair to say that the honeymoon of psychology and linguistics ended sometime after 1970 . . . One reason is the disappointing outcome of the psychological experimentation that stemmed from Chomsky's 1965 theory . . . As the Chomskian revolution receded, the pervasive influence of semantic and pragmatic factors grew increasingly evident. . . . Many psycholinguists concluded that a satisfactory model of how people use their syntactic knowledge will not be forthcoming until we have a theory of how context influences language use (Lachman, Lachman, & Butterfield, 1979, p. 404).

In fact, the more one studied syntax, the more it seemed to become intertwined with all of cognitive psychology.

Quotations of Cognitive Psychologists

1. The scientific study of cognitive psychology has moved dramatically forward under the pretheoretical commitments of the information-processing approach. Great progress is reflected in the way our discipline has refocused its research effort toward accounting for intelligent human behavior. This refocusing required a revolution: The significant issues simply could not be addressed adequately within the framework of neobehavioristic psychology (Lachman, Lachman, & Butterfield, 1979, p. 525).

2. We do not feel that we were behaviorists, at least not in the sense J. B. Watson defined the term, yet we were much more concerned . . . with what people did than with what they knew. Our emphasis was upon processes lying immediately behind action, but not with action itself. On the other hand, we did not consider ourselves introspective psychologists . . . yet we were willing to pay attention to what people told us about their ideas and plans. How does one characterize a position that seems to be a mixture of elements usually considered incompatible? Deep in the middle of this dilemma it suddenly occurred to us that we were subjective behaviorists (Miller, Galanter, & Pribram, 1960, p. 211).

3. A really satisfactory theory of the higher mental processes can only come into being when we also have theories of motivation, personality, and social interaction. The study of cognition is only one fraction of psychology, and it cannot stand alone (Neisser, 1966, p. 305).

4. The study and explanation of complex human behavior is to proceed as follows:

1. Behavior is to be explained by specifying programs that will, in fact, produce the behavior. These programs consist of systems of elementary information processes.

2. Elementary information processes are to be explained by showing how they can be reduced to known physiological processes in the central nervous system and its appendages (Newell and Simon, 1961, p. 156).

Cognitive Psychology: Description and Assessment

A review of three of its many research areas can hardly do justice to all of cognitive psychology. The review can, however, convey a flavor that offers insight into cognitive psychology as a paradigm. Because cognitive psychology has yet to achieve a high level of integration or run its historical course, it can best be considered as "a paradigm, an approach to constructing theories, a style of theorizing. It cannot be correct or incorrect, only more or less productive" (Hayes, 1978).

The core assumption in cognitive psychology that sets it apart from stimulus-response neobehaviorism, is that in order to relate environmental events (stimuli) to behavior (response) it becomes necessary to postulate an extensive number of *mental structures* and *processes.* This emphasis on postulating a model of the mind was deemed essential to understanding the so-called higher mental processes which stimulus-response psychologists had carefully labeled as *reasoning, problem solving* and *verbal behavior,* to avoid any taint of a subjective mentalism. No general agreement prevailed among cognitive psychologists about the strategy to follow in identifying the mental structures and processes required for constructing a cognitive theory. Common sense, naive phenomenology, computer analogy, and intuition, were all considered reasonable sources for theoretical ideas. Such tolerance was deemed justified because the ultimate rationale for a theoretical hypothesis, either in reference to a mental structure or process, was its contribution in explaining empirical evidence.

Three theoretical constructs played a central role in establishing cognitive psychology as an independent paradigm: *knowledge, representation,* and *processing.* Initially, their meanings were defined informally with the expectation that empirical research would make each more precise. *Knowledge* is information, what is known; *representation* is a coded form of knowledge, *processing* modifies the form of knowledge. These concepts could easily be applied to the entire spectrum of psychological activities from sensation and perception, to personality and social psychology, and even to psychotherapy. For example, the four dots of Figure 7.1 on page 184 can be conceptualized as incoming information that is processed as a configuration that represents the corners of a square. A student who learns he has failed a course processes the information as an illustration of the maxim, "There are no poor students, only poor teachers." The goals of cognitive therapy (e.g., Beck, 1976) are the examination of a faulty self-representation, and an increase in the patient's ability to realistically process knowledge about the world and oneself.

The maturing of cognitive psychology has been accompanied by an increasing proliferation of theoretical concepts. Enlarging the theoretical vocabulary has proved to be the paradigm's strength and its weakness. It has permitted a theoretical flexibility that enables the cognitive psychologists to interpret psychological phenomena with apparent ease, thus encouraging an enormous amount of research. Is that a virtue? The ability of a paradigm to be prolific is often perceived as a valuable asset. Others, including some cognitive psychologists, disagree; modern psychology is drowning in an overabundance of research evidence. Empirical data, taken alone, have no value. Unless they can be integrated into some general theory that covers a reasonable empirical range, the data have minimal significance at best. The fundamental question facing present-day cognitive theory is whether its data fit together in a significant theoretical way or are merely superficially integrated by a common technical vocabulary. Is there any chance, even in the distant future, of a general theory of cognition capable of explaining a truly broad spectrum of cognitive phenomena, or can we only hope for effective theories for fairly narrow topics?

Cognitive psychology has changed over the years. Reservations are now being expressed about the *black-box* strategy that governed the early days of cognitive psychology. Two of its leaders, Endel Tulving (1985) and Michael Posner (1984) are actively engaged in trying to formulate neurophysiological interpretations of cognitive phenomena. Tulving's ternary theory of memory suggested different neurophysiological systems for each of the postulated memory systems and speculated that each developed at different stages of biological evolution. Posner, who was instrumental in developing a Cognitive Neuropsychology Laboratory, insists that progress in cognitive psychology will be blocked if it remains isolated from neurophysiology:

> The separation between mind and brain has seemed a bar to progress in psychology. I believe a major accomplishment of the next generation of psychologists will be to create the conditions that will effectively by-pass this separation (Posner, 1984, p. 241).

Second, a realization has grown that developmental psychology must be brought into the center stage of cognitive psychology. The initial research interests of experimental cognitive psychologists were mainly concerned with the higher mental processes of adult humans, primarily college students. These processes, however, emerge, as Piaget sought to demonstrate, from cognitive processes at earlier stages of life; that is, adult cognition cannot be fully understood independently of its developmental history. One cognitivist (Schlesinger, 1984) offers the "rather unorthodox thesis that in the last analysis, every theory in Cognitive Psychology must be a developmental theory."

The same logic can also be employed to conclude that every theory in cognitive psychology must be a comparative theory because the cognitive abilities of humans are an outgrowth of evolutionary changes. We should remember that human cognition has not evolved to play chess but rather to help meet biological needs, including reproduction. Although cognitive psychologists, for the most part, initially adopted the working hypothesis that human cognition is discontinuous with animal behavior, that view is coming to be seen as shortsighted. For example, the adaptive processes of infants and children resemble in many ways the associative learning that is revealed in animal learning, particularly in conditioning. To fully understand linguistic and conceptual representations it becomes necessary to unravel the evolutionary links between human vision, which was inherited from the acute, three-dimensional color vision of primates, and human language which tends to be richly endowed with words that can be visualized (Lachman & Lachman, 1981). In sum, cognitive psychology, in order to achieve its goal of understanding adult human cognition, must expand its horizons to include both the study of developmental psychology of humans and comparative psychology of animals. Some cognitive psychologists, over the objection of others, are encouraging these new directions.

What changes in cognitive psychology can be expected in the future? One of the most puzzling and controversial problems is the relationship between the traditional link of cognitive psychology that employs experimental tests of theoretical hypotheses and the approach that attempts to simulate human cognition with computers. Do they represent two methodologically distinct cognitive psychologies or are their theoretical efforts commensurable in the sense that a computer simulation of human cognition can be translated into a conventional theory and evaluated by the methods of experimental psychology, and vice versa? The aforementioned difficulties of abstracting theories from complex programs suggest that, for the time being, the two approaches differ in a fundamental way. Luce (1985), one of the most sophisticated mathematical psychologists, observes that computer simulation is becoming a much more popular method of constructing cognitive theories than the conventional mode of developing a mathematical model based on experimental results. Luce suggests that the reason for the preference for computer simulations is that:

> complex options are easy to build in. Subjects seem to have available many alternative ways of behaving and it seems less stressful to most theorists to try to embody this in computer programs (Simon & Newell, 1974). I am yet to be convinced that this use of computer programs is really solving any problem. The difficulties we are having in cognitive psychology may

be conceptual or experimental or both. We may be asking the wrong questions, given our current understanding, and we may not be getting under experimental control enough of what goes on in the typical cognitive experiment . . . In any event, I think some cognitive psychologists may have thrown over mathematics for computer programs a bit too fast (Luce, 1985, pp. 670–671).

In spite of his expressed reservations about the strategy of employing computer simulation in preference to mathematical theorizing, Luce, a committed deductivist when it comes to scientific explanation, concludes, "Still, mathematics and computer simulation are really the only games in town if you want to understand and predict data." But by distinguishing between the two, Luce is implying a possible methodological difference.

The ultimate impact of computer technology on society and science is yet to be known. For the time being, the research programs of artificial intelligence and computer simulation of human cognition will continue to expand, as will traditional attempts at mathematical theorizing. Developments in these research programs should ultimately provide the necessary information about whether computer science represents a radically new path to scientific understanding.

Computer science does differ from the traditional theoretical approach in being more oriented toward practical concerns. For the most part, theoretical psychology in America, from the days of Titchener, has been an ivory tower psychology, the first goal of which is to formulate a theory based upon general principles that might later be applied to the solution of practical problems. Some computer scientists (e.g., Reitman, 1984) question this grand strategy of theory construction simply because it has not worked. The life spans of cognitive theories are extremely brief: "Today's theories are unlikely to go anywhere useful tomorrow." Consequently, Reitman argues, artificial intelligence procedures should be employed to solve practical problems and general theorizing postponed until later, a strategy that bears some resemblance to the one proposed by Kurzweil. Reitman expresses his idea in a blunt and pragmatic fashion:

> A strange new power is moving among us now. Conjoined with the scientist's urge to understand and explain, we now have found the most powerful and reliable motive in the world: the urge to make a buck. If you can figure how a doctor diagnoses diseases, or an attorney thinks about tax laws, with enough knowledge about artificial intelligence, you can try to convert the information into dollars, by building an "expert system" that supports the doctor or lawyer sufficiently well so that he will pay you for your efforts. The profit motive has made protocol analysis, artificial intelligence and programming (now known as "knowledge engineering"), the hottest profession in the market (Reitman, 1984, pp. 125–126).

In essence, Reitman argues, cognitive psychologists should develop the highest possible level of artificial intelligence to meet the needs of a complex technological society. Ignore the problem of simulating human thought. By so doing, the chances of future success will increase.

One major issue that has generated much debate is whether the emphasis on cognition in cognitive psychology does not represent a gigantic obstacle to the achievement of a truly comprehensive human psychology. By emphasizing rational cognitive processes, cognitive psychology has subordinated noncognitive processes, such as motivation and emotion, and has minimized, if not ignored, the problem of a theory of action. A theory of knowledge by itself is both interesting and important, but it will have little practical significance unless we know the principles that govern the conversion of ideas into action.

A Debate about Cognitive Psychology

Moderator: Both of the participants in this debate have to assume a special responsibility. The history of cognitive psychology is incomplete. You, therefore, must be modest in your historical extrapolation and tentative in your evaluation.

Pro: Your requests are appropriate and I will try to abide by them. Cognitive psychology solved the problem that was destabilizing psychology from the time of Wundt; the mind-body problem. Directly examining consciousness failed to yield reliable knowledge. Behaviorism offered only a pseudosolution in that it generated reliable knowledge only about mindless behavior. Cognitive psychology solved the mind-body problem by retaining the mind in psychology without abandoning objective methods of research. Cognitivists formulated a model of the mind that was evaluated by natural science modes of inquiry. Their success is demonstrated by a solid body of knowledge in research areas that previously were practically ignored or investigated by methods doomed to failure: psycholinguistics, thinking, memory, decision making, imagery, text comprehension, and other mental activities that characterized us as human. In addition to including psychological activities that behaviorists tried to excommunicate from psychology, cognitive psychology sensibly did not aspire to formulate a general theory that would integrate all of psychology but instead let different research areas develop at their own rate and left it to the future to decide when efforts for a general theory should be initiated. I feel compelled to add that attempts to formulate a general theory of cognition should be made, but we should be aware that success is not guaranteed. Physics is not a theoretically integrated science and there is no reason to believe that psychology will achieve that status. Cognitive psychology offers a realistic conception of psychological theorizing in place of the romantically unrealistic conceptions of neobehaviorists like Hull.

Con: Unfortunately, your rosy commentary is inaccurate on several counts. First, it ignores the fact that the resolution of the mind-body problem that most cognitive psychologists adopted was not original with cognitive psychology, but essentially was an adaptation of the strategy that Tolman devised and even Wundt practiced at times. Second, your claim that cognitive psychology returned to psychology problems that were excommunicated by neobehaviorism conveniently fails to mention that the enthusiasm for investigating the higher mental processes during the early days of cognitive psychology effectively excommunicated neuropsychology and animal psychology from cognitive psychology. Some contemporary cognitivists are now realizing that ignoring these two research areas, intimately related to Darwin's evolutionary theory, creates obstacles in the development of cognitive psychology. Third, cognitive psychology has exaggerated its claims of theoretical successes. Hull may have been right in suggesting that once mentalistic concepts are brought into a psychological theory, a false sense of understanding is generated. It is interesting to note that his proposal that a behaving organism should be conceptualized "as a completely self-maintaining robot, constructed of materials as unlike ourselves as may be" is consistent with the conception that underlies computer simulation of behavior. I am 99 percent sure that if Hull lived three or four decades later, he would have become a computer scientist but not a cognitive psychologist. Fourth, the attempt of some cognitive theorists to include areas of psychology that initially were rejected as a primary concern—motivation, neurophysiology, animal psychology—should be recognized not as progress but as a retreat to the position of the stimulus-response mediational theory. It is too bad that historical experiments cannot be conducted. What would have happened if the stimulus-response mediational approach had been pursued with the same number of psychologists and with the same vigor as had cognitive psychology? The so-called higher mental processes may not have been penetrated as much but perhaps a more solid foundation of facts and theories could have been achieved which would have had greater promise of future success than is offered by the muddle that is presently cognitive psychology. Fifth, and finally, mention should be made of Neisser, whose book *Cognitive Psychology* (1967) did so much to launch the paradigm of the same name. Neisser (1976) has been disappointed in the way that cognitive psychology has developed; it has generated too much research that is isolated from real life. Neisser now argues that it is necessary to conduct "ecologically valid research" the results of which will be relevant to life outside of the laboratory and consistent with the evolutionary principles that have generally been ignored by cognitive psychology.

Moderator: My cognition tells me to terminate this debate at this point.

SUMMARY

Cognitive psychology represents a confluence of many different ideas from the history of psychology as well as from related disciplines. The theoretical technique of inferring mental events from experimental results that was employed by Wundt (e.g., mental chronometry) has been absorbed into cognitive psychology. The distinction between mental structures and cognitive processes, which has historical antecedents in functionalism, Gestalt psychology, Tolman's cognitive behaviorism, Bartlett's reconstructivist theory of memory, and Piaget's development theory of intelligence, has all been assimilated, in one form or another, into cognitive psychology. Similarly, George Miller's interpretation of short-term memory and his mentalistic concepts of *chunking* and *plan*, human engineering's interpretation of information-flow through a man-machine system, and signal-detection theory's conception of humans as information transmitters and decision makers, have all influenced the development of cognitive psychology. At least of equal importance to cognitive psychology has been ideas from related disciplines: communication engineering, Chomsky's linguistic theory, and computer science.

    Cognitive psychology was considered to be a revolutionary redirection of psychology from radical behaviorism. Other forms of stimulus-response psychology, however, such as Woodworth's S-O-R conception and the mediational S-R formulation that emerged from the Hullian framework, were moving in the direction of developing mediational mechanisms to account for human cognition. The vast majority of psychologists interested in the higher mental processes concluded that stimulus-response language with its antimentalistic bias was too restrictive to be used fruitfully in the interpretation of human cognition. A model of the mind was needed that actually reflected mental structures and cognitive processes. To accomplish this goal, a mentalistic oriented language was deemed necessary for the development of cognitive psychology.

Simple descriptive definitions of the subject matter of cognitive psychology are "how the mind works" and "the functional organization of the mind." The aim of most cognitive psychologists is to analyze the structures and processes of particular subsystems of the mind (e.g., memory, decision-making). When the functioning of each subsystem is comprehended, then attempts will be made to interpret the functioning of the mind as an integrated whole.

The mind has been conceptualized in a variety of ways by different cognitive psychologists, the most common being as a set of mental structures and processes that intervene between stimulus input and response output. Other metaphors that are popular are to equate the mediational events that compose the mind with a computer program, or an electronic communication system, or as the human brain. The question that has been raised is whether these different preconceptions of the mediational processes lead to different conceptions of cognition or whether the various models will mesh as reliable knowledge is discovered.

Numerous methods of investigation have been employed by cognitive psychology mainly because of the variety of psychological traditions that have been absorbed into cognitive psychology: verbal learning, mental chronometry, psycholinguistics, and computer simulation of cognitive processes. The methodological orientation of most cognitive psychologists is that of methodological behaviorism, but this orientation does not clearly fit the efforts of Piaget, Chomsky, and Simon and Newell.

Most cognitive psychologists employ the criterion of truth of deductive explanation but some critics suggest that this standard is sometimes confused with the intuitive knowing that is generated by the appealing mentalistic descriptions and flowcharts of cognitive processes.

The strategy adopted by cognitive psychology was for the most part in opposition to neobehavioristic tactics: Broad general theories were renounced in preference to narrow theoretical models with limited empirical implications, animal research tended to be ignored, and greater interest was paid to fields related to psychology such as linguistics, engineering, and computer science.

Cognitive psychology has generated an enormous amount of research that cannot be incorporated simply into any general conception of cognition. The distinctive *mentalistic* approach of cognitive psychology is illustrated in the classic study that demonstrates that the rotation of mental images in consciousness operates in a similar fashion as the physical rotation of a physical object in physical space. The study of memory suggests that a mental structure, a sensory register, stores incoming stimulation for a brief period of time in its original form. The duplex theory proposes that information from the sensory register then is transferred, if not forgotten, to a short-term memory store with a limited storage capacity (seven units of information plus or minus two). If the information is rehearsed in short-term memory store then it can be transferred to the long-term memory store in a variety of encoded forms. Because of the enormous amount of information present in the long-term storage, retrieval cues are needed to recover information. A competing theory to the duplex model hypothesizes that the major variable in remembering is the manner in which the information is processed (e.g., by perceptual features, specific meaning, or meaningfully integrated into a large body of knowledge). More recently, Tulving has argued against the notion of considering memory as a single set of structures or processes. He proposes that memory is composed of three integrated systems (procedural, semantic, episodic), which are correlated with different phenomenological experiences and neurophysiological processes that are related in an evolutionary order.

The task of simulating human cognition with computer programs raises many methodological and theoretical issues. Of prime importance is the distinction between artificial intelligence that simulates human cognition and artificial intelligence that does not. The basic assumption governing the conclusion that human cognition has been simulated by a computer program is that the match beween the output of each is identical or very close. Current issues in the debate include the criteria of a satisfactory match and the variety of problems that a computer program must simulate to qualify as a truly human simulation. At present, both computer scientists and psychologists disagree as to whether computer simulation of human cognition has been achieved, and if not, the best strategy for achieving the goal.

Although Chomsky's linguistic theory was the main force in molding the new field of psycholinguistics, the formulation experienced great difficulty in incorporating newly discovered empirical evidence. A spin-off from research designed to teach anthropoid apes a human language revealed the absence of any clear-cut meaning of a universal grammar, the core concept in Chomsky's theory. In addition, developmental research and experimental studies failed to support the Chomskian hypothesis, that the syntax of a human language was genetically preprogrammed. Developmental research suggested the absence of any general principles that governed the development of childhood grammar, primarily because nonsyntactical variables influence the acquisition of grammar.

Cognitive psychology is not a highly integrated paradigm and therefore can be considered as "an approach to constructing theories, a style of theorizing . . . [that is] not correct or incorrect, only more or less productive" (Hayes, 1978). The core assumption of cognitive psychology is the requirement of a model of the mind with mental structures and cognitive processes to account for human cognition. Three theoretical constructs—*knowledge (information)*, *representation*, and *processing* have played central roles in cognitive theories and research. The large amount of cognitive research has encouraged the proliferation of theoretical concepts, which has proved to be the strength and weakness of cognitive psychology. The numerous structures and processes have provided a vast number of theoretical tools to interpret almost any form of behavior. At the same time numerous facts of cognitive psychology frequently appear isolated from others, suggesting a field of knowledge that lacks integration. The future of cognitive psychology will depend upon the ability of its theorists to provide a unity that is presently absent.

Within the brief history of cognitive psychology, a shift has occurred in the direction of considering neurophysiology, developmental psychology, and comparative psychology of greater importance than initially thought.

The research area of artificial intelligence represents the greatest puzzle within cognitive psychology. Is it one of several component areas of cognitive psychology or does it represent a unique approach to human cognition?

Perhaps the most common criticism directed at cognitive psychology is that noncognitive processes (e.g., motivation) are ignored, thus precluding the development of a complete psychology.

SUGGESTED READINGS

Students who wish to pursue their interest in cognitive psychology have a variety of choices. My favorite is Lachman, Lachman, and Butterfield's *Cognitive Psychology and Information Processing: An Introduction* (1979), because it proposes a sophisticated methodological-historical analysis of its subject. The historical classics, Miller, Galanter, and Pribram's *Plans and the Structure of Behavior*, (1960) and Neisser's *Cognitive Psychology* (1960) are excellent sources for gaining knowledge about the emergence of cognitive psychology. A brief book by a distinguished cognitivist, Michael I. Posner, entitled *Cognition: An Introduction* (1973) is well worth reading. *The Process of Cognition* by Blumenthal (1977), is an interesting and ambitious book because its attempt to formulate a broad conception of cognition that interprets phenomena varying from visual perception to concept formation.

So many books have been written about verbal learning, memory, human engineering, communication engineering, psycholinguistics, and computer science that it would be impossible to list the good ones without serious omissions. Your teacher could offer good recommendations if you desire to pursue your interests in any of these fields.

12

Humanistic Psychology

In 1964 a group of psychologists, including Carl Rogers (born 1902), Abraham Maslow (1908–1970), Rollo May (born 1909), Gordon Allport (1897–1967), and some humanists like Jacques Barzun, a historian with broad philosophical interests, met in Old Saybrook, Connecticut, and launched a movement that became known as humanistic psychology.

> That conference developed out of the groundswell of protest against the theory of man of behaviorism on the one side and orthodox psychoanalysis on the other. That is why we are often called the Third Force. There was a feeling on all sides among different psychologists that neither of these two versions dealt with human beings as human. Nor did they deal with real problems of life. They left great numbers of people feeling alienated and empty. At that conference we discussed what the chief elements of humanistic psychology would be (May, in Gilbert, 1975, p. 4).

Like most revolutionary movements, the participants were more in agreement about what they opposed than what they accepted. Subsequent events demonstrated that sharing the common name, *humanistic psychology*, did not guarantee agreement about what humanistic psychology is.

HISTORICAL ROOTS

The historical roots of humanistic psychology are manifold. Our primary concern will be with *humanism* as a philosophical movement, *human sciences* as a scientific methodology, and the relationships between humanistic psychology and the psychology of personality and Gestalt psychology.

Humanism

Humanism originally referred to the views of the major thinkers during the Italian Renaissance that emerged during the second half of the fourteenth century. They extolled the intrinsic virtues of the human spirit that prevailed during the classical period in Greece and were suppressed during the Middle Ages. Then and now, humanism assumes that humans are the measure of all things, that is, everything—government, traditions, laws, art, science—must be judged in relation to its impact on individual men and women, and not in terms of some future heavenly paradise or utopian ideal.

A dominant theme in humanism was the exaltation of freedom; humans should be given the freedom to decide their own fate instead of having their future dictated to them by church or state. The emphasis on free choice, which permeates all humanism, is captured by Pico della Mirandola (1463–1494) in the famous passage he attributes to God in the *Oration on the Dignity of Man:*

> I have given you Adam, neither a predetermined place nor a particular aspect nor any special prerogatives, in order that you may take and possess these through your own decision and choice. The limitations on the nature of other creatures are contained within my prescribed laws. You shall determine your own nature without constraint from any barrier, by means of the freedom to whose power I have entrusted you. I have placed you at the center of the world so that from that point you might see better what is in the world. I have made you neither heavenly nor earthly, neither mortal nor immortal so that, like a free and sovereign artificer, you might mold and fashion yourself into that form you yourself have chosen (Quoted from Abbagnano, translated by Langiulli, 1967, p. 70).

Within the philosophy of humanism in its original Renaissance form were certain ideals: happiness and pleasure are preferable to asceticism, the active life is superior to the contemplative life, religion should serve a civil function of creating happiness and encouraging altruism, spontaneity is more desirable than conformity, and goodness can be an expression of natural desires and not a defense against evil urges.

Because humanism was opposed to all forms of dogmatism, it was expressed in undogmatic fashion to allow individuals freedom to interpret it in their own enlightened way. As the impact of the Middle Ages faded, a variety of humanisms developed, all sharing, to some degree, the concern with human values, the respect for classical knowledge, and the veneration of human freedom.

Modern Forms of Humanism. Some varieties of contemporary humanism are worth describing because of their impact on humanistic psychology: *Transcendental humanism* can be considered an outgrowth of New England Transcendentalism, primarily a literary movement headed by such distinguished Americans as Ralph Waldo Emerson (1803–1882) and Henry David Thoreau (1817–1862). A basic assumption of transcendentalism is that important ideas need not be based on empirical observations. Two possible sources of such ideas are the intuitions of the mind and mystical experience. Emerson favored the first alternative; a Transcendentalist is one who has a "tendency to respect intuitions." Other transcendental humanists favored mystical interpretations of life.

Transcendental humanism is more a state of mind than a systematic philosophy, and is distinguished mainly by its romantic and idealistic attachment to the principles that human spirit is godlike and the ultimate authority of a person's conduct is his or her own conscience. The New England Transcendentalists were liberal in outlook and persistent in their opposition to slavery, cultural philistinism, and political and religious dogmatism. This liberal attitude has persisted in most contemporary forms of humanism.

Secular humanism rejects the religious principle that God created man in his own image and proposes instead that man created God in his own image. This view enrages fundamentalist and evangelical preachers who accuse secular humanism of committing the sin of putting "man above God." The accusation is correct in the sense that the secular humanist rejects any moral absolutes or traditional beliefs that are justified only by religious or biblical authority. Because of their intrinsic freedom, people are capable of arriving at moral principles and a philosophy of life in the absence of any dogmatic claims of some higher authority. By exploring the humanities—literature, art, philosophy, history—an intimate understanding of human nature will be realized which in turn can be used in planning a workable and tolerant society for all.

Existential humanism stresses the principle that the only universe that actually exists resides in human subjective experience. Kierkegaard (1813–1855) sought to release people from "the illusion of objectivity" by denying that science and formal systems of philosophy can provide valid information about how one should live. Jean-Paul Sartre (1905–1980), the French playwright and novelist, did much to popularize existentialism. Living involves *conscious* choices that cannot be avoided if one truly desires to control one's own fate. One popular existential interpretation is that the entire universe was created by an accident and, therefore, life is absurd; human beings are simply products of physical and biological evolution that has neither plan nor purpose. In order to cope with this existential crisis each individual—*nobody else*—must give meaning to his or her own life.

Human Sciences

A dominant question throughout psychology's history has been its scientific status. Most, but certainly not all, psychologists at leading American universities think of psychology as a natural science. For them, science is a method of controlled empirical inquiry designed to interpret and predict phenomena, psychological as well as physical.

A contrasting view dates back to the conception of Giambattista Vico (1668–1774), a Neapolitan philosopher of history, social theorist, and jurist who insisted that the study of history needs a method that is distinct from physics because the objects of inquiry, human beings, are intrinsically different from inanimate objects; they possess consciousness. Comprehending human action requires sharing a person's conscious experience. For Vico, an historian, a human studying human events is capable of *empathizing* with those who made history and therefore can achieve an intimate acquaintance with the subject matter that is denied the physical scientist when dealing with physical phenomena (Gardiner, 1967).

Vico laid the ground work for a discipline that became known as a human science. Subsequent developments in philosophy and psychology made it clear that human science contained more than a single method. In recognition of that fact we presently refer to the human sciences (Polkinghorne, 1983), which differ among themselves on such fundamental issues as the relationship between human sciences and natural science and the criterion of understanding. In spite of these differences, an underlying agreement prevails about the central concern in all human sciences. Polkinghorne, the president of a graduate school in humanistic psychology, states that "my position [is] that methods and research design for the human sciences must be able to yield information about being human as we experience it."

Human sciences will be described in relation to some of their basic ideas: *attributes of consciousness, intentionality, Husserl's phenomenology, and verstehen.* While becoming acquainted with the methodology of the human sciences keep in mind some basic questions. Does an unbridgeable chasm exist between natural science and the human sciences so that knowledge from one is incompatible with the other? Or does the knowledge they each yield complement each other, thus offering the possibility of a complete psychology that is denied to a natural science or human science interpretation alone?

Attributes of Consciousness. Consciousness can be conceptualized in different ways. Titchener considered consciousness as a set of processes or elements that could be directly observed by a trained introspector, thus producing a veridical account of consciousness.

Consciousness could also be observed by the method of naive phenomenology, the "unbiased scrutiny of experience." Within the history of experimental psychology, naive phenomenology was primarily considered as an essential first step in psychological research, not as an end in itself. Once phenomena (e.g., Purkinje effect, insight) were described phenomenologically, the researcher would be in a better position to experimentally investigate them.

The view of consciousness within humanistic psychology has been shaped by clinical considerations. The humanistic therapist seeks an empathic understanding of the patient, particularly in regard to various features of his or her self-concept: self-image, self-esteem, social self, and so forth. The concern with the self stems from the belief that therapeutic success, to various degrees, is a consequence of improving a patient's self-image in the direction of healthier, more realistic reactions. Thus the phenomenological orientation of humanistic psychology, although sharing similarities with the naive phenomenology of some experimental psychologists, differs in that phenomenological analysis is considered as an end in itself.

Intentionality. Franz Brentano's concept of intentionality—that consciousness creates objects, strivings, and goals—encouraged the development of human sciences. Although the concept of intentionality generates much philosophical controversy (e.g., Quine, 1960), it has influenced the human sciences in four important ways. First, intentionality justifies the human sciences. Intentionality characterizes the mental; physical objects like atoms and stars do not have intentions. Consequently, psychology, conceptualized as a mental science, is a different kind of science than is physics. Second, because the mind intentionally creates subjective goals, we should not treat humans as objects in a manner analogous to a physicist seeking to understand how crystals form. If we do, we rob humans of an essential feature of their humanity. Third, because physical objects lack intentionality, their activities are strictly controlled by natural laws. Intentionality implies a capacity to make choices, thus suggesting that human behavior is not strictly causal in the same sense that physical phenomena are. Fourth, the emphasis that intentionality assigns to goals has encouraged humanistic psychologists to be concerned with human strivings toward meaningful life goals.

Husserl's Phenomenology. A dictionary definition states that *phenomenology* is the branch of science that deals with the description of phenomena in the absence of all interpretation, explanation, and evaluation. Edmund Husserl (1859–1938), who was greatly influenced by Brentano, founded a school of philosphy known as *phenomenology*, which was dedicated to a descriptive study of consciousness completely free of preconceptions, especially those stemming from a naturalistic view of the world. Thus, objects of pure imagination, such as a unicorn or a gargoyle, are as legitimate objects for phenomenological examination as are natural events like eclipses or the behavior of animals. In essence, Husserl was arguing against psychophysical analyses of consciousness, as practiced by Weber and Fechner, believing that the study of consciousness must be restricted to consciousness itself; phenomenology copes with the *essence* of subjective experience and not its relation to physical events. Husserl was proposing a radical theory of subjectivity that had its impact upon humanistic psychology by emphasizing the phenomenology of one's self, the conscious experience of one's own individuality. Near the end of his career, Husserl vigorously argued that people in the Western world, by perceiving natural science as the only source of facts, severed themselves from their own consciousness and a human-centered view of life.

Verstehen (Understanding). Wilhelm Dilthey (1833–1911), a German philosopher, played a key role in emphasizing the distinction between natural and human sciences. He rejected the notion that human life could be reduced to biological processes used to interpret animal behavior. Human life must be understood in terms of human consciousness. Dilthey assumed that humans experience life as meaningful and that meaning, whether it applies to a particular situation or to the entire theme of one's existence, is the prime source of human action.

A fundamental concept in Dilthey's systematic interpretation of human experience is the method of *verstehen,* the German equivalent for *understanding.* One can understand the actions of others if one can share their experience, including the underlying meaning they assign to their lives. Dilthey's conception of a human science shares many procedures with natural science—observation, description, induction, deduction, hypothesis testing, and so forth—to achieve verstehen of the actions of others.

Understanding human action requires three prerequisites: (1) One must be intimately acquainted with human consciousness and its outward behavioral manifestations. Living a full life, including reading great literature and important biographies, can enhance one's sensitivities to human experiences. (2) A deeper understanding of a person's experience can be achieved when one understands the social milieu in which that person lives. One can better understand Freud, for example, by comprehending the social and intellectual life of Vienna during his lifetime. (3) Verstehen is also facilitated by knowing the language in which the attitudes and ideas of a person are expressed. In sum, the more one knows about the context in which a person lives, the deeper is the understanding that can be achieved.

The Psychology of Personality

Personality seems to be a different kind of research area from the more traditional experimental fields such as perception, learning, and cognition. The difference is expressed in the following comment:

> Nobody in his private life seriously doubts that personality exists. Indeed we take the personalities of ourselves and others into account a good deal in day-to-day decisions and activities. But, once we try to specify the nature of personality in some precise, objective way, it seems to evaporate before our eyes, leaving us frustrated and uncertain. This has even happened to some psychologists, with the result that they have seriously contended that personality does not exist (Maddi, 1980, p. 4).

John B. Watson (1924) reduced personality to "The end product of our habit systems." That is, the psychologist would not have to refer to an individual's personality if all his habits could be specified. B. F. Skinner

(1953) takes the same tack; to him personality is an "explanatory fiction." Instead of employing the concepts of *personality*, one should analyze behavior to identify "functionally unified systems of responses." An exhaustive study of the literature about fifty years ago (Allport, 1937) revealed about fifty different definitions of personality, some completely at odds with others. If psychologists cannot agree about the meaning of personality, and the last half of the century has not increased the degree of concurrence, the concept might be best abandoned.

Humanistic psychologists, in contrast, insist that the concept of personality is essential for psychology for two major reasons. First, personality is a holistic concept which cannot be reduced to the sum of its parts. An intrinsic unity operates in personality which makes every person unique. William Stern (1871–1939), the founder of *personalistic psychology* said: "The person is a living whole, individual, unique, striving toward goals, self contained and yet open to the world around him; he is capable of having experience" (Stern, 1938). This emphasis on gestalt (holism) and phenomenology (experience) is retained in humanistic psychology. Second, the psychology of personality requires the concept of self, even though Skinner would dismiss it as an "explanatory fiction." Humanistic psychology followed James's lead by insisting that personality could not be understood without reference to the self.

Alfred Adler and Carl Jung. Both Alfred Adler and Carl Jung, important figures in the psychoanalytic movement, anticipated humanistic psychology by suggesting that humans sought positive goals—mastery and harmony according to Adler and self-realization according to Jung— while simultaneously deemphasizing the role of biological factors in human conduct.

Gordon Allport. Strictly speaking, Gordon Allport (1897–1967) was not a humanistic psychologist, even though he participated in its creation as an independent orientation. He shared many of its ideas while retaining more traditional views. His reputation as a professor of psychology at Harvard University and as the president of the American Psychological Association was primarily based on his contribution to the development of personality tests and to the definition and assessment of *traits*, measurable and relatively stable characteristics of personality that predispose the individual to respond in a systematic fashion. In spite of Allport's research, designed to measure personality objectively, he entertained strong doubts about borrowing too much from the methods of the natural sciences for psychology. He believed a natural science orientation tends to encourage continuities that are psychologically false. Adult humans cannot be conceptualized as machines, or animals, or even as children. Trying to force psychologists to define concepts precisely may be self-defeating by freezing the meaning of terms before enough is known about them. Allport's critics accused him of preferring artistically out-of-focus terms to rigorously defined constructs.

FIGURE 12.1   Gordon W. Allport

Archives of The History of American Psychology

Allport's ambivalence toward natural science was expressed in his rejection of the notion that a single department of psychology could encompass all of psychology. Immediately after World War II, psychology was divided into two independent entities at Harvard. The traditional department of psychology was composed of experimental psychologists whose research interests ranged from sensory processes to learning. The newly formed department of social relations was composed of personality and social psychologists, clinical psychologists, sociologists, and cultural anthropologists. Allport was appointed the first chairperson, partially in recognition of his spearheading the separation between a strictly natural science department of psychology and a humanistically oriented one.

Several of Allport's substantive notions were sympathetically received by humanistic psychologists:

The distinction between normal and neurotic personalities.   Allport disagreed with the Freudian assumption that a theory of normal personality could be derived from studying neurotic patients; they were not on the same psychological continuum. To understand normal personalities required studying normal, not neurotic individuals. Normal individuals could be understood by analyzing their present conduct without considering their pasts or their childhoods. In addition, the normal personality is not controlled by unconscious urges. Instead, one's own conscious feelings, attitudes, and intentions are the best source of information for predicting one's behavior.

Nomethetic versus idiographic research methods. Allport distinguished between two major methods of investigating personality. The *nomethetic* method studies large groups of individuals with the aim of abstracting basic principles of personality that would apply to all individuals. The *idiographic* method is designed to study an individual as an isolated phenomenon in order to identify the distinctive and unique characteristics of his or her personality. Allport (1946) acknowledged both methods to be legitimate modes of investigation but favored the individual (idiographic) approach because "as long as psychology deals only with the universal and not with particulars, it won't deal with much—least of all with human personality."

The self.

One of the striking phenomena of the past sixty years in psychology has been the demise and subsequent rebirth of self and ego concepts. Perhaps no other psychologist has had so influential a role in restoring and purifying the ego concept as Allport. Not only has he placed the concept in historical context but he has also attempted persistently to show the functional necessity of employing some such concept in a discriminating way in any attempt to represent normal, complex, human behavior (Hall & Lindzey, 1957, p. 289).

Allport's conception had such an impact that when practicing clinical psychologists were asked in 1951 which personality theorist was most valuable in their clinical efforts, the name of Freud led all others, but Allport was considered the second most influential (Schafer, Berg, & McCandless, 1951).

Becoming. Three common themes of humanistic psychology are expressed in Allport's essay with the provocative title of *Becoming* (1955). First is the emphasis on the uniqueness of human personality: "I venture the opinion that all the animals in the world are psychologically less distinct from one another than one man is from other men." Second, human motivation is tied to the future not to the past: "People, it seems, are busy leading their lives, whereas psychology, for the most part, is busy tracing them in the past." Third is *becoming*, the growth of personality toward an integrative system. Allport criticizes traditional theories for their failure to cope with personality growth toward ideal goals:

I wish to show that an adequate personality of becoming cannot be written exclusively in terms of stimulus, emotional excitement, association, and response. It requires subjective and inner principles of organization of the sort frequently designated by the terms self or ego (Allport, 1955, p. 60).

Growth or becoming is not aimless. It is directed toward meaningful goals that have human value, such as becoming a good mechanic, flower arranger, or a creative scientist. These goals may not be completely obtainable, but the motive itself is important, "the stretching toward this limit, whatever it is, is as much a triumph for a life of slight potential as for a life whose potentials are great." Allport offers an image of man that is not simply satisfied with achieving biological homeostasis or enduring pleasure, but is instead a motive to become human in the highest sense of the word:

> Every man, whether he is religiously inclined or not, has his own ultimate presuppositions. He finds he cannot live his life without them, and for him they are true. Such presuppositions, whether they be called ideologies, philosophies, notions, or merely hunches about life, exert creative pressures upon all conduct that is subsidiary to them (which is to say, upon nearly *all* of man's conduct) (Allport, 1955, p. 95–96).

Gestalt Psychology

One cannot avoid discussing the relationship between Gestalt psychology and humanistic psychology if only to clarify popular misconceptions. The assumption that they are practically equivalent was fostered by a humanistic therapy known as *gestalt therapy* formulated by Fritz Perls (1893–1970), who admitted that he never read Wertheimer, Koffka, or Köhler, and employed the term *gestalt* because he believed it to be intrinsic to the concept of human nature.

In spite of the dissociation between Gestalt psychology and gestalt therapy, Gestalt psychology and humanistic psychology do share important philosophical ideas, namely *holism, moral optimism,* and *antipositivism.* Personality, for humanistic psychologists, was more than a sum of a person's motives, cognitions, and habits in the same sense that a melody for the Gestalt psychologists could not be reduced to the sum of its notes. Psychological events must be conceptualized as wholes. Both Gestalt psychology and humanistic psychology share the optimistic view that humans are morally good, if they are not denied the opportunity to achieve their potentialities. And finally both reject the positivistic position that all knowledge is based upon a foundation of sensory observation. Pure rationalism and phenomenological analysis are sometimes essential ingredients of truth and knowledge.

These shared ideas did not, however, equate humanistic psychology with Gestalt psychology. Wertheimer, Koffka, and Köhler were primarily concerned with laboratory psychology, particularly perception, learning, and thinking. Köhler's admission that he and his gestalt colleagues were not as rigorous experimentalists and theorists as some American behaviorists indicated his desire for Gestalt psychology to meet the demands of natural science methodology. Thus, Gestalt psychology diverges from humanistic psychology by operating within the arena of natural science, not the human sciences.

METHODOLOGICAL ASSUMPTIONS

Although humanistic psychologists disagree about important methodological issues, attention will be mainly focused on the common themes that unite the human sciences in their protest against a natural science interpretation of human psychology.

The Subject Matter of Psychology

Conscious experience is the central concern of humanistic psychology. How do humanistic psychologists deal with this subject that has generated so much controversy and confusion since the beginning of psychology as an independent discipline? By rejecting the tenets of natural science which place such a heavy reliance on public (objective) observations, humanistic psychologists feel free to accept verbal reports of self-observation as reflecting the inner experiences of a person. This does not mean that they reject the possibility that somebody would deliberately lie about socially unacceptable feelings. It means that in most cases self-reports are fairly accurate representations of consciousness. And when not, a sensitive psychologist can detect the dissimilitude. In sum, the core subject matter of humanistic psychology is conscious experience but the methodological requirements for observing and interpreting mental events is more relaxed—a humanistic psychologist might say less compulsive—than the criteria employed by natural science psychologists.

Methods of Investigation

Humanistic psychology places no limits on psychological research. Some humanistic psychologists encourage objective research that they assume reflects conscious experience. At the same time, other humanistic psychologists stress self-reports of conscious experience as the ultimate evidence on which to base psychological principles.

The spectrum of research topics investigated by humanistic psychologists is as broad as that explored by more traditional experimentalists. The research interests of humanistic psychologists, however, are definitely weighted in the direction of personality, clinical psychology, and social psychology.

Criterion of Truth

One of the key issues distinguishing the human sciences from the natural sciences is the criterion of truth. This view was originally expressed in Vico's argument that human scientists achieve a different kind of understanding than natural scientists. The distinction between the two disciplines is briefly expressed in the proposition that the natural sciences investigate phenomena from the outside with the aim of identifying their causes, whereas human sciences study human phenomena from the inside with the goal of revealing subjective meaning.

Implicit in this distinction is that natural sciences deal with an outside reality; the laws of nature can, in principle, be understood with absolute certainty. Thus we can with complete conviction expect the apple to fall downward from the tree, the mating of two blue eyed people to produce a blue-eyed offspring, and deafness to result from severing the auditory nerve. Although natural scientists know that they only observe reality indirectly through sense experiences, they nevertheless accept the existence of reality and so strive to understand the principles that govern it. In contrast, human scientists acknowledge the fact that the conscious experience of another cannot be known or experienced with absolute certainty and therefore are more tolerant when evaluating competing theories because truth can only be approximated. This elastic conception of truth in humanistic psychology can even lead to the acceptance of apparently contradictory views. When psychoanalysis is conceptualized as a human science, it is argued, different *story lines* could be effectively employed with the same patient as long as they are meaningful, *true*, to the patient.

Unfortunately the nice neat dichotomy between a reality oriented natural science and subjectively meaningful human science is not as clear as just described. Most sharp distinctions, when closely examined, are fuzzy at the boundaries. Some philosophers and scientists deny the possibility that absolute, valid knowledge about reality can ever be achieved. The theories of Galileo, Newton, and Einstein represent successively improved approximations. But although psychological knowledge can only be approximately determined, the understanding employed by natural science psychology is based on public criteria—deductive explanation and/or behavioral control—while humanistic psychology is willing to accept private judgments of interpretive consistency and/or intuitive knowing.

STRATEGY

By adopting the firm position that psychology must deal with human experience, humanistic psychology encouraged the development of different strategies to reveal the essence of human consciousness. Perhaps the dominant strategy that most humanistic psychologists adopted is that life, as experienced, is more clearly reflected in the clinic, or even in literature, than in the laboratory.

DIFFERENT FORMS OF HUMANISTIC PSYCHOLOGY

Carl R. Rogers proposed his ideas about humanistic psychology in direct competition to traditional forms of natural science psychology. Although he finally left university life because of what he considered to be a stifling atmosphere, he nevertheless behaved as a traditional academic by engaging in philosophical debates, particularly with Skinner, while pursuing an active and influential career as a clinical psychologist. Thus Rogers is a natural choice to be considered a central figure in the analysis of humanistic psychology as long as one heeds Rogers's own warning: "It is too diversified, its boundaries too vague, for me to endeavor to be a spokesman" (Rogers, 1964).

Rogers's Self Theory

Like Freud, Rogers's own life appears to have shaped his psychological views.

Carl R. Rogers (born 1902)

Rogers was raised in the Midwest in a strict, loving, Christian household, in which dancing, playing cards, attending movies, smoking, and exhibiting sexual interests were not tolerated. He studied agriculture first, but soon recognized that religion was his major interest. In his junior year at the University of Wisconsin he was selected as one of ten American students to attend the World Student Christian Federation Conference in Peking, China.

After receiving his bachelor's degree in history, Rogers enrolled in the Union Theological Seminary in New York City, a move that did not please his parents, who preferred a more conservative religious institution. The modern, liberal religion to which Rogers was exposed included clinical work which he found "exciting." During his second year, Rogers took courses in philosophy of education and clinical psychology at Teachers College of Columbia University, located across the street from the Union Seminary. Rogers soon concluded that religion was an inadequate vehicle to accomplish what he passionately desired, to help others by communicating with them in an undogmatic way.

FIGURE 12.2 Carl R. Rogers

Courtesy of Carl Rogers

While working on his doctorate at Teachers College, Rogers was awarded a fellowship at the Institute for Child Guidance where he gained both experience and confidence as a clinical psychologist. He recalls being shocked once by Alfred Adler who, in his lecture, rejected the traditional procedure of collecting an extensive case history of each patient. At that time Rogers routinely took case histories of fifty to seventy pages in length.

Rogers's next job was at the Rochester Child Guidance Clinic, where he stayed for twelve years. During that time his clinical experiences encouraged him to formulate his own ideas about the psychology of personality. He soon became disenchanted with psychoanalysis because of its apparent ineffectiveness. He recalled the case of a pyromaniac whose problems were traced to sexual difficulties, but who set fire to a building after his therapy was completed. Rogers began questioning the effectiveness of interviewing techniques in revealing the source of a patient's problems. One case proved particularly instructive. An intelligent mother of a problem child refused, after many interviews, to accept Rogers's interpretation that she had rejected her son. They both agreed to terminate the therapy but before leaving, the mother surprised Rogers with the question, "Do you ever take adults for counseling here?" Rogers agreed to treat her and was surprised to see a complete change in her behavior. Instead of offering sterile memories of herself and her son, she poured out her despair and unhappiness.

> Real therapy began then . . . and ultimately it was highly successful—for her and her son. This incident . . . helped me to experience the fact—only realized later—that it is the *client* who knows what hurts, what directions to go, what problems are crucial, what experiences have been deeply buried. It began to occur to me that unless I had a need to demonstrate my own cleverness and learning, I would do better to rely upon the client for the direction of movement in the process (Rogers, 1967, p. 359).

Ohio State University, influenced by the publication of Rogers's *The Clinical Treatment of the Problem Child* (1939), offered him a full professorship of psychology. Rogers's seminars and practicums in counseling and psychotherapy proved immensely popular and established the precedent of supervised training in therapy, which included reviewing tape recordings of previous therapy sessions. In 1945, Rogers went to the University of Chicago, where he established a counseling center that also served as a center for research and the training of graduate students. Rogers then wrote *Client-centered Therapy* (1951), which was based upon the assumption that "we cannot teach another person directly; we can only facilitate his learning."

Rogers became president of the American Psychological Association in the 1946–1947 year and over the next two years suffered a "period of personal distress." The distress was brought on by treating a "deeply disturbed client . . . and I somehow gave up *my* self in the relationship." He realized that he was "on the edge of a complete breakdown," and that he *"had* to escape." After a couple of months away he returned to Chicago, underwent therapy, and "worked through to a point where I could value myself, even like myself, and was much less fearful of receiving or giving love" (Rogers, 1967).

The University of Wisconsin was so desirous of attracting Rogers to its campus that it asked him to prepare the complete specifications of an ideal job. He was then offered the position, which he could not refuse. The psychology department "was highly laboratory oriented and very distrustful of clinical psychology." He soon became completely dissatisfied with graduate psychology training and in 1964, a year before leaving Wisconsin, he wrote what is described by a science reporter, as:

> "a passionate statement" on graduate education in psychology, in which he criticized a long list of assumptions that he felt were doing out-right "damage" to students in graduate training: the assumption

. . . that they could not be trusted to pursue their own learning; that teaching meant showering incontrovertible "facts" on the heads of the students, who were treated as "passive objects"; that they were supposed to "learn by being threatened . . . with catastrophic failure." . . . [This statement] carried the message, which Rogers still believes pertains, that higher education is a conservative bastion filled with defensive people who resist sharing their power with students, hide behind status to avoid revealing their fallibility, and put too high a premium on cognitive learning and devalue subjective knowledge (Holden, 1977, p. 32).

In 1964 Rogers abandoned university life to become a member of the California-based Western Behavioral Sciences Institute, an organization "devoted to humanistically oriented research in interpersonal relations, with a particular focus on the manner in which constructive change in interpersonal relationships comes about" (Rogers, 1967). Although initially captivated by his new surroundings peopled with humanistically oriented scholars from a variety of disciplines, he soon became disenchanted with the limited amount of action resulting from an excessive amount of discussion. With much regret, he left the Western Behavioral Sciences Institute to establish the Center for the Studies of the Person while simultaneously admitting that all such institutes should self-destruct in five years. At the age of eighty-two, he bemoaned the fact that humanistic psychology has not had more of an impact on mainstream psychology but nevertheless refused to abandon his goal, which his friends have described as, "giving people permission to be themselves." The University of Santa Clara awarded him an honorary degree with the citation, "You have made it respectable to be human."

Knowing. Rogers distinguishes among three kinds of knowing:

Subjective knowing. Psychophysics can illustrate subjective knowing. When lifting two successive weights, 40 and 40.5 grams respectively, you examine your conscious experience to determine which is heavier. You may initially hypothesize that the second weight is heavier and then become convinced that your conjecture is correct. The same hypothesis testing operates when you deal with more significant phenomena: "Do I really love her?" or "Do I really hate him?" As you mature you usually become more precise and accurate in interpreting your own feelings: "Any one who has experienced psychotherapy will have lived through this way of sharpening or of contradicting previously held inner hypotheses" (Rogers, 1964).

Like James, Rogers admits these self-reports can be fallible; you may make mistakes in observing your inner experiences. He also admits that because subjective "knowing is not infallible and does not lead to publicly validated knowledge, little attention is given to it today " (Rogers, 1964). But Rogers strongly condemns this negative attitude. We all have to deal with our own conscious experience—we have to live with and adjust to it. This demands, Rogers argues, that psychology deal with it.

Objective knowing. In this form of knowing, hypotheses are based on an external, an *outer* frame of reference. To understand the statement that "an intermittent reinforcement schedule creates greater resistance of extinction," the psychologist has to know the method employed to investigate the relationship and the evidence that justifies the empirical law. According to Rogers, one understands this law when one has an "empathic" ability to understand the frame of reference of experimental psychologists.

Rogers insists, properly, that objective knowing involves subjective observation. Operant behavior of rats is observed in the experimenter's consciousness. The only difference between the observational foundations of subjective knowing and objective knowing is that the former is *intra*subjective and the latter *inter*subjective. You are the *only one* who can observe your own feelings while many individuals can observe whether a rat presses a bar. Both kinds of observations are subjective; the difference between them is the number of people that can make the observation.

Rogers argues that objective knowing is also fallible. The history of science, physics as well as psychology, is filled with examples of empirical laws and theoretical conclusions that were initially thought to be true, that is objectively *known,* only later to be discovered to be false.

Although Rogers suggests similarities such as subjective observation and fallibility, between subjective and objective knowing, he stresses an important difference. Subjective knowing stems from observing human consciousness, while objective knowing depends on observing objects. "Am I really falling in love?" demands subjective knowing. Knowing whether intermittent reinforcements create greater resistance to extinction treats organisms as objects because no reference is made to consciousness.

Interpersonal knowing. This third mode of knowing, which falls in between the other two, "applies primarily to knowledge of human beings" (Rogers, 1964). This kind of knowledge is based upon the ability of one person to make correct hypotheses about the inner world of another person. Interpersonal knowing, or what Rogers sometimes calls "phenomenological knowledge," is based on the assumptions that getting "inside" another person's mind (e.g., "He despises himself,") is possible. This assumption is valid under ideal conditions:

> I may—and here is the essence of my experience in psychotherapy—create a climate which makes it psychologically safe and rewarding for you to reveal your internal frame of reference. Then you can find that you can

share with me your unsatisfied ambition, the disgust you feel with your-self, your pattern of beliefs, or any other aspect of your world of personal meaning. In psychotherapy we have found this way of knowing to be most fruitful. Utilizing empathic inference to the fullest, checking our hypotheses against the phenomenal world of the client, we have gained knowledge which has led to the formulation of psychological principles related to personality change (Rogers, 1964, pp.115–116).

The criteria of interpersonal knowing is whether the person confirms the hypothesis and/or whether others arrive at the same conclusion, thus suggesting that consensual agreement can prevail about another person's phenomenology.

The Relationship among the Three Ways of Knowing. Rogers adopts a position about the relationships among the three modes of knowing—subjective, objective, and interpersonal—that would be rejected by many humanistic psychologists as well as by natural science psychologists. His thesis is that all three modes of knowing in proper proportions are required for a mature science of psychology. The mature psychologist, according to Rogers, trusts his own experiences (subjective knowing) and the hypotheses it generates about others. The mature psychologist also forms significant hypotheses from his empathic relationships with others (interpersonal knowing). Finally, he recognizes that all hypotheses are put to their "most severe test" in the objective world (objective knowing).

While implying that objective knowledge is primary, Rogers is careful to point out that none of the three kinds of knowledge is intrinsically superior to the other two. As previously noted, all of the three kinds of knowledge are fallible. In addition, when one or two kinds of knowledge are stressed to the exclusion of the other forms, gross distortions of a psychology will occur. Rogers suggests that behaviorists, by scorning subjective and interpersonal knowing, have proposed a deformed image of man which has hampered the development of a truly human psychology. Similarly, those human scientists who trust only phenomenological (subjective and interpersonal) knowledge will inevitably prevent psychology from obtaining reliable knowledge (objective knowing), the hallmark of natural science psychology.

Rogers's Theory. Now that Rogers's modes of psychological knowing have been explained, his theory of the self can be described. In considering the theory, it becomes important to judge whether the conception meets the criteria of knowing that Rogers himself established.

Client-centered counseling. Rogers dislikes both the words *patient* and *therapist* when describing his mode of psychological treatment. The term *client* is deliberately chosen in preference to *patient* to emphasize the client's autonomy and independence. Rogers also rejects the term *therapist* because it implies attempts at imposing a solution to the client's problems, whereas Rogers believes counseling is effective only when it creates an environment conducive to the client's learning. Thus, Rogers chose the term *facilitator* to designate the counselor. Another important feature of client-centered therapy, which is captured in the designation *nondirective therapy*, is that the facilitator never encourages the client to discuss a particular topic, such as the client's relationships with her father; the client always decides the topic for discussion.

The client-centered facilitator is interested in creating an understanding atmosphere that will encourage the client to clarify present feelings and attitudes. The client is regarded as an individual behaving in the present without regard to the past. Client-centered therapy stresses the phenomenological experience of the client. The client is not considered as a sick patient in need of treatment, but rather as a person who is isolated and incapable of communicating openly with others, thus prevented from realizing his or her full potential.

During the initial interviews, clients talk a good deal about their difficulties, describing their symptoms and problems. The facilitator tries to reflect back to the client the feelings expressed so that the client will determine the direction of the therapy. For example, to the client's comment, "I'm always depressed" the facilitator might respond with, "You constantly feel unhappy?" Although such a nondirective response could leave the client without much to say, clients are not aware of the facilitator's strategy and pursue their own line of thought, which ultimately results in a fuller exposure of their experiential problems.

In line with Rogers's desire for objective knowing, he tried to get a handle on the events that transpire during psychotherapy. The therapy sessions were recorded so that an empirical analysis of the verbal behavior could be made. One early research finding (Seeman, 1949) was that as therapy proceeded through successive sessions, there were fewer client reports of symptoms and descriptions of problems, and more expressions of understanding their difficulties.

Core Ideas of Rogers's Self Theory. Rogers's theory of personality emerged from his clinical experience, although it must be noted that it meshes with his philosophy of life. Several core principles of his theory of the self can be briefly summarized:

People are basically good. A human being is analogous to a plant. If given a satisfactory environment, including adequate sunshine and nutrients, a plant will grow and achieve its full potential. Similarly, humans are basically good; they become deformed only when denied the opportunities for inner fulfillment. Such a person is like the plant whose growth is stunted because it is denied full access to sunlight.

The phenomenological self is at the center of personality growth and change. Self-acceptance and self-knowledge permit the normal growth of personality. If a person fails to develop normally, then the task becomes one of changing the feelings toward the self. This emphasis on the self is expressed in Rogers's view of therapy:

> The individual and not the problem is the focus. The aim is not to solve one particular problem, but to assist the individual to *grow,* so that he can cope with the present problem and later problems in a better-integrated fashion. If he can gain enough integration to handle one problem in more independent, more responsible, less confused, better organized ways, then he will also handle new problems in that manner (Rogers, 1942, pp. 28–29).

Implicit in this view is that the best therapist is the *client,* the person who potentially has the greatest wisdom for discovering the most effective course of treatment.

Psychological conditions for personality growth. The therapeutic situation is not insulated from real life problems. The client essentially has not grown normally and thus requires assistance to get back on the right track. The client may still be behaving like a child, seeking help for problems he or she should solve. Rogers identifies several characteristics of the facilitator that will encourage growth in the clinical situation: empathetic listening, accepting the client as a person, and being nonjudgmental.

If acceptance, empathy, and openness are important in the clinic, they are equally important at home. Good parents, according to Rogers, empathize with their children, keep open channels of communication, and accept them in a nonjudgmental manner. Rogers believes it is important to treat children as equals in order for them to develop a positive image of themselves that will enable them to control their choices and grow into psychologically healthy individuals.

Experiential Groups. In the 1960s, humanistic psychology underwent a change as a consequence of a new form of group interaction variously described as *experiential groups, T-groups* (T standing for training), *encounter groups, sensitivity training groups, personal growth groups,* and the like. Characterizing these groups is difficult chiefly because they have no systematic character; their common goals are to improve individuals' sensitivity to themselves and others; to do whatever is required to enable the participants to live fully; to achieve personal growth; to produce a free, spontaneous, flexible person who is more closely in touch with his or her feelings; and to raise consciousness. These goals are consistent with those of Carl Rogers, who endorsed the experiential group movement. Rogers said that "the encounter group or intensive group experience . . . is, I believe, one of our most successful modern inventions for dealing with the feeling of unreality, of impersonality, and of distance and separation that exists in so many people in our culture" (Quoted by Smith, 1984, p. 157).

Experiential groups reached their height of popularity during the 1960s and 1970s. At the time, a strong counterculture developed in the United States as a consequence of the anti-Vietnam War movement. The methods of some experiential groups became dominated by the alienated, hedonistic, drug-oriented features of the counterculture that operated on the principle, "If it feels good, do it." Intimate methods were adopted in experiential groups, such as massage techniques, nude bathing, physical expressions of aggression, and intense verbal exchanges, hostile or friendly. In addition some leaders of the experiential groups movement expressed antiscientific, arational, and mystical attitudes; "it seemed to me that much of the leadership of the humanistic psychology movement was running away from the human in search of the supernatural and divine" (Smith, 1982).

Experiential groups are obviously controversial. In evaluating humanistic psychology, it is important to distinguish between those groups that function essentially as group therapy from those that serve as social protests and/or hedonistic outlets in the guise of achieving personal growth. The interesting question is whether the radical forms of experiential groups are an aberrant form of humanistic psychology or an inevitable consequence of its subjective orientation.

Maslow's Theory of Self-Actualization

Rogers's and Maslow's humanistic theories of personality share much in common but they also differ in important respects. Both conceive of humanistic psychology as a third force, in opposition to both behaviorism and psychoanalysis. But Maslow was not as opposed to psychoanalytic theory and therapy as was Rogers. His theory doesn't deny the Freudian picture of man but instead supplements it, adding the healthy half of personality to Freud's description of the sick half. Maslow, although trained in experimental psychology, was never as committed to achieving some rapprochement with traditional objective psychology as was Rogers. While Rogers extolled the virtues of objective knowing as an essential component of a complete understanding of psychological phenomena and encouraged research in psychotherapy, Maslow operated more like a humanistic philosopher who expansively theorized about human nature and human morality without any strong commitment to obtain supporting empirical evidence.

Maslow's Motivation Theory. Maslow (1970) postulated a hierarchy of inborn human needs represented in the form of a step ladder (Figure 12.4) to highlight the assumption that the motives at the higher levels do not operate until those lower down are satisfied. At the lowest levels are the basic physiological goadings of hunger, thirst, and sex. Immediately above are the safety needs—searching for security and stability, and

FIGURE 12.3 Abraham H. Maslow

avoiding fear. At the next-highest level are the needs for social belonging as expressed by the desire for affectionate relationships. Then comes the need for self-esteem, to respect one's self, to believe that one is successful as a person. At the top rung is the need for self-actualization, "the desire to become more and more what one is, to become everything that one is capable of becoming" (Maslow, 1954).

Self-Actualization and a Humanistic Theory of Values. Maslow's theory of motivation became involved in one of the most controversial topics of humanistic psychology—the ability of humanistic psychology to discover "moral principles common to the entire human species, which can be scientifically confirmed" (Goble, 1971). Maslow suggested that by examining self-actualizing people it becomes possible to discover a scientifically valid ethical system. His rationale for this argument is that self-actualizing individuals are the healthiest, having achieved the highest level of human potential:

> You can find the values by which mankind must live, and for which man has always sought, by digging into the best people in depth. I believe . . .

FIGURE 12.4 Maslow's Hierarchy of Needs

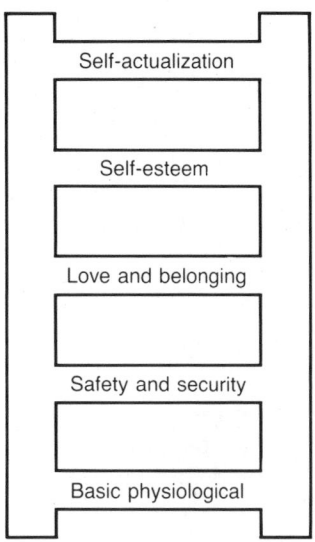

Self-actualization

Self-esteem

Love and belonging

Safety and security

Basic physiological

Maslow's hierarchy of human motives shown schematically in the form of a step ladder. According to Maslow's theory, the needs at any rung of the ladder do not operate until some prior satisfaction of the motives below. (Adapted from Maslow, 1970.)

that I can find ultimate values which are right for mankind by observing the best of mankind . . . If under the best conditions and in the best specimens I simply stand aside and describe in a scientific way what these human values are, the old values of truth, goodness, and beauty and some additional ones as well—for instance, gaiety, justice, and joy (Maslow, 1961, pp. 5–6).

According to Maslow's line of reasoning, the search for valid ethical principles throughout history has been misguided. We have sought a universal standard of morality by virtue of divine authority or philosophical assumptions when actually moral imperatives reside in both human phenomenology and behavior. Maslow implemented his ideas by collecting information about a group of individuals he judged to be self-actualized because they had realized their true potentialities. The group he studied included Jefferson, Lincoln, Einstein, Eleanor Roosevelt, Jane Addams, and some of his own friends and acquaintances. Maslow described them as individuals who identified with mankind and who were realistic, accepting of themselves, spontaneous, and humorous in a philosophical sense as opposed to a hostile sense. In addition, self-actualized people report peak experiences, feelings that they are fused into one with the rest of the world, are at the height of their power, and are living fully in the present, emancipated from thoughts of the past and future.

More than any other systematic approach to psychology, humanistic psychology has been most concerned with the task of offering a moral code that is right for mankind. Other systematic positions, Wundtian (Chapter 2), Gestalt (Chapter 7), and radical behaviorism (Chapter 10) all offered suggestions about what is good and bad. But only the humanistic psychologists have been fully committed to prescribing moral values for humanity.

Other Conceptions of Humanistic Psychology

Although both Rogers and Maslow are the best known humanistic psychologists, each having been elected to the presidency of the American Psychological Association, their ideas do not offer a complete picture of all forms of humanistic psychology.

Existential Psychology.　Existential psychology is seen by some to be just as much a philosophy of life as a systematic psychological position. This is true because it directly encourages a certain mode of living. Viktor E. Frankl (born 1905) was born in Vienna and was heavily influenced by Freudian ideas both in medical school and thereafter. But he began to feel that orthodox psychoanalysis misconceived the problems humans face. Frankl proposes that the central psychological issue is discovering the meaning in life and accepting responsibility for oneself. Failure to achieve a meaningful understanding of life will make one unable to cope with the problems of existence; finding meaning will enable one to tolerate the worst life can offer. Nietzsche expressed a similar thought: "He who has a *why* to live can bear with almost any *how.*"

Existential psychology stresses the power of humans to rise above their surroundings. This point is dramatically underlined by Frankl's experiences in a German concentration camp during World War II. During this time his wife, father, mother, and brother either died or were murdered in concentration camps. In spite of the hopelessness, humiliation, and senseless suffering, Frankl and his fellow prisoners had the freedom to give their lives meaning by religious faith, taking responsibility for others, valuing their own talents, and even by dying with dignity. In other words, regardless of the past and in spite of the present, a human being can always choose to give life meaning.

Frankl's method (1963) consists neither of moral exhortation nor persuasion to assign a particular meaning to life. Rather, his aim is to broaden each person's consciousness so he or she can see life in the proper perspective. Frankl's task is like that of an ophthalmologist who provides his patients with a clear perception of the world to replace the previously distorted one. To see life accurately requires that each individual discover for himself life's meaning and fully accept responsibility for that choice.

From an entirely different social background, Rollo May (born 1909), an American existential psychologist, also emphasizes the view that human life requires meaning. Like Rogers, May studied to be a minister, and still practices the Christian faith, but does not believe that religious belief per se automatically leads to self-fulfillment. May's existential position revolves about three fundamental sociopsychological problems: the empty values of Western civilization, the frustration of our basic human needs for love and beauty, and the need to experience deep despair before creating meaning for life.

May attributes some of the difficulties with which we are confronted to our failure to study the classics. He claims that the university, with its technological bias in favor of the natural sciences, computer science, and business, has relegated the classics to an insignificant part of modern education, thus depriving students of exposure to the eternal values of the arts and humanities. Technology can be admired but only arts and the humanities can be loved: "The musicians have something to love. You can like accounting. I don't see how you can *love* accounting." (May, as reported by Cunningham, 1985b). A society that idolizes competitive success and money erects an obstacle to loving people. People are thrust along the path to achieve conventional goals and thus passively adapt to an existence without meaning. Only by facing up to and acknowledging the emptiness and despair of existence will a real choice become possible between a senseless and a meaningful life. May, in line with Nietzsche and Kierkegaard, the Danish philosopher who influenced existentialism, argues that

> we are not going to get out of our predicament unless we are willing to face life nakedly, unless we are willing to live without grabbing for other supports, other substitutes, or an old-time Christianity. We have to keep our freedom and our determinism, so that we are facing our problems directly (May, as reported by Cunningham, 1985b, p. 17).

Politically Oriented Forms of Humanistic Psychology. Self-fulfillment, the maximal realization of one's potentialities, is a dominant theme that pervades all of humanistic psychology. Although acknowledging its importance, humanistic psychologists disagree about the conditions that prevent an individual from becoming fulfilled. The major obstruction to self-fulfillment, for Rogers, is the development of an inadequate *self,* which hinders normal psychological growth. Maslow shared a similar view except that he hypothesized that self-actualization is prevented by the failure to satisfy lower drives in the hierarchy of motives, such as the search for security. For both Rogers and Maslow, the failure to become fulfilled is *primarily* psychological in nature.

Existential psychologists, like Frankl and May, also stress the importance of fulfillment, but assign more elasticity to its meaning. Maslow gives the impression that within each of us is a genetic blueprint of the ideal self that can be attained. Thus, if Beethoven became a talented pianist but not a great composer, he would not have been actualized. For existential psychologists, fulfillment is analogous to creating meaning in one's life, but a variety of meanings will lead to self-fulfillment. Within

May's existential view is the notion that failure to achieve fulfillment may not simply stem from psychological difficulties, but primarily from intrinsic defects in society. A society that emphasizes materialism and ignores the humanities encourages demoralization, stripping from life the meaning that is essential for an adequate psychological adjustment.

An explicit form of humanistic psychology that embraces a specific political and economic view is that of Erich Fromm (1900–1980), who can be described as a *humanistic psychoanalyst* or as a *dialectical humanist*. He was one of the early members of the Frankfurt Institute of Social Research, founded in 1923 in Germany as a center for interdisciplinary research in the social sciences. The orientation was neo-Marxist; it believed that a rational and compassionate society could be planned on the basis of Marxian principles, even though the failure of Stalin's Russia was readily acknowledged.

Fromm was a neo-Freudian who rejected the libido theory, based upon innate biological drives of sex and aggression, while stressing the essential roles of self, interpersonal relations, society and culture in personality development. As they mature, humans recognize their animal component but then learn to appreciate the uniqueness of their humanity which dominates their existence (Fromm, 1941). Freedom is essential for human fulfillment, but people pay a price for freedom in loneliness that breeds anxiety. To escape from this anxiety, some people forego their freedom by conforming excessively to the restrictive conventions of society or by affiliating with an authoritarian political movement that dictates the choices its members should make. To allow people an opportunity for self-fulfillment requires a society in tune with human nature, one that seeks to eliminate punishment, intolerance, poverty, authoritarianism, prejudice, alienation, and so on. In order to enhance a person's opportunities for self-fulfillment, clinical psychologists and psychiatrists must help build a better society. Fromm believed that would take the form of a socialist state.

Quotations of Humanistic Psychologists

1. It should be noted that this basic actualizing tendency is the only motive which is postulated in [my] theoretical system. It should also be noted that it is the organism as a whole, and only the organism as a whole, which exhibits this tendency (Rogers, 1959, p. 196).

2. The model of science in general, inherited from the impersonal sciences of things, objects, animals, and part processes, is limited and inadequate when we attempt to know and to understand whole and individual persons and cultures . . . But only recently has it been demonstrated just how and where this impersonal model failed with the personal, and unique, the holistic (Maslow, 1966, p. xii).

3. To venture causes anxiety, but not to venture is to lose oneself (Kierkegaard, cited in May, 1977, p. 234).

4. Thus, the mode of life, as it is determined for the individual by the peculiarity of an economic system, becomes the primary factor in determining his whole character structure, because the imperative need for self-preservation forces him to accept the conditions under which he has to live. This does not mean that he cannot try, together with others, to effect certain economic and political changes; but primarily his personality is molded by the particular mode of life . . . which represents all the features that are typical of a particular society or class (Fromm, 1941, p. 18).

CONTRIBUTIONS AND ASSESSMENT OF HUMANISTIC PSYCHOLOGY

By now, it should be clear that the evaluation of any systematic approach in psychology depends upon the frame of reference that is employed. If judged within the general philosophical position of humanism and the human sciences, humanistic psychology will *generally* receive high grades because it is designed to conform to humanistic standards. For the very same reasons, humanistic psychology will be judged as lacking objectivity by the standards of natural science. What is required to judge humanistic psychology is some independent perspective. This need can be met by considering humanistic psychology from a historical perspective.

Experiential Psychology

In making the choice between the mind or behavior as the primary subject matter of psychology, humanistic psychology clearly selects the mind. Humanistic psychologists argue that the essence of being human is represented by human self-consciousness and therefore their subject matter must be experiential psychology. Implied in their position is that methodological considerations, such as the search for reliable knowledge, must initially be ignored. The subject matter comes first and the methodology has to be adapted to it. By combining experiential psychology with philosophical humanism, humanistic psychology offers a distinctive form of psychology.

Image of Man

By deciding that the essence of humanity is conscious experience, humanistic psychologists posed a question that is ignored by natural science psychologists: "What does it *mean* to be human?" This question is important to humanistic psychology because of their need to map out the field of their inquiry so as not to ignore important qualities of being human. Humanistic psychologists stress *seeking meaning*, the importance of the *self*, and the *ability to make choices.* In addition, some, like Rogers, suggest that human beings are basically good.

Existential psychologists, in considering the image of man, have been more concerned with the nature of human existence than with a specific ideal image. They stress that life, in addition to providing opportunities for happiness, has unavoidable tragic features. For example, everyone has to cope with dying. It has even been proposed that authentic living can only be achieved when one fully recognizes the inevitability of one's own death. Dying is the last act of living and should be conducted, as all life should, with human dignity.

> It is said that when Sir Thomas More . . . was led to the block during the reign of King Henry VIII to have his head chopped off, he told his executioners two things: one, to make the stroke clean, and two, not to worry that anyone would take revenge on him for what he was about to do. . . . More wanted to make sure his style of dying would reflect his style of living . . . it was therefore important to die in such a way as to exemplify the values he held in life . . . not only pity and charity but forgiveness as well (Pollio, 1982, p. 413).

Natural science psychologists are perplexed by the intense concern of humanistic psychologists with the issue of *the image of man.* From their vantage point, the *image of man* is something to be discovered, not proclaimed. They also find it difficult to accept the optimistic claim that humans are basically good. Natural science psychologists find that this idealistic preconception is falsified by the realities of human history, with its bloody wars and as many examples of man's inhumanity to man as of man's goodness. The natural science psychologists conceptualize the problem of the image of man solely within a research framework. Those conditions that promote altruism, compassion, cooperation, and other forms of behavior that are considered good must be discovered, just as those variables that encourage hostility, aggression, violence, and other reactions that are judged to be bad need to be identified.

The Role of Values in Psychology

No issue divides psychologists as much as the relationships between psychological facts, on one hand, and moral principles and social policies on the other. From the days of Wundt, the idea has been advanced that psychological facts can be employed to justify ethical principles and social policies.

Wundt formulated a theory of cultural development which led to the conclusion that cultures that emphasize moral principles of heroism, duty, and spiritual ideas are superior to those that are primarily concerned with materialism, pragmatism, and commercialism. In a more indirect manner, Skinner proposes that a utopian society can be erected on the principles of operant conditioning. Maslow explicitly proposed that his research on self-actualization prescribes a set of valid ethical imperatives. All three share the view that psychological facts can dictate morality and social aims.

Many scientists, including psychologists, reject the notion that empirical results can reveal a valid moral principle or a correct social policy. To understand the logic of their position, consider an oversimplified hypothetical case.

Suppose an experiment is conducted in kindergarten classes to determine the effects of training children to be polite. The results reveal that the training is effective in encouraging politeness but has the side effect of reducing spontaneity. Let us also assume that repetitions of the experiment produce the same results. Should the new training procedures to encourage politeness be introduced in kindergarten classes? In spite of agreeing about the validity of the empirical evidence, two people could reasonably disagree about the policy that should be adopted, namely, whether to encourage politeness at the risk of inhibiting spontaneity. Policy conclusions, the argument would go, whether social or moral, cannot logically be *deduced* from data; "a policy decision is determined in light of facts, but is not deduced from them" (Passmore, 1953). If politeness is valued more than spontaneity, then the new training procedure should be instituted; if spontaneity is judged more important, then the new training procedure should not be implemented.

This example illustrates the *descriptive position* in the relationship between facts and values; psychologists should not *prescribe right* or *correct* or *valid* moral principles or social policies. To be more specific, the discipline of psychology enjoys no special moral insight into such issues as capital punishment, bilingual education, nuclear weapons, affirmative action, or abortion-on-demand. The only contribution psychologists can make is to describe the consequences of such social policies, for example, that capital punishment reduces or does not affect the incidence of murder; bilingual, in comparison to monolingual education, results in superior or inferior education, and so forth. But psychologists, with their facts, have no moral authority to dictate the correct course of action.

The *descriptive* position of the relationship between facts and values is obviously at odds with the prescriptive stance of Wundt, Skinner, and Maslow. To clarify the issues in dispute, reexamine the concept of self-actualization which plays such a central role in many humanistic conceptions.

Plato believed that people would realize their potentialities by conforming to the ideal model of the human soul. Thomas Aquinas suggested that human fulfillment could be secured by the practice of virtue and allegiance to the Church and its sacraments. Johann Fichte (1762–1814), a German idealist, assigned different meanings to self-realization as he grew older. Initially, it was attained by the acceptance of an austere moral code, then by accepting the will of God, and finally by identifying with the will of German nationalism. This latter position anticipated the extreme national chauvinism of Nazism; self-fulfillment for Germans would be achieved in conquering the world. And today many terrorists justify their actions by appealing to the need for self-fulfillment. They argue that self-fulfillment is an unobtainable goal in many societies and therefore those governments must be destroyed before a society is erected that will allow its citizens the opportunity to attain fulfillment.

Obviously, the meaning of self-fulfillment is not fixed. A person could achieve fulfillment according to one criterion, but not according to another. The reason for this difference seems obvious. Plato, Aquinas, and Fichte disagreed about the meaning of *goodness* and the *purpose* of life. In short, they were committed to different ethical goals. The significant question that is raised by this brief historical review is whether psychology can define self-fulfillment in empirical terms independent of personal and moral judgments.

Natural science psychologists would answer no, and point to Maslow's presumed scientifically confirmed set of values to justify their conclusions. The link between Maslow's behavioral and experiential characteristics of self-actualizers and the right set of values is not as direct as some might like to believe. In fact, the relationship could be simply tautological. Self-actualizers share Maslow's own value system; Maslow labels such people as the best and therefore their ethical commitments—his own, basically—become the "ultimate values which are right for mankind." Another psychologist, more enamored with pragmatists, might consider Henry Kissinger, Thomas Edison, Neil Simon, and Andrew Carnegie as examples of self-actualized individuals. Or perhaps another psychologist, fascinated with the irony of life, would suggest that both Groucho Marx and W. C. Fields were fulfilled.

Can differences about the meaning of self-actualization be resolved by empirical means? No, say natural science psychologists. The reason is that Maslow adopted a set of ethical principles in the same manner as do others who rely on some outside authority such as church or state. In truth, Maslow substituted the authority of the psychologists, in this case, himself, for that of God or government. This failing, it must be underlined, is not with the values Maslow chose to adopt, because psychologists, like other people, are entitled to choose values they consider best. The fault is with the manner in which Maslow chose to justify his value system. By insisting that his value system is demanded by psychological facts and is a consequence of a scientific analysis, Maslow misled himself as well as his audience.

Humanistic psychologists are not of one mind concerning the relationship between facts and values. A former president of the Division of Humanistic Psychology of the American Psychological Association admits that:

> there is indeed no major bridge between facts and values. No more than anyone else can psychologists prove the preferability of particular values by considerations of fact (M.B. Smith, 1978, p. 194).

Nevertheless, many humanistic psychologists argue that phenomenological reports and clinical evidence offer special insights into ethical principles. One supportive argument is that a major characteristic of people who seek psychotherapy is that they are "demoralized" (Frank, 1972). Being uncommitted to a set of values that provides life with meaning prevents them from making choices that control their destiny and hence they are forced to seek psychological help. Consequently, humanistic psychologists argue that a set of values that encourages psychological growth is intrinsically good. Although such a conclusion seems eminently reasonable it suffers from a source of ambiguity. The meaning of *psychological growth* is fairly clear when applied to early life and adolescence, but disagreements abound about its interpretation during adulthood. A child grows psychologically when becoming toilet trained, an adolescent when becoming capable of making mature decisions. Humanistic psychology, for the most part, implies an adult form of psychological maturity that is heavily weighed with value judgments. This point is expressed in May's previously quoted comment, "The musicians have something to love. You can like accounting. I don't see how you can *love* accounting." Why not? Does everybody have to share the intellectual and artistic inclinations of May and other like-minded humanistic psychologists to be considered psychologically mature? It is one thing to hypothesize that psychological growth, as Allport suggested, is directed toward meaningful goals, such as becoming a good mechanic, but quite another thing to suggest that true maturity is limited to those who share those specific values that May and Maslow hold dear.

Now that the distinction between the prescriptive and descriptive assumptions have been made and analyzed, it becomes necessary to point out that neither group, humanistic or natural science psychologists, are in complete agreement as to the appropriate stance to take in regard to the relationship between facts and values. Skinner, as one example of the natural science approach to psychology, adopts the prescriptive stance, but has been criticized for his view. At the same time, some leading humanistic psychologists question the logic of the prescriptive assumption. But for the most part, a large segment of the humanistic psychology movement accepts some form of the prescriptive assumption while the descriptive position is generally thought to be more consistent with the canons of natural science.

Contributions to Clinical and Counseling Psychology

Humanistic psychology seeks to raise people's consciousness about humanistic concerns and thereby help them cope with life's problems without sacrificing their humanity. Many techniques have been developed to achieve these goals, and they in turn have had a strong impact on three important topics: the self, the measurement of the effectiveness of psychotherapy, and the emphasis on humanistic concerns.

The Self. Humanistic psychology's emphasis on the self has assigned a central importance to the concept both in personality theory and in psychotherapy. However, this emphasis is not limited to humanistic psychology. A similiar view was reached independently by a neopsychoanalytic orientation known as ego psychology. A leading exponent of this view was Heinz Kohut (1913–1981), a German psychoanalyst, whose views bear important similarities to those of Carl Rogers.

> Both [Kohut and Rogers] have placed an important emphasis on the concept of the self, which as a perceiving, experiencing entity, is able to make choices and control its destiny. Both have been concerned with self-enhancement in the therapeutic process—Kohut in his goal of bringing the "constituents" of the self to maturity and Rogers in his attempt to bring about a greater "congruence" of the self, that is, a fuller access to the self of the experiences present in the organism. Kohut sought to remove society's derogatory attitude toward self-love (narcissism) and Rogers . . . too, has written about the "apologetic attitude" in our culture toward self-enjoyment. Finally, both, in their therapeutic work, have focused more on the self than on the self in relation to others (Kahn, 1985, p. 894).

In sum, humanistic psychology has encouraged the general view that a person's self-concept is a sort of theory about oneself. The self represents a conception of oneself that includes one's competence, morality, worth, effectiveness, and so forth. The theory can vary in terms of validity from accuracy to distortion. It can vary in generality, fluctuating from situation to situation, or remaining steady. Most of us possess at the core of our personality a fairly stable overall evaluation of ourselves. Largely because of it, we cannot change ourselves. The implication of the self theory is that personality modification requires changes in the self concept.

The Measurement of the Effectiveness of Psychotherapy. The concern with evaluating the effects of psychotherapy began with psychotherapy. Freud (1963) recognized the problem of obtaining objective indexes of the effectiveness of psychoanalysis but concluded that the task was too complex. Obtaining inadequate evidence, Freud thought, would be more misleading than no evidence at all. Behind this position was

Freud's subjective conviction that psychoanalysis was effective in most cases. Rogers, in spite of his confidence in subjective knowing, believed that objective evaluation of psychotherapy is essential, not only to measure the outcome of psychotherapy (whether improvement occurred), but perhaps more importantly, to discover what was happening during psychotherapy. Along with others, Rogers encouraged the view that psychotherapists had an obligation to objectively evaluate psychotherapy as well as to develop procedures by which this goal could be accomplished. He definitely represented a minority view among psychotherapists, especially among psychoanalysts.

Rogers's enthusiasm for, and involvement with, attempts to evaluate psychotherapy in an objective fashion have diminished with the years. His endorsement of experiential groups—"one of our most successful modern inventions"—was made without any objective evidence. In general, humanistic psychologists have ignored any need, beyond subjective testimonials, to evaluate experiential groups and other forms of therapy.

Rogers's contributions to the efforts to objectively evaluate psychotherapy are important, but it is also important to know why he abandoned this mission. Perhaps the heavy emphasis on subjectivity, which pervades humanistic psychology, became so dominant that Rogers's initial concern with objective knowing evaporated. Many humanistic psychotherapists, and others as well, believe that the subjective opinions of therapist and patient, or facilitator and client, are the truest measure of therapeutic success. This is not surprising considering that conscious experience is at the core of humanistic psychology.

Humanistic Psychology and Humanistic Concerns. Regardless of one's evaluation of humanistic psychology, one has to acknowledge its influence in shifting attention to significant problems of life that had been relatively ignored. By being committed to the goal of a natural science interpretation of behavior, traditional academic psychologists have flocked to the laboratory to conduct research in rigorously controlled experimental situations that were designed presumably to reveal basic principles of psychology—associative learning, perception, memory, motivation—but which, according to humanistic psychologists, generated findings that were far removed at best, and irrelevant at worst, to the significant experiences of human life, including the search for meaning, love, happiness, marriage, art, divorce, even dying. Admittedly, these towering human events are complex, but that is not reason, humanistic psychologists argue, that they should be ignored. Nor should it be simply assumed that they will ultimately be understood by experimental means. Perhaps they are beyond experimental clarification. If so, cannot psychologists offer insights by phenomenology, naturalistic observations, and clinical interactions?

A distinction must be made between humanistic psychology and the psychological issues that it focuses on. Natural science psychologists can admit that humanistic psychologists made an important contribution in the history of psychology by directing attention to significant psychological problems, but nevertheless deny that their treatment of the problems has any real value. This point returns us to the differences between natural and human sciences and the contributions they can each make to personal adjustment and social planning.

Human Sciences and Natural Sciences

In judging the contributions of humanistic psychology, one is ultimately forced to compare the kind of knowledge the human sciences produce with natural science information. In previous analyses the simple distinction that has been suggested is that natural science psychology has been concerned with viewing organisms from the outside (objective) with the aim of identifying the causes of their behavior while, in contrast, the goal of human science is to observe humans from the inside in order to provide a meaningful interpretation of their conscious experience. The understanding that is achieved by natural science is a deductive explanation and/or behavior control while human sciences offer a sense of understanding that results in intuitive knowing or interpretive consistency.

By proposing that a complete understanding of psychological events requires objective knowing, Rogers represents a faction of humanistic psychology that seeks to maintain ties with natural science psychology. He does this by proposing that an objective evaluation is essential for understanding psychotherapy. In spite of differences between the therapeutic methods of humanistic and other forms of psychotherapy (e.g., behavior modification), their relative effectiveness can be put to empirical test. In sum, the importance of various forms of therapy and specific techniques, such as establishing an empathic relationship, can be determined by the methods of natural science as long as objective methods of measurement are employed.

If, however, humanistic psychology adopts a purely subjective criterion of psychotherapy, then the common meeting ground between humanistic psychology and natural science psychology disappears. Each discipline then goes its own separate way and employs a conception of understanding opposed to that adopted by the other, not only for judging psychotherapy but for interpreting all psychological phenomena.

A Debate about Humanistic Psychology

Moderator: I do not expect much agreement in this debate but I do hope that the arguments will be kept within the bounds of propriety and that the differences will not be exaggerated.

Pro: I frankly believe that your suggestions cannot be heeded for the simple reason that the differences are so broad and so fundamental that they cannot be exaggerated. The fact is that the so-called natural science psychology has deceived itself, and more importantly, society, about the nature of psychology. By promising a psychology that is similar to physics, they have misled people into believing that human behavior can be precisely predicted and controlled. But after more than 100 years of psychology, these promises have not even been approached, much less fulfilled. We have no exact, effective methods of child rearing, no powerful educational techniques, no guaranteed procedures of dealing with mental health problems. Why? Because human beings are different from inanimate objects and therefore cannot be analyzed by the methods of natural science. We possess free will, a capacity to make our own choices, and therefore are beyond a strictly deterministic analysis. Instead of trying to impose an inappropriate, foreign, interpretive frame of reference on human beings, one should first recognize the uniqueness of the human mind, found not only in our consciousness but most importantly, in an awareness of ourselves as unique individuals. And within this self-consciousness, enhanced by knowledge of great art and literature, lies a capacity to know others as we know ourselves. By sharing self-knowledge the human race is capable of creating a better life for all, one in which fulfillment becomes a realizable goal.

Con: I must confess that it is incomprehensible to me that such vague and unbridled romanticism can be advocated in a serious discussion about natural science psychology and humanistic psychology. I will try to extract the meaningful points in your sermon and examine their implications. Prediction and control varies along a dimension of success from zero probability to the probability of one, from chance to a strict determinism. Natural science psychology asserts that behavior is predictable and controllable, with the level of probability being determined by the complexity of the phenomenon. Natural science psychology has developed many useful techniques to help rear children, improve education, and treat behavior disorders, although admittedly none operates at a level of absolute certainty. And it should also be noted that the application of psychological knowledge has been hampered by outside forces over which psychology has no control. For example, insufficient funds have prevented the utilization of many effective educational techniques. In addition, society is unclear about desirable behavioral outcomes: Should our educational system be planned to produce knowledgeable or well-adjusted or socially adept students? If the desired behavioral outcome is clear—to acquire mathematical skills, to design machines that are user efficient, to improve memory, to measure aptitudes for different jobs, to eliminate maladaptive forms of behavior—natural science psychology can offer much.

To suggest that humanistic psychology, with the aid of phenomenological examination, can validate moral principles and social policies represents not only a gross distortion but a socially irresponsible claim. One merely has to look at the radical forms of humanistic encounter groups to illustrate how subjective criteria of morality can spin out of control to justify an egocentric, shallow, hedonistic approach to life that is antithetical to humanistic philosophy.

I would also add that only natural science psychology meets the needs of the citizens of a political democracy who desire reliable knowledge about the consequences of competing social policies before deciding which political and social program to support. And finally, I would note that a tough-minded and clear-headed approach that resists confusing facts and values, the objective and subjective, can be more useful in achieving *humanistic* goals than would a psychology that *dictates* so-called humanistic values. Humanism is a fine philosophy of life, and I find secular humanism and existential philosophy particularly attractive not because I am a natural science psychologist, but because I find humanism's ideas and ideals congenial. But I insist that the scientific analysis of psychology and humanistic principles are unrelated and I know better than to conflate the two. One is a method of inquiry designed to understand psychological events, the other is a philosophy of life. By trying to combine them you destroy both.

Pro: Aren't you being inconsistent by rejecting offhand the moral principles underlying radical encounter groups while simultaneously rejecting the notion that natural science psychologists cannot prescribe appropriate values? In spite of your efforts to dehumanize psychology you cannot escape from your own conscious experience, which finds certain kinds of moral principles repellent. I'm not arguing that human consciousness is an absolute litmus test that distinguishes all good from all evil. But I am convinced that the consciousness of healthy humans will judge the golden rule—do unto others as you have them do unto you—to be good, and treating people differently because of their race, religion, or gender, to be morally repugnant. To suggest that psychology is incapable of discovering a psychologically sound, moral principle is to deny psychology the opportunity to make a basic contribution to society and the world.

Moderator: This debate seems endless but I will terminate it now.

SUMMARY

Humanistic psychology was launched by a group of psychologists who referred to their movement as a Third Force because of their opposition to both behaviorism and psychoanalysis, neither of which they believed interpreted human beings as truly human. The historical roots of humanistic psychology can be found in the philosophical position of *humanism*, that stresses the importance of freedom, life's meaning, and the human spirit revealed in the classics, literature, and the arts; *human sciences*, a methodological orientation that seeks to understand conscious experience; the *psychology of personality*, with special stress on the concept of the self; and *Gestalt psychology's* commitments to holism, moral optimism, and antipositivism.

The subject matter of humanistic psychology is conscious experience, but it is readily acknowledged that the experience of another person can only be approximated; it can never be known with certainty. Humanistic psychologists investigate a broad range of phenomena but mostly study personality, clinical psychology, and social psychology. The criterion of truth employed by humanistic psychology is whether the empathic interpretation of another person's conscious experience is intuitively compelling, subjectively convincing. The strategy of humanistic psychology is to develop methodological techniques appropriate to the study of human experience. A dominant strategy is that conscious experience can be more effectively studied in the clinic than in the laboratory.

Humanistic psychology does not have an official spokesman because "It is too diversified, its boundaries too vague" (Rogers, 1964). Carl Rogers, because of his professional prestige, and innovative client-centered therapy, became one of the leaders of humanistic psychology during its early stages. He distinguished among three kinds of knowing: *subjective knowing* (knowing one's own consciousness), *objective knowing* (understanding external phenomena within a natural science framework), and *interpersonal knowing* (knowledge of another person's inner experience). Rogers suggested that each kind of knowing is fallible, while maintaining that a full understanding of psychological events requires all three kinds of knowing.

Rogers's self theory emerged from his clinical experience. Finding traditional forms of psychotherapy (e.g., psychoanalysis) to be inadequate, Rogers formulated a method of treatment known as client-centered therapy (nondirective therapy) designed to create an understanding atmosphere that will encourage the client (patient) to clarify present feelings and attitudes in order to obtain a deeper self-understanding. As a result of interactions with the facilitator (therapist), the client will ultimately make choices that will lead to self-fulfillment. Rogers also developed objective methods to evaluate the effectiveness of psychotherapy.

The core ideas of Rogers's self theory are that people are basically good, the phenomenological self is the central concept in personality, and empathic understanding, open communication channels, and nonjudgmental reactions encourage the development of positive self-images.

Experiential groups became a popular form of humanistic psychology during the 1960s. A variety of techniques were employed, all of them presumably effective in raising consciousness and in achieving personal growth. Although Rogers endorsed these groups' methods, some forms of encounter groups were criticized as being more concerned with mystical experiences or pure hedonism than with psychological adjustment.

Maslow's motivational theory postulated a hierarchy of inborn needs ranging from the lowest order of physiological goadings (e.g., hunger, sex) to the highest level, the tendency for self-actualization ("to become everything that one is capable of becoming"). Maslow concluded that self-actualized people were the psychologically healthiest and therefore the moral principles they adopted are scientifically valid.

Existential psychology stresses the importance of people giving meaning to their own lives. Other forms of humanistic psychology are politically oriented in that only in certain kinds of societies will self-fulfillment be possible.

Evaluating humanistic psychology depends upon the frame of reference employed. A historical analysis indicates that the core of humanistic psychology is conscious experience. Proponents argue that experience can be effectively investigated by the methods of the human sciences. Many humanistic psychologists postulate an image of man that stresses the importance of the self, ability to make choices, and the search for a meaningful life. Natural science psychologists reject such proposals, suggesting that humanistic psychologists are behaving like ministers without collars instead of scientists. They suggest that the scientific question is to identify variables that determine different forms of behavior. Humanistic psychology, for the most part, endorses the prescriptive stance in regard to psychology's ability to propose valid moral values and social policies, while most natural science psychologists uphold the position that psychology should serve society by describing the psychological consequences of different ethical and social policies, but not prescribing, *as psychologists*, what is good or bad. The major contributions of humanistic psychology in clinical and counseling psychology is the stress placed on the importance of the self-image in psychotherapy, the early emphasis on objective measurements of the effectiveness of psychotherapy, the focus on humanistic concerns such as life's meaning, and the employment of a human science approach to psychology. The critical historical question is whether natural science and humanistic science methodologies are mutually opposed or whether they complement each other.

SUGGESTED READINGS

Insight into the variety of positions within humanistic psychology can be captured by reading Carl Rogers's *On Becoming a Person* (1961), Erich Fromm's *Escape from Freedom* (1941), and Fritz Perls's *In and Out of the Garbage Pail* (1969). Some textbooks representing a humanistic orientation are C. Bühler and M. Allen's *Introduction to Humanistic Psychology* (1972), J. Shaffer's *Humanistic Psychology,* (1978), and one that seeks to reconcile humanistic psychology with natural science psychology, H. R. Pollio's *Behavior and Existence: An Introduction to Empirical Humanistic Psychology* (1981).

Donald Polkinghorne's *Methodology for the Human Sciences* (1983) is a difficult but informative introduction to the nature of the human sciences. A series of papers, edited by T. Wann, entitled *Behaviorism and Phenomenology: Contrasting Bases for Modern Psychology* (1964), and H. H. Kendler's *Psychology: A Science in Conflict* (1981), offer a variety of answers to the relationships between the methodologies of natural science and human sciences.

13

The Legacies of the Past and Projections into the Future

The history of psychology can be likened to a road that extends over time, beginning with the founding of the first psychological laboratory by Wilhelm Wundt in 1879 and ending in the present. Our task now will be to construct a retrospective map of this road by identifying the major junctures that forced psychologists to make choices as to the direction psychology would take. One consequence of our task will be to discover whether psychology, after more than 100 years, has reached a common destination. In addition, our retrospective road map will provide clues about the directions psychology will take in the future.

THE MIND-BODY PROBLEM

Almost 300 years before Wundt established psychology as an independent discipline, Descartes anticipated four fundamental questions that would challenge psychologists: (1) Is psychology a science of the mind or behavior or both? (2) Is psychology a natural science or a human science, or some sort of hybrid science? (3) Is psychology a strictly deterministic science or must the influence of free will be acknowledged? (4) How do the mind and body interact?

The Subject Matter of Psychology

Although the mind-body dichotomy implied two subject matters—mind and behavior—it became apparent only after Wundt launched psychology as an independent science that the choice was far more complex than the mere selection of one of the two alternatives. Once psychology began operating as an independent empirical science, intricate problems came to the fore that could not have been anticipated, especially by those arm-chair philosophers who had speculated about the psychological nature of man for centuries.

The etymology of *psychology*—which in Greek means the science of the human soul or mind—would seem to dictate that psychology would begin as a mental discipline. The metaphysical and romantic *Zeitgeist* of Germany, destined to be the birthplace of the new science of psychology, also encouraged the view that psychology should be based upon the em-pirical foundations of self-observation, the direct examination of mental events. To understand the historical development of psychology requires the recognition that antimentalistic conceptions of psychology were ex-pressed in the eighteenth and nineteenth centuries, but not with suffi-cient persuasion to counteract the dominance of a mentalistic outlook.

By conceptualizing human beings as machines, the eighteenth cen-tury French philosopher, La Mettrie, expressed the belief that psychic activity has no independent reality; it is an epiphenomenon, a conse-quence of the action of the brain and the nervous system. If psychologists really desire to understand the mind, they must look into the brain. La Mettrie anticipated the views of the Russian physiologists Sechenov and later Pavlov and Bekhterev who maintained the reductionist thesis that mental events could only be understood in terms of materialistic processes within the nervous system. These three Russian physiologists influenced the development of American behaviorism by their commit-ment to a physiological reflexology and objective methods of research.

On a more sophisticated level, in the nineteenth century Comte re-jected the idea that psychology, as a mental discipline based on *observa-tions from within*, could be a natural science. Natural science methodology, the only procedure for discovering *valid facts*, demanded *objective* obser-vation, hypotheses, and experimentation. Therefore, if psychology were to aspire to the status of a natural science, psychological phenomena must be *observed from the outside*.

Thus, the first choice confronting early psychologists was that be-tween two conceptions of psychology, as the science of the mind or the science of behavior. All early psychologists chose the turn that led to a mental science, while a few philosophers and physiologists on the side-lines warned not only that the wrong choice was being made, but also that the road chosen would lead to a quagmire.

Immediately after choosing to study the mind, psychologists were faced with a new choice between competing conceptions of the *appropriate* scientific method for studying consciousness.

The Nature of Science

The views of Comte and others who believed that the methods of self-observation created serious obstacles to the pursuit of scientific knowl-edge about consciousness were more or less ignored by those who were predisposed to consider psychology as the science of the mind. Their in-difference to Comte's concerns expressed two prevailing attitudes: an op-timism that observations of consciousness could be as accurate as observations of physical events and a feeling that the scientific method, which was successful in the physical sciences, could be adapted to the psychology of the mind. At that time, science was generally considered a method for obtaining *valid* knowledge, but the method itself was not clearly understood.

Two major interpretations of the scientific method are possible, sci-ence as a single basic method or as a collection of different methods each specially designed to discover valid knowledge in different disciplines. The single-science view considers the scientific method to be a systematic mode for arriving at warranted empirical conclusions that transcends the border of different scientific disciplines. Regardless of different investi-gatory procedures used (e.g., balls rolling down an inclined plane, chem-ical reactions, comprehending a story), the criteria of empirical truth remains constant.

Scientific method can also be conceived as a set of methods, each designed to meet the special needs of specific discipline. Vico, as early as the eighteenth century, insisted that the social sciences require a different method from the physical sciences because physical events must be ob-served from the outside while human events can be observed from the inside by empathizing with, by *sharing*, the experiences of others.

The distinction between two kinds of sciences became important in Germany in the middle of the nineteenth century. *Wissenchaft* (science) was generally considered to be a disciplined research method to reveal empirical truth. The term *Geisteswissenschaften* was coined to represent the human or social sciences and to distinguish it from the traditional *Naturwissenschaften* (natural sciences). This difference has threaded its way through the entire history of psychology, beginning with Wundt and persisting to the present day in the form of a similar distinction between the *natural* and *human sciences.* Although the exact difference between the methods is subject to much debate, natural science methodology is con-sidered to be, as just noted, "A systematic mode for arriving at warranted empirical conclusions" while human sciences seek to understand con-sciousness as "we experience it."

PSYCHOLOGY AS A SCIENCE OF CONSCIOUSNESS

The decision to study mental events raised two basic questions: What method—natural or human sciences—should be used to study conscious-ness? What should be the nature, or what is technically known as the *epistemological status,* of the forthcoming evidence? Although not all the early psychologists consciously entertained these questions, their efforts provided the information for history to answer them.

Self-Observation

Descartes' suggestion that the method of self-observation, the direct examination of one's consciousness, be employed to study the mind appears to be a simple and reasonable proposal, but it failed to convey the complexities of such a method.

Wundt thought that self-observation required training and thus initiated the tradition of trained introspection. He assumed that introspection could be as valid as the physicist's perception of the outer world, an assumption that two of his more important students, Titchener and Külpe, willingly adopted. But they disagreed markedly about the requirements for accurate introspection. Wundt, for example, restricted introspection to a repeatable experimental situation in which the introspector was exposed to a constant source of physical stimulation, while both Titchener and Külpe rejected such criteria, both permitting introspective analysis of thought. The assumption of introspective accuracy was shattered by numerous competing accounts of conscious content, the most famous one being the controversy about imageless thought.

The failure to resolve the imageless thought controversy and similar conflicts produced by conflicting introspective analyses could stem from two possible sources. Either the introspective method, as employed by Wundt, Titchener, and their followers, was an inadequate method of self-observation; or no method of self-observation could yield reliable knowledge. The first alternative left open the possibility that natural science methodology could be used for the direct examination of consciousness, while the second alternative denied that possibility. William James, the "unsystematic psychologist" was to agree with each alternative.

James coined the name *the psychologist's fallacy* to refer to the "confusion of the [psychologist's] own standpoint with that of the mental fact." The discovery of discrete mental processes or elements in Wundt's laboratory did not persuade James that these basic mental processes or elements were in the mind originally. Instead, he suggested that the preconceptions of the introspectors encouraged them to appear in consciousness. Employing an orientation nearer to what would be called *phenomenology*—"unbiased scrutiny of experience" and "disciplined naiveté"—that assumes that consciousness can be accurately observed in the absence of introspective training, James failed to discover that his mental world contained assemblages of basic mental elements (processes). Instead, his stream of consciousness, as the Gestalt psychologists were to report, consisted of integrated wholes.

Unlike Wundt and Titchener, James did not assume that with proper training introspection would automatically yield a veridical account of consciousness; he said that "introspection is difficult and fallible." But he claimed that ultimately, the inevitable errors would be eliminated, as they have been in the natural sciences. Finally, according to James, consensual agreement would be reached. This historical prediction has never been confirmed. Why? Perhaps the *psychologist's fallacy* is justified in a much broader context than James originally intended. The direct examination of consciousness is *always* biased by the preconceptions of the self-observer, whether by the method of trained introspection, naive phenomenology, or any other method that seeks to examine consciousness directly. Theoretical preconceptions, cultural attitudes, linguistic orientations, and other factors govern the outputs of self-observation. As long as consciousness can only be observed by a single individual, the influence of the observer from what is observed can never be separated.

James was unable to cope decisively with the difficult methodological issue he faced by identifying the subject matter of psychology to be the mind, self-observation to be the method, and a natural science psychology to be the goal. Finally, almost in desperation, James admitted to doubts about the natural science status of psychology: psychologists should never "forget that the natural science assumptions with which we started are provisional and revisable things."

In essence, James was questioning the choice that early psychologists, such as Wundt, Titchener, and Külpe had made that natural science methodology was appropriate for the direct examination of consciousness. One can speculate that the methodological stresses and strains within psychology forced James to flee from psychology to the safe haven of philosophy, where he could deal with all facets of human experience and behavior without being restricted by empirical considerations.

Although James fled from psychology, his functional orientation, with its broad range of interests, persisted. Although generally accepting the notion that psychology was the science of the mind, consciousness was conceptualized differently by the functionalist than by the structuralists. Whereas Titchener was interested in the experiential qualities of consciousness—its content—James and the functionalists viewed consciousness more as an activity with adaptive functions. Carr, who was the most empirically productive of the Chicago functionalists, described psychology as "primarily concerned with the study of mental activity." He hastened to add that "mental acts may be subjectively or objectively observed." Carr admitted that each form of observation has advantages and disadvantages. Self-observation can provide "intimate . . . knowledge of mental events," but such observations are impossible to verify because of their private nature. Behavioral data, although meeting the standards of objective evidence, fail to be a valid source of subjective experience. Carr, true to the pragmatism of functionalism, resolves the conflict by adopting the position that "Psychology, like the other sciences, utilizes any fact that is significant for its purposes, irrespective of how or where or by whom it was obtained (1925)." But he overlooked the possibility that when judging psychological theories, one form of data—private examination of conscious experience or public observation of behavior—must have priority.

To continue the retrospective analysis of the method of self-observation, reference must be made to Freudian psychology and related psychoanalytic systems that are within the traditions of mental psychology that employ self-observation as the primary investigatory procedure. The mind, admittedly much more complex than the one envisioned by academic psychologists, is the subject matter of psychology and, in principle, could be accurately observed with proper training. In addition, Freud shared with Wundt, Titchener, and James the assumption that the direct examination of mental processes could be conducted according to the methods of natural science. "Psychoanalysis is a part of the mental science of psychology [which] . . . is a natural science. What else can it be?" (1933) Finally, it should be noted that psychoanalysis expanded the implications of the criticism of the *psychologist's fallacy*. Any kind of self-observation, introspection, or phenomenology, could be distorted by unconscious processes. But, so can psychoanalytic reports. Freud recognized the danger of oversuggesting ideas to patients, but nevertheless insisted that it was the psychoanalyst's responsibility to "boldly demand confirmation" by patients of the sexual etiology of their psychological disorders. Thus, Freud implicitly recognized the dangers of committing the psychologist's fallacy, but minimized the tendency of psychoanalytic techniques to encourage such errors.

Finally, it becomes necessary to mention the views of William Dilthey to complete our retrospective analysis of self-observation. He essentially suggests that training *is necessary* to practice naive phenomenology. To understand a person's consciousness demands an intimate acquaintance with the social and cultural context in which that person lives.

Self-Observation: A Summing Up.   Looking back down the road it seems that those psychological systems that chose the mind as the object of inquiry and self-observation as the method of investigation met another major junction—whether to go the way of trained introspection or naive phenomenology. But soon after making this choice, regardless of which it was, the road forked again and again because of the numerous options each method offered. Because the results of self-observation are influenced by the *specific* method of trained introspection or naive phenomenology, the essential nature of conciousness and the mind was never even crudely approximated by the variety of the methods employed. Two interrelated factors are responsible for this failure. First and foremost is the intrinsic privacy of any method of self-observation; only the experiencing individual can observe his or her consciousness. Second is the psychologist's fallacy; observation of mental events is contaminated by preconceptions about the nature of the mind, and it may be that preconceptions are unavoidable.

PSYCHOLOGY AS A BEHAVIORAL SCIENCE

The failure of the general method of self-observation to yield reliable knowledge encouraged the development of methodological behaviorism.

At the most elementary level, behaviorism replaced the mind with behavior as the object of observation. By so doing, psychology became a science that employed intersubjective, in place of intrasubjective, observations, and thereby began to resemble the natural sciences.

The Role of the Mind in Methodological Behaviorism

Replacing the mind with behavior did not, however, generate agreement on the role of conciousness in a behavioristic psychology, as a brief review of behaviorism, and the neobehaviorisms it spawned, will illustrate. Although Watson had initially acknowledged that conciousness is "the instrument or tool with which all scientists work," later, in his effort to completely extirpate the mind from psychology, he adopted the absurd position of metaphysical behaviorism—that conciousness does not exist.

Hull, like Watson during his early days, recognized that conciousness played an essential role in scientific observations but was suspicious of its possible role in scientific explanation. Employing common sense mentalistic interpretations, Hull argued, would place insurmountable obstacles in the way of judging scientific theories. To avoid any subjective contamination of objective theoretical explanations, Hull proposed to regard the behaving organism, human or subhuman, "as a completely self-maintaining robot, constructed of materials as unlike ourselves as may be."

Tolman (1932) offered a form of cognitive behaviorism that directly opposed Watson's antimentalism and Hull's mechanistic strategy without abandoning methodological behaviorism. He illustrated how a behaviorist could employ common sense phenomenology as a core of a theory. But the criterion of a theory's validity was not how well it reflected inner experience but rather how capable it was of generating logical deductions that agreed with behavioral evidence.

While rejecting all traditional forms of self-observation, Skinner insists that radical behaviorism does "consider events taking place in the private world within the skin." Private events for Skinner are qualitatively similar to overt behavior. Therefore, laws that govern overt behavior will also govern inner behavior. In essence, Skinner offers the unusual argument that mental events cannot be understood unless behavior is understood.

Hebb denies any contradiction in the idea that psychologists must study the mind and behavior. "All psychology has become behavioristic in the sense that it depends for its facts on the objective record," (Hebb, 1966). For Hebb, the *mind* is a theoretical construct to be explained by the operating characteristics of the brain.

The important point for those natural science psychologists, who believe that a model of the mind is necessary, is to heed the advice of Kurt Koffka, one member of the triumvirate that launched the phenomenologically oriented Gestalt psychology:

> Although psychology was reared as the science of consciousness or mind, we shall use behaviour as our keystone. . . . if we start with behaviour it is easier to find a place for consciousness and mind than it is to find a place for behaviour if we start with mind or consciousness (Koffka, 1935, p. 25).

In line with the gestalt research strategy it should also be noted that phenomenological analysis need not be considered to be in opposition to methodological behaviorism. Gestalt psychology, as well as those early sensory physiologists such as Hering and Purkinje, illustrated that the phenomenological description of experience can serve as a useful *starting point* in constructing objective behavioral theories. In sum, the juncture faced by psychologists between studying the mind or behavior does not mean that the choice of behavior as the dependent variable excludes any consideration of mental processes. Behavior can be the object of inquiry while a theoretical model of the mind can serve as the essential link in interpreting and predicting behavior.

The early psychologists, as well as modern humanistic psychologists, assign primacy to the direct examination of consciousness in preference to overt behavior. But overt behavior can and has been used by Wundt and modern humanistic therapists to infer mental processes. Such inferences, however, are judged by different standards than those employed by methodological behaviorists, including most cognitive psychologists, when evaluating theoretical models of the mind. The former are concerned with whether the inferred mental states accurately reflect consciousness while the latter are interested in whether specific models of the mind accurately predict behavior.

UNDERSTANDING

Another major crossroad occurs at the point where a choice is made about the criteria of *understanding*. Strikingly different choices have been made, none of which can be claimed to reach the destination of *ultimate truth*. The history of psychology has been dominated by four different views of psychological truth:

1. *Deductive explanation*—understanding is achieved when an event is deduced from one or more general propositions—is the form of comprehension commonly associated with natural science methodology. The essential characteristic of a deductive scientific theory is that the formulation is capable of generating deductions (predictions or postdictions) that can be judged in a public manner as to their consistency with empirical evidence. Deductive theories vary in two basic ways: First, they vary in the logical rigor of the deductive process. Hull was the most forceful exponent of the strategy that deductive theories must be formulated in a strictly mathematical fashion even though his own efforts fell short of his stated objective. The Hullian conception of deductive theories is presently being pursued by those psychologists (e.g., Luce, 1985) who are explicitly committed to mathematical representation of psychological processes. Sharing this allegiance to logical rigor are those theorists who formulate theories in the form of computer programs, although the exact relationship between such theories and those that employ mathematical representation is a subject of debate.

The second point at issue among deductive theorists is whether a theory should interpret psychological events with a neurophysiological frame of reference (e.g., Hebb) or merely represent abstract psychological processes completely isolated from neurophysiology (e.g., Tolman).

Finally, it should be noted that some early mental psychologists (e.g., Wundt) occasionally employed a deductive form of understanding to interpret mental processes by inferring them from experimental results, a theoretical procedure that was adopted later by Tolman and cognitive psychologists.

2. *Behavioral control*—behavior is understood when it can be controlled—is the form of understanding that is mostly associated with radical behaviorism. Although most experimental psychologists find this conception shallow, they nevertheless acknowledge that it is consistent with the canons of natural science, because propositions about controlling behavior can be publicly evaluated.

3. *Interpretive consistency*—understanding is achieved by interpreting phenomena within a coherent conception that is immune to any possible falsification—raises many complex issues, primarily because it reveals the vague border line that separates natural from human sciences. A formulation that is incapable of being falsified does not mean that it cannot, in principle, be modified to qualify as a natural science theory. Thus, the hope springs eternal for many psychoanalytically oriented psychologists that Freudian theory and the numerous variations it generated can be formulated into a deductive theory that can be evaluated by its capacity to predict empirical evidence. At the same time, other psychoanalytically oriented psychologists frankly reject any attempt to modify psychoanalytical theories in the direction of natural science formulations. These psychologists frankly reject "naively objectivist" interpretations. Psychoanalytical formulations, for them, offer meaningful interpretations of human existence which cannot be matched or even approached by deductive natural science theories. In essence, they are proposing that the test of a psychological theory is not in its ability to rigorously integrate empirical evidence, but instead to offer a compelling, meaningful interpretation of the human condition that is relevant to an individual's life.

4. *Intuitive knowing*—a subjective conviction of understanding—represents pure understanding in the absence of any independent criterion. It is based on a conviction that some propositions—such as people are basically good—are true because phenomenological experience confirms it. Intuitive knowing, as a form of understanding, is implicit in the oft-repeated phrase, "Psychology is an art," and justifies the position that some psychologists are endowed with special insight into the minds of others.

Consensual Agreement and Modes of Understanding

History has demonstrated that psychologists have employed different standards of understanding. To insist that one form of understanding is more valid than others would be impossible to confirm because of the absence of any absolute criterion of understanding. This conclusion does not mean that the different conceptions of understanding are equally good or valuable; it only suggests that they are fundamentally different.

The four forms of understanding can be differentiated in terms of the public nature of the criteria employed. *Deductive explanation* and *behavioral control* emphasize public criteria that yield a higher level of consensual agreement than do the subjectively based form of *interpretive consistency* and *intuitive knowing.* This does not mean that consensual agreement is always forthcoming if *deductive explanation* or *behavioral control* is adopted as a criterion of understanding, but with time, effort, and technical developments, the goal tends to be approached. By the same token, the purely subjective characteristic of *interpretive consistency* and *intuitive knowing* prevents consensual agreement. Nevertheless, they serve the need of some psychologists to provide insights into human experience better than *deductive explanation* or *behavioral control.*

PSYCHOLOGY AND SOCIETY

Another important juncture in the road that represents the history of psychology is between two different social roles. Should psychology adopt the epistemological principle that facts and values are *logically* dissociated and the consequence that psychology cannot prescribe a set of valid ethical principles and correct social policies? Or is psychology a *prescriptive* science, with special techniques and privileged information that permits the identification of valid ethical beliefs and correct social policies? The role of psychology has recently become a dominant issue as a result of psychology's rapid growth as a profession and government's reliance on scientific knowledge in the formulation of social policy.

Descriptive versus Prescriptive Views of Psychology

From its beginnings as an independent discipline, psychology was concerned with the problem of judging moral and social values. Wilhelm Wundt sponsored a prescriptive psychology that recommended ethical imperatives for nations. His prescriptive stance was an outgrowth of his commitment to German idealistic philosophy and his conception of social psychology as a human science. His analysis of historical events led him to conclude that evolutionary principles govern cultural development. Cultures could be judged by the organic unity that was achieved in balancing the needs of the state and its citizens. Applying this criterion, he argued that Germany had achieved a level of unity higher than both Great Britain and the United States, because heroism, duty, and spiritual ideals are superior to materialism, pragmatism, and commercialism.

Numerous attempts have been made by psychologists (e.g., Maslow, Skinner) to recommend moral principles and social policies as psychologically true or scientifically valid. At the same time, vigorous opposition to the prescriptive stance has been enunciated by others; scientists "best serve the public by living within the ethics of science, not those of politics" (Handler, 1980), and "My central and harsh thesis is that it is *wrong* . . . for [psychologists] to imply or suggest or not to deny that the discipline of psychology enjoys special standing in the realm of moral discourse. It is wrong because it is fraudulent" (Robinson, 1984). Accurate description of empirical results, not prescription of social policies and moral principles, is the responsibility of a psychologist in society.

GENERAL HISTORICAL CONCLUSIONS

The analysis of the history of psychology indicates a variety of methodological approaches, particularly in regard to its subject matter, criterion of truth, and social role. The variety raises the question as to whether psychology is a unified discipline or a collection of different disciplines. One possible argument in favor of retaining the unity of psychology is that various segments, when combined, offer a complete version that is beyond the grasp of any individual component. Only by studying the mind and behavior, and achieving understanding by deductive explanation, interpretive consistency, behavioral control, and intuitive knowing can one achieve a full sense of psychological understanding.

This holistic conception has had little appeal. Leading psychologists like Wundt, James, Carr, Freud, and Rogers attempted some form of reconciliation of divergent methodological orientations but none have been widely accepted.

All of them, in one way or another, failed to provide any compelling resolution of the methodological conflicts between the private observation of consciousness and the public observation of behavior. Nor were they able to propose a satisfactory solution to apparently incompatible forms of understanding, such as deductive explanation and/or behavioral control versus interpretive consistency and/or intuitive knowing. What would be true for one form of understanding, subjective or objective, would be false or meaningless for the other.

When a unified conception of psychology is rejected, one is confronted with a "volitional bifurcation" (Reichenbach, 1938) that requires a choice between forms of psychology that lead to different kinds of knowledge and social application. The decisions themselves cannot be judged in terms of their truth; they are choices, basically, of alternative life styles within psychology. One major choice is some form of natural science psychology, which some would equate with methodological behaviorism, that can range from one extreme of a mechanistic conception that totally ignores mental processes to the other extreme of a model of the mind that is inferred from behavioral evidence. The other major choice is a humanistic conception of human life as experienced.

THE FUTURE

An understanding of the past provides a glimpse into the future. By identifying significant historical trends and charting their course, one can conjecture about some of the directions that psychology will take in decades to come. Four important topics will now be discussed with the full realization that they represent only a small segment of psychology's future.

Cognitive Psychology

Cognitive psychology is presently the dominant theoretical orientation. There is every reason to believe that its preeminent position will be retained for decades to come although the enthusiasm the new paradigm originally evoked is being tempered by the grim challenges it faces. Will cognitive psychology ever achieve a theoretical unity? The boundless number of cognitive minitheories have failed to coalesce into more general conceptions that are needed to transform the isolated trees in the landscape into an integrated forest. Will this transformation occur or do the intrinsic properties of cognitive psychology encourage isolated minitheories at the expense of general conceptions?

Serious attempts are being made at formulating more general conceptions and the future should answer whether any of the strategies will prove successful. One of several strategies is to simply consider the contemporary plethora of minitheories as a normal historical development. Self-conscious efforts to formulate general theories before sufficient progress has been made with minitheories will only yield failure. Time and talent will ultimately overcome the extreme specificity of cognitive theories.

Another general strategy is to equate cognitive psychology with computer programming of information processing with the expectation that the rigorousness of such an approach will yield more general theories. In attaining this goal, two computer strategies have been suggested: either attempt to simulate human cognition or develop the most effective forms of artificial intelligence with the expectation that the information gained will throw light on human mental processes.

Recently, it has been proposed that the narrowness of cognitive theories is an inevitable outcome of the limited control researchers have over basic cognitive processes. In other words, *black box* theories, however ingenious they may be, can only yield crude empirical laws that cannot support a general theoretical formulation. To formulate a general cognitive theory demands more direct *control* over information processing. This requires knowledge about how the brain processes information. When that relationship is understood, a general cognitive theory will become possible. In reaching such a goal, the suggestion has been offered that collaboration with other cognitive scientists—such as mathematicians, neuroscientists, and physicists—will be required.

Neuropsychology

Psychology and physiology are obviously related. Consciousness depends on brain function; when a person suffers an intense blow to the head or is asphyxiated the experience of consciousness disappears. The hallucinating schizophrenic regains contact with reality when given an appropriate neuroleptic drug, a medication with antipsychotic properties. Similarly other drugs, like LSD, can induce hallucinations in a person who never suffered from them. Behavior is intimately related to neurophysiology; damage to parts of the general area of the lateral frontal side of the cortex produces disordered language behavior known as aphasia. For example, a specific brain injury has been known to eliminate a person's ability to speak or understand a foreign language but not his ability in his native tongue. Some brain lesions result in expressive aphasia; a person cannot say what he wants to say even though capable of identifying one of several sentences that expresses his idea. One kind of receptive aphasia produced by lesions in a specific area of the brain makes it possible to hear speech sounds, but the words are as incomprehensible as if they were in a strange language.

Evidence of this sort suggests that psychology requires a neurophysiological orientation. But some psychologists have rejected this position, insisting that psychology should be studied independently of neurophysiology. The independence of the two disciplines has been stressed both by psychologists who are concerned with the mind (e.g., Titchener, Rogers) and those who study behavior (e.g., Skinner). The justification for treating consciousness independently of neurophysiology is simply that the essence of conscious experience is not revealed by the underlying neurophysiological processes. Although mood controlling drugs such as antidepressants can control conscious experiences, such knowledge of the relationship, the argument goes, contributes nothing to the description of the experience itself. In a somewhat different vein, black box behaviorists argue that an interpretation of behavior does not require any knowledge of neurophysiological changes.

These negative views about the role of physiology in understanding psychological events have always had their supporters, from the time of Wundt on. However, the historical trend in recent decades, especially due to gigantic advances in biotechnology and psychopharmacology, has definitely been in the direction of shifting neurophysiology onto the center stage of psychology. While the argument that knowledge of the relationship between neurophysiology and the mind fails to illuminate the essence of consciousness is still persuasive, the position that the study of behavior can ignore neurophysiology is steadily being weakened. For example, psychophysical research in sensory psychology was popular during the first half of the twentieth century, but today the theoretical analysis of sensory processes demands consideration of neurophysiological mechanisms. Recent history suggests that the same situation will soon prevail for other fields as well (e.g., perception, learning, behavior pathology). In fact, the argument can be advanced that the neuroscientific approach to psychology must be encouraged if psychologists adopt James's pragmatic evaluation of the *cash value* of ideas. Six and one half *billion* dollars were saved in mental health costs in the first decade following the introduction of the neuroleptic drug, lithium (Reifman & Wyatt, 1980), which has proved effective in the treatment of manic and depressive reactions.

The projection into the future is clear in regard to theories of behavior; they will become increasingly involved with neurophysiological processes. And one may also speculate that in spite of the sharp distinction between phenomenology and neurophysiology, research on psychoactive drugs will offer interesting insights into conscious experience.

Psychotherapy

In spite of continuing controversies about the effectiveness of psychotherapy—talk therapy—this form of psychological treatment is destined to retain some of its popularity. Why is psychotherapy so popular? If the notion that behavior that is rewarding persists, is valid, then the conclusion is inevitable that psychotherapy is reinforcing in spite of the absence of compelling evidence in favor of psychotherapy's effectiveness. There are several possible reasons for this popularity:

1. A successful and widely respected artist, on a well-known talk show, readily admitted that his psychoanalysis had not modified his anxiety, tics, and other forms of neurotic behavior, but nevertheless it made him feel better and enabled him to unleash his creativity. Patients, for the most part, offer positive phenomenological evidence in support of psychotherapy. As long as patients judge psychological treatment in a subjective manner, a need will prevail for psychotherapists.

2. Various forms of psychological treatment, ranging from one-on-one psychotherapy to experiential groups, function sometimes as a form of spiritual guidance, or an exposure to a new life style, rather than a direct form of treatment. Psychotherapy can offer meaningful interpretations of human existence as illustrated by the suggestion that Freud gives a picture of the human condition that has an essential validity. However persuasive Freud's conception is, some people will be drawn to other interpretations of the human condition such as those offered by Jung, Adler, Maslow, Rogers, or some pop psychologists, many of whom appear on television. Psychotherapists have offered pictures of the human condition varying in complexity, depth, and ethical commitment, and they all have been successful in finding an audience that considers their particular interpretation to possess an essential validity. The popularity of psychological treatment may be due in part to the common search for a convincing picture of the meaning of life:

> "we are witnessing the rise of the psychotherapist as the new shaman, explanation giver, the guru. Psychology flourishes as the new myth system" (Albee, 1977, p. 151).

3. Psychological treatment, particularly experiental groups, provide opportunities for strong emotional and mystical experiences that many people seek. Furthermore, experiential groups can be fun and lead to close relationships. And, if the person who wants to participate cannot accept a hedonistic interpretation of experiential groups, he or she can always justify them in terms of their own need for personal growth (Back, 1972).

Evaluation Research

Social psychology can play an important role in society by providing reliable knowledge about the psychological consequences of different social policies, a form of investigation that is known as *evaluation research.*

Psychologists who adopt a descriptive stance in which facts and values are logically dissociated bemoan the failure of society and government to fully appreciate the potential contributions of psychological research for efficient and effective social planning. Evidence from psychological research makes possible a sophisticated evaluation of a social program that is in force or before it is widely implemented.

More likely than not however, evaluation research of any program, such as bilingual education, will yield results that are neither simple nor unequivocal. Social phenomena of the sort that evaluation research seeks to understand are exceedingly complex, typically involving a variety of behavioral outcomes. For example, bilingual education may produce lower efficiency in communicating in English while increasing ethnic identification. Society then has to decide which factor is more important and whether some new technique can be introduced to retain the beneficial results while minimizing or eliminating undesirable outcomes. But, regardless of what the results are, the importance of evaluation research is that social planning will be based on *informed* decision making.

One possible scenario that may gain acceptance in the future is the appointment of a select committee of distinguished psychologists to make recommendations to government. A review of available evidence and/or the results of new research can yield useful information about the psychological consequences of a particular social program. The select committee procedure has been successfully employed in the health sciences in solving such medical problems as identifying dangerous carcinogens in food additives. The same procedure for social decisions can yield a rich harvest for both society and psychology.

A FINAL THOUGHT

Wilhelm Wundt considered psychology to be the propaedeutic science. By this, he meant that psychology served as the foundation of the physical sciences because scientific knowledge is based upon human observation and subjective mental processes. In a similar sense, psychology is basic to all the social sciences because in one way or another they each involve the activities of human minds. One can easily accept Wundt's judgment of the importance of psychology without necessarily ascribing to his conception of psychology. Psychology, conceptualized as the science of mind or behavior, or both, is at the center of human concerns. Everything—art, literature, science, politics, society, education, existence—contains a psychological core.

The importance of psychology cannot be denied. Unfortunately, importance does not automatically generate understanding. In spite of the development of an arsenal of sophisticated research techniques that have and will continue to add to our ever increasing body of knowledge, a universally accepted, integrated view of psychology has yet to be achieved. Two major obstacles to this goal have been the overwhelming complexity of psychological phenomena and the unsettled debate about the nature of psychology itself.

Whether psychology should strive in the future for unity or readily admit to a fundamental disunity is a source of much controversy. Regardless of what the future brings, psychology, as a science and profession, will always retain its intrinsic interest and vital importance, and therefore will continually challenge the human intellect and spirit.

REFERENCES

ABBAGNANO, N. (1967). Humanism (N. Langiulli, Trans.). In P. Edwards (Ed.), *The encyclopedia of philosophy.* (Vol. 4). New York: Macmillan & The Free Press.

ADLER, A. (1930). Individual psychology. In C. Murchison (Ed.), *Psychologies of 1930.* Worcester, MA: Clark University Press.

ALBEE, G. (1977). The protestant ethic, sex, and psychotherapy. *American Psychologist, 32,* 150–161.

ALLEN, G. W. (1967). *William James: A biography.* New York: Viking.

ALLPORT, G. W. (1937). *Personality: A psychological interpretation.* New York: Holt, Rinehart & Winston.

ALLPORT, G. W. (1946). Geneticism *versus* ego-structure in theories of personality. *British Journal of Educational Psychology, 16,* 57–58.

ALLPORT, G. W. (1955). *Becoming.* New Haven, CT: Yale University Press.

AMSEL, A. (1962). Frustrative nonreward in partial reinforcement and discrimination learning. *Psychological Review, 69,* 306–328.

AMSEL, A. & RASHOTTE, M. E. (1984). *Mechanisms of adaptive behavior: Clark L. Hull's theoretical papers with commentary.* New York: Columbia University Press.

ANGELL, J. R. (1904). *Psychology.* New York: Holt, Rinehart & Winston.

ANGELL, J. R. (1907). The province of functional psychology. *Psychological Review, 14,* 61–91.

ANGELL, J. R. (1920). *An introduction to psychology.* New York: Holt, Rinehart & Winston.

ANGELL, J. R. (1932). James Rowland Angell. In C. Murchison (Ed.), *A history of psychology in autobiography.* New York: Russell.

ANGELL, J. R. & MOORE, A. W. (1896). Reaction time: A study in attention and habit. *Psychological Review, 3,* 245–258.

ASCH, S. E. (1968a). Wolfgang Köhler: 1887–1967. *The American Journal of Psychology, 81,* 110–119.

ASCH, S. E. (1968b). Gestalt theory. In D. L. Sills (Ed.), *International encyclopedia of the social sciences,* Vol. 6. New York: Macmillan & The Free Press.

ATKINSON, R. C. (1977). Reflections on psychology's past and concerns about its future. *American Psychologist, 32,* 205–210.

ATKINSON, R. C. & SHIFFRIN, R. M. (1977). Human memory: A proposed system and its control processes. In G. H. Bower (Ed.), *Human memory: Basic processes.* New York: Academic Press.

ATTNEAVE, F. (1954). Some informational aspects of visual perception. *Psychological Review, 61,* 183–193.

BABKIN, B. P. (1949). *Pavlov: A biography.* Chicago: University of Chicago Press.

BACK, K. W. (1972). *Beyond words. The story of sensitivity training and the encounter movement.* New York: Basic Books.

BAKAN, D. (1958). *Sigmund Freud and the Jewish mystical tradition.* Princeton, NJ: Van Nostrand-Reinhold.

BAKAN, D. (1966). Behaviorism and American urbanization. *Journal of the History of the Behavioral Sciences, 2*, 5–28.

BARTLETT, F. C. (1932). *Remembering: A study in experimental and social psychology.* Cambridge: Cambridge University Press.

BECK, A. T. (1976). *Cognitive therapy and the emotional disorders.* New York: International Universities Press.

BERGMANN, G. (1943). Psychoanalysis and experimental psychology: A review from the standpoint of scientific empiricism. *Mind, 52*, 122–140.

BERGMANN, G. (1956). The contributions of John B. Watson. *Psychological Review, 63*, 265–276.

BIRCH, H. G. (1945). The relation of previous experience to insightful problem-solving. *Journal of Comparative Psychology, 38*, 367–383.

BLIGHT, J. G. (1981). Must psychoanalysis retreat to hermeneutics? Psychoanalytic theory in the light of Popper's evolutionary epistemology. *Psychoanalysis and Contemporary Thought, 4*, 147–205.

BLUMENTHAL, A. L. (1970). *Language and psychology: Historical aspects of psycholinguistics.* New York: John Wiley & Sons.

BLUMENTHAL, A. L. (1975). A reappraisal of Wilhelm Wundt. *American Psychologist, 11*, 1081–1088.

BLUMENTHAL, A. L. (1977). *The process of cognition.* Englewood Cliffs, NJ: Prentice-Hall.

BLUMENTHAL, A. L. (1985). Wilhelm Wundt: Psychology as the propaedeutic science. In C. E. Buxton (Ed.), *Points of view in the modern history of psychology.* New York: Academic Press.

BOAG, P. T. & GRANT, P. R. (1981). Intense natural selection in a population of Darwin's Finches (geospizinae) in the Galápagos. *Science, 214*, 82–85.

BOE, E. E. & CHURCH, R. M. (1967). Permanent effects of punishment during extinction. *Journal of Comparative and Physiological Psychology, 63*, 486–492.

BORING, E. G. (1929). *A history of experimental psychology.* New York: Appleton-Century-Crofts.

BORING, E. G. (1942). *Sensation and perception in the history of experimental psychology.* New York: Appleton-Century-Crofts.

BORING, E. G. (1950). *A history of experimental psychology* (2nd ed.). Englewood Cliffs, NJ: Prentice-Hall.

BOUSFIELD, W. A. (1953). The occurrence of clustering in the recall of randomly arranged associates. *Journal of General Psychology, 49*, 229–240.

BRELAND, K. & BRELAND, M. (1961). The misbehavior of organisms. *American Psychologist, 16*, 681–684.

BRELAND, K. & BRELAND, M. (1966). *Animal behavior.* New York: Macmillan.

BRENTANO, F. (1874/1925). Psychologie vom empirischen standpunkt (3rd ed.). [Psychology from an empirical standpoint] Leipzig: F. Meiner, 1925.

BREUER, J. & FREUD, S. (1895). *Studies in hysteria.* Leipzig: Franz Deuticke.

BRILL, A. A. (Ed.). (1938). *The basic writings of Sigmund Freud.* New York: Modern Library.

BRINGMANN, W. & TWENEY, R. D. (1980). *Wundt studies: A centennial collection.* Toronto: C. J. Hogrefe.

BROWN, R. W. (1973). *A first language; the early stages.* Cambridge, MA: Harvard University Press.

BRUNER, J. S. (1980). Jerome S. Bruner. In G. Lindzey (Ed.), *A history of psychology in autobiography.* Vol. 7. San Francisco: W. A. Freeman.

BRUNER, J. S., GOODNOW, J. J., & AUSTIN, G. A. (1956). *A study of thinking.* New York: John Wiley & Sons.

BÜHLER, C. & ALLEN, M. (1972). *Introduction to humanistic psychology.* Monterey, CA: Brooks/Cole.

CARR, H. (1917a). The nature of mental process. *Psychological Review, 24,* 181–187.

CARR, H. (1917b). The relation between emotion and its expression. *Psychological Review, 24,* 369–375.

CARR, H. (1925). *Psychology.* New York: Longmans, Green and Co.

CATTELL, J. McK. (1928). Early psychological laboratories. In M. L. Reymert (Ed.), *Feelings and emotions; the Wittenberg Symposium.* Worcester, MA: Clark University Press.

CHAPANIS, A., GARNER, W. R. & MORGAN, C. T. (1949). *Applied experimental psychology.* New York: John Wiley & Sons.

CHOMSKY, N. (1959). A review of B. F. Skinner's *Verbal Behavior. Language, 35,* 26–58.

CHOMSKY, N. (1964). *Current issues in linguistic theory.* The Hague: Mouton.

CHOMSKY, N. (1965). *Aspects of the theory of syntax.* Cambridge, MA: MIT Press.

CHOMSKY, N. (1968). *Language and mind.* New York: Harcourt Brace Jovanovich.

CLARK, R. W. (1980). *Freud: The man and the cause.* New York: Random House.

CONRAD, D. G., ELSMORE, T. F., & SODETZ, F. J. (1972). Tetrahydrocannabinol: Dose-related effects on timing behavior in chimpanzees. *Science, 175,* 547–550.

CONRAD, R. (1964). Acoustic confusions and memory span for words. *Nature, 197,* 1029–1030.

COOPER, L. A. & SHEPARD, R. N. (1973). Chronometric studies of the rotation of mental images. In W. G. Chase (Ed.), *Visual information processing.* New York: Academic Press.

CORDES, C. (1984). Easing toward perfection at Twin Oaks. *APA Monitor, 15*(11), 1–31.

COX, C. M. (1926). *Genetic studies of genius. Vol. 2. The early mental traits of three hundred geniuses.* Stanford, CA: Stanford University Press.

CRAIK, F. I. M. & LOCKHART, R. S. (1972). Levels of processing: A framework for memory research. *Journal of Verbal Learning and Verbal Behavior, 11,* 671–684.

CRESPI, L. P. (1942). Quantitative variation of incentive and performance in the white rat. *American Journal of Psychology, 55,* 467–517.

CUNNINGHAM, S. (1985a). Humanists celebrate gains, goals. *APA Monitor, 16,*(5), 16 & 18.

CUNNINGHAM, S. (1985b). Rollo May: the case for love, beauty and the humanities. *APA Monitor, 16,*(5), 17.

DANZIGER, K. (1979). The positivist repudiation of Wundt. *Journal of the History of the Behavioral Sciences, 15,* 205–230.

DANZIGER, K. (1980a). The history of introspection reconsidered. *Journal of the History of the Behavioral Sciences, 16,* 241–262.

DANZIGER, K. (1980b). Wundt's theory of behavior and volition. In R. W. Rieber (Ed.), *Wilhelm Wundt and the making of a scientific psychology.* New York: Plenum Press.

DARWIN, F. (1887). *The life and letters of Charles Darwin,* including an autobiographical chapter (3 vols.). London: John Murray.

DE GROOT, A. (1965). *Thought and choice in chess.* The Hague: Mouton.

DEWEY, J. (1886). *Psychology.* New York: Harper.

DEWEY, J. (1896). The reflex arc concept in psychology. *Psychological Review, 3,* 357–370.

DEWEY, J. (1900). Psychology and social practice. *Psychological Review, 7,* 105–124.

DEWEY, J. & DEWEY, E. (1915). *Schools of to-morrow.* New York: E. P. Dutton.

DIAMOND, S. (1980a). Wundt before Leipzig. In R. W. Rieber (Ed.), *Wilhelm Wundt and the making of scientific psychology.* New York: Plenum Press.

DIAMOND, S. (1980b). Francis Galton and American psychology. In R. W. Rieber & K. Salzinger (Eds.), *Psychology: Theoretical-historical perspectives.* New York: Academic Press.

DOLLARD, J. & MILLER, N. E. (1950). *Personality and psychotherapy.* New York: McGraw-Hill.

DULANY, D. E. (1968). Awareness, rules and propositional control: A confrontation with S-R behavior theory. In T. R. Dixon & D. L. Horton (Eds.), *Verbal behavior and general behavior theory.* Englewood Cliffs, NJ: Prentice-Hall.

EBBINGHAUS, H. (1885/1964). *Memory: A contribution to experimental psychology.* New York: Dover.

EFRON, A. (1985). The sexual body: An interdisciplinary perspective. *The Journal of Mind and Behavior, 6,* 1 & 2.

ELLENBERGER, H. F. (1970). *The discovery of the unconscious.* New York: Basic Books.

ELLIS, W. D. (1950). *A source book of gestalt psychology.* New York: The Humanities Press.

ERICSSON, K. A. & SIMON, H. A. (1984). *Protocol analysis: Verbal reports as data.* Cambridge, MA: MIT Press.

ESTES, W. K. (1944). An experimental study of punishment. *Psychological Monographs, 57,* 263.

ESTES, W. K. (1959). The statistical approach to learning theory. In S. Koch (Ed.), *Psychology: A study of a science.* Vol. 2. New York: McGraw-Hill.

EVANS, R. B. (1972). Titchener and his lost system. *Journal of the History of the Behavioral Sciences, 8,* 168–180.

EVANS, R. I. (1968). *B. F. Skinner: The man and his ideas*. New York: Putnam.

EYSENCK, H. J. (1967). New ways in psychotherapy. *Psychology Today, 1*(2), 39–47.

FANCHER, R. E. (1973). *Psychoanalytic psychology: The development of Freud's thought*. New York: Norton.

FANCHER, R. E. (1979). *Pioneers of psychology*. New York: Norton.

FECHNER, G. (1860/1966). *Elements of psychophysics* (H. Adler, Trans.). Leipzig: Briet Kopf & Härtel. New York: Holt, Rinehart & Winston.

FEIGENBAUM, E. A. (1970). Information processing and memory. In D. A. Norman (Ed.), *Models of human memory*. New York: Academic Press.

FEINSTEIN, H. M. (1984). *Becoming William James*. Ithaca, NY: Cornell University Press.

FERSTER, C. B. & DE MYER, M. K. (1961). The development of performance in autistic children in an automatically controlled environment. *Journal of Chronic Diseases, 13*, 312–345.

FERSTER, C. B. & SKINNER, B. F. (1957). *Schedules of reinforcement*. New York: Appleton-Century-Crofts.

FLAVELL, J. H. & DRAGUNS, J. A. (1957). Microgenetic approach to perception and thought. *Psychological Bulletin, 54*, 197–217.

FRAISSE, P. (1970). French origins of the psychology of behavior: The contributions of Henri Piéron. *Journal of the History of the Behavioral Sciences, 6*, 111–119.

FRANK, J. P. (1972). The bewildering world of psychotherapy. *Journal of Social Issues, 22*, 27–43.

FRANKL, V. E. (1963). *Man's search for meaning: An introduction to logotherapy*. Boston: Beacon Press.

FREEDMAN, A. M., KAPLAN, H. I. & SADOCK, B. J. (1972). *Modern synopsis of comprehensive textbook of psychiatry*. Baltimore, MD: Williams & Wilkins.

FREUD, S. (1895/1954). *The origins of psycho-analysis. Letters to Wilhelm Fliess, drafts and notes: 1887–1902*. New York: Basic Books.

FREUD, S. (1933). *New introductory lectures on psycho-analysis*. New York: W. W. Norton.

FREUD, S. (1938). *A general introduction to psychoanalysis*. Garden City, NY: Garden City Publishing Co.

FREUD, S. (1947). *Leonardo da Vinci: A study in psychosexuality*. New York: Random House.

FREUD, S. *The standard edition of the complete psychological works of Sigmund Freud*. Translated from the German under the general editorship of J. Strachey, in collaboration with Anna Freud. London: Hogarth Press.

    (1893–1895). *Studies on hysteria* (Vol. 2).

    (1898). *Sexuality in the aetiology of the neuroses* (Vol. 3).

    (1900). *The interpretation of dreams* (Vol. 4 & 5).

    (1901). *The psychopathology of everyday life* (Vol. 6).

    (1905). *On psychotherapy* (Vol. 7).

    (1910a). *Five lectures on psycho-analysis* (Vol. 11).

    (1910b). *'Wild' psychoanalysis* (Vol. 11).

(1916–1917). *Introductory lectures on psychoanalysis* (Vol. 15 & 16).

(1920) *Beyond the pleasure principle* (Vol. 18).

(1925). *An autobiographical study* (Vol. 20).

(1930). *Civilization and its discontents* (Vol. 21).

(1933). *New introductory lectures on psycho-analysis* (Vol. 22).

(1940). *Some elementary lessons in psycho-analysis* (Vol. 23).

FROMM, E. (1941). *Escape from freedom.* New York: Rinehart & Co.

GALTON, F. (1869/1952). *Hereditary genius: An inquiry into its laws and consequences.* New York: Horizon Press.

GALTON, F. (1908). *Memories of my life.* London: Methuen.

GARDINER, P. (1967). Vico, Giambattista. In P. Edwards (Ed.), *The encyclopedia of philosophy* (Vol. 8). New York: Macmillan & The Free Press.

GARDNER, B. T. & GARDNER, R. A. (1971). Two-way communication with an infant chimpanzee. In A. Schrier & F. Stollnitz (Eds.), *Behavior of nonhuman primates.* New York: Academic Press.

GARNER, W. R. (1962). *Uncertainty and structure as psychological concepts.* New York: John Wiley & Sons.

GILBERT, R. (Ed.). (1975). *Edited transcript AHP Theory Conference,* Tucson, Arizona, April 4–6, 1975. San Francisco, CA: Association for Humanistic Psychology.

GLEITMAN, H. (1985). Some trends in the study of cognition. In S. Koch & D. E. Leary (Eds.), *A century of psychology as science.* New York: McGraw-Hill.

GOBLE, F. (1971). *The third force.* New York: Pocket Books.

GOETHE, J. W. (1810/1840). *Zur Farbenlehre* (Translated into *Theory of colours*). London: Murray.

GREEN, D. M. & SWETS, J. A. (1966). *Signal detection theory and psychophysics.* New York: John Wiley & Sons.

GREENSPOON, J. (1955). The reinforcing effect of two spoken sounds on the frequency of two responses. *American Journal of Psychology, 68,* 409–416.

GREGG, L. & SIMON, H. A. (1967). Process models and stochastic theories of simple concept formation. *Journal of Mathematical Psychology, 4,* 246–276.

GRÜNBAUM, A. (1984). *The foundations of psychoanalysis: A philosophical critique.* Berkeley: University of California Press.

GUTHRIE, E. R. (1935). *The psychology of learning.* New York: Harper & Row.

HALL, C. S. & LINDZEY, G. (1957). *Theories of personality.* New York: John Wiley & Sons.

HALL, M. H. (1967). An interview with "Mr. Behaviorist" B. F. Skinner. *Psychology Today, 1*(5), 20–23, 68–71.

HANDLER, P. (1980). Public doubts about science. *Science, 208,* 1093.

HARLOW, H. F. & HARLOW, M. (1962). Learning to love. *American Psychologist, 17,* 1–9.

HARRIS, B. (1979). Whatever happened to little Albert. *American Psychologist, 34,* 151–160.

HARTMANN, E. VON (1878/1931). *The philosophy of the unconscious.* New York: Harcourt Brace & Jovanovich.

HAYES, P. J. (1978). Cognitivism as a paradigm. *The Behavioral and Brain Sciences, 1,* 238–239.

HEARST, E. (1979a). One hundred years: Themes and perspectives. In E. Hearst (Ed.), *The first century of experimental psychology.* Hillsdale, NJ: Erlbaum.

HEARST, E. (1979b). *The first century of experimental psychology. Hillsdale, NJ: Erlbaum.*

HEBB, D. O. (1949). *The organization of behavior.* New York: John Wiley & Sons.

HEBB, D. O. (1955). C.N.S. (Conceptual Nervous System). *Psychological Review, 62,* 243–254.

HEBB, D. O. (1959). A neuropsychological theory. In S. Koch (Ed.), *Psychology: A study of a science* (Vol. 1). New York: McGraw-Hill.

HEBB, D. O. (1966). *A textbook of psychology* (2nd ed.). Philadelphia: Saunders.

HEBB, D. O. (1972). *Textbook of psychology* (3rd ed.). Philadelphia: Saunders.

HEBB, D. O. (1974). What psychology is about. *American Psychologist, 29,* 71–79.

HEBB, D. O. (1980). D. O. Hebb. In G. Lindzey (Ed.), *A history of psychology in autobiography* (Vol. 7). San Francisco: W. A. Freeman.

HEIDBREDER, E. (1933). *Seven psychologies.* Englewood Cliffs, NJ: Prentice-Hall.

HELSON, H. (1964). *Adaptation-level theory.* New York: Harper & Row.

HENLE, M. (1961). *Documents of Gestalt psychology.* Berkeley, CA: University of California Press.

HENLE, M. (1978). One man against the Nazis—Wolfgang Köhler. *American Psychologist, 33,* 939–951.

HERBART, J. F. (1816/1891). *A text-book in psychology.* New York: D. Appleton.

HERBART, J. F. (1824–25). *Psychologie als wissenschaft.* [*Psychology as a science*] Könisberg: A. W. Unzer.

HERGENHAHN, B. R. (1976). *An introduction to theories of learning.* Englewood Cliffs, NJ: Prentice-Hall.

HERRNSTEIN, R. J. (1958). The Skinnerian Method. Paper delivered at *Symposium on The Future of Contemporary Learning Theories.* Meeting of the American Association for the Advancement of Science, Washington, DC, December 29.

HERRNSTEIN, R. J. & BORING, E. G. (1966). *A source book in the history of psychology.* Cambridge, MA: Harvard University Press.

HILGARD, E. R. (1961). Introduction to a new edition of C. L. Hull's *Hypnosis and suggestibility.* New York: Appleton-Century-Crofts.

HILGARD, E. R. & BOWER, G. H. (1975). *Theories of learning* (4th ed.). Englewood Cliffs, NJ: Prentice-Hall.

HILGARD, E. R. & MARQUIS, D. G. (1940). *Conditioning and Learning.* New York: Appleton-Century-Crofts.

HOLDEN, C. (1977). Carl Rogers: Giving people permission to be themselves. *Science, 198,* 31–35.

HOOK, S. (1959). *Psychoanalysis, scientific method and philosophy.* New York: New York University Press.

HULL, C. L. (1920). Quantitative aspects of the evolution of concepts. *Psychological Monographs, 28*(123).

HULL, C. L. (1924). The influence of tobacco smoking on mental and motor efficiency. *Psychological Monographs, 33*(150).

HULL, C. L. (1928). *Aptitude testing.* New York: World.

HULL, C. L. (1932). The goal gradient hypothesis and maze learning. *Psychological Review, 39,* 25–43.

HULL, C. L. (1933). *Hypnosis and suggestibility.* New York: Appleton-Century-Crofts.

HULL, C. L. (1943). *Principles of behavior.* New York: Appleton-Century-Crofts.

HULL, C. L. (1951). *Essentials of behavior.* New Haven: Yale University Press.

HULL, C. L. (1952a). Clark L. Hull. In E. G. Boring, H. S. Langfeld, H. Werner, R. M. Yerkes (Eds.). *A history of psychology in autobiography.* Worcester, MA: Clark University Press.

HULL, C. L. (1952b). *A behavior system.* New Haven: Yale University Press.

HULL, C. L., HOVLAND, C. I., ROSS, R. T., HALL, M., PERKINS, D. T., & FITCH, F. B. (1940). *Mathematico-deductive theory of rote learning.* New Haven: Yale University Press.

HUMPHREY, G. (1951). *Thinking: An introduction to its experimental psychology.* London: Methuen.

HUNTER, W. S. (1913). *Delayed reaction in animals and children.* New York: Holt, Rinehart & Winston.

HURVICH, L. M. & JAMESON, D. (1957). An opponent-process theory of color vision. *Psychological Review, 64,* 384–404.

ISAACS, W., THOMAS, J. & GOLDIAMOND, I. (1960). Application of operant conditioning to reinstate verbal behavior in psychotics. *Journal of Speech and Hearing Disorders. 25,* 8–12.

JACOBSON, E. (1932). Electrophysiology of mental activities. *American Journal of Psychology, 44,* 677–694.

JACOBSEN, E. (1938). *Progressive relaxation.* Chicago: The University of Chicago Press.

JAMES, H. (Ed.). (1920). *The letters of William James,* Vol. 1. Boston: Atlantic Monthly Press.

JAMES, W. (1875). Review of *Grundzüge der Physiologischen Psychologie.* [*Principles of physiological psychology*] *North American Review, 121,* 195–201.

JAMES, W. (1884). What is an emotion? *Mind, 9,* 188–205.

JAMES, W. (1890). *The principles of psychology, Vols. 1 and 2.* New York: Henry Holt & Co.

JAMES, W. (1892a). *Psychology: The briefer course.* New York: Holt, Rinehart & Winston.

JAMES, W. (1892b). A plea for psychology as a natural science. *Philosophical Review, 1,* 146–153.

JAMES, W. (1899). *Talks to teachers.* New York: Holt, Rinehart & Winston.

JAMES, W. (1902/1928). *The varieties of religious experience.* New York: Longmans, Green & Co.

JAMES, W. (1907). *Pragmatism.* New York: Longmans, Green & Co.

JAMES, W. (1909a). *The meaning of truth.* New York: Longmans, Green & Co.

JAMES, W. (1909b). *A pluralistic universe.* New York: Longmans, Green & Co.

JAMES, W. (1912). *Essays in radical empiricism* (R. W. Perry, ed.). London: Longmans, Green & Co.

JERSILD, A. T. & LAZAR, E. A. (1962). *The meaning of psychotherapy in the teacher's life and work.* New York: Bureau of Publications, Teachers College, Columbia University.

JONES, E. (1953). *The life and work of Sigmund Freud Vol. 1.* New York: Basic Books.

JONES, M. C. (1924). A laboratory study of fear: The case of Peter. *Pedagogical Seminary, 31,* 308–315.

JONES, M. C. (1974). Albert, Peter, and John B. Watson. *American Psychologists, 29,* 581–583.

JUNG, C. G. (1912). *The psychology of the unconscious.* Leipzig: Franz Deuticke.

JUNG, C. G. (1963). *Memories, dreams, reflections.* London: Collins & Routledge & Kegan Paul.

KAHN, E. (1985). Heinz Kohut and Carl Rogers: A timely comparison. *American Psychologist, 40,* 893–904.

KANNER, J. H. (1954). A test of whether the "nonrewarded" animals learned as much as the "rewarded" animals in the California latent learning study. *Journal of Experimental Psychology, 48,* 175–183.

KANT, I. (1781/1950). *Critique of pure reason* (K. Smith, Trans.). New York: The Humanities Press.

KATZ, D. (1935). *The world of colour.* London: Routledge.

KELLER, F. S. & SHERMAN, J. G. (1974). *PSI: The Keller plan handbook.* Menlo Park, CA: Benjamin.

KENDLER, H. H. (1947). A comparison of learning under motivated and satiated conditions in the white rat. *Journal of Experimental Psychology, 37,* 545–549.

KENDLER, H. H. (1981). *Psychology: A science in conflict.* New York: Oxford.

KENDLER, H. H. (1984). Evolutions or revolutions. In K. M. J. Lagerspetz & P. Niemi (Eds.), *Psychology in the 1990's.* Amsterdam: Eisevier Science Publishers B.V. (North Holland).

KENDLER, H. H. (1985). Behaviorism and psychology: An uneasy alliance. In S. Koch & D. Leary (Eds.), *A century of psychology as science.* New York: McGraw-Hill.

KENDLER, H. H. & KENDLER, T. S. (1962). Vertical and horizontal processes in problem solving. *Psychological Review, 69,* 1–16.

KENDLER, H. H. & KENDLER, T. S. (1975). From discrimination learning to cognitive development: A neobehaviorist odyssey. In W. K. Estes (Ed.), *Handbook of learning and cognitive processes* (Vol. 1). Hillsdale, NJ: Erlbaum.

KIMBLE, G. A. (1961). *Hilgard and Marquis' conditioning and learning* (2nd ed.). New York: Appleton-Century-Crofts.

KOCH, S. (1959). *Psychology: A study of a science* Vol. 2. New York: McGraw-Hill.

KOCH, S. (1964). Psychology and emerging conceptions of knowledge as unitary. In T. W. Wann (Ed.), *Behaviorism and phenomenology.* Chicago: University of Chicago Press.

KOFFKA, K. (1924). *The growth of the mind.* New York: Harcourt Brace Jovanovich.

KOFFKA, K. (1935). *Principles of gestalt psychology.* New York: Harcourt Brace Jovanovich.

KÖHLER, W. (1918/1950). Simple structural functions in the chimpanzee and in the chicken. In W. D. Ellis (Ed.), *A source book of Gestalt psychology.* New York: The Humanities Press.

KÖHLER, W. (1920/1950). Physical gestalten. In W. D. Ellis (Ed.), *A source book of gestalt psychology.* New York: The Humanities Press.

KÖHLER, W. (1925). *The mentality of apes.* New York: Harcourt Brace Jovanovich.

KÖHLER, W. (1929). *Gestalt psychology.* New York: Liveright.

KÖHLER, W. (1938). *The place of value in a world of facts.* New York: Liveright.

KÖHLER, W. (1944). Value and fact. *Journal of Philosophy, 41,* 197–212.

KÖHLER, W. (1947/1964). *Gestalt psychology* (rev. ed.). New York: Mentor Books.

KÖHLER, W. (1959). Gestalt psychology today. *American Psychologist, 14,* 727–734.

KRAFFT-EBING, R. F. VON (1886). *Psychopathia sexualis.* Stuttgart: F. Enke.

KRECHEVSKY, I. (1932). "Hypotheses" versus "chance" in the pre-solution period in sensory discrimination-learning. *University of California Publications in Psychology, 6,* 27–44.

KRECHEVSKY, I. (1933). Hereditary nature of "hypotheses." *Journal of Comparative Psychology, 16,* 89–116.

KUENNE, M. R. (1946). Experimental investigation of the relation of language to transposition behavior in young children. *Journal of Experimental Psychology, 36,* 471–490.

KUHN, T. S. (1962). *The structure of scientific revolutions.* Chicago: University of Chicago Press.

KURZWEIL, R. (1985). What is artificial intelligence anyway? *American Scientist, 73,* 258–264.

LACHMAN, J. L. & LACHMAN, R. (1981). General process theory, ecology, and animal-human continuity: A cognitive perspective. *The Behavioral and Brain Sciences, 4,* 149–150.

LACHMAN, R., LACHMAN, J. L., & BUTTERFIELD, E. C. (1979). *Cognitive psychology and information processing: An introduction.* Hillsdale, NJ: Erlbaum.

LA METTRIE, J. DE (1748/1960). *L'homme Machine; A study in the origins of an idea.* Princeton: Princeton University Press.

LARSON, C. (1979). Highlights of Dr. John B. Watson's career in advertising. *The Industrial-Organizational Psychologist, 16*(3), 3–5.

LASHLEY, K. S. (1929). *Brain mechanisms and intelligence: A quantitative study of injuries to the brain.* Chicago: University of Chicago Press.

LEAHEY, T. H. (1979). Something old, something new: Attention in Wundt and modern cognitive psychology. *Journal of the History of the Behavioral Sciences, 15,* 242–252.

LEAHEY, T. H. (1980). *A history of psychology.* Englewood Cliffs, NJ: Prentice-Hall.

LEWIN, K. (1935). *A dynamic theory of personality.* New York: McGraw-Hill.

LEWIN, K. (1948). *Resolving social conflicts.* New York: Harper & Row.

LEWIN, K. (1951). *Field theory in social science.* New York: Harper & Row.

LITTMAN, R. A. (1979). Social and intellectual origins of experimental psychology. In E. Hearst (Ed.), *The first century of experimental psychology.* Hillsdale, NJ: Erlbaum.

LOGAN, F. A. (1968). Clark L. Hull. In D. L. Sills (Ed.), *International encyclopedia of the social sciences.* (Vol. 6. pp. 535–539). New York: Macmillan & The Free Press.

LUBORSKY, L., CHANDLER, M., AUERBACH, A. H., COHEN, J., & BACHRACH, H. M. (1971). Factors influencing the outcome of psychotherapy: A review of quantitative research. *Psychological Bulletin, 75,* 145–185.

LUCE, R. D. (1985). Mathematical modeling of perceptual learning and cognitive processes. In S. Koch & D. E. Leary (Eds.), *A century of psychology as science.* New York: McGraw-Hill.

MACCORQUODALE, K. (1969). Skinner's verbal behavior: A retrospective appreciation. *Journal of the Experimental Analysis of Behavior, 12,* 831–841.

MACCORQUODALE, K. & MEEHL, P. E. (1953). Preliminary suggestions as to a formalization of expectancy theory. *Psychological Review, 60,* 55–63.

MACCORQUODALE, K. & MEEHL, P. E. (1954). Edward C. Tolman. In W. K. Estes, S. Koch, K. MacCorquodale, P. E. Meehl, C. E. Mueller, W. N. Schoenfeld, & W. S. Verplanck (Eds.), *Modern Learning Theory.* New York: Appleton-Century-Crofts.

MCDOUGALL, W. (1905). *Physiological Psychology.* London: J. M. Dent & Sons.

MCDOUGALL, W. (1908). *An introduction to social psychology.* London: Methuen.

MCDOUGALL, W. (1923). *Outline of psychology.* New York: Charles Scribner's Sons.

MCDOUGALL, W. (1930). The hormic psychology. In C. Muchison (Ed.), *Psychologies of 1930.* Worcester, MA: Clark University Press.

MCGUIRE, W. (Ed.). (1974). *The Freud/Jung letters: The correspondence between Sigmund Freud and C. G. Jung.* London: Hogarth Press and Routledge & Kegan Paul.

MACLEOD, R. B. (1968). Phenomenology. In D. L. Sills (Ed.), *International encyclopedia of the social sciences* (Vol. 12). New York: Macmillan & The Free Press.

MADDI, S. R. (1980). *Personality theories: A comparative analysis* (4th ed.). Homewood, IL: Dorsey Press.

MALCOLM, J. (1982). *Psychoanalysis: The impossible profession.* New York: Vintage Books.

MALCOLM, J. (1984). *In the Freud archives.* New York: Alfred A. Knopf.

MALTHUS, T. R. (1872/1976). *An essay on the principle of population.* New York: W. W. Norton.

MANDLER, G. (1979). Emotion. In E. Hearst (Ed.), *The first century of experimental psychology.* Hillsdale, NJ: Erlbaum.

MARX, M. H. & HILLIX, W. A. (1979). *Systems and theories in psychology.* New York: McGraw-Hill.

MASLOW, A. H. (1954). *Motivation and personality.* New York: Harper & Row.

MASLOW, A. H. (1961). "Eupsychia-the good society." *Journal of Humanistic Psychology, 1*(2), 1–11.

MASLOW, A. H. (1966). *The psychology of science.* New York: Harper & Row.

MASLOW, A. H. (1970). *Motivation and personality* (2nd ed.). New York: Harper & Row.

MASSON, J. (1984). *The assault on truth: Freud's suppression of the seduction theory.* New York: Farrar, Straus and Giroux.

MATTHIESSEN, F. O. (1961). *The James family: Including selections from the writings of Henry James, Senior, William, Henry, and Alice James.* New York: Alfred A. Knopf.

MAY, R. (1977). *Meaning of anxiety* (rev. ed.). New York: W. W. Norton.

MAYER, A. & ORTH, J. (1901). Zur qualitativen untersuchung der associationen. [Qualitative investigations of associations] *Zeitschrift für Psychologie, 26,* 1–13.

MAX, L. W. (1937). Experimental study of the motor theory of consciousness: IV Action-current responses in the deaf during awakening, kinesthetic imagery and abstract thinking. *Journal of Comparative Psychology, 24,* 301–344.

MEEHL, P. E. (1970). Some methodological reflections on the difficulties of psychoanalytic research. In M. Radner & S. Winokur (Eds.), *Minnesota Studies in the Philosophy of Science* (Vol. 4). Minneapolis: University of Minnesota Press.

MILLER, G. A. (1956). The magical number seven, plus or minus two. *Psychological Review, 63,* 81–97.

MILLER, G. A. (1962). *Psychology: The science of mental life.* New York: Harper & Row.

MILLER, G. A., GALANTER, E. & PRIBRAM, K. H. (1960). *Plans and the structure of behavior.* New York: Holt, Rinehart & Winston.

MILLER, N. E. (1944). Experimental studies in conflict. In J. McV. Hunt (Ed.), *Personality and the Behavior Disorders.* New York: Ronald Press.

MILLER, N. E. (1948). Theory and experiment relating psychoanalytic displacement to stimulus-response generalization. *Journal of Abnormal and Social Psychology, 43,* 155–178.

MILLER, N. E. (1951). Learnable drives and rewards. In S. S. Stevens (Ed.), *Handbook of Experimental Psychology* (pp. 435–472). New York: John Wiley & Sons.

MILLER, N. E. (1959). Liberalization of basic S-R concepts: Extensions to conflict behavior, motivation and social learning. In S. Koch (Ed.), *Psychology: A Study of a Science* (Vol. 2). New York: McGraw-Hill.

MILLER, N. E. & DOLLARD, J. (1941). *Social learning and imitation.* New Haven: Yale University Press.

MORGAN, C. L. (1894). *An introduction to comparative psychology.* London: Scott.

MURPHY, G. (1949). *Historical introduction to modern psychology.* New York: Harcourt Brace Jovanovich.

NAFE, J. P. (1924). An experimental study of the affective qualities. *American Journal of Psychology, 35,* 507–544.

NAGEL, E. (1959). Methodological issues in psychoanalytic theory. In S. Hook (Ed.), *Psychoanalysis, scientific method, and philosophy.* New York: New York University Press.

NAGEL, E. (1961). *The structure of science.* New York: Harcourt Brace Jovanovich.

NEISSER, U. (1966). *Cognitive psychology.* New York: Appleton-Century-Crofts.

NEISSER, U. (1976). *Cognition and reality.* San Francisco: W. A. Freeman.

NELSON, K. (1973). Structure and strategy in learning to talk. *Monographs of the Society for Research in Child Development,* Serial No. 149.

NIETZSCHE, F. (1878/1984). *Humans, all too human.* Lincoln, NE: University of Nebraska Press.

NIETZSCHE, F. (1886/1955). *Beyond good and evil.* Chicago: Henry Regnery.

NEWELL, A. & SIMON, H. (1961). The simulation of human thought. In *Current Trends in Psychological Theory.* Pittsburgh, PA: The University of Pittsburgh Press.

OLDS, J. & MILNER, P. (1954). Positive reinforcement produced by electrical stimulation of septal area and other regions of rat brain. *Journal of Comparative and Physiological Psychology, 47,* 419–427.

OSGOOD, C. E. (1957). A behavioristic analysis of perception and language as cognitive phenomena. *Contemporary approaches to cognition: A symposium held at the University of Colorado.* Cambridge, MA: Harvard University Press.

OSGOOD, C. E., SUCI, G. J. & TANNENBAUM, P. H. (1957). *The measurement of meaning.* Urbana, IL: University of Illinois Press.

PASSMORE, J. A. (1953). Can the social sciences be value-free? In H. Feigl & M. Brodbeck (Eds.), *Readings in the Philosophy of Science.* New York: Appleton-Century-Crofts.

PAVLOV, I. P. (1927). *Conditioned reflexes* (G. V. Anrep, Trans.). London: Oxford.

PEARSON, K. (1914–1930). *The life, letters and labours of Francis Galton* (3 vols in 4). Cambridge, England: University Press.

PENFIELD, W. (1975). *The mystery of the mind.* Princeton, NJ: Princeton University Press.

PERIN, C. T. (1942). Behavior potentiality as a joint function of the amount of training and degree of hunger at the time of extinction. *Journal of Experimental Psychology, 30,* 93–113.

PERKY, C. W. (1910). An experimental study of imagination. *American Journal of Psychology, 21,* 422–452.

PERLS, F. (1969). *In and out of the garbage pail.* Lafayette, CA: Real People Press.

POLKINGHORNE, D. (1983). *Methodology for the human sciences.* Albany, NY: State University of New York Press.

POLLIO, H. R. (1982). *Behavior and existence: An introduction to empirical humanistic psychology.* Monterey, CA: Brooks/Cole.

POSNER, M. I. (1973). *Cognition: An introduction.* Glenview, IL: Scott, Foresman.

POSNER, M. I. (1984). Neural systems and cognitive processes. In K. M. J. Lagerspetz & P. Niemi (Eds.), *Psychology in the 1990's.* Amsterdam: North Holland.

POSNER, M. I. & KEELE, S. W. (1967). Decay of visual information from a single letter. *Science, 158,* 137–139.

QUINE, W. V. O. (1960). *Words and objects.* Cambridge, MA: MIT Press.

REICHENBACH, H. (1938). *Experience and prediction.* Chicago: University of Chicago Press.

REIFMAN, A. & WYATT, R. J. (1980). Lithium: A brake in the rising costs of mental illness. *Archives of General Psychiatry, 37,* 385–388.

REITMAN, W. (1984). Machines, architecture, intelligence, and knowledge: Changing conceptions of the cognitive psychologist's data source. In K. M. J. Lagerspetz & P. Neimi (Eds.), *Psychology in the 1990's.* Amsterdam: North-Holland.

RIEBER, R. W. (Ed.). (1980). *Wilhelm Wundt and the making of a scientific psychology.* New York: Plenum Press.

RIGGS, L. A. (1968). Hunter, Walter S. In D. L. Sills (Ed.), *International encyclopedia of the social sciences* (Vol. 7). New York: Macmillan & The Free Press.

RILEY, D. A. (1968). *Discrimination learning.* Boston: Allyn & Bacon.

ROBACK, A. A. (1964). *A history of American psychology* (rev. ed.). New York: Collier.

ROBINSON, D. N. (1981). *An intellectual history of psychology* (rev. ed.). New York: Macmillan.

ROBINSON, D. N. (1984). Ethics and advocacy. *American Psychologist, 39,* 787–793.

ROGERS, C. R. (1939). *The clinical treatment of the problem child.* Boston: Houghton Mifflin.

ROGERS, C. R. (1942). *Counseling and psychotherapy: Newer concepts in practice.* Boston: Houghton Mifflin.

ROGERS, C. R. (1951). *Client-centered therapy, its current practice, implications, and theory.* Boston: Houghton Mifflin.

ROGERS, C. R. (1959). A theory of therapy, personality, and interpersonal relationships as developed in the client-centered framework. In S. Koch (Ed.), *Psychology: A study of a science* (Vol. 3). New York: McGraw-Hill.

ROGERS, C. R. (1961). *On becoming a person: A therapist's view of psychotherapy.* Boston: Houghton Mifflin.

ROGERS, C. R. (1964). Toward a science of the person. In T. W. Wann (Ed.), *Behaviorism and phenomenology.* Chicago: The University of Chicago Press.

ROGERS, C. R. (1967). Carl R. Rogers. In E. G. Boring and G. Lindzey (Eds.), *A history of psychology in autobiography.* New York: Naiburg Publishing Corporation.

ROGERS, C. R. & SKINNER, B. F. (1956). Some issues concerning the control of human behavior. *Science, 124,* 1057–1066.

RUJA, H. (1956). Productive psychologists. *American Psychologists, 11,* 148–149.

SAHAKIAN, W. S. (1975). *History and systems of psychology.* New York: Halsted Press.

SAMELSON, F. (1974). History, origin, myth, and ideology: Comte's 'discovery' of social psychology. *Journal for the Theory of Social Behavior, 4,* 217–231.

SAMELSON, F. (1980). J. B. Watson's litle Albert, Cyril Burt's twins, and the need for a critical science. *American Psychologist, 35,* 619–625.

SCHACHTER, S. (1971). *Emotion, obesity, and crime.* New York: Academic Press.

SCHAFER, R. (1984). The pursuit of failure and the idealization of unhappiness. *American Psychologist, 39,* 398–405.

SCHAFER, R., BERG, I. & McCANDLESS, B. (1951). Report on survey of current psychological testing practices. *Supplement to Newsletter Division of Clinical and Abnormal Psychology, American Psychology Association, 4*(5).

SCHLESINGER, I. (1984). *What is a theory of language development a theory of? (Unpublished paper.)*

SCHLOSBERG, H. (1954). Three dimensions of emotions. *Psychological Review, 61,* 81–88.

SCRIVEN, M. (1956). A study of radical behaviorism. In H. Feigl & M. Scriven (Eds.), *Minnesota Studies in the Philosophy of science* (Vol. 1). Minneapolis: University of Minnesota Press.

SEARS, R. R. (1943). *Survey of objective studies of psychoanalytic concepts.* New York: Social Science Research Council Bulletin (No. 51).

SECHENOV, I. M. (1863/1935). *Reflexes of the brain.* Moscow and Leningrad: State Publishing House for Biological and Medical Literature.

SEEMAN, J. (1949). A study of the process of non-directive therapy. *Journal of Consulting Psychology, 13,* 157–168.

SHAFFER, J. (1978). *Humanistic psychology.* Englewood Cliffs, NJ: Prentice-Hall.

SHANNON, C. E. (1948). A mathematical theory of communicaton. *Bell Systems Technical Journal, 27,* 379–423, 623–656.

SIDMAN, M. (1960). *Tactics of scientific research.* New York: Basic Books.

SILVERMAN, L. H. (1976). Psychoanalytic theory: "The reports of my death are greatly exaggerated." *American Psychologist, 31,* 621–637.

SIMON, H. A. (1965). *The shape of automation for men and management.* New York: Harper & Row.

SIMON, H. A. & NEWELL, A. (1958). Heuristic problem solving: The next advance in operations research. *Operations Research, 6,* 7–8.

SIMON, H. A. & NEWELL, A. (1964). Information processing in computer and man. *American Scientist, 52,* 281–300.

SIMON, H. A. & NEWELL, A. (1971). Human problem solving: The state of the theory in 1970. *American Psychologist, 26,* 145–159.

SIMON, H. A. & NEWELL, A. (1974). Thinking processes. In D. H. Krantz, R. C.

Atkinson, R. D. Luce, & P. Suppes (Eds.), *Contemporary developments in mathematical psychology* (Vol. 1). San Francisco: W. A. Freeman.

SKINNER, B. F. (1938). *The behavior of organisms: An experimental analysis.* New York: Appleton-Century-Crofts.

SKINNER, B. F. (1945). Rejoinders and second thoughts: Part V. *Psychological Review, 52,* 291–294.

SKINNER, B. F. (1948). *Walden Two.* New York: Macmillan.

SKINNER, B. F. (1950). Are theories of learning necessary? *Psychological Review, 57,* 193–216.

SKINNER, B. F. (1953). *Science and human behavior.* New York: Macmillan.

SKINNER, B. F. (1956). A case history in scientific method. *American Psychologist, 11,* 221–233.

SKINNER, B. F. (1957). *Verbal behavior.* New York: Appleton-Century-Crofts.

SKINNER, B. F. (1958). Teaching machines. *Science, 128,* 969–977.

SKINNER, B. F. (1959). John Broadus Watson, Behaviorist. *Science, 129,* 197–198.

SKINNER, B. F. (1960). Pigeons in a pelican. *American Psychologist, 15,* 28–37.

SKINNER, B. F. (1961). *Cumulative Record.* New York: Appleton-Century-Crofts.

SKINNER, B. F. (1967). B. F. Skinner. In E. G. Boring and G. Lindzey (Eds.), *A history of psychology in autobiography.* New York: Naiburg Publishing Corporation.

SKINNER, B. F. (1969). *Contingencies of reinforcement: A theoretical analysis.* New York: Appleton-Century-Crofts.

SKINNER, B. F. (1971). *Beyond freedom and dignity.* New York: Alfred A. Knopf.

SKINNER, B. F. (1974). *About behaviorism.* New York: Alfred A. Knopf.

SKINNER, B. F. (1976). *Particulars of my life.* New York: Alfred A. Knopf.

SKINNER, B. F. (1981). Selection by consequences. *Science, 213,* 499–504.

SKINNER, B. F. (1983a). Intellectual self-management in old age. *American Psychologist, 3,* 239–244.

SKINNER, B. F. (1983b). *A matter of consequences.* New York: Alfred A. Knopf.

SMITH, E. E. (1978). Theories of semantic memory. In W. K. Estes (Ed.), *Handbook of learning and cognitive processes* (Vol. 6). Hillsdale, NJ: Erlbaum.

SMITH, M. B. (1978). Psychology and values. *Journal of Social Issues, 34,* 181–199.

SMITH, M. B. (1982). Psychology and humanism. *Psi Chi Newsletter, 8,*(1), 1, 3–7.

SMITH, M. B. (1984). Humanistic psychology. In R. J. Corsini (Ed.), *Encyclopedia of psychology* (Vol. 2). New York: John Wiley & Sons.

SOKAL, M. M. (Ed.). (1981). *An education in psychology. James McKeen Cattell's Journal and letters from Germany and England, 1880–1888.* Cambridge, MA: MIT Press.

SPENCE, K. W. (1936). The nature of discrimination learning in animals. *Psychological Review, 43,* 427–449.

SPENCE, K. W. (1937). The differential response in animals to stimuli varying within a single dimension. *Psychological Review, 44,* 430–444.

SPENCE, K. W. (1950). Cognitive versus stimulus-response theories of learning. *Psychological Review, 57*, 159–172.

SPENCE, K. W. (1956). *Behavior theory and conditioning.* New Haven: Yale University Press.

SPERLING, G. (1960). The information available in brief visual presentations. *Psychological Monographs, 74,*(498).

SPIELBERGER, C. D. & DeNIKE, L. D. (1966). Descriptive behaviorism in verbal operant conditioning. *Psychological Review, 73*, 303–326.

STADDON, J. E. R. & SIMMELHAG, V. L. (1971). The "superstition" experiment: A reexamination of its implications for the principles of adoptive behavior. *Psychological Review, 78*, 3–43.

STERN, W. (1938). *General psychology from the personalistic viewpoint.* New York: Macmillan.

THIGPEN, C. H. & CLECKLEY, H. M. (1957). *The three faces of Eve.* New York: McGraw-Hill.

THORNDIKE, E. L. (1898). Animal intelligence: An experimental study of the associative process in animals. *Psychological Monographs, 2*(8).

THORNDIKE, E. L. (1911). *Animal intelligence: Experimental studies.* New York: Macmillan.

THORNDIKE, R. L. & HAGEN, E. (1961). *Measurement and evaluation in psychology and education* (2nd ed.). New York: John Wiley & Sons.

THURSTONE, L. L. (1948). Psychological implications of factor analysis. *American Psychologists, 3*, 402–406.

THURSTONE, L. L. (1959). *The measurement of values.* Chicago: University of Chicago Press.

THURSTONE, L. L. & THURSTONE, T. G. (1941). Factorial studies of intelligence. *Psychometric Monographs.* No. 2.

TITCHENER, E. B. (1898). The postulates of a structural psychology. *The Philosophical Review, 1*, 449–465.

TITCHENER, E. B. (1896/1921). *An outline of psychology.* (New Edition with additions.) New York: Macmillan.

TITCHENER, E. B. (1899). Discussion: Structural and functional psychology. *Philosophical Review, 8*, 290–299.

TITCHENER, E. B. (1901–1905). *Experimental Psychology.* New York: Macmillan.

TITCHENER, E. B. (1908/1973). *Lectures on the elementary psychology of feeling and attention.* New York: Arno Press.

TITCHENER, E. B. (1909). *Lectures on the experimental psychology of the thought-processes.* New York: Macmillan.

TITCHENER, E. B. (1910). *A text-book of psychology.* New York: Macmillan.

TITCHENER, E. B. (1912). The schema of introspection. *American Journal of Psychology, 23*, 486–508.

TITCHENER, E. B. (1913). *A primer of psychology.* (rev. ed.), New York: Macmillan.

TITCHENER, E. B. (1921). Review of Wundt's Erlebtes und Erkanntes. *American Journal of Psychology, 32*, 575–580.

TITCHENER, E. B. (1923). *A textbook of psychology.* New York: Macmillan.

TITCHENER, E. B. (1925). Experimental psychology: A restrospect. *American Journal of Psychology, 36,* 313–323.

TITCHENER, E. B. (1929/1972). *Systematic psychology: Prolegomena.* Ithaca, NY: Cornell University Press.

TOLMAN, E. C. (1922). A new formula for behaviorism. *Psychological Review, 29,* 44–53.

TOLMAN, E. C. (1932). *Purposive behavior in animals and men.* New York: Appleton-Century-Crofts.

TOLMAN, E. C. (1938). The determiners of behavior at a choice point. *Psychological Review, 45,* 1–41.

TOLMAN, E. C. (1942). *Drives toward war.* New York: Appleton-Century-Crofts.

TOLMAN, E. C. (1949). There is more than one kind of learning. *Psychological Review, 56,* 144–155.

TOLMAN, E. C. (1952). Edward Chace Tolman. In E. G. Boring, H. S. Langfeld, H. Werner, & R. M. Yerkes (Eds.), *A history of psychology in autobiography* (Vol. 4). Worcester, MA: Clark University Press.

TOLMAN, E. C. (1959). Principles of purposive behavior. In S. Koch (Ed.), *Psychology: A study of a science* (Vol. 2). New York: McGraw-Hill.

TOLMAN, E. C. & HONZIK, C. H. (1930). Introduction and removal of reward and maze performance of rats. *University of California Publications in Psychology, 4,* 257–275.

TRYON, R. C. (1940). Genetic differences in maze-learning ability in rats. *39th Yearbook of National Society Studies in Education.* Part 1. pp. 111–119.

TUDDENHAM, R. D. (1962). The nature and measurement of intelligence. In L. Postman (Ed.), *Psychology in the making: Histories of selected research problems.* New York: Alfred A. Knopf. © 1982 by Alfred A. Knopf.

TULVING, E. (1985). How many memory systems are there? *American Psychologist, 40,* 385–398.

TULVING, E. & PEARLSTONE, Z. (1966). Availability vesus accessibility of information in memory for words. *Journal of Verbal Learning and Verbal Behavior, 5,* 381–391.

WANN, T. W. (1964). *Behaviorism and phenomenology: Contrasting bases for modern psychology.* Chicago: University of Chicago Press.

WARREN, H. C. (1921). *A history of the association psychology.* New York: Charles Scribner's Sons.

WATSON, J. B. (1907). Kinaesthetic and organic sensations: Their role in the reactions of the white rat to the maze. *Psychological Review, Monograph Supplements, 8*(33).

WATSON, J. B. (1908). The behavior of noddy and sooty terns. *Carnegie Institution Publications, 103,* 187–255.

WATSON, J. B. (1913). Psychology as a behaviorist views it. *Psychological Review, 20,* 158–177.

WATSON, J. B. (1914). *Behavior: An introduction to comparative psychology.* New York: Holt, Rinehart & Winston.

WATSON, J. B. (1919). *Psychology from the standpoint of a behaviorist.* Philadelphia, PA: Lippincott.

WATSON, J. B. (1924). *Behaviorism.* New York: W. W. Norton.

WATSON, J. B. (1926). Experimental studies on the growth of the emotions. In C. Murchison (Ed.), *Psychologies of 1925.* Worcester, MA: Clark University Press.

WATSON, J. B. (1928). *Psychological care of the infant and child.* New York: W. W. Norton.

WATSON, J. B. (1930). Behaviorism (rev. ed.). New York: W. W. Norton.

WATSON, J. B. (1936). Autobiography. In C. Murchison (Ed.), *A history of psychology in autobiography* (Vol. 3). Worcester, MA: Clark University Press.

WATSON, J. B. & McDOUGALL (1929). *The battle of behaviorism.* New York: Norton.

WATSON, J. B. & MORGAN, J. J. B. (1917). Emotional reactions and psychological experimentation. *American Journal of Psychology, 28,* 163–174.

WATSON, J. B. & RAYNER, R. (1920). Conditioned emotional reactions. *Journal of Experimental Psychology, 3,* 1–14.

WATSON, J. R. (1950). Letter to the editors. *Life, 29*(3:8).

WATSON, R. I. (1978). *The great psychologists* (4th ed.). Philadelphia: Lippincott.

WEAVER, W. (1958). Communicative accuracy. *Science, 127,* 499.

WEISS, J. M. (1972). Psychological factors in stress and disease. *Scientific American, 226*(6), 104–114.

WEIZENBAUM, J. (1976). *Computer power and human reasons.* San Francisco: W. H. Freeman.

WERTHEIMER, M. (1945). *Productive thinking.* New York: Harper & Row.

WERTHEIMER, M. (1950). Gestalt theory. In W. D. Ellis (Ed.), *A source book of gestalt psychology.* New York: Humanities Press.

WERTHEIMER, M. (1961). On truth. In M. Henle (Ed.), *Documents of gestalt psychology.* Berkeley, CA: University of California Press.

WERTHEIMER, MICHAEL (1978). Max Wertheimer, Gestalt prophet. Draft of a presidential address to Division 26, Division of the History of Psychology of the *American Psychological Association,* Toronto, Canada, August 31.

WITTELS, F. (1924). *Sigmund Freud: His personality, his teachings, and his school.* London: George Allen and Unwin.

WOLPE, J. (1958). *Psychotherapy by reciprocal inhibition.* Stanford, CA: Stanford University Press.

WOODS, E. L. (1915). An experimental analysis of the process of recognizing. *American Journal of Psychology, 26,* 313–387.

WOODWORTH, R. S. (1938). *Experimental Psychology.* New York: Holt, Rinehart & Winston.

WOODWORTH, R. S. (1958). *Dynamics of behavior.* New York: Holt, Rinehart & Winston.

WOODWORTH, R. S. (1959). John Broadus Watson: 1878–1958. *American Journal of Psychology, 72,* 301–310.

WUNDT, W. (1897). *Outlines of psychology* (C. H. Judd, Trans.). Leipzig: Wilhelm Engelmann.

WUNDT, W. (1900–1920). *Völkerpsychologie* [Folk psychology] (10 Volumes). Leipzig: W. Engelmann.

WUNDT, W. (1906). Die Entwicklung des Willens. In *Essays* (2nd ed.). Leipzig: W. Engelmann.

WUNDT, W. (1910). *Principles of physiological psychology* (Vol. 1). New York: Macmillan.

WUNDT, W. (1912/1973). *An introduction to psychology* (Rudolf Pintner, Trans.). New York: Arno Press.

WUNDT, W. (1916). *Elements of folk psychology.* New York: Macmillan.

WUNDT, W. (1980). Selected texts from writings of Wilhelm Wundt (translated with commentary notes by Solomon Diamond) in R. W. Rieber (Ed.), *Wilhelm Wundt and the making of a scientific psychology.* New York: Plenum Press.

ZEAMAN, D. (1949). Response latency as a function of the amount of reinforcement. *Journal of Experimental Psychology, 39,* 446–483.

ZURIFF, G. E. (1985). *Behaviorism: A conceptual reconstruction.* New York: Columbia University Press.

Author Index

i

Subject Index

ABOUT THE AUTHOR

Howard H. Kendler's career has been varied and distinguished. He received his B.A. from Brooklyn College and his M.A. and Ph.D. from the University of Iowa. He served in the U.S. Army during World War II and was Chief Clinical Psychologist at Walter Reed General Hospital. From 1946 to 1948 he was an assistant professor at the University of Colorado and from 1948 to 1963 he was associated with New York University, where in 1951 he became Professor of Psychology and Chairman of the Department of Psychology of University College. Since 1963 he has been Professor of Psychology at the University of California, Santa Barbara. Dr. Kendler has been a Fellow at the Center for Advanced Studies in the Behavioral Sciences as well as a Visiting Professor at the University of California, Berkeley and the Hebrew University in Jerusalem. He is the author of *Basic Psychology* and *Psychology: A Science in Conflict*; is the co-editor of *Essays in Neobehaviorism: A Memorial Volume to Kenneth W. Spence*; and has written more than 100 professional articles. In addition to serving as consultant to numerous governmental agencies, Dr. Kendler has held the offices of President of the Western Psychological Association, Chairman of the Board of Governors of the Psychonomic Association, and President of both the Division of General Psychology and Division of Experimental Psychology of the American Psychological Association. He is also a member of the Society of Experimental Psychologists.

A Note on the Type

The text of this book was set in 10/12 Palatino using a film version of the face designed by Hermann Zapf that was first released in 1950 by Germany's Stempel Foundry. The face is named after Giovanni Battista Palatino, a famous penman of the 16th century. In its calligraphic quality, Palatino is reminiscent of the Italian Renaissance type designs, yet with its wide, open letters and unique proportions it still retains a modern feel. Palatino is considered one of the most important faces from one of Europe's most influential type designers.

Composition by Weimer Typesetting, Indianapolis, Indiana.

Printed and bound by Vail-Ballou Press, Inc., Binghamton, New York.